英语语境语法 3

教师参考用书

（第四版）

Grammar in Context

TEACHER'S ANNOTATED EDITION

4TH EDITION

SANDRA N. ELBAUM

HILARY GRANT

北京大学出版社
PEKING UNIVERSITY PRESS

著作权合同登记　图字：01-2006-4114 号

图书在版编目（CIP）数据

英语语境语法 3 教师参考用书(第四版)＝Grammar in Context 3 Teacher's Annotated Edition (Fourth Edition)/
桑德拉·艾尔鲍姆(Sandra N. Elbaum)，希拉里·格兰特(Hilary Grant)．—影印本．—北京：北京大学出版
社，2006.8

（英语语境语法系列丛书）

ISBN 7-301-11017-0

Ⅰ.英…　Ⅱ.①桑…　②希…　Ⅲ.英语–语法–高等学校–教学参考资料　Ⅳ.H314

中国版本图书馆 CIP 数据核字（2006）第 100673 号

SANDRA N. ELBAUM/HILARY GRANT

Grammar in Context 3 Teacher's Annotated Edition （Fourth Edition）

EISBN：1-4130-0821-6

书　　　　名：英语语境语法 3 教师参考用书（第四版）
　　　　　　　Grammar in Context 3 Teacher's Annotated Edition（Fourth Edition）
著作责任者：桑德拉·艾尔鲍姆（Sandra N. Elbaum）希拉里·格兰特（Hilary Grant）
责 任 编 辑：胡　娜
标 准 书 号：ISBN 7-301-11017-0/H·1678
出 版 发 行：北京大学出版社
地　　　址：北京市海淀区成府路 205 号　100871
网　　　址：http://www.pup.cn
电　　　话：邮购部 62752015　发行部 62750672　编辑部 62767347　出版部 62754962
电 子 邮 箱：zbing@pup.pku.edu.cn
印 刷 者：北京中科印刷有限公司
经 销 者：新华书店
　　　　　　889 毫米×1194 毫米　16 开本　34 印张　858 千字
　　　　　　2006 年 8 月第 1 版　2006 年 8 月第 1 次印刷
定　　　价：68.00 元

导　言

北京大学英语系教授　王逢鑫

一

语言由语音、词汇和语法三个要素组成。学习一门外语，必须掌握这三个要素，缺一不可。有人认为只要记住单词，能读出音来，就行了，而语法可有可无。其实这是一种误解。语法是组词造句的法则，十分重要。传统英语语法细分为词法(morphology)和句法(syntax)。词法解释词分为哪些种类，即词类；告诉人们每个词类有什么特点，即词性；说明一个词与别的什么词可以联系在一起使用，即在句子里起什么作用。英语词汇形态与汉语有很大的区别。例如，名词有单、复数之分，还有可数与不可数之分。人称代词有主格、宾格和所有格之分。动词有现在式、过去式和过去分词三种不同形式；还有不定式、现在分词、过去分词和动名词等非谓语动词形式。形容词有原级、比较级和最高级三种形式。数词有基数词和序数词之分。以上词类大都是规则变化，但是也有很多不规则变化的例外情况。例如英语有一百来个不规则动词，其中多数是常用动词。介词后面跟人称代词要用宾格，跟动词要用动名词形式。英语的冠词更是难学。有人学了多年英语，还是弄不清楚什么时候用定冠词，什么时候用不定冠词，什么时候不用任何冠词。虽然不定冠词仅有 a 和 an 两种形式，但是有人把 an hour 写成 a hour，把 a university 写成 an university。这些繁杂的内容都是初学者必须掌握的，使用不当就要犯错误。

英语句法分析句子的种类、结构和功能。英语句法比汉语复杂。英语有各种各样的时态，每种时态有自己固定的形式，不能用错。句法规则繁多，几乎没有什么道理可讲。例如，在一般现在时里，单数第三人称的动词要加-s。情态动词和助动词后面要跟原形动词。英语句子讲究人称和时态前后呼应，左右照顾。诸如此类的条条框框都是初学者的"拦路虎"。

国内外的语言学家和英语教师，曾经尝试使用各种各样的方法来教英语语法。时代不同，学习目的不同，教学对象不同，教材不同，学习方法不同，使得人们很难找到学习英语语法的一个最佳方案。但是，我们了解一下国内外英语语法教学的来龙去脉，或许有助于我们吸取教训，总结经验，寻找有效的学习英语语法的途径。

传统法(traditional method)强调以语法为纲，以语法为教学中心。学生按部就班学习语法规则，先是死记硬背条条框框，然后做大量的机械性(mechanical)练习，基本上是没有上下文的单句翻译、语法填空和造句练习。追求的是语法形式正确无误，而不管在什么情况下使用语言。学习语法，不是为了交际，而是为了阅读内容艰深的文章，分析复杂的句法结构。我国解放前和解放初期的英语专业大学生，是通过传统法学习英语语法的，虽然有一些弊端，例如引导学生重视阅读和笔译，而忽视口头表达能力的培养。但是这种方法也并非一无是处。学生中不乏精通英语的成功者。传统法强调阅读小说、诗歌、戏剧和散文等文学作品，认为文学语言是最好的语言。通过对语句和篇章细致的句法分析，学生获得对语句和篇章结构,尤其是繁杂结构的精确理解。今天我们强调学习语言是为了交流思想,重视口头表达能力,传统法是难当此任的。

听说法(audio-visual method)将英语分成许多基本句型(sentence pattern),将语法教学与句型教学结合在一起。要求学生熟练掌握句型,反复口头练习,达到不假思索,脱口而出的程度。掌握了句型,就等于掌握了语法。20世纪60年代初,听说法引入我国,在当时的英语专业大学生中间曾经奏效。学生反复练习没有上下文的基本句型,虽然枯燥无味,但是在当时的历史环境下,多数学生能够不厌其烦地做大量的机械性口头练习,而取得较好的学习效果。现在的学生要求在学习过程中有更多的独立自主,对死记硬背基本句型不太感兴趣。利用听说法学习英语语法似乎不太合乎时宜了。

语言学家和英语教师总是想方设法改进语法教学。他们先是将以单句练习为主的机械性句型练习,扩充为共有两句话的二人对话,构成一个简单的情景,使所练习的句型变得有意义。再往后,进一步将二人对话扩大为围绕一个主题的、有上下文的情景会话(situational conversation)。这样,学生可以在一定的语境(context)之中通过句型学习英语语法。最初的语境是为了练习某个语言点,或为了掌握某种意念功能而编造的,具有人为的成分。20世纪80年代初,国内外兴起交际法(communicative method)。这种教学法的目标是让学生不仅学会听、说、读、写的语言能力 (linguistic competence), 还要掌握交际能力(communicative competence)。交际法从交流的目的出发,既要求语法正确(correct in grammar),更要求语用得体(appropriate in use)。因而在教学中引进了社会与文化因素。学习内容不再是干巴巴的基本句型,而是人们关注的社会问题和文化现象。学生不再为学习语法而学习语法,而是为了交际来学习语法。他们希望能够使用语法正确、语用得体的语言,就人们关注的社会问题和文化现象进行交流。这样就需要在一定的社会环境和文化语境里学习语言,包括学习语法。在学习语言的同时,必须了解英语国家的文化背景, 以及中外文化差异。只有学习了相关的文化背景知识, 才能更好地掌握语言。这套名为 *Grammar in Context* (《英语语境语法》)的教材,在上述背景下应运而生。

二

这套《英语语境语法》的编者 Sandra N. Elbaum 女士,是美国的一位英语教师,专门教授从世界各地到美国的移民,他们是以英语为第二语言的学生。Elbaum 女士幼年随父母由波兰移民到美国,语言差异和文化差异经常使她的父母感到困惑。Elbaum 女士在移民聚居的社区中成长,深知一个外国移民在美国生存,不仅要逾越语言障碍,更要克服文化差异。她有一个信念,就是通过语境学习语法。她不但在教学中身体力行,通过语境教英语语法,而且亲自编写教材,体现这一理念。

这套英语教材名曰《英语语境语法》,实际上是教给学生通过语境学习英语语言。这套教材的宗旨是:让学习者在语境中学习语法,以便学到更多东西,记住更多东西,更加有效地运用语言。

这套教材有如下突出特点:

1. 教给学生进行口头交流和书面交流所必需的语法知识。按照循序渐进原则安排语法点,讲解后面的语法内容都联系和复习前面的语法内容,使整个语法系统构成一个有机的整体。解释每个语法点,都使用形象的语法图表(grammar chart),一目了然。每个语法图表提供有语境的精选例句,并给出清晰的解释,还配以语言提示(language note),增强学习者对所学语法结构的理解。每个语法点还以图表方式解释其形式、用途、语序、主语、相关结构、描述与定义、所需介词搭配、肯定句、否定句和疑问句及回答等项目。每个项目都配有大量的口头和笔头练习。

2. 不是为教语法而教语法，而是通过语法教学，给学习者提供有用的（useful）、有意义的（meaningful）技能和基本文化知识。在课堂上，教师不是局限于让学生做机械性练习，而是让他们通过二人对话、小组活动、游戏、讨论等多种形式的扩展活动（expansion activity），互相启发，互相帮助，学以致用。通过阅读、作文、独立思考的练习等方式，学习者拓展自己的语言知识和交际能力，最终达到既能有效使用语言，又有信心正确使用语言进行交流的双重目的。

3. 教材将英语语法学习和美国文化语境结合起来。全套教材分为1、2、3三级，每级又分为两个分册，共有1A、1B、2A、2B、3A、3B等6个分册。1级和2级各有14课；3级有10课。每课内容，包括语法讲解和练习、阅读课文和扩展活动，都围绕美国社会的一个热门话题，构成一个语境。从语言学习角度，涉及一个语法点；从文化学习角度，涉及一个话题。二者巧妙结合。1级有学校生活、美国政府、美国节日、美国人及其住宅、家庭与姓名、美国人生活方式、婚礼、飞行、购物、营养与健康、伟大女性、美国地理、约会与婚姻、实习等14个话题。2级有宠物、老年生活、改善生活、婚礼、感恩节与印第安人、健康、移民、租房、上网搜索、找工作、交友、体育、法律、货币等14个话题。3级有工作、好莱坞、灾难与悲剧、消费者警告、肯尼迪家族、计算机与互联网、帮助他人、来到美国、关爱儿童、科学与科幻小说等10个话题。这些语境概括了美国社会的方方面面，是了解美国文化和在美国生存所必需的基本知识。这些语境有助于学习者掌握必需的文化背景知识，使他们懂得美国文化在语言、信仰和日常生活情景等方面的重要作用。

这是一套通过语境学习英语的好教材。使用这套教材，学习者不仅可以熟练掌握英语语法，运用英语语言；而且可以学习美国文化背景知识，在语境中学习英语，在语境中使用英语。希望学习者喜欢这套教材，并通过学习这套教材学好英语。

Contents

Lesson 1   1

Lesson 4   137

Lesson 7   273

Appendices

In memory of
Meyer Shisler—teacher, scholar, inspiration

Acknowledgments

Many thanks to Dennis Hogan, Jim Brown, Sherrise Roehr, Yeny Kim, and Sally Giangrande from Thomson Heinle for their ongoing support of the *Grammar in Context* series. I would especially like to thank my editor, Charlotte Sturdy, for her keen eye to detail and invaluable suggestions.

And many thanks to my students at Truman College, who have increased my understanding of my own language and taught me to see life from another point of view. By sharing their observations, questions, and life stories, they have enriched my life enormously. —*Sandra N. Elbaum*

Heinle would like to thank the following people for their contributions:

Marki Alexander
Oklahoma State
 University
Stillwater, OK

Joan M. Amore
Triton College
River Grove, IL

**Edina Pingleton
Bagley**
Nassau Community
 College
Garden City, NY

Judith A. G. Benka
Normandale Community
 College
Bloomington, MN

**Judith Book-
Ehrlichman**
Bergen Community
 College
Paramus, NJ

Lyn Buchheit
Community College of
 Philadelphia
Philadelphia, PA

Charlotte M. Calobrisi
Northern Virginia
 Community College
Annandale, VA

Sarah A. Carpenter
Normandale Community
 College
Bloomington, MN

Jeanette Clement
Duquesne University
Pittsburgh, PA

Allis Cole
Shoreline Community
 College
Shoreline, WA

**Jacqueline M.
Cunningham**
Triton College
River Grove, IL

Lisa DePaoli
Sierra College
Rocklin, CA

Maha Edlbi
Sierra College
Rocklin, CA

Rhonda J. Farley
Cosumnes River College
Sacramento, CA

Jennifer Farnell
University of Connecticut
American Language
 Program
Stamford, CT

**Abigail-Marie
Fiattarone**
Mesa Community College
Mesa, AZ

Marcia Gethin-Jones
University of Connecticut
American Language
 Program
Storrs, CT

Linda Harlow
Santa Rosa Junior
 College
Santa Rosa, CA

Suha R. Hattab
Triton College
River Grove, IL

Bill Keniston
Normandale Community
 College
Bloomington, MN

Walton King
Arkansas State
 University
Jonesboro, AR

Kathleen Krokar
Truman College
Chicago, IL

John Larkin
NVCC-Community and
 Workforce
 Development
Annandale, VA

Michael Larsen
American River College
Sacramento, CA

Bea C. Lawn
Gavilan College
Gilroy, CA

Rob Lee
Pasadena City College
Pasadena, CA

**Oranit
Limmaneeprasert**
American River College
Sacramento, CA

Gennell Lockwood
Shoreline Community
 College
Shoreline, WA

Linda Louie
Highline Community
 College
Des Moines, WA

Melanie A. Majeski
Naugatuck Valley
 Community College
Waterbury, CT

Maria Marin
De Anza College
Cupertino, CA

Karen Miceli
Cosumnes River College
Sacramento, CA

Jeanie Pavichevich
Triton College
River Grove, IL

Herbert Pierson
St. John's University
New York City, NY

Dina Poggi
De Anza College
Cupertino, CA

Mark Rau
American River College
Sacramento, CA

John W. Roberts
Shoreline Community
 College
Shoreline, WA

Azize R. Ruttler
Bergen Community
 College
Paramus, NJ

Ann Salzmann
University of Illinois,
Urbana, IL

Eva Teagarden
Yuba College
Marysville, CA

Susan Wilson
San Jose City College
San Jose, CA

Martha Yeager-Tobar
Cerritos College
Norwalk, CA

A word from the author

It seems that I was born to be an ESL teacher. My parents immigrated to the U.S. from Poland as adults and were confused not only by the English language but by American culture as well. Born in the U.S., I often had the task as a child to explain the intricacies of the language and allay my parents' fears about the culture. It is no wonder to me that I became an ESL teacher, and later, an ESL writer who focuses on explanations of American culture in order to illustrate grammar. My life growing up in an immigrant neighborhood was very similar to the lives of my students, so I have a feel for what confuses them and what they need to know about American life.

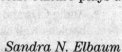

ESL teachers often find themselves explaining confusing customs and providing practical information about life in the U.S. Often, teachers are a student's only source of information about American life. With *Grammar in Context, Fourth Edition,* I enjoy sharing my experiences with you.

Grammar in Context, Fourth Edition connects grammar with American cultural context, providing learners of English with a useful and meaningful skill and knowledge base. Students learn the grammar necessary to communicate verbally and in writing, and learn how American culture plays a role in language, beliefs, and everyday situations.

Enjoy the new edition of *Grammar in Context!*

Sandra N. Elbaum

Grammar in Context

Students learn more, remember more, and use language more effectively when they learn grammar in context.

Learning a language through meaningful themes and practicing it in a contextualized setting promote both linguistic and cognitive development. In *Grammar in Context,* grammar is presented in interesting and culturally informative readings, and the language and context are subsequently practiced throughout the chapter.

New to this edition

- **New and updated readings** on current American topics such as Instant Messaging and eBay.
- **Updated grammar charts** that now include essential language notes.
- **Updated exercises and activities** that provide contextualized practice using a variety of exercise types, as well as additional practice for more difficult structures.
- **New lower-level** *Grammar in Context Basic* for beginning level students.
- **New wrap-around Teacher's Annotated Edition** with page-by-page, point-of-use teaching suggestions.
- **Expanded Assessment CD-ROM** with *ExamView® Pro* Test Generator now contains more questions types and assessment options to easily allow teachers to create tests and quizzes.

Distinctive Features of *Grammar in Context*

Students are prepared for academic assignments and everyday language tasks.

Discussions, readings, compositions, and exercises involving higher-level critical thinking skills develop overall language and communication skills.

Students expand their knowledge of American topics and culture.

The readings in *Grammar in Context* help students gain insight into and enrich their knowledge of American culture and history. Students gain ample exposure to the practicalities of American life, such as writing a résumé, dealing with telemarketers, junk mail, and getting student internships. Their new knowledge helps them adapt to everyday life in the U.S.

Students learn to use their new skills to communicate.

The exercises and Expansion Activities in *Grammar in Context* help students learn English while practicing their writing and speaking skills. Students work together in pairs and groups to find more information about topics, to make presentations, to play games, and to role-play. Their confidence in using English increases, as does their ability to communicate effectively.

Grammar in Context Student Book Supplements

Audio Program

* Audio CDs and Audio Tapes allow students to listen to every reading in the book as well as selected dialogs.

More Grammar Practice Workbooks

* Workbooks can be used with *Grammar in Context* or any skills text to learn and review the essential grammar.
* Great for in-class practice or homework.
* Includes practice on all grammar points in *Grammar in Context.*

Teacher's Annotated Edition

* New component offers page-by-page answers and teaching suggestions.

Assessment CD-ROM with *ExamView® Pro* Test Generator

* Test Generator allows teachers to create tests and quizzes quickly and easily.

Interactive CD-ROM

* CD-ROM allows for supplemental interactive practice on grammar points from *Grammar in Context.*

Split Editions

* Split Editions provide options for short courses.

Instructional Video/DVD

* Video/DVD offers teaching suggestions and advice on how to use *Grammar in Context.*

Web Site

* Web site gives access to additional activities and promotes the use of the Internet.

Welcome to *Grammar in Context, Fourth Edition*

Students learn more, remember more, and use language more effectively when they learn grammar in context.

Grammar in Context, Fourth Edition connects grammar with rich, American cultural context, providing learners of English with a useful and meaningful skill and knowledge base.

An **Audio Program** allows students to hear the readings and dialogs, and provides an opportunity to practice their listening skills.

Readings on American topics such as Instant Messaging, eBay, and The AIDS Ride present and illustrate the grammatical structure in an informative and meaningful context.

Grammar charts offer clear explanations and provide contextualized examples of the structure.

Language Notes refine students' understanding of the target structure.

CHARLIE CHAPLIN

Before You Read
1. Have you ever heard of Charlie Chaplin?
2. Have you ever seen a silent movie? Do you think a silent movie can be interesting today?

Charlie Chaplin, 1889–1977

Read the following article. Pay special attention to participles used as adjectives.

Charlie Chaplin was one of the greatest actors in the world. His **entertaining** silent movies are still popular today. His **amusing** character "Little Tramp" is well **known** to people throughout the world. Chaplin had an **amazing** life. His idea for this poor character in worn-out shoes, round hat, and cane probably came from his childhood experiences.

Born in poverty in London in 1889, Chaplin was abandoned by his father and left in an orphanage by his mother. He became **interested** in acting at the age of five. At ten, he left school to travel with a British acting company. In 1910, he made his first trip to America. He was talented, athletic, and **hard-working**, and by 1916 he was earning $10,000 a week. He was the **highest-paid** person in the world at that time. He produced, directed, and wrote the movies he starred in.

Even though "talkies" came out in 1927, he didn't make a movie with sound until 1940, when he played a comic version of the **terrifying** dictator, Adolf Hitler.

As Chaplin got older, he faced **declining** popularity as a result of his politics and personal relationships. After he left the U.S. in 1952, Chaplin was not allowed to re-enter because of his political views. He didn't return to the U.S. until 1972, when he was given a special Oscar for his lifetime of **outstanding** work.

Did You Know?
Reagan did not want Chaplin to be allowed back into the U.S.

Passive Voice; Participles Used as Adjectives; *Get* + Participles and Adjectives   77

2.10 | Participles Used as Adjectives to Show Feelings

The participles of a verb can be used as adjectives.

Chaplin's movies **entertained** people.
(verb)

His movies are **entertaining**.
(present participle)

People are **entertained**.
(past participle)

Chaplin's movies **interest** us.
(verb)

Chaplin's movies are **interesting**.
(present participle)

We are **interested** in his movies.
(past participle)

Examples	Explanation
The movie **bored** us. (*bored* = verb)	In some cases, both the present participle (a) and the past participle (b) of the same verb can be used as adjectives.
a. The movie was **boring**. I left the **boring** movie before it was over.	The present participle (a) gives an active meaning. The movie *actively* caused a feeling of boredom.
b. Some people were **bored**. The **bored** people got up and left.	The past participle (b) gives a passive meaning. It describes the receiver of a feeling. The people were bored by the movie.
a. Chaplin had an **interesting** life. He was poor and then became very rich. b. I am **interested** in Chaplin. I would like to know more about him.	A person can cause a feeling in others or he can receive a feeling. Therefore, a person can be both *interesting* and *interested*, *frightening* and *frightened*, etc.
a. The main character in *Friday the Thirteenth* is a **frightening** man. b. I was **frightened** and couldn't sleep after seeing the movie.	
The book is **interesting**. (never *interested*) The movie is **entertaining**. (never *entertained*)	An object (like a book or a movie) doesn't have feelings, so a past participle cannot be used to describe an object.

Language Notes:

1. The following pictures show the difference between a *frightening* man and a *frightened* man.

a. The man is frightening the children. = He's a *frightening* man.

b. The man is frightened by the robber. = He's a *frightened* man.

78   Lesson 2

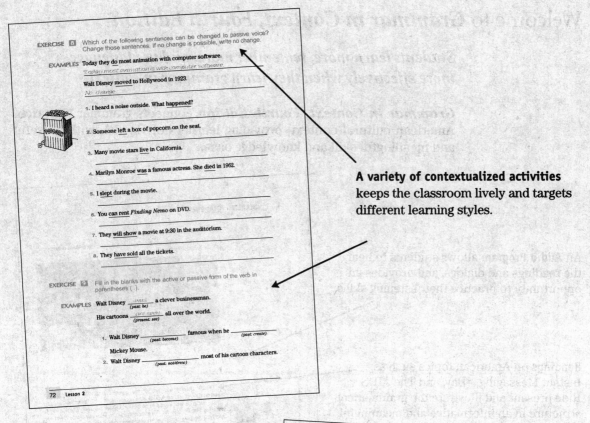

EXERCISE 8 Which of the following sentences can be changed to passive voice? Change those sentences. If no change is possible, write no change.

EXAMPLES Today they do most animation with computer software.
Today most animation is done with computer software.

Walt Disney moved to Hollywood in 1923.
No change.

1. I heard a noise outside. What happened?

2. Someone left a box of popcorn on the seat.

3. Many movie stars live in California.

4. Marilyn Monroe was a famous actress. She died in 1962.

5. I slept during the movie.

6. You can rent *Finding Nemo* on DVD.

7. They will show a movie at 9:30 in the auditorium.

8. They have sold all the tickets.

EXERCISE 9 Fill in the blanks with the active or passive form of the verb in parentheses ( ).

EXAMPLES Walt Disney _____was_____ a clever businessman.
(past: be)

His cartoons ___are seen___ all over the world.
(present: see)

1. Walt Disney _____ famous when he _____
(past: become)   (past: create)
Mickey Mouse.

2. Walt Disney _____ most of his cartoon characters.
(past: not/draw)

72   Lesson 2

A variety of contextualized activities keeps the classroom lively and targets different learning styles.

A **Summary** provides the lesson's essential grammar in an easy-to-reference format.

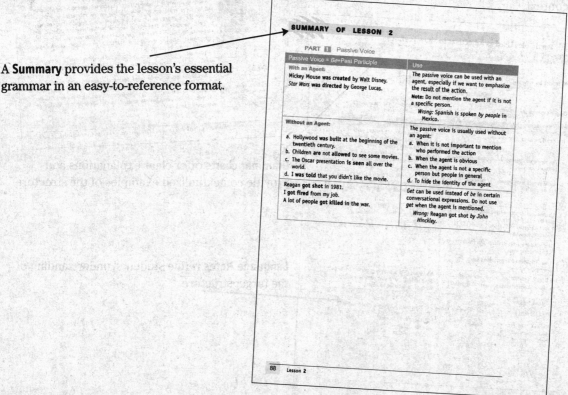

SUMMARY OF LESSON 2

PART 1   Passive Voice

Passive Voice = Be+Past Participle	Use
With an Agent: Mickey Mouse **was created** by Walt Disney. *Star Wars* **was directed** by George Lucas.	The passive voice can be used with an agent, especially if we want to emphasize the result of the action. **Note:** Do not mention the agent if it is not a specific person. *Wrong:* Spanish is spoken *by people* in Mexico.
Without an Agent: a. Hollywood **was built** at the beginning of the twentieth century. b. Children **are not allowed** to see some movies. c. The Oscar presentation **is seen** all over the world. d. I **was told** that you didn't like the movie.	The passive voice is usually used without an agent: a. When it is not important to mention who performed the action b. When the agent is obvious c. When the agent is not a specific person but people in general d. To hide the identity of the agent
Reagan got shot in 1981. I **got fired** from my job. A lot of people **got killed** in the war.	*Get* can be used instead of *be* in certain conversational expressions. Do not use *get* when the agent is mentioned. *Wrong:* Reagan got shot *by John Hinckley.*

88   Lesson 2

Editing Advice gives students pre-writing practice by alerting them to common errors.

Test/Review at the end of each lesson provides a chance to review and/or assess the grammar from the lesson.

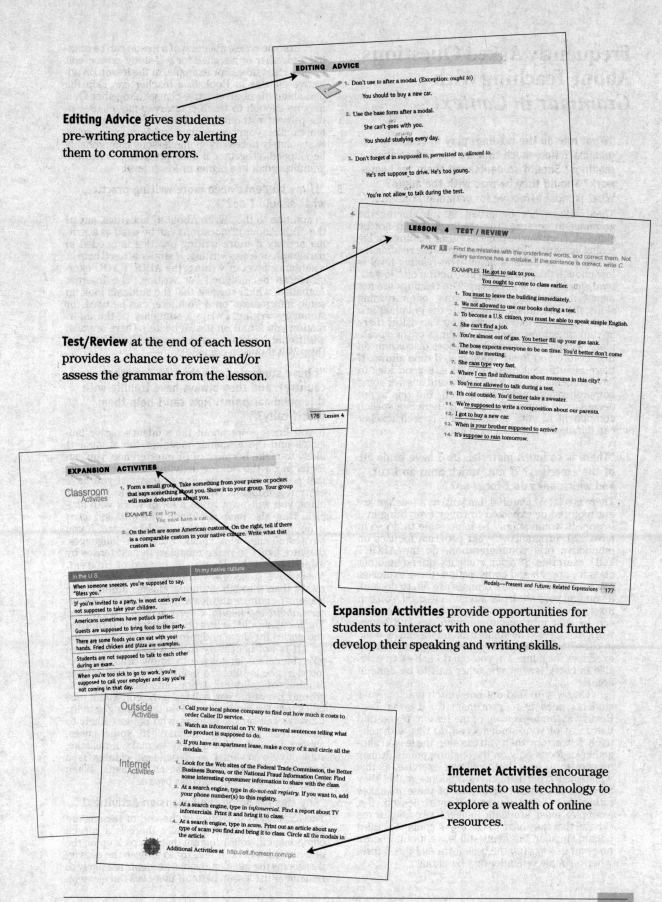

EDITING ADVICE

1. Don't use *to* after a modal. (Exception: *ought to*)

   You should to buy a new car.

2. Use the base form after a modal.

   She can't goes with you.

   You should studying every day.

3. Don't forget *d* in *supposed to, permitted to, allowed to*.

   He's not suppose to drive. He's too young.

   You're not allow to talk during the test.

176 Lesson 4

LESSON 4 TEST / REVIEW

PART 1 Find the mistakes with the underlined words, and correct them. Not every sentence has a mistake. If the sentence is correct, write *C*.

EXAMPLES He got to talk to you.

You ought to come to class earlier. *C*

1. You must to leave the building immediately.
2. We not allowed to use our books during a test.
3. To become a U.S. citizen, you must be able to speak simple English.
4. She can't find a job.
5. You're almost out of gas. You better fill up your gas tank.
6. The boss expects everyone to be on time. You'd better don't come late to the meeting.
7. She cans type very fast.
8. Where I can find information about museums in this city?
9. You're not allowed to talk during a test.
10. It's cold outside. You'd better take a sweater.
11. We're supposed to write a composition about our parents.
12. I got to buy a new car.
13. When is your brother supposed to arrive?
14. It's suppose to rain tomorrow.

Modals—Present and Future; Related Expressions **177**

EXPANSION ACTIVITIES

Classroom Activities

1. Form a small group. Take something from your purse or pocket that says something about you. Show it to your group. Your group will make deductions about you.

   EXAMPLE car keys
   You must have a car.

2. On the left are some American customs. On the right, tell if there is a comparable custom in your native culture. Write what that custom is.

In the U.S.	In my native culture
When someone sneezes, you're supposed to say, "Bless you."	
If you're invited to a party, in most cases you're not supposed to take your children.	
Americans sometimes have potluck parties. Guests are supposed to bring food to the party.	
There are some foods you can eat with your hands. Fried chicken and pizza are examples.	
Students are not supposed to talk to each other during an exam.	
When you're too sick to go to work, you're supposed to call your employer and say you're not coming in that day.	

Outside Activities

1. Call your local phone company to find out how much it costs to order Caller ID service.
2. Watch an infomercial on TV. Write several sentences telling what the product is supposed to do.
3. If you have an apartment lease, make a copy of it and circle all the modals.

Internet Activities

1. Look for the Web sites of the Federal Trade Commission, the Better Business Bureau, or the National Fraud Information Center. Find some interesting consumer information to share with the class.
2. At a search engine, type in *do-not-call registry*. If you want to, add your phone number(s) to this registry.
3. At a search engine, type in *infomercial*. Find a report about TV infomercials. Print it and bring it to class.
4. At a search engine, type in *scam*. Print out an article about any type of scam you find and bring it to class. Circle all the modals in the article.

Additional Activities at http://elt.thomson.com/gic

Expansion Activities provide opportunities for students to interact with one another and further develop their speaking and writing skills.

Internet Activities encourage students to use technology to explore a wealth of online resources.

Welcome to *Grammar in Context*

Frequently Asked Questions About Teaching with *Grammar in Context*

1. "What role do the readings play in teaching grammar? How much time do I spend on the readings? Should students read them for homework? Should they be read with the audio? What is most effective for grammar students?"

The readings are important in introducing the grammar in context. The readings should not be skipped. They can be done as either readings or listening activities. To save class time, the reading/listening can be done at home. The reading level is low enough that classroom instruction on "how to" read should not be necessary. The readings are not meant to challenge and improve one's reading skills; they are meant to illustrate the grammar in a stimulating context. In class, you can ask if there are any questions about the readings or the vocabulary within. There can be a short discussion on the "Before You Read" questions, if time allows. If there is sufficient class time, it is a good idea to have students listen to the audio and answer some comprehension questions as well. But this is not necessary in a grammar class. If there is a speech component in your program, the speech teacher can handle the listening activity.

2. "There is so much material. Do I have to do all of the exercises? If not, which ones do I cut, and which ones do I focus on?"

There is a lot of material, but you, as a teacher, are not required or expected to cover everything in a lesson. It would simply be impossible to do so in most ESL programs. If your program focuses on interactive oral communication, do the ABOUT YOU exercises. If your students attend another class for speech and conversation, these exercises can be skipped. These exercises are fun to do, and, if you find your students' attention waning, you can insert one of these activities. The other exercises can be split into classroom exercises and homework exercises. The simpler exercises can be done in class, leaving the more challenging combination exercises for home. Or, you can do half of an exercise in class, leaving the other half to be done at home.

One way to find out how much practice your students need is to give them the Lesson Test/Review at the *beginning* of the lesson. If you find that most of your students can do this with relatively few errors, then you can skip the lesson altogether or focus only on the sticking points. It may be enough to only do the editing exercise, as this will reveal typical mistakes students make; they may just need to be reminded of these mistakes rather than being taught the entire lesson. For example, most students in level two and three "know" that they have to use the -s ending for third person singular, but many still leave it out. There's no point in *teaching* the base form and the -s form when a simple reminder may be enough.

In some cases, a section of a lesson can be omitted altogether or assigned for self-study extra credit to save class time. For example, in the lesson on adjective clauses in Book 3, a teacher can skip the part about the nonrestrictive clauses altogether. Or it may be enough to teach contrary-to-fact clauses in the present without getting into the past or mixed tenses. Let your curriculum guide you on what is absolutely necessary. Some lessons can probably be skipped altogether if your program teaches the grammar point in a higher or lower level.

3. "If my students need more writing practice, what should I do?"

In addition to the "Write About it" activities, any of the "Talk About it" questions can be used as a writing activity if more writing practice is needed in paragraph or essay writing. If students need help at a sentence level of writing, the ABOUT YOU exercises can be assigned for writing. The Internet Activities, which suggest that the students look up some information on a Web site, can be used for summary writing. (Write a summary of the information you found on the Web site.) There are also additional writing activities on the Web site (http://elt.thomson.com/gic).

4. "I have students from the UAE (or other country), and they always have trouble with this grammar point. How can I help them specifically?"

If you know a lot about the student's native language and the grammar mistakes the student is likely to make because of L1 interference, you can focus in on the editing activities that correct for that particular mistake. For example, if you have eastern Europeans (Russians, Poles, etc.) in your class, you will want to do a lot of work with articles. They also have confusion with *that* and *what* in noun clauses: *I know what you like pizza.* If you have students who speak Ethiopian languages, they are likely to make mistakes in past tenses by using the verb *be: He was go* instead of *He went.* Near-native speakers who learned English by ear rather than through grammar classes are likely to leave off endings and leave out words: *I am concern about my health. I been here for two hours.* The focus should be less on grammatical terms and categories for them and more on error correction.

It is not necessary to be a native speaker of your students' languages to know what kind of interference is likely to occur; if you have a large number of students from one language background, over time you will learn the consistent mistakes that are made. When I do the editing activity, I always call on the student who is most likely to make that particular mistake. In some cases, almost all students are likely to make a mistake; subject/verb reversal in dependent clauses is a common mistake for almost all students: *When arrived the teacher, the class began.*

5. "Any tips for doing the Expansion Activities?"

The Expansion Activities at the end of lessons are fun, but time is limited. Ideally, there is a speech component in your program that can pick up on the oral activities here. If not, try to choose the activity that seems the most enjoyable. Students are likely to remember the lesson better if there is a fun element.

LESSON

1

GRAMMAR
The Present Perfect
The Present Perfect Continuous[1]

CONTEXT : The Law
Job Résumé and Cover Letter
Where Have All the Jobs Gone?
The *Occupational Outlook Handbook*

1

Lesson Overview

GRAMMAR

1. Activate students' prior knowledge. Ask students to name as many verb tenses in English as they can.
2. Write *past, present, future* on the board. Ask: *Which word means what is happening right now?* (present) *Which one means what happened before now?* (past) *Which one means what is going to happen next?* (future)
3. Ask: *What tenses will we study in this lesson?* (present perfect and present perfect continuous) Give several examples of sentences using the present perfect and present perfect continuous tenses (*I have worked here since 2002. I have been teaching English for six years.*). Have volunteers give examples. Write several examples for each tense on the board.

CONTEXT

1. Ask: *What will we learn about in this lesson?* (jobs, looking for a job, résumés, cover letters) Elicit students' prior knowledge. Ask: *What do you know about looking for a job in the United States?*
2. Have students share their knowledge and personal experiences.

Photo

1. Direct students' attention to the photo. Ask: *Where are the people?* (in a warehouse) *Who are they?* (employees of the warehouse)
2. Have students share their workplace experiences.

⏱ To save class time, have students do the Test/Review at the end of the lesson, or administer a lesson test generated from the Assessment CD-ROM with *ExamView® Pro*. Skip sections of the lesson that students have already mastered. You may also assign some sections for self-study for extra credit.

Expansion

Theme The topic for this lesson can be enhanced with the following ideas:

1. Résumés and cover letters, either your own or samples (from résumé books, the Internet, etc.)
2. Job applications from several workplaces
3. Job aptitude inventories
4. Timelines showing the history of an industry, company, or other employment-related series of events

1.1 | An Overview

1. Have students look at grammar chart **1.1**. Ask: *What is the subject of a sentence?* (the person or thing the sentence is about) *What is the complement?* (words or phrases that follow the verb)
2. Ask: *What differences do you see between the present perfect and the present perfect continuous?* (the present perfect uses the past participle; the present perfect continuous uses *been* and the present participle)
3. Have students look at the sentences you wrote on the board earlier. Have them identify the subject, tense, and complement in each sentence.
4. Review the example sentences in the grammar chart. Say that we use these tenses for actions that began in the past and continue to, or are still important in, the present.

Job Résumé and Cover Letter (Reading)

1. Have students look at the photo. Ask: *Where are the people?* (in a hotel) *Who is the man behind the counter?* (the front desk clerk) *Who is the other man?* (a hotel guest) *What is happening?* (The guest is checking out of the hotel. The clerk is handing the guest his bill.)
2. Have students look briefly at the résumé on page 3. Ask: *What is this document called?* (a job résumé) *Who wrote this document?* (Daniel Mendoza) *Why?* (to help him look for a job) Have students make predictions about what will be included in the résumé.
3. Preteach any essential vocabulary words your students may not know, such as *summary, professional, coordinated, proficiency, Master of Science, Bachelor of Science,* and *affiliation.*

BEFORE YOU READ

1. Have students discuss the questions in pairs. Try to pair students of different cultures together.
2. Ask a few volunteers to share their answers with the class.

To save class time, skip "Before You Read" or have students prepare answers for homework ahead of time.

1.1 | An Overview

Present Perfect Tense			
Subject	*Has / Have*	Past Participle	Complement
Daniel	has	had	several jobs.
We	have	been	in the U.S. for three years.
You	have	seen	the manager.

Present Perfect Continuous Tense				
Subject	*Has / Have*	*Been*	Present Participle	Complement
Daniel	has	been	living	in the U.S. for many years.
We	have	been	studying	English for three years.
You	have	been	working	hard this year.

JOB RÉSUMÉ AND COVER LETTER

Before You Read
1. Do you have a résumé?
2. Do you have a job now? What do you do? How did you find your job?
3. How can you find and apply for a new job?

Read the résumé and cover letter on the next two pages. In the cover letter, pay special attention to the present perfect and present perfect continuous tenses.

2   Lesson 1

Grammar Variation

Have students make a chart similar to grammar chart **1.1** in their notebooks. Have students write the sentences from the board in their charts.

Culture Note

Explain that *résumé* is a French word used in English to mean a short history or summary of a person's experience, education, and qualifications for a job, usually when the person is applying for a new job. Ask: *Do you know any other words used for* résumé? *(curriculum vitae, vita, CV)*

Daniel Mendoza
6965 Troy Avenue
Chicago, Illinois 60659
773-555-1946
E-mail: dmendoza@srv.com

Summary: Hotel professional with proven management skills and successful experience in improving operations, upgrading properties, building teams, and improving customer relations.

Professional Experience

- Developed sales/marketing plans geared towards business travelers
- Handled customer relations, correspondence, and communication
- Coordinated, organized, and supervised front desk operations and food service
- Assisted guests and groups in planning tours and arranging transportation, restaurant accommodations, and reservations
- Designed and maintained hotel Web site
- Managed hotel bookkeeping

Employment History

2004–Present	Town and Country Hotel, Front Office Manager	Chicago, IL
2002–2004	Mid-Town Hotel, Bookkeeper (part-time)	Evanston, IL
1998–2002	Travel Time Hotel, Front Desk Clerk (part-time)	Champaign, IL
1994–1998	Hotel Mendoza, Front Desk Clerk	Mexico City, Mexico

Technical Proficiencies

- Microsoft Office (Word, Excel, Access, PowerPoint); Quicken; Photoshop; Dreamweaver; Flash; Fireworks; Front Page; HTML

Education

- Master of Science: Business Administration, Northwestern University, 2004
- Bachelor of Science: Business Administration, University of Illinois, 2002
- Degree in Hotel Management: National University of Mexico, 1998

Professional Affiliations

- Travel & Tourism Research Association (TTRA)
- Association of Travel Marketing Executives (ATME)
- International Association of Convention & Visitor Bureaus (IACVB)

1. Have students first read the text silently. Tell them to pay special attention to the dates in the reading. Then play the audio and have students read along silently.
2. Check students' comprehension. Ask questions such as: *When did Daniel start working in a hotel?* (1994) *How many hotels has Daniel worked in?* (four) *How many universities has Daniel attended?* (three) *What are some things Daniel has done in his jobs?* (supervised front desk operations, helped guests, designed a hotel Web site)

The Present Perfect; The Present Perfect Continuous   3

Reading Variation

To practice listening skills, have students first listen to the audio alone. Ask a few comprehension questions. Repeat the audio if necessary. Then have them open their books and read along as they listen to the audio.

Reading Glossary

affiliation: membership in or belonging to an organization

Bachelor of Science (B.S.) or **Bachelor of Arts (B.A.):** a university degree, usually after four years of study

coordinate: manage; direct; supervise

Master of Science (M.S.) or **Master of Arts (M.A.):** a university degree following a Bachelor's degree, usually after two more years of study

professional: (as a noun) person who has a life-long career, usually with education or training; (as an adjective) job or career; by occupation

proficiency: skill or ability

summary: a short version of a longer document or description, including only the most important information

Reading (cont.)

3. Have students look briefly at the cover letter on page 4. Ask: *What is this document called?* (a cover letter) *Who wrote this document?* (Daniel Mendoza) *Why?* (to apply for a job at the Paradise Hotel) Have students make predictions about what will be included in the cover letter.

4. Preteach any essential vocabulary words your students may not know, such as *fluent, plus, aspect,* and *now that.*

5. Have students first read the text silently. Tell them to pay special attention to the present perfect and present perfect continuous tenses. Then play the audio and have students read along silently.

6. Check students' comprehension. Ask questions such as: *How many languages does Daniel speak?* (two—Spanish and English)

🕐 To save class time, have students do the reading for homework ahead of time.

EXERCISE 1

1. Tell students that this exercise is about Daniel's work experience and his job search. Have students read the direction line. Ask: *What do* true *and* false *mean?* (correct and not correct)

2. Model the exercise. Direct students to the examples in the book. Ask: *Is the first example true or false?* (true) *How do you know?* (In the cover letter, Daniel says that he worked in his family's hotel in high school.) *Is the second example true or false?* (false) *How do you know?* (Daniel doesn't mention California in his résumé.)

3. Have students complete the rest of Exercise 1 individually. Then have them check their answers in pairs and confirm their answers with information from the reading. Circulate and observe the pair work. If necessary, check the answers as a class.

4. Assess students' performance. If necessary, review grammar chart 1.1 on page 2.

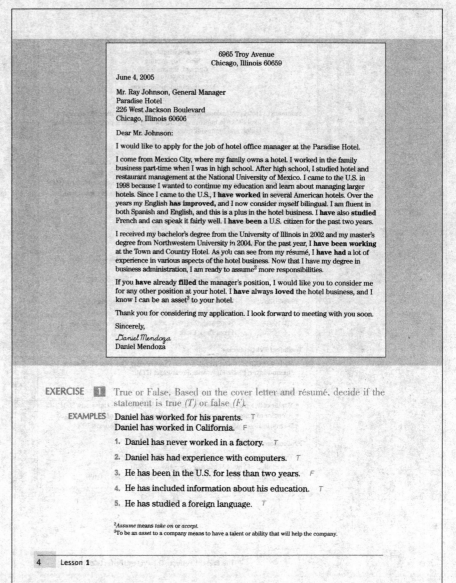

6965 Troy Avenue
Chicago, Illinois 60659

June 4, 2005

Mr. Ray Johnson, General Manager
Paradise Hotel
226 West Jackson Boulevard
Chicago, Illinois 60606

Dear Mr. Johnson:

I would like to apply for the job of hotel office manager at the Paradise Hotel.

I come from Mexico City, where my family owns a hotel. I worked in the family business part-time when I was in high school. After high school, I studied hotel and restaurant management at the National University of Mexico. I came to the U.S. in 1998 because I wanted to continue my education and learn about managing larger hotels. Since I came to the U.S., I **have worked** in several American hotels. Over the years my English **has improved,** and I now consider myself bilingual. I am fluent in both Spanish and English, and this is a plus in the hotel business. I **have** also **studied** French and can speak it fairly well. I **have been** a U.S. citizen for the past two years.

I received my bachelor's degree from the University of Illinois in 2002 and my master's degree from Northwestern University in 2004. For the past year, I **have been working** at the Town and Country Hotel. As you can see from my résumé, I **have had** a lot of experience in various aspects of the hotel business. Now that I have my degree in business administration, I am ready to assume[2] more responsibilities.

If you **have** already **filled** the manager's position, I would like you to consider me for any other position at your hotel. I **have** always **loved** the hotel business, and I know I can be an asset[3] to your hotel.

Thank you for considering my application. I look forward to meeting with you soon.

Sincerely,

Daniel Mendoza
Daniel Mendoza

EXERCISE 1 True or False. Based on the cover letter and résumé, decide if the statement is true *(T)* or false *(F)*.

EXAMPLES Daniel has worked for his parents. *T*
Daniel has worked in California. *F*

1. Daniel has never worked in a factory. *T*
2. Daniel has had experience with computers. *T*
3. He has been in the U.S. for less than two years. *F*
4. He has included information about his education. *T*
5. He has studied a foreign language. *T*

[2]*Assume* means *take on* or *accept.*
[3]To be an *asset* to a company means to have a talent or ability that will help the company.

4　Lesson 1

Reading Variation

To practice listening skills, have students first listen to the audio alone. Ask a few comprehension questions. Repeat the audio if necessary. Then have them open their books and read along as they listen to the audio.

Reading Glossary

aspect: part; area
fluent: able to speak a language easily; able to express all of one's ideas in a language
now that: because something is now true; because of something that has changed
plus: (as a noun) an advantage; an extra skill

Culture Note

Explain that a résumé usually includes contact information, work history, educational history, and organizational memberships.

6. He has had experience in several hotels. *T*

7. He has already met with Mr. Johnson. *F*

8. He has included his age and marital status in his résumé. *F*

1.2 | The Present Perfect Tense—Forms

Affirmative

Subject	*Have*	Past Participle	Complement	Explanation
I	have	been	in the U.S. for three years.	To form the present perfect, use:
You	have	had	a lot of experience.	*I, you, we, they,* plural noun + *have* + past participle.
We	have	written	a job résumé.	
They	have	seen	the application.	
My parents	have	given	me encouragement.	

Subject	*Has*	Past Participle	Complement	Explanation
My sister	has	been	a doctor for two years.	To form the present perfect, use:
She	has	had	a lot of experience.	*he, she, it,* singular noun + *has* + past participle.
My father	has	visited	me in the U.S.	
It	has	rained	a lot this month.	

Negative

Subject	*Have / has*	Not	Past Participle	Complement	Explanation
He	has	not	found	a job.	To form the negative, put *not* between the auxiliary verb (*has / have*) and the past participle.
The teacher	has	not	given	a test yet.	
We	have	not	done	Lesson Two yet.	
I	have	not	applied	for a job lately.	

With an Adverb

Subject	*Have / has*	Adverb	Past Participle	Complement	Explanation
You	have	never	worked	in a factory.	You can put an adverb between the auxiliary verb (*have / has*) and the past participle.
We	have	always	wanted	to learn English.	
They	have	already	found	a job.	
My uncle	has	just	arrived	in the U.S.	
The plane	has	probably	arrived	already.	

The Present Perfect; The Present Perfect Continuous   5

Grammar Variation

Copy several of the sentences from the grammar chart on the board so that the parts line up in columns, as in the chart, but mix the order of the complements. Have students figure out which complement is correct for each sentence.

1.2 | The Present Perfect Tense—Forms

1. Have students find examples of the present perfect tense in the cover letter on page 4. Ask students to use the sentences to give information about Daniel (do not include the sentence using the present perfect continuous or the sentence about the manager's position). Write the six sentences on the board. For example, write: *He has worked in several American hotels.* Below that, write: *Over the years, his English has improved.* Make sure the subject, *has,* and the participle line up. Ask: *What do all of the sentences have?* (subject + *has* + past participle) Write these labels above the sentences.

2. Ask students to make sentences about themselves similar to the ones on the board.

3. Have students look at the first two sections of grammar chart 1.2. Ask: *What is the difference between the first chart and the second chart?* (subjects in the second chart are *he* and *she*, with *has* instead of *have*) Review the example sentences.

4. Review the third section of chart **1.2.** Ask: *Where do we put* not *in a negative sentence with the present perfect tense?* (between the auxiliary verb and the past participle) Review the example sentences.

5. Review the fourth section of chart **1.2.** Ask: *Where do we put adverbs in a sentence with the present perfect tense?* (between the auxiliary verb and the past participle) If necessary, review the meanings of adverbs in the chart, such as *just* (a very short time ago) and *probably* (likely, almost surely). Review the example sentences.

1. Tell students that this exercise is about looking for a job in the United States. Have students read the direction line. Ask: *What words do we underline?* (present perfect tense verbs)
2. Direct students to the underlined words in the first line. Ask: *Why is* have been *underlined?* (it is a present perfect tense verb form)
3. Have students complete Exercise 2 individually. Then have them check their answers in pairs. Circulate and observe the pair work. If necessary, check the answers as a class.
4. Assess students' performance. If necessary, review grammar chart **1.2** on page 5.

1.3 | The Past Participle

1. Have students cover up the grammar chart. Draw a three-column chart, similar to the one on page 7, on the board. Have volunteers call out the base forms of 10 or 12 verbs; write (or have a student write) the verbs on the board in the left column. Then elicit the past form of each verb; write (or have a student write) the past forms in the middle column. Finally, elicit the past participle of each verb; write (or have a student write) the past participles in the right column.
2. Ask students to say what they observe about the rules for forming past forms and past participles. If students have difficulty, say: *With regular verbs, the past form and the past participle are the same, and end in -d or -ed. With irregular verbs, the past participle is sometimes the same as the past form and sometimes different, and can be formed in several ways.*
3. Have students look at grammar chart **1.3**. Review the verbs and explanations.

EXERCISE 2 Read the following paragraph. Underline all present perfect tense verbs.

I am looking for a job. I <u>have been</u> an electrical engineer for the past eight years. I arrived in the U.S. a few months ago, so I <u>have not had</u> much experience with American job interviews. I don't think my English is a problem, because I <u>have studied</u> English since I was a child. But in my country, I found a job right after I graduated from college. I stayed at the same job until I came here. The process of finding a job in the U.S. is a bit different. To learn about this process, I <u>have used</u> the Internet. I <u>have</u> also <u>taken</u> a course at a nearby college on how to prepare for an interview. So far, I <u>have had</u> three interviews, but I <u>have not done</u> well on them. I hope that each interview will help me do better on the next one, and soon I hope to find a good job.

1.3 | The Past Participle

The past participle is the third form of the verb. We use it to form the present perfect tense.

Forms			Explanation
Regular Verbs			
BASE FORM	PAST FORM	PAST PARTICIPLE	The past participle of regular verbs ends in -ed. The past form and the past participle of regular verbs are the same.
work	worked	worked	
improve	improved	improved	
Irregular Verbs			
BASE FORM	PAST FORM	PAST PARTICIPLE	The past participle of irregular verbs is sometimes the same as the past form and sometimes different.
have	had	had	
leave	left	left *(same as past)*	
write	wrote	written	
drive	drove	driven *(different from past)*	

6   Lesson **1**

Expansion

Exercise 2 Tell students that the writer has had some good experiences and some problems looking for a job. Have students tell you which things that have happened to the writer are good (his or her English is good) and which things are problems (he or she hasn't done well on interviews).

For some verbs, the past participle is different from the past form.		
Base Form	Past Form	Past Participle
become	became	become
come	came	come
run	ran	run
blow	blew	blown
draw	drew	drawn
fly	flew	flown
grow	grew	grown
know	knew	known
throw	threw	thrown
swear	swore	sworn
tear	tore	torn
wear	wore	worn
break	broke	broken
choose	chose	chosen
freeze	froze	frozen
speak	spoke	spoken
steal	stole	stolen
begin	began	begun
drink	drank	drunk
ring	rang	rung
sing	sang	sung
sink	sank	sunk
swim	swam	swum
arise	arose	arisen
bite	bit	bitten
drive	drove	driven
ride	rode	ridden
rise	rose	risen
write	wrote	written
be	was / were	been
do	did	done
eat	ate	eaten
fall	fell	fallen
forget	forgot	forgotten
forgive	forgave	forgiven
get	got	gotten
give	gave	given
go	went	gone
lie	lay	lain
mistake	mistook	mistaken
prove	proved	proven (or proved)
see	saw	seen
shake	shook	shaken
show	showed	shown (or showed)
take	took	taken

Note: For an alphabetical list of irregular past tenses and past participles, see Appendix M.

1.3 | The Past Participle (*cont.*)

4. Ask students to cover up page 7. Have students work in groups. Ask each group to quickly list ten verbs on a piece of paper. When each group has ten verbs, ask groups to write the past form and past participle for each verb as quickly as they can. When every group is finished, have groups exchange lists and check each other's work. The group that finishes first with correct forms is the winner.

5. Have students look at the grammar chart on page 7. Review the forms in the chart. Ask students to try to identify the pattern in each of the first six sections of the chart.

6. Draw students' attention to the last section of the chart. Tell students that irregular past participles like these do not conform to rules and must be learned individually.

7. Have students look at the alphabetical list of irregular verbs in Appendix M.

Expansion

Grammar Brainstorm with students methods for memorizing irregular past forms and past participles. Possibilities include quizzing one another, using flashcards, filling in worksheets on paper or on grammar quiz Web sites, and computer software.

1. Tell students that this exercise provides practice with irregular participles. Have students read the direction line. Ask: *What are you going to write?* (past participles)
2. Model the exercise. Do #1 with the class. Ask a volunteer to give an answer.
3. Have students complete the exercise individually. Then have them check their answers in pairs. Circulate and observe the pair work. If necessary, check the answers as a class.
4. If necessary, review grammar chart **1.3** on pages 6–7.

1. Tell students that this exercise is about Daniel's experiences looking for a job. Have students read the direction line.
2. Direct students to the example. Ask: *What is has sent?* (the present perfect tense of *send*)
3. Have students complete the exercise individually. Then have them check their answers in pairs. Circulate and observe the pair work. If necessary, check the answers as a class.
4. Assess students' performance. If necessary, review grammar chart **1.3** on pages 6–7.

🕐 To save class time, have students do half of the exercise in class and complete the other half for homework. Or assign the entire exercise for homework.

EXERCISE 3 Fill in the blanks with the past participle of the verb shown.

1. eat	eaten	11. find	found	21. ride	ridden
2. go	gone	12. listen	listened	22. hid	hidden
3. read	read	13. think	thought	23. look	looked
4. drive	driven	14. live	lived	24. leave	left
5. work	worked	15. make	made	25. fall	fallen
6. see	seen	16. write	written	26. feel	felt
7. believe	believed	17. grow	grown	27. choose	chosen
8. swim	swum	18. begin	begun	28. lose	lost
9. drink	drunk	19. be	been	29. do	done
10. steal	stolen	20. study	studied	30. understand	understood

EXERCISE 4 Fill in the blanks with the correct form of the verb in parentheses ( ) to form the present perfect tense.

EXAMPLE Daniel ___has sent___ three résumés this week.
(send)

1. He ___has had___ several interviews.
(have)

2. Mr. Johnson ___has gottten___ a letter from Daniel.
(get)

3. There ___have been___ many applicants for the job.
(be)

4. Daniel's parents ___have always been___ in the hotel business.
(always/be)

5. Daniel ___has recently graduated___ from college.
(recently/graduate)

6. I ___have read___ Daniel's résumé.
(read)

7. Daniel ___has never worked___ as a programmer.
(never/work)

8. He ___has sent___ his résumé to many companies.
(send)

9. The company ___has interviewed___ 20 applicants so far.
(interview)

8   Lesson 1

Expansion

Exercise 4 Have students use Daniel's résumé and cover letter to write three additional sentences about experiences Daniel has had.

1.4 | The Present Perfect—Contractions

Examples	Explanation
I've had a lot of experience. **It's** been hard to find a job. **There's** been a change in my plans.	We can make a contraction with subject pronouns and *have* or *has*. I have = I've He has = He's You have = You've She has = She's We have = We've It has = It's They have = They've There has = There's
My father**'s** taught me a lot about the hotel business. The manager**'s** had many job applications.	Most singular nouns can contract with *has*.
I **haven't** had experience in the restaurant business. Mr. Johnson **hasn't** called me.	Negative contractions: *have not = haven't* *has not = hasn't*

Language Note:
The *'s* in *he's*, *it's*, and *there's* can mean *has* or *is*. The word following the contraction will tell you what the contraction means.
   He*'s* working. = He **is** working
   He*'s* worked. = He **has** worked.

EXERCISE ☐4 Make a contraction with the subject to fill in the blanks. Use *hasn't* or *haven't* for negative consequences.

EXAMPLE   You _'ve_____ already sent your application.

1. I _'ve_____ applied for many jobs.

2. We _'ve_____ seen Daniel's résumé.

3. His father _'s_____ never come to the U.S.

4. It _'s_____ been hard for Daniel to find a job.

5. Daniel _'s_____ had several jobs so far.

6. Mr. Johnson (not) _____hasn't_____ looked at all the résumés.

7. They (not) _____haven't_____ made a decision yet.

Expansion

Exercise 5 Have students look back at Exercise 2 on page 6 and change the underlined present perfect tense verbs and their subjects to contractions whenever possible.

1.4 | The Present Perfect—Contractions

1. Have students cover the grammar chart. Demonstrate how to form contractions of *have* and *has*. On the board, write: *I have had some interesting jobs.* Ask: *How can we make a contraction with the subject and* have*?* (subject + *'ve*) Write: *I've had some interesting jobs.* Elicit contractions for *you, he, she,* and *they.* Write them on the board.

2. Demonstrate how to form the negative. Write: *I have had a lot of different jobs.* Ask: *How can we make this sentence negative?* (add *not* after *have*) Write: *I have not had a lot of different jobs.* Then ask: *How can we make a contraction?* (*have* + *n't*) Write: *I haven't had a lot of different jobs.*

3. Have students look at grammar chart **1.4.** Review the forms and explanations in the chart.

4. Draw students' attention to the Language Note. Write additional examples on the board, such as *She's arriving soon* and *She's arrived.* Ask students what each *'s* means. (*has* or *is*)

EXERCISE 5

1. Tell students that this exercise is about job hunting. Have students read the direction line.

2. Model the exercise. Direct students to the example in the book. Ask: *What is* you've *a contraction of?* (*you* + *have*) Then do #1 with the class. Ask a volunteer to give an answer.

3. Have students complete Exercise 5 individually. Then have them compare their answers in pairs. Finally, check the answers as a class.

4. Assess students' performance. If necessary, review grammar chart **1.4.**

1.5 | The Present Perfect—Question Formation

1. Have students cover up grammar chart **1.5**. Elicit from students two sentences about things Daniel has done, such as *Daniel has worked in Mexico and in the U.S.* and *Daniel has applied for three jobs.* Write the sentences on the board. Elicit the help of volunteers to write questions about the statements, such as *Where has Daniel worked?* and *How many jobs has Daniel applied for?*

2. Have students look at the first section of grammar chart **1.5**. Review the example sentences in the grammar chart. Draw students' attention to the difference between questions with *what* as subject (*What has happened?*) and questions with *what* and a subject (*What have you learned?*).

3. Have students look at the second section of grammar chart **1.5**. Review the example sentences. If appropriate, give students an opportunity to ask you questions beginning with *Why haven't you . . .*, such as *Why haven't you given us a test?*

EXERCISE 6

CD 1, Track 2

1. Tell students that this exercise is a job interview with Daniel. Have students read the direction line.
2. Model the exercise. Direct students to the first line in the interview.
3. Have students complete Exercise 6 individually. Have them compare their answers in pairs. Finally, check the answers as a class.
4. Assess students' performance. If necessary, review grammar chart **1.5**.

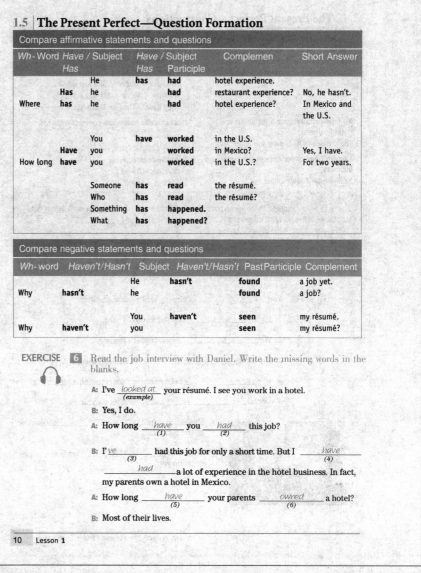

1.5 | The Present Perfect—Question Formation

Compare affirmative statements and questions

Wh- Word	Have / Subject Has	Have / Subject Has	Past Participle	Complement	Short Answer
		He	has	had	hotel experience.	
	Has	he		had	restaurant experience?	No, he hasn't.
Where	has	he		had	hotel experience?	In Mexico and the U.S.
		You	have	worked	in the U.S.	
	Have	you		worked	in Mexico?	Yes, I have.
How long	have	you		worked	in the U.S.?	For two years.
		Someone	has	read	the résumé.	
		Who	has	read	the résumé?	
		Something	has	happened.		
		What	has	happened?		

Compare negative statements and questions

Wh- word	Haven't/Hasn't	Subject	Haven't/Hasn't	Past Participle	Complement
		He	hasn't	found	a job yet.
Why	hasn't	he		found	a job?
		You	haven't	seen	my résumé.
Why	haven't	you		seen	my résumé?

EXERCISE 6 Read the job interview with Daniel. Write the missing words in the blanks.

A: I've _looked at_ your résumé. I see you work in a hotel.
    (example)

B: Yes, I do.

A: How long __have__ you __had__ this job?
           (1)   (2)

B: I'__ve__ had this job for only a short time. But I ____
     (3)   __have__
                                                    (4)
    ___had___ a lot of experience in the hotel business. In fact, my parents own a hotel in Mexico.

A: How long __have__ your parents __owned__ a hotel?
           (5)   (6)

B: Most of their lives.

10   Lesson 1

Exercise 6 Variation

To provide practice with listening skills, have students close their books and listen to the audio. Repeat the audio as needed. Ask comprehension questions, such as: *Where does Daniel work?* (in a hotel) *How long has he had this job?* (only for a short time) Then have students open their books and complete Exercise 6.

Expansion

Exercise 6 Have students write three questions they could ask a classmate, using the present perfect tense. Have students exchange papers and answer each other's questions.

Exercise 6 Put students in groups. Ask groups to write several questions they have been asked in job interviews in the U.S. Ask groups to share their lists with the class.

A: _____*Have*_____ you seen your parents recently?
         (7)

B: My mother _____*has*_____ _____*comelbeen*_____ to the U.S. a few
              (8)   (9)

times to see me. But my father _____*has*_____ never
                                        (10)

_____*comelbeen*_____ here because someone has to stay at the
         (11)

hotel all the time. He's _____*told*_____ me many times, "When
                               (12)

you are an owner of a business, you don't have time for vacations."
But I don't want to be an owner now. I just want a job as a manager.

_____*Have*_____ you filled the position yet?
         (13)

A: No, I haven't. I' *ve* _____ already _____*interviewed*_____
                        (14)   (15)

several people and will interview a few more this week. When we
make our decision, we'll let you know.

1.6 | Uses of the Present Perfect Tense—An Overview

Examples	Explanation
Daniel **has been** in the U.S. since 1998. He **has had** his present job for a short time. He **has** always **loved** the hotel business.	The action started in the past and **continues** to the present.
He **has sent** out 20 résumés so far. He **has had** three interviews this month.	The action **repeats** during a period of time that started in the past and continues to the present.
Mr. Johnson **has received** Daniel's letter. He **hasn't made** his decision yet. **Has** Daniel ever **worked** in a restaurant? Daniel **has studied** French, and he speaks it fairly well.	The action occurred at an **indefinite time** in the past. It still has importance to a present situation.

EXERCISE **7**   Fill in the blanks with appropriate words to complete each
statement. (Refer to the résumé and cover letter on pages 3–4.)

EXAMPLE   Daniel has included _____*his phone number*_____ in his résumé.

1. Daniel has been _____*in the U.S.*_____ since 1998.
2. He has had his job at the Town and Country Hotel for _____*one year*_____
3. He has studied in _____*three*_____ universities.
4. He has never worked in _____*Answers will vary.*_____

The Present Perfect; The Present Perfect Continuous   **11**

1.6 | Uses of the Present Perfect Tense—An Overview

1. Have students cover up grammar chart **1.6.** Ask: *When do we use the present perfect tense?* Elicit answers; discuss the idea that we use the present perfect tense for actions that began in the past and continue to, or are still important in, the present.
2. Have students uncover and review grammar chart **1.6.**
3. Review the example sentences. Tell students that they will study each of these uses of the present perfect tense in detail in this lesson.

EXERCISE 7

1. Tell students that this exercise is about Daniel's experience and qualifications. Have students read the direction line. Ask: *Where will you get the information?* (from Daniel's résumé and cover letter)
2. Model the exercise. Direct students to the example in the book. Then do #1 with the class. Ask a volunteer to give an answer. Tell students that different answers are possible.
3. Have students complete Exercise 7 individually. Then have them compare their answers in pairs. Finally, check the answers as a class.
4. Assess students' performance. If necessary, review grammar chart **1.6.**

Culture Note

At job interviews in the U.S., interviewers often ask applicants if there are any questions they would like to ask. It is a good idea to come prepared to ask one or two questions. Questions such as *Are there any training opportunities?* are appropriate. Direct questions about money, such as *When can I get a raise?* are usually not considered appropriate.

Grammar Variation

After students have reviewed the example sentences in the grammar chart, have them go back to Exercise 2 on page 6 and identify which explanation applies to each underlined present perfect tense verb in the exercise.

5. He has had a lot of experience in ____hotels____.

6. In his résumé, he has not included ___Answers will vary.___

7. So far, he has worked in ____four____ hotels.

8. He hasn't ____found____ a job yet.

9. Why ___hasn't he found___ a job yet?

10. ____Has he____ ever organized group transportation?

11. Daniel has ____done____ hotel bookkeeping.

12. ___Has he___ finished his master's degree yet? Yes, he ___has___.

13. How long ___has he been___ a member of a travel association? He's been a member for several years.

14. How many times ____has he____ worked with business travelers?

15. He has lived in ____three____ cities in Illinois. He has never ____lived____ in New York.

16. He has ____studied____ French and speaks it fairly well.

Expansion

Exercise 7 Have students convert #1 through #5 to questions. If students have difficulty, review grammar chart **1.5** on page 10.

1.7 | The Present Perfect with Continuation from Past to Present

We use the present perfect tense to show that an action or state started in the past and continues to the present.

Examples	Explanation
a. Daniel has been a U.S. citizen **for two years.**	a. Use *for* + amount of time.
b. His parents have been in the hotel business **all their lives.**	b. Omit *for* with an expression beginning with *all*.
c. He has had his job **for the past few years.**	c. You can say *for the past / last* + time period.
Daniel has been in the U.S. **since 1998.** I have been a citizen **since last March.**	Use *since* + date, month, year, etc. to show when the action began.
I have had my car **since** I *came* **to the U.S.** He has wanted to manage hotels **ever since** he *was* **a teenager.**	Use *since* or *ever since* to begin a clause that shows the start of a continuous action. The verb in the *since*-clause is in the simple past tense.
Daniel went to Chicago in 2002. He has been there **ever since.** My grandfather gave me a watch when I was five years old. I have had it **ever since.**	You can put *ever since* at the end of the sentence. It means "from the past time mentioned to the present."
How long has he been in the U.S.? **How long** have you known your best friend?	Use *how long* to ask an information question about length of time.
Daniel has **always** loved the hotel business. I have **always** wanted to start my own business. I have **never** liked cold weather.	We use the present perfect with *always* and *never* to show that an action began in the past and continues to the present.
Daniel has **never** written to Mr. Johnson before.	We often use *before* at the end of a *never* statement.

```
                 1998              now
  past  ←————————————————————————————————————→ future
               ┌─────────────────┐
               │ He has been in the │
               │ U.S. since 1998    │
               └─────────────────┘
```

EXERCISE 8 Fill in the blanks with the missing word(s). Not every sentence needs a word.

EXAMPLE   I'*ve*_____ been in the U.S. for three years.

1. Daniel has _*been/lived*_ in Chicago _*since*_ 2002.

2. How _*long*_ has he been in the U.S.? He'*s*___ been in the U.S. _*for*_ many years.

Variation

Exercise 8 Have students work in groups to make a timeline of Daniel's life, using the information in the Examples column of chart **1.7.** Have groups use a horizontal line for their timeline, vertical marks for each date, and horizontal arrows between vertical marks for periods of time.

1.7 | The Present Perfect with Continuation from Past to Present

1. Have students cover grammar chart **1.7.** Ask: *What two time words do we often use with the present perfect tense? (since, for) How are they different? (Since* is used with a specific time or event, e.g., *1998, Monday, I came to the U.S.; for* is used with a period of time, e.g., *five years, 10 minutes,* or *a long time.)*

2. Draw a timeline on the board. Make a vertical mark at the right and label it for this year. Ask: *When did Daniel come to the U.S.?* (1998) Make a vertical mark in the center of the timeline; label it *1998.* Draw an arrow between the two marks. Say: *Daniel came to the U.S. in 1998, and he's still here today. He has been here since 1998.* Ask: *How long has Daniel loved the hotel business?* (always) Draw an arrow from the far left of the timeline to this year's mark. Say: *Daniel has always loved the hotel business, and he still loves it today.*

3. Have students look at grammar chart **1.7.** Review the example sentences and explanations carefully.

4. Make several statements about yourself, similar to those in the grammar chart, such as *I have had this job for two years* or *I have had long hair ever since I was a teenager.* Ask students to make statements about themselves.

EXERCISE 8

1. Tell students that this exercise is about Daniel's life in the past and in the present. Have students read the direction line. Point out that some sentences do not need a word in the blank.

2. Model the exercise. Direct students to the example in the book. Then do #1 with the class. Ask a volunteer to give the answer.

3. Have students complete Exercise 8 individually. Then have them compare their answers in pairs. Finally, check the answers as a class.

1. Tell students that this exercise is about their personal thoughts and interests. Have students read the direction line.
2. Direct students to the example in the book.
3. Have students read the prompts silently and think about their answers for a few minutes. Encourage students to make notes. Then have students interview each other in pairs. Say: *Now read the requests to your partners and write down their answers.* Ask volunteers to share their answers with the class.

🕐 To save class time, have students do this exercise in writing for homework.

1. Tell students that this exercise is about their experiences and lives. Have students read the direction line.
2. Direct students to the examples in the book. Model the exercise with your own answers.
3. Have students complete the exercise individually. Ask volunteers to share their answers with the class.

🕐 To save class time, have students do half of the exercise in class and complete the other half for homework. Or assign the entire exercise for homework.

---

3. He found a good job in 2004. He _____has_____ worked at the same job ever _____since_____.

4. He has worked at a hotel ever _____since_____ he _____graduated_____ from high school.

5. His parents have lived in Mexico _____∅_____ all their lives.

6. Daniel has had his apartment for the _____last_____ ten months.

7. _____Have_____ you always worked in a hotel?

8. _____How_____ long have you had your job?

9. Daniel _____has_____ been in the U.S. since he _____graduated_____ from college.

10. He has wanted to manage a hotel _____ever/∅_____ since he was a child.

EXERCISE 9 ABOUT YOU Make statements with *always*.

EXAMPLE Name something you've always thought about.
I've always thought about my future.

Answers will vary.
1. Name something you've always disliked.
2. Name something you've always liked.
3. Name something you've always wanted to own.
4. Name something you've always wanted to do.
5. Name something you've always believed in.

EXERCISE 10 ABOUT YOU Write four **true** sentences telling about things you've always done or ways you've always been. Share your answers with the class.

EXAMPLES *I've always worked very hard.*
I've always been very thin.

1. _____ Answers will vary. _____
2. _____
3. _____
4. _____

Expansion

Exercises 9 and 10 Have students work in groups. Have each group make a list of new answers to some of the prompts in each exercise, such as *Minh has always wanted to learn to ice skate.* Have groups share their most interesting answers with the class.

EXERCISE 11 ABOUT YOU Make statements with *never*.

EXAMPLE   Name a machine you've never used.
I've never used a sewing machine.

Answers will vary.
1. Name a food you've never tried.
2. Name something you've never drunk.
3. Name something you've never owned.
4. Name something you've never done.
5. Name something your teacher has never done in class.
6. Name a job you've never had.

EXERCISE 12 ABOUT YOU Write four **true** sentences telling about things you've never done but would like to. Share your answers with the class.

EXAMPLES   *I've never gone to Paris, but I'd like to.*
I've never flown in a helicopter, but I'd like to.

1. _____ Answers will vary. _____
2. _____
3. _____
4. _____

1.8 | Negative Statements with *Since, For,* and *In*

We can use *since, for,* and *in* with negative statements.

Examples	Explanation
Daniel hasn't worked in Mexico **since** 1998.	He worked in Mexico until 1998. He stopped in 1998.
Daniel hasn't seen his parents **for** three years. OR Daniel hasn't seen his parents **in** three years.	He saw his parents three years ago. That was the last time. In negative statements, you can use either *for* or *in*.
Language Note: We often say in ages to mean "in a long time." Hi Daniel! I haven't seen you **in ages!**	

Expansion

Exercises 9, 10, 11 and 12 Have students work in groups. Have each group make a list of answers to the exercises for their group, such as *Roberto has always liked folk music.* Collect the groups' papers. Design a 4 × 4 or 5 × 5 grid with interesting answers from students in each box, such as:

has always liked folk music	

In a later class, copy the grid on the board. Have students each make a copy. Then have students circulate around the room, asking *Have you always liked folk music?* until they find someone who answers *yes*. Students write that person's name in that box. The first student with a name in every box is the winner.

1. Tell students that this exercise is about their own experiences. Have students read the direction line.
2. Direct students to the example in the book. Model the exercise with your own answers.
3. Have students read the prompts silently and think about their answers for a few minutes. Encourage students to make notes. Then have students interview each other in pairs. Say: *Now read the requests to your partner and write down his or her answers.* Ask volunteers to share their answers with the class.

🕐 To save class time, have students do this exercise in writing for homework.

1. Tell students that this exercise is about their thoughts and interests. Have students read the direction line.
2. Direct students to the examples in the book. Point out the phrase *but I'd like to*; say that this phrase does not require a verb at the end of the sentence.
3. Have students complete the exercise individually. Ask volunteers to share their answers with the class.
4. Assess students' performance. If necessary, review grammar chart 1.6.

🕐 To save class time, have students do half of the exercise in class and complete the other half for homework. Or assign the entire exercise for homework.

1.8 | Negative Statements with *Since, For,* and *In*

1. Have students review the examples and explanations in the grammar chart.
2. Draw students' attention to *in*. Note that *in* can be used in the same way as *for* in negative statements with the present perfect tense, but not with positive statements.

1. Tell students that this exercise is about their personal histories. Have students read the direction line.
2. Direct students to the examples in the book. Read the request in the example to the class. Ask one or two volunteers to respond.
3. Give students a few minutes to think about their answers. Then have pairs of students interview each other to complete the exercise.

1.9 | The Present Perfect vs. the Simple Present

1. Have students review the examples and explanations in the grammar chart.
2. Draw students' attention to the name of the present perfect tense. Say: *Even though this tense has* present *in its name, it is not used to talk just about the present. It's used to connect the past to the present.*

1. Tell students that this exercise is a series of conversations between two friends. Have students read the direction line.
2. Model the exercise. Direct students to the examples in the book. Then do #1 with the class.
3. Have students complete Exercise 14 individually. Then have them check their answers in pairs by practicing the dialogues. Circulate and observe the pair work. If necessary, check the answers as a class.

EXERCISE 13 ABOUT YOU Name something.

EXAMPLE Name something you haven't eaten in a long time.
I haven't eaten fish in a long time.

Answers will vary.

1. Name someone you haven't seen in a long time.
2. Name a place you haven't visited in a long time.
3. Name a food you haven't eaten in a long time.
4. Name a subject you haven't studied since you were in high school.
5. Name a game you haven't played since you were a child.
6. Name something you haven't had time to do since you started to study English.

1.9 | The Present Perfect vs. the Simple Present

Examples	Explanation
I **am** in the U.S. now. I **have been** in the U.S. *for* two years.	The simple present refers only to the present time. The present perfect with *for*, *since*, *always*, or *never* connects the past to the present.
He **has** a car. He **has had** his car *since* March.	
I **love** my job. I **have** always **loved** my job.	
I **don't like** to wake up early. I **have** never **liked** to wake up early.	

EXERCISE 13 Fill in the blanks to complete the following conversations. Some answers may vary.

EXAMPLES A: Do you have a computer?
B: Yes, I do.
A: How long ___have you___ had your computer?
B: I '*ve had*___ my computer for three years.

1. A: Do you have a car?
   B: Yes, I do.
   A: How long ___have you had___ your car?
   B: I '*ve had*___ my car for six months.

2. A: Is your sister married?
   B: Yes, she is.
   A: How long ___has she been___ married?
   B: She '*s been married*___ since 1995.

16   Lesson 1

Expansion

Exercise 13 Ask students to interview a new partner and record their partners' answers. Ask volunteers to share their partners' answers with the class.

3. A: Do you have a bike?

   B: Yes, I _____ do _____.

   A: How long _____ have you had _____ your bike?

   B: I _____ 've had _____ my bike _____ for _____

      the past _____ Answers will vary. _____

4. A: Do you want to learn English?

   B: Of course, I do.

   A: _____ How _____ long _____ have you wanted _____ to learn English?

   B: I _____ 've wanted _____ to learn English ever since I

      _____ was _____ a child.

5. A: Does your mother have a driver's license?

   B: Yes, she _____ does _____.

   A: How _____ long has she had _____ her driver's license?

   B: She _____ 's had _____ her driver's license since _____ Answers will vary. _____

6. A: _____ Is _____ Ms. Foster your teacher?

   B: Yes, she is.

   A: How long _____ has she been _____ your teacher?

   B: For _____ Answers will vary. _____

7. A: Does your school have a computer lab?

   B: Yes, it _____ does _____.

   A: _____ How _____ long _____ has it had _____ a computer lab?

   B: It _____ has had _____ a computer lab since _____ Answers will vary. _____

8. A: Do you know your friend Mark very well?

   B: Yes, I _____ do _____.

   A: How long _____ have you known _____ each other?

   B: We _____ 've known _____ each other ever

      _____ since _____ we _____ were _____ in elementary school.

9. A: _____ Does _____ your son _____ have _____ a cell phone?

   B: Yes, he _____ does _____.

   A: How long _____ has he had it /one _____ ?

   B: He bought one when he started going to college and he

      _____ has had _____ it ever _____ since _____

      _____ Answers will vary. _____

The Present Perfect; The Present Perfect Continuous   **17**

Expansion

Exercise 14 Have students work in pairs to write conversations with the simple present and present perfect tenses. Pairs should use the conversations in Exercise 14 as a model. Have pairs perform their conversations for the class.

EXERCISE 15

1. Tell students that this exercise is a chance to ask you some questions about your experience and interests. Have students read the direction line. Ask: *What word do we add to the questions? (always)*
2. Direct students to the example in the book. Review the example, and then ask a volunteer to answer #1.
3. Have students complete the exercise in writing individually. Ask volunteers to ask you the questions. Answer the questions, if possible contrasting the simple present with the present perfect (e.g., *English is easy for me now, but English hasn't always been easy for me.*).

🕐 To save class time, have students write out the questions for homework. Students may then ask you the questions in class. Or they may work in pairs and role-play the conversation between the teacher and a student.

EXERCISE 16

1. Tell students that this exercise is a chance to ask questions about each other. Have students read the direction line.
2. Direct students to the example in the book. Review the example, and then ask a volunteer to answer #1 with you.
3. Have students complete the exercise in pairs. Circulate and observe the pair work. If possible, participate in the exercise as you circulate
4. Assess students' performance. If necessary, review grammar charts **1.5** on page 10 and **1.9** on page 16.

🕐 To save class time, have students do half of the exercise. Or if students do not need speaking practice, the entire exercise may be skipped.

---

10. A: Do you like to dance?
    B: Yes, I _____ *do* _____ .
    A: _____ *Have* _____ you always _____ *liked* _____ to dance?
    B: Yes. I've always liked to dance. But my wife _____ *has* _____ never _____ *liked* _____ to dance.

EXERCISE **15** Read each statement about your teacher. Then ask your teacher a question beginning with the words given. Include *always* in your question. Your teacher will answer.

EXAMPLE You're a teacher. Have you _____ *always been a teacher?* _____
No. I was a nurse before I became a teacher. I've only been a teacher for five years.

1. You teach adults. Have you *always taught adults?*
2. You work with ESL students. Have you *always worked with ESL students?*
3. You're a teacher at this school. Have you *always been a teacher at this school?*
4. You think about grammar. Have you *always thought about grammar?*
5. English is easy for you. Has English *always been easy for you?*
6. Your last name is _____ . Has your last name _____ *always been . . . ?*
7. You live in this city. Have you *always lived in this city?*
8. You like teaching. Have you *always liked teaching?*

EXERCISE **16** ABOUT YOU Ask a present tense question. Another student will answer. If the answer is *yes*, ask *Have you always . . . ?*

EXAMPLE A: Are you interested in learning English?
B: Yes, I am.
A: Have you always been interested in learning English?
B: Yes. I've been interested in learning English since I was a small child.

Answers will vary.
1. Are you a good student?
2. Do you wear glasses?
3. Do you like to travel?
4. Are you interested in politics?
5. Do you like American movies?
6. Are you an optimist?
7. Do you think about your future?

18   Lesson 1

Exercise 15 Variation

Complete steps 1, 2, and 3 above. Divide the class in half. Have one half ask you the questions and the other half record your answers. Pair students from the two halves to check their work.

Expansion

Exercise 16 Have students write their own lists of present tense statements about themselves. Have students exchange lists and interview each other. Circulate and observe the pair work. Give help when needed. Ask students to report interesting activities to the class (e.g., *Katrina has always been good at languages.*).

8. Do you live in an apartment?

9. Are you a friendly person?

10. Do you use credit cards?

11. Do you work hard?

12. Do you want a college degree?

WHERE HAVE ALL THE JOBS GONE?

Before You Read

1. Do you know anyone who has lost a job?

2. Do you think some jobs are more secure than others? Which ones?

 Read the following article. Pay special attention to the present perfect and present perfect continuous tenses.

Have you ever **called** an American company for service and **gotten** an answer from someone in another country? Many American companies **have been moving** customer service and technology jobs overseas. Using workers in other countries is called "outsourcing." India is the leading country used in outsourcing. Why India? Because India has a high level of information technology (IT) workers, and many Indians speak English well.

(continued)

The Present Perfect; The Present Perfect Continuous   19

Expansion

Theme The topic for this lesson can be enhanced with the following ideas:

1. Classified advertising section from a local newspaper
2. An article from a newspaper or a magazine about job security, new jobs, job losses, or new businesses opening in your area

Reading Variation

To practice listening skills, have students first listen to the audio alone. Ask a few comprehension questions. Repeat the audio if necessary. Then have students open their books and read along as they listen to the audio.

Culture Note

Ask students if they have ever bought items or services that list a phone number or Web site customers can use if they have questions or complaints about the product or service. Ask volunteers to describe their experiences with customer service phone lines, or describe your own.

Where Have All the Jobs Gone? (Reading)

1. Have students look at the photo. Ask: *Where are the people?* (in a call center) *What are they doing?* (talking on the phone and using computers) *What country do you think this is?* (India)
2. Preteach any vocabulary words your students may not know, such as *customer service, information technology, cut, manufacturing, call center, go to, benefit, overseas,* and *impact.*

BEFORE YOU READ

1. Activate students' prior knowledge about job security. Ask: *What does* job security *mean?* (knowing that you will not lose your job) *When do jobs become less secure?* (when there are changes in the economy)
2. Have students discuss the questions in pairs. Try to pair students of different cultures.
3. Ask a few volunteers to share their answers with the class.

To save class time, skip "Before You Read" or have students prepare answers for homework ahead of time.

Reading CD 1, Track 3

1. Have students first read the text silently. Tell them to pay special attention to the present perfect and present perfect continuous tense verbs in the reading. Then play the audio and have students read along silently.
2. Check students' comprehension. Ask questions such as: *What is outsourcing?* (using workers in another country) *Who has been benefiting from outsourcing?* (U.S. companies and employees in some other countries) *Who has not?* (some U.S. workers)

To save class time, have students do the reading for homework ahead of time.

Discuss the information about wages with the class. Ask: *Why do you think the wages are so different in these two countries?*

1.10 | The Present Perfect Continuous

1. Have students find sentences from the reading on pages 19 and 20 that contain present perfect continuous tense verbs. Write several of the sentences on the board. For example, write: *Many American companies have been moving customer service and technology jobs overseas.*

2. Have students review the example sentences in the first section (Forms) of the grammar chart. Ask: *How is the present perfect continuous tense different in form from the present perfect tense?* (The present perfect continuous uses *been* and the present participle with *-ing*.)

3. Draw students' attention to the Language Notes. Explain how to form the negative and negative contractions.

4. Ask volunteers to make statements about themselves using the present perfect continuous tense; give one or two examples of your own (e.g., *I have been living at the same address for five years.*).

5. Have students review the example sentences and explanations in the second section (Uses) of the grammar chart.

Why **has** this shift[4] **occurred?** By using lower wages[5] overseas, U.S. companies can cut labor costs by 25% to 40%. In addition, service is available to customers 24 hours a day by phone or online.

Years ago, American companies started using foreign labor for manufacturing jobs. But college educated workers thought they had nothing to worry about. Then companies started to move call centers abroad[6] to cut costs. But more and more of the jobs going abroad today go to highly skilled, educated people.

Many American workers who **have been working** at the same company for years are losing their jobs. Many educated workers **have had** to take jobs at a lower pay or get more training or education. While U.S. companies **have been benefiting** from outsourcing, American workers **have been losing**. While some American workers in some fields **have become** more insecure about their jobs, educated Indian workers **have become** more confident.

U.S. companies are expected to send 3.4 million jobs overseas by 2015. The U.S. government **has been studying** the impact of outsourcing on the American economy.

Did You Know?
A computer programmer in the U.S. who makes $80,000 a year can be replaced with an Indian worker at $11,000 a year.

1.10 | The Present Perfect Continuous

Forms				
Subject	*Have / Has*	*Been*	Past Participle	Complement
I	have	been	working	in a call center.
Workers	have	been	losing	their jobs.
You	have	been	getting	more job experience.
Companies	have	been	moving	jobs overseas.
The U.S.	has	been	studying	the effects of outsourcing.
Daniel	has	been	working	at a hotel.
He	has	been	living	in the U.S.

Language Notes:
1. To form the negative, put *not* between *have* or *has* and *been*.
   You **have *not*** been studying.   She **has *not*** been working hard.
2. We can make contractions for negative forms.
   have not = haven't   has not = hasn't

[4] A *shift* is a change.
[5] *Wages* means pay for a job.
[6] *Abroad* means beyond the boundaries of one's country.

20   Lesson 1

Reading Glossary

benefit: gain; become better; get an advantage
call center: telephone customer service office
customer service: jobs related to helping customers in a store or by phone or e-mail
cut: reduce, lower
go to: be given to
impact (noun): result, changes made by
information technology (IT): work related to developing and using computers and technology to make information available
manufacturing: making things for customers or businesses
overseas: in another country, usually a country separated from yours by a sea or ocean

---

Uses

Examples	Explanation
I **have been working** at the same job since 2001. American companies **have been using** workers in foreign countries for many years.	We use the present perfect continuous to talk about an action that started in the past and continues to the present. We use *for* and *since* to show the time spent at an activity.
He **has been working** as a programmer for the past few years. OR He **has worked** as a programmer for the past few years.	With some verbs, we can use either the present perfect or the present perfect continuous with actions that began in the past and continue to the present. There is very little difference in meaning.
He's working now. → He **has been working** for the past eight hours.	If the action is still happening, use the present perfect continuous, not the present perfect.
I have **always** worked as a programmer. I have **never** had another career.	Do not use the continuous form with *always* and *never*.
Americans **have become** insecure about their jobs. (*Not: have been becoming*) I **have known** my friend for 10 years. (*Not: I have been knowing*)	We do not use a continuous tense with nonaction verbs. (See below for a list of nonaction verbs.)

Action: I **have been thinking** *about* starting a new career.
Nonaction: I **have** always **thought** *that* an educated person can find a good job.
	Think can be an action or nonaction verb, depending on its meaning.
	    Think about = action verb
	    Think that = nonaction verb

Nonaction: Daniel **has had** a lot of experience in hotels. Action: Daniel **has been having** problems finding a job.	*Have* is usually a nonaction verb. However, *have* is an action verb in these expressions: *have experience, have a hard time, have a good time, have difficulty, have trouble.*

Nonaction verbs:

like	prefer	understand	taste	have (for possession)
love	know	remember	feel	
hate	believe	see	seem	
want	think(that)	smell	cost	
need	care (about)	hear	owm	

EXERCISE 17 Fill in the blanks with the present perfect continuous form of the verb in parentheses ( ).

EXAMPLE   Bob _____has been working_____ as a programmer for the past ten years.
                             (work)

1. His company _____has been sending_____ jobs to India since 2001.
                           (send)

2. He and his coworkers _____have been worrying_____ about losing their jobs.
                                  (worry)

1. Tell students that this exercise is about an employee who is worried about his job security. Have students read the direction line. Ask: *What form of the verb do we write?* (present perfect continuous)
2. Direct students to the example in the book.
3. Have students complete the exercise in writing individually. Ask volunteers to share their answers with the class.

Grammar Variation

Have students match the verbs in boldface in the reading on pages 19 and 20 to the appropriate explanation in the grammar chart.

1. Tell students that this exercise is a series of conversations between two friends. Have students read the direction line.
2. Model the exercise. Direct students to the example in the book. Point out the photo of the man playing the guitar. Repeat the conversation with a volunteer. Then do #1 with the class.
3. Have students complete Exercise 18 individually. Then have them check their answers in pairs by practicing the dialogues. Circulate and observe the pair work. If necessary, check the answers as a class.

🕐 To save class time, have students do half of the exercise in class and complete the other half for homework. Or assign the entire exercise for homework.

---

3. Bob __'s been taking__ classes for the past two years to get retrained.
      (take)

4. He __'s been reading__ a lot of articles about outsourcing.
      (read)

5. He __'s been working__ on his résumé for the past two days.
      (work)

6. His friends __have been advising__ him to see a job counselor.
      (advise)

EXERCISE 18 Fill in the blanks in the following conversations. Some answers may vary.

EXAMPLE A: Do you __play__ a musical instrument?
B: Yes. I play the guitar.
A: How long __have__ you __been playing__ the guitar?
B: I __'ve been playing__ the guitar since I __was__ ten years old.

1. A: Do you work with computers?
B: Yes, I do.
A: How long __have__ you __been working__ with computers?
B: I __'ve been working__ with computers since 1998.

2. A: __Does__ your father study English?
B: Yes, he does.
A: How long __has__ he been __studying English__ ?
B: He __'s been studying__ since he __camelmoved__ to the U.S.

3. A: Does your teacher have a lot of experience?
B: Yes, she __does__ .
A: How long __has she been__ teaching English?
B: She __'s been teaching__ English for 20 years.

Expansion

Exercise 18 Put students in groups. Ask students to make true or false statements about themselves, using the present perfect continuous. Have the other students guess if the statements are true or false. Model an example. Say: *I've been thinking about learning Japanese. True or false?* Students guess if you're telling the truth.

4. A: Do you wear glasses?

   B: Yes, I _____do_____.

   A: How long _____have you been wearing_____ glasses?

   B: I _'ve been wearing_____ glasses since I ____was____ in high school.

5. A: _____Do_____ your parents live in this city?

   B: Yes, they _____do_____.

   A: How long _____have they been living_____ in this city?

   B: For ___Answers will vary.___.

6. A: Is your roommate preparing to take the TOEFL[7] test?

   B: Yes, he _____is_____.

   A: How long _____has he been preparing_____ to take this test?

   B: Since _____Answers will vary._____.

7. A: _____Are_____ you studying for your chemistry test?

   B: Yes, I _____am_____.

   A: How long _____have you been studying_____ for your chemistry test?

   B: I _____have been studying_____ all week.

8. A: _____Is_____ your roommate using the computer now?

   B: Yes, he _____is_____.

   A: How long _____has he been using_____ it?

   B: He started to use it when he woke up and ___he has been using___ it ever ____since____.

9. A: _____Is_____ it raining now?

   B: Yes, it _____is_____.

   A: How long _____has it been raining_____?

   B: It _____has been raining_____ since ___Answers will vary.___.

10. A: _____Is_____ she talking about her children again?

    B: Yes, she _____is_____.

    A: How long _____has she been talking_____ about them?

    B: For the past _____Answers will vary._____.

---

[7]The *TOEFL* is the Test of English as a Foreign Language. Many U.S. colleges and universities require foreign students to take this test.

Expansion

Exercise 18 Have pairs of students choose one of the dialogues in Exercise 18. Ask them to write two additional sentences to continue the dialogue. Ask volunteers to present their dialogues to the class.

1. Tell students that this exercise is about things that are happening around them right now. Have students read the direction line. Ask: *What kind of statement do we make?* (a true statement)
2. Direct students to the example in the book. Then have a volunteer complete #1.
3. Have students complete the exercise individually. Ask for volunteers to share their answers with the class.
4. Assess students' performance. If necessary, review grammar chart **1.10** on pages 20 and 21.

To save class time, have students do half of the exercise in class and complete the other half for homework. Or assign the entire exercise for homework.

EXERCISE **25** ABOUT YOU Fill in the blanks to make a true statement about the present. Then make a statement that includes the past by changing to the preset perfect continuous form with *for* or *since*.

EXAMPLE I'm studying _____ *French.*
___ *I've been studying French for two semesters.*

1. I work in / as _____
   _____ *I've been working . . .*

2. I live _____
   _____ *I've been living . . .*

3. I attend _____
   _____ *I've been attending . . .*

4. I'm trying to _____
   _____ *I've been trying to . . .*

5. I'm wearing _____
   _____ *I've been wearing . . .*

6. The teacher is explaining _____
   _____ *He/She has been explaining . . .*

7. I'm thinking about _____
   _____ *I've been thinking about . . .*

8. I'm using _____
   _____ *I've been using . . .*

9. I'm studying _____
   _____ *I've been studying . . .*

10. We're using _____
    _____ *We've been using . . .*

Exercise 19 Variation

Have students complete only the first statement in each item in the exercise. Then have students work in pairs. Have one partner read his or her statement, and the other partner ask a question with *how long* (e.g., *How long have you been working at that job?*). Have students use the present perfect continuous in their answers.

1.11 | The Present Perfect vs. the Simple Past

Examples	Explanation
How long **have** you **had** your present car? I**'ve had** my present car for three months. How long **have** you **been working** at your present job? I**'ve been working** at my present job for two years.	Use *how long* and *for* with the present perfect or present perfect continuous to include the present.
How long **did** you **have** your last car? I **had** my last car for six years. How long **did** you **work** at your last job? I **worked** at my last job for five years.	Use *how long* and *for* with the simple past tense when you are not including the present.
When did you **come** to the U.S.? I **came** to the U.S. a few years **ago**.	A question that asks *when* usually uses the simple past. A sentence that uses *ago* uses the simple past.
I **came** to this city on January 15. I **have been** in this city since January 15. I **have been living** in this city since January 15.	Use the past tense to refer to a past action that does not continue. Use the present perfect (continuous) to show the continuation of an action from past to present.

EXERCISE 20 Fill in the blanks with the simple past, the present perfect, or the present perfect continuous, using the words in parentheses ( ).

EXAMPLES How long ___*has she had*___ her present computer?
                        (she/have)

When ___*did she buy*___ her computer?
           (she/buy)

1. How long ___*was Lincoln*___ president of the U.S.?
                        (be/Lincoln)

2. Lincoln ___*was*___ president from 1861 to 1865.
                  (be)

3. How long ___*has ... been*___ president of the U.S.?
              (be/use the name of the current president)

4. He ___*has been*___ president since ___Answers will vary.___
              (be)

5. I ___*have been studying/have studied*___ English since I was in high school.
           (study)

6. When I was a child, I ___*studied*___ German.
                               (study)

7. Albert Einstein died in 1955. He ___*lived*___ in the U.S. for
                                          (live)
   22 years.

8. I ___*have lived*___ in this city for ___Answers will vary.___ years.
           (live)

The Present Perfect; The Present Perfect Continuous   25

1.11. | The Present Perfect vs. the Simple Past

1. On the board, write a pair of sentences that contrasts the past and present perfect tenses. For example, write:
   1. Mina had a job for two years.
   2. Mina has had a job for two years.
   Ask: *In #1, does Mina still have the job?* (no) *In #2, does Mina still have the job?* (yes)
2. Have students draw a timeline for each of the two sentences. Ask for volunteers to draw their timelines on the board. Make sure that the timeline for #1 shows a period of two years that ended in the past, and that the timeline for #2 shows a period of two years that includes the present date.
3. Have students look at grammar chart **1.11.** Review the example sentences and explanations in the grammar chart.

EXERCISE 20

1. Tell students that this exercise is about events in the past and present. Have students read the direction line.
2. Direct students to the examples in the book. Review the examples with the class.
3. Have students complete the exercise individually and then check their work in pairs. Review the answers as a class.

Grammar Variation

On the board, draw a timeline with two vertical marks, one near the left end and one near the right end. Label the mark on the left *January 15* (or another appropriate date), and label the mark on the right with today's date. Write on the board: *I _____ to this city on January 15. I _____ in this city since January 15.* Ask students to help complete the sentences (*came, moved; have been, have been living, have lived*). Ask: *Why do we use the simple past in the first sentence and the present perfect in the second sentence?* (because the first action is finished and the second action is continuing)

🎧 *CD 1, Track 4*

1. Tell students that this exercise is a conversation between two friends. Have students read the direction line.
2. Model the exercise. Direct students to the example in the book. Then complete the examples with the class. Point out the picture of the waitperson on page 27.
3. Have students complete Exercise 21 individually. Then have them check their answers in pairs by practicing the dialogue. Circulate and observe the pair work. If necessary, check the answers as a class.
4. Assess students' performance. If necessary, review grammar chart **1.11** on page 25.

🕐 To save class time, have students do half of the exercise in class and complete the other half for homework. Or assign the entire exercise for homework.

---

9. When ___*did you buy*___ your car?
   (you/buy)
10. I ___*bought*___ my car two years ago.
   (buy)
11. How long ___*have you had*___ your driver's license?
   (you/have)
12. I ___*have had*___ my driver's license since May.
   (have)
13. How long ___*have you known*___ our English teacher?
   (you/know)
14. I ___*have known*___ our teacher for six months.
   (know)
15. When ___*did you meet*___ the English teacher?
   (you/meet)
16. I ___*met*___ her in September.
   (meet)
17. How long ___*did you study*___ English in your previous school?
   (you/study)
18. How long ___*have you studied*___ English in this school?
   (you/study)

EXERCISE 21 🎧 Two friends meet on the street. Fill in the blanks in their conversation below. Use the present perfect, the present perfect continuous, or the past. Fill in any other necessary words.

A: Hi, Ivan. I ___*haven't seen*___ you ___*in*___ ages. Where ___*have you been*___?
   (example: not/see) (1) (2 you/be)

B: I ___*have been looking*___ for a job for the last few weeks.
   (3 look)

A: What ___*happened*___ to your old job?
   (4 happen)

B: My company is outsourcing, and I ___*got*___ laid off last
   (5 get)
   month. I'm getting depressed. I ___*haven't had*___ a paycheck
   (6 not/have)
   ___*for*___ four weeks.
   (7)

A: Don't lose hope. You're young and educated and healthy.
B: I know. But jobs here are disappearing, even for educated people.

A: That's true. Look at me. I ___*have always wanted*___ to be an actor, but
   (8 always/want)
   I ___*have been waiting*___ tables in a restaurant for the last three
   (9 wait)
   years. My friend, Ron, has a degree in accounting, and he
   ___*has been driving*___ a taxi for the ___*last/past*___ two years.
   (10 drive) (11)

B: At least you're earning some money now. For the last month, I
   ___*have been spending*___ money but I ___*haven't been earning*___ any.
   (12 spend) (13 not/earn)

26   Lesson 1

Exercise 21 Variation

To provide practice with listening skills, have students close their books and listen to the audio. Repeat the audio as needed. Ask comprehension questions, such as: *What has Ivan been doing for the last few weeks?* (looking for a job) *What happened to Ivan's old job?* (His company is outsourcing, and he got laid off.) Then have students open their books and complete Exercise 21.

Culture Note

Explain that in the U.S., employment is not automatic after graduation from a university or college. Ask students what jobs the people in Exercise 21 and their friends are doing, and why. Use yourself or a friend or acquaintance as an example to illustrate paths Americans sometimes take in finding a career.

A: If you want, I can ask my boss if there are any openings for a waitperson in the restaurant.

B: I *have never worked* in a restaurant, and I don't really want to.
   (14 never/work)

A: It would just be temporary, until you can find a computer job.

B: Temporary? Like your job? You *graduated* from
   (15 graduate)
   college three years ago and you *have been waiting* tables
   (16 wait)
   ever *since* .
   (17)

A: But I *have never given* up hope of becoming a famous actor.
   (18 never/give)

1.12 | The Present Perfect with Repetition from Past to Present

Examples	Explanation
Daniel is looking for a job. He **has had** three interviews *this month*. We **have studied** two lessons *this semester*.	We use the present perfect to talk about the repetition of an action in a time period that includes the present. The time period is open, and there is a possibility for more repetition to occur. Open time periods include: *today, this week, this month, this year, this semester*.
My company is laying off workers. Three workers **have lost** their jobs *so far*. We are planning to buy a house. *So far*, we **have looked** at five houses. *Up to now*, she **has had** three jobs.	*So far* and *up to now* mean "including this moment." We use these expressions with the present perfect to show that another repetition may occur.
Daniel **has worked** at *several* hotels. You **have had** *a lot of* experience with computers. I **have learned** *many* new words.	We can use *several, many, a lot of,* or a number to show repetition from past to present.
How many interviews **have** you **had** this year? *How much* money **have** you **spent** on career counseling so far?	We can ask a question about repetition with *how many* and *how much.*
I **haven't spent** *any* money *at all* on career counseling.	A negative statement with "*any . . . at all*" means the number is zero.
We've **studied** two lessons so far. *Not*: We've **been studying** two lessons so far.	Do not use the continuous form for repetition.

```
                                    now
past ←━━━━━━━━━━━━━━━━━━━━━━━━━━━━━━━━━━━━━━━━━━━━━→ future
      ┌──────────────────────┐
      │ He has had three interviews
      │ this month.          │
      └──────────────────────┘
```

1. Have students cover the grammar chart. Draw a timeline on the board. Make a vertical mark on the timeline and label it with today's date (e.g., *10/17*). Make three vertical marks to the left and label them with earlier dates in this month (e.g., *10/2, 10/8, 10/14*). Next to each date, write: *interview*.

2. Ask: *When did Daniel have his first interview?* (on October 2); ask about the second and third interviews.

4. Ask: *What can you say about Daniel's interviews?* Elicit and write: *Daniel has had three interviews this month.* Ask: *Is the month finished?* (no) *Is it possible for Daniel to have more interviews this month?* (yes) Say: *To talk about a repeating action that may continue, we use the present perfect tense.*

5. Have students review the example sentences and explanations in the grammar chart.

6. Ask volunteers to make statements about themselves using the present perfect tense with repetition; give one or two examples of your own (e.g., *I have taught this class three times; My parents have visited me twice this year.*).

Expansion

Exercise 21 Have students practice the conversation in pairs. Have volunteers act out the conversation for the class.

Grammar Variation

Have students review the example sentences and explanations first. Then have students write statements about themselves with repetition—one statement about jobs they've had, one about places they've visited in the U.S., and one about things they've learned in class this semester.

EXERCISE 22

1. Tell students that this exercise is a series of short conversations between two classmates or friends. Have students read the direction line.
2. Model the exercise. Direct students to the example in the book; repeat the conversation with a volunteer. Then do #1 with the class.
3. Have students complete the rest of the exercise individually. Then have them check their answers in pairs by practicing the dialogues. Circulate and observe the pair work. Check the answers as a class.

EXERCISE 23

1. Tell students that this exercise is about their personal experiences in this city. Have students read the direction line. Ask: *What question are we answering?* (How many)
2. Model the exercise. Direct students to the examples in the book.
3. Have students complete the rest of the exercise individually. Then have them check their answers in pairs and as a class.

To save class time, have students do half of the exercise in class and complete the other half for homework. Or assign the entire exercise for homework.

EXERCISE 22 Fill in the blanks in the following conversations.

EXAMPLE A: How many pages have we ___done___ in this book so far?
B: We ___'ve___ done 50 pages so far.

1. A: How many tests ___have___ we had so far this semester?
   B: So far we ___have had___ two tests this semester.
2. A: How many compositions have we ___written___ this semester?
   B: We ___have written___ two compositions this semester.
3. A: How many times have you ___been___ absent this semester?
   B: I ___have been___ absent one time this semester.
4. A: How many times ___has___ the teacher been absent this semester?
   B: The teacher ___hasn't been___ absent at all this semester.
5. A: How much money have we ___spent___ this week?
   B: We ___have spent___ about $100 so far this week. We need to save more.
6. A: How ___many___ phone calls ___has she made___ so far today?
   B: She ___has___ made ten phone calls so far today.
7. A: How ___much___ water have you ___drunk___ today?
   B: I ___have drunk___ two glasses of water so far today.
8. A: How ___many___ TV shows ___have___ the children ___watched___ today?
   B: They ___have watched___ three TV programs today.
9. A: How many ___times___ have you ___brushed___ your teeth today?
   B: I ___have brushed___ my teeth twice so far today.
10. A: How many meals have you ___eaten___ in a restaurant this week?
    B: I ___have not eaten___ in a restaurant at all this week.

EXERCISE 23 ABOUT YOU Write a statement to tell how many times you have done something in this city. (If you don't know the exact number, you may use a *few, several,* or *many.*)

EXAMPLES live in / apartment(s)
I've lived in one apartment in this city.

get lost / time(s)
I've gotten lost a few times in this city.

Exercise 23 Variation

Have students write a question for each item in the exercise, such as: *How many apartments have you lived in in this city?* Have pairs of students use the questions to interview each other. Then have each student write sentences about his or her partner based on his or her answers (e.g., *Ali has lived in three apartments in this city.*).

1. **have / job(s)**
   I've had OR I haven't had any jobs in this city.

2. **have / job interview(s)**
   I've had OR I haven't had any job interviews in this city.

3. **have / traffic ticket(s)**
   I've had OR I haven't had any traffic tickets.

4. **buy / car(s)**
   I've bought OR I've never bought OR I haven't bought any cars in this city.

5. **attend / school(s)**
   I've attended OR I've never attended school in this city.

6. **live in / apartment(s)**
   I've lived in OR I've never lived in any OR I haven't lived in any apartments in this city.

7. **go downtown / time(s)**
   I've gone downtown OR I've never gone downtown in this city.

EXERCISE 24   ABOUT YOU Ask a question with *How much . . . ?* or *How many . . . ?* and the words given. Talk about today. Another student will answer.

EXAMPLES   coffee / have

A: How much coffee have you had today?
B: I've had three cups of coffee today.

glasses of water / drink

A: How many glasses of water have you drunk today?
B: I haven't drunk any water at all today.

1. **tea / have** *How much tea have you had today?*

2. **glasses of water / have** *How many glasses of water have you had today?*

3. **cookies / eat** *How many cookies have you eaten today?*

4. **glasses of cola / have** *How many glasses of cola have you had today?*

5. **times / check your e-mail** *How many times have you checked your e-mail today?*

6. **miles / walk or drive** *How many miles have you walked/driven today?*

7. **money / spend** *How much money have you spent today?*

8. **coffee / have** *How much coffee have you had today?*

1. Tell students that this exercise is about what they've done so far today. Have students read the direction line.
2. Direct students to the examples in the book. Model the first example with a student. Then have two other students model the second example.
3. Ask: *What is the difference between the first example and the second example?* (*Coffee* is a noncount noun; *glasses* is a count noun; we use *how much* with noncount nouns and *how many* with count nouns.)
4. Have students complete the exercise in pairs, alternating asking and answering the questions.
5. Assess students' performance. If necessary, review grammar chart **1.12** on page 27.

🕐 To save class time, have students do half of the exercise in class and complete the other half in writing for homework, answering the question about themselves. Or assign the entire exercise for homework as a written assignment about themselves.

Expansion

Exercise 24 Have students write their own questions with *How much* or *How many* and the present perfect tense. Have students choose another student to ask their questions as the class listens. Then ask the class if they believe the answers are true or false.

1.13 | Present Perfect vs. Simple Past with Repetition

1. Have students cover the grammar chart. Write on the board: *Chris is 21 years old. He has had four jobs. George is 70 years old. He had four jobs.* Ask: *What do the verb tenses tell you about Chris and George?* (Chris will probably have more jobs; George is finished working.)
2. Have students review the example sentences and explanations in the grammar chart.
3. Have students cover the right side of the chart. For each pair of example sentences in the grammar chart, ask students to explain in their own words why one sentence uses a simple past tense verb and the other uses a present perfect tense verb.
4. Ask volunteers to give sentences about themselves using the present perfect tense with repetition; give one or two examples of your own (e.g., *I have seen my favorite movie five times.*).

EXERCISE 25

🎧 *CD 1, Track 5*

1. Tell students that this exercise is a conversation between two friends about job hunting. Have students read the direction line.
2. Direct students to the example in the book. Then complete the first two lines with the class.
3. Have students complete Exercise 25 individually. Then have them check their answers in pairs by practicing the dialogues. Circulate and observe the pair work. If necessary, check the answers as a class.
4. Assess students' performance. If necessary, review grammar chart **1.13**.

1.13 | Present Perfect vs. Simple Past with Repetition

Examples	Explanation
How many interviews **have** you **had** this month? I **have had** two interviews **so far** this month. How many times **have** you **been** absent this semester? I **have been** absent twice **so far**.	To show that there is possibility for more repetition, use the present perfect. *This month* and *this semester* are not finished. *So far* indicates that the number given may not be final.
How many interviews **did** you **have** last month? I **had** four interviews last month. How many times **were** you absent last semester? I **was** absent four times last semester.	To show that the number is final, use the simple past tense and a past time expression (*yesterday, last week, last year, last semester,* etc.).
Compare: a. I **have seen** my counselor twice this week. b. I **saw** my counselor twice this week. a. I **have made** five phone calls today. b. I **made** five phone calls today.	With a present time expression (such as *today, this week,* etc.), you may use either the present perfect or the simple past. a. The number may not be final. b. The number seems final.
Compare: a. My grandfather died in 1998. He **had** several jobs in his lifetime. b. My father is a programmer. He **has had** five jobs so far.	a. If you refer to the experiences of a dead person, you must use the simple past tense because nothing more can be added to that person's experience. b. A living person can have more of the same experience.
Compare: a. In my country, I **had** five jobs. b. In the U.S., I **have had** two jobs.	a. To talk about a closed phase of your life, Iuse the simple past tense. For example, if you do not plan to live in your native country again, use the simple past tense to talk about your experiences there. b. To talk about your experiences in this phase of your life, you can use the present perfect tense.

EXERCISE 25 🎧 In the conversation below, fill in the blanks with the correct form of the verb in parentheses ( ).

A: I'm very frustrated about finding a job. I ___have sent___ out 100
(example: send)

B: résumés so far. And I ___have made___ dozens of phone calls to
(1 make)
companies.

B: Have you ___had___ any answers to your letters and calls?
(2 have)

A: Yes. Last week I ___had___ six interviews. But so far, nobody
(3 have)
___has offered___ me a job.
(4 offer)

Grammar Variation

Have students cover grammar chart **1.13**. Write pairs of sentences from or similar to those in the chart on the board, without the verbs (e.g., *In my country, I _____ five jobs. In the U.S., I _____ two jobs.* Or *I _____ three interviews last month. I _____ three interviews this month.*). Ask students how they would complete each sentence and why. Then have students uncover and review the chart.

Exercise 25 Variation

To provide practice with listening skills, have students close their books and listen to the audio. Repeat the audio as needed. Ask comprehension questions, such as: *How many résumés has person A sent out so far?* (100) *How many interviews did person A have last week?* (six) *Has anyone offered him a job?* (no) Then have students open their books and complete Exercise 25.

B: You should call those companies.

A: I know I should. But this week, I ___have been___ very busy getting
(5 be)

career counseling. I ___have seen___ my counselor several times in
(6 see)

the past few weeks.

B: Has your counselor ___given___ you any advice about looking
(7 give)

for a job?

A: Yes. Last week she ___gave___ me a lot of advice. But looking for a
(8 give)

job is so strange in the U.S. I feel like I have to sell myself.

B: Don't worry. You ___haven't had___ much work experience in
(9 not/have)

the U.S. so far. I'm sure you'll get used to the process of finding a job.

A: I don't know. I ___have talked___ to a lot of other people
(10 talk)

looking for work. Even though English is their native language, they

___haven't had___ much luck either.
(11 not/have)

B: ___Was it___ easy for you to find a job when you lived
(12 it/be)

in your native country?

A: In my native country, I ___never had___ this problem. After I
(13 never/have)

___graduated___ from college, I ___found___ a job immediately
(14 graduate)   (15 find)

and ___worked___ in the same place for many years.
(16 work)

B: In the U.S., people change jobs often. Take me, for example.

I ___have had___ six jobs, and I'm only 28 years old.
(17 have)

A: I'm 40 years old. But when I lived in my native country, I ___had___
(18 have)

the same job for ten years. And I ___lived___ in the same apartment
(19 live)

for many years until I came to the U.S. My parents ___lived___ in the
(20 live)

same apartment from the time they got married until the time they
died.

B: Get used to it! Life today is about constant change.

Expansion

Exercise 25 Have students practice the conversation in pairs. Have volunteers act out the conversation for the class.

Culture Note

Tell students that according to the U.S. government, the average person born in the U.S. between 1957 and 1964 held 10 jobs between age 18 and age 38. Young people between the ages of 18 and 22 changed jobs the most often, with 71 percent of these jobs ending in under one year.

Ask students to talk about how easy it is to find a job, and how long people usually keep jobs, in their native countries. Ask volunteers to share their experiences with jobs in their countries and jobs in the U.S.

The *Occupational Outlook Handbook* (Reading)

1. Have students look at the photo. Ask: *Who are the two people?* (a career counselor and a student) *What do you think they are talking about?* (possible future careers for the student)
2. Preteach any vocabulary words your students may not know, such as *major, field, publication, nature,* and *check out.*

BEFORE YOU READ

1. Activate students' prior knowledge about job counseling, employment services, and accessing job information. Ask: *How did you find your last job? What do employment agencies do?* (help people find jobs) *How can you find out about jobs that are available in your area?*
2. Have students discuss the questions in pairs. Try to pair students of different cultures.
3. Ask a few volunteers to share their answers with the class.

🕐 To save class time, skip "Before You Read" or have students prepare answers for homework ahead of time.

Reading 🎧 CD 1, Track 6

1. Have students first read the text silently. Explain that this is a conversation between a college student and her counselor. Tell them to pay special attention to the present perfect and present perfect continuous tense verbs in the reading. Then play the audio and have students read along silently.
2. Check students' comprehension. Ask questions such as: *What is the relationship between the two people?* (a college counselor and a student) *Why is the student thinking about changing majors?* (It might be difficult to make a living as an artist.) *What does the counselor suggest?* (looking at the *Occupational Outlook Handbook*)

🕐 To save class time, have students read the reading for homework.

THE *OCCUPATIONAL OUTLOOK HANDBOOK*

Before You Read
1. Have you ever seen a counselor about finding a job?
2. What careers interest you? What are some jobs you wouldn't want to have?

🎧 Read the following conversation between a college student (S) and her counselor (C). Pay special attention to the present perfect tense and the present perfect continuous tense.

C: I see you're majoring in art. **Have** you **thought** about a career yet for your future?

S: **I've thought** about it, but I'm still not sure what I'm going to do when I graduate. **I've** always **loved** art, but my parents are worried that I won't be able to make a living as an artist. Lately **I've been thinking** about changing majors.

C: What major **have** you **been considering**?

S: Graphic design or commercial art.

C: **Have** you **taken** any courses in these fields?

S: **I've** already **taken** a course in graphic design. But I don't know much about the future of this career. Are there a lot of jobs for graphic artists?

C: **Have** you ever **used** the *Occupational Outlook Handbook*?

S: No, I **haven't**. **I've** never even **heard** of it. What is it?

C: It's a government publication that gives you a lot of information about jobs in the U.S. You can find it in the library or on the Internet. If you look up "graphic designer" in this publication, it will tell you the nature of the work, where the jobs are, what salary you can expect, what kind of training you need, what the future will be for graphic designers, and much more.

S: Thanks for the information. Can I come back and see you in a few weeks after I have a chance to check out the *Occupational Outlook Handbook*?

C: Yes, please come back.

32   Lesson 1

Expansion

Theme The topic for this lesson can be enhanced with the following ideas:

1. A college catalog or Web page listing majors
2. The *Occupational Outlook Handbook* online, at http://www.bls.gov/oco/home.htm
3. The U.S. Bureau of Labor Statistics' career information page for young adults, at http://stats.bls.gov/k12/index.htm

Reading Variation

To practice listening skills, have students first listen to the audio alone. Ask a few comprehension questions. Repeat the audio if necessary. Then have students open their books and read along as they listen to the audio.

> *(A few weeks later)*
>
> **C:** Hi. **Have** you **looked** at the *Occupational Outlook Handbook* yet?
>
> **S:** Yes. Thanks for telling me about it. **I've looked** at many jobs in the art field, but so far I **haven't decided** on anything yet. But I have some ideas.
>
> **C:** **Have** you **talked** to your parents lately? **Have** you **told** them that you're planning on changing majors?
>
> **S:** Oh, yes. They're very happy about it. They don't want me to be a starving[8] artist.

1.14 | The Present Perfect with Indefinite Past Time—An Overview

We use the present perfect to refer to an action that occurred at an indefinite time in the past that still has importance to a present situation.

Questions	Short Answers	Explanation
Has she **ever visited** a counselor? **Have** you **ever used** the *Occupational Outlook Handbook*? **Have** you **ever taken** an art history course?	Yes, she **has**. No, I never **have**. No, I **haven't**.	A question with *ever* asks about any time between the past and the present. Put *ever* between the subject and the main verb in a question.
Have you **decided** on a major **yet**? **Has** she **told** her parents about her decision **yet**?	No, not **yet**. Yes, she **already** has.	*Yet* and *already* refer to an indefinite time in the near past. There is an expectation that an activity took place a short time ago.
Have you **talked** to your parents **lately**? **Have** you **seen** your counselor **recently**?	No, I **haven't**. Yes, I **have**.	Questions with *lately* and *recently* refer to an indefinite time in the near past.

```
                            now
past ←——————————————————————|————————————————————→ future
              ┌─────────────────────────┐
              │ Have you ever seen a     │
              │ job counselor?           │
              └─────────────────────────┘
```

[8]*Starving* means hungry, not having enough to eat.

1.14 | The Present Perfect with Indefinite Past Time—An Overview

1. Have students look at the reading and underline the present perfect and present perfect continuous tense verbs. Ask students if they can say exactly when the actions in the present perfect sentences took place (no, the present perfect doesn't tell exactly when an action happened).
2. Have students look at the grammar chart. Review the example sentences and explanations.
3. Have students look back at the reading and underline *ever, yet, already,* and *lately*.
4. Have students write and ask each other questions with *Have you ever . . . .*

Reading Glossary

check out: look at; investigate; get more information about
field: area of study or area of employment
major: specialization in college or at a university; the field a student chooses to study
nature: character or characteristics
publication: book, magazine, or other written material sold or given away by a company or individual

Culture Note

Explain that *starving artist* is a stereotype of a young or beginning artist who doesn't make much money, but chooses to live frugally, rather than give up the work he or she loves.

Grammar Variation

Have students underline *yet, ever, already,* and *lately* in the reading before they look at the grammar chart.

CD 1, Track 7

1. Tell students that this exercise is about preparing to look for a new job. Have students read the direction line. Ask: *What tenses do we underline?* (present perfect and present perfect continuous)
2. Direct students to the example in the first sentence.
3. Have students complete the exercise individually. Check the answers as a class.
4. Assess students' performance. If necessary, review grammar chart **1.14** on page 33.

1.15 | Questions with *Ever*

1. Have students look at grammar chart **1.15**. Say: *We use* ever *in a question when we want to ask about any time in the past.* Review the example sentences in the grammar chart.
2. Point out the negative short answer: *No, I never have.* Ask: *Where do we put* never? (between the subject and *have*) Remind students not to use a negative verb with *never*. Write on the board:
Correct: No, I never have.
Incorrect: No, I never haven't.

EXERCISE 26 Read the following conversation. Underline the present perfect and present perfect continuous tenses.

EXAMPLE A: There's going to be a job fair at the college next week. <u>Have</u> you ever <u>gone</u> to one?

B: What's a job fair?

A: Representatives from different companies come to one place. You can meet these people, find out about their companies, and give them your résumé. Lately <u>I've been going</u> to a lot of job fairs. And <u>I've been looking</u> for jobs online. <u>I've just rewritten</u> my résumé too. <u>I haven't found</u> a job yet, but I'm hopeful.

B: But you have a good job as an office manager.

A: I'm going to quit in two weeks. <u>I've already given</u> my employer notice. <u>I've worked</u> there for two years, and <u>I haven't had</u> a raise yet. <u>I've realized</u> that I can make more money doing something else. <u>I've talked</u> to a career counselor and <u>I've taken</u> a test to see what I'm good at. <u>I've also taken</u> more courses to upgrade my skills.

B: <u>Have</u> you <u>decided</u> what you want to do?

A: Yes. <u>I've decided</u> to be a legal assistant.

1.15 | Questions with *Ever*

Examples	Explanation

Have you ever **seen** a job counselor?
  Yes, I **have**. **I've seen** a job counselor a few times.
Have you ever **used** the Internet to find a job?
  Yes, **I've used** the Internet many times.
Have you ever **worked** in a restaurant?
  No, I never **have**.
	We use *ever* to ask a question about any time in the past.

Have you ever **written** a résumé?
  a. Yes, I **have**.
  b. Yes. I **wrote** my résumé two weeks ago.
Has he ever **taken** a design course?
  a. Yes. He **has taken** several design courses.
  b. Yes. He **took** one last semester.
	You can answer an *ever* question with the present perfect or the simple past.
	a. Use the **present perfect** to answer with no reference to time.
	b. Use the **simple past** to answer with a definite time (*last week, last semester, last Friday, two weeks ago*).

Exercise 26 Variation

To provide practice with listening skills, have students close their books and listen to the audio. Repeat the audio as needed. Ask comprehension questions, such as: *What's happening at the college next week?* (There's going to be a job fair.) *What can you do at a job fair?* (meet representatives from different companies, find out about their companies, and give them your résumé) Then have students open their books and complete Exercise 26.

Expansion

Exercise 26 Have students make a list of all of the things the speaker has done to try to find a better job.

EXERCISE **27** ABOUT YOU Ask question with *Have you ever . . . ?* and the words given. Use the past participle of the verb. Another student will answer. If the answer is *yes,* ask for more specific information. To answer with a specific time, use the simple past tense. To answer with a frequency response, use the present perfect tense.

EXAMPLE   eat a hot dog

A: Have you ever eaten a hot dog?
B: Yes, I have.
A: When did you eat a hot dog?
B: I ate one at a picnic last summer.

1. find money on the street
   Have you ever found money on the street?
2. go to a garage sale
   Have you ever gone to a garage sale?
3. meet a famous person
   Have you ever met a famous person?
4. study art history
   Have you ever studied art history?
5. get a ticket for speeding
   Have you ever gotten a ticket for speeding?
6. be on television
   Have you ever been on television?
7. win a contest or a prize
   Have you ever won a contest or a prize?
8. lend money to a friend
   Have you ever lent money to a friend?
9. lose your keys
   Have you ever lost your keys?
10. break an arm or a leg
    Have you ever broken an arm or a leg?
11. go to a football game
    Have you ever gone to a football game?
12. go to court
    Have you ever gone to court?
13. hear of[6] Martin Luther King, Jr.
    Have you ever heard of Martin Luther King, Jr.?
14. eat in a Vietnamese restaurant
    Have you ever eaten in a Vietnamese restaurant?
15. order products over the Internet
    Have you ever ordered products over the Internet?
16. get lost in this city
    Have you ever gotten lost in this city?
17. tell a lie
    Have you ever told a lie?
18. go to Canada
    Have you ever gone to Canada?
19. travel by train
    Have you ever traveled by train?
20. eat pizza
    Have you ever eaten pizza?
21. be on a roller coaster
    Have you ever been on a roller coaster?
22. see a play in this city
    Have you ever seen a play in this city?
23. eat Chinese food
    Have you ever eaten Chinese food?
24. use a digital camera
    Have you ever used a digital camera?
25. go camping
    Have you ever gone camping?
26. use a scanner
    Have you ever used a scanner?

EXERCISE **28**   Work with a partner. Use *ever* to write four questions to ask your teacher. Your teacher will answer.

EXAMPLES   *Have you ever eaten raw fish?*

Have you ever written a poem?

1. _____ Answers will vary. _____
2. _____
3. _____
4. _____

[6]*Hear of* means to recognize a name.

_____

The Present Perfect; The Present Perfect Continuous   35

---

1. Tell students that this exercise is about personal and life experiences. Have students read the direction line. Ask: *What word do we add to the questions?* (*ever*) Ask: *What are some frequency responses?* (*often, many times, a few times,* etc.)
2. Direct students to the example in the book. Ask several students the question. Point out the pictures of the person getting a speeding ticket, the football player, and the roller coaster.
3. Have students complete the exercise in pairs, alternating asking and answering questions every four or five questions. Have the student who is answering questions cover the exercise in his or her book.

EXERCISE   28

1. Tell students that this exercise is a chance to ask you some questions about your experiences. Have students read the direction line. Ask: *What word do we add to the questions?* (*ever*)
2. Direct students to the examples in the book.
3. Have students complete the exercise in pairs. Ask volunteers to ask you the questions. Answer the questions.

To save class time, have students write the questions for homework. Then have a few volunteers ask you questions in class.

Expansion

Exercise 27 Have students write their own lists of things they have done. Tell students not to include when or how often they did the activity. Collect the lists and pass them out again. Have students stand and move around the room questioning one another until they locate the student whose list they have. Ask students to report interesting experiences to the class.

_____

Expansion

Exercise 28 Have students write *Have you ever . . .* questions they would like to ask a famous person. Have students tell the class whom they would like to address their question to and why.

1. Tell students that this exercise is a series of conversations between friends about life experiences. Have students read the direction line. Ask: *What tenses will we use in the sentences?* (present perfect and simple past) Review the example in the book. Complete the example with a volunteer.

2. Have students complete the exercise individually. Point out the picture of the boy with the broken leg. Collect for assessment or have students read their sentences to a partner.

🕐 To save class time, have students do half of the exercise in class and complete the other half for homework. Or assign the entire exercise for homework.

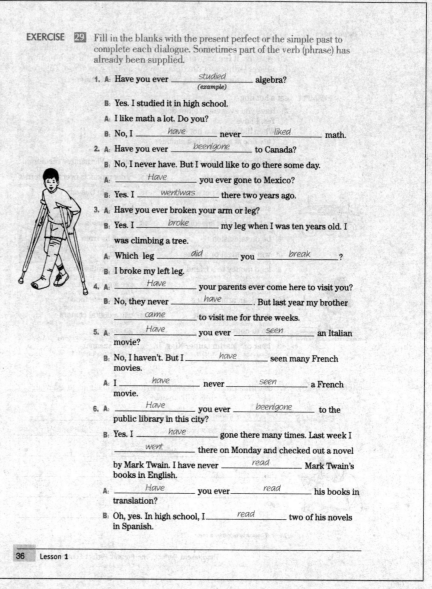

EXERCISE 29 Fill in the blanks with the present perfect or the simple past to complete each dialogue. Sometimes part of the verb (phrase) has already been supplied.

1. A: Have you ever _____studied_____ algebra?
        (example)

   B: Yes. I studied it in high school.

   A: I like math a lot. Do you?

   B: No, I ___have___ never ___liked___ math.

2. A: Have you ever ___been/gone___ to Canada?

   B: No, I never have. But I would like to go there some day.

   A: ___Have___ you ever gone to Mexico?

   B: Yes. I ___went/was___ there two years ago.

3. A: Have you ever broken your arm or leg?

   B: Yes. I ___broke___ my leg when I was ten years old. I was climbing a tree.

   A: Which leg ___did___ you ___break___?

   B: I broke my left leg.

4. A: ___Have___ your parents ever come here to visit you?

   B: No, they never ___have___. But last year my brother ___came___ to visit me for three weeks.

5. A: ___Have___ you ever ___seen___ an Italian movie?

   B: No, I haven't. But I ___have___ seen many French movies.

   A: I ___have___ never ___seen___ a French movie.

6. A: ___Have___ you ever ___been/gone___ to the public library in this city?

   B: Yes. I ___have___ gone there many times. Last week I ___went___ there on Monday and checked out a novel by Mark Twain. I have never ___read___ Mark Twain's books in English.

   A: ___Have___ you ever ___read___ his books in translation?

   B: Oh, yes. In high school, I ___read___ two of his novels in Spanish.

Expansion

Exercise 29 Have pairs of students write their own conversations using the first sentence of one of the items in Exercise 29, and continuing with their own words. Have volunteers perform their conversations for the class.

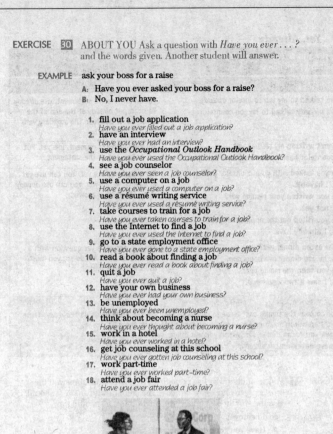

EXERCISE **30** ABOUT YOU Ask a question with *Have you ever ... ?* and the words given. Another student will answer.

EXAMPLE ask your boss for a raise

A: Have you ever asked your boss for a raise?
B: No, I never have.

1. fill out a job application
   Have you ever filled out a job application?
2. have an interview
   Have you ever had an interview?
3. use the *Occupational Outlook Handbook*
   Have you ever used the Occupational Outlook Handbook?
4. see a job counselor
   Have you ever seen a job counselor?
5. use a computer on a job
   Have you ever used a computer on a job?
6. use a résumé writing service
   Have you ever used a résumé writing service?
7. take courses to train for a job
   Have you ever taken courses to train for a job?
8. use the Internet to find a job
   Have you ever used the Internet to find a job?
9. go to a state employment office
   Have you ever gone to a state employment office?
10. read a book about finding a job
    Have you ever read a book about finding a job?
11. quit a job
    Have you ever quit a job?
12. have your own business
    Have you ever had your own business?
13. be unemployed
    Have you ever been unemployed?
14. think about becoming a nurse
    Have you ever thought about becoming a nurse?
15. work in a hotel
    Have you ever worked in a hotel?
16. get job counseling at this school
    Have you ever gotten job counseling at this school?
17. work part-time
    Have you ever worked part-time?
18. attend a job fair
    Have you ever attended a job fair?

The Present Perfect; The Present Perfect Continuous   **37**

1. Tell students that this exercise is about their experiences looking for a job. Have students read the direction line. Ask: *What word will we use in the questions?* (*ever*) Review the example in the book.
2. Have students complete the exercise in pairs. Point out the picture of the job fair. Circulate and observe the pair work. Ask pairs to share interesting information about their partners with the class.
3. Assess students' performance. If necessary, review grammar chart **1.15** on page 34.

🕐 To save class time, have students do half of the exercise in class and complete the other half in writing, answering the questions about themselves, for homework. Or if students do not need speaking practice, the entire exercise may be skipped.

Expansion

Exercise 30 Have students survey the class to see how many students answer *yes* to each question. If possible, have each student take responsibility for one question. Have students prepare a graph showing how many students answered *yes* for each question.

1.16 | Yet, Already

1. Have students cover up the grammar chart. Write on the board: *Have you visited the career office? Have you visited the career office yet?* Ask: *What is the difference between these two questions?* (With *yet*, the questioner is expecting you to visit the career office. Without *yet*, the questioner is just asking about what you have done.)
2. Have students look at the grammar chart. Review the example sentences and explanations.
3. Draw students' attention to the Language Note. Tell students that many people use the simple past with *already* and *yet* in informal conversations.

EXERCISE 31

1. Tell students that this exercise is about their learning about a new city. Have students read the direction line. Ask: *What word are we using in the questions?* (yet)
2. Model the exercise with a student who has arrived recently. Direct students to the example in the book.
3. Have students work in groups. Have each group identify the student who has moved to the area the most recently by asking *How long have you lived here?* Then have members of the group take turns asking that student the questions. Have groups report back to the class.

1.16 | Yet, Already

Use *yet* and *already* with the present perfect to show an expectation that something took place.

Examples	Explanation
I **have talked** to my job counselor *already*. I **have** *already* **talked** to my job counselor.	For an affirmative statement, use *already*. You can put *already* at the end of the sentence or between the auxiliary verb and the main verb.
I **haven't written** my résumé *yet*. The counselor **hasn't answered** my e-mail *yet*.	For a negative statement, use *yet*. Put *yet* at the end of the statement.
Have you **talked** with your counselor *yet*? 　No, I **haven't**. **Have** you **written** your résumé *yet*? 　No, **not yet**. **Have** you **filled** out the application *yet*? 　Yes, I *already* **have**.	For questions, use *yet*. You can use *yet* in a negative answer. You can use *already* in an affirmative answer.
Has he **eaten** dinner *yet*? 　Yes, he **ate** dinner *two hours ago*. **Have** you **seen** the movie *yet*? 　Yes, I **saw** it *two weeks ago*.	You can answer a *yet* question with a specific time. If you do so, you must use the simple past.

Language Note:
You often hear the simple past tense in questions with *yet* and statements with *already*. There is no difference in meaning between the present perfect and the past.
　Have you **eaten** dinner *yet*? = **Did** you **eat** dinner *yet*?
　I **have eaten** dinner *already*. = I **ate** dinner *already*.

EXERCISE **31** Ask a student who has recently moved here questions with the words given and *yet* or *already*. The student who answers should use the simple past tense if the answer has a specific time.

EXAMPLE　go downtown
　A: Have you gone downtown yet?
　B: Yes. I went downtown three weeks ago.

1. buy a computer
　Have you bought a computer yet?
2. find an apartment
　Have you found an apartment yet?
3. get a library card
　Have you gotten a library card yet?
4. use public transportation
　Have you used public transportation yet?
5. visit any museums
　Have you visited any museums yet?
6. meet any of your neighbors
　Have you met any of your neighbors yet?

Expansion

Exercise 31 Have groups write a short paragraph about the student they interviewed, using the present perfect tense, *yet*, and *already*.

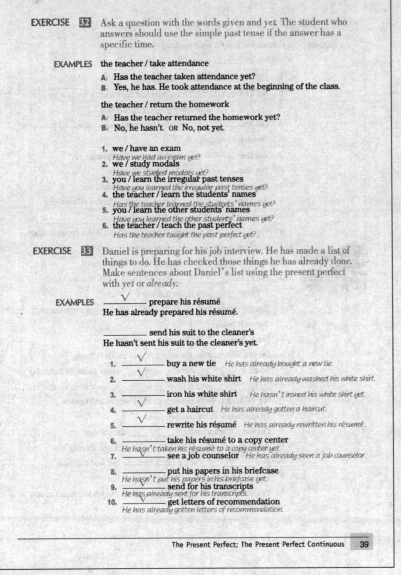

EXERCISE 32   Ask a question with the words given and *yet*. The student who
answers should use the simple past tense if the answer has a
specific time.

EXAMPLES   the teacher / take attendance

A: Has the teacher taken attendance yet?
B: Yes, he has. He took attendance at the beginning of the class.

the teacher / return the homework

A: Has the teacher returned the homework yet?
B: No, he hasn't. OR No, not yet.

1. we / have an exam
Have we had an exam yet?
2. we / study modals
Have we studied modals yet?
3. you / learn the irregular past tenses
Have you learned the irregular past tenses yet?
4. the teacher / learn the students' names
Has the teacher learned the students' names yet?
5. you / learn the other students' names
Have you learned the other students' names yet?
6. the teacher / teach the past perfect
Has the teacher taught the past perfect yet?

EXERCISE 33   Daniel is preparing for his job interview. He has made a list of
things to do. He has checked those things he has already done.
Make sentences about Daniel's list using the present perfect
with *yet* or *already*.

EXAMPLES   _____√_____ prepare his résumé
He has already prepared his résumé.

_____ send his suit to the cleaner's
He hasn't sent his suit to the cleaner's yet.

1. ___√___ buy a new tie   *He has already bought a new tie.*
2. ___√___ wash his white shirt   *He has already washed his white shirt.*
3. _____ iron his white shirt   *He hasn't ironed his white shirt yet.*
4. ___√___ get a haircut   *He has already gotten a haircut.*
5. ___√___ rewrite his résumé   *He has already rewritten his résumé.*
6. _____ take his résumé to a copy center
He hasn't taken his résumé to a copy center yet.
7. ___√___ see a job counselor   *He has already seen a job counselor.*
8. _____ put his papers in his briefcase
He hasn't put his papers in his briefcase yet.
9. ___√___ send for his transcripts
He has already sent for his transcripts.
10. ___√___ get letters of recommendation
He has already gotten letters of recommendation.

1. Tell students that this exercise is
about their experiences so far in
class. Have students read the
direction line.
2. Ask two volunteers to model the
exercise. Direct students to the
examples in the book.
3. Have students complete the
exercise in pairs. If necessary, check
answers with the class.

EXERCISE 33

1. Tell students that this exercise is
about Daniel's preparations for a job
interview. Have students read the
direction line. Ask: *What did Daniel
make a list of?* (things to do to get
ready for a job interview)
2. Model the exercise using the
examples in the book.
3. Have students complete the exercise
individually. Then have them
compare their answers in pairs.
Finally, check the answers as a
class.

⏱ To save class time, have
students do half of the exercise
in class and complete the other half in
writing for homework. Or if students
do not need speaking practice, the
entire exercise may be skipped or done
in writing.

Expansion

Exercise 33 Have students make lists of things they do every day, and then check off the
ones they have already done today. Have volunteers report to the class (e.g., *I have already
cleaned the kitchen. I haven't picked up my children yet.*).

1. Tell students that this exercise is a series of conversations between friends. Have students read the direction line.
2. Model the exercise. Direct students to the example in the book. Point out the picture of Niagara Falls.
3. Have students complete Exercise 34 individually. Then have them check their answers in pairs by practicing the dialogues. Circulate and observe the pair work. If necessary, check the answers as a class.
4. Assess students' performance. If necessary, review grammar chart **1.16** on page 38.

🕐 To save class time, have students do half of the exercise in class and complete the other half for homework. Or assign the entire exercise for homework.

EXERCISE 34 Fill in the blanks to complete each conversation.

EXAMPLE A: Have you bought your textbook yet?
  B: No. I _haven't_ bought it _yet._

1. A: Have you _eaten/had_ dinner yet?
   B: No, I haven't. I _ate/had_ lunch at 2:30, so I'm not hungry now.

2. A: _Has_ your sister gotten married yet?
   B: Yes. She _got_ married two weeks ago. She _had_ a beautiful wedding.
   A: Has she _gotten_ back from her honeymoon yet?
   B: Yes. She _got_ back last Thursday.

3. A: Have your parents _found_ an apartment yet?
   B: No. They _haven't_ found one yet. They're still looking.

4. A: I'm going to rent the movie *Titanic*. Have you _seen_ it yet?
   B: Yes, I _saw_ it a couple of years ago, but I'd like to see it again.

5. A: What are you going to do during summer vacation?
   B: I haven't _thought_ about it yet. It's only April.
   A: I've already _made_ plans. I'm going to Niagara Falls.
      I _bought/got_ my ticket last week.

6. A: Has the movie _began/started_ yet? I want to buy some popcorn before it begins.
   B: Shhh! It _begun/started_ ten minutes ago.

7. A: Do you want to go to the museum with me on Saturday?
   B: Sorry. I _have_ already _made_ other plans for Saturday.

8. A: _Has_ your brother _gotten_ back from Mexico yet?
   B: No, he hasn't. We're expecting him to arrive on Tuesday.

9. A: I'd like to talk to the teacher, please.
   B: I'm sorry. She's already _left_ for the day.
   A: But she told me to call her before 4 o'clock and it's only 3:30.
   B: She _left_ at 2 o'clock because her son was sick.

10. A: Is that a good book?
    B: Yes, it is. I haven't _finished_ it yet, but when I finish it, you can have it.

Expansion

Exercise 34 Have students work in pairs. Draw students' attention to items 4, 5, and 7. Have students use the first question for each to write their own conversations. Have volunteers read their conversations to the class.

Culture Note

Draw students' attention to item 7 in Exercise 34. Explain that *I've already made other plans* is a polite way to decline an invitation.

1.17 | Questions with *Lately* and *Recently*

Questions with *lately* and *recently* ask about an indefinite time in the near past. We can answer a *lately* or *recently* question with the present perfect or the simple past.

Examples	Explanation
Have you **seen** your parents lately? 　No, I **haven't**. **Have** you **gotten** a raise recently? 　No. I **haven't gotten** a raise recently.	When the answer is *no*, we usually use the present perfect.
Have you **seen** any good movies lately? 　Yes. I **saw** a great movie last week. **Have** you **gone** to the library recently? 　Yes. I **went** to the library two days ago.	When the answer is *yes*, we usually give a specific time and use the simple past tense.

EXERCISE 35 ABOUT YOU Ask a *yes / no* question with the words given. Another student will answer. A past-tense statement may be added to a *yes* answer.

EXAMPLE　go swimming recently

　　A: Have you gone swimming recently?
　　B: Yes, I have. I went swimming yesterday.

1.　write to your family lately
　　Have you written to your family lately?
2.　go to the library recently
　　Have you gone to the library recently?
3.　go to the zoo lately
　　Have you gone to the zoo lately?
4.　see any good movies lately
　　Have you seen any good movies lately?
5.　receive any letters lately
　　Have you received any letters lately?
6.　be absent lately
　　Have you been absent lately?
7.　have a job interview lately
　　Have you had a job interview lately?
8.　read any good books recently
　　Have you read any good books recently?
9.　make any long-distance calls lately
　　Have you made any long-distance calls lately?
10.　take any tests recently
　　Have you taken any tests recently?

1.17 | Questions with *Lately* and *Recently*

1. Have students cover the grammar chart. Say: *We use* lately *or* recently *and the present perfect to ask questions about what someone has done at an indefinite time in the near past.* Ask a volunteer: *Have you been to (a place in your area) recently? When did you go there? What movies have you seen lately?*
2. Have students uncover and review the grammar chart. Ask: *When do we answer with the simple past?* (when the answer is *yes*) *When do we answer with the present perfect?* (when the answer is *no*)

EXERCISE 35

1. Tell students that this exercise is about their recent activities. Have students read the direction line. Ask: *When will we add a statement in the simple past?* (when the answer to the question is *yes*)
2. Direct students to the example in the book. Model the exercise with a student.
3. Have students complete the rest of the exercise in pairs. Circulate and observe the pair work. Have volunteers share information about their partners with the class.

Expansion

Exercise 35 Have students create new statements from the prompts. Model an example: *I haven't written to my family lately, but I called them last weekend.*

1. Tell students that this exercise is a chance to ask you some questions about your recent activities. Have students read the direction line. Ask: *What word do we use in the questions?* (*lately* or *recently*)
2. Direct students to the example in the book.
3. Have students complete the exercise in pairs. Ask volunteers to ask you the questions. Answer the questions. When possible, add an explanation using the present perfect or past tense as appropriate.

🕐 To save class time, have students write the questions for homework. Then have a few volunteers ask you questions in class.

1. Tell students that this exercise is a series of conversations between friends about recent activities. Have students read the direction line. Ask: *Which tenses do we use in the answers?* (simple past or present perfect)
2. Direct students to the example in the book. Ask: *Which tense do we use in the answer?* (the simple past) *Why?* (because the answer is *yes* and a time is given)
3. Have students complete the exercise in pairs. Point out the picture of the person who is getting a massage. Circulate and observe the pair work. If necessary, review the answers as a class.
4. Assess students' performance. If necessary, review grammar chart **1.17** on page 41.

🕐 To save class time, have students do half of the exercise in class and complete the other half for homework. Or assign the entire exercise for homework.

EXERCISE 36 Work with a partner. Write four questions to ask your teacher about what he or she has done lately. Your teacher will answer.

EXAMPLE _Have you taken a vacation lately (or recently)?_

1. _____ Answers will vary. _____
2. _____
3. _____
4. _____

EXERCISE 37 Fill in the blanks with the correct verb forms.

EXAMPLE A: Have you ___gotten___ a letter from your parents lately?
(get)
B: Yes. I ___got___ a letter from them yesterday.

1. A: Have you ___taken___ any pictures lately?
(take)
B: No, I ___haven't___. My camera is broken.

2. A: Have you ___seen___ any good movies lately?
(see)
B: Yes. I ___saw___ a great movie last weekend.

3. A: Have you ___gone___ for a walk lately?
(go)
B: Yes. I ___went___ for a walk yesterday.

4. A: Have you ___bought___ yourself a gift lately?
(buy)
B: Yes. I ___bought___ myself a new CD player last week.

5. A: Have you ___had___ a good conversation with a friend lately?
(have)
B: No. I ___haven't had___ time to talk with my friends lately.

6. A: Have you ___had___ a massage lately?
(have)
B: No. I ___have___ never ___had___ a massage.

7. A: Have you ___done___ the laundry lately?
(do)
B: Yes. I ___did___ it this morning.

8. A: Have you ___gone___ to any parties lately?
(go)
B: No, I ___haven't___. I've been too busy lately.

42   Lesson 1

Expansion

Exercise 37 Have students write an alternate answer with the opposite response (*yes* or *no*) to the items in the exercise.

1.18 | The Present Perfect Continuous with Ongoing Activities

Examples	Explanation
Many American companies **have been sending** jobs abroad. American companies **have been benefiting** from outsourcing. Lately I **have been thinking** about changing majors. My English **has been improving** a lot lately.	We use the present perfect continuous to show that an activity has been ongoing or in progress from a time in the near past to the present. Remember, do not use the continuous form with nonaction verbs: She **has been** absent a lot lately.

EXERCISE 38 ABOUT YOU Fill in the blanks with *have* or *haven't* to tell about yiur experiences lately. (You may add a sentence telling why.)

EXAMPLE I ___*haven't*___ been reading a lot lately. *I haven't had much time.*

Answers will vary.

1. I _____ been getting a lot of sleep recently.

2. I _____ been getting together with my friends lately.

3. I _____ been watching the news a lot lately.

4. I _____ been studying a lot lately.

5. I _____ been learning a lot about English grammar lately.

6. I _____ been worrying a lot lately.

7. I _____ been looking for a job recently.

8. I _____ been watching a lot of TV recently.

9. I _____ been having a lot of problems with my car lately.

10. I _____ been spending a lot of money recently.

11. I _____ been absent a lot lately.

12. I _____ been using a computer a lot lately.

1.18 | The Present Perfect Continuous with Ongoing Activities

1. Tell students about something you have been doing a lot lately (e.g., *I've been exercising a lot lately.*). Have students give examples of their own with *lately* or *recently*.
2. Have students review the examples and explanation in the grammar chart.

EXERCISE 38

1. Tell students that this exercise is about their lives lately. Have students read the direction line. Ask: *What words will we use in the sentences?* (*have* or *haven't*) Review the example in the book. Point out the sentence telling why.
2. Have students complete the exercise individually. Have students read their sentences to a partner.
3. Assess students' performance. If necessary, review grammar chart **1.18**.

Expansion

Exercise 38 After students complete the exercise, have them work in pairs to ask each other about their statements with *why* or *why not*:

A: *I haven't been getting a lot of sleep recently.*

B: *Why not?*

A: *Because we have a new baby.*

1. Tell students that this exercise is about things that they have been doing lately. Have students read the direction line.
2. Direct students to the example in the book. Have volunteers read the examples. Ask: *Is this true for you?*
3. Have students complete the exercise. Ask volunteers to share their answers with the class.

🕐 To save class time, have students do half of the exercise in class and complete the other half for homework. Or assign the entire exercise for homework.

1.19 | The Present Perfect with No Time Mentioned

1. Have students cover the grammar chart. On the board, write a statement about yourself using the present perfect tense with no time mentioned (e.g., *I've studied French, but I still don't speak it well.*). Ask: *Do you know when I studied French?* (no) Ask: *Why do we use the present perfect tense in this sentence?* (because we don't say when the action (studying) happened, but it's still important now (because I still don't speak it well))
2. Have students uncover and review the example sentences and explanations in the grammar chart.
3. Ask volunteers to give sentences about themselves using the present perfect tense with no time mentioned.

1. Tell students that this exercise is about things that they have been done at some time in the past. Have students read the direction line.
2. Direct students to the example in the book. Ask: *Is this true for you?*
3. Have students complete the exercise. Ask volunteers to share their answers with the class.

EXERCISE **39** ABOUT YOU Fill in the blanks to make true statements about yourself.

EXAMPLES _____My pronunciation_____ has been getting better.

_____My eyesight_____ has been getting worse.

1. _____Answers will vary._____ has been improving.

2. _____ has been getting worse.

3. _____ has been increasing.

4. _____ has been helping me with my studies.

5. _____ has been making me tired.

1.19 | The Present Perfect with No Time Mentioned

Examples	Explanation
I **have thought** about my career. **Have** you **told** your parents that you're changing majors? Many educated workers **have lost** their jobs. Many American workers **have become** more insecure about their jobs.	We can use the present perfect to talk about the past without any reference to time. The time is not important or not known or imprecise. Using the present perfect, rather than the past, shows that the past is relevant to a present situation.

EXERCISE **40** ABOUT YOU Fill in the blanks to make a true statement about yourself.

EXAMPLE I've eaten _____pizza_____, and I like it a lot.

1. I've visited _____Answers will vary._____, and I would recommend it to other people.

2. I've tried _____, and I like this food a lot.

3. I've seen the movie _____, and I would recommend it to others.

4. The teacher has said that _____, but some of us forget.

5. I've studied _____, and it has really helped me in my life.

6. I've had a lot of experience with _____ and can help you with it, if you need me to.

Expansion

Exercise 39 Have students work in pairs. Ask students to write about their partners (e.g., *Leyla's roommate has been helping her with her studies.*).

Exercise 40 Ask: *What activity have you done or place have you visited in this city?*

EXERCISE **41** ABOUT YOU Place a check mark (✓) next to the work-related experiences you've had. Then at the bottom, write three more things you've done at your present or former job. Write things that would impress an interviewer.

Answers will vary.

1. _____ I've worked on a team.
2. _____ I've taken programming courses.
3. _____ I've had experience talking with customers on the phone.
4. _____ I've worked overtime when necessary to finish a project.
5. _____ I've worked and gone to school at the same time.
6. _____ I've helped my family financially.
7. _____ I've given oral presentations.
8. _____ I've done research.
9. _____ I've created a Web site.
10. _____ I've done physical labor.
11. _____ I've been in charge of a group of workers.
12. _____ I've traveled as part of my job.
13. _____
14. _____
15. _____

EXERCISE **42** Fill in the blanks with the present perfect (for no time mentioned) or the simple past (if the time is mentioned) of the verb in parentheses ( ).

I _have had_ many new experiences since I moved here. I
(example: have)

have tried some foods for the first time in my life. I _have eaten_
(1 try)   (2 eat)

pizza, but I don't like it much. Yesterday, I _tried_ Chinese food
(3 try)

for the first time and thought it was delicious.

I _have met_ a lot of new people and have some new friends.
(4 meet)

I _have seen_ some new behaviors. For example, there's a guy in my
(5 see)

math class who wears torn jeans every day. Yesterday I _asked_ him
(6 ask)

The Present Perfect; The Present Perfect Continuous   45

EXERCISE 41

1. Tell students that this exercise is about work-related experiences they have had at some time in the past. Have students read the direction line. Ask: *What do we write for numbers 13 to 15?* (three more things we've done at a job)
2. Have students complete the first statement together. Ask: *How many people made a check mark?*
3. Have students complete the exercise individually. Ask volunteers to share their answers with the class.

EXERCISE 42

🎧 *CD 1, Track 8*

1. Tell students that this exercise is about one person's experiences in the U.S. Have students read the direction line. Ask: *Which tenses do we use?* (the present perfect or simple past)
2. Direct students to the example. The have students complete the second statement together.
3. Have students complete the exercise individually. Ask volunteers to share their answers with the class.

🕐 To save class time, have students do half of the exercise in class and complete the other half for homework. Or assign the entire exercise for homework.

Expansion

Exercise 41 Have students use their own experience to make longer statements, such as: *I've worked on a team, but I haven't been in charge of a group of workers.*

Have students ask each other questions about the items, such as: *Have you given an oral presentation?* and for a *yes* answer, *When did you give an oral presentation?*

Exercise 42 Variation

To provide practice with listening skills, have students close their books and listen to the audio. Repeat the audio as needed. Ask comprehension questions, such as: *Does the person like pizza?* (no, not much) *What new type of food did the person try yesterday?* (Chinese food) Then have students open their books and complete Exercise 42.

1.20 | The Present Perfect vs. the Present Perfect Continuous with No Time Mentioned

1. Have students cover the explanations column in the grammar chart. Ask: *What is the difference between the (a) examples and the (b) examples?* (The (a) examples are present perfect; the (b) examples are present perfect continuous.) Ask: *Why are the (b) examples present perfect continuous?* (because the activity is not finished yet)
2. Have students uncover and review the explanations.

EXERCISE 43

1. Tell students that this exercise is about whether people's activities are finished or ongoing. Have students read the direction line.
2. Direct students to the example in the book. Ask: *Why is the second choice correct?* (because the people are still making noise)
3. Model the activity. Complete #1 with the class.
4. Have students complete the exercise individually. Ask volunteers to share their answers, and the reasons they chose them, with the class.
5. Assess students' performance. If necessary, review grammar chart **1.20**.

---

if he needs money for new clothes, but he just laughed and said, "Torn clothes are in style."

I ___have visited___ some interesting places. I ___have gone___ to the art
    (7 visit)   *(8 go)*

museum and the science museum. I ___have taken___ a boat ride on a
                                      (9 take)

nearby river. I ___have even gone___ to the top of the tallest building.
              (10 even/go)

I ___have learned___ about looking for a job. I ___have written___ résumés and
   (11 learn)   *(12 write)*

___have had___ job interviews. I ___have gone___ to job fairs. I ___have even used___
(13 have)   *(14 go)*   *(15 even/use)*

the Internet for my job search. Last week I ___went___ to see a job counselor
                                            (16 go)

at my college, and she ___gave___ me some help with interviewing
                      (17 give)

techniques.

1.20 | The Present Perfect vs. the Present Perfect Continuous with No Time Mentioned

We can use both the present perfect and the present perfect continuous with no time mentioned.

Examples	Explanation
a. My counselor **has helped** me with my résumé. b. My family **has been helping** me a lot.	The (a) examples are present perfect. They refer to a single occurrence at an indefinite time in the past.
a. I **have applied** for a job in New York. b. I **have been applying** for jobs all over the U.S.	The (b) examples are present perfect continuous. They refer to an ongoing activity that is not finished. The activity is still in progress.
a. **Have** you **eaten** in a restaurant lately? b. I**'ve been eating** in restaurants a lot lately.	

EXERCISE **43** Check (✓) the sentence or clause that best completes the idea.

EXAMPLE I can't sleep. The people in the next apartment . . .

    _____ have made a lot of noise.

    ___✓___ have been making a lot of noise.

Grammar Variation

Have students close their books. Draw timelines on the board to illustrate the (a) examples (drawing a single mark on the "past" section of the timeline to show the action was a single occurrence) and the (b) examples (drawing a continuous line with an arrow to the present to show the action is an ongoing activity that is not finished). Ask students to form sentences to describe these actions. Elicit the (a) and (b) example sentences from the grammar chart. Then have students open their books and review the grammar chart.

1. She's been sick all week.
   - ———— She's stayed in bed.
   - √ She's been staying in bed.

2. She is unhappy.
   - √ She has just lost her job.
   - ———— She has been losing her job.

3. She lost her job three weeks ago. She hasn't had much free time lately because . . .
   - ———— she has looked for a new job.
   - √ she has been looking for a new job.

4. My writing has been improving a lot because . . .
   - ———— I have written compositions.
   - √ I have been writing compositions.

5. At first she planned to move, but now she doesn't want to.
   - √ She has changed her mind.
   - ———— She has been changing her mind.

6. I meet new people everywhere: in my neighborhood, at my job, at school.
   - ———— I have met new people.
   - √ I have been meeting new people.

7. Now I can pay for my car repair because I . . .
   - √ have received a check from my insurance company.
   - ———— have been receiving a check from my insurance company.

8. Every week I put 20 percent of my salary in the bank. I plan to buy a house as soon as I can.
   - ———— I have saved my money.
   - √ I have been saving my money.

9. I'm going to become an engineer.
   - √ I have made my decision.
   - ———— I have been making my decision.

10. A: Have you been outside today?
    - B: ———— No, I have worked on my composition.
    - √ No, I have been working on my composition.

Expansion

Exercise 43 Have students complete the following dialogue:

A: Have you found a job yet?
B: No, I haven't.
A: Why not?
B: Well, I've been busy. I've been . . .

Then ask a few volunteers to act out the dialogue for the class.

EXERCISE 44

1. Tell students that this exercise is about whether people's job experiences are finished or ongoing. Have students read the direction line. Ask: *How many tenses can we use?* (three)
2. Direct students to the example in the book. Ask: *Why is this answer correct?* (because it is a single event in the past)
3. Model the activity. Complete #1 with the class. Point out the pictures of the pilot and the kindergarten teacher.
4. Have students complete the exercise individually. Ask volunteers to share their answers, and the reasons they chose them, with the class.
5. Assess students' performance. If necessary, review grammar chart **1.20** on page 46.

To save class time, have students do half of the exercise in class and complete the other half for homework. Or assign the entire exercise for homework.

EXERCISE **44** Fill in the blanks with the simple past, the present perfect, or the present perfect continuous of the verb in parentheses ( ). In some cases, more than one answer is possible.

EXAMPLE I ___*worked*___ as a cashier when I was in high school.
(work)

1. I think I'm qualified for the job of driver because I ___*have worked*___ as a driver before.
(work)

2. I ___*worked*___ as a pilot many years ago. My job as a pilot
(work)
___*took*___ me away from home much of the time.
(take)

3. I don't like the sight of blood, so I ___*have never thought/never thought*___
(never/think)
about becoming a doctor.

4. I'm a hair stylist. I ___*have been cutting*___ people's hair for 15 years.
(cut)

5. I'm afraid of the interview process because I ___*have never had*___ a job interview before.
(never/have)

6. Many years ago, I ___*worked*___ as a kindergarten
(work)
teacher. Now I have my own day care center.

7. I'm a car mechanic. I ___*have been*___ a mechanic for three
(be)
years. I ___*have had*___ a lot of experience working with
(have)
American cars, but I ___*haven't had*___ much experience with
(not/have)
foreign cars.

8. I'm 62 years old and I like my job as a lab technician, but I
___*have been thinking*___ about retiring soon.
(think)

9. When I was in my native country, I ___*was*___ an
(be)
engineer, but now I'm a salesperson.

Expansion

Exercise 44 Have students use the items in the exercise to write their own sentences about their job experience, job-hunting experience, and thoughts on jobs and work.

10. People ___have often asked___ me why I want to be a funeral
        (often/ask)
    director when I graduate.

11. Lately I ___have been using___ the Internet a lot to get
        (use)
    information about jobs.

SUMMARY OF LESSON 1

Compare the Simple Present and the Present Perfect.

Simple Past	Present Perfect
She **has** a job.	She **has had** her job for six months.
She **is** a lab technician.	She **has been** a lab technician since May.

Compare the Present Continuous and the Present Perfect Continuous.

Present Continuous	Present Perfect Continuous
He **is working** now.	He **has been working** for three hours.
She **is sleeping** now.	She **has been sleeping** for 20 minutes.

Compare the Simple Past and the Present Perfect.

Simple Past	Present Perfect
Daniel **worked** in Mexico City from 1994 to 1998.	He **has worked** in the U.S. since 1998.
He **found** a job in 2004.	He **has had** his present job since January, 2004.
He **bought** his car when he came to Chicago.	He **has had** his car since he came to Chicago.
When **did** he **come** to Chicago?	How long **has** he **been** in Chicago?
He **had** three interviews last month.	He **has had** two interviews this month.
He **studied** business in college.	He **has studied** French and speaks it well.
He **went** to New York in July.	He **has gone** to Los Angeles many times.
Did you **go** to the job fair last week?	**Have** you ever **gone** to a job fair?

Summary of Lesson 1

1. **Compare the Simple Present and the Present Perfect.** Have students make statements about themselves in the simple present and then add a sentence in the present perfect with details (e.g., *I have a dog. I've had my dog for seven years.*).
   If necessary, have students review:
   1.9 The Present Perfect vs. the Simple Present (p. 16).

2. **Compare the Present Continuous and the Present Perfect Continuous.** Have students make statements about events in the news or weather, classroom events, or events going on in their lives (e.g., *My family is visiting me.*). Have volunteers ask questions with *how long* (e.g., *How long has your family been visiting you?*), and have students answer.
   If necessary, have students review:
   1.10 The Present Perfect Continuous (pp. 20–21).

3. **Compare the Simple Past and the Present Perfect.** Have students work in pairs to ask each other questions about the examples in the chart. Model the activity: *Why do we use the present perfect in the sentence* He has worked in the U.S. since 1998? (The action started in the past and continues to the present.)
   If necessary, have students review:
   1.11 The Present Perfect vs. the Simple Past (p. 25)
   1.13 Present Perfect vs. Simple Past with Repetition (p. 30).

Summary Variation

Write phrases in the present perfect, simple present, and simple past on the board (e.g., *I have had . . .; I was . . .; I go . . .*). In pairs, have students talk about themselves using the phrases in statements.

Summary of Lesson 1 (cont.)

4. **Compare the Present Continuous and the Present Perfect Continuous.** Have students make statements about themselves based on the examples in the chart, such as: *I have worked as a cashier for the past six months; I have been living with my sister for the past three years.*
If necessary, have students review:
1.1 An Overview (p. 2)
1.10 The Present Perfect Continuous (pp. 20–21)
1.20 The Present Perfect vs. the Present Perfect Continuous with No Time Mentioned (p. 46).

Editing Advice

For each item, have students provide the grammar rule behind the editing advice. This can be done as an individual, a pair, a group, or a class activity.

1. Use the present participle (with *-ing*) with the present perfect continuous.
   Use the past participle with the present perfect tense.
2. Use *for* with periods of time and *since* with specific times.

Compare the Present Perfect and the Present Perfect Continuous.

Present Perfect	Present Perfect Continuous
Ron **has worked** as a programmer for the past five years. *(This sentence has the same meaning as the one on the right.)*	Ron **has been working** as a programmer for the past five years. *(This sentence has the same meaning as the one on the left.)*
I **have lived** in three American cities. *(This sentence refers to a repetition from past to present.)*	I **have been living** in this city for the past two years. *(This sentence shows a continuation from past to present.)*
How many apartments **have** you **had** in this city? *(This question asks about a repetition from past to present.)*	How long **have** you **been living** in your present apartment? *(This question asks about a continuation from past to present.)*
Dan **has studied** French. *(This sentence shows only past activity, with no indication of a continuation.)*	The U.S. government **has been studying** the effect of outsourcing. *(This sentence shows an activity that is still in progress.)*
I **have thought** about changing majors. *(This sentence tells about a time in the indefinite past.)*	I **have been thinking** a lot about my future. *(In this sentence, the phrase "a lot" indicates that this activity is still in progress.)*

EDITING ADVICE

1. Don't confuse the *-ing* form and the past participle.
   taking
   I've been ~~taken~~ English courses for several years.
   been
   Have you ever ~~being~~ in Texas?

2. Don't confuse *for* and *since*.
   for
   He's been in Chicago ~~since~~ three years.

50   Lesson 1

---

3. Use the simple past, not the present perfect, with a specific past time and in questions and statements with *when*.

> *wrote*
> He ~~has written~~ a book five years ago.

> She has bought a car when she has found a job.

> *did he get*
> When ~~has he gotten~~ his driver's license?

4. Use the present perfect (continuous), not the present tense, if the action started in the past and continues to the present.

> *have been*
> I'm working in a factory for six months.

> *have   had*
> How long ~~do you have~~ your computer?

5. Don't use the continuous form for repetition.

> *eaten*
> How many times have you ~~been eating~~ pizza?

6. Use the simple past in a *since*-clause.

> *came*
> He's had three jobs since he ~~has come~~ to the U.S.

7. Use correct word order.

> *never been*
> He has ~~been never~~ in New York.

> *ever eaten*
> Have you ~~eaten ever~~ Chinese food?

8. Use *yet* in negative statements. Use *already* in affirmative statements.

> *yet*
> I haven't finished the book ~~already~~.

> *already*
> I've finished the book ~~yet~~.

9. Use *how long* for a question about length of time. Don't include the word *time*.

> How long ~~time~~ have they been working in a restaurant?

10. If the main verb is *have*, be sure to include the auxiliary verb *have* for the present perfect.

> *has*
> He had his job since March.

Editing Advice (*cont.*)

3. With *when*, and with a specific past time, use the simple past tense, not the present perfect.

4. If an action started in the past and continues to the present, use the present perfect or present perfect continuous tense.

5. For repetition, don't use the present perfect continuous.

6. Use the simple past, not the present perfect, after *since*.

7. Put *never* between *have* or *has* and the participle in a sentence; put *ever* between the subject and the participle in questions.

8. Use *yet* in negative statements and *already* in affirmative statements.

9. Don't use *time* after *how long* in a question.

10. With the present perfect, remember to use the auxiliary verb *have*, even when the main verb is *have*.

Lesson 1 Test/Review

For additional practice, review, and assessment materials, see Assessment CD-ROM with *ExamView Pro*, *More Grammar Practice* Workbook 3, Interactive CD-ROM, and Web site http://elt.thomson.com/gic

PART 1

1. Part 1 may be used as an in-class test to assess student performance, in addition to the Assessment CD-ROM with *ExamView Pro*. Have students read the direction line. Ask: *Does every sentence have a mistake?* (no)
2. Collect for assessment.
3. If necessary, have students review: **Lesson 1.**

PART 2

1. Part 2 may also be used as an in-class test to assess student performance, in addition to the Assessment CD-ROM with *ExamView Pro*. Tell students that this is a conversation between two people. Words and phrases are missing. Review the example. Then do the next sentence as a class. Ask: *What goes in the first blank?* (don't have)
2. Collect for assessment.
3. If necessary, have students review: **Lesson 1.**

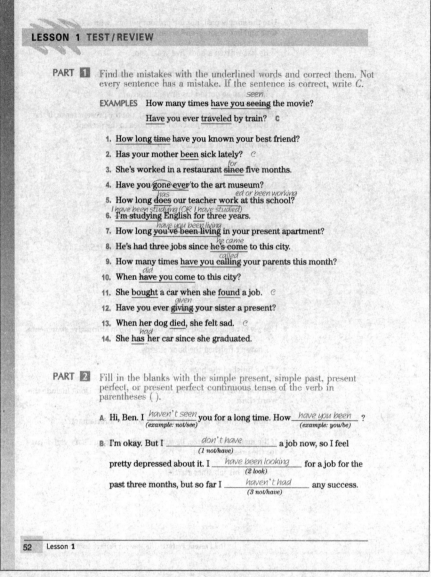

LESSON 1 TEST/REVIEW

PART 1 Find the mistakes with the underlined words and correct them. Not every sentence has a mistake. If the sentence is correct, write *C*.

EXAMPLES How many times have you seeing the movie? *seen*

Have you ever traveled by train? *C*

1. How long time have you known your best friend?
2. Has your mother been sick lately? *C*
3. She's worked in a restaurant since five months. *for*
4. Have you gone ever to the art museum?
5. How long does our teacher work at this school? *has ... ed or been working*
6. I'm studying English for three years. *I have been studying (OR I have studied)*
7. How long you've been living in your present apartment? *have you been living*
8. He's had three jobs since he's come to this city. *he came*
9. How many times have you calling your parents this month? *called*
10. When have you come to this city? *did*
11. She bought a car when she found a job. *C*
12. Have you ever giving your sister a present? *given*
13. When her dog died, she felt sad. *C*
14. She has her car since she graduated. *had*

PART 2 Fill in the blanks with the simple present, simple past, present perfect, or present perfect continuous tense of the verb in parentheses ( ).

A: Hi, Ben. I __*haven't seen*__ you for a long time. How __*have you been*__ ?
     (example: not/see)   (example: you/be)

B: I'm okay. But I __*don't have*__ a job now, so I feel
                     (1 not/have)

pretty depressed about it. I __*have been looking*__ for a job for the
                              (2 look)

past three months, but so far I __*haven't had*__ any success.
                                  (3 not/have)

52 Lesson 1

Lesson Review

To use Part 1 as a review, assign it as homework or use it as an in-class activity to be completed individually or in pairs. Check answers and review errors as a class. Reteach grammar points that students haven't mastered. Then student learning may be assessed using a test generated from the Assessment CD-ROM with *ExamView Pro*.

A: My best friend _____graduated_____ from college last year, and
(4 graduate)

he _____hasn't found_____ a job yet. A lot of American jobs
(5 not/find)

_____have disappeared/have been disappearing_____ in recent years. Many jobs
(6 disappear)

_____have gone/have been going_____ to India and other countries.
(7 go)

B: That's terrible. My family _____came_____ to the U.S. last
(8 come)

year to find better jobs, but it's not easy anymore.

A: But it's not impossible. _____Have_____ you ever _____used_____ the
(9 use)

Occupational Outlook Handbook?

B: No, I never _____have_____ .
(10 have)

A: You can find it on a Web site. It lists information about professions in

the U.S. My counselor _____told_____ me about it when I
(11 tell)

_____started_____ taking courses. I _____have_____ a good job now.
(12 start)   (13 have)

I _____work_____ as a dental assistant.
(14 work)

B: How long _____have you worked/have you been working_____ there?
(15 you/work)

A: Since I _____got_____ my certificate two years ago. I don't have
(16 get)

to worry about outsourcing. You can't look in people's mouths from
another country.

B: You're lucky to have such a good job.

A: It's not luck. I _____chose_____ this job carefully before I started
(17 choose)

taking courses. And I _____studied_____ hard when I
(18 study)

was in the dental program. Now when I _____go_____ to work
(19 go)

every day, I _____feel_____ good because I am helping people and
(20 feel)

making good money. Also I _____have_____ good benefits. In
(21 have)

addition, I _____have gotten_____ two salary increases so far.
(22 get)

Lesson Review

To use Part 2 as a review, have students complete the conversation individually. Check
answers and review errors as a class. Then practice the conversation in pairs. Circulate to
observe pair work. Give help as needed. Reteach grammar points that students haven't
mastered. Then student learning may be assessed using a test generated from the Assessment
CD-ROM with *ExamView Pro*.

Expansion Activities

These expansion activities provide opportunities for students to interact with one another and further develop their speaking and writing skills. Encourage students to use grammar from this lesson whenever possible.

🕐 To save class time, assign parts of the activities as homework. Then use class time for interaction and communication. If students do not need additional speaking practice, some of the activities may be assigned as writing activities for homework, or skipped altogether.

CLASSROOM ACTIVITIES

1. Tell students that this activity is about experience. Ask: *What tense do we use to talk about experience?* (the present perfect tense) Review question formation with the present perfect tense with students. If necessary, provide the option of writing out the questions before asking a partner. When students have finished, have them report their results as a class. Ask: *Who has been exercising a lot lately?*

2. Tell students that this activity is about interviewing for a job. Ask each pair to decide on a workplace and type of job for their interview before they begin. Have pairs switch roles and repeat the activity.

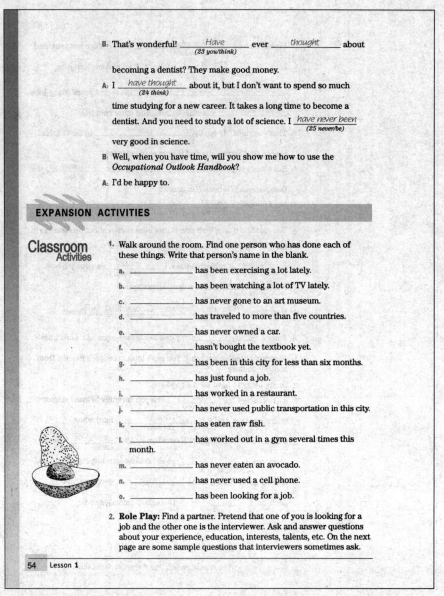

B: That's wonderful! _____Have_____ ever _____thought_____ about
(23 you/think)

becoming a dentist? They make good money.

A: I _____have thought_____ about it, but I don't want to spend so much
(24 think)

time studying for a new career. It takes a long time to become a

dentist. And you need to study a lot of science. I _____have never been_____
(25 never/be)

very good in science.

B: Well, when you have time, will you show me how to use the
Occupational Outlook Handbook?

A: I'd be happy to.

EXPANSION ACTIVITIES

Classroom Activities

1. Walk around the room. Find one person who has done each of these things. Write that person's name in the blank.

   a. _____ has been exercising a lot lately.

   b. _____ has been watching a lot of TV lately.

   c. _____ has never gone to an art museum.

   d. _____ has traveled to more than five countries.

   e. _____ has never owned a car.

   f. _____ hasn't bought the textbook yet.

   g. _____ has been in this city for less than six months.

   h. _____ has just found a job.

   i. _____ has worked in a restaurant.

   j. _____ has never used public transportation in this city.

   k. _____ has eaten raw fish.

   l. _____ has worked out in a gym several times this
   month.

   m. _____ has never eaten an avocado.

   n. _____ has never used a cell phone.

   o. _____ has been looking for a job.

2. **Role Play:** Find a partner. Pretend that one of you is looking for a job and the other one is the interviewer. Ask and answer questions about your experience, education, interests, talents, etc. On the next page are some sample questions that interviewers sometimes ask.

54   Lesson 1

Classroom Activities Variation

Activity 2 After pairs have finished their interviews, ask each interviewer whether he or she will hire the applicant. Have interviewers say why they made the decisions they did.

- Why did you leave your last job?
- Why are you applying for this position?
- Where would you like to be five years from now?
- What are your strengths?
- What are your weaknesses?
- Why should we hire you?

3. **Game—True-True-False:** Form a small group. On a piece of paper, write two unusual things you have done in the past. Write one false statement about your past. (Use the present perfect with no mention of time.) Read your statements to the other members of your group. The other members have to guess which is the false statement.

EXAMPLES I've flown in a helicopter.
I've worked on a farm.
I've met the president of my native country.

4. Fill in the blanks and discuss your answers.
   a. I've learned _____ from my experiences in the U.S.
   b. I've thought a lot about _____.
   c. Most people in my native country have never _____.
   d. In the U.S., it's been hard for me to _____.

Talk About it

1. How is looking for a job in the U.S. different from looking for a job in other countries?

2. How is the work environment in your present job different from the work environment in a previous job you had?

3. In other countries, how do people usually select a career? Are there career counselors to help people make a decision?

4. Have you ever used the Internet to search for jobs? Has it been helpful?

5. Look at the list of jobs below. Which ones do you think are interesting and why? What do you think are some good or bad aspects of these jobs?

airplane pilot	funeral director	librarian
architect	gardener	musician
bus driver	immigration officer	newspaper reporter
circus clown	lawyer	police officer
firefighter	letter carrier	veterinarian

3. Ask: *Which tense do we use to ask questions about what people have done in the past?* (present perfect) Tell students to write false statements that are unusual but possible.

4. Tell students this activity is about change. Have students fill in the blanks and then share their answers with a partner. Discuss interesting answers as a class. If necessary, have students explain vocabulary or customs from their past that students might not understand.

TALK ABOUT IT

Have students work in groups. Either assign or have each group choose one or more of the topics to discuss. Review language for agreeing, checking for agreement, and disagreeing (e.g., *I think so, too. Are you sure that's right? I'm not sure I agree.*). Set a time limit for discussion. Then have groups talk about their topics. If appropriate, have groups report back to the class; have each group appoint a spokesperson.

Talk About it Variation

Activity 5 Have students choose one of the jobs listed (or another job) to give an oral report on. Instruct students to find out some basic facts, such as the salary, required education and qualifications, and hours. Then have students present their findings to the class. Students may use the *Occupational Outlook Handbook* or other library or Internet resources for their research.

1. Review the use of the present perfect and the simple past in discussing work experience. Have students write a paragraph about their work experience. Collect for assessment and/or have students review each other's work.
2. Have students brainstorm careers they have heard of and think would be interesting, and why they think so. Have students choose one career to write about. Collect for assessment and/or have students present their paragraph to a group.
3. Have students brainstorm jobs they would like to have and jobs they would not like to have, and why. Say: *A job I would never want to have is . . . because . . .* Have students write a paragraph on a job they would not want to have. Collect for assessment and/or have students present their paragraph to a group.
4. Review language for giving advice (e.g., *I think you should. Maybe you should. It's best if you . . .*). Have students brainstorm outlines for their articles. Collect for assessment and/or have students review each other's work.

OUTSIDE ACTIVITIES

Instruct students to interview a friend, family member, or acquaintance outside the class, using the questions in the book and others, if possible. If necessary, provide the option of writing out the questions before the interview.

INTERNET ACTIVITIES

1. Check that students are familiar with terms such as *search engine* and *hits*.
2. Brainstorm search terms to use to find career counseling Web sites.
3. Have students share information they find. Ask: *Which advice do you think is good advice? Why?*
4. Have students share want ads for jobs they find interesting. Discuss abbreviations commonly used in want ads (*FT, PT, req.*, etc.).
5. Have students find out what applicants should bring with them to a job fair (e.g., a résumé).
6. Have students report back to the class on information they find.
7. Have students tell the class why they chose the companies they did and what types of information were available on the Web sites.

Write About It

1. Write about your past work experience.
2. Write about a career that you think is interesting. Explain why you think this career is interesting.
3. Write about a job you would never want to have. Tell why.
4. Write an article giving advice to somebody looking for a job.

Outside Activity

Interview someone about his or her job. Find out the following information and report it to the class.

- how long he or she has been working at this job
- what his / her job responsibilities are
- if he / she likes this job
- how he / she found this job

NOTE: It is not polite to ask about salary.

Internet Activities

1. Type *career* or *jobs* in a search engine. See how many "hits" come up.
2. Find some career counseling Web sites. Find a sample résumé in your field or close to your field. Print it out and bring it to class. What's the difference between a chronological résumé and a functional résumé?
3. From one of the Web sites you found, get information on one or more of the following topics:
   - how to write a cover letter
   - how to find a career counselor
   - how to plan for an interview
   - how to network
   - what questions to ask the interviewer
4. See if your local newspaper has a Web site. If it does, find the Help Wanted section.
5. Type in *job fair* and the name of your city. Are there any jobs fairs near you?
6. Type in *Occupational Outlook Handbook*. Find information about a job that interests you.
7. Many businesses have pages on the Internet that give information about the company and offer job listings. Find information about a company that interests you.

Additional Activities at http://elt.thomson.com/gic

Write About it Variation

Have students exchange first drafts with a partner. Ask students to help their partners edit their drafts. Refer students to Editing Advice on pages 50–51.

Outside Activity Variation

As an alternative, you may invite a guest to your classroom (e.g., an administrator, a librarian, or a service worker at your school) and have students do a class interview. Students should prepare their interview questions ahead of time.

Internet Activities Variation

Activities 2–6 If students don't have access to the Internet, they may find the information needed in books at a local public library.

Activity 3 Have students use the information they find to write a cover letter, plan for an interview, or make a networking contact. Have students talk about how they might use their letter, plan, or contact in the job hunt.

Activity 6 If students don't have access to the Internet, they may find a copy of the *Occupational Outlook Handbook* at a local public library.

LESSON

2

GRAMMAR

Passive Voice
Participles Used as Adjectives
Get + Participles and Adjectives

CONTEXT: Hollywood

The Oscars
The History of Animation
Charlie Chaplin
Being Famous

57

Lesson Overview

GRAMMAR

1. Activate students' prior knowledge. Write *active voice* and *passive voice* on the board. Ask students what they can say about each one.
2. Ask: *What will we study in this lesson?* (passive voice, participles used as adjectives, and *get* with participles and adjectives) Give several examples of sentences using the passive voice (e.g., *This watch was given to me by my son. This book was published in 2005.*). Have volunteers give examples. Write two or three examples using the passive voice on the board.

CONTEXT

1. Ask: *What will we learn about in this lesson?* (Hollywood, the Oscars, animation, Charlie Chaplin, being famous) Elicit students' prior knowledge. Ask: *What do you know about the history of movies? About movie-making in the U.S.?*
2. Have students share their knowledge and personal experiences.

Photo

1. Direct students' attention to the photo montage. Ask: *Who are the people?* (clockwise from top left: Tim Robbins, Halle Berry, Denzel Washington, Adrian Brody, Nicole Kidman) *Where are they?* (at the Academy Awards) *What are they holding?* (Oscar statuettes)
2. Have students share information.

🕐 To save class time, have students do the Test/Review at the end of the lesson, or administer a lesson test generated from the Assessment CD-ROM with *ExamView® Pro*. Skip sections of the lesson that students have already mastered. You may also assign some sections for self-study for extra credit.

Expansion

Theme The topic for this lesson can be enhanced with the following ideas:

1. Entertainment section from a local newspaper showing movie listings
2. Newspaper article about a local movie theater
3. List of top 100 films of all time
4. Timelines showing the history of still photography and motion pictures

Culture Note

Explain that terms for movies include *film* and *motion picture*. Say that *motion picture* is an older term for *movie*; ask: What does *motion* mean? (*movement, moving*) Show that *motion picture* and *movie* are related terms. Say that *movie* usually refers to commercial entertainment; *film* is sometimes used for less commercial, more artistic productions and in business and educational contexts.

2.1 | Passive Voice—An Overview

1. Have students cover grammar chart **2.1.** Write two example sentences that can be converted to the passive voice on the board, such as: *A lot of people saw this movie.* Elicit or present and write the passive statement (*This movie was seen by a lot of people.*). Elicit the names of the parts of the sentences (*subject/agent, verb, object*). Draw arrows between the two statements, as in the grammar chart, to show the relationship between the passive and active sentences.
2. Have students uncover and review the grammar chart. Ask: *Where are American films made?* (in Hollywood) *What will be announced?* (the winner's name) *What is sold in movie theaters?* (popcorn)
3. Ask: *Is the passive voice a tense?* (No; sentences in many tenses use the passive voice. Voice is a perspective.) Draw students' attention to the use of *agent* in naming the person who performed the action in sentences in the passive voice.

The Oscars (Reading)

1. Have students look at the picture on the right. Ask: *What is this? What does it stand for?* (an Oscar statuette; for an award in the U.S. movie industry)
2. Have students look briefly at the reading. Have students look at the title of the reading. Ask: *What is the reading about? How do you know?* Have students make predictions.
3. Preteach any essential vocabulary words your students may not know, such as *recognize, present, nominate,* and *sealed.*

BEFORE YOU READ

1. Have students discuss the questions in pairs. Try to pair students of different language backgrounds.
2. Ask for a few volunteers to share their answers with the class.

To save class time, skip "Before You Read" or have students prepare answers for homework ahead of time.

2.1 | Passive Voice—An Overview

Examples	Explanation
American films **are made** in Hollywood. The winner's name **will be announced.** Popcorn **is sold** in movie theaters.	Passive = a form of *be* + past participle
Subject Verb Object Active: The children **saw** the movie. Subject Verb by agent Passive: The movie **was seen** by the children.	Compare active and passive. The object of the active sentence (*movie*) is the subject of the passive sentence. If the agent of the action (the person who performs the action) is mentioned, it follows *by*.

THE OSCARS

Before You Read

1. Who is your favorite actor? Who is your favorite actress?
2. What movies have you seen recently?

Read the following article. Pay special attention to verbs in the passive voice.

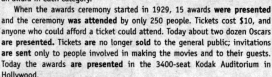

The Academy Awards **are given** out every year to recognize outstanding work of movie actors, directors, and others who are part of the movie-making industry. These awards, called Oscars, **are presented** in a formal ceremony in Hollywood. Several people **are nominated** in specific categories, such as Best Movie, Best Actor, Best Music, Best Costumes. One person **is chosen** to receive an award in each category.

When the awards ceremony started in 1929, 15 awards **were presented** and the ceremony **was attended** by only 250 people. Tickets cost $10, and anyone who could afford a ticket could attend. Today about two dozen Oscars **are presented.** Tickets **are** no longer **sold** to the general public; invitations **are sent** only to people involved in making the movies and to their guests. Today the awards **are presented** in the 3400-seat Kodak Auditorium in Hollywood.

Until 1941, the winners' names **were** already **known** before the ceremony and **published** in newspapers the night before the ceremony. Now the winners' names **are placed** in sealed envelopes and the envelopes **are not opened** until the night of the ceremony.

Since 1953, Oscar night **has been televised** and **broadcast** all over the world. This show **is seen** by hundreds of millions of people. Viewers watch as their favorite movie stars arrive looking beautiful and hopeful.

Did You Know?

Walt Disney has won the most Oscars ever: 26.

58   Lesson 2

Expansion

Theme The topic for this lesson can be enhanced with the following ideas:

1. List of recent Oscar winners or an Oscar ballot
2. Photos of guests and/or award winners at an Academy Awards ceremony
3. Photo and article about Walt Disney

Reading Variation

To practice listening skills, have students first listen to the audio alone. Ask a few comprehension questions. Repeat the audio if necessary. Then have students open their books and read along as they listen to the audio.

Reading Glossary

nominate: to recommend or suggest a person for an award, honor, or public office
present: give out, distribute, especially in public or in front of other people in a ceremony
recognize: praise publicly, bring to others' attention
seal: close securely, usually with glue, wax, tape, etc.

2.2 | Passive Voice—Form

Both the active voice and the passive voice can be used with different tenses and with modals. The tense of the passive sentence is shown in the verb *be*. Use the past participle with every tense. Compare active voice and passive voice in different tenses.

Tense	Active	Passive = *Be* + Past Participle
Simple Present	A committee **chooses** the best actor.	The best actor **is chosen** by a committee.
Present Continuous	They **are presenting** an award now.	An award **is being presented** now.
Future	They **will pick** the best movie. They **are going to pick** the best movie.	The best movie **will be picked.** The best movie **is going to be picked.**
Simple Past	They **announced** the winner's name.	The winner's name **was announced.**
Past Continuous	They **were taking** photographs.	Photographs **were being taken.**
Present Perfect	They **have chosen** the best movie.	The best movie **has been chosen.**
Modal	They **should announce** the winner's name.	The winner's name **should be announced.**

Examples	Explanation
Before 1941, the winners' names **were** *already* **known** before the ceremony. Today the winners **are** *never* **announced** ahead of time.	An adverb can be placed between the auxiliary verb and the main verb.
Affirmative: The movie **was filmed** in the U.S. *Negative:* It **wasn't filmed** in Canada. Question: **Was it filmed** in Hollywood? Short Answer: No, it **wasn't.** *Wh-* Question: Where **was it filmed?**	Observe affirmative statements, negative statements, and questions with the passive voice. Never use do, does, or did with the passive voice. (*Wrong:* The movie **didn't filmed** in Canada.)
The Oscar ceremony **is televised and seen** by millions of people.	If two verbs in the passive voice are connected with *and*, do not repeat *be*.
Active: **She** saw **him.** Passive: **He** was seen by **her.** Active: **They** helped **us.** Passive: **We** were helped by **them.**	Notice the difference in pronouns in an active sentence and a passive sentence. After *by*, the object pronoun is used.

Culture Note

Ask students to name other awards they are familiar with, such as Nobel prizes, Pulitzer prizes, and other entertainment awards (Grammy awards, Latin Grammys, Emmys, etc.). If appropriate, ask students to name awards given in their native countries.

Reading 🎧 *CD 1, Track 9*

1. Have students first read the text silently. Tell them to pay special attention to the verbs in boldface in the reading. Then play the audio and have students read along silently.
2. Check students' comprehension. Ask questions such as: *What are the Academy Awards?* (awards given to actors and others in the movie business) *Who can attend the Academy Awards ceremony?* (only people involved in making movies and their guests) *What is Oscar Night?* (the night the Academy Awards are given out)

🕐 To save class time, have students do the reading for homework ahead of time.

DID YOU KNOW ?

Explain that Walt Disney was one of the most famous U.S. film-makers. Disney was born in Chicago in 1901 and made his first animated cartoon in 1920. His company made some of the most famous animated films in the U.S. Disney was also responsible for the famous amusement parks Disneyland in California and Walt Disney World in Florida. Disney died in 1966.

2.2 | Passive Voice—Form

1. Have students cover the center and right columns of the first section of the grammar chart. Review the names of the tenses in the left column. Ask: *When do we use the simple present?* (to talk about habits, everyday events, etc.)
2. Have students uncover and review the examples in the first section. Have students identify the form of *be* and the past participle in each passive sentence. Ask: *Do we use the past participle in the passive with all the tenses?* (yes)
3. Ask students to say what they observe about the rules for forming the passive voice.
4. Draw students' attention to the first example. Ask: *What is the agent?* (a committee) Point out that in the other examples, the agent is not given. Tell students that they will study agents in later sections of the lesson.
5. Have students review the second section of the grammar chart. If necessary, review the meaning of *pronoun* and *object pronoun*.

1. Tell students that this exercise is about the Academy Awards and some aspects of the awards ceremony. Have students read the direction line. Ask: *What do we write?* (*A* for *active* or *P* for *passive*)
2. Model the exercise. Direct students to the examples in the book. Ask: *Is the first example active or passive?* (active) *How do you know?* (there is no past participle) *Is the second example active or passive?* (passive) *How do you know?* (there is a past participle)
3. Have students complete the rest of Exercise 1 individually. Then review language for checking work (*What do you have for #3?*) and have them check their answers in pairs and confirm their answers with information from the readings. Circulate and observe the pair work. Then check the answers as a class.
4. Assess students' performance. If necessary, review grammar charts **2.1** on page 58 and **2.2** on page 59.

1. Tell students that this exercise is about movies and awards in the United States. Have students read the direction line. Ask: *What verbs do we use in the sentences?* (the verbs in parentheses)
2. Direct students to the example. Then complete #1 with the class. Ask: *How many words do we write?* (two) *Why?* (there are two blanks in the sentence)
3. Have students complete Exercise 2 individually. Then have them check their answers in pairs. Circulate and observe the pair work. If necessary, check the answers as a class.
4. Assess students' performance. If necessary, review grammar chart **2.2** on page 59.

🕑 To save class time, have students do half of the exercise in class and complete the other half for homework. Or assign the entire exercise for homework.

EXERCISE 1 Read the following sentences. Decide if the underlined verb is active (A) or passive (P).

EXAMPLES   The actress received an Oscar.   *A*

The actress was given an Oscar.   *P*

1. The actress wore a beautiful gown.   *A*
2. The gown was designed by Anne Klein.   *P*
3. Julia Roberts presented an Oscar.   *A*
4. Julia Roberts was presented an Oscar.   *P*
5. Julia Roberts has been seen in many movies.   *P*
6. The director has been nominated many times.   *P*
7. The movie was filmed in black and white.   *P*
8. Many actors live in California.   *A*
9. Movies are made in Hollywood.   *P*
10. The names of the winners will be printed in tomorrow's newspaper.
11. The actress thanked all the people who helped her win.   *A*
12. The actress was driven to the ceremony in a white limousine.   *P*
13. Hollywood was built at the beginning of the twentieth century.   *P*
14. Hollywood has become the movie capital of the U.S.   *A*
15. Movie reviewers make predictions about the winners.   *A*

EXERCISE 2 Fill in the blanks with the passive voice of the verb, using the tense given.

EXAMPLE   (simple present: *give*)

The best actor ___is given___ an Oscar.

1. (simple present: *see*)

The awards ceremony ___is___ ___seen___ by millions of people.

2. (future: *choose*)

Which actor ___will___ ___be___ ___chosen___ next year?

Expansion

Exercise 1 Ask students questions related to appropriate items, such as (for #1): *Can you name an actress who wears beautiful clothes?*; (for #7): *Can you name a movie that was filmed in black and white?*

3. (modal: *can / see*)

The movie __can__ __be__ __seen__ at many theaters.

4. (present perfect: *make*)

Many movies __have__ __been__ __made__ about World War II.

5. (simple past: *give*)

James Cameron __was__ __given__ an award in 1997 for Best Director, for *Titanic*.

6. (present continuous: *show*)

A good movie __is__ __being__ __shown__ at a theater near my house.

7. (simple past: *make*)

Star Wars __was__ __made__ in 1977.

8. (present perfect: *show*)

The movie __has__ __been__ __shown__ on TV many times.

9. (present perfect: *give*)

Over 2,000 Academy Awards __have__ __been__ __given__ out since 1929.

10. (simple past: *give*)

In 1929, only one award __was__ __given__ to a woman.

11. (simple past: *add*)

When __was__ sound __added__ to movies?

It __was__ __added__ in 1927.

12. (simple present: *often / make*)

Movies __are__ __often__ __made__ in Hollywood.

13. (present perfect: *film*)

How many movies __have__ __been__ __filmed__ in black and white?

Expansion

Exercise 2 Bring in a list of famous movies or a list of Oscar nominees or winners. Have students make sentences with the new information similar to number 5 or number 7.

2.3 | Passive and Active Voice—Uses

1. Have students look at the pictures in the left-hand column of the grammar chart. Ask: *What is the difference between these two people?* (One is eating, one is being eaten.)
2. Review the example sentences and explanations with the class. Ask: *What do we focus on in an active voice sentence?* (the person who does the action) *What do we focus on in a passive voice sentence?* (the receiver or result of the action)
3. Ask: *In examples B and C, who is the agent?* (We don't know.) Write on the board: *In some passive voice sentences, the agent is not given.* Ask: *Who is the agent in this sentence?* (We don't know.)

EXERCISE 3

1. Tell students that this exercise provides practice with deciding when to use the passive voice. Have students read the direction line. Ask: *Do these sentences have the same meaning?* (no) Check that students understand that they are not converting an active voice sentence to a passive voice sentence in this exercise.
2. Model the exercise. Do #1 with the class.
3. Have students complete the exercise in groups. Circulate and observe the group work. Check and compare answers as a class.
4. If necessary, review grammar chart **2.3**.

2.3 | Passive and Active Voice—Uses

Examples	Explanation
Compare: Active: The man **ate** the fish. Passive: The man **was eaten** by the fish.	When the verb is in the active voice, the subject performs the action. When the verb is in the passive voice, the subject receives the action.
A. Active: I **see** the Academy Awards ceremony every year. Passive: The Academy Awards ceremony **is seen** by millions. B. Active: **Do** you **know** the winners' names? Passive: The winners' names **are not known** until the night of the ceremony. C. Active: The Academy **presents** awards to the best actors and directors. Passive: The awards **are presented** every year.	The active voice focuses on the person who does the action. The passive voice focuses on the receiver or the result of the action. Sometimes the passive voice mentions the agent, the person who does the action (A). Sometimes it is not necessary to mention the agent (B and C).

EXERCISE 3 Write an active sentence and a passive sentence for each subject. Choose an appropriate tense.

EXAMPLE *Active:* The test _____ has 12 questions. _____

Passive: The test _____ will be given in a large auditorium. _____

1. *Active:* My textbook _____ Answers will vary. _____
   Passive: My textbook _____
2. *Active:* My best friend _____
   Passive: My best friend _____
3. *Active:* Some students _____
   Passive: Some students _____
4. *Active:* I _____
   Passive: I _____
5. *Active:* Actors _____
   Passive: Actors _____
6. *Active:* Movies _____
   Passive: Movies _____

62   Lesson 2

Grammar Variation

After step 1, provide additional examples of active and passive sentences with very different meanings (*My dog chased a cat. My dog was chased by a cat. John loved Mary. John was loved by Mary.*). Then continue with steps 2 and 3.

2.4 | The Passive Voice Without an Agent

The passive voice is used more frequently without an agent than with an agent.

Examples	Explanation
The invitations **have been sent** out. The winners' names **are placed** in envelopes.	The passive voice is used when it is not important to mention who performed the action.
A. Active: *Someone* **stole** my wallet. Passive: My wallet **was stolen** last week. B. Active: *Someone* **told** me that you like movies. Passive: I **was told** that you like movies.	The passive voice is used when we do not know the agent (A) or when we prefer not to mention the agent (B).
a. One person **is chosen** to receive the award. b. Oscar night **has been televised** since 1953.	The passive voice is used when the agent is obvious and doesn't need to be mentioned. a. It is obvious that the Academy chooses the winner. b. It is obvious that TV studios have televised Oscar night.
Compare Active (A) and Passive (P): A. *You* **can rent** DVDs at many stores. P. DVDs **can be rented** at many stores. A. *They* **sell** popcorn in movie theaters. P. Popcorn **is sold** in movie theaters.	In conversation, the active voice is often used with the impersonal subjects *people, you, we,* or *they.* In more formal speech and writing, the passive is used with no agent.

EXERCISE **4**   Fill in the blanks with the passive voice of the verb in parentheses ( ). Choose an appropriate tense.

EXAMPLE   Hollywood _____was built_____ in the early 1900s.
                                  (build)

1. Most American movies _____are made_____ in Hollywood.
                                        (make)

2. Let's get some popcorn. It's fresh. It _____is being made_____ right now.
                                                    (make)

3. Movie listings _____can be found_____ in the newspaper.
                              (can/find)

4. Children _____are not allowed_____ to see some movies.
                        (not/allow)

5. Hurry! The winners _____are going to/will be announced_____ in ten minutes.
                                      (announce)

Grammar Variation

After students have reviewed the examples and explanations in the grammar chart, have them go back to the reading on page 58 to identify which explanation is appropriate for each of the passive voice verbs in the reading.

2.4 | The Passive Voice Without an Agent

1. Ask students to cover the right column of the grammar chart. Ask questions about the agent in the first three example sentences, such as: *Who sent out the invitations?* (We don't know.) *Is it important?* (no) *Who told you that I like movies?* (I don't want to say.). For the last row in the chart, ask: *Which sentences do you think people say? Which sentences do you think people write?* (the active voice sentences; the passive voice sentences)

2. Have students uncover and review the explanations in the grammar chart.

3. Draw students' attention to the last section of the chart. Ask: *Have you noticed Americans' use of* you *to mean everyone or anyone?* Tell students that Americans frequently use *you* and *they* to mean people in general.

4. Provide several examples about students in the class, or about your school (e.g., *They built our school in 1928.*). Ask students to convert the sentences to the passive voice (e.g., *Our school was built in 1928.*).

EXERCISE   4

1. Tell students that this exercise is about making and seeing movies. Have students read the direction line.

2. Direct students to the example. Ask: *What tense do we use?* (the simple past) *Why?* (because the event is finished)

3. Model the exercise. Complete #1 with the class. Have students complete the exercise individually. Then have them check their answers in pairs. Circulate and observe the pair work. If necessary, check the answers as a class.

4. Assess students' performance. If necessary, review grammar chart **2.4**.

6. In 1929, only fifteen Oscars ___were presented___
   (present)

7. Before 1941, the winners' names ___were published___ in
   (publish)
   newspapers the night before the ceremony.

8. A new theater ___is being built___ near my house at this time.
   (build)

9. We can't get into the movie theater because all the tickets
   ___have been sold___ already.
   (sell)

10. Did you see the movie *Jaws*? Where ___was___ it
    ___filmed___?
    (film)

11. I went to the lobby to buy popcorn, and my seat
    ___was taken___.
    (take)

12. No one knows why the award ___is called___ "Oscar."
    (call)

13. *Lord of the Rings* ___was chosen___ as the best film of 2004.
    (choose)

14. In a movie theater, coming attractions[1] ___are shown___
    (show)
    before the feature film begins.

15. Sound ___was added___ to movies in 1927.
    (add)

16. The Kodak Theater, where the awards ___are presented___
    (present)
    each year, ___was built___ in 2001.
    (build)

[1]*Coming attractions* are short previews of new movies. Theaters show coming attractions to get your interest in returning to the theater to see a new movie.

Expansion

Exercise 4 Bring in the entertainment section with movie listings of a local newspaper. Have students review the listings and report on a movie they'd like to see, e.g., Dancing Tigers *is being shown at the Muviplex at 7:15.*

Exercise 4 Have students work in groups to brainstorm vocabulary and phrases they know related to movies, theaters, and Hollywood. Have them include the vocabulary from the exercise and from the reading on page 58. If appropriate, set a time limit and have groups compete to make the longest list.

Culture Note

Ask students about movies and theaters in their native countries. Ask: *Are food and drinks sold in movie theaters, or cinemas, in your country?* Discuss the various ways that students have seen American movies—in their countries, on television, at home on video or on DVD, etc. Ask students if U.S. movies influence the impressions people in their countries have of life in the U.S.

2.5 | The Passive Voice with an Agent

Sometimes the passive voice is used with an agent.

Active	Passive
Active: Billy Crystal **has hosted** the Oscar ceremony many times. Passive: The Oscar ceremony **has been hosted** by Billy Crystal many times. Active: Ralph Lauren **designs** many of the actresses' gowns. Passive: Many of the actresses' gowns **are designed** by Ralph Lauren.	When the sentence has a strong agent (a specific person: Billy Crystal, Ralph Lauren), we can use either the active or the passive voice. The active voice puts more emphasis on the person who performs the action. The passive voice puts more emphasis on the action or the result. In general, the active voice is more common than the passive voice when an agent is mentioned. Billy Crystal
Active: *The first Oscar ceremony* **took** place in 1929. Passive: *It was attended* by 250 people. Active: *The Oscar ceremony* **is** popular all over the world. Passive: *It is seen* by millions of viewers each year.	Sometimes the passive voice is used to continue with the same subject of the preceding sentence.
Active: Steven Spielberg **directed** *Star Wars*, didn't he? Passive: No. *Star Wars* **was directed** by George Lucas.	We can use the passive voice to shift the emphasis to the object of the preceding sentence.
Passive: The dress **was designed** by Vera Wang. Passive: The music **was composed** by Bob Dylan. Passive: The movie camera **was invented** by Thomas Edison.	We often use the passive voice when the agent *made, discovered, invented, designed, built, wrote, painted,* or *composed* something.
The 2004 Oscar ceremony **was hosted** *by Billy Crystal.* The 2003 ceremony **was not hosted** *by him.* It was hosted by Steve Martin.	When the agent is included, use *by* + noun or object pronoun.

2.5 | The Passive Voice with an Agent

1. On the board, write a pair of sentences that contrasts the active and passive voices with an agent. For example, write:
   1. Peter Jackson directed The Lord of the Rings.
   2. The Lord of the Rings was directed by Peter Jackson.
   Ask: *In #1, which part of the sentence is emphasized?* (Peter Jackson)
   In #2, which part of the sentence is emphasized? (*The Lord of the Rings*) Say that the passive voice puts more emphasis on the action, or on the result.
2. Have students look at grammar chart **2.5.** Review the example sentences and explanations.
3. Draw students' attention to the 4th section of the chart. Provide several examples of famous inventions, books, movies, or works of art (electricity (invention), *Moby Dick* (book), *Gone with the Wind* (movie), *Mona Lisa* (work of art)) Ask students to make sentences in the passive voice using the inventor, the writer, etc. (e.g., *Moby Dick* was written by Herman Melville.).

Culture Note

Ask students who they think the best movie actors are and what the best movies are, and why. Ask: *Who are some famous movie stars in your country?* Say that in the U.S., movie fans (people who love movies) sometimes wait in line for days to see a new movie.

1. Tell students that this exercise is about famous inventions, plays, and works of art and the people who created them. Have students read the direction line. Ask: *What do we write on the line?* (one of the names from the box)
2. Model the exercise. Complete #1 with the class. Ask a volunteer to give an answer.
3. Have students complete the exercise individually. Then have them compare their answers in pairs. Finally, check the answers as a class.

1. Tell students that this exercise is about making and seeing movies. Have students read the direction line.
2. Review the examples. Be sure that students are aware of the different tenses used in the exercise. Model the exercise. Complete #1 as a class.
3. Have students complete Exercise 6 individually. Have them compare their answers in pairs. Finally, check the answers as a class.
4. Assess students' performance. If necessary, review grammar chart **2.5**.

EXERCISE 5 *Test Your Knowledge.* Fill in the blanks with the past tense passive voice and the name of the agent. Choose an agent from the box below.

Pablo Picasso	Christopher Columbus	Leonardo Da Vinci
Alexander Graham Bell	Thomas Edison	William Shakespeare
Celine Dion	Barbra Streisand	Steven Spielberg
George Lucas	Walt Disney	Mark Twain

1. Mickey Mouse _____was created_____ by ____Walt Disney____.
   (create)

2. The *Mona Lisa* _____was painted_____ by ____Leonardo Da Vinci____.
   (paint)

3. America _____was discovered_____ by ____Christopher Columbus____.
   (discover)

4. The electric light _____was invented_____ by ____Thomas Edison____.
   (invent)

5. *Romeo and Juliet* _____was written_____ by ____William Shakespeare____.
   (write)

6. The telephone _____was invented_____ by ____Alexander Graham Bell____.
   (invent)

7. *My Heart Will Go On* _____was sung_____ by ____Celine Dion____.
   (sing)

8. *Star Wars* _____was directed_____ by ____George Lucas____.
   (direct)

EXERCISE 6 Fill in the blanks with the active or passive of the verb in parentheses ( ). Use the tense indicated.

EXAMPLES I _____saw_____ an old movie on TV last night.
   (past: see)

The movie _____was filmed_____ in black and white.
   (past: film)

It _____will be shown_____ again on TV tonight.
   (future: show)

1. Many movies _____are made_____ in Hollywood.
   (present: make)

2. Steven Spielberg _____has made_____ many movies.
   (present perfect: make)

3. We ____are going to / will rent____ a DVD this weekend.
   (future: rent)

4. Vera Wang _____designs_____ beautiful dresses.
   (present: design)

66   Lesson 2

Expansion

Exercise 5 Students may not be familiar with all of the names in Exercise 5. If they are not, assign a different name to each member of the class. Have students research the names on the Internet or at the library and report back to the class.

5. The actress _____was wearing_____ a dress that
   (past continuous: wear)
   _____was designed_____ by Ralph Lauren.
   (past: design)

6. Who _____wrote_____ the music for the movie? The music
   (past: write)
   _____was written_____ by Randy Newman.
   (past: write)

7. The first Academy Awards presentation _____had_____
   (past: have)
   250 guests.

8. I _____have never seen_____ Star Wars.
   (present perfect: never/see)

9. Computer animation _____is used_____ in many movies.
   (present: use)

10. Movie reviewers _____predict_____ the winners weeks
    (present: predict)
    before the Oscar presentation.

11. Oscar winners _____always thank_____ the people who helped them.
    (present: always/thank)

2.6 | Verbs with Two Objects

Some verbs have two objects: a direct object (D.O.) and an indirect object (I.O.).

Examples	Explanation
I.O. D.O. Active: They gave Spielberg an award. Passive 1: *Spielberg* was given an award. Passive 2: *An award* was given to Spielberg.	When an active sentence has two objects, the passive sentence can begin with either object. Notice that if the direct object (*an award*) becomes the subject of the passive sentence, *to* is used before the indirect object.

Some verbs that use two objects are:

bring	lend	pay	serve	teach
give	offer	sell	show	tell
hand	owe	send	take	write

EXERCISE **7**   Change the following sentences to passive voice in two ways. Omit the agent.

EXAMPLE   They gave the actress an award.

The actress was given an award.

The award was given to the actress.

2.6 | Verbs with Two Objects

1. Have students cover grammar chart 2.6. Write an example sentence with a direct and an indirect object on the board, such as: *Someone gave these tickets to Rosa.* Ask students to identify the parts of the sentence (subject, verb, direct object, indirect object). Tell students that in this sentence, *tickets* is the direct object and *Rosa* is the indirect object (the person or thing to or for which the action in the sentence is done). Say: *We can write this sentence in the passive voice in two ways.* Write: *These tickets were given to Rosa. Rosa was given these tickets.*

2. Have students review the examples and explanations in the grammar chart.

3. Direct students' attention to the verb list at the bottom of the chart. Clarify any vocabulary students are unfamiliar with.

EXERCISE 7

1. Tell students that this exercise is about alternate ways that actions can be described. Have students review the direction line. Ask: *What does* omit *mean?* (take out; don't include)

2. Model the exercise. Direct students to the example in the book. Then do #1 with the class.

3. Have students complete Exercise 7 individually. Then have them compare their answers in pairs. Finally, check the answers as a class.

4. Assess students' performance. If necessary, review grammar chart 2.6.

Grammar Variation

After students have reviewed the examples in the grammar chart, have them work in groups. Have each group write sentences with three of the verbs in the second section of the chart. Have the groups exchange sentences and underline the direct and indirect objects in each other's sentences.

The History of Animation (Reading)

1. Have students look at the graphics on pages 68 and 69. Ask: *What do you see?* (drawing of a cartoon; photo of Walt Disney; photo of a girl manipulating a cartoon on a computer)
2. Have students look quickly at the reading. Ask: *What is the reading about? How do you know?* Have students use the title and the graphics to make predictions about the reading.
3. Preteach any vocabulary words your students may not know, such as *cartoon, animate, background, illusion,* and *technique.*

BEFORE YOU READ

1. Activate students' prior knowledge about animation. Ask: *What is animation?* (a word for movies or films made with drawings, not with actors) *What is a cartoon?* (a humorous animated movie or short film) *Do you like animated films? Can you name a famous animated film or cartoon?*
2. Have students discuss the questions in pairs. Try to pair students of different language backgrounds.
3. Ask a few volunteers to share their answers with the class.

   To save class time, skip "Before You Read" or have students prepare answers for homework ahead of time.

---

1. They handed the actress an Oscar.
   The actress was handed an Oscar.
   The Oscar was handed to the actress.

2. Someone served the guests dinner.
   The guests were served dinner.
   Dinner was served to the guests.

3. Someone told the students the answers.
   The students were told the answers.
   The answers were told to the students.

4. Someone will send you an invitation.
   You will be sent an invitation.
   An invitation wil be sent to you.

5. They have shown us the movie.
   We have been shown the movie.
   The movie has been shown to us.

6. They will give the winners flowers.
   The winners will be given flowers.
   Flowers will be given to the winners.

7. Someone has given you the key.
   You have been given the key.
   The key has been given to you.

THE HISTORY OF ANIMATION

Before You Read

1. Do you like cartoons? Which cartoons do you like?
2. Do you know how cartoons are created?
3. Are cartoons just for children? Do adults enjoy cartoons too?

Gertie the Dinosaur
Winsor McCay

68   Lesson 2

Expansion

Theme The topic for this lesson can be enhanced with the following ideas:

1. A drawing of Mickey Mouse or another famous cartoon character
2. A page from the entertainment section of the newspaper showing an ad for an animated feature or cartoon

Read the following article. Pay special attention to active and passive verbs.

Animated movies **have changed** a lot over the last 100 years. Winsor McCay **is considered** the father of animation. In the early 1900s, McCay **animated** his films by himself. He **drew** every picture separately and had them photographed, one at a time. Hundreds of photographs **were needed** to make a one-minute film. Sometimes it would take him more than a year to make a five-minute cartoon.

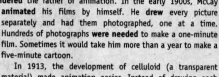

Walt Disney

In 1913, the development of celluloid (a transparent material) made animation easier. Instead of drawing each picture separately, the animator could make a drawing of the background, which **remained** motionless, while only the characters **moved.**

Walt Disney **took** animation to a new level. He **created** Mickey Mouse, **added** sound and music to his movies, and **produced** the first full-length animated film, *Snow White and the Seven Dwarfs*. Many people think he was a great cartoonist, but he wasn't. Instead, he was a great story editor and clever businessman who had other artists do most of the drawings.

Today most animated films **are** not **drawn** by hand. The animation **is done** by computer software. Also special effects for movies, such as *Star Wars*, **are done** by computer animation. To create the illusion of move-ment, an image **is put** on the computer and then quickly **replaced** by a similar image with a small change. While this technique is similar to hand-drawn animation, the work **can be done** much faster by computer. In fact, anyone with a home compu-ter and special software can create a simple animation.

Passive Voice; Participles Used as Adjectives; *Get* + Participles and Adjectives   69

Reading 🎧 *CD 1, Track 10*

1. Have students first read the text silently. Tell them to pay special attention to the active and passive verbs in the reading. Then play the audio and have students read along silently.
2. Check students' comprehension. Ask questions such as: *How is animation done?* (by making small changes in drawings or images and then filming them) *Who is famous for making animated films and cartoons popular in the U.S.?* (Walt Disney)

🕐 To save class time, have students do the reading for homework.

Reading Variation

To practice listening skills, have students first listen to the audio alone. Ask a few comprehension questions. Repeat the audio if necessary. Then have students open their books and read along as they listen to the audio.

Reading Glossary

animate: to make pictures appear to move
background: the color or image you can see behind the main subject of a picture or an image
cartoon: animated film for children, or humorous animated film
illusion: an image which fools or misleads the viewer
technique: way of doing something; method

Culture Note

Movies often are categorized by their length: a full-length or feature film is usually 90 to 120 minutes long, a short feature or "short" can be 10 to 30 minutes long. Movie types include documentaries (nonfiction), docudramas (dramatic telling of a real story), and biopics (biographical docudramas).

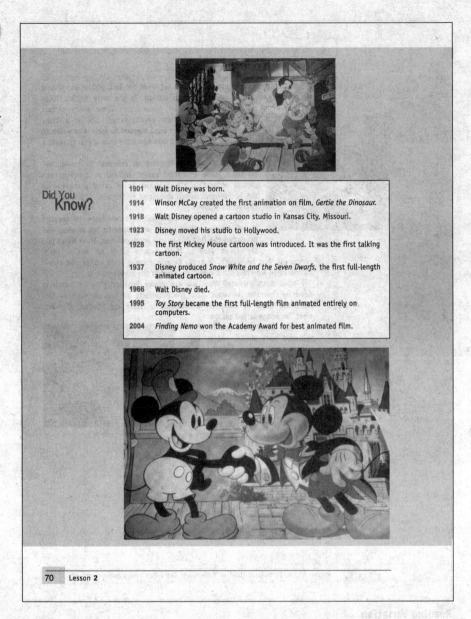

Did You Know?

1901	Walt Disney was born.
1914	Winsor McCay created the first animation on film, *Gertie the Dinosaur.*
1918	Walt Disney opened a cartoon studio in Kansas City, Missouri.
1923	Disney moved his studio to Hollywood.
1928	The first Mickey Mouse cartoon was introduced. It was the first talking cartoon.
1937	Disney produced *Snow White and the Seven Dwarfs,* the first full-length animated cartoon.
1966	Walt Disney died.
1995	*Toy Story* became the first full-length film animated entirely on computers.
2004	*Finding Nemo* won the Academy Award for best animated film.

70   Lesson 2

2.7 | Transitive and Intransitive Verbs

Examples	Explanation
Compare: verb object Active: McCay **created** the first animated film. Passive:The first animated film **was created** in 1913. verb object Active: Walt Disney **didn't draw** his cartoons. Passive:His cartoons **were drawn** by studio artists.	Most active verbs are followed by an object. They can be used in the active and passive voice. These verbs are called *transitive* verbs.
Active only: Disney **lived** in Hollywood most of his life. He **became** famous when he created Mickey Mouse. He **worked** with many artists. What **happened** to the first Mickey Mouse cartoon? I'd like to see it.	Some verbs have no object. We cannot use the passive voice with these verbs. agree die look seem arrive fall occur sleep be go rain stay become happen recover walk come live remain work These are called *intransitive* verbs.
Compare: a. Disney **left** Kansas City in 1923. b. The books **were left** on the floor.	*Leave* can be intransitive or transitive, depending on its meaning. In sentence (a), *leave* means "go away from." It is an intransitive verb. It has no passive form. In sentence (b), leave means "not taken." It is a transitive verb. It has a passive form.
Compare: a. Cartoons **have changed** a lot over the years. b. The light bulb **was changed** by the janitor. a. In a cartoon, it looks like the characters **are moving**, but they are not. b. The chairs **were moved** to another room.	*Change* and *move* can be intransitive or transitive. When a change happens through a natural process (a), it is intransitive. When someone specific causes the change (b), it is transitive.
Compare: Walt Disney **was born** in 1901. He **died** in 1966.	Notice that we use *was / were* with *born,** but we don't use the passive voice with *die*.
Note: **Born* is not a verb. It is a past participle used as an adjective.	

2.7 | Transitive and Intransitive Verbs

1. Have students cover the grammar chart. On the board, write simple sentences with direct objects, such as: *Winsor McCay made the first cartoons* and *Walt Disney employed many artists.* Ask: *What are the direct objects in these sentences?* (*the first cartoons; many artists*) Have volunteers write passive voice sentences for each example (*The first cartoons were made by Winsor McCay. Many artists were employed by Walt Disney.*). Say: *The verbs* make *and* employ *are transitive verbs; they take a direct object.*

2. Have students look at the first section of grammar chart **2.7**. Review the example sentences and explanation.

3. Draw students' attention to the second section of the chart. Review the list of verbs that cannot be used with the passive voice.

4. Have students look at the final three sections of the grammar chart. Review the example sentences and explanations carefully.

5. Provide several additional examples with verbs from the list in the chart, such as: *We walked to the theater* or *It rained for two days.* Ask: *Can these sentences be re-written in the passive voice?* (no)

Grammar Variation

Have students go back to the reading on page 69. Have learners say whether each verb is in the active or passive voice; for sentences in the passive voice, have students give an equivalent sentence using the active voice.

EXERCISE 8

1. Tell students that this exercise is about movies. Have students read the direction line. Ask: *Do we change every sentence?* (no)
2. Model the exercise. Direct students to the examples in the book. Then do #1 with the class. Ask a volunteer to give the answer. Point out the picture of the box of popcorn.
3. Have students complete the exercise individually. Then have them compare their answers in pairs. Finally, check the answers as a class.

EXERCISE 9

1. Tell students that this exercise is about animation and Walt Disney. Have students read the direction line.
2. Model the exercise. Direct students to the examples in the book. Then do #1 with the class. Ask a volunteer to give the answer.
3. Have students complete the exercise individually. Then have them compare their answers in pairs. If necessary, check the answers as a class.
4. Assess students' performance. If necessary, review grammar chart 2.7 on page 71.

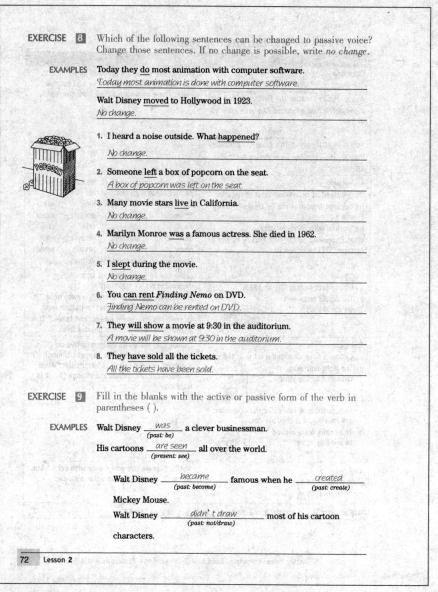

EXERCISE 8   Which of the following sentences can be changed to passive voice? Change those sentences. If no change is possible, write *no change*.

EXAMPLES   Today they <u>do</u> most animation with computer software.
Today most animation is done with computer software.

Walt Disney <u>moved</u> to Hollywood in 1923.
No change.

1. I heard a noise outside. What <u>happened</u>?
   No change.
2. Someone <u>left</u> a box of popcorn on the seat.
   A box of popcorn was left on the seat.
3. Many movie stars <u>live</u> in California.
   No change.
4. Marilyn Monroe <u>was</u> a famous actress. She died in 1962.
   No change.
5. I <u>slept</u> during the movie.
   No change.
6. You <u>can rent</u> *Finding Nemo* on DVD.
   Finding Nemo can be rented on DVD.
7. They <u>will show</u> a movie at 9:30 in the auditorium.
   A movie will be shown at 9:30 in the auditorium.
8. They <u>have sold</u> all the tickets.
   All the tickets have been sold.

EXERCISE 9   Fill in the blanks with the active or passive form of the verb in parentheses ( ).

EXAMPLES   Walt Disney ___was___ a clever businessman.
                        (past: be)
His cartoons ___are seen___ all over the world.
                        (present: see)

Walt Disney ___became___ famous when he ___created___
                        (past: become)   (past: create)
Mickey Mouse.
Walt Disney ___didn't draw___ most of his cartoon
                        (past: not/draw)
characters.

72   Lesson 2

Expansion

Exercise 8 After students complete the exercise, have them work in pairs. Have pairs use the answer to each item to begin a short conversation of two or three lines. Have pairs perform their conversations for the class.

3. Most of his cartoons ___were drawn___ by studio artists.
   (past: draw)

4. Walt Disney ___was given___ 26 Oscars.
   (past: give)

5. Walt Disney ___moved___ his studio to Hollywood.
   (past: move)

6. Walt Disney ___lived___ in Hollywood most of his life.
   (past: live)

7. Disney ___died___ in 1966.
   (past: die)

8. Today's animations ___are created___ by computer.
   (present: create)

9. Cartoon characters look like they ___are moving___
   (present continuous: move)

10. Even today, Disney's old cartoons ___look___ beautiful.
    (present: look)

EXERCISE 10 Fill in the blanks with the active or passive form of the verb in parentheses ( ). Use the past tense.

Ronald Reagan ___was elected___ president of the United States in
(example: elect)
1980. Before he ___became___ president, he was governor of
(example: become)
California. Even before that, he ___worked___ as a Hollywood
(1 work)
actor. He ___appeared___ in 53 Hollywood movies between 1937
(2 appear)
and 1964. He ___wasn't considered___ a great actor, and he never
(3 not/consider)
___won___ an Oscar.
(4 win)

On March 20, 1981, the day the Oscar ceremony ___was scheduled___
(5 schedule)
to take place, something terrible ___happened___. Reagan
(6 happen)
___was shot___ in an assassination attempt. Fortunately, he
(7 shoot)
___didn't die___ from his wounds. However, one of his
(8 past: not die)
aides, who was with him at the time, ___was wounded___. Out
(9 wound)

Passive Voice; Participles Used as Adjectives; *Get* + Participles and Adjectives **73**

EXERCISE 10

1. Tell students that this exercise is about a famous American. Have them scan the reading quickly. Ask: *Who is the reading about?* (Ronald Reagan) Have students read the direction line.
2. Direct students to the examples in the book. Point out the photos of Ronald Reagan as president and as an actor.
3. Have students complete the exercise individually. Ask volunteers to share their answers with the class.

To save class time, have students do half of the exercise in class and complete the other half for homework. Or assign the entire exercise for homework.

Expansion

Exercises 8, 9, and 10 Have students work in groups to make two lists—one list of all the verbs in Exercises 8, 9, and 10 that are used with the passive voice and another list of all the verbs that are not used with the passive voice.

Culture Note

After students have finished Exercise 10, ask: *What happened to the Academy Awards ceremony after Reagan was shot?* (It was postponed.) Public events in the U.S. are frequently postponed or cancelled after a disaster or tragic event. Ask students if such events affect entertainment or sporting events in their countries.

EXERCISE 11

1. Tell students that this exercise is about going to the movies. Have students read the direction line. Ask: *Does every sentence have a mistake?* (no)

2. Direct students to the examples in the book. Remind students that they are editing, or correcting, the sentences.

3. Have students complete the exercise individually. Ask volunteers to share their answers with the class.

🕐 To save class time, have students do half of the exercise in class and complete the other half for homework. Or assign the entire exercise for homework.

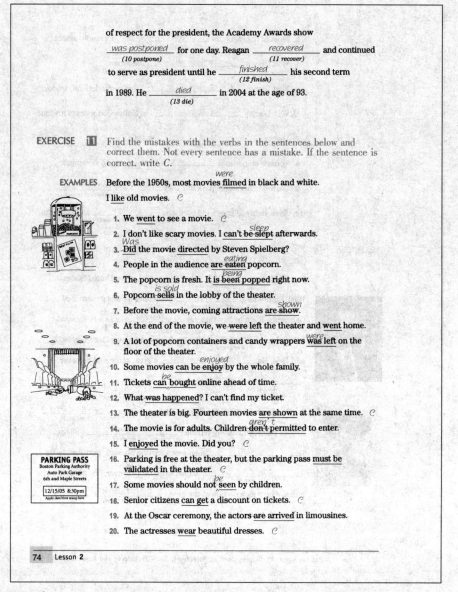

of respect for the president, the Academy Awards show

___*was postponed*___ for one day. Reagan ___*recovered*___ and continued
(10 postpone)   (11 recover)

to serve as president until he ___*finished*___ his second term
                               (12 finish)

in 1989. He ___*died*___ in 2004 at the age of 93.
            (13 die)

EXERCISE 11 Find the mistakes with the verbs in the sentences below and correct them. Not every sentence has a mistake. If the sentence is correct, write *C*.

EXAMPLES
Before the 1950s, most movies <u>filmed</u> in black and white. *(were)*

I <u>like</u> old movies. *C*

1. We <u>went</u> to see a movie. *C*

2. I don't like scary movies. I can't be <u>slept</u> afterwards. *(sleep)*

3. <u>Did</u> the movie <u>directed</u> by Steven Spielberg? *(Was)*

4. People in the audience are <u>eaten</u> popcorn. *(eating)*

5. The popcorn is fresh. It is <u>been</u> popped right now. *(being)*

6. Popcorn <u>sells</u> in the lobby of the theater. *(is sold)*

7. Before the movie, coming attractions are <u>show</u>. *(shown)*

8. At the end of the movie, we <u>were</u> left the theater and went home.

9. A lot of popcorn containers and candy wrappers <u>was</u> left on the floor of the theater. *(were)*

10. Some movies can be <u>enjoy</u> by the whole family. *(enjoyed)*

11. Tickets can <u>bought</u> online ahead of time. *(be)*

12. What <u>was</u> happened? I can't find my ticket.

13. The theater is big. Fourteen movies <u>are shown</u> at the same time. *C*

14. The movie is for adults. Children <u>don't</u> permitted to enter. *(aren't)*

15. I enjoyed the movie. Did you? *C*

16. Parking is free at the theater, but the parking pass <u>must be validated</u> in the theater. *C*

17. Some movies should not <u>seen</u> by children. *(be)*

18. Senior citizens <u>can get</u> a discount on tickets. *C*

19. At the Oscar ceremony, the actors <u>are arrived</u> in limousines.

20. The actresses <u>wear</u> beautiful dresses. *C*

PARKING PASS
Boston Parking Authority
Auto Park Garage
6th and Maple Streets

12/15/05 8:30pm
Apply date/time stamp here

74   Lesson 2

Expansion

Exercise 11 After students complete the exercise, go back to the items that were incorrect. Have students work in pairs to determine why each item was incorrect. Have students use grammar chart **2.7** on page 71 as a reference.

2.8 | Passive with *Get*

Examples	Explanation
Actors **get paid** a lot of money. I don't like violent movies. A lot of people **get shot** and **killed.**	In conversation, we sometimes use *get* instead of *be* with the passive. 　*get paid* = *are paid* 　*get shot* = *are shot* 　*get killed* = *are killed* We usually omit the agent after *get.* Compare: 　He **was shot** by a cowboy. 　He **got shot** three times.
How much **do** actors **get paid** for a movie? She **didn't get paid** last Friday.	When *get* is used with the passive voice, questions and negatives are formed with *do, does, did,* and other auxiliaries. *Be* is not used with *get.* 　*Wrong:* She *wasn't* get paid last Friday.
She **got hired** for the job. He **got laid off** last month.	*Get* is frequently used with: *killed, injured, wounded, paid, hired, fired, laid off.*

EXERCISE 12 Fill in the blanks ith *get* + the past participle of the verb in parentheses ( ).

EXAMPLE Who ___got chosen___ for the part in the movie?
　　　　　　　　(choose)

1. Reagan ___got shot___ on the day of the Oscars.
　　　　　(shoot)

2. No one ___got killed___ .
　　　　　　(kill)

3. Did you ___get hired___ for the job?
　　　　　　(hire)

4. How often do you ___get paid___ ?
　　　　　　　　　(pay)

5. His car ___got stolen___ from in front of his house.
　　　　　(steal)

6. The little boy told a lie, and he ___got punished___ .
　　　　　　　　　　　　　　(punish)

2.8 | Passive with *Get*

1. Have students cover the grammar chart. Write one or two examples using the passive with *get* on the board, such as: *I get paid every two weeks* or *My backpack got stolen last year.* Ask: *Are these sentences in the passive voice?* (yes) *Do you think these are formal written sentences or informal spoken sentences?* (informal spoken)

2. Have students review the grammar chart. Then ask them to convert each example with *get* to a passive voice sentence with a form of *be.*

EXERCISE 12

1. Tell students that in this exercise they will practice using the passive voice informally in conversation. Have students read the direction line.

2. Direct students to the example in the book. Complete the first item with the class.

3. Have students complete the exercise individually. Check answers as a class.

4. Assess students' performance. If necessary, review grammar chart **2.8.**

Expansion

Exercise 12 After students have finished the exercise, have them convert each sentence to a more formal written passive sentence with a form of *be* and the past participle.

2.9 | Participles Used as Adjectives

1. On the board, write: *This movie looks interesting; are you interested in going with me?* Tell students that while *interested* and *interesting* look similar, they are used differently in sentences. Ask: *Which one is the present participle?* (*interesting*) *Which one is the past participle?* (*interested*)

2. Have students review the examples and explanations in the grammar chart. Draw students' attention to the formation of present and past participles in the top section of the chart. If necessary, review the definition of an adjective (a word used to modify a noun).

7. We have so much to do, but I'm not worried. Everything will _____get done_____ little by little.
   (do)

8. The results of the exam _____got sent_____ to the wrong
   (send)
   person by mistake.

9. One student _____got caught_____ cheating on the exam.
   (catch)

10. If you leave your car in a no-parking zone, it might
   _____get towed_____.
   (tow)

2.9 | Participles Used as Adjectives

A present participle is verb + -*ing*. A past participle is the third form of the verb (usually -*ed* or -*en*). Both present participles and past participles can be used as adjectives.

Examples	Explanation
We saw an **entertaining** movie. *Star Wars* is an **exciting** movie. *The Matrix* has **amazing** visual effects.	In these examples, a *present participle* is used as an adjective.
The winners' names are placed in **sealed** envelopes. I wasn't **bored** during the movie. Are you **interested** in action movies? Do you like **animated** films?	In these examples, a *past participle* is used as an adjective.

76   Lesson 2

Grammar Variation

Have prepared, on the board or on an overhead, the example sentences from the grammar chart with the adjectives removed. Ask students to provide adjectives for each sentence; try to elicit a variety of responses. Then have students review the grammar chart.

CHARLIE CHAPLIN

Before You Read

1. Have you ever heard of Charlie Chaplin?
2. Have you ever seen a silent movie? Do you think a silent movie can be interesting today?

Charlie Chaplin, 1889–1977

Read the following article. Pay special attention to participles used as adjectives.

Charlie Chaplin was one of the greatest actors in the world. His **entertaining** silent movies are still popular today. His **amusing** character "Little Tramp" is well **known** to people throughout the world. Chaplin had an **amazing** life. His idea for this poor character in worn-out shoes, round hat, and cane probably came from his childhood experiences.

Born in poverty in London in 1889, Chaplin was abandoned by his father and left in an orphanage by his mother. He became **interested** in acting at the age of five. At ten, he left school to travel with a British acting company. In 1910, he made his first trip to America. He was talented, athletic, and hard-**working**, and by 1916 he was earning $10,000 a week. He was the highest-**paid** person in the world at that time. He produced, directed, and wrote the movies he starred in.

Even though "talkies" came out in 1927, he didn't make a movie with sound until 1940, when he played a comic version of the **terrifying** dictator, Adolf Hitler.

As Chaplin got older, he faced **declining** popularity as a result of his politics and personal relationships. After he left the U.S. in 1952, Chaplin was not allowed to re-enter because of his political views. He didn't return to the U.S. until 1972, when he was given a special Oscar for his lifetime of **outstanding** work.

Did You Know?

President Ronald Reagan did not want Chaplin to be allowed back into the U.S.

Passive Voice; Participles Used as Adjectives; *Get* + Participles and Adjectives 77

Expansion

Theme The topic for this lesson can be enhanced with the following ideas:

1. Photos of tramps from the early 1900s in the U.S.
2. A short biography of Charlie Chaplin from a Web site, film history, or encyclopedia

Reading Variation

To practice listening skills, have students first listen to the audio alone. Ask a few comprehension questions. Repeat the audio if necessary. Then have students open their books and read along as they listen to the audio.

Reading Glossary

abandon: leave; give up

decline: reduce; become less

tramp: beggar, hobo, homeless person, especially in the early part of the twentieth century in the U.S.

version: variation; different form

view: opinion

Charlie Chaplin (Reading)

1. Have students look at the photos. Ask: *Who is the man?* (Charlie Chaplin) *What is his occupation?* (He's an actor.) *What time period do you think his films are from?* (early twentieth century)
2. Have students look quickly at the reading. Ask: *What is the reading about? How do you know?* Have students use the title and photos to make predictions about the reading.
3. Preteach any vocabulary words your students may not know, such as *tramp, abandoned, version, declining,* and *views.*

BEFORE YOU READ

1. Activate students' prior knowledge about Charlie Chaplin and silent movies. Ask: *What were the first movies like?* (silent, black and white)
2. Have students discuss the questions in pairs. Try to pair students of different language backgrounds.
3. Ask a few volunteers to share their answers with the class.

To save class time, skip "Before You Read" or have students prepare answers for homework ahead of time.

Reading ⏱ CD 1, Track 11

1. Have students first read the text silently. Tell them to pay special attention to participles used as adjectives. Then play the audio and have students read along silently.
2. Check students' comprehension. Ask questions such as: *Where was Charlie Chaplin from?* (London, England) *What else did Charlie Chaplin do besides acting?* (He also produced, directed, and wrote his movies.)

To save class time, have students do the reading for homework ahead of time.

DID YOU KNOW?

When Charlie Chaplin returned to the U.S. in 1972 to receive a special Oscar, Ronald Reagan was the governor of California, where the Oscar ceremonies are held. Although Chaplin lived in America for many years, he never became a U.S. citizen.

2.10 | Participles Used as Adjectives to Show Feelings

1. On the board, rewrite the sentences from grammar chart **2.9** with blanks: *Chaplin's movies are _____. We are_____in his movies.* Write *interesting* and *interested* on the board. Ask: *Which one goes in which sentence?* Review the difference between present and past participles; refer to grammar chart **2.9** if necessary.
2. Review the grammar chart with students. Draw students' attention to the explanation of causes and recipients of feelings.
3. Provide pairs of students with cues for practice. Ask students to make simple sentences with both forms, e.g., *frightened* (I am frightened by thunder.) and *frightening* (The cost of college is frightening.); alternate forms.

2.10 | Participles Used as Adjectives to Show Feelings

The participles of a verb can be used as adjectives.

Chaplin's movies entertained people.
(verb)

His movies are entertaining. → People are entertained.
(present participle) (past participle)

Chaplin's movies interest us.
(verb)

Chaplin's movies are interesting. → We are interested in his movies.
(present participle) (past participle)

Examples	Explanation
The movie *bored* us. (*bored* = verb)	In some cases, both the present participle (a) and the past participle (b) of the same verb can be used as adjectives.
a. The movie was **boring.** I left the **boring** movie before it was over.	The present participle (a) gives an active meaning. The movie *actively* caused a feeling of boredom.
b. Some people were **bored.** The **bored** people got up and left.	The past participle (b) gives a passive meaning. It describes the receiver of a feeling. The people were bored by the movie.
a. Chaplin had an **interesting** life. He was poor and then became very rich. b. I am **interested** in Chaplin. I would like to know more about him. a. The main character in *Friday the Thirteenth* is a **frightening** man. b. I was **frightened** and couldn't sleep after seeing the movie.	A person can cause a feeling in others or he can receive a feeling. Therefore, a person can be both *interesting* and *interested, frightening* and *frightened,* etc.
The book is **interesting.** (never *interested*) The movie is **entertaining.** (never *entertained*)	An object (like a book or a movie) doesn't have feelings, so a past participle cannot be used to describe an object.

Language Notes:

1. The following pictures show the difference between a *frightening* man and a *frightened* man.

a. The man is frightening the children. = He's a *frightening man.*

b. The man is frightened by the robber. = He's a *frightened man.*

Grammar Variation

Write: *I am* _____ on the board twice. Pantomime a bored person—yawn, look at the clock, look around the room, etc. Ask: *What can you say about me?* (You are bored.) Fill in the first sentence. Then play the part of a long-winded presenter or entertainer; talk in incomplete sentences or in unnecessary detail about a small issue; ask: *What can you say about me?* (You are boring.) Ask: *Are these two sentences the same?* (no) Then review the grammar chart with students.

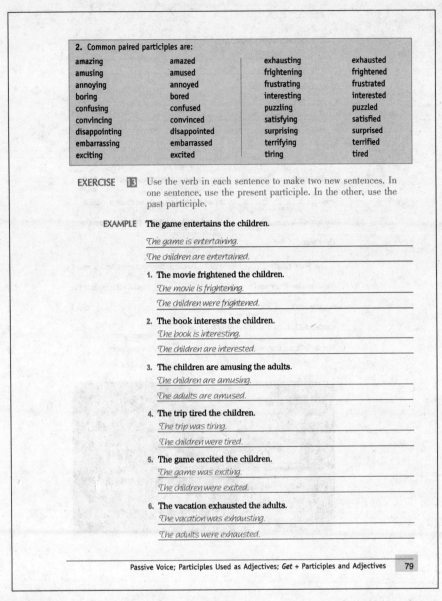

2. Common paired participles are:

amazing	amazed	exhausting	exhausted
amusing	amused	frightening	frightened
annoying	annoyed	frustrating	frustrated
boring	bored	interesting	interested
confusing	confused	puzzling	puzzled
convincing	convinced	satisfying	satisfied
disappointing	disappointed	surprising	surprised
embarrassing	embarrassed	terrifying	terrified
exciting	excited	tiring	tired

EXERCISE 13 Use the verb in each sentence to make two new sentences. In one sentence, use the present participle. In the other, use the past participle.

EXAMPLE The game entertains the children.

The game is entertaining.

The children are entertained.

1. The movie frightened the children.

   The movie is frightening.

   The children were frightened.

2. The book interests the children.

   The book is interesting.

   The children are interested.

3. The children are amusing the adults.

   The children are amusing.

   The adults are amused.

4. The trip tired the children.

   The trip was tiring.

   The children were tired.

5. The game excited the children.

   The game was exciting.

   The children were excited.

6. The vacation exhausted the adults.

   The vacation was exhausting.

   The adults were exhausted.

Passive Voice; Participles Used as Adjectives; *Get* + Participles and Adjectives   79

2.10 | Participles Used as Adjectives to Show Feelings (*cont.*)

4. Direct students to the Language Notes. Review the list of paired participles with the class. Check that students are comfortable with the meaning of each pair. Review the preposition used with each, e.g., *disappointed in, surprised by,* and *tired of.*

EXERCISE 13

1. Tell students that this exercise is about feelings. Have students read the direction line.
2. Direct students to the example in the book.
3. Model the exercise. Complete #1 with the class.
4. Have students complete the exercise individually. Review the answers as a class.

Expansion

Exercise 13 Have students write their own pairs of sentences, similar to those in Exercise 13, using other participle pairs from grammar chart **2.10** on page 79. Ask volunteers to share their sentence pairs with the class.

1. Tell students that this exercise is about one person's opinion of a new movie. Have students read the direction line.
2. Direct students to the example in the book.
3. Have students complete the rest of the exercise individually. Then have them check their answers in pairs. Circulate and observe the pair work. If necessary, check the answers as a class.

---

7. The movie bored the adults.
   The movie was boring.
   The adults were bored.

8. Chaplin interests me.
   Chaplin is interesting.
   I'm interested (in Chaplin).

EXERCISE **14** Fill in the blanks with the correct participle, present or past, of the verb in parentheses ( ).
🎧

Last night my friend and I went to see a new movie. We thought it

was _____*boring*_____ . It had a lot of stupid car chases, which
          (example: bore)

were not _____*exciting*_____ at all. And I didn't like the characters.
          (1 excite)

They weren't very _____*convincing*_____ .
          (2 convince)

We were pretty _____*disappointed*_____ because the reviewers said it was a
          (3 disappoint)

good movie. They said it had _____*amazing*_____ visual effects. But for
          (4 amaze)

me, it wasn't _____*interesting*_____ at all. I was _____*annoyed*_____ that I
          (5 interest)   (6 annoy)

wasted $10 and a whole evening for such a _____*disappointing*_____ movie.
          (7 disappoint)

The only thing that was _____*satisfying*_____ was the popcorn.
          (8 satisfy)

Exercise 14 Variation

To provide practice with listening skills, have students close their books and listen to the audio. Repeat the audio as needed. Ask comprehension questions, such as: *Did the person like the new movie?* (no) *Why not?* (The car chases weren't exciting; the characters weren't very convincing.) *What did the reviewers say about the movie?* (It was a good movie.) Then have students open their books and complete Exercise 14.

Expansion

Exercise 14 Ask students to describe a really terrible movie they have seen. Encourage students to use the exercise as a model. Then ask students to describe a really good movie they have seen.

EXERCISE **15** Fill in the blanks and discuss your answers.

EXAMPLE I'm interested in _____ *sports* _____.

1. I'm interested in _____ Answers will vary. _____ movies.
2. Now I'm worried about _____.
3. In the past, I was worried about _____.
4. In my opinion, _____ is an amazing (*choose one*) actor / athlete / politician.
5. Married people _____ than single people.
6. Children shouldn't be allowed to _____.
7. I'm not interested in _____.
8. I'm annoyed when people _____.
9. _____ is a boring subject for me.
10. I feel frustrated when _____.
11. I am amazed that _____ in the U.S.
12. It's not surprising that _____ in the U.S.
13. Sometimes I feel embarrassed when I _____.
14. I was very excited when _____.
15. When I came to this school, I was surprised _____.

1. Tell students that this exercise is a chance to talk about their feelings. Have students read the direction line.
2. Direct students to the example in the book. Ask several volunteers how they would complete the sentence in the example.
3. Have students complete the exercise individually. Have students work in pairs to read their answers to each other. Ask volunteers to share interesting information about their partners.
4. Tell students that you will answer questions they have about your answers; students may ask you, for example: *What is your answer to #7?* Answer the questions.

To save class time, have students do half of the exercise in class and complete the other half for homework. Or assign the entire exercise for homework.

Expansion

Exercise 15 Have students write interview questions using participles as adjectives to show feelings. For example: *What is the most frightening movie you have ever seen? Have you ever been embarrassed by your parents?* Have students use their questions to interview one another, and report interesting answers to the class.

2.11 | Other Past Participles Used as Adjectives

1. On the board, write: *My DVD player is broken.* Ask: *What is* broken *in this sentence?* (an adjective and a participle) Say: *I don't know who broke it or when, but it's not really important now.* Say that in this sentence, what is important is the result—the DVD player is broken and doesn't work.
2. Have students review the grammar chart. In the first section, review each example and its explanation together.
3. Provide additional practice by having students complete sentences such as: *I am done with _____.* Or *_____ is related to _____.*

2.11 | Other Past Participles Used as Adjectives

Some sentences look passive (*be* + past participle), but there is no action in the sentence. The past participles are used as adjectives.

Examples	Explanation
  a. No one knows the winners' names because the envelope is **sealed**. b. Is this seat **taken**? c. Chaplin was **born** in England. d. The dress is **made** of silk. e. The door is **locked** now. f. He bought a **used** car.	In some cases, we are looking at the result of a previous action. We no longer know or care about the agent of the action or even the action.[2] a. **Previous Action:** Someone *sealed* the envelope. b. **Previous Action:** Someone *took (occupied)* the seat. c. **Previous Action:** His mother *bore* a child. d. **Previous Action:** The dress *was made* by someone. e. **Previous Action:** The door *was locked* by the janitor. f. **Previous Action:** The car *was used* by another owner.
Many people are **involved** in making a movie. Hollywood is **located** in California. Is Geraldine Chaplin **related** to Charlie Chaplin? We are **done** with the video. When you are **finished** with the video, return it to the store. Is the theater **air-conditioned**? The theater was very **crowded**.	In some cases, we use a past participle as an adjective even though there is no previous action. The sentences to the left have no equivalent active form.
a. The glass is **broken**. b. Don't touch the **broken** glass. a. The child is **lost** in the park. b. Let's take the **lost** child to the park office. a. The child seems **tired**. b. Let's put the **tired** child to bed.	Past participles can be used: a. after *be* and other linking verbs (*seem, look, feel, sound,* etc.). OR b. before a noun.

[2]These forms are sometimes called "stative passives."

82   Lesson **2**

Grammar Variation

Write several sentences with participles used as adjectives on the board with the nouns missing, such as: _____ *isn't allowed in school* or _____ *is made from* _____. Have students provide examples of their own by filling in the blanks.

Ask: *What are* allowed *and* made? (adjectives) *What words do they come from* (allow, make) *What form are they?* (past participles) Say that past participles are often used as adjectives. Then review the grammar chart as a class.

Examples	Explanation
Chaplin was a *well known* actor. He was a *highly paid* actor. He was *well liked* by millions.	To emphasize and further describe the adjectives used as past participles, an adverb can be added. Common phrases include: • a well known actor • a highly paid actor • a well educated person • a closely watched experiment • a well behaved child • a slightly used book • a well dressed woman • closely related languages • a well fed dog

The following are some common combinations of *be* + past participle:

be air-conditioned	be filled (with)	be married
be accustomed (to)	be finished	be permitted (to)
be allowed (to)	be gone	be pleased
be born	be injured	be prepared
be broken	be insured	be related (to)
be closed	be interested (in)	be taken (*occupied*)
be concerned (about)	be involved (in)	be used
be crowded	be known	be used to
be divorced	be located	be worried (about)
be done	be locked	be wounded
be dressed	be lost	
be educated	be made (of, in)	

EXERCISE 16   Underline the past participle in the following sentences.

EXAMPLE   Movie theaters are crowded on Saturday night.

1. The movie theater is closed in the morning.
2. Where is the movie theater located?
3. Charlie Chaplin was married several times.
4. Chaplin was not an educated man.
5. Children are not allowed to see some movies.
6. Many movies are made in Hollywood.
7. How many people were involved in making *Toy Story*?
8. Chaplin was a well paid actor.
9. Chaplin was born in England.
10. He was well known all over the world.
11. Ronald Reagan was involved in movies before he became a politician.

2.11 | Other Past Participles Used as Adjectives (*cont.*)

4. Have students review the fourth section of the grammar chart. Ask volunteers to make sentences from each of the phrases in the explanation column, e.g., *Ronald Reagan was a well-known actor.*
5. Direct students' attention to the list at the bottom of the chart. Clarify any vocabulary students are unfamiliar with. Ask volunteers to give sentences about themselves using the combinations; give one or two examples of your own (e.g., *My son is involved in the theater at his school. I don't like going to the mall; it's always crowded.*).

EXERCISE 16

1. Tell students that this exercise is about movies and theaters. Have students read the direction line. Ask: *What do we underline?* (the past participle)
2. Direct students to the example in the book. Point out the photo of the scene from the movie *Toy Story*.
3. Have students complete the exercise individually. Check answers as a class.

Expansion

Grammar   Bring in several newspapers and divide them among groups of students. Have students find and list examples of participles used as adjectives and phrases with an adverb and a participle. Have groups share their lists with the class.

EXERCISE 17

1. Tell students that this exercise is also about movies and theaters. Have students read the direction line.
2. Direct students to the examples in the book.
3. Have students complete the exercise in writing individually, and then check their work in pairs. Circulate during pair work. If necessary, check answers as a class.
4. Assess students' performance. If necessary, review grammar chart **2.11** on pages 82 and 83.

🕐 To save class time, have students do half of the exercise in class and complete the other half for homework. Or assign the entire exercise for homework.

Being Famous (Reading)

1. Have students look at the photos. Ask: *Who are the people?* (Elizabeth Taylor and Richard Burton; Arnold Schwarzenegger) *Are they famous people?* (yes)
2. Have students look quickly at the reading. Ask: *What is the reading about? How do you know?* Have students use the title and photos to make predictions about the reading.
3. Preteach any vocabulary words your students may not know, such as: *glamour, on top,* and *cosmetic surgery.*

BEFORE YOU READ

1. Activate students' prior knowledge about the lives of famous people. Ask: *What do you think it's like to be really famous? Do you think it's easier or more difficult than being an ordinary person? Why?*
2. Have students discuss the questions in pairs. Try to pair students of different language backgrounds.
3. Ask a few volunteers to share their answers with the class.

🕐 To save class time, skip "Before You Read" or have students prepare answers for homework ahead of time.

EXERCISE **17** Find the mistakes and correct them. Not every sentence has a mistake. If the sentence is correct, write *C*.

EXAMPLES The theater located near my house.
(is)

Are you interested in action movies? *C*

1. Is Julia Roberts marry? *married*
2. I'm concerned about the violence in movies. *C*
3. Movie theaters crowded on Friday nights. *are*
4. Children aren't allow to enter some movies. *^allowed*
5. How many people are involved in making a movie? *C*
6. Walt Disney born in 1901. *was*
7. When you're finish with the DVD, please return it to the video store. *^finished*
8. Is the Oscar make of gold? *made*

BEING FAMOUS

Before You Read
1. In the U.S., movie stars get divorced a lot. Is this true in other countries?
2. Is the divorce rate for Hollywood stars higher than for average people?
3. Do you think being famous would be fun?

Culture Note

The movie rating system used in the U.S. is managed by the Motion Picture Association of America. It includes ratings of G (for general audiences, or everyone); PG (parental guidance; parents should check the movie before they let their children see it); PG-13 (parents may not want children under 13 to see the movie); R (restricted; children under 17 must have a parent or adult with them to see the movie); NC-17 (children under 17 may not see the movie), and X (children under 17 may not see the movie). Movie theaters and rental movie boxes show the rating a movie received.

Expansion

Theme The topic for this lesson can be enhanced with the following ideas:

1. A fan magazine or Web site printout
2. Tabloid newspapers with stories about and pictures of stars
3. A map of stars' homes in Hollywood, or a newspaper story about over-zealous fans

Read the following article. Pay special attention to *be* and *get* before past participles and adjectives.

Becoming a Hollywood star is a dream for many. Glamour, money, beauty, and even power make the occupation very attractive. However, actually living the Hollywood star life can **be difficult** and **challenging,** both personally and professionally.

Hollywood stars are known for their short and frequent marriages—and divorces. Elizabeth Taylor **got married** eight times. In fact, she married the same man (Richard Burton) twice—and divorced him twice. Britney Spears **got married** one day and **got divorced** the next day. One Hollywood couple is an exception—Paul Newman and Joanne Woodward. They **have been married** since 1958. What few people know is that Newman **was married** once before, from 1949 to 1958.

Why is being famous so difficult? Some actors **get rich** overnight and don't handle their sudden wealth and fame easily. Life can **be difficult** in the public eye, when reporters record an actor's every moment. Also, Hollywood stars need to look great to stay on top. They do not like to **get old.** Many Hollywood stars use cosmetic surgery to look young. Many work out with a personal trainer because they don't want to **get fat** or out of shape.

Some Hollywood actors go into politics when they **get tired** of acting. They use their popularity as actors to win elections. Ronald Reagan and Arnold Schwarzenegger both went from being actors to becoming governor of California. Ronald Reagan went on to become president of the U.S.[3] A famous wrestler, Jessie Ventura, even got to be governor of Minnesota.

Life in the public eye seems wonderful, but it can be difficult at times.

Passive Voice; Participles Used as Adjectives; *Get* + Participles and Adjectives   **85**

 Reading CD 1, Track 13

1. Have students first read the text silently. Tell them to pay special attention to *be* and *get* before past participles and adjectives. Then play the audio and have students read along silently.

2. Check students' comprehension. Ask questions such as: *What are some things the article says Hollywood stars do?* (get married often, and for a short time; have cosmetic surgery; work out with a personal trainer; go into politics, etc.) *What does* in the public eye *mean? (*always being followed by reporters; always of interest to the public)

🕑 To save class time, have students do the reading for homework ahead of time.

Reading Variation

To practice listening skills, have students first listen to the audio alone. Ask a few comprehension questions. Repeat the audio if necessary. Then have students open their books and read along as they listen to the audio.

Reading Glossary

cosmetic surgery: surgery to change a person's appearance, especially to make a person look younger or thinner
glamour: style; attractiveness; star quality
on top: in the public eye; popular; more popular than others

2.12 | Past Participles and Other Adjectives with *Get*

1. Have students cover grammar chart **2.12**. Ask: *When were Paul Newman and Joanne Woodward married?* (1958); write the answer on the board: *Paul Newman and Joanne Woodward were married in 1958.* Then erase *were* and ask: *What word do we usually use here?* (*get*) Ask: *What is their marital status?* (They are married.); *What does status mean?* (condition) Say: *When we talk about the point when a status begins or began, we can use get. What are some other phrases with get and a participle?* (*get divorced, get rich, get old*) *What does get mean?* (become)
2. Have students look at grammar chart **2.12**. Review the example sentences and explanations.
3. Direct students' attention to the Usage Note. Review the examples. Then ask volunteers to talk about themselves using the examples as models (*I am married. I have been married to . . . , etc.*).
4. Direct students' attention to the list at the bottom of the page. Clarify any vocabulary students are unfamiliar with.

2.12 | Past Participles and Other Adjectives with *Get*[4]

Examples	Explanation
a. **Is** Julia Roberts **married?** b. When did she **get married?**	a. *Be* + past participle describes the status of a noun over a period of time.
a. The actress **is divorced.** b. She **got divorced** soon after she **got married.**	b. *Get* + past participle shows the specific point at which this status began. There is no reference to the continuation of this status.
a. You're yawning. I see you **are tired.** b. When Arnold Schwarzenegger **got tired** of acting, he went into politics.	
a. Movie stars **are rich.** b. A lot of people buy a lottery ticket because they want to **get rich** quickly.	a. *Be* + adjective describes the status of a noun over a period of time.
a. Paul Newman **is old.** b. Most stars don't want to **get old.** They want to look young forever.	b. *Get* + adjective shows the specific point at which this status began. *Get* means *become*.

Usage Note:
Notice the difference between *to be married, to marry, to get married.*
Paul Newman **is married.** He **has been married** to the same woman for many years. (status)
He **married** Joanne Woodward in 1958. (The verb *marry* is followed by an object.)
Paul and Joanne **got married** in 1958. (*Get married* is not followed by an object.)

Past Participles with *get*		Adjectives with *get*	
get accustomed to	get hurt	get angry	get old
get acquainted	get lost	get dark	get rich
get bored	get married	get fat	get sleepy
get confused	get scared	get hungry	get upset
get divorced	get tired	get nervous	get well
get dressed	get used to		
get engaged	get worried		

[4]For a list of expressions with *get*, see Appendix C.

Grammar Variation

Have students review the reading on page 85 and list all of the phrases with *get*. Ask: *What do you think* get *means?* (become) *When we use* get, *what are we showing?* (the point at which a status or condition began or begins) Then introduce grammar chart **2.12** above.

Expansion

Grammar Have students work in groups. Ask each group to write a sentence about each member of the group, using the phrases in the chart at the bottom of page 86. Have each group present their lists to the class.

EXERCISE 18 Circle the correct words to complete this conversation between two young men.

A: Jennifer Lopez is my favorite actress. When she (was /**got**) married a
   (example)
   few years ago, I felt so sad. But then she (was /**got**) divorced just a
   (1)
   year later. I was so happy.

B: Happy? Sad? Do you think Jennifer (**is** / gets) interested in you? She
   (2)
   doesn't even know you!

A: I keep sending her letters. I would like to (be /**get**) acquainted with
   (3)
   her.

B: She's not going to answer your letters. She (**is** / gets) too rich and
   (4)
   famous to pay attention to you.

A: Well, I'm an actor too, you know.

B: Mostly you're just a waiter.

A: I'm not always going to be a waiter. When acting studios discover
   me, I'm going to (**get** / be) famous, and Jennifer will notice me.
   (5)

B: You will be an old man by the time you (**get** / are) famous.
   (6)

A: That doesn't matter. Someday it will happen, and I'll meet Jennifer.

B: By that time, she (**will be** / will get) old and you won't be interested
   (7)
   in her anymore.

A: I will always (get /**be**) interested in her. She's my one true love.
   (8)

B: Oh really? What does your girlfriend have to say about that?

A: I never talk to her about Jennifer. One time I told her how much
   I like Jennifer, and she (was /**got**) angry.
   (9)

B: I don't think your girlfriend has anything to worry about.

Passive Voice; Participles Used as Adjectives; *Get* + Participles and Adjectives   87

EXERCISE 18

CD 1, Track 14

1. Tell students that this exercise is a
   conversation between two friends
   about hopes and dreams. Have
   students read the direction line.
2. Model the exercise. Direct students
   to the example in the book. Then do
   #1 with the class.
3. Have students complete the
   exercise individually. Then have
   them check their answers in pairs
   by practicing the conversation.
   Circulate and observe the pair work.
   If necessary, check the answers as a
   class.

Exercise 18 Variation

To provide practice with listening skills, have students close their books and listen to the
audio. Repeat the audio as needed. Ask comprehension questions, such as: *When did person A
feel sad?* (when Jennifer Lopez got married a few years ago) *When did he feel happy?* (when
she got divorced just a year later) *Does Jennifer Lopez know person A?* (no) Then have
students open their books and complete Exercise 18.

Expansion

Exercise 18 Ask students to describe the two young men. Ask: *Do you have friends like
this?* Then have students write several sentences or a short paragraph, as appropriate,
describing one of the two friends in the conversation. Collect for assessment.

Culture Note

Tabloid newspapers have stories about famous people and movie stars, and photographs of
them. Many of these are unauthorized paparazzi, or photographers who chase famous people
to try to take their pictures, usually for money.

Summary of Lesson 2

PART 1

Passive Voice Provide a series of cues and have students make complete sentences using the passive voice (*got lost, was written, was made, have been told, is shown*, etc.).

If necessary, have students review:
2.2 Passive Voice—Form (p. 59)
2.3 Passive and Active Voice—Uses (p. 62)
2.4 The Passive Voice Without an Agent (p. 63)
2.5 The Passive Voice with an Agent (p. 65)
2.8 Passive with *Get* (p. 75).

SUMMARY OF LESSON 2

PART 1 Passive Voice

Passive Voice = *Be* + Past Participle	Use
With an Agent: Mickey Mouse **was created** by Walt Disney. *Star Wars* **was directed** by George Lucas.	The passive voice can be used with an agent, especially if we want to emphasize the result of the action. **Note:** Do not mention the agent if it is not a specific person. *Wrong:* Spanish is spoken *by people* in Mexico.
Without an Agent: a. Hollywood **was built** at the beginning of the twentieth century. b. Children **are** not **allowed** to see some movies. c. The Oscar presentation **is seen** all over the world. d. I **was told** that you didn't like the movie.	The passive voice is usually used without an agent: a. When it is not important to mention who performed the action b. When the agent is obvious c. When the agent is not a specific person but people in general d. To hide the identity of the agent
Reagan **got shot** in 1981. I **got fired** from my job. A lot of people **got killed** in the war.	*Get* can be used instead of *be* in certain conversational expressions. Do not use *get* when the agent is mentioned. *Wrong:* Reagan got shot *by John Hinckley.*

Summary Variation

Write on the board phrases used in passive voice sentences (*was built, is known for, are made, is located*, etc.). Have students write sentences about the history of, places in, or facts about their native countries. Have students share their information with the class.

PART 2 Participles Used as Adjectives

Examples	Explanation
Silent movies are very **interesting**. We are **interested** in the life of Charlie Chaplin.	Use the present participle to show that the noun produced a feeling. Use the past participle to show that the noun received a feeling.
I'm tired of your **broken** promises. Is this seat **taken?**	Use the past participle to show the result of a previous action. **Previous Actions:** Someone *broke* the promise. Someone *took* the seat.
The child is **lost**. The bus is **crowded**. Where is Hollywood **located?**	Some past participles are not related to a previous action.
She **got confused** when the teacher explained participles. I **got lost** on my way to your house. She **got upset** when she couldn't find her keys.	Use *get* with past participles and other adjectives to mean *become*.

EDITING ADVICE

PART 1 Passive Voice

1. Use *be*, not *do / does / did* to make negatives and questions with the passive voice.

          wasn't
   My watch didn't made in Japan.

        was
   When did the movie filmed?

2. Don't use the passive voice with intransitive verbs.

   The accident was happened at 10:30 p.m.

   Her grandfather was died three years ago.

3. Don't confuse the *-ing* form with the past participle.

         eaten
   The candy was eating by the child.

4. Don't forget the *-ed* ending for a regular past participle.

        ed
   The floor was wash by the janitor.

Passive Voice; Participles Used as Adjectives; *Get* + Participles and Adjectives   **89**

PART 2

Participles Used as Adjectives Have students make statements about life in the U.S., using pairs of words from the verb chart on page 79 (e.g., *Some traffic laws in the U.S. are confusing. I'm confused about what* yield *means on traffic signs.*).
If necessary, have students review:
2.9   Participles Used as Adjectives (p. 76)
2.10 Participles Used as Adjectives to Show Feelings (p. 78)
2.11 Other Past Participles Used as Adjectives (p. 82)
2.12 Past Participles and Other Adjectives with *Get* (p. 86).

Editing Advice

For each item, have students provide the grammar rule behind the editing advice. This can be done as an individual, a pair, a group, or a class activity.

PART 1

1. For negative statements and questions in the passive voice, use forms of *be*, not *do, does,* or *did*.
2. The passive voice cannot be used with intransitive verbs (verbs that do not take a direct object).
3. Use the past participle, not the *-ing* form, with the passive voice.
4. Regular past participles end in *-ed*.

Summary Variation

Write a list of participles used as adjectives on the board (e.g., *upset, pleased, used to, tired,* and *amused*). Have students talk about themselves using the adjectives.

PART 1 (cont.)

5. Passive sentences must include a form of *be*.

6. When the agent is mentioned in a passive sentence, use *by*.

7. When the agent is named, use the object pronoun after *by*, not the subject pronoun.

8. For negative statements and questions in the passive with the informal *get*, use *do, does,* or *did*—not a form of *be*.

PART 2

1. Regular past participles have a *-d* or *-ed* ending.

2. When a participle is used as an adjective after a noun, remember to use a verb (usually a form of *be*) before the participle.

3. Use *be*, not *do*, with participles used as adjectives.

5. Don't forget to use a form of *be* in a passive sentence.

      was
  The movie seen by everyone in my family.

6. Use *by* to show the agent of the action.

      by
  Tom Sawyer was written for Mark Twain.

7. Use an object pronoun after *by*.

            her
  My mother prepared the soup. The salad was prepared by she too.

8. Use *do, does,* or *did* when you use *get* in questions and negatives with the passive voice.

      Did
  Were you get fired from your job?

PART **2** Participles and Other Adjectives

1. Don't forget the *-ed* ending for past participles used as adjectives.

          d
  I'm very tire now. I have to go to sleep.

            ied
  When did you get marry?

2. Don't forget to include a verb (usually *be*) before a participle used as an adjective.

      is
  My college located on the corner of Broadway and Wilson Avenues.

      was
  The movie boring, so we left.

3. Participles used as adjectives are used with *be*, not *do*.

      isn't
  My sister doesn't married.
  Are
  Do you bored in your math class?

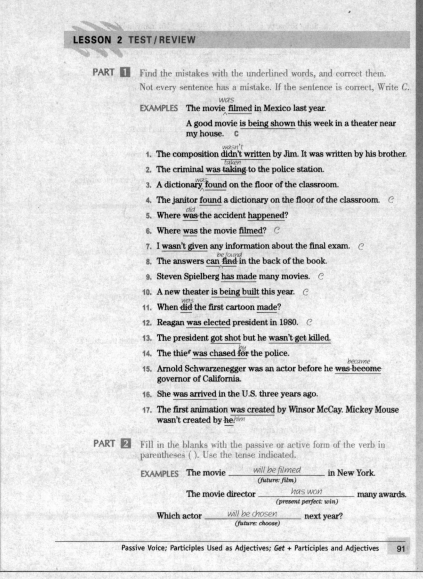

LESSON 2 TEST/REVIEW

PART 1 Find the mistakes with the underlined words, and correct them. Not every sentence has a mistake. If the sentence is correct, Write *C*.

EXAMPLES   The movie ~~filmed~~ ^was^ in Mexico last year.

A good movie is being shown this week in a theater near my house.   **C**

1. The composition ~~didn't written~~ ^wasn't^ by Jim. It was written by his brother.
2. The criminal was ~~taking~~ ^taken^ to the police station.
3. A dictionary found ^was^ on the floor of the classroom.
4. The janitor found a dictionary on the floor of the classroom.   **C**
5. Where ~~was~~ the accident ^did^ happened?
6. Where was the movie filmed?   **C**
7. I wasn't given any information about the final exam.   **C**
8. The answers can ~~find~~ ^be found^ in the back of the book.
9. Steven Spielberg has made many movies.   **C**
10. A new theater is being built this year.   **C**
11. When ~~did~~ the first cartoon ^was^ made?
12. Reagan was elected president in 1980.   **C**
13. The president got shot but he wasn't get killed.
14. The thief was chased ^by^ for the police.
15. Arnold Schwarzenegger was an actor before he ~~was become~~ ^became^ governor of California.
16. She was arrived in the U.S. three years ago.
17. The first animation was created by Winsor McCay. Mickey Mouse wasn't created by ~~he.~~ ^him^

PART 2 Fill in the blanks with the passive or active form of the verb in parentheses ( ). Use the tense indicated.

EXAMPLES   The movie ___*will be filmed*___ in New York.
　　　　　　　　　　　(future: film)

The movie director ___*has won*___ many awards.
　　　　　　　　　　　(present perfect: win)

Which actor ___*will be chosen*___ next year?
　　　　　　　　(future: choose)

Passive Voice; Participles Used as Adjectives; *Get* + Participles and Adjectives   **91**

Lesson 2 Test/Review

For additional practice, review, and assessment materials, see Assessment CD-ROM with *ExamView Pro*, *More Grammar Practice* Workbook 3, Interactive CD-ROM, and Web site http://elt.thomson.com/gic

PART 1

1. Part 1 may be used as an in-class test to assess student performance, in addition to the Assessment CD-ROM with *ExamView Pro*. Have students read the direction line. Ask: *Does every sentence have a mistake?* (no)
2. Collect for assessment.
3. If necessary, have students review: **Lesson 2.**

PART 2

1. Part 2 may also be used as an in-class test to assess student performance, in addition to the Assessment CD-ROM with *ExamView Pro*. Tell students to choose the passive or active form of the verb, and to use the tense shown. Review the examples. Then do #1 as a class. Ask: *What goes in the first blank?* (*will be chosen*)
2. Collect for assessment.
3. If necessary, have students review: **Lesson 2.**

Lesson Review

To use Part 1 as a review, assign it as homework or use it as an in-class activity to be completed individually or in pairs. Check answers and review errors as a class. Reteach grammar points that students haven't mastered. Then student learning may be assessed using a test generated from the Assessment CD-ROM with *ExamView Pro*.

2. Julia Roberts _____*has been seen*_____ in many movies.
   (present perfect: see)

3. My sister _____*doesn't eat*_____ popcorn during movies.
   (simple present: not/eat)

4. A new movie _____*is being made*_____ about World War II.
   (present continuous: make)

5. I _____*didn't see*_____ the Oscar presentation last year.
   (past: not/see)

6. The audience _____*enjoyed*_____ the movie.
   (past: enjoy)

7. We _____*will buy*_____ our tickets tomorrow.
   (future: buy)

8. Her parents _____*don't permit*_____ her to watch adult movies.
   (present: not/permit)

9. While the movie _____*was being made*_____, one of the actors
   (past continuous: make)
   _____*was hurt*_____.
   (past: hurt)

10. *Star Wars* is a great movie. It _____*should be seen*_____ on a large
    (should/see)
    screen, not on a TV screen.

11. Today's animation _____*is done*_____ on a computer. It
    (simple present: do)
    _____*isn't drawn*_____ by hand.
    (simple present: not/draw)

12. Charlie Chaplin _____*became*_____ interested in acting at
    (past: become)
    the age of five.

13. Chaplin _____*left*_____ the U.S. in 1952 and
    (past: leave)
    _____*returned*_____ in 1972.
    (past: return)

14. President Lincoln _____*was shot*_____ while he
    (past: shoot)
    _____*was watching*_____ a play. He _____*died*_____ a
    (past continuous: watch) *(past: die)*
    few days later. The killer _____*was caught*_____.
    (past: catch)

Lesson Review

To use Part 2 as a review, assign it as homework or use it as an in-class activity to be completed individually or in pairs. Check answers and review errors as a class. Reteach grammar points that students haven't mastered. Then student learning may be assessed using a test generated from the Assessment CD-ROM with *ExamView Pro*.

PART **3** Find the mistakes with the underlined words, and correct them. Not every sentence has a mistake. If the sentence is correct, write *C*.

EXAMPLES Are you ~~worry~~ *ied* about your children?
When did they get divorced? **C**

1. You look like you don't understand the lesson. Are you confuse? *d*
2. I *'m* very tired now. I just want to go to sleep.
3. I come from Miami. I'm not accustomed to cold weather. *C*
4. Last week we saw a very boring movie. *C*
5. My cousin was excited about coming to the U.S. *C*
6. Do you have an interesting job? *C*
7. I am surprised to find out that you don't like ice cream. *C*
8. When did you get married? *C*
9. I'm not ~~satisfy~~ *satisfied* with my grade in this course.
10. The teacher's office *is* located on the second floor.
11. The library ~~doesn't~~ *isn't* crowded at 8 a.m.
12. ~~Do~~ *Are* you disappointed with your grade?

PART **4** Fill in the blanks with the present participle or the past participle of the verb in parentheses ( ).

EXAMPLES The movie wasn't very good. In fact, it was __boring__.
(bore)

I had a great meal. I feel very __satisfied__.
(satisfy)

1. We read an __interesting__ story about Charlie Chaplin.
(interest)

2. He became __interested__ in acting when he was a child.
(interest)

3. He was well __known__ all over the world.
(know)

4. When he left the U.S. in 1952, he was not __allowed__ to re-enter.
(allow)

5. Chaplin was __married__ four times.
(marry)

6. He was an __entertaining__ actor.
(entertain)

7. I am never __bored__ during one of his movies.
(bore)

Passive Voice; Participles Used as Adjectives; *Get* + Participles and Adjectives   **93**

PART 3

1. Part 3 may also be used as an in-class test to assess student performance, in addition to the Assessment CD-ROM with *ExamView Pro*. Have students read the direction line. Ask: *Does every sentence have a mistake?* (no)
2. Collect for assessment.
3. If necessary, have students review: **Lesson 2.**

PART 4

1. Part 4 may also be used as an in-class test to assess student performance, in addition to the Assessment CD-ROM with *ExamView Pro*. Have students read the direction line. Ask: *What do we write?* (the present participle or past participle)
2. Collect for assessment.
3. If necessary, have students review: **Lesson 2.**

Lesson Review

To use Parts 3 and 4 as a review, assign them as homework or use them as in-class activities to be completed individually or in pairs. Check answers and review errors as a class. Reteach grammar points that students haven't mastered. Then student learning may be assessed using a test generated from the Assessment CD-ROM with *ExamView Pro*.

Expansion Activities

These expansion activities provide opportunities for students to interact with one another and further develop their speaking and writing skills. Encourage students to use grammar from this lesson whenever possible.

To save class time, assign parts of the activities as homework. Then use class time for interaction and communication. If students do not need additional speaking practice, some of the activities may be assigned as writing activities for homework, or skipped altogether.

CLASSROOM ACTIVITIES

1. Tell students that this activity is about famous discoveries and creations. Have students cover the answers in the box below the lists. Ask: *What do we match?* (an item from the left column with a name from the right column) Review with students language for agreeing, checking for agreement, and disagreeing (e.g., *I think so too. Are you sure that's right? I'm not sure I agree.*). Then have groups work together to complete the task. Have groups report their results as a class.

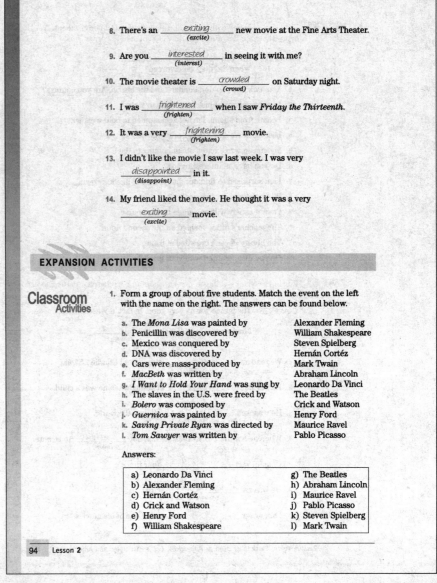

8. There's an _____exciting_____ new movie at the Fine Arts Theater.
   (excite)

9. Are you _____interested_____ in seeing it with me?
   (interest)

10. The movie theater is _____crowded_____ on Saturday night.
    (crowd)

11. I was _____frightened_____ when I saw *Friday the Thirteenth*.
    (frighten)

12. It was a very _____frightening_____ movie.
    (frighten)

13. I didn't like the movie I saw last week. I was very
    _____disappointed_____ in it.
    (disappoint)

14. My friend liked the movie. He thought it was a very
    _____exciting_____ movie.
    (excite)

EXPANSION ACTIVITIES

Classroom Activities

1. Form a group of about five students. Match the event on the left with the name on the right. The answers can be found below.

   a. The *Mona Lisa* was painted by — Alexander Fleming
   b. Penicillin was discovered by — William Shakespeare
   c. Mexico was conquered by — Steven Spielberg
   d. DNA was discovered by — Hernán Cortéz
   e. Cars were mass-produced by — Mark Twain
   f. *MacBeth* was written by — Abraham Lincoln
   g. *I Want to Hold Your Hand* was sung by — Leonardo Da Vinci
   h. The slaves in the U.S. were freed by — The Beatles
   i. *Bolero* was composed by — Crick and Watson
   j. *Guernica* was painted by — Henry Ford
   k. *Saving Private Ryan* was directed by — Maurice Ravel
   l. *Tom Sawyer* was written by — Pablo Picasso

   Answers:

a) Leonardo Da Vinci	g) The Beatles
b) Alexander Fleming	h) Abraham Lincoln
c) Hernán Cortéz	i) Maurice Ravel
d) Crick and Watson	j) Pablo Picasso
e) Henry Ford	k) Steven Spielberg
f) William Shakespeare	l) Mark Twain

94   Lesson **2**

Expansion

Classroom Activities When students have completed activity 1, ask which items were difficult. Then assign individuals or groups to research each item using the library or the Internet. Have students bring one additional fact about the item they researched back to the class (e.g., *The* Mona Lisa *is now in the Louvre museum in Paris.*).

2. Fill in the blanks. Then find a partner. Discuss your answers with your partner.

a. _____ is an interesting place in this city.

b. _____ is an interesting actress.

c. _____ is a boring topic in our grammar class.

d. A surprising fact about the U.S. is _____.

e. _____ is a relaxing activity.

f. I feel relaxed when _____.

g. I get bored when I _____.

h. I get angry when _____.

i. You know you're getting old when _____.

j. I get confused when _____.

k. People in my native country who _____ can get rich.

l. One of the main reasons people get divorced is _____.

3. In a small group of people give your opinions about the best actors and actresses.

Talk About it

1. Is it important to give awards to actors and actresses? Why or why not?

2. Have you ever seen an Academy Awards ceremony? What did you think of it?

3. How are American films different from films made in other countries?

4. What are some of your favorite movies? What movies have you seen lately?

5. Who are your favorite actors and actresses?

6. What American movies have been popular in your native country?

2. Have students complete the activity individually and then compare and discuss answers with a partner. Have pairs report to the class (*I get angry when I'm stuck in traffic. Joel gets angry when he can't find his keys.*).

3. If necessary, remind students of polite language for agreeing and disagreeing, as in #1 above, before they begin the activity. Circulate and assist groups as necessary.

TALK ABOUT IT

Have students work in groups. Either assign or have each group choose one or more of the topics to discuss. Review language for agreeing, checking for agreement, and disagreeing (e.g., *I think so too. Are you sure that's right? I'm not sure I agree.*). Set a time limit for discussion. Then have groups talk about their topics. If appropriate, have groups report back to the class; have each group appoint a spokesperson.

Classroom Activities Variation

Activity 3 After groups have finished their discussions, have the class hold a vote on the best actors and actresses. Have groups nominate their choices, and allow a few minutes for groups to say why they think their choices are best. Then hold either a voice vote (voting aloud) or a secret ballot (voting on paper).

Talk About it Variation

Have students work in pairs. Have members of the pairs interview each other using the questions in the activity, alternating interviewers. Have the interviewers take notes on their partners' responses.

Items 1 and 3 Have students debate item 1 or item 3. Divide the class into two teams. Tell each team to list five reasons supporting its view. Have each team present its arguments. Then give each team an opportunity to respond to the other team's arguments. At the end of the debate, survey the class to see which opinion is more popular.

WRITE ABOUT IT

Review the use of participles as adjectives to show feelings. Have students write a paragraph about their experiences. Collect for assessment and/or have students review each other's work.

OUTSIDE ACTIVITIES

1. Before the activity, brainstorm with students the kinds of signs they may see (e.g., Parking Prohibited). Make a class list of the sentences students bring in. Review the language in the signs; clarify any difficult items.
2. If some students are unable to rent and view movies at home, consider bringing a Charlie Chaplin movie to class to view together to complete the activity.

INTERNET ACTIVITIES

1. If appropriate, encourage students to research an actor or actress from their native countries.
2. Brainstorm search terms to use to find information about the most recent Oscars.
3. Have students share the processes they used to find the information (e.g., *First, I click on . . .*).
4. Have students share the reasons they chose their movies. Ask if anyone has seen the movie; ask what he or she thought about it.
5. Have students report their results using the correct participles and phrases (*was born in, died in*).

Write About it

Write about an entertainment event that you have recently attended (such as a movie in a theater, a concert, an art fair, a museum exhibit). Did you enjoy it? Why or why not? Was there anything surprising or unusual about it?

Outside Activities

1. Look for signs, headlines, and captions that use passive constructions. (Remember, sometimes the verb *be* is omitted in a sign.) Copy the passive sentences and bring them to class.
2. Rent and watch a Charlie Chaplin movie. Summarize the story.

Internet Activities

1. On the internet, find information about an actor or actress that interests you. Print out this information and bring it to class.
2. Find out who won the Oscars most recently in these categories: Best Actor, Best Actress, Best Picture, Best Director.
3. Check to see if your local newspaper has a Web site. If it does, are there movie listings?
4. At a search engine, type in *movies*. Find a summary of a movie that interests you. Print it and bring it to class.
5. Choose two of these famous actors. Find out when they were born and when they died.

Humphrey Bogart	Spencer Tracy	John Wayne
Marilyn Monroe	Henry Fonda	Gary Cooper
Clark Gable	Vivien Leigh	Audrey Hepburn
Cary Grant	Grace Kelly	Mary Pickford
Katherine Hepburn	Natalie Wood	Jack Lemmon

 Additional Activities at http://elt.thomson.com/gic

Write About it Variation

Have students exchange first drafts with a partner. Ask students to help their partners edit their drafts. Refer students to Editing Advice on pages 89–90.

Internet Activities Variation

Activity 2 Hold an Oscar-type ceremony in class. Have students suggest appropriate categories (best actor, best singer, best supporting actress, best original excuse for missing class, best clothing, etc.) and nominate their classmates. Have groups prepare ballots, hold a vote, choose a master of ceremonies (MC) and plan a ceremony. If appropriate, invite outside guests to attend the classroom Oscars.

If students don't have access to the Internet, they may find the information needed in books, newspapers, etc., at a local public library.

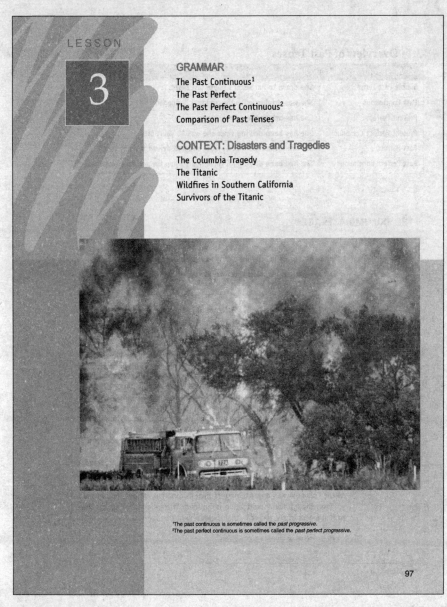

GRAMMAR

The Past Continuous[1]
The Past Perfect
The Past Perfect Continuous[2]
Comparison of Past Tenses

CONTEXT: Disasters and Tragedies

The Columbia Tragedy
The Titanic
Wildfires in Southern California
Survivors of the Titanic

[1]The past continuous is sometimes called the *past progressive*.
[2]The past perfect continuous is sometimes called the *past perfect progressive*.

97

Lesson 3

Lesson Overview

GRAMMAR

1. Activate students' prior knowledge. Ask: *What tenses did we study in Lesson 1?* (the present perfect and present perfect continuous) Write an example with each tense on the board, such as: *We have already studied the present perfect tense. Lately we have been studying the passive voice.*

2. Ask: *What will we study in this lesson?* (the past continuous, the past perfect, the past perfect continuous, comparison of past tenses) Give several examples of sentences using the past continuous and the past perfect (e.g., *The phone was ringing when I walked in the door. When I got home at 8, my husband had already made dinner.*). Have volunteers give examples. Write one or two examples on the board.

3. Draw students' attention to the alternate names for the past continuous and past perfect continuous at the bottom of page 97.

CONTEXT

1. Elicit students' prior knowledge. Ask: *What will we learn about in this lesson?* (disasters and tragedies—the Columbia tragedy, the Titanic, and wildfires in southern California) Ask: *What do you know about the Columbia? The Titanic? Wildfires in California?*

2. Have students share their knowledge and personal experiences.

Photo

1. Direct students' attention to the photo. Ask: *What do you see in the photo? What is happening? What do you think is going to happen next?*

2. Have students talk about what they know about wildfires and what causes them.

🕐 To save class time, have students do the Test/Review at the end of the lesson, or administer a lesson test generated from the Assessment CD-ROM with *ExamView® Pro.* Skip sections of the lesson that students have already mastered. You may also assign some sections for self-study for extra credit.

Expansion

Theme The topic for this lesson can be enhanced with the following ideas:

1. Newspaper or magazine articles about natural disasters or disaster relief
2. A disaster relief appeal from a humanitarian organization
3. Examples from quoted speech, notes, letters, or other informal writing showing the simple past tense used when the past perfect would normally be expected

Culture Note

Explain that *disaster* is often used to describe an event in nature, such as an earthquake or hurricane, or a large-scale accident, that affects people or the environment in a very bad way. *Tragedy* is often used to describe very terrible or sad events, whether caused by nature or by people, and focuses on our feelings about the event.

3.1 | Overview of Past Tenses

1. Have students look at grammar chart **3.1**. Ask: *How many tenses are listed in the chart?* (six) *Which ones have we already studied?* (the simple past, present perfect, and present perfect continuous)
2. Have students look at the examples in the chart. Ask: *How many of these tenses are you comfortable using? We will learn more about all of these tenses in this lesson.*
3. On the board, write sentences using the tenses presented in the chart. Ask students which tense each sentence is in.

The Columbia Tragedy (Reading)

1. Have students look at the photo on page 99. Ask: *What is this? What is it doing?* (It's a U.S. space shuttle taking off to travel into space.)
2. Have students look briefly at the reading. Ask: *What is the reading about? How do you know?* Have students use the title and photo to make predictions about the reading.
3. Preteach any essential vocabulary words your students may not know, such as *mission, orbiting, aboard, tragic, concluded, lift off, gases,* and *astronaut.*

BEFORE YOU READ

1. Have students discuss the questions in pairs. Try to pair students of different language backgrounds.
2. Ask for a few volunteers to share their answers with the class.

   To save class time, skip "Before You Read" or have students prepare answers for homework ahead of time.

Reading 🎧 *CD 1, Track 15*

1. Have students first read the text silently. Tell them to pay special attention to the verbs in boldface. Then play the audio and have students read along silently.

DID YOU KNOW ?

The first rocket with liquid fuel was launched in 1926 by Dr. Robert H. Goddard in Massachusetts. Before the space shuttle, astronauts traveled in much smaller capsules, and the rockets that carried them into space burned before the astronauts returned.

3.1 | Overview of Past Tenses

In this lesson, we will be looking at all the past tenses.

Simple Past Tense	She **drove** to her sister's house last night.
Past Continuous	She **was driving** when the accident happened.
Present Perfect	She **has driven** there many times.
Present Perfect Continuous	She **has been driving** since she was 18 years old.
Past Perfect	She knew the road well because she **had driven** it many times.
Past Perfect Continuous	She **had been driving** for three hours when the accident happened.

THE COLUMBIA TRAGEDY

Before You Read
1. What well-known accidents do you remember from history?
2. Do you remember what you were doing when a famous event occurred?

Read the following article. Pay special attention to the past continuous and the simple past-tense verbs.

Did You Know?
The Columbia was the first reusable space vehicle. Before the Columbia, manned space flight had been limited to rockets, which could only be used once, making the space program much more expensive.

On January 16, 2003, the Columbia space shuttle **left** on a science mission orbiting the Earth, with seven crew members aboard. It **stayed** in space for 16 days. On February 1, 2003, it **was traveling** back to Earth after completing its mission. NASA (the National Aeronautics and Space Administration) **received** its last communication from the Columbia on February 1, 2003, at 9 a.m. While the Columbia **was flying** over east Texas just 16 minutes from its landing in Florida, it **disintegrated**[3]. Families who **were** happily **waiting** for the return of their relatives at the Kennedy Space Center in Florida **received** the tragic news. People all over the world **were shocked** and **saddened** by this tragic loss of lives.

NASA **studied** the causes of this disaster. The investigation **concluded** that a piece of the left wing **fell** off as the Columbia **was lifting off.** This **created** a hole in the wing, and super-hot gases **entered** the wing's interior. As the Columbia **was approaching** its final destination, its left wing **burned.**

Even though the investigation is finished, farmers and hunters continue to find pieces of the rocket in their fields and nearby forests.

[3] *To disintegrate* means to break into small pieces.

98   Lesson **3**

Expansion

Theme The topic for this lesson can be enhanced with the following ideas:

1. Photos of the Columbia and Challenger space shuttles and their crews; photos of the Mir space station
2. Articles about the investigation into the Columbia and Challenger disasters
3. Map of the U.S. to show Texas and Florida
4. Pictures of early space

Reading Variation

To practice listening skills, have students first listen to the audio alone. Ask a few comprehension questions. Repeat the audio if necessary. Then have students open their books and read along as they listen to the audio.

The Columbia **was** the United States' second major disaster in space. The first one **was** in January 1986, when the space shuttle Challenger **exploded** 73 seconds after liftoff, killing all seven crew members.

NASA **was going to send** another rocket into space in March 2003, but this mission **was** postponed. Safety issues of future astronauts in space **needed** to be studied before another mission could take place.

1957	The USSR[4] puts the first satellite in space to orbit the Earth.
1961	The USSR puts the first man into space.
1966 (January)	The USSR lands a spacecraft on the moon.
1969	The first astronauts walk on the moon (Americans).
1970s and 1980s	The USSR and the U.S. explore Venus, Mars, Jupiter, and Saturn in fly-bys.
1986	The USSR launches the space station *Mir*.
1986	The U.S. spacecraft *Challenger* explodes shortly after liftoff. All seven crew members die.
1995	U.S. astronauts meet Russian cosmonauts at space station *Mir*.
2003	Seven U.S. astronauts are killed in the *Columbia* shuttle disaster.
2004	The U.S. lands a spacecraft on Mars.

[4] The USSR no longer exists as a country. In 1991, it broke up into 15 countries, the largest of which is Russia.

The Past Continuous; The Past Perfect; The Past Perfect Continuous; Comparison of Past Tenses   99

Reading (cont.)

2. Check students' comprehension. Ask questions such as: *What happened to the space shuttle Columbia?* (It burned and disintegrated in 2003.) *What happened to the space shuttle Challenger?* (It exploded in flight in 1986.)
3. Review the timeline with the class. Clarify vocabulary if necessary. Point out that the verbs in the timeline are in the simple present tense, even though the events are in the past. Say that timelines are often written in the simple present tense.

To save class time, have students do the reading for homework ahead of time.

Reading Glossary

aboard: on a ship, airplane, train or other vehicle
astronaut: space traveler
conclude: arrive at a decision
gases: vapors, fumes
lift off: take off from the ground vertically
mission: a trip or travel with a purpose, e.g., exploration
orbit: go around something in a circular path
tragic: extremely sad; horrible

Culture Note

In the 1950s through the 1980s, the U.S. and the U.S.S.R. competed for "firsts" in space. The U.S.S.R. put the first satellite in space; the U.S. put the first astronauts on the moon.

3.2 | The Past Continuous—Forms

1. Have students cover page 100. Give an example about yourself using the past continuous (*In 2003, I was living in . . .*). Write your example on the board. Ask: *What tense is this?* (the past continuous) Ask: *In 2003, where were you living?* Have several volunteers answer.

2. Have students uncover the chart and review the first section. Ask students to say what they observe about the rules for forming the past continuous. Ask: *What is the present participle?* (verb + -*ing*)

3. Draw students' attention to the Language Notes. Review the use of negatives, contractions, and adverbs.

4. Have students review the examples in the second and third sections of the chart. Draw students' attention to the short answers in the second section.

3.2 | The Past Continuous—Forms

Subject	was / were	Present Participle	Complement	Explanation
I She He It The rocket	was			To form the past continuous, use *was* or *were* + present participle (verb + -*ing*).
		traveling	fast.	
We You They The astronauts	were			

Language Notes:
1. To make the negative, put *not* between *was / were* and the present participle.
   I **was** *not* **living** in the U.S. in January 2003.
   Americans **were** *not* **expecting** this tragedy.
2. The contraction for *were not* is *weren't*. The contraction for *was not* is *wasn't*.
3. An adverb can be placed between *was / were* and the present participle.
   You **were** *probably* **watching** the news.

Questions and Short Answers

Question Word	was / wasn't were / weren't	Subject	Present Participle	Complement	Short Answer
	Was	the rocket	traveling	fast?	Yes, it was.
How fast	was	it	traveling?		
	Weren't	they	flying	over Florida?	No, they weren't.
Where	were	they	flying?		
	Were	you	watching	it on TV?	No, I wasn't.
Why	weren't	you	watching	it on TV?	
Who	was		watching	it on TV?	

Passive

Subject	was / were	being	Past Participle	Complement
The landing	was	being	filmed.	
Experiments	were	being	done	in space.

Grammar Variation

Have students underline the past continuous verbs in the reading before they look at the grammar chart.

EXERCISE **1** Fill in the blanks with the correct form of the verb in parentheses ( ). Use the past continuous.

EXAMPLE The Columbia _____was approaching_____ Florida.
(approach)

1. Family members _____were waiting_____.
(wait)

2. The Columbia _____was traveling_____ over Texas.
(travel)

3. It _____wasn't traveling_____ over Florida.
(not/travel)

4. It _____was returning_____ to Earth after a successful mission.
(return)

5. The astronauts _____were looking_____ forward to seeing their families.
(look)

6. Reporters _____were preparing_____ to interview the astronauts.
(prepare)

7. How many people _____were waiting_____?
(wait)

8. Where _____were they waiting_____?
(they/wait)

9. Pieces of the Columbia _____were being collected_____ and
(passive: collect)
_____were being put_____ together.
(passive: put)

The Past Continuous; The Past Perfect; The Past Perfect Continuous; Comparison of Past Tenses | 101

EXERCISE 1

1. Tell students that this exercise is about what happened when the space shuttle Columbia burned. Have students read the direction line.
2. Model the exercise. Direct students to the example in the book. Ask: *What tense is the verb?* (past continuous)
3. Have students complete the rest of Exercise 1 individually. Then have them check their answers in pairs. Circulate and observe the pair work. Check the answers as a class.
4. Assess students' performance. If necessary, review grammar chart **3.2** on page 100.

Expansion

Exercise 1 Have students write questions for the items in Exercise 1. Write questions for the first few items as a class (*What were the family members doing? Where was the Columbia traveling?*). Then have students finish the activity individually.

Lesson 3   **101**

3.3 | The Past Continuous Tense—Uses

1. Have students cover the grammar chart. Tell the class about what you or a friend were doing when you heard about the Columbia disaster, or another disaster or major event. For example, say: *We were eating breakfast and listening to the radio when we heard about the Columbia.* Draw a small timeline on the board, with a horizontal line for time and a vertical line at the left. Label the vertical line (e.g., *start breakfast*). Draw an arrow toward the right to show continuation. Then draw a second vertical line labeled *Columbia.* Say: *This event (hearing about the disaster) happened when we were in the middle of this event (eating and listening to the radio).*

2. Have students uncover and review the grammar chart. Review each section with its explanation.

3. Draw students' attention to examples in the 6th row of the chart. Clarify the meaning of *carry out;* ask: *Did these events happen?* (No, they didn't. They weren't carried out.)

4. Have students look at the Punctuation Note. Make sure that students understand the meanings of *clause* and *comma.*

3.3 | The Past Continuous Tense—Uses

Examples	Explanation
What **were** you **doing** at 9 a.m. on February 1, 2003? I **was watching** TV. My brother **was sleeping.**	The past continuous is used to show that an action was in progress at a specific past time. It didn't begin at that time.
The Columbia **disintegrated** while it **was traveling** back to the Earth. Family members **were waiting** in Florida when the Columbia accident **happened.** The Columbia **was approaching** the Earth when it **lost** communication with NASA.	We use the past continuous together with the simple past tense to show the relationship of a longer past action to a shorter past action.
While the Columbia **was approaching** its Florida destination, family members **were waiting** for the astronauts. While the astronauts **were orbiting** the Earth, they **were doing** scientific studies.	The past continuous can be used in both clauses to show that two past actions were in progress at the same time.
Compare *when* and *while.* a. **While (When)** the Columbia *was flying* over Texas, it disintegrated. b. The Columbia was flying over Texas **when** it **disintegrated.**	The meaning of sentences (a) and (b) is basically the same. a. *While* is used with a past continuous verb (*was flying*). In conversation, many people use *when* in place of *while*. b. *When* is used with the simple past tense (*disintegrated*).
As the Columbia was approaching its final destination, its left wing burned. **While** the Columbia was approaching its final destination, its left wing burned.	*As* and *while* have the same meaning.
The astronauts **were going to** return with scientific data. Family members **were going to** celebrate with the astronauts. NASA **was going to** send astronauts into space in March 2003, but this mission was postponed.	*Was / were going to* means that a past plan was not carried out.

Punctuation Note:
If the time clause precedes the main clause, separate the two clauses with a comma.
The Columbia was flying over Texas when it disintegrated. (No comma)
When the Columbia disintegrated, it was flying over Texas. (Comma)

102 Lesson 3

Grammar Variation

Have students work in groups. Assign each group to review one of the sections of the grammar chart. Have groups review the examples and explanations in their sections, and then have each group present its section to the class.

Have students look back at the reading on pages 98 and 99 and try to match the past continuous verbs with the explanations in the grammar chart.

EXERCISE **2** ABOUT YOU Ask and answer. Ask the student next to you what he or she was doing at this particular time.

EXAMPLE   at 4 a.m.

A: What were you doing at 4 a.m.?
B: I was sleeping, of course.

1. at 10 p.m. last night
   What were you doing at 10 p.m. last night?
2. at 7 a.m. this morning
   What were you doing at 7 a.m. this morning?
3. at 2 a.m. last night
   What were you doing at 2 a.m. last night?
4. when the teacher entered the classroom today
   What were you doing when the teacher entered the classroom today?
5. at _____ (*your choice of time*)
   What were you doing at (answers will vary)?
6. while the teacher was explaining the past continuous
   What were you doing while the teacher was explaining the past continuous?

EXERCISE **3** Fill in the blanks with the simple past or the past continuous form of the verb in parentheses ( ).

EXAMPLE   We _were watching_ cartoons on TV when we _heard_ the bad news.
           (watch)   (hear)

1. While the Columbia _was returning_ to Earth, it _disintegrated_.
                        (return)   (disintegrate)

2. My sister _was sleeping_ when I _woke_ her up to tell
             (sleep)   (wake)
   her about the accident.

3. A hunter _was walking_ near the forest when he
            (walk)
   found a piece of metal.
   (find)

4. When he _was going_ to pick up the piece of metal, his
           (go)
   friend _told_ him not to.
          (tell)

5. When I _heard_ about the accident, I _was driving_ to work.
          (hear)   (drive)

6. My sister _was watching_ a TV program when the disaster
             (watch)
   happened.
   (happen)

7. While the Columbia _was returning_ to Earth, family
                        (return)
   members _were waiting_ in Florida.
           (wait)

8. What _were you doing_ when the accident _happened_?
         (you/do)   (happen)

9. The Challenger _was lifting_ off when it _exploded_ in 1986.
                   (lift)   (explode)

The Past Continuous; The Past Perfect; The Past Perfect Continuous; Comparison of Past Tenses   103

EXERCISE **2**

1. Tell students that this exercise is about what they were doing at various times. Have students read the direction line. Model the example with a volunteer.
2. Have students complete Exercise 2 in pairs; have pairs take turns asking and answering. Circulate and observe the pair work; have students ask you the questions.
3. Have volunteers share interesting answers with the class.

EXERCISE **3**

1. Tell students that this exercise is about the Columbia disaster. Have students read the direction line. Ask: *What tenses do we write?* (simple past or past continuous)
2. Model the exercise. Direct students to the example in the book. Then do #1 with the class. Ask a volunteer to give the answer.
3. Have students complete the rest of the exercise individually. Then have them compare their answers in pairs. Finally, check the answers as a class.
4. Assess students' performance. If necessary, review grammar chart **3.3** on page 102.

To save class time, have students do half of the exercise in class and complete the other half for homework. Or assign the entire exercise for homework.

Expansion

Exercise 3 Ask students what they were doing when they heard about a recent or famous event.

3.4 | The Past Continuous or the Simple Past

1. Have students look at the first section of the grammar chart. Review the examples. Say: *There are three actions in the first pair of sentences. What are they?* (*watching TV, heard the news, called my sister*) Ask: *Which happened first? Second? Third?* (starting to watch TV, heard the news, called) Repeat with the second pair of sentences.
2. Tell students that the second section of the chart is a news story or summary of what happened when the Columbia was lost. Ask students to identify actions in the story that were in progress and those that took place after 9:00.

EXERCISE 4

🎧 *CD 1, Track 16*

1. Tell students that this exercise consists of two interviews with people about the Columbia disaster. Have students read the direction line. Ask: *What tenses do we use?* (simple past and past continuous)
2. Direct students to the example. Then fill in the first two blanks in part 1 as a class.
3. Have students complete the exercise individually. Then have them check their answers in pairs. Circulate and observe the pair work. If necessary, check the answers as a class.

3.4 | The Past Continuous or the Simple Past

Examples	Explanation
Compare: a. What **were** you **doing** when you heard the news? I was watching TV. b. What **did** you **do** when you heard the news? I called my sister.	a. Use the past continuous to show what was in progress **at** the time a specific action occurred. b. Use the simple past to show what happened **after** a specific action occurred.
a. She **was driving** to work when she had an accident. b. She **called** the police when she had an accident.	
a. On February 1, 2003, relatives **were waiting** in Florida for the astronauts. They **were getting** ready to celebrate. Camera crews **were preparing** to take pictures of the landing. Suddenly, at 9 a.m., just minutes before the landing, NASA lost communication with the Columbia.	a. Use the past continuous to show the events **leading up to** the main event of the story.
b. A NASA official **announced** the tragedy to the public. The president **went** on TV to express his sadness. NASA **began** an investigation of the accident. Investigators **went** to Texas to talk with witnesses.	b. Use the simple past tense to tell what happened **after** the main event of the story.

EXERCISE 4 Fill in the blanks to complete these conversations.

🎧 1. *A reporter is interviewing a family in Texas after the Columbia disaster.*

A: What <u>were you doing</u> at 9 a.m. on February 1, 2003?

    (example: you/do)

B: I <u>was sleeping</u>, A loud noise <u>woke</u> me up. I

    (1 sleep)   *(2 wake)*

<u>jumped</u> out of bed and <u>ran</u> outside.

  (3 jump)   *(4 run)*

I saw my husband outside. He <u>was fixing</u> our car. We

                                   (5 fix)

thought it was an earthquake. Then we <u>saw</u> pieces

                                    (6 see)

of metal on our property. I <u>was going</u> to pick up a piece,

                             (7 go)

Grammar Variation

Have students look back at the reading on pages 98 and 99. Ask students to identify actions in the reading that were in progress and those that took place after 9:00 a.m. on February 1, 2003.

Exercise 4 Variation

To provide practice with listening skills, have students close their books and listen to the audio. Repeat the audio as needed. Ask comprehension questions, such as: *What did the woman do when the loud noise woke her up?* (She jumped out of bed and ran outside.) *What did she see outside?* (her husband) *What was her husband doing?* (fixing their car) Then have students open their books and complete Exercise 4.

but my husband told me not to. Instead we ___called___ the
(8 call)

police. They told us not to touch anything.

2. *A reporter is interviewing a member of NASA after the Columbia disaster.*

A: How fast ___was the Columbia traveling___ when the accident
(9 the Columbia/travel)

___happened___ ?
(10 happen)

B: It ___was traveling___ at 12,500 m.p.h. We ___were communicating___
(11 travel) (12 communicate)

with the Columbia when, suddenly, communication ___stopped___ .
(13 stop)

A: What ___did you do___ when you ___realized___ that the crew
(14 you/do) (15 realize)

members were lost?

B: We ___notified___ the family members and the press. Many
(16 notify)

of the family members ___were waiting___ at the Kennedy Space
(17 wait)

Center in Florida when the accident ___happened___ .
(18 happen)

A: What ___happened___ after that?
(19 happen)

B: An investigation ___began___ . We ___started___ to look
(20 begin) (21 start)

for the pieces of the rocket and ___tried___ to understand
(22 try)

the reason for the accident.

A: ___Did you find___ all the pieces?
(23 you/find)

B: No, of course not. Many of the people of East Texas ___called___
(24 call)

to tell us about finding pieces on their land. Hunters ___called___
(25 call)

to tell us that while they ___were hunting___ in forests, they ___found___
(26 hunt) (27 find)

pieces of metal. We ___found___ enough pieces to come to
(28 find)

a conclusion about the cause of the accident.

The Past Continuous; The Past Perfect; The Past Perfect Continuous; Comparison of Past Tenses   105

Expansion

Exercise 4 When students have completed and checked the exercise, have them match each sentence in the interviews with the appropriate explanation in Grammar Chart **3.4**.

CD 1, Track 17

1. Tell students that this exercise is about stories people tell about a series of events. Have students read the direction line.
2. Model the exercise. Direct students to the examples in the book. Ask: *In the examples, which action was in progress?* (walking to school) *When did the police come?* (after the accident)
3. Have students complete the rest of the exercise individually. Then have them compare their answers in pairs. Finally, check the answers as a class.
4. Assess students' performance. If necessary, review grammar chart **3.4** on page 104.

To save class time, have students do half of the exercise in class and complete the other half for homework. Or assign the entire exercise for homework.

EXERCISE **5** Fill in the blanks with the simple past or the past continuous of the verb in parentheses ( ).

EXAMPLES I ___was walking___ to school when I ___saw___ a car accident.
(walk)   (see)

The police ___came___ and ___gave___ a ticket to one of the drivers.
(come)   (give)

1. I ___was getting___ ready for bed when someone ___came___
(get)   (come)

to my door. I ___opened___ the door and saw my neighbor.
(open)

He ___was standing___ in front of me with a video in his hand. He said,
(stand)

"I just rented a movie. Would you like to watch it with me?" I didn't

want to be impolite, so I said yes. While we ___were watching___ the
(watch)

movie, I ___fell___ asleep.
(fall)

2. While the baby ___was sleeping___ , the babysitter ___was watching/watched___
(sleep)   (watch)

TV. Suddenly the baby ___started___ to cry, and the babysitter
(start)

___ran___ into the room to see what had happened. She
(run)

___picked___ up the baby and started to rock her. Then she
(pick)

___put___ her back to bed.
(put)

3. When I ___got___ home, my sister and brothers
(get)

___were watching___ TV. I said, "I'm hungry. Let's eat." But they
(watch)

___didn't turn___ off the TV. I ___started___ to cook dinner. They
(not/turn)   (start)

all ___came___ into the kitchen to see what I ___was cooking___ .
(come)   (cook)

4. She ___was listening___ to the radio while she ___was working___ on
(listen)   (work)

the computer. Suddenly she ___heard___ the news of a terrible
(hear)

accident. She ___went___ to the TV to find out more information.
(go)

Exercise 5 Variation

To provide practice with listening skills, have students close their books and listen to the audio. Repeat the audio as needed. Ask comprehension questions, such as: *In conversation 1, why did the neighbor come to the person's door?* (He wanted to watch a video together.) *Why did the person agree to watch the video?* (The person didn't want to be impolite.) Then have students open their books and complete Exercise 5.

5. While Sam ___was driving___ , his cell phone ___rang___ . He
(drive)   (ring)

___was talking___ on his phone when he ___had___ a car
(talk)   (have)

accident. He ___hit___ a light post. Fortunately,
(hit)

he ___was wearing___ his seatbelt, so he wasn't hurt.
(wear)

6. When the storm ___began___ last night, we ___were watching___
(begin)   (watch)

a scary movie. The lights went out, so we ___had___ to
(have)

use candles. While I ___was looking___ for matches and candles,
(look)

my little brother suddenly ___entered___ the room with a
(enter)

flashlight and a scary mask. He really ___scared___ me.
(scare)

7. While I ___was looking___ for my gloves in a drawer, I
(look)

___found___ an old photograph of me. In this photo, I
(find)

___was wearing___ a silly looking bathing suit. I can't even remember
(wear)

who ___took___ the picture.
(take)

8. I ___was typing___ my composition on the computer when
(type)

suddenly we ___lost___ electrical power. When the power
(lose)

___came___ back on, I ___turned___ on the computer,
(come)   (turn)

but all my work was gone. I know how important it is to save my

work. I ___went___ to save it on a disk, but I didn't have any.
(go)

So I ___lost___ everything and ___had___ to start
(lose)   (have)

all over.

The Past Continuous; The Past Perfect; The Past Perfect Continuous; Comparison of Past Tenses   107

Expansion

Exercise 5 Have students write a story of their own about a series of events. Have students use the stories in the exercise as models. Remind students to use the simple past and past continuous tenses. Have students share their stories with the class.

Exercise 5 Have students look at the illustration and say which item it illustrates (#6). Be sure that students understand what the boy is doing (wearing a mask and holding a flashlight under his face) and why (to look scary).

Culture Note

In the U.S., some children wear masks and costumes on Halloween (October 31) and go from door to door collecting candy from neighbors. This practice is called "trick-or-treating."

The Titanic (Reading)

1. Have students look at the photo. Ask: *What is this?* (the ocean liner Titanic)
2. Have students look quickly at the reading. Ask: *What is the reading about? How do you know?* Have students use the title and photos to make predictions about the reading.
3. Preteach any vocabulary words your students may not know, such as: *voyage, third-class, emigrants, mild,* and *lifeboats.*

BEFORE YOU READ

1. Activate students' prior knowledge about the Titanic. Ask: *What kind of ship was the Titanic?* (a luxury ocean liner) *What happened to it?* (It sank.) *Did anyone survive?* (yes)
2. Have students discuss the questions in pairs. Try to pair students of different language backgrounds.
3. Ask a few volunteers to share their answers with the class.

🕐 To save class time, skip "Before You Read" or have students prepare answers for homework ahead of time.

Reading 🎧 CD 1, Track 18

1. Have students first read the text silently. Tell them to pay special attention to the past perfect tense verbs in boldface. Then play the audio and have students read along silently.
2. Check students' comprehension. Ask questions such as: *What was special about the Titanic?* (It was the most modern and luxurious ship that had ever been built.) *What two groups of passengers were on the Titanic?* (rich passengers and emigrants coming to the U.S.) *Why weren't there enough lifeboats for everyone?* (Some of them had been removed to make the ship look better.)

🕐 To save class time, have students do the reading for homework ahead of time.

THE TITANIC

Before You Read
1. Have you ever traveled by ship? Where did you go? What was the trip like?
2. Did you see the 1997 movie *Titanic*? If so, did you enjoy it? Why or why not?

 Read the following article. Pay special attention to the past perfect tense.

The year was 1912. The radio **had** already **been invented** in 1901. The Wright brothers **had** already **made** their first successful flight in 1903. The Titanic—the ship of dreams—**had** just **been built** and was ready to make its first voyage from England to America with its 2,200 passengers.

The Titanic was the most magnificent ship that **had** ever **been built**. It had luxuries that ships **had** never **had** before: electric light and heat, electric elevators, a swimming pool, a Turkish bath, libraries, and much more. It was built to give its first-class passengers all the comforts of the best hotels.

But rich passengers were not the only ones traveling on the Titanic. Most of the passengers in third class were emigrants who **had left** behind a complete way of life and were coming to America with hopes of a better life.

108   Lesson 3

Expansion

Theme The topic for this lesson can be enhanced with the following ideas:

1. Photos of the interior of the Titanic or of passengers
2. Flyers or pages from a Web site advertising cruises or boat tours
3. A copy of the movie *Titanic* in its box

Reading Variation

To practice listening skills, have students first listen to the audio alone. Ask a few comprehension questions. Repeat the audio if necessary. Then have students open their books and read along as they listen to the audio.

The Titanic began to cross the Atlantic Ocean on April 10. The winter of 1912 **had been** unusually mild, and large blocks of ice **had broken** away from the Arctic region. By the fifth day at sea, the captain **had received** several warnings about ice, but he was not very worried; he didn't realize how much danger the ship was in. On April 14, at 11:40 p.m., an iceberg was spotted[5] straight ahead. The captain tried to reverse the direction of his ship, but he couldn't because the Titanic was traveling too fast and it was too big. It hit the iceberg and started to sink.

The Titanic **had** originally **had** 32 lifeboats, but 12 of them **had been removed** to make the ship look better. While the ship was sinking, rich people were put on lifeboats. Women and children were put on the lifeboats before men. By the time the third-class passengers were allowed to come up from their cabins, most of the lifeboats **had** already **left.**

Several hours later, another ship arrived to help, but the Titanic **had** already **gone** down. Only one-third of the passengers survived.

[5] *To spot* means *to see suddenly.*

The Past Continuous; The Past Perfect; The Past Perfect Continuous; Comparison of Past Tenses 109

Reading Glossary

emigrant: a person who leaves his or her own country permanently to go to another country

lifeboat: a small boat on board a larger boat, to be used for rescue in an emergency

mild: warm; not severe or too cold

third-class: the least expensive, least comfortable, and most crowded accommodations on a ship or train

voyage: a long trip, especially across an ocean

3.5 | The Past Perfect Tense—Forms

1. Make a chart on the board with five unlabelled columns, similar to the chart on page 110 without the explanation column. Have students find examples of the past perfect tense in the reading on page 108. Ask students to read their examples aloud. Write each example in the chart on the board, putting the parts of the sentence in the appropriate columns. Ask: *What do all of the sentences have?* (subject + *had* + past participle) Write these labels above the columns.

2. Have students review the example sentences in the grammar chart.

3. Draw students' attention to the Language Notes. Ask: *Where do we put* not *in a negative sentence with the past perfect tense?* (between *had* and the past participle) *Where do we put adverbs?* (between *had* and the past participle) If necessary, review the meaning of *originally* (in the beginning; at first).

4. Draw students' attention to item #2 in the Language Notes. Write additional examples on the board, such as *He'd wanted to* and *He'd like to*. Ask students what each *'d* means.

5. Have students look at the list of irregular past tenses and past participles in Appendix M.

6. Have students review the final two sections of the chart.

7. Draw students' attention to examples in the first and second sections of the chart that have *had* as a past participle. Tell students that in sentences in which *had* appears twice, one is the auxiliary and the second is the past participle of *have*.

3.5 | The Past Perfect Tense—Forms

Subject	*Had*	*Not/* Adverb	Past Participle	Complement	Explanation
The captain	had		received	several warnings.	To form the past perfect, use *had* + past participle.
He	had	not	paid	attention.	
The winter	had		been	unusually mild.	
The ship	had	originally	had	32 lifeboats.	
They	had	never	been	on a ship before.	

Language Notes:
1. The pronouns (except *it*) can be contracted with *had*: *I'd, you'd, she'd, he'd, we'd, they'd*.
   He'd received several warnings.
2. Apostrophe + *d* can be a contraction for both *had* or *would*. The word following the contraction will tell you what the contraction means.
   He'd spoken. = He *had* spoken.
   He'd speak. = He *would* speak.
3. For a negative contraction, use *hadn't*.
   He hadn't paid attention.
4. For an alphabetical list of irregular past tenses and past participles, see Appendix M.

Questions					
Question Word	*Had*	Subject	Past Participle	Complement	Short Answer
	Had	the Titanic	crossed	the ocean before?	No, it **hadn't**.
How much experience	had	the captain	had?		
Who	had		heard	of the Titanic before?	

Passive				
Subject	*Had*	Adverb	*Been*	Past Participle
Lifeboats	had		been	removed.
The survivors	had		been	found.
The airplane	had	already	been	invented.

EXERCISE **6** Fill in the blanks with the past perfect of the verb in parentheses ( ) plus any other included words.

EXAMPLE When we read about the Titanic, the story was not new to me because I ___had seen___ the movie.
(see)

1. The captain of the Titanic ___had made___ a serious mistake
(make)
when he didn't listen to the warnings.

2. When the Titanic disaster occurred, how much experience
___had the captain had___ ?
(the captain/have)

3. I didn't realize that airplanes ___had been invented___ by the time
(passive: invent)
of the Titanic.

4. In 1912, World War I ___had not begun yet___ .
(not/yet/begin)

5. The story about the Titanic was new to me because I
___had never read___ an article about it before.
(never/read)

6. ___Had you already heard___ this story before we read
(you/already/hear)
about it in class?

7. How many lifeboats ___had the Titanic originally had___ ?
(have/the Titanic/originally)

Why ___had they been removed___ ?
(they/passive: remove)

The Past Continuous; The Past Perfect; The Past Perfect Continuous; Comparison of Past Tenses 111

1. Tell students that this exercise is about the Titanic. Have students read the direction line.
2. Model the exercise. Direct students to the example.
3. Have students complete the rest of Exercise 6 individually. Have them compare their answers in pairs. Finally, check the answers as a class.
4. Assess students' performance. If necessary, review grammar chart **3.5** on page 110.

Expansion

Exercise 6 Ask students what they heard or read about the Titanic before they read about it in the textbook. Remind students to give their answers in the past perfect tense.

3.6 | The Past Perfect—Use

1. Have students cover grammar chart **3.6.** Ask review questions about the reading. Ask: *Did a rescue ship arrive?* (yes) *Did it arrive before or after the Titanic went down?* (after) Then draw a timeline on the board similar to the timeline in the grammar chart. Say: *To show that one event happened after the other, we use the past perfect.* Elicit students' help to write the sentence: *When the rescue ship arrived, the Titanic had already gone down.* Say: *We use* already *to show the time relationship.*

2. Have students review the first section of the grammar chart. Then have students draw a timeline to illustrate the second example.

3. Have students look at the remaining sections of grammar chart **3.6.** Review the example sentences and explanations carefully.

4. Make several statements about yourself similar to those in the grammar chart, such as *Before I came here, I had never lived in a city* or *When I got my master's degree in 1990, I had already taught for three years.*

5. Ask students to use one of the examples in the grammar chart or one of the examples on the board to make statements about themselves.

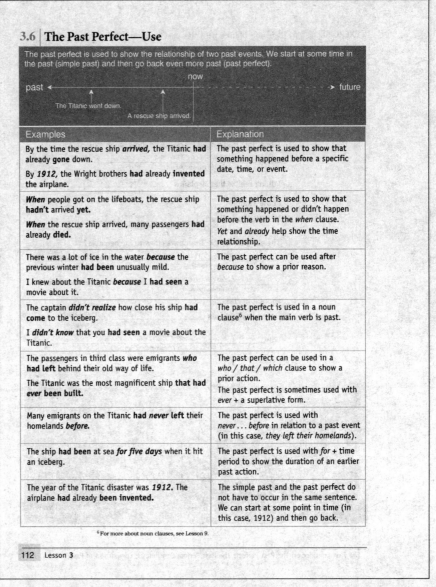

3.6 | The Past Perfect—Use

The past perfect is used to show the relationship of two past events. We start at some time in the past (simple past) and then go back even more past (past perfect).

past ← ——————————————— now ——————————————— → future

The Titanic went down.

A rescue ship arrived.

Examples	Explanation
By the time the rescue ship *arrived,* the Titanic **had** already **gone** down. By *1912,* the Wright brothers **had** already **invented** the airplane.	The past perfect is used to show that something happened before a specific date, time, or event.
When people got on the lifeboats, the rescue ship **hadn't** arrived **yet.** *When* the rescue ship arrived, many passengers **had** already **died.**	The past perfect is used to show that something happened or didn't happen before the verb in the *when* clause. *Yet* and *already* help show the time relationship.
There was a lot of ice in the water *because* the previous winter **had been** unusually mild. I knew about the Titanic *because* I **had seen** a movie about it.	The past perfect can be used after *because* to show a prior reason.
The captain *didn't realize* how close his ship **had come** to the iceberg. I *didn't know* that you **had seen** a movie about the Titanic.	The past perfect is used in a noun clause[6] when the main verb is past.
The passengers in third class were emigrants *who* **had left** behind their old way of life. The Titanic was the most magnificent ship *that had* **ever been built.**	The past perfect can be used in a *who / that / which* clause to show a prior action. The past perfect is sometimes used with *ever* + a superlative form.
Many emigrants on the Titanic **had never** left their homelands *before.*	The past perfect is used with *never...before* in relation to a past event (in this case, *they left their homelands*).
The ship **had been** at sea *for five days* when it hit an iceberg.	The past perfect is used with *for* + time period to show the duration of an earlier past action.
The year of the Titanic disaster was *1912.* The airplane **had** already **been invented.**	The simple past and the past perfect do not have to occur in the same sentence. We can start at some point in time (in this case, 1912) and then go back.

[6] For more about noun clauses, see Lesson 9.

112   Lesson 3

Grammar Variation

Prepare a handout with three timelines similar to the one in grammar chart **3.6,** but without labels on the vertical lines. Have students review the grammar chart individually or in pairs. Then have students make timelines for the second, third, and twelfth example sentences. Check the timelines on the board as a class. Then review any difficulties as a class.

Examples	Explanation
a. **Before** the Titanic hit the iceberg, the captain **tried** to turn the ship around. b. **Before** the Titanic hit the iceberg, the captain **had tried** to turn the ship around. a. The captain *realized* that he **made** a mistake. b. The captain *realized* that he **had made** a mistake. a. He failed the test *because* he **didn't study.** b. He failed the test *because* he **hadn't studied.**	In some cases, either the simple past (a) or the past perfect (b) can be used if the time relationship is clear. This is especially true with *before, after, because,* and in a noun clause (after *knew, realized, understood,* etc.).

EXERCISE 7 Fill in the blanks with the simple past or the past perfect of the verb in parentheses ( ).

EXAMPLE The Titanic had luxuries that ships _had never had_ before.
(never/have)

1. By 1912, the radio _had already been invented_.
(passive: already/invent)

2. The Titanic was the biggest ship that _had ever been built_.
(passive: ever/build)

3. The Titanic _originally had_ 32 lifeboats.
(originally/have)

4. When the Titanic _left_ England, many of the
(leave)
lifeboats _had been removed_.
(passive: remove)

5. By April 1912, pieces of ice _had broken_ away from
(break)
the Arctic region.

6. The captain of the Titanic _didn't pay_ attention
(not/pay)
to the warnings he _had received_.
(receive)

7. When the Titanic _hit_ an iceberg, it _had been_
(hit)   (be)
at sea for four days.

8. By the time the poor emigrants _were_ allowed to
(be)
come up from their cabins, most of the lifeboats _had already left_.
(already/leave)

9. By the time the rescue ship _arrived_,
(arrive)
the Titanic _had already sunk_.
(already/sink)

Culture Note

The simple past is frequently used instead of the past perfect in informal speech in the U.S.

1. Tell students that this exercise is also about the Titanic. Have students read the direction line. Ask: *Which tense do we write?* (the simple past or past perfect)
2. Model the exercise. Direct students to the example in the book. Then do #1 with the class.
3. Have students complete Exercise 7 individually. Then have them compare their answers in pairs. Finally, check the answers as a class.

EXERCISE 8

1. Tell students that this exercise is about their day. Have students read the direction line.
2. Direct students to the example in the book. Ask: *What is the difference between these two statements?* (The first student arrived after the teacher collected the homework; the second student arrived before the teacher collected the homework.) Ask several volunteers which answer is appropriate for them.
3. Have students complete the exercise individually. Then have them check their answers in pairs. Circulate to observe pair work. Finally, ask volunteers to report their partners' information to the class.

🕐 To save class time, have students do half of the exercise in class and complete the other half in writing for homework. Or if students do not need speaking practice, the entire exercise may be skipped or done in writing.

EXERCISE 9

1. Tell students that this exercise is about space travel and the space shuttle Columbia. Have students read the direction line.
2. Model the exercise. Direct students to the example in the book. Then do #1 with the class.
3. Have students complete the exercise individually. Then have students check their answers in pairs. Circulate to observe pair work. If necessary, check answers as a class.

🕐 To save class time, have students do half of the exercise in class and complete the other half for homework. Or assign the entire exercise for homework.

EXERCISE **8** ABOUT YOU Tell if the following had already happened or hadn't happened yet by the time you got to class.

EXAMPLE   the teacher / collect the homework
By the time I got to class, the teacher had already collected the homework.
OR
When I got to class, the teacher hadn't collected the homework yet.

Answers will vary. 1. the teacher / arrive

2. most of the students / arrive

3. the class / begin

4. the teacher / take attendance

5. I / do the homework

6. the teacher / hand back the last homework

7. the teacher / explain the past perfect

EXERCISE **9** Fill in the blanks with the simple past or the past perfect of the verb in parentheses ( ).

EXAMPLE By the time the U.S. ___sent___ a man into space (1962), the Russians
(send)
___had already put___ a man in space (1961).
(already/put)

1. When an American astronaut ___stepped___ on the moon in
(step)
1969, no person ___had ever walked___ on the moon before.
(ever/walk)

2. By 2003, NASA ___had completed___ hundreds of successful spaceflights.
(complete)

3. When the Columbia mission took off in 2003, NASA ___had had___
(have)
only two serious accidents in its space program.

4. By the time the U.S. ___sent___ a mission to Mars, the
(send)
reasons for the Columbia accident ___had already been discovered___.
(already/passive: discover)

5. By the time the 16 days were up, the Columbia crew
___had done___ all its scientific experiments.
(do)

6. Until 9 a.m. on February 1, NASA ___had had___ good
(have)
communication with the Columbia.

7. At first, NASA couldn't understand what ___had happened___.
(happen)

114   Lesson 3

Expansion

Exercise 8 Write on the board: *Before I came to the U.S., I had never . . .* Have volunteers complete the statement for themselves.

8. When they lost communication with the Columbia, they were
afraid that all of the astronauts _____had died_____ .
                                        (die)

9. The original date for the Columbia mission was July 2002. The date
was postponed until 2003 because cracks in the fuel line
_____had been found_____ .
        (passive: find)

10. NASA _____knew_____ that the Columbia _____had lost_____ a
              (know)   (lose)
piece of its wing on liftoff, but they didn't think it would be a problem.

11. They _____didn't realize_____ that this problem _____had created_____ a
              (not/realize)   (create)
hole in the wing.

12. By the time the investigation _____ended_____ in April 2003, NASA
                                       (end)
_____had collected_____ 40 percent of pieces of the Columbia.
     (collected)

3.7 | *When* with the Simple Past or the Past Perfect

Sometimes *when* means *after*. Sometimes *when* means *before*.	
Examples	**Explanation**
a. When the captain saw the iceberg, he **tried** to turn the ship around. b. When the captain saw the iceberg, the ship **had been** at sea for five days.	If you use the simple past in the main clause (a), *when* means *after*. If you use the past perfect in the main clause (b), *when* means *before*.
a. When the Columbia lifted off, it **lost** a piece of its wing. b. When the Columbia lifted off in January 2003, it **had had** 27 successful missions.	

Compare	
When means *after*.	*When* means *before*.
When I came home, my wife and I **ate** dinner.	When I came home, my wife **had eaten** dinner.

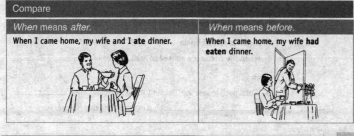

The Past Continuous; The Past Perfect; The Past Perfect Continuous; Comparison of Past Tenses   115

3.7 | *When* with the Simple Past or the Past Perfect

1. Have students cover grammar chart **3.7**. Write on the board: *When I got home, I had already heard the news.*
When I got home, I heard the news.
For both sentences, ask: *Does* when *in this sentence mean before or after?*

2. Have students uncover and review the grammar chart.

3. Ask for volunteers to give examples about themselves using the simple past or past perfect, beginning with *When I came home. . . .*

Expansion

Exercise 9 When students have completed Exercise 9, have them look back at grammar chart **3.6** and match each item in Exercise 9 with the appropriate explanation in the grammar chart.

EXERCISE 10

1. Tell students that this exercise is about the order in which events happen. Have students read the direction line.
2. Model the exercise. Direct students to the examples in the book. Then do #1 with the class.
3. Have students complete the exercise individually. Check answers as a class.
4. If necessary, review grammar chart 3.7 on page 115.

EXERCISE 11

1. Tell students that this exercise is about the Titanic and Columbia disasters. Have students read the direction line. Ask: *What tenses do we use?* (the simple past or the past perfect)
2. Model the exercise. Direct students to the examples in the book. Then do #1 with the class. Ask a volunteer to give an answer.
3. Have students complete Exercise 11 individually. Then have them compare their answers in pairs. Finally, check the answers as a class.
4. Assess students' performance. If necessary, review grammar chart 3.7 on page 115.

To save class time, have students do half of the exercise in class and complete the other half for homework. Or assign the entire exercise for homework.

EXERCISE 10 Write numbers to show which action happened first.

EXAMPLES

When she got home, she took an aspirin.
(1) (2)

When she got home, she had already taken an aspirin.
(2) (1)

1. When they came into the room, their son left.
(1) (2)
2. When they came into the room, their son had just left.
(2) (1)
3. When I got home from school, I did my homework.
(1) (2)
4. When I got home from school, I had already done my homework.
(2) (1)
5. When she got to my house, she had eaten dinner.
(2) (1)
6. When she got to my house, she ate dinner.
(1) (2)
7. The teacher gave a test when Linda arrived.
(2) (1)
8. The teacher had already given a test when Linda arrived.
(1) (2)

EXERCISE 11 Fill in the blanks with the verb in parentheses ( ). Use the simple past to show that *when* means *after*. Use the past perfect to show that *when* means *before*.

EXAMPLES

When I saw the movie *Titanic*, I __told__ my friends about it.
(tell)

When I saw the movie *Titanic*, I __had never heard__ of this ship before.
(never/hear)

1. When the Titanic sank, a rescue ship __came__ to pick up the survivors.
(come)

2. When the ship hit an iceberg, the captain __had received__ several warnings.
(receive)

3. When the ship was built, people __were__ amazed at how beautiful it was.
(be)

4. When the ship left England, 12 lifeboats __had been removed__.
(passive: remove)

5. When the passengers heard a loud noise, they __ran__ to get on the lifeboats.
(run)

6. When the Arctic ice started to melt, pieces of ice __broke__ away.
(break)

7. When people saw the Titanic for the first time, they __had never seen__ such a magnificent ship before.
(never/see)

Expansion

Exercise 11 Have students look back at Exercise 10 of Lesson 2 (page 73). Work together, or have students work in groups, to write sentences about Ronald Reagan with *when*. If necessary, write several cues on the board: *When Reagan became president, . . .* ; *When Reagan was shot, . . .* ; etc.

8. When the rescue ship arrived, many passengers ___had already died___
   (already/die)

9. When the Columbia accident happened, people ___were___ shocked.
   (be)

10. When the Columbia accident happened, the astronauts ___had been___ in space for 16 days.
    (be)

11. When relatives heard the news, they ___started___ to cry.
    (start)

12. When people in east Texas heard a loud sound, they ___thought___ it was an earthquake.
    (think)

13. For months after the accident, farmers in east Texas found pieces of the Columbia that ___had fallen___ in their fields.
    (fall)

WILDFIRES IN SOUTHERN CALIFORNIA

Before You Read

1. Do you know about any fires that burned for a long time?

2. Do you know anyone who has lost a home because of a natural disaster?

Read the following article. Pay special attention to the past perfect and the past perfect continuous tenses.

Did You Know?

San Francisco had a major earthquake in 1906. At least 1,000 people died.

In October 2003, wildfires in San Diego County burned out of control. Many residents had to leave their homes as they were warned of the approaching fire. They watched and waited as firefighters battled the fire.

One of the fires was started accidentally by a lost hunter in a forest, who **had been trying** to signal his location. Strong winds spread the fire quickly. The San Diego area **had had** very little rain or humidity, and there were millions of dry dead trees that caught fire quickly.

The fire **had been burning** for a week by the time firefighters got it under control. Many residents returned only to find that they **had lost** their homes and all their possessions. "We **had been living** in the same house for the past 26 years when we lost our home," said a San Diego woman, whose family went to stay with relatives nearby. "Now we have nothing, not even a photograph of our former lives."

(continued)

The Past Continuous; The Past Perfect; The Past Perfect Continuous; Comparison of Past Tenses   117

Expansion

Theme The topic for this lesson can be enhanced with the following ideas:

1. Pictures of an area after a wildfire
2. A page from a disaster preparedness Web site, especially a page on food and supplies to have on hand in case of an emergency
3. A flyer on services for the homeless in your area

Reading Variation

To practice listening skills, have students first listen to the audio alone. Ask a few comprehension questions. Repeat the audio if necessary. Then have students open their books and read along as they listen to the audio.

Reading Glossary

contain: control; hold in place
former: before now; finished in the past
out of control: impossible to stop; uncontrollable
under control: possible to manage or take care of; controllable

Wildfires in Southern California (Reading)

1. Have students look at the photos on pages 118–119. Ask: *Where is this man? What is he doing? What do you think happened to this man? What do you see in the pictures?*
2. Have students look briefly at the reading. Have students look at the title of the reading. Ask: *What is the reading about? How do you know?* Have students make predictions.
3. Preteach any vocabulary words your students may not know, such as: *out of control, under control, former,* and *contain.*

BEFORE YOU READ

1. Activate students' prior knowledge about wildfires. Ask: *Are wildfires a danger in your native country? What kinds of conditions make fires more dangerous?*
2. Have students discuss the questions in pairs. Try to pair students of different language backgrounds.
3. Ask a few volunteers to share their answers with the class.

To save class time, skip "Before You Read" or have students prepare answers for homework ahead of time.

Reading ∩ CD 1, Track 19

1. Have students first read the text silently. Tell them to pay special attention to the past perfect and past perfect continuous tense verbs in the reading. Then play the audio and have students read along silently.
2. Check students' comprehension. Ask questions such as: *Why did the fires spread so quickly?* (There had been very little rain or humidity.) *How long did it take to control the fire?* (a week) *How many buildings were destroyed?* (over 2,400)

To save class time, have students do the reading for homework ahead of time.

DID YOU KNOW?

The San Francisco earthquake of 1906 happened at around five o'clock in the morning. The earthquake lasted almost a minute and was felt as far away as Oregon and Nevada. The earthquake destroyed 28,000 buildings.

3.8 | The Past Perfect Continuous—Forms

1. Have students find sentences from the reading on pages 117–118 that contain past perfect continuous tense verbs. Simplify and write several of the sentences on the board, e.g., *One fire was started by a hunter who had been trying to signal his location.*
2. Have students review the example sentences in the first section of the grammar chart. Ask: *How is the past perfect continuous tense different in form from the past perfect tense?* (the past perfect continuous uses *been* and the present participle with -*ing*)
3. Have students review the example sentences and explanations in the second section of the grammar chart (Questions and Short Answers). Ask: *Where does the subject go in a question with the past perfect continuous?* (between *had* and *been*)

Many of the firefighters were exhausted because they **had been working** around the clock to get the fire under control. Firefighters from other areas in the U.S. came to help contain the fire. By the time the fire was brought under control, over 2,400 homes and businesses **had been destroyed** and 16 people **had died.**

3.8 | The Past Perfect Continuous—Forms

Subject	Had	Not / Adverb	Been	Present Participle	Complement	Explanation
We	had		been	living	in the same house.	To form the past perfect continuous, use: *had + been + verb* -*ing*.
Firefighters	had		been	working	around the clock.	
California	had	not	been	getting	much rain.	
A hunter	had	probably	been	trying	to send a signal.	

Questions and Short Answers						
Question Word	Had	Subject	Been	Present Participle	Complement	Short Answer
	Had	it	been	raining?		No, it **hadn't.**
How long	had	the fire	been	burning?		
	Had	you	been	living	in the same house?	Yes, we **had.**
Who	had		been	living	in that house?	

EXERCISE 12   Fill in the blanks with the past perfect continuous tense.

EXAMPLE   I ___had been driving___ for two hours when I had an accident.
                   (drive)

1. The fire ___had been burning___ for two days by the time firefighters
           (burn)
   put it out.

2. We ___had been living___ in a refugee camp for three months
       (live)
   when we got permission to come to the U.S.

3. He ___had been climbing___ the mountain for three hours when he fell.
       (climb)

4. The Titanic ___had been traveling___ for five days when it sank.
               (travel)

5. By the time he retired, he ___had been working___ at the same job
                              (work)
   for 36 years.

6. Why ___had the hunter been trying___ to send a signal?
       (the hunter/try)

The Past Continuous; The Past Perfect; The Past Perfect Continuous; Comparison of Past Tenses   119

EXERCISE 12

1. Tell students that this exercise provides practice in forming the past perfect continuous. Have students read the direction line. Ask: *What form of the verb do we write?* (past perfect continuous)
2. Direct students to the example in the book.
3. Have students complete the exercise individually. Ask volunteers to share their answers with the class.
4. Assess students' performance. If necessary, review grammar chart **3.8**.

Culture Note

Refugees are different from immigrants. According to the U.S. government, refugees are people who were persecuted in their native countries, or have a "well-founded fear" that they will be persecuted because of their race, religion, nationality, social group, or political views. The U.S. allows a certain number of refugees to enter the country each year.

3.9 | The Past Perfect Continuous—Uses

1. Have students cover grammar chart **3.9**. Ask review questions about the reading. Ask: *Was the fire brought under control?* (yes) *How long had the firefighters been working?* (for a week) *How did they feel?* (They were exhausted.) Then draw a timeline for these events on the board, similar to the timeline in the grammar chart. Say: *To show that one event was happening before another event happened, we use the past perfect continuous.* Elicit students' help to write the sentence: *By the time the fire was brought under control, the firefighters were exhausted because they had been working for a week.*
2. Have students review the first section of the grammar chart. Then have students draw a timeline to illustrate the second example.
3. Have students look at the remaining section of grammar chart **3.9**. Review the example sentences and explanations carefully.
4. Make several statements about yourself similar to those in the grammar chart, such as *Before I came here, I had been living in New York* or *By the time I went to the doctor's office, I had been feeling sick for three days.* Write the examples on the board.
5. Ask students to use one of the examples in the grammar chart or on the board as a model to make a statement about themselves.

EXERCISE 13

1. Tell students that this exercise is about one person's journey to the U.S. Have students read the direction line.
2. Model the exercise. Direct students to the example in the book. Then do #1 with the class.
3. Have students complete the rest of Exercise 13 individually. Then have them check their answers in pairs. Circulate and observe the pair work. If necessary, check the answers as a class.
4. If necessary, review grammar chart **3.9** on page 120.

3.9 | The Past Perfect Continuous—Uses

Examples	Explanation
The fire **had been burning** *for a week* by the time it was controlled.	The past perfect continuous tense is used to show the connection of a continuous action that was completed before another past action. The amount of time of the continuous action is expressed with *for*.
We **had been living** in the same house *for 26 years* when we lost our home.	
One of the fires was started by a lost hunter who **had been trying** to call attention to his location.	
Compare:	We use the past perfect continuous:
a. By the time the fire was controlled, it **had been burning** for over a week.	a. When an action took place over a period of time, such as *over a week*
	We use the past perfect with:
b. When the fire started, Southern California **had had** very little rain.	b. Nonaction verbs
c. When residents returned, they found out that their homes **had been destroyed.**	c. An action of no duration
d. By the time the fire ended, 16 people **had died.**	d. A multiple or repeated action

EXERCISE 13 Fill in the blanks with the simple past tense or the past perfect continuous tense of the verb in parentheses ( ).

EXAMPLE When I ___came___ to the U.S., I ___had been studying___ English for three
        (come)   _(study)_
        years.

1. I ___had been waiting___ for two years when I ___got___
      (wait)   _(get)_
   a chance to leave my country.

2. I ___had been living___ in the same house all my life when I
      (live)

   ___left___ my city.
      (leave)

3. I ___felt___ very sad when I left my job because I
      (feel)

   ___had been working___ with the same people for ten years.
      (work)

120 Lesson 3

Grammar Variation

Put students in groups. Ask students to write true or false statements about themselves at age 15, using the past perfect continuous. The other students guess if the statements are true or false. Model an example. Say: *By the time I was 15, I had been cooking dinner for my family every night for five years. True or false?* Then the other students guess if the statement is true or false.

4. I ___had been studying___ to be a nurse for six months when a
(study)

war ___broke out___ in my country.
(break out)

5. When I ___left___ my country, the war
(leave)

___had been going on___ for three years.
(go on)

6. My family ___had been waiting___ in Germany for three months
(wait)

before we ___got___ permission to come to the U.S.
(get)

7. By the time I ___got___ to the U.S., I
(get)

___had been traveling___ for four days.
(travel)

EXERCISE 14 Fill in the blanks with the past perfect continuous for a
continuous action. Fill in the blanks with the past perfect for a
one-time action, multiple or repeated actions, or a nonaction verb.

In the year 1800, the population of Chicago was only 5,000. But the

population ___had been growing___ steadily since the beginning of the century.
(example: grow)

In 1871, Chicago ___had recently passed___ St. Louis to become the fourth
(example: recently/pass)

largest city in the U.S. Chicago ___had reached___ a place of
(I reach)

importance when the Great Chicago Fire began on October 8, 1871.

The Past Continuous; The Past Perfect; The Past Perfect Continuous; Comparison of Past Tenses   121

🎧 **CD 1, Track 20**

1. Tell students that this exercise is about a historic fire in Chicago. Have students read the direction line. Ask: *What tenses do we use?* (the past perfect or the past perfect continuous)
2. Model the exercise. Direct students to the examples in the book. Then do #1 with the class.
3. Have students complete Exercise 14 individually. Then have them check their answers in pairs. Check the answers as a class. For each item, ask students to explain their choice of tenses.

🕐 To save class time, have students do half of the exercise in class and complete the other half for homework. Or assign the entire exercise for homework.

Expansion

Exercise 13 Ask students if any of the items in Exercise 13 are like their experiences. Have students use the statements in the exercise as models to write statements about their own experiences. Ask volunteers, if appropriate, to share their statements with the class.

Exercise 14 Variation

To provide practice with listening skills, have students close their books and listen to the audio. Repeat the audio as needed. Ask comprehension questions, such as: *What happened in 1871?* (Chicago had recently passed St. Louis to become the fourth largest city in the U.S.) *When did Chicago reach a place of importance?* (when the Great Chicago Fire began on October 8, 1871) Then have students open their books and complete Exercise 14.

That October was especially dry because there ___had been___
(2 be)

very little rain. At that time, most of the streets, sidewalks, bridges, and buildings were made of wood. On Sunday night, a fire broke out in a barn. The firefighters were exhausted that night because they

___had been fighting___ a fire since the day before. Strong winds
(3 fight)

from the south quickly spread the fire to the center of the city. When the firefighters finally arrived at the fire, the fire

___had spread___ out of control. It wasn't until two days later,
(4 spread)

when rain began to fall, that the fire finally died out. By this time, almost

300 people ___had died___ and more than one hundred
(5 die)

thousand Chicagoans ___had lost___ their homes.
(6 lost)

Millionaires, who ___had been living___ in mansions,
(7 live)

as well as poor laborers, found themselves homeless. Chicagoans, rich

and poor, who ___had never had___ contact with each other,
(8 have/never)

gathered in parks and wondered how they would rebuild their lives.

Because of its great location for industry, Chicago remained strong

after the fire. By 1873, the city ___had been rebuilt___, this time
(9 passive: rebuild)

with brick instead of wood. Chicago continued to grow as a commercial

center, and, by 1890, its population ___had reached___ more
(10 reach)

than one million. Today Chicago is the third largest city in the U.S.

Expansion

Exercise 14 Ask students if they had heard about the Chicago fire before they read the reading. Ask what information in the reading surprised them.

Culture Note

The Great Chicago Fire destroyed four square miles of the city's business district. A long-standing legend says that the fire was started when a cow belonging to a Mrs. O'Leary kicked over an oil lamp.

3.10 | The Past Perfect (Continuous) or the Present Perfect (Continuous)

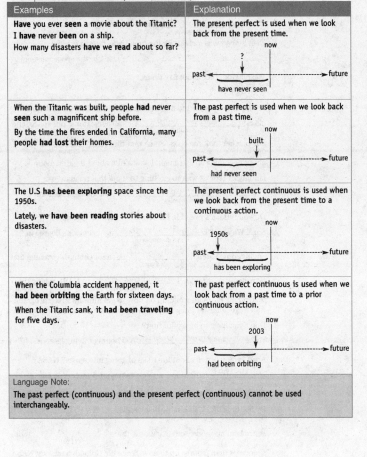

Examples	Explanation
Have you ever **seen** a movie about the Titanic? I **have** never **been** on a ship. How many disasters **have** we **read** about so far?	The present perfect is used when we look back from the present time.
When the Titanic was built, people **had** never **seen** such a magnificent ship before. By the time the fires ended in California, many people **had lost** their homes.	The past perfect is used when we look back from a past time.
The U.S **has been exploring** space since the 1950s. Lately, we **have been reading** stories about disasters.	The present perfect continuous is used when we look back from the present time to a continuous action.
When the Columbia accident happened, it **had been orbiting** the Earth for sixteen days. When the Titanic sank, it **had been traveling** for five days.	The past perfect continuous is used when we look back from a past time to a prior continuous action.

Language Note:
The past perfect (continuous) and the present perfect (continuous) cannot be used interchangeably.

The Past Continuous; The Past Perfect; The Past Perfect Continuous; Comparison of Past Tenses   123

3.10 | The Past Perfect (Continuous) or the Present Perfect (Continuous)

1. Have students cover up grammar chart **3.10**. Review the present perfect and present perfect continuous tenses with students. Write statements on the board based on the reading. For example, write: *We have read about two fires. We have been studying the past perfect tense since (Tuesday).* Then have students write questions in their notebooks for the statements. Check answers with the class. (*How many fires have we read about? How long have we been studying the past perfect tense?*)

2. Have students review the example sentences and explanations in the first two sections of the grammar chart. Ask: *How is the present perfect tense different in form from the past perfect tense?* (the present perfect tense uses *have* and the past perfect tense uses *had*)

3. Have students review the example sentences and explanations in the third and fourth sections of the grammar chart. Ask: *How is the present perfect continuous tense different in form from the past perfect continuous tense?* (the present perfect continuous tense uses *have* and the past perfect continuous tense uses *had*)

4. Draw students' attention to the Language Note. If necessary, clarify the meaning of *interchangeably* (in one another's place).

Grammar Variation

Have students write a question for each of the statements in the grammar chart (e.g., *Have you ever been on a ship?*). Have pairs of students work together to ask and answer the questions.

CD 1, Track 21

1. Tell students that this exercise is a conversation between two friends about a dream job. Have students read the direction line. Ask: *How many different tense choices are there?* (four)
2. Direct students to the example in the book. Review the example, and then ask a volunteer to answer #1.
3. Have students complete the exercise individually. Check answers as a class.
4. Assess students' performance. If necessary, review grammar chart **3.10** on page 123.

EXERCISE 15 Fill in the blanks with the present perfect, the present perfect continuous, the past perfect, or the past perfect continuous of the verb in parentheses ( ).

A: I'm really interested in space exploration.

B: How long __*have you been*__ interested in it?
    (example: you/be)

A: Ever since I was a child. By the time I was ten years old, I
    __*had gone*__ to the space museum in
    (1 go)
    Washington, D.C. about five times.

B: Who took you?

A: My parents took me most of the time. But one time my fifth grade
    class __*had been studying*__ all semester about space, and
    (2 study)
    our teacher took the class. Since that time, I __*have always dreamed*__
    (3 always/dream)
    about becoming an astronaut. I saw a film about the first moon
    landing in 1969. It was so exciting to think that no man
    __*had ever walked*__ on the moon before.
    (4 ever/walk)

B: Do you think it's possible for you to become an astronaut?

A: Sure. Why not? I __*have already gotten*__ my bachelor's degree in
    (5 already/get)
    engineering. Lately I __*have been reading*__ a lot about the training that
    (6 read)
    astronauts go through. I __*have already written*__ to NASA asking them
    (7 already/write)
    to send me more information on how to get into the space program.
    And next semester I'm going to enter a master's program in physics.

B: Don't you have to be a pilot first?

A: Yes. I __*have already taken*__ 500 hours of flying lessons.
    (8 already/take)

B: Aren't you worried about the risks of going into space? NASA
    __*has had*__ several major disasters so far.
    (9 have)

A: Of course, there are risks. But the space program needs to continue.
    By the time of the Columbia disaster, it __*had already had*__ 27
    (10 already/have)
    successful missions. And in general, there __*have been*__ more
    (11 be)
    successes than failures up to now. Since the Columbia tragedy, NASA
    __*has been studying*__ ways to improve the safety of its astronauts.
    (12 study)

Exercise 15 Variation

To provide practice with listening skills, have students close their books and listen to the audio. Repeat the audio as needed. Ask comprehension questions, such as: *What is person A interested in?* (space exploration) *What kind of film did person A see?* (a film about the first moon landing in 1969) Then have students open their books and complete Exercise 15.

Expansion

Exercise 15 Have students work in groups to write two lists of facts about speaker A in the conversation. For the first list, have them complete the sentence: *By the time he/she was an adult, he/she had . . .* For the second list, have them complete the sentence: *Recently, he/she has . . .*

Exercise 15 Ask students: *Did you have a dream job when you were young? What inspired your dream? Do you still have the same dream? Have you done anything about it?*

SURVIVORS OF THE TITANIC

Before You Read

1. Why do you think the Titanic disaster is still interesting today?
2. If you could ask a survivor of the Titanic any question, what would you ask him or her?

 Read the following article. Pay special attention to past tense verbs (simple past, past continuous, past perfect, past perfect continuous, and present perfect).

People **have been** fascinated with the Titanic disaster for about 100 years. Several movies **have been made** giving fictitious[7] stories of the passengers who died. But their real experiences are not known. However, approximately 700 people **survived** the Titanic disaster and **lived** to tell their stories to newspapers.

Philip Zanni, an Assyrian emigrant, **was traveling** to the U.S. in third class. He **was sleeping** when he **heard** a crash. He immediately **ran** to the upper deck[8] where he **saw** great confusion. Men **were lowering** the lifeboats, and Zanni **tried** to jump into one of them. But an officer with a gun **stopped** him, yelling, "Women and children first." Moments later, the officer **turned** away, and Zanni **jumped** on. He **was hiding** under one of the seats when the boat **pulled** away. There **were** 20 women and three men in the boat. They **had** to row quickly because the ship **was sinking.** When they were about two miles away, they **saw** the Titanic sink. It **wasn't** until five in the morning that they **saw** a rescue ship arrive. Zanni **reported** that while the survivors **were being raised** to the rescue ship, a woman **begged** Zanni to save her dog, which she **had been carrying** since leaving the Titanic.

Mary Davis, a second-class passenger, **was traveling** to visit her sister in New York. She **had saved** the money for the trip by working as a maid in London. She **was sleeping** when she **heard** a noise. She **was told** that there was no danger, and so she **returned** to bed. A few minutes later, she **was told** to go to the highest deck because the ship **was sinking.** Two men **helped** her get on a lifeboat, and then it **was lowered.** In the morning, the rescue ship **found** her boat and **pulled** the people aboard. When Ms. Davis **died** in 1987 at the age of 104, she **had lived** to be older than any other Titanic survivor.

[7] *Fictitious* means not real.
[8] A *deck* is a floor of a ship.

The Past Continuous; The Past Perfect; The Past Perfect Continuous; Comparison of Past Tenses   125

Expansion

Theme The topic for this lesson can be enhanced with the following ideas:
1. A Web site about Titanic survivors
2. A list of Web sites related to the Titanic and articles, art, and music related to the sinking, e.g., http://seawifs.gsfc.nasa.gov/titanic.html
3. A synopsis of the plot of the movie *Titanic*

Reading Variation

To practice listening skills, have students first listen to the audio alone. Ask a few comprehension questions. Repeat the audio if necessary. Then have students open their books and read along as they listen to the audio.

Reading Glossary

fascinate: be very interesting; hold people's attention for a long time
row: use oars (long paddles) to move a boat through the water
turn away: turn around; turn one's back; stop paying attention

Survivors of the Titanic (Reading)

1. Have students look at the photo. Ask: *Where are the people?* (in a lifeboat) *What do you think happened to them?* (They left a ship that was sinking.)
2. Have students look quickly at the reading. Ask: *What is the reading about? How do you know?* Have students make predictions.
3. Preteach any vocabulary words your students may not know, such as *fascinated, turned away,* and *row.*

BEFORE YOU READ

1. Activate students' prior knowledge about survivors of the Titanic. Ask: *Have you every seen a movie about the Titanic? Do you think what happened in the movie is what really happened? Why or why not?*
2. Have students discuss the questions in pairs. Try to pair students of different language backgrounds.
3. Ask a few volunteers to share their answers with the class.

To save class time, skip "Before You Read" or have students prepare answers for homework ahead of time.

Reading CD 1, Track 22

1. Have students first read the text silently. Tell them to pay special attention to the past tense verbs. Then play the audio and have students read along silently.
2. Check students' comprehension. Ask questions such as: *How did Philip Zanni survive?* (He got into a lifeboat while the officers weren't looking and hid under a seat.) *Why did Mary Davis go back to bed instead of trying to leave the ship?* (She had been told that there was no danger.)

To save class time, have students do the reading for homework ahead of time.

3.11 | Comparison of Past Tenses

1. Have students cover the right-hand column of the grammar chart. Review each set of examples with the class. Ask: *Which tense is used in these examples? Why?* Elicit the explanation for each set of examples from the class. Have students uncover and look at each explanation as you finish its section.

3.11 | Comparison of Past Tenses

Examples	Explanation
a. The Titanic **left** England on April 10, 1912. b. Mary Davis, a survivor of the Titanic, **lived** until she was 104 years old. c. I **saw** a movie about the Titanic last year. d. I **read** several articles about the space program last month.	The **simple past tense** shows an action that started and ended in the past. It does not show the relationship to another past action. It can be used for a short action (a) or a long action (b). It can be used for a single action (c) or repeated actions (d).
Many passengers **were sleeping** at 11:40 p.m. The Titanic **was crossing** the Atlantic when it sank. The Columbia **was returning** from its mission when the accident happened.	The **past continuous tense** shows that something was in progress at a specific time in the past.
a. When the rescue ship arrived, 1,500 passengers of the Titanic **had** already **died**. b. When the Columbia accident happened, it **had** already **had** 27 successful missions.	The **past perfect** shows the relationship of an earlier past action to a later past action. a. earlier = *had died;* later = *arrived* b. earlier = *had had;* later = *happened*
The Titanic **had been traveling** for five days when it sank. The fires in California **had been burning** for about a week when they were controlled.	The **past perfect continuous** is used with the amount of time of a continuous action that happened before another past action. *For* is used to show the amount of time.
People **have been** fascinated with the Titanic for about a hundred years. **Have** there **been** any space missions lately? California **has had** many disasters, including fires and earthquakes.	The **present perfect** uses the present time as the starting point and looks back.
We **have been talking** about the Titanic for several days. We **have been studying** past tenses for a few days. NASA **has been exploring** space since the 1950s.	The **present perfect continuous** uses the present time as the starting point and looks back at a continuous action that is still happening.
Compare: a. When my sister came home, I **ate** dinner. (simple past) b. When my sister came home, I **was eating** dinner. (past continuous) c. When my sister came home, I **had eaten** dinner. (past perfect)	Be especially careful with *when.* In sentence (a), I ate *after* my sister came home. In sentence (b), I was in the process of eating *when* my sister came home. In sentence (c), my dinner was finished *when* my sister came home.

Grammar Variation

Divide students into teams. At random, choose example sentences from the left side of the grammar chart to read aloud. Give a point to the first team to correctly identify the tense in the sentence you have read. The team with the most points is the winner.

Language Notes:

1. Sometimes the past continuous and the past perfect continuous can be used in the same case. The past perfect continuous is more common with a *for* phrase.

   The Titanic **was traveling** across the Atlantic when it hit an iceberg.

   The Titanic **had been traveling** *for five days* when it hit an iceberg.

2. Sometimes the simple past or the past perfect can be used in the same case.

   Some lifeboats **were** removed before the Titanic left.

   Some lifeboats **had been** removed before the Titanic left.

EXERCISE 16 Read a survivor's account of the night of the Titanic disaster.[9] Fill in the blanks with the simple past, the past perfect, or the past continuous of the verb in parentheses.

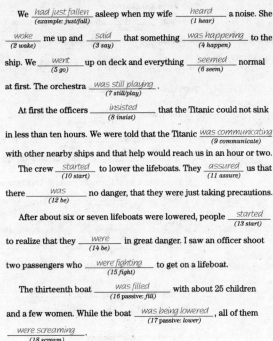

We __had just fallen__ asleep when my wife __heard__ a noise. She
(example: just/fall)   (1 hear)

__woke__ me up and __said__ that something __was happening__ to the
(2 wake)   (3 say)   (4 happen)

ship. We __went__ up on deck and everything __seemed__ normal
(5 go)   (6 seem)

at first. The orchestra __was still playing__ .
(7 still/play)

At first the officers __insisted__ that the Titanic could not sink
(8 insist)

in less than ten hours. We were told that the Titanic __was communicating__
(9 communicate)

with other nearby ships and that help would reach us in an hour or two.

The crew __started__ to lower the lifeboats. They __assured__ us that
(10 start)   (11 assure)

there __was__ no danger, that they were just taking precautions.
(12 be)

After about six or seven lifeboats were lowered, people __started__
(13 start)

to realize that they __were__ in great danger. I saw an officer shoot
(14 be)

two passengers who __were fighting__ to get on a lifeboat.
(15 fight)

The thirteenth boat __was filled__ with about 25 children
(16 passive: fill)

and a few women. While the boat __was being lowered__ , all of them
(17 passive: lower)

__were screaming__ .
(18 scream)

[9] Adapted from *The Bulletin* San Francisco, April 19, 1912.

3.11 | Comparison of Past Tenses (*cont.*)

2. Draw students' attention to the Language Notes. Review the examples and explanations.

EXERCISE 16

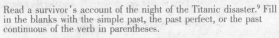 **CD 1, Track 23**

1. Tell students that this exercise is one man's story of surviving the sinking of the Titanic. Draw students' attention to the footnote at the bottom of page 127. Ask: *What does* adapted *mean?* (*made* or *changed*, in this case from a true story) Have students read the direction line.

2. Direct students to the example in the book. Review the example, and then ask a volunteer to answer items 1 through 4 with you.

3. Have students complete the exercise individually, and then check their answers in pairs. Circulate and observe the pair work. Check answers as a class. Where students had difficulty, ask volunteers to explain their choice of the three tenses.

4. Assess students' performance. If necessary, review grammar chart **3.11** on pages 126–127.

Exercise 16 Variation

To provide practice with listening skills, have students close their books and listen to the audio. Repeat the audio as needed. Ask comprehension questions, such as: *Why did the man's wife wake up?* (She heard a noise.) *When the man and his wife went up on deck, what was happening?* (Everything was normal; the orchestra was playing.) *Why did the crew start to lower the lifeboats?* (because they were taking precautions) Then have students open their books and complete Exercise 16.

1. Tell students that this exercise is about the sinking of the Titanic and our fascination with it. Have students read the direction line. Ask: *Does every item have only one possible answer?* (No; some have more than one.)

2. Direct students to the example in the book.

3. Have students complete the exercise individually.

4. Collect the exercise for assessment, or check answers as a class. Where students had difficulty, ask volunteers to explain their answers.

5. Assess students' performance. If necessary, review grammar chart **3.11** on pages 126–127.

🕐 To save class time, have students do half of the exercise in class and complete the other half for homework. Or assign the entire exercise for homework.

I _____*knew*_____ one of the officers on the Titanic because I
(19 know)

__*had traveled*__ with him before on another ship. He __*pushed*__ me into
(20 travel)   (21 push)

the thirteenth boat and __*ordered*__ me to take care of the children.
(22 order)

As our boat __*was leaving*__, we __*heard*__ the orchestra
(23 leave)   (24 hear)

playing a religious song.

I will never forget the terrible scene as our boat __*moved*__ away.
(25 move)

Husbands and fathers __*were waving*__ and __*throwing*__ kisses to
(26 wave)   (27 throw)

their wives and children.

The ship __*sank*__ only three hours after it __*had hit*__
(28 sink)   (29 hit)

the iceberg.

EXERCISE 17 Fill in the blanks with the correct past tense. Use the passive voice where indicated. In some cases, more than one answer is possible.

EXAMPLE The Titanic __*sank*__ in 1912.
(sink)

1. The Titanic __*was built*__ in Ireland.
(passive: build)

2. When the captain __*saw*__ the iceberg, he
(see)

__*tried*__ to turn the ship around.
(try)

3. There was a lot of ice in the water in 1912 because the previous

winter __*had been*__ mild.
(be)

4. The Titanic __*was traveling*__ fast when it __*hit*__ an iceberg.
(travel)   (hit)

5. Many people __*had been / were sleeping*__ when they __*heard*__ a loud noise.
(sleep)   (hear)

6. When they __*heard*__ the noise, they __*woke*__ up.
(hear)   (wake)

7. When third-class passengers __*went*__ to the top deck,
(go)

most of the lifeboats __*had already left*__.
(already/leave)

8. A few hours later, another ship __*arrived*__, but the Titanic
(arrive)

__*had already sunk*__.
(already/sink)

Expansion

Exercise 16 Have students go back to the questions they proposed in item 2 of Before You Read on page 125. Ask if any of the answers to their questions appear in the survivor's account in Exercise 16. Have students write two or three additional questions they would like to ask this survivor.

Culture Note

In 1985, a team led by explorer Dr. Robert Ballard located the wreck of the Titanic. It had been lost underwater for 73 years. Thousands of artifacts have been brought up. In 2004, Dr. Ballard visited the shipwreck again and broadcast a television special from the site.

9. The rescue ship _____picked_____ up the people in the lifeboats.
   (pick)

10. The Titanic _____was making_____ its first voyage when it _____sank_____.
    (make)   (sink)

11. In 1985, the ship _____was finally found_____ in the North Atlantic.
    (passive: finally/find)

12. People are still interested in the Titanic. People _____have been_____
    (be)
    interested in it for almost a hundred years.

13. Many articles and books _____have been written_____ about the Titanic
    (passive: write)
    over the years.

14. Several movies _____have been made_____ about the Titanic.
    (passive: make)

15. In 1912, the sinking of the Titanic was the worst tragedy that
    _____had ever occurred_____.
    (ever/occur)

16. I was going to invite my friends to come over and watch the video
    Titanic last month, but most of them _____had already seen_____ the movie.
    (already/see)

EXERCISE 18 Fill in the blanks with the correct past tense of the verb in
parentheses ( ). In some cases, more than one answer is possible.

A: I loved the movie *Titanic*. I _____saw_____ it for the first time when it
   (see)
   came out. Since then, I _____have rented_____ it two more times.
   (1 rent)
   _____Have you ever seen_____ it?
   (2 you/ever/see)

B: Do you mean the movie with Leonardo DiCaprio? Actually, I
   _____have never seen_____ it. But I _____saw_____ a 1950s
   (3 never/see)   (4 see)
   movie about the Titanic a few years ago.

A: The DiCaprio version was great. You should rent it.

B: You know, I _____rented_____ it about six months ago, but I only watched
   (5 rent)
   about 15 minutes of it. While I _____was watching_____ it, there was a
   (6 watch)
   power failure in my area and the electricity _____went_____
   (7 go)
   out for several hours. I _____had to_____ return the video that night.
   (8 have to)
   Up to now, I _____had forgotten_____ all about it—until you mentioned it.
   (9 forget)

The Past Continuous; The Past Perfect; The Past Perfect Continuous; Comparison of Past Tenses   129

🎧 *CD 1, Track 24*

1. Tell students that this exercise is a conversation between two friends about the movie *Titanic*. Have students read the direction line.
2. Model the exercise. Direct students to the example in the book; then do #1 with the class.
3. Have students complete Exercise 18 individually.
4. Collect the exercise for assessment, or check answers as a class. Where students had difficulty, ask volunteers to explain their answers.
5. Assess students' performance. If necessary, review grammar chart 3.11 on pages 126–127.

🕐 To save class time, have students do half of the exercise in class and complete the other half for homework. Or assign the entire exercise for homework.

Expansion

Exercise 17 Have students write questions related to items 1, 2, 3, 10, 11, and 12, such as: *Where was the Titanic built?*

Exercise 18 Variation

To provide practice with listening skills, have students close their books and listen to the audio. Repeat the audio as needed. Ask comprehension questions, such as: *How many times has person A seen* Titanic? (three times) *Why did person B only watch 15 minutes of the movie?* (because there was a power failure and the electricity went off for several hours) Then have students open their books and complete Exercise 18.

Summary of Lesson 3

1. **Showing the relationship between two past actions** Have students find a sentence from the readings in the lesson to illustrate each of the relationships in the chart.

If necessary, have students review:
Lesson 3.

A: You should rent it again. It was a great story.

B: But everyone knows how the story ___ended___ . The ship
    (10 end)

___sank___ and a lot of people ___died___ .
    (11 sink)   (12 die)

A: But there was also a great love story. It's a story about a woman
named Rose. She ___was planning / had been planning / had planned___ to marry a rich man when she
    (13 plan)

___met___ Jack and ___fell___ in love with him. Jack was a poor
    (14 meet)   (15 fall)

man who ___was traveling___ in third class. When Rose was with Jack, she
    (16 travel)

___felt___ freer than she ___had ever felt___ before. But when
    (17 feel)   (18 ever/feel)

Rose's fiancé ___found out___ that Rose was in love with
    (19 find out)

another man, he ___became___ very angry.
    (20 become)

B: Stop! Don't tell me more. I think I'll rent the movie this weekend.

A: If you do, let me know. I'd like to watch it with you.

SUMMARY OF LESSON 3

1. Showing the relationship between two past actions

The Past Perfect	
The reference point is past.	Another action is more past.
When the rescue ship **arrived,** In **1912,**	many people **had died.** the airplane **had** already **been invented.**

The Past Perfect Continuous	
The reference point is past.	A continuous action preceded it.
A woman wanted to save the dog	that she **had been carrying** since she left the Titanic.
The captain couldn't turn the ship around	because it **had been traveling** so fast.

The Past Continuous	
An action was in progress . . .	. . . at a specific time or when a shorter action occurred.
They **were sleeping** We **were watching** TV	at 11:40 p.m. when the Columbia accident occurred.

130   Lesson **3**

Expansion

Exercise 18 After students complete the exercise, ask: *Has person A seen the DiCaprio movie* Titanic? (yes) *Has person B seen it?* (no) *Why not?* (After he/she had watched 15 minutes, the power went out.) *Do you think person B will invite person A to see the movie this weekend? Why/why not?*

Summary Variation

Item 1 Have students review a newspaper story or magazine article about a recent series of events in your area. Have students write sentences showing the relationship between actions in the article using the tenses in item 1. Have volunteers present their sentences to the class.

2. Relating the past to the present

The Present Perfect	The Present Perfect Continuous
Have you ever **seen** the movie *Titanic*? I **have** never **seen** it, but I'd like to. I **have seen** two movies so far this month. I've always **been** interested in space exploration.	She is watching the movie now. She **has been watching** it for 45 minutes. I've **been reading** a book about space exploration.

3. Describing the past without relating it to another past time

The Simple Past Tense
I **rented** a movie last week. I **liked** the movie so much that I **watched** it twice. Mary **lived** in England all her life. The Columbia accident **happened** in 2003.

EDITING ADVICE

1. Don't use *be* to form the simple past tense.
   came
   He was come home at 6 o'clock last night.

2. Don't forget *be* in a past continuous sentence.
   was
   I ^ walking on the icy sidewalk when I fell and broke my arm.

3. Do not use a present tense for an action that began in the past. Use the present perfect (continuous).
   have been
   I am married for ten years.
   has been
   She is working at her present job for seven months.

4. Don't forget *have* with perfect tenses.
   have
   I ^ been living in the U.S. for six months.

5. Don't confuse the present perfect and the past perfect. The past perfect relates to a past event. The present perfect relates to a present situation.
   had
   When I started college, I have never used a computer before.
   has
   She's a teacher now. She had been a teacher for 15 years.

The Past Continuous; The Past Perfect; The Past Perfect Continuous; Comparison of Past Tenses   **131**

Summary Variation

Item 2 Have students give examples of things they have done or thought about doing to help victims of a global disaster or local emergency.

Item 3 Have students work in groups to make a list of sentences telling about natural events, both disasters and nondisasters, they know about (e.g., *Mount St. Helens eruption in 1980.*).

Summary of Lesson 3 (*cont.*)

2. **Relating the past to the present**
   Have students use the present perfect tense to make statements about experiences they have had or heard about related to natural disasters (*I've never seen a wildfire, thank goodness, but my brother has.*). Ask: *Have you been thinking about making an emergency plan? Getting together a disaster kit? Buying some emergency supplies?*
   If necessary, have students review:
   3.1 Overview of Past Tenses (p. 98)
   3.10 The Past Perfect (Continuous) or the Present Perfect (Continuous) (p. 123)
   3.11 Comparison of Past Tenses (pp. 126–127).

3. **Describing the past without relating it to another past time**
   Have students work in groups to write a sentence in the simple past about each of the disasters they have read about in the lesson. Have groups share their sentences with the class.
   If necessary, have students review:
   3.11 Comparison of Past Tenses (pp. 126–127).

Editing Advice

For each item, have students provide the grammar rule behind the editing advice. This can be done as an individual, a pair, a group, or a class activity.

1. Use the simple past tense form of a verb alone, without *be*.
2. Use a form of *be* (*was* or *were*) with the past continuous.
3. If an action started in the past and continues to the present, use the present perfect or present perfect continuous tense.
4. Use *have* or *has* with the present perfect and present perfect continuous tenses.
5. Use the past perfect to talk about related events in the past. Use the present perfect to talk about the past as it relates to the present.

Editing Advice (cont.)

6. Clauses with *ago* name a specific time and use the simple past.
7. For actions that happened once and did not continue, use *when*.
8. Clauses with *since* give a period of time and use the simple past.
9. When a single action is repeated, don't use the continuous forms.
10. Use the past participle with the present perfect and past perfect tenses, not the present participle, with *-ing*.
11. To choose between the simple past and present perfect after a clause with *when*, determine whether *when* means *after* or *before*.
12. Use the passive when the object of an action is emphasized.

Lesson 3 Test/Review

For additional practice, review, and assessment materials, see Assessment CD-ROM with *ExamView Pro*, *More Grammar Practice* Workbook 3, Interactive CD-ROM, and Web site http://elt.thomson.com/gic

PART 1

1. Part 1 may be used as an in-class test to assess student performance, in addition to the Assessment CD-ROM with *ExamView Pro*. Have students read the direction line. Ask: *Does every sentence have a mistake?* (no)
2. Collect for assessment.
3. If necessary, have students review:
   3.11 Comparison of Past Tenses (pp. 126–127)
   Summary of Lesson 3 (pp. 130–131).

---

6. Use the simple past with *ago*.
   came
   He was coming to the U.S. four years ago.

7. Use *when*, not *while*, for an action that has no continuation.
   when
   I was washing the dishes while I dropped a plate.

8. Use the simple past, not the present perfect, in a *since* clause.
   came
   She has had her car ever since she has come to the U.S.

9. Don't use the continuous form for a repeated action.
   drunk
   By the time I got to work, I had been drinking four cups of coffee.

10. Don't confuse the *-ing* form with the past participle.
    seen
    When he moved to Chicago, he had never seeing a skyscraper before.

11. Be careful to choose the correct past tense in a sentence with *when*.
    came
    When I left my hometown, I had come to New York.
    had begun
    When I arrived in class, the test began already.

12. Don't confuse active and passive.
    found
    In 1985, the Titanic was finding.

LESSON 3 TEST/REVIEW

PART 1 Find the mistakes with the underlined words, and correct them. Not every sentence has a mistake. If the sentence is correct, write *C.*

EXAMPLES   I couldn't answer the phone when it rang because I <u>took</u> *was taking* a shower.
She <u>found</u> a job last week. C

1. I <u>was work</u> when the fire <u>started</u>. *was working*
2. How long <u>do you live</u> in this city? *have you lived*
3. They <u>were getting</u> married five years ago. *got*
4. When he <u>came</u> to the U.S., he <u>had never studied</u> English before. *C*
5. Have you ever <u>seeing</u> the mayor of this city? *seen*
6. By the time he got divorced, he <u>has been</u> married for ten years. *had*

Lesson Review

To use Part 1 as a review, assign it as homework or use it as an in-class activity to be completed individually or in pairs. Check answers and review errors as a class. Reteach grammar points that students haven't mastered. Then student learning may be assessed using a test generated from the Assessment CD-ROM with *ExamView Pro*.

7. She <u>left</u> her dictionary in the library yesterday. *C*

8. When she <u>came</u> to the U.S., she <u>had never spoken</u> English before. *C*

9. My sister is in medical school. She <u>has wanted</u> to be a doctor ever since she <u>has been</u> a little girl. *was*

10. My grandparents <u>were living</u> in Germany when World War II <u>started</u>. *C*

11. I <u>been working</u> as a computer programmer for five years. I love my job. *have*

12. My sister is a nurse. She <u>had been</u> a nurse for ten years. *has*

13. When we <u>finished</u> dinner, we <u>washed</u> the dishes. *C*

14. An accident <u>was happened</u> in front of my house early this morning.

15. Last year when the landlord <u>raised</u> my rent, I <u>decided</u> to move. *C*

16. I wasn't injured in the car accident because I <u>had been wearing</u> my seat belt. *was*

17. By the time my sister <u>came</u> to the U.S., our father <u>had</u> already <u>died</u>. *C*

18. We <u>had been driven</u> for three hours when we had a flat tire. *driving*

19. When he came to the U.S., he <u>had never met</u> an American before. *C*

20. Fifteen hundred people <u>died</u> on the Titanic. *C*

21. Have you ever <u>traveled</u> by ship? No, I never <u>have</u>. *C*

22. When they <u>came</u> to the U.S., they <u>saw</u> the Statue of Liberty for the first time. *C*

23. She was eating lunch <u>while</u> the phone rang. *when*

PART **2** Fill in the blanks with the simple past or the past perfect form of the verb in parentheses ( ).

EXAMPLE   When Mary Davis ____*came*____ to America, she
                                    (come)

____*had never left*____ England before.
        (never/leave)

1. I registered late for this class. The class ____*had already had*____
                                                        (already/have)

    a test on the review lesson by the time I ____*registered*____.
                                                        (register)

2. She ____*wanted*____ to go to Paris for vacation last year
            (want)

    because she ____*had never gone*____ there before.
                        (never/go)

3. I got to class late. By the time I ____*got*____ to class, the
                                            (get)

    teacher ____*had already explained*____ the homework.
                    (already/explain)

PART 2

1. Part 2 may also be used as an in-class test to assess student performance, in addition to the Assessment CD-ROM with *ExamView Pro*. Tell students that this is about time relationships between events. Review the example. Then do the next sentence as a class. Ask: *What goes in the first blank? (had already had)*

2. Collect for assessment.

3. If necessary, have students review:

   3.5 The Past Perfect Tense—Forms (p. 110)

   3.6 The Past Perfect—Uses (pp. 112–113)

   3.7 *When* with the Simple Past or the Past Perfect (p. 115)

   3.11 Comparison of Past Tenses (pp. 126–127)
   Summary of Lesson 3 (pp. 130–131).

Lesson Review

To use Part 2 as a review, assign it as homework or use it as an in-class activity to be completed individually or in pairs. Check answers and review errors as a class. Reteach grammar points that students haven't mastered. Then student learning may be assessed using a test generated from the Assessment CD-ROM with *ExamView Pro*.

1. Part 3 may be used as an in-class test to assess student performance, in addition to the Assessment CD-ROM with *ExamView Pro*. Have students read the direction line. Ask: *How many tenses do we choose from?* (six)
2. Collect for assessment.
3. If necessary, have students review: **Lesson 3.**

4. When she got to work, she ___realized___ that she
   (realize)
   ___had left___ the stove on, so she had to go back home.
   (leave)

5. When my mother came to the U.S., she ___was___ afraid to speak
   (be)
   English because she ___had never spoken___ English with
   (never/speak)
   an American before.

6. When I ___started___ English lessons, I
   (start)
   ___had never studied___ a foreign language before.
   (never/study)

7. Many people ___died___ when they
   (die)
   ___jumped___ into the water because the water was so cold.
   (jump)

8. Many of the survivors of the Titanic ___had already died___
   (already/die)
   of old age when the ship ___was found___ in 1985.
   (passive: find)

9. He ___called___ the fire department
   (call)
   when the fire ___started___.
   (start)

10. When the fire department came, the house ___had already burned___
    (already/burn)
    down.

PART 3 Fill in the blanks with one of the past tenses: simple past, past continuous, present perfect (continuous), or past perfect (continuous). In some cases, more than one answer is possible.

A: What ___happened___ to your car?
   (happen)

B: I ___had___ an accident yesterday.
   (1 have)

A: How ___did___ it ___happen___?
   (2 happen)

B: I ___was driving___ to work when a dog ___ran___ in front of my car.
   (3 drive)   (4 run)

   I ___stopped___ my car suddenly, and the car behind me ___hit___
   (5 stop)   (6 hit)

   my car because the driver ___had been following___ me too closely.
   (7 follow)

Lesson Review

To use Part 3 as a review, assign it as homework or use it as an in-class activity to be completed individually or in pairs. Check answers and review errors as a class. Reteach grammar points that students haven't mastered. Then student learning may be assessed using a test generated from the Assessment CD-ROM with *ExamView Pro*.

A: ___Did you get___ a ticket?
(8 you/get)

B: No, but the driver who hit me did.

A: Who will pay to have your car fixed?

B: The other driver. When he ___hit___ me, he ___got___ out of
(9 hit)   (10 get)

his car and ___gave___ me his insurance card. He's a new driver. He
(11 give)

___has only had___ his driver's license for two months.
(12 only/have)

A: You're a new driver too, aren't you?

B: Oh, no. I ___have been driving___ for twenty years.
(13 drive)

A: I thought you ___had gotten___ your driver's license a few months ago.
(14 get)

B: In this state, I have a new license. But I ___had had___
(15 have)

a driver's license for many years before I ___moved___ here.
(16 move)

A: ___Have___ you ever ___gotten___ a ticket?
(17 get)

B: One time. I ___was driving___ about 65 miles an hour on the
(18 drive)

highway when a police officer ___stopped___ me. She said that the speed
(19 stop)

limit was only 55. She ___gave___ me a ticket for speeding. She also
(20 give)

gave me a ticket because I ___was not wearing___ my seat belt.
(21 not/wear)

EXPANSION ACTIVITIES

Classroom
Activities

1. In a small group or with the entire class, turn to the person next to you and say a year. The person next to you has to tell a short story about his / her life at or before that time.

EXAMPLES 1996
I had just graduated from high school. I was living with my parents. I hadn't thought about coming to the U.S. at that time.

Expansion Activities

These expansion activities provide opportunities for students to interact with one another and further develop their speaking and writing skills. Encourage students to use grammar from this lesson whenever possible.

🕐 To save class time, assign parts of the activities as homework. Then use class time for interaction and communication. If students do not need additional speaking practice, some of the activities may be assigned as writing activities for homework or skipped altogether.

CLASSROOM ACTIVITIES

1. Tell students that this activity is about telling a story about a time in the past. Review the examples. Ask: *What tenses are used in the examples?* (past perfect and past continuous) Then begin the activity.

Classroom Activities Variation

Activity 1 As pairs work, have them make notes about their partners' statements. Then have students report interesting stories from their partners' lives to the group, as appropriate.

2. Tell students that this activity is about learning more about their classmates. Pass out blank index cards or slips of paper. When each student has written a statement, collect the cards and read them to the class one by one. Have students guess whose card each one is.

TALK ABOUT IT

Have students work in groups. Either assign or have each group choose one of the topics to discuss. Review with students language for agreeing, checking for agreement, and disagreeing (e.g., *I think so too. Are you sure that's right? I'm not sure I agree.*). Set a time limit for discussion. Then have groups talk about their topics. If appropriate, have groups report back to the class; have each group appoint a spokesperson.

WRITE ABOUT IT

Have students review the topics carefully before choosing. Encourage students to organize their thoughts and make notes about their topics before they begin to write. Ask: *Which tenses will you most likely use? Why?* When students have finished, collect for assessment and/or have students review each other's work.

OUTSIDE ACTIVITY

If some students are unable to rent and view movies at home, consider bringing one of the movies to class, if possible, to view a few scenes together.

INTERNET ACTIVITIES

Brainstorm search terms to use to find each type of information. Decide, or have the class decide, which items to assign to which students. Have students bring their articles to class; for activities 1 and 4, have students share the information they found. For activities 2 and 3, have students write on the board any past tense verbs they had questions about. Clarify with the class as necessary.

1963
I hadn't been born yet.

1997
I had just had my second child. I was living with my wife's parents.

2. On an index card, write the following sentence, filling in the blank to make a **true** statement about yourself. The teacher will collect the cards and read the sentences. Try to guess who wrote the sentences.

> EXAMPLE When I came to this school, I had never _____ before.
> When I came to this school, I had never paid so much for a textbook before.

Talk
About it

1. Why do you think that women and children were put on lifeboats before men?

2. Do you think the space program should continue?

Write
About it

Choose one of the following topics and write a short composition.

1. An accident or unusual experience that happened to you

2. How you met your spouse or a new friend

3. An important event in the history of your native country

4. A famous person who died in an accident, assassination, or another unusual way

5. Write about a tragedy in recent history. Tell what you *were doing* when you heard the news. Tell what you *did* when you heard the news.

Outside
Activity

Rent the movie *Titanic* (1997) and/or *A Night to Remember* (1957). Write a summary of one of these movies.

Internet
Activities

1. Find Web sites that tell about the Titanic. Find personal accounts of survivors. Report one of these to the class.

2. Find an article about the California fires of 2003. Bring it to class. Circle all the past tenses in the article.

3. Find an article about the Columbia tragedy of 2003. Bring it to class. Circle all the past tenses in the article.

4. Find an article about the Tsunami disaster of 2004. Bring it to class and report on a personal account.

Additional Activities at http://elt.thomson.com/gic

Talk About it Variation

1. Have students work in pairs. Have members of the pairs interview each other using the questions in the activity, alternating interviewers. Have the interviewers take notes on their partners' responses.

2. Have students debate one or both of the items. Divide the class into two teams. Tell each team to list five reasons supporting its view. Have each team present its arguments. Then give each team an opportunity to respond to the other team's arguments. At the end of the debate, survey the class to see which opinion is more popular.

Write About it Variation

Have students exchange first drafts with a partner. Ask students to help their partners edit their drafts. Refer students to Editing Advice on pages 131–132.

Internet Activities Variation

If students don't have access to the Internet, they may find the information needed at a local public library.

LESSON

4

GRAMMAR

Modals—Present and Future
Related Expressions

CONTEXT : Consumer Warnings

Sweepstakes or Scam?
Telemarketing
Infomercials
My Elderly Neighbor

Congratulations
Sweepstakes USA
Corporate Headquarters
Somewhere, TX 12345
Pay to: Ms. Jackie Goldman
Official Sweepstakes Winner
$1,000,000
$1,000,000
One Million Dollars
Grand Prize Awarded
Winner

137

Lesson 4

Lesson Overview

GRAMMAR

1. Activate students' prior knowledge. Write *modals* on the board. Ask students to name as many modals as they can. List the modals on the board.
2. Ask: *What will we study in this lesson?* (modals with the present and future and related expressions) Use the modals students suggested in #1 to provide a few examples of your own (*I can ice skate, but I can't swim; It might snow tomorrow.*). Have volunteers give examples. Write an example using each modal on the board.

CONTEXT

1. Elicit students' prior knowledge. Ask: *What will we learn about in this lesson?* (sweepstakes and scams, telemarketing, and infomercials) *What are sweepstakes?* (contests, usually of chance, not skill) *What is telemarketing?* (marketing or sales by telephone)
2. Have students share their knowledge and personal experiences.

Picture

1. Direct students' attention to the picture. Ask: *What is this woman's name?* (Jackie Goldman) *How do you think she feels? Why does she feel that way? Why are there a house and a car in the picture?*
2. Have students talk about their experience with a lottery or sweepstakes. Ask: *Have you ever bought a lottery ticket or entered a sweepstakes? Do businesses use telemarketing or sweepstakes in your native country?*

To save class time, have students do the Test/Review at the end of the lesson, or administer a lesson test generated from the Assessment CD-ROM with *ExamView® Pro*. Skip sections of the lesson that students have already mastered. You may also assign some sections for self-study for extra credit.

Expansion

Theme The topic for this lesson can be enhanced with the following ideas:

1. An ad for lottery tickets from a newspaper or a convenience store
2. A copy of the driver's handbook for your state
3. The FTC's Top Ten Consumer Complaints Web site, at: http://www.ftc.gov/opa/2004/01/top10.htm

Culture Note

Television shows sometimes give a lot of publicity to sweepstakes and other contest winners. They may become celebrities for a short time. The chances of winning a sweepstakes or lottery, however, are very small.

4.1 | Overview of Modals and Related Expressions

1. Have students cover the grammar chart. Draw students' attention to the list of modals and the sentences on the board from the Grammar Overview. If any of the nine modals from the top section of the chart is missing, add it to the list on the board, along with an example sentence.

2. Have students look at grammar chart **4.1.** Review the examples and explanation in each section of the chart.

3. Draw students' attention to the sentences labeled *wrong* in the explanation column. Ask: *What are the two rules?* (the modal comes before the base verb; modals never have an -s ending)

4. Draw students' attention to the Language Note. Ask the class several similar questions: *Can you drive a truck? Why shouldn't you believe everything you read? When will we finish this lesson?*

4.1 | Overview of Modals and Related Expressions

Modals = *can, could, shall, should, will, would, may, might, must*

Examples	Explanation
She **should** leave. (advice) She **must** leave. (necessity) She **might** leave. (possibility)	Modals add meaning to the verbs that follow them.
He **can help** you. They **should eat** now. You **must pay** your rent.	The base form follows a modal. *Wrong:* He can *helps* you. *Wrong:* They should *eating* now. *Wrong:* You must *to pay.* The modal never has an -s ending. *Wrong:* He *cans* help you.
You **should not** leave now. He **cannot** speak English	To form the negative, put *not* after the modal. *Cannot* is written as one word.
A pen **should be used** for the test. The movie **can be seen** next week. He **must** go to court. = He **has to** go to court. You **must** not park your car there. = You **are not supposed to** park your car there. He **can** speak English well. = He **is able to** speak English well.	A modal can be used in passive voice: modal + *be* + past participle The following expressions are like modals in meaning: *have to, have got to, be able to, be supposed to, be allowed to, had better.*
British: We **shall** study modals. American: We **will** study modals.	For the future tense, *shall* is more common in British English than in American English. Americans sometimes use *shall* in a question to make a suggestion or invitation. *Shall we dance?*

Language Note:
Observe statements and questions with modals:
Affirmative: He *can* speak German.
Negative: He *can't* speak French.
Yes / No **Question:** *Can* he speak English?
Short Answers: Yes, ha *can.* / No, he *can't.*
Wh- **Question:** Why *can't* he speak French?
Subject Question: Who *can* speak French?

Grammar Variation

Elicit the nine modals at the top of the grammar chart from students; provide any modals that students do not provide. Write the modals on the board. Point to the modals at random; ask for a volunteer to provide a sentence about himself or herself using that modal. Ask students to say what they observe about the rules for modals. Assess students' performance; note areas of special difficulty for later in the lesson. Then review the grammar chart as a class.

SWEEPSTAKES OR SCAM?

Before You Read

1. Do you get a lot of junk mail?
2. What do you do with these pieces of mail?

Read the following article. Pay special attention to *might, may, have to, must, should, be supposed to,* and *ought to.*

Jack Goldman
123 Lucky Drive
Anytown, NY 01234

Congratulations

Congratulations, Jack Goldman.
You're a winner!
Choose your prize of *$25,000,*
a new car, or an exotic vacation.
You can't afford to miss this offer!
Simply call 800-555-5555 today!

Did you ever get a letter with your name printed on it telling you that you have won a prize or a large amount of money? Most people in the U.S. get these letters.

We often get mail from sweepstakes companies. A sweepstakes is like a lottery. To enter a sweepstakes, you usually **have to** mail a postcard. Even though the chances of winning are very small, many people enter because they have nothing to lose and **might** even win something.

Are these offers of prizes real? Some of them are. Why would someone give you a prize for doing nothing? A sweepstakes is a chance for a company to promote its products, such as magazines. But some of these offers **might** be deceptive,[1] and you **should** read the offer carefully. The government estimates that Americans lose more than one billion dollars every year through "scams," or tricks to take your money. You **should** be careful of letters, e-mails, and phone calls that tell you:

* You **must** act now or the offer will expire.
* You **may** already be a winner. To claim your gift, you only **have to** pay postage and handling.
* You've won! You **must** call a 900 number to claim your prize.
* You've won a free vacation. All you **have to** do is pay a service fee.

You **shouldn't** give out your credit card number or Social Security number if you are not sure who is contacting you about the sweepstakes.

Senior citizens **should** be especially careful of scams. Eighty percent of the victims of scams are 65 or older. They often think that they **have to** buy something in order to win a prize and often spend thousands of dollars on useless items. Or they think that their chances of winning **might** increase if they buy the company's product. But in a legitimate sweepstakes, you **don't have to** buy anything or send any money. The law states that "no purchase necessary" **must** appear in big letters. In addition, the company **is supposed to** tell you your chances of winning.

How can you avoid becoming the victim of a scam? If you receive a letter saying you are a guaranteed winner, you **ought to** read it carefully. Most people just throw this mail in the garbage.

[1]Something that is deceptive tries to make you believe something that is not true.

Modals—Present and Future; Related Expressions   139

Expansion

Theme The topic for this lesson can be enhanced with the following ideas:

1. Sweepstakes or other direct mail or junk mail solicitations
2. An article or story from the news about sweepstakes fraud
3. The Federal Citizen Information Center's Web site on scams and frauds, at: http://www.pueblo.gsa.gov/scamsdesc.htm

Reading Variation

To practice listening skills, have students first listen to the audio alone. Ask a few comprehension questions. Repeat the audio if necessary. Then have students open their books and read along as they listen to the audio.

Reading Glossary

legitimate: honest; legal; real
lottery: a contest of chance you can enter by buying a ticket
nothing to lose: without risk; no financial investment
promote: advertise; publicize

Sweepstakes or Scam? (Reading)

1. Have students look at the documents. Ask: *What are these? Who were they sent to?* (a sweepstakes letter and envelope; Jack Goldman) Have students look at the picture. Ask: *What is she doing? What is she thinking?* (opening a sweepstakes envelope; thinking that she might win a lot of money)
2. Have students look briefly at the reading. Ask: *What is the reading about? How do you know?* Have students make predictions.
3. Preteach any essential vocabulary words your students may not know, such as *lottery, nothing to lose, promote,* and *legitimate.*

BEFORE YOU READ

1. Have students discuss the questions in pairs. Try to pair students of different language backgrounds.
2. Ask for a few volunteers to share their answers with the class.

To save class time, skip "Before You Read" or have students prepare answers for homework ahead of time.

Reading CD 1, Track 25

1. Have students first read the text silently. Tell them to pay special attention to the modals in the reading. Then play the audio and have students read along silently.
2. Check students' comprehension. Ask questions such as: *What is a scam?* (a trick to take someone's money) *Which people are especially likely to be the victims of a scam?* (senior citizens—people 65 or older) *Name two things you should do if you receive a sweepstakes letter.* (Read it carefully. Throw it out.)

To save class time, have students do the reading for homework ahead of time.

4.2 | Possibilities—*May, Might, Could*

1. Have students look at the three examples in the first section of the grammar chart. For each example, ask: *Is this example about the past, the present, or the future?* (the present; the future; the present) Say: *We use* may, might, *and* could *to talk about possibilities in the present and in the future.*
2. Review the remaining examples and explanations as a class.
3. Draw students' attention to the last section of the chart. Provide several examples of sentences with *maybe* for students to convert to sentences with *may,* such as: *Maybe it's a scam. Maybe isn't true.* (It may be a scam. It may not be true.)

EXERCISE 1

🎧 **CD 1, Track 26**

1. Tell students that this exercise is a conversation between two friends about plans and possibilities. Have students read the direction line. Ask: *What do we write?* (appropriate verbs)
2. Model the exercise. Direct students to the example in the book. Then do #1 with the class.
3. Have students complete Exercise 1 individually. Then have them check their answers in pairs by practicing the dialogue. Circulate and observe the pair work. If necessary, check the answers as a class.
4. If necessary, review grammar chart **4.2.**

4.2 | Possibilities—*May, Might, Could*

Examples	Explanation
You **may** already be a winner. You **might** win a prize. This **could** be your lucky day!	Use *may, might, could* to show possibilities about the present or future.
She **may not** know that she is a winner. I **might not** come to class tomorrow.	For negative possibility, use *may not* or *might not.* Don't use *could not.* It means *was / were not able to.* Do not make a contraction with *may not* or *might not.*
Do you think I **might** win? **Do you think** I **could** get lucky?	To make questions about possibility with *may, might, could,* say, "Do you think . . . *may, might, could* . . .?" The clause after *Do you think* uses statement word order.
Compare: a. **Maybe** you are right. b. You **may be** right. a. **Maybe** he is a winner. b. He **may be** a winner.	*Maybe,* written as one word (a), is an adverb. It is usually put before the subject. *May be,* written as two words (b), is a modal + verb. The meaning of (a) and (b) is the same, but notice that the word order is different.

EXERCISE 1 Fill in the blanks with appropriate verbs to complete this conversation.

🎧

A: What are you going to do this summer?

B: I haven't decided yet. I might ___go___ back to Peru, or I may
(example)
___stay___ here and look for a summer job. What about you?
(1)

A: I'm not sure either. My brother might ___come___ here. If he
(2)
does, we might ___visit___ some interesting places in the U.S. I
(3)
received a letter a few days ago telling me that if I mail in a postcard,
I could ___win___ a trip for two to Hawaii.
(4)

B: I don't believe those letters. When I get those kinds of letters, I just throw them away.

A: How can you just throw them away? You could ___be___
(5)
a winner.

B: Who's going to give us a free trip to Hawaii for doing nothing?

Grammar Variation

Have students match the verbs in boldface in the reading on page 139 to the appropriate explanations in the grammar chart.

Exercise 1 Variation

To provide practice with listening skills, have students close their books and listen to the audio. Repeat the audio as needed. Ask comprehension questions, such as: *What did person A get in the mail a few days ago?* (a letter) *According to the letter, what happens if person A mails the postcard?* (could win a trip for two to Hawaii) *What does person B do with those kinds of letters?* (throws them away) Then have students open their books and complete Exercise 1.

Expansion

Exercise 1 Have students act out the conversation. Encourage actors to figure out and use the feelings appropriate for each actor (e.g., disdain, longing, or resignation).

A: Well, I suppose you're right. But someone has to win those prizes. It
could _____be_____ me. And if I buy a lot of magazines from this
   (6)
company, my chances of winning might _increase/get better/improve_.
                                                      (7)

B: That's not true. Those letters always say, "No Purchase Necessary."

A: I really want to go to Hawaii with my brother.

B: Then I suggest you work hard and save your money.

A: I might _____be_____ 90 years old by the time I have enough money.
     (8)

EXERCISE 2 Answer these questions by using the word in parentheses ( ).

EXAMPLE Is the company legitimate? (*might*)
It might be legitimate.

1. Does the company give out prizes? (*may*)
   It may give out prizes.
2. Are the prizes cheap? (*could*)
   They could be cheap.
3. Will I be chosen as a winner? (*might*)
   You might be chosen as a winner.
4. Will this company take my money and give me nothing? (*might*)
   It might take your money and give you nothing.
5. Will I win a trip? (*could*)
   You could win a trip.

EXERCISE 3 ABOUT YOU Fill in the blanks with possible results for the
following situations.

EXAMPLE If I pass this course, _I might take a computer course next semester._

1. If I don't pay my rent, _____Answers will vary._____
2. If I save a lot of money, _____
3. If I drink a lot of coffee tonight, _____
4. If I eat a lot of sugar, _____
5. If I drive too fast, _____
6. If I exercise regularly, _____
7. If I increase my computer skills, _____
8. If I win a lot of money, _____
9. If I come late to class, _____
10. If I don't do my homework, _____

Modals—Present and Future; Related Expressions   **141**

Expansion

Exercise 2 After students complete the exercise, say: *These questions have two possible
answers.* Model a longer answer with both possibilities, for example,
A: *Is the company legitimate?*
B: *It might be legitimate, or it might not be legitimate.*
Have students repeat the exercise using longer answers with two possibilities.

Exercise 3 Have students write their answers to one item on a card or piece of paper; tell
students that their answers will not be private. Collect the cards and read them to the class.
Have the class guess who wrote each sentence.

4.3 | Necessity and Urgency with *Must, Have To, Have Got To*

1. Have students cover up the grammar chart. Ask: *What does* necessity *mean?* (something that must be done) *What does* urgency *mean?* (something really important, in a hurry) *What does* obligation *mean?* (responsibility, something we don't have a choice about)
2. Provide examples with *must, have to,* and *have got to* (e.g., *I have to help my children with their homework tonight. Books must be checked out at the desk.*). Ask: *What differences have you observed between the way people use* must *and the way people use* have to? (*Must* is used on signs and in other official language; people usually use *have to* to talk about their own responsibilities.)
3. Have students uncover and review the examples and explanations in grammar chart **4.3**.
4. Draw students' attention to the Pronunciation Note; review the examples. Then have students read the earlier examples in grammar chart **4.3** aloud using the pronunciations shown in the note.

EXERCISE 4

1. Tell students that this exercise is about rules regarding sweepstakes companies. Have students read the direction line. Ask: *Is more than one answer possible?* (yes)
2. Direct students to the example. Ask: *What is the meaning of* obey? (follow) Complete #1 with the class.
3. Have students complete the exercise individually. Then have them check their answers in pairs. Check the answers as a class.

4.3 | Necessity and Urgency with *Must, Have To, Have Got To*

Modal	Explanation
Individuals and companies **must** (or **have to**) obey the law. Sweepstakes companies **must** (or **have to**) tell you the truth. "No Purchase Necessary" **must** (or **has to**) appear in big letters.	For legal obligation, use *must* and *have to*. *Must* has a very official tone. It is often used in court, in legal contracts (such as rental agreements) and in rules books.

You **must** act now! Don't wait or you will lose this fabulous offer!
 	
 You**'ve got to** act now!
 	
 You **have to** act now!
	Must, have to, and *have got to* express a sense of urgency. All three sentences to the left have the same meaning.
	
	 Have got to is usually contracted:
	     I have got to = I've got to
	     He has got to = He's got to

I**'ve got to** help my sister on Saturday. She **has to** study for a test.	Avoid using *must* for personal obligations. It sounds very official or urgent and is too strong for most situations. Use *have to* or *have got to*.

Pronunciation Note:
In fast, informal speech,
- *have to* is often pronounced "hafta."
- *has to* is pronounced "hafta."
- *have got to* is often pronounced "gotta." (*Have* is often not pronounced before "gotta.")

EXERCISE **4** Fill in the blanks with an appropriate verb to talk about sweepstakes rules. Answers may vary.

EXAMPLE Sweepstakes companies must ___*obey*___ the law.

1. Sweepstakes companies must ___*write*___ "No Purchase Necessary" in big letters in the information they send to you.
2. Sweepstakes companies sometimes tell people that they must ___*call*___ a 900 number to win a prize.
3. Sweepstakes companies often tell people, "You must ___*act/answer/reply/respond*___ now. Don't wait."
4. Companies must ___*tell*___ the truth about the conditions of the contest.
5. If a sweepstakes company tells you that you must ___*buy/purchase*___ something, it is not a legitimate sweepstakes.

142   Lesson 4

Grammar Variation

Have students cover the grammar chart. Dictate several sentences using the informal pronunciations shown in the Pronunciation Note, such as: *I gotta help my sister. She hasta study for a test.* Have students try to write what you say. Then have students uncover the chart and review the examples, the explanation, and the Pronunciation Note.

Culture Note

A 900 number is a telephone number which you must pay to call. An 800 or 888 number is toll-free; the person who calls does not have to pay for the call.

EXERCISE **5** Fill in the blanks with an appropriate verb (phrase) to talk about driving rules. Answers may vary.

EXAMPLE Drivers must ___stop___ at a red light.

1. A driver must ___have___ a license.
2. In a car, you must ___put___ a baby in a special car seat.
3. You must _pull over and stop / slow down_ when you hear a fire truck siren.
4. In many cities, drivers must ___put___ a city sticker on their windshields.
5. A car must ___display / have___ a license plate.

EXERCISE **6** ABOUT YOU Fill in the blanks with words that describe personal obligations. Answers may vary.

EXAMPLE I have to _call my parents_ once a week.

1. After class, I've got to _Answers will vary._
2. This weekend, I have to _____
3. Before the next class, we've got to _____
4. Every day I have to _____
5. Once a month, I've got to _____
6. When I'm not sure of the spelling of a word, I have to _____
7. Before I go to sleep at night, I have to _____
8. A few times a year, I've got to _____
9. My English isn't perfect. I have to _____
10. Before I take a test, I've got to _____

EXERCISE **7** ABOUT YOU Make a list of personal obligations you have to do on the weekends.

EXAMPLE _On Saturdays, I have to take my sister to ballet lessons._
Answers will vary.

Modals—Present and Future; Related Expressions 143

Expansion

Exercises 6 and 7 Have students write and present examples of obligations they have, listing the reasons they have them, such as: *I have to take medicine because my cholesterol is too high. I have to study a lot because English isn't easy for me.*

EXERCISE 8

1. Tell students that this exercise is about their personal obligations at work, at school, and/or at home. Have students read the direction line. Ask: *What modals do we use?* (*have to, have got to*)
2. Model the exercise. Direct students to the example in the book. Provide an example of your own; then ask volunteers to provide examples of their own.
3. Have students complete the exercise individually. Then have volunteers share their answers with the class.
4. Assess students' performance. If necessary, review grammar chart 4.3 on page 142.

🕐 To save class time, have students do half of the exercise in class and complete the other half for homework. Or assign the entire exercise for homework.

4.4 | Obligation with *Must* or *Be Supposed To*

1. Ask students to cover grammar chart 4.4. Say the four sentences in the second section of the chart aloud. After each sentence, ask: *Who do you think is saying this?* Elicit the difference between *must* (an official requirement) and *be supposed to* (a reminder).
2. Have students uncover and review the grammar chart. Point out the use of *supposed to* when a rule or law is broken.
3. Draw students' attention to the Pronunciation Note. Have students practice saying the examples in the grammar chart without pronouncing the *-d* in *supposed to*.

EXERCISE **8** ABOUT YOU Make a list of obligations you have at your job, at your school, or in your house.

EXAMPLE *At work, I've got to answer the phone and fill out orders.*

Answers will vary.

_____

_____

_____

_____

4.4 | Obligation with *Must* or *Be Supposed To*

Examples	Explanation
"No Purchase Necessary" **must** appear in big letters. This is the law.	*Must* has an official tone.
The sweepstakes company **must** tell you your chances of winning.	
People who win money **must** pay taxes on their winnings.	
Compare: a. Police officer to driver: "You **must** wear your seat belt." b. Driver to passenger: "You're **supposed to** wear your seat belt." a. Teacher to student: "You **must** write your composition with a pen." b. Student to student: "You **are supposed to** write your composition with a pen."	a. A person in a position of authority (such as a police officer, parent, or teacher) can use *must*. The tone is very official. b. Avoid using *must* if you are not in a position of authority. Use *be supposed to* to remind someone of a rule.
Companies **are supposed to** follow the law, but some of them don't. Drivers **are supposed to** use a seat belt, but they sometimes don't. Students **are supposed to** be quiet in the library, but some talk.	*Be supposed to*, not *must*, is used when reporting on a law or rule that is broken.
Pronunciation Note: The *d* in *supposed to* is not pronounced.	

144 Lesson 4

Grammar Variation

Tell students three things students or staff at your school are supposed to do (e.g., *Teachers are supposed to park in the back. Students are supposed to pay 25 cents for a cup of coffee,* etc.). Ask: *Does everyone follow these rules?* (no) Ask students to name some other rules that are sometimes broken.

EXERCISE 9 A teenager is talking about rules his parents gave him and his sister. Fill in the blanks with *be supposed to* + an appropriate verb.

EXAMPLE I *'m supposed to babysit* for my little sister when my parents aren't home.

1. I *'m supposed to do/finish* my homework before I watch TV.
2. I (not) *'m not supposed to talk* on the phone with my friends for more than 30 minutes.
3. I *'m supposed to clean* my room once a week. My mother gets mad when I leave it dirty.
4. If I go to a friend's house, I *'m supposed to tell* my parents where I am so they won't worry.
5. I have a part-time job. I *'m supposed to put* some of my money in the bank. I (not) *'m not supposed to spend* my money on foolish things.
6. I *'m supposed to help* my parents with jobs around the house. For example, I *'m supposed to wash* the dishes once a week. I *'m supposed to take out* the garbage every day.
7. My sister *is supposed to put* her toys away when she's finished playing.
8. She (not) *'s not supposed to touch* the stove.
9. She (not) *'m not supposed to watch* TV after 8 p.m.
10. She *'s supposed to go* to bed at 8:30.

EXERCISE 10 ABOUT YOU Report some rules in one of the following places: in your apartment, in court, in traffic, in a library, in class, on an airplane, or in the airport.

EXAMPLES *In my apartment, the landlord is supposed to provide heat in the winter.*

I'm supposed to pay my rent by the fifth of the month.

_____ Answers will vary. _____

_____

_____

_____

_____

Modals—Present and Future; Related Expressions   **145**

Expansion

Exercise 9 Ask students how the obligations this teenager has compare to the obligations they had as teenagers at home or the obligations they have now.

1. Tell students that this exercise is about children's obligations at home. Have students read the direction line. Ask: *Who is talking in this exercise?* (a teenager)
2. Model the exercise. Direct students to the example in the book. Then do #1 with the class.
3. Have students complete the rest of Exercise 9 individually. Then have them check their answers in pairs. Circulate and observe the pair work. If necessary, check the answers as a class.

EXERCISE 10

1. Tell students that this exercise is about rules at different places in the community. Have students read the direction line.
2. Direct students to the examples in the book. If necessary, review the difference between habit (*usually* + simple present) and obligation (*be supposed to*).
3. Have students complete the exercise individually. Ask volunteers to share their answers with a partner; then have students share their partners' answers with the class.

To save class time, have students do half of the exercise in class and complete the other half for homework. Or assign the entire exercise for homework.

1. Tell students that this exercise is about obligations that we forget or ignore. Ask: *Do you ever forget or decide not to do something you're supposed to do? Why or why not?* Then have students read the direction line.
2. Review the example with the class. Ask students if these ever happen at their homes.
3. Have students write their answers individually. Then have students tell a partner about their answers. Ask volunteers to share their answers with the class.
4. Assess students' performance on Exercises 10 and 11. If necessary, review grammar chart **4.4** on page 144.

🕐 To save class time, have students do half of the exercise in class and complete the other half for homework. Or assign the entire exercise for homework.

4.5 | Advice with *Should, Ought To,* and *Had Better*

1. Have students cover the grammar chart. Ask: *What modal do we use to tell people that something is a good idea, or that something isn't a good idea?* (*should* or *shouldn't*) Give a few examples of your own (*I should get more exercise. People shouldn't give out their Social Security numbers.*). Elicit a few examples from students; write several examples on the board. Ask: *What other words mean the same thing as* should? Elicit or present *ought to* and *had better.* Say: *If something is a good idea, we can say that it's advisable.*
2. Have students uncover and review the grammar chart. Point out the use of contractions (*shouldn't; 'd better*).
3. Draw students' attention to the pronunciation suggestions for *ought to* and *'d better* (e.g., *you better, we better*). Have students practice saying the examples in the grammar chart with the reduced pronunciation of *ought to* and without the *-d* in *'d better.*

EXERCISE **11** ABOUT YOU Tell about an obligation you or a member of your family has that is often not done.

EXAMPLE *My sister is supposed to finish her homework before watching TV,*

but she usually watches TV as soon as she gets home from school.

I'm supposed to wash the dishes in my house, but I often leave them

in the sink for the next day.

_____ Answers will vary. _____

4.5 | Advice with *Should, Ought To,* and *Had Better*

Examples	Explanation
Senior citizens **should** be careful of scams.	*Should* shows advisability. It is used to say that something is a good idea.
You **should** read the offer carefully to see what the conditions are.	
You **shouldn't** give your credit card number to people you don't know.	*Shouldn't* means that something is a bad idea. The action is not advisable.
You **shouldn't** believe every offer that comes in the mail.	
If you receive a letter saying you are a winner, you **ought to** throw it away.	*Ought to* has the same meaning as *should.* Ought is the only modal followed by *to.*
You **ought to** work hard and save your money. Don't expect to get rich from a sweepstakes.	Don't use *ought to* for negatives and questions. Use *should.*
You **ought to** turn off the TV and do your homework.	*Ought to* is pronounced /ɔtə/.
I'm expecting an important phone call. I**'d better** leave my cell phone on so I won't miss it.	*Had better (not)* is used in conversation to show caution or give a warning. A negative consequence may result.
You**'d better not** give your credit card number to strange callers, or they might use it to make purchases in your name.	Use *'d* to contract *had* with a pronoun. In some fast speech, *'d* is omitted completely.
Compare: a. Companies and individuals **must** obey the law. b. You **should** read the letter carefully.	a. Use *must* for rules, laws, and urgent situations. b. Use *should* for advice.

Expansion

Exercises 10 and 11 Have students use the examples in Exercise 11 to write several examples of things people are supposed to do, but don't always do, in one of the locations listed in Exercise 10.

EXERCISE **12** Give advice to people who are saying the following.

EXAMPLES   I'm lonely. I don't have any friends.

You should get a dog or a cat for companionship.

I'm so tired. I've been working hard all day.

You ought to get some rest.

1. I've had a headache all day.

Answers will vary.

2. The teacher wrote something on my paper, but I can't read it.

3. Every time I write a composition and the teacher finds mistakes, I have to write it all over again.

4. I got a letter telling me that I won a million dollars.

5. My old TV doesn't work well anymore. It's too expensive to repair.

6. I received an offer for a new job. It pays double what I get now.

7. My car is making a strange noise. I wonder what it is.

8. I sit at a desk all day. I don't get enough exercise. I'm gaining weight.

9. Whenever I tell my personal problems to my coworker, he tells other people.

10. I have to write a résumé, but I don't have any experience with this.

Modals—Present and Future; Related Expressions   147

Expansion

Exercise 12 After pairs perform their conversations for the class, have students write about several of them (e.g., *Gina's car is making a strange noise. She should take it to a mechanic.*).

EXERCISE 12

1. Tell students that this exercise is about giving advice. Have students read the direction line. Ask: *Which modals do we use?* (*should, shouldn't, ought to, 'd better, 'd better not*)
2. Model the exercise. Direct students to the examples. Elicit several different responses to the cues.
3. Before students begin the exercise, have them read the items. Encourage students to make notes as they read. Then have students complete the exercise in pairs, alternating giving cues and giving advice. Finally, ask pairs to perform one of the items for the class.

EXERCISE 13

1. Tell students that this exercise is about customs and good manners in their native cultures. Ask: *What does* social situation *mean?* (any situation where people interact—in public, in the workplace, in someone's home, etc.) Have students read the direction line. Ask: *Which modal do we use?* (should/shouldn't)

2. Direct students to the example in the book. Say: *This is good advice in the U.S. Is this good advice in your country?* Elicit several other responses from the class.

3. Give students a few minutes to read through and think about the situations. Then complete the exercise as a class. If students are surprised by or interested in their classmates' responses, encourage questions (*What is a good gift to bring?*) or comments (*Really? In my culture, you should . . .*).

🕐 To save class time, have students do half of the exercise in class and complete the other half for homework. Or assign the entire exercise for homework.

EXERCISE 14

1. Tell students that this exercise is a series of conversations between friends. Have students read the direction line. Ask: *Which modal do we use?* ('d better, 'd better not)

2. Model the exercise. Direct students to the example in the book. Then do #1 with the class.

3. Have students complete Exercise 14 individually. Then have them check their answers in pairs by practicing the dialogues. Try to pair students from different countries. Circulate and observe the pair work. If necessary, check the answers as a class.

4. Assess students' performance. If necessary, review grammar chart **4.5.**

🕐 To save class time, have students do half of the exercise in class and complete the other half for homework. Or assign the entire exercise for homework.

EXERCISE 13 ABOUT YOU Give advice about what people should do or say in the following social situations in your native culture. Share your answers with the class.

EXAMPLE If you are invited to someone's house for dinner, _you should bring a small gift._

1. If you invite a friend to eat in a restaurant, _____

2. If you bump into someone, _____

3. If you don't hear or understand what someone says, _____

4. If someone asks, "How are you?" _____

5. If you want to leave the dinner table while others are still eating, _____

6. If a woman with a small child gets on a crowded bus, _____

7. If you're invited to someone's house for dinner, _____

8. If you meet someone for the first time, _____

EXERCISE 14 Give a warning by using *you'd better (not)* in the following conversations.

EXAMPLE A: Someone's at the door. I'll go and open it.
B: You _'d better not open it_ if you don't know who it is.

1. A: The caller wants my Social Security number.
   B: Do you know who the caller is?
   A: No.
   B: You _'d better not give_ him your Social Security number then.

Expansion

Exercise 13 Have students complete the advice again in writing, in class or as homework. Collect for assessment.

2. A: I got a letter about a sweepstakes. Do you think I should enter?

   B: You've probably got nothing to lose. But you _'d better read_ the letter carefully to make sure that it's legitimate.

3. A: This offer says the deadline for applying is Friday.

   B: You _'d better hurry_ . You don't have much time.

4. *(phone conversation)*

   A: Hello?

   B: Hello. I'd like to speak with Mrs. Green.

   A: Speaking.

   B: You are a winner! You _'d better hurry_ or you might lose this offer. You don't have much time.

   A: You keep calling me and telling me the same thing. You _'d better stop calling me_ , or I'll report you.

5. A: You are the only person in the office who wears jeans.

   B: What's wrong with that?

   A: You _'d better dress_ appropriately, or you might lose your job.

6. A: I don't like my supervisor's attitude. I'm going to tell her about it.

   B: You _'d better not tell her_ . She might not like it.

7. A: I typed my composition on the computer, but I forgot to bring a disk to save it. I'll just print it.

   B: Here. Use my disk. You _'d better save it_ in case you have to revise it.

8. *(a driver and a passenger in a car)*

   A: I'm getting sleepy. Can you drive for a while?

   B: I can't. I don't have my driver's license yet. You _'d better stop and rest_ for a while.

Expansion

Exercise 14 Have students work in pairs to write their own conversations and advice similar to those in Exercise 14. Have volunteers perform their conversations for the class.

Culture Note

Cultures vary in standards for who may give advice to whom, and for who may confront whom. A worker who is having trouble with a supervisor usually goes through official channels (complaint or grievance procedures). Students may be interested in hearing each others' responses to #6 in Exercise 14.

Telemarketing (Reading)

1. Have students look at the photo. Ask: *Where is this woman? How does she feel? Why?*
2. Have students look briefly at the reading. Have students look at the title of the reading. Ask: *What is the reading about? How do you know?* Have students make predictions.
3. Preteach any vocabulary items your students may not know, such as *registry, charities, go into effect, in the meantime,* and *screens.*

BEFORE YOU READ

1. Activate students' prior knowledge about telemarketing and telemarketing laws. Ask: *What is telemarketing?* (phone calls trying to sell you something) *How do you feel about these calls? Is there anything you can do about them?* (sign up for the Do-Not-Call registry)
2. Have students discuss the questions in pairs. Try to pair students of different language backgrounds.
3. Ask a few volunteers to share their answers with the class.

Reading 🎧 CD 1, Track 27

1. Have students first read the text silently. Tell them to pay special attention to *may, can, be permitted to, be allowed to,* and other modals. Then play the audio and have students read along silently.
2. Check students' comprehension. Ask questions such as: *What is the Do-Not-Call registry?* (a list of people who do not want to be called by telemarketers) *Who can still call you, even if you sign up for the registry?* (political organization, charities, and companies with which you do business)
3. Brainstorm a list of polite ways to say no to telemarketers (*I'm sorry; I don't do any business over the phone.*).

DID YOU KNOW ?

The U.S. government has a number of services designed to help consumers protect themselves from unwanted solicitations. One resource is at http://www.pueblo.gsa.gov/cfocus/cfprivacy02/focus.htm

---

TELEMARKETING

Before You Read

1. Do you ever get calls from people who are trying to sell you something?
2. How do you respond to these calls?

 Read the following article. Pay special attention to *may, can, be permitted to, be allowed to,* and other modals.

You have just sat down to dinner when, suddenly, the phone rings. Someone is trying to sell you a magazine, a long-distance phone service, or a vacation. Has this ever happened to you?

Salespeople place about 100 million calls a year. They use an automatic dialer to call hundreds of homes at the same time. Some of these calls might offer you a better long-distance telephone service or let you know about a special rate for cable or DSL service. But sometimes these calls can be very annoying. Now there is something you can do about it.

In 2003, the U.S. government[2] created a "Do Not Call" registry. You can register your phone number online or by phone. If you do so, most telemarketers **are not permitted to** call you for five years. However, some telemarketers **can** still call you: political organizations and charities. Also, companies with which you do business, such as your bank, **may** call you to offer you a new product or service. However, when they call, you can ask them not to call you again. If you make this request, they **are not allowed to** call you again.

You **can** register up to three numbers on the "Do Not Call" national registry, including your cell phone number. It may take three months before the "do not call" order goes into effect. In the meantime, here are some suggestions for dealing with telemarketers:

- You could get a Caller ID to see who is calling. (About 40% of households have them.)
- You could ask your phone company if they have a "privacy manager," a service that screens unidentified phone calls. The phone will not even ring in your house unless the caller identifies himself.
- If you are not interested in the offer, you can try to end the phone call quickly. But you shouldn't get angry at the caller. He or she is just trying to make a living.
- If you do decide to buy a product or service, remember, you should never give out your credit card number if you are not sure who the caller is.

[2] The Federal Trade Commission (FTC) is the government department that created this registry.

Did You Know?
Many telemarketing calls you receive come from call centers in India, Mexico, and other countries, where callers are paid much less than in the U.S.

150   Lesson 4

Expansion

Theme The topic for this lesson can be enhanced with the following ideas:

1. The national Do-Not-Call registry's home page at: https://www.donotcall.gov/default.aspx
2. A flyer or mailing from a phone company showing services offered, e.g., privacy screening or caller ID

Reading Variation

To practice listening skills, have students first listen to the audio alone. Ask a few comprehension questions. Repeat the audio if necessary. Then have students open their books and read along as they listen to the audio.

Reading Glossary

charity: an organization, supported by donations, that helps people, animals, etc.
go into effect: start working; become a rule or the law
in the meantime: while you are waiting
registry: list you can sign up for (ask to be on)
screen: identify phone numbers, or listen to calls on an answering machine, before you answer them

4.6 | Permission and Prohibition

Examples	Explanation
Political organizations **may** call you. (They **are permitted to** call you.) Charities **can** call you. (They **are allowed to** call you.)	Use *may* or *can* to show that something is permitted. Alternate forms are *be allowed to* and *be permitted to*.
If you put your phone number on a "Do Not Call" registry, companies **may not** call you for five years. If you ask a company to stop calling you, this company **cannot** call you again.	Use *may not* or *cannot* (*can't*) to show that something is prohibited. *Cannot* is written as one word. *May not* has no contraction form.
You **can** wear jeans to class. We **can** call our teacher by his first name.	In addition to legal permission, *can* also has the meaning of social acceptability.

Language Note:
The meaning of *cannot* or *may not* (not permitted) is very similar to the meaning of *must not* (prohibited).
Compare:

   a. You *can't* talk during a test.
   b. You *may not* talk during a test.
   c. You *must not* talk during a test.

   a. You *can't* bring food into the computer lab.
   b. You *may not* bring food into the computer lab.
   c. You *must not* bring food into the computer lab.

EXERCISE 15   Fill in the blanks to talk about what is and isn't permitted.

EXAMPLE   We can _____*talk*_____ in the hall, but we can't _____*talk*_____ in the library.

1. If you put your name on a "Do Not Call" registry, companies may

   not _____ Answers will vary. _____.

2. In the library, you may not _____.

3. During a test, we can _____ but we cannot

   _____.

4. Books, CDs, and DVDs are protected by law. We are not permitted

   to _____.

5. In this building, we may not _____.

Modals—Present and Future; Related Expressions   151

4.6 | Permission and Prohibition

1. Have students cover up the grammar chart. Ask: *What does* permission *mean?* (being allowed to do something; having the OK) *What does* prohibition *mean?* (not being allowed to do something; being told *no*)

2. Have students cover the grammar chart. Elicit from students sentences about things telemarketers can and can't do, such as *Telemarketers can't call you if you are on the Do-Not-Call registry. Charities can still call you.* Write the sentences on the board.

3. Have students uncover the grammar chart; review the examples and explanations. Ask: *What is* can't? (contraction for *cannot*) *When do we use* can't *instead of* cannot? (*can't* is more informal)

4. Draw students' attention to the Language Note. Ask: *Which one sounds the most formal?* (*must not*) *Which one sounds the most informal?* (*can't*)

EXERCISE 15

1. Tell students that this exercise is about rules and laws. Have students read the direction line.

2. Direct students to the example in the book. Review the example, and then ask a volunteer to complete #1.

3. Have students complete the exercise individually and then check their work in pairs. Review the answers as a class.

Grammar Variation

After students have reviewed the example sentences in the grammar chart, have them go back to the reading on page 150 and identify which explanation applies to each of the words or phrases in bold in the reading.

EXERCISE 16

1. Tell students that this exercise is about rules and laws in their native countries. Have students read the direction line. Ask: *What words do we use?* (*may, can, can't, may not, permitted to, not permitted to*)
2. Direct students to the examples in the book. Review the examples, and then ask a volunteer to answer #1.
3. Have students complete the exercise and then compare their answers in pairs. Try to pair students from different countries. Circulate and observe the pair work. If possible, participate in the exercise as you circulate. Have volunteers share their answers with the class.

🕐 To save class time, have students do half of the exercise in class and complete the other half for homework. Or assign the entire exercise for homework.

EXERCISE 16 ABOUT YOU Fill in the blanks with an appropriate permission word to talk about what is or isn't permitted in your native country.

EXAMPLES A man _____*isn't permitted*_____ to have more than one wife.

Teachers _____*can*_____ talk about religion in public schools.

1. People _____Answers will vary._____ own a gun.

2. People under 18 _____ get married.

3. Children _____ work.

4. Children _____ see any movie they want.

5. A man _____ have more than one wife.

6. A married woman _____ get a passport without her husband's permission.

7. Teachers _____ talk about religion in public schools.

8. Teachers _____ hit children.

9. People _____ travel freely.

10. People _____ live anywhere they want.

Expansion

Exercise 16 When students have completed the exercise, have the class compile the results into a graph, with columns showing the number of countries in which each action is and is not permitted.

EXERCISE **17** Write about what is or isn't permitted in these places. Use *can*, *may*, *be allowed to*, or *be permitted to*.

EXAMPLES In the U.S., _____*children may sue their parents.*_____

In a theater, _____*you can't yell "fire."*_____

1. In the U.S., _____Answers will vary._____

2. In the computer lab, _____

3. In this classroom, _____

4. In a courtroom, _____

5. In my house / apartment building, _____

6. In an airplane, _____

7. In an airport, _____

8. In this city, _____

EXERCISE **18** ABOUT YOU Tell if these things are socially acceptable in your country or native culture.

EXAMPLES Students can call their teachers by their first names.
In my country, students can't call their teachers by their first names. It's very impolite.

Answers will vary.

1. Parents can take small children to a party for adults.

2. If you are invited to a party, you can invite your friends.

3. Students can wear jeans to class.

4. Students can use a cell phone in class.

5. Students can remain seated when the teacher enters the room.

6. Students can call their teachers by their first names.

7. Students can talk to each other during a test.

8. Students can argue with a teacher about a grade.

9. Men and women can kiss in public.

10. Men and women can hold hands in public.

1. Tell students that this exercise is about things we are and aren't permitted to do. Have students read the direction line.
2. Direct students to the examples in the book. Elicit several other responses from the class.
3. Have students complete the exercise in writing individually. Ask volunteers to share their answers with the class.

To save class time, have students do half of the exercise in class and complete the other half for homework. Or assign the entire exercise for homework.

1. Tell students that this exercise is about customs in their native countries. Have students read the direction line. Ask: *What does* socially acceptable *mean?* (something that is generally OK to do; polite behavior.)
2. Direct students to the example in the book. Elicit several other responses from the class. Then have volunteers complete #1.
3. Have students read the items. Then have them work in pairs to tell a partner about their countries. Try to pair students from different countries. Circulate and observe the pair work. Have partners share information about each other's countries with the class.
4. Assess students' performance. If necessary, review grammar chart **4.6** on page 151.

To save class time, have students do half of the exercise in class and complete the other half in writing for homework. Or if students do not need speaking practice, the entire exercise may be skipped or done in writing.

Expansion

Exercise 18 Have students give their own examples of things that are socially acceptable in their countries, and things that are not.

Exercise 18 Have students ask each other questions about the items, such as: *In your country, can employees argue with supervisors?*

Culture Note

Talk about the difference between socially acceptable actions governed by law (Men can't have more than one wife.) and those governed by custom (Men and women can't hold hands in public.).

4.7 | Comparing Negative Modals

1. Have students cover grammar chart **4.7.** Write the negative modals (*must not, be not supposed to, cannot, may not, shouldn't, 'd better not, don't have to*) on the board. Read the meanings in grammar chart **4.7** in random order; ask students to match them with a modal, e.g., *Which one means it's a bad idea? (shouldn't)*
2. Have students uncover the chart and review the examples and explanations carefully.
3. Review the chart again. For each section, ask volunteers to provide a sentence (e.g.,*You must not let small children ride in the front seat of a car.*).
4. Draw students' attention to the Language Note. Point out the difference in meaning between *don't have to* and *must not*. Provide additional examples (e.g.,*You must not eat on the subway. We don't have to take the subway; we can walk.*).

4.7 | Comparing Negative Modals

Examples	Explanation
You **must not** talk during the test. You **must not** bring food into the computer lab. If you are involved in a traffic accident, you **must not** leave.	It's prohibited. You have no choice in the matter. *Must not* has an official tone.
You **are not supposed to** talk during the test. You **are not supposed to** bring food into the lab. Shh! You**'re not supposed to** talk in the library.	*Be supposed to* is used as a reminder of a rule. It has an unofficial tone. Often the rule has already been broken.
Telemarketers **cannot** call you if you place your phone number on a "do not call" list. Telemarketers **may not** call you if you ask them to take you off their list.	It's prohibited. The meaning is similar to *must not*.
You **shouldn't** give strange callers your credit card number. You **shouldn't** buy products that you don't need.	It's a bad idea. This is advice.
You**'d better not** arrive late for the exam, or you won't have time to finish it. You**'d better not** call your friend late at night. She might be asleep. You might wake her up.	This is a warning. A negative consequence is stated or implied.
a. You **don't have to** buy magazines to enter a sweepstakes. b. I **don't have to** work on Saturday. It's my day off. c. We **don't have to** type our compositions. We can write them by hand.	a. It's not necessary. It is your choice to do it or not. b. It is not required. c. There are other choices or options.

Language Note:
Even though *must* and *have to* are similar in meaning in affirmative statements, they are completely different in meaning in negative statements.
  You *must* obey the law. = You *have to* obey the law.
  You *must not* talk during the test. = This is prohibited.
  You *don't have to* use a pen for the the test. = It is not necessary, You have a choice. You can use a pencil.

Grammar Variation

Have students cover the left column of grammar chart **4.7.** Read the examples from the left column in random order. Have students say which explanation each example goes with. Then review the grammar chart as a class as above.

EXERCISE **19** ABOUT YOU Tell if students in this school or another school you have attended have to or don't have to do the following.

EXAMPLES wear a uniform
Students in my school don't have to wear a uniform.

take final exams
Students in my school have to take final exams.

Answers will vary.
1. stand up to answer a question
2. go to the chalkboard to answer a question
3. call the teacher by his or her title (for example, "Professor")
4. buy their own textbooks
5. pay tuition
6. attend classes every day
7. have a written excuse for an absence
8. get permission to leave the classroom
9. study a foreign language
10. attend graduation

EXERCISE **20** ABOUT YOU Tell if you have to or don't have to do the following.

EXAMPLES work on Saturdays
I have to work on Saturdays.

wear a suit to work
I don't have to wear a suit to work.

Answers will vary.
1. pay rent on the first of the month
2. study English
3. get up early on Sundays
4. cook every day
5. wear formal clothes (a suit, a dress, a uniform) to work / school
6. come to school on Saturdays

Modals—Present and Future; Related Expressions **155**

EXERCISE 19

1. Tell students that this exercise is about rules at school. Have students read the direction line. Ask: *What modals do we use?* (*have to* and *don't have to*)
2. Direct students to the examples in the book. Then have a volunteer complete #1. Point out that students should use examples in the present time.
3. Have students complete the exercise by telling their information to a partner. Check answers as a class.

EXERCISE 20

1. Tell students that this exercise is about obligations. Have students read the direction line.
2. Model the exercise. Direct students to the examples. Elicit additional responses to the cues.
3. Ask for volunteers to respond to each cue. For students who use *don't have to*, ask for an explanation (e.g., *I don't have to cook every day because my mother cooks sometimes.*).

To save class time, have students do half of the exercise in class and complete the other half in writing for homework. Or if students do not need speaking practice, the entire exercise may be skipped or done in writing.

Expansion

Exercise 20 Have students work in groups. Have each group write a report of how many people in the group have to and don't have to do each item. Have groups compare results.

1. Tell students that this exercise is about the difference between prohibition and having a choice. Have students read the direction line. Ask: *What do we write?* (*don't have to* or *must not*)
2. Model the exercise. Direct students to the example in the book. Then complete #1 with the class.
3. Have students complete Exercise 21 individually. Then have them check their answers in pairs. Circulate and observe the pair work. If necessary, check the answers as a class.

🕐 To save class time, have students do half of the exercise in class and complete the other half for homework. Or assign the entire exercise for homework.

1. Tell students that this exercise is about the public library. Have students read the direction line.
2. Model the exercise. Direct students to the examples in the book. Then do #1 with the class.
3. Have students complete the rest of the exercise individually. Have them check their answers in pairs. If necessary, check answers as a class.
4. Assess students' performance. If necessary, review grammar chart **4.7** on page 154.

🕐 To save class time, have students do half of the exercise in class and complete the other half for homework. Or assign the entire exercise for homework.

EXERCISE **21** Fill in the blanks with *don't have to* or *must not*.

EXAMPLE   If you receive a sweepstakes postcard, you _don't have to_ send it back.

1. You _don't have to_ buy anything to win. No purchase is necessary.
2. Sweepstakes companies _must not_ break the law.
3. In a legitimate sweepstakes, you _don't have to_ call a 900 number to win a prize.
4. Passengers on an airplane _must not_ use a computer while the plane is taking off and landing.
5. Passengers on an airplane _must not_ carry a weapon.
6. Passengers on an airplane _must not_ walk around when the airplane is taking off or landing.
7. Passengers on an airplane _don't have to_ wear their seat belt after the seat belt sign is turned off.
8. Students _must not_ copy answers from each other during a test.
9. The students in this class _don't have to_ bring their dictionaries to class.
10. Teachers _don't have to_ teach in the summer if they don't want to.
11. Teachers in American schools _must not_ hit children. It is prohibited.

EXERCISE **22** Fill in the blanks with *don't have to* or *must not* to describe situations in a public library.

EXAMPLES   You _must not_ write in a library book.

You _don't have to_ know the name of the author to find a book. You can find the book by the title.

1. You _don't have to_ wait until the due date to return a book. You can return it earlier.
2. You _don't have to_ return your books to the circulation desk. You can leave them in the book drop.
3. You _don't have to_ study in the library. You can study at home.
4. You _must not_ eat in the library.
5. You _must not_ tear a page out of a book.
6. You _must not_ make noise in the library.

Expansion

Exercise 22 Have students identify one or more locations in their community (e.g., a hospital or clinic, the Social Security office, their children's school, etc.) and write statements with *don't have to* and *must not* for them.

EXERCISE **23** ABOUT YOU Work with a partner. Use *be (not) supposed to* to write a list of rules the teacher has for this class. Use affirmative and negative statements.

EXAMPLES *We're not supposed to use our books during a test.*

We're supposed to write five compositions this semester.

<u>Answers will vary.</u>

_____

_____

_____

_____

_____

EXERCISE **24** Write a list of driving rules. Use *must not* or *can't.* (Use *you* in the impersonal sense.)

EXAMPLE *You must not pass a car when you're going up a hill.*

<u>Answers will vary.</u>

_____

_____

_____

_____

EXERCISE **25** Circle the correct words to complete these sentences.

EXAMPLES We (shouldn't, don't have to) talk loudly in the library.

We (shouldn't, don't have to) bring our dictionaries to class.

1. The teacher says we (can't, don't have to) use our books during a test.

2. The teacher says we (shouldn't, don't have to) sit in a specific seat in class. We can sit wherever we want.

3. We (can't, don't have to) talk to each other during a test. It's not permitted.

4. We (must not, don't have to) type our compositions. We can write them by hand.

Expansion

Exercise 23 Have students work in groups to make a poster of class or classroom rules. If possible, have groups type and post their lists.

Exercise 24 If students disagree or are unsure about driving rules in Exercise 24, assign students to research the rules outside of class, using the Internet, public library, or state or local driving authority.

1. Tell students that this exercise is about the rules in their classroom. Have students read the direction line.
2. Model the exercise. Direct students to the examples in the book. Elicit one or two additional examples.
3. Have students complete the exercise in pairs. Circulate to observe pair work. Have pairs volunteer to share their statements with the class.

1. Tell students that this exercise is about driving rules. Have students read the direction line. Ask: *What does* you *mean in driving rules?* (The impersonal *you* means *everyone* or *people*.)
2. Direct students to the example. Elicit one or two additional rules from the class.
3. Have students complete the exercise individually, and then share their answers with the class.

To save class time, have students do half of the exercise in class and complete the other half for homework. Or assign the entire exercise for homework.

1. Tell students that this exercise is about the difference between negative modals. Have students read the direction line. Ask: *What do we do?* (circle one of the choices)
2. Direct students to the examples in the book; then complete #1 with the class.
3. Have students complete the rest of the exercise individually. Then have them check their answers in pairs. Circulate and observe the pair work. If necessary, check the answers as a class.
4. Assess students' performance. If necessary, review grammar chart 4.7.

To save class time, have students do half of the exercise in class and complete the other half for homework. Or assign the entire exercise for homework.

5. We (shouldn't, can't) speak our native language in class. It's not a good idea.

6. We (don't have to, aren't supposed to) come back after the final exam, but we can in order to pick up our tests.

7. Parents often tell children, "You (shouldn't, don't have to) talk to strangers."

8. Parents (aren't supposed to, don't have to) send their kids to public schools. They can send them to private schools.

9. Teachers (aren't supposed to, don't have to) teach summer school if they don't want to.

10. English teachers (shouldn't, don't have to) talk fast to foreign students.

11. A driver who is involved in an accident must report it to the police. He (must not, doesn't have to) leave the scene of the accident.

12. I'm warning you. You (don't have to, 'd better not) spend so much time talking to your co-workers, or you might lose your job.

13. Drivers (don't have to, must not) go through red lights.

14. You (shouldn't, don't have to) make noise and disturb your neighbors.

15. Most American students (don't have to, had better not) study a foreign language in college. They have a choice.

16. I have a test tomorrow morning. I ('d better not, must not) stay out late tonight, or I won't be alert in the morning.

17. Some students (shouldn't, don't have to) pay tuition because they have a scholarship.

18. You (may not, don't have to) bring food into the computer lab. It's against the rules.

19. You (shouldn't, may not) talk on a cell phone while driving. Even though it's permitted, it's not a good idea.

20. You (don't have to, shouldn't) leave your cell phone on in class. It might disturb the class.

21. Those students are talking in the library. They should be quiet. They (must not, are not supposed to) talk in the library.

Culture Note

Many public places have signs asking people to turn off cell phones and other electronic devices. Ask students where they have seen these signs (doctors' offices, movie theaters, etc.). Review the language used in these signs. Ask students to make note of the language on signs about electronic devices to bring to class.

EXERCISE 26 Fill in the blanks to make true statements.

EXAMPLE I don't have to _make an appointment to see the teacher_.

1. In this class, we aren't supposed to ____ Answers will vary. ____.
2. In this class, we don't have to ____.
3. The teacher doesn't have to ____, but he / she does it anyway.
4. In this building, we must not ____.
5. You'd better not ____, or the teacher will get angry.
6. We're going to have a test next week, so you'd better ____ the night before.
7. When another student doesn't know the answer, you shouldn't ____. You should let him try to find it himself.
8. You can't ____ in the computer lab. It's not permitted.
9. Teachers should be patient. They shouldn't ____ when students don't understand.
10. You don't have to ____ to win a sweepstakes prize.

EXERCISE 27 In your opinion, what laws should be changed? What new laws should be created? Fill in the blanks to complete these statements, using _must / must not, have to / don't have to, can / can't, should / shouldn't._ You may work with a partner or in small groups.

EXAMPLES There ought to be a law that says _you can't use your cell phone while driving._

There ought to be a law that says _that people who want to have a baby must take a course in parenting._

1. There ought to be a law that says ____ Answers will vary. ____

2. There ought to be a law that says ____

1. Tell students that this exercise is about rules and customs at school. Have students read the direction line.
2. Model the exercise. Direct students to the example. Ask one or two volunteers for their responses to the cue. Complete #1 as a class.
3. Have students complete the exercise individually. Check answers as a class.
4. Assess students' performance. If necessary, review grammar chart 4.7 on page 154.

To save class time, have students do half of the exercise in class and complete the other half for homework. Or assign the entire exercise for homework.

1. Tell students that this exercise is about people's opinions about laws. Have students read the direction line.
2. Direct students to the examples in the book. Elicit several additional responses from the class.
3. Have students complete the exercise individually, and then share their answers in pairs or groups. Have pairs or groups share interesting ideas with the class.

To save class time, have students do half of the exercise in class and complete the other half for homework. Or assign the entire exercise for homework.

Expansion

Exercise 27 Have students create three new rules for your classroom (e.g., You must turn your cell phone ringer off during class.).

4.8 | Making Suggestions

1. Have students cover the grammar chart. Tell students about a problem someone is having (you, a friend, or a family member), such as: *My kids don't eat enough vegetables* or *My friend needs a new car.* Ask: *Which modals do we use to make suggestions?* (*can* and *could*)
2. Have students uncover and review the grammar chart.
3. Draw students' attention to *could.* Say: *The modal* could *has the same form as the past tense of* can, *but the meaning is different. As a modal, it's used to offer suggestions.*
4. Draw students' attention to *should* and *shouldn't.* Ask: *To give advice, which is stronger:* could *or* should? (*should*)

EXERCISE 28

1. Tell students that this exercise is about making suggestions. Have students read the direction line.
2. Direct students to the example in the book. Elicit several additional responses from the class.
3. Have students complete the exercise in pairs, or individually if appropriate. Then have volunteers share their suggestions with the class.
4. Assess students' performance. If necessary, review grammar chart **4.8** on page 160.

---

3. There ought to be a law that says _____

4. There ought to be a law that says _____

5. There ought to be a law that says _____

4.8 | Making Suggestions

Examples	Explanation
How **can** I deal with telemarketing calls? You **could** use Caller ID to see who's calling. You **can** put your telephone number on a "do not call" list. You **could** end the call quickly.	*Can* and *could* are used to offer suggestions. More than one choice is acceptable. *Can* and *could* have the same meaning in offering suggestions. *Could* does not have a past meaning in offering suggestions.

Compare *can / could* and *should* :
 a. I'm having a problem with annoying telemarketing calls.
     You **could** get Caller ID. Or you **can** just hang up. Or you **can** put your phone number on a "Do Not Call" registry.
 b. A caller asked for my credit card number.
     You **should** be careful. You **shouldn't** give out your credit card number to strangers.
	a. Use *could* or *can* to offer one or more of several possibilities.
	
	 b. Use *should* or *shouldn't* when you feel that there is only one right way.

EXERCISE 28   Offer at least two suggestions to a person who says each of the following statements. You may work with a partner.

EXAMPLE   I need to find a book about American history.

You could go to a bookstore. You can get one at the public library.

You could try an online bookstore.

1. I'm leaving for vacation tomorrow, and I need to find out about the weather in the city where I'm going.

Answers will vary.

---

160   Lesson 4

Expansion

Exercise 28 As homework, have students write situations of their own similar to those in Exercise 28. Have students bring their situations to class; collect and distribute them. Ask students to provide suggestions in writing for the situation they receive. Or ask students to think about the situation, and then present their solutions to the class (e.g., *This person wants to get more exercise, but she never has time. She could try walking when she goes to school or to the store, or she could ride a bike.*).

2. I type very slowly. I need to learn to type faster.

_____

_____

3. My landlord is raising my rent by $50, and I can't afford the increase.

_____

_____

4. I'd like to learn English faster.

_____

_____

5. I want to know the price of an airline ticket to my country.

_____

_____

6. I need to buy a new computer, and I want to compare prices.

_____

_____

7. I'm going to a party. The hostess asked each guest to bring
something to eat.

_____

_____

8. I need to lose ten pounds.

_____

_____

Culture Note

If you are asked to dinner at an American's home, it's always polite to ask if you can bring
anything. Even when the host says no, guests often bring something to drink or flowers. When
the host says that a party is potluck, each guest is expected to bring a dish (a food item, not an
empty dish). Sometimes a host will ask guests to bring a certain type of food (e.g., a salad or
a dessert). Office parties are frequently potluck parties.

Infomercials (Reading)

1. Have students look at the photo. Ask: *Who are these people? What are they doing? Who is the man standing up with the microphone?*
2. Have students look briefly at the reading. Have students look at the title of the reading. Ask: *What is the reading about? How do you know?* Have students make predictions.
3. Preteach any vocabulary words your students may not know, such as *products* and *informative*.

BEFORE YOU READ

1. Activate students' prior knowledge about infomercials. Ask: *Have you ever watched a program on TV that you thought was information, only to discover later that it was a long commercial? How can you tell a real program from an infomercial?*
2. Have students discuss the questions in pairs. Try to pair students of different language backgrounds.
3. Ask a few volunteers to share their answers with the class.

To save class time, skip "Before You Read" or have students prepare answers for homework ahead of time.

Reading 🎧 *CD 1, Track 28*

1. Have students first read the text silently. Tell them to pay special attention to *be supposed to* in the reading. Then play the audio and have students read along silently.
2. Check students' comprehension. Ask questions such as: *Where does the word* infomercial *come from?* (a combination of *information* and *commercial*) *What kinds of products are sometimes sold on infomercials?* (health and beauty products, exercise machines, diet foods, etc.)

To save class time, have students do the reading for homework ahead of time.

INFOMERCIALS

Before You Read
1. Do you think TV commercials are interesting?
2. Do you believe what you see in commercials?

 Read the following conversation. Pay special attention to *be supposed to*.

 We sometimes see "programs" on TV for products that **are supposed to** make our lives better. These look like real, informative TV shows, but they are not. They are called "infomercials" (*information + commercial*).

You**'re supposed to** think that you are watching an informative TV show and getting advice or information from experts and celebrities. These "shows" usually last 30 minutes, like regular TV shows. And they have commercial breaks, like regular TV shows, to make you believe they are real shows. These "shows" tell you that their products **are supposed to** make you thin, young, rich, or beautiful. For example, you may see smiling people with great bodies using exercise equipment. You**'re supposed to** believe that it's easy and fun to lose weight if you buy this equipment. But weight loss takes hard work and a lot of time.

Be careful when buying products from infomercials, because the results may not be what you see on TV.

162   Lesson 4

Expansion

Theme The topic for this lesson can be enhanced with the following ideas:

1. Ads from the mail or from a newspaper showing products with "As seen on TV" noted in the ad
2. A copy of TV listings for your area, including "paid programming"
3. The Federal Citizen Information Center's Web page on tips for shopping from home, at: http://www.consumeraction.gov/caw_shopping_general_tips.shtml

Reading Variation

To practice listening skills, have students first listen to the audio alone. Ask a few comprehension questions. Repeat the audio if necessary. Then have students open their books and read along as they listen to the audio.

Reading Glossary

informative: providing information
product: an item for sale; an item someone produces

4.9 | Expectations with *Be Supposed To*

Be supposed to is used to show that we have an expectation about something based on information we were given, In the examples on the left, we have an expectation because of a schedule.

Examples	Explanation
This diet pill **is supposed to** make you thinner in 30 days. This cream **is supposed to** grow hair in 30 days.	In the examples on the left, we expect something after watching an infomercial.
Let's rent *The Matrix* this weekend. It's **supposed to** be a good movie. Let's go to Mabel's Restaurant. The food there **is supposed to** be very good. I was just listening to the radio. It's **supposed to** rain this weekend, but tomorrow **is supposed to** be a nice day. I want to take Ms. King's class. She's **supposed to** be a good teacher.	In the examples on the left, we expect something because we heard it or learned it from a friend, TV, radio, a newspaper, the Internet, etc.
The movie **is supposed to** begin at 8 p.m. The plane **is supposed to** arrive at 7:25.	

Be supposed to is used to show that something is expected of the subject of the sentence because of a rule, requirement, custom, or commitment (promise).

Examples	Explanation
Sweepstakes companies **are supposed to** tell you your chances of winning. Drivers **are supposed to** wear seat belts. We're **not supposed to** talk during the test. You're **not supposed to** talk in the library, but some students do anyway.	A person is expected to do something because of a law or rule. (See 4.4)
I'm **supposed to** write a paper for my class. I'm **supposed to** write about my favorite TV commercial.	A person is expected to meet a requirement (in these cases, by the teacher).
In many cultures, you're **supposed to** take off your shoes before you enter a house. In the U.S., a bride and groom **are supposed to** send thank-you notes for their gifts.	A person is expected to behave in a certain way because of a custom.
I can't come to class tomorrow. I'm **supposed to** take my mom to the doctor. My friends are moving on Saturday. I'm **supposed to** help them.	A person is expected to do something because he has made a promise or commitment.

4.9 | Expectations with *Be Supposed To*

1. Have students cover the grammar chart. Write on the board: *Fat-B-Gone* and *Hairy Magic* or similar invented products. Ask: *What do you think these products are supposed to do?* (make you lose weight, grow hair) Ask: *What is the weather supposed to be like tomorrow? How do you know?* (from a weather report; from something we've heard) Then ask: *What are we supposed to do when we leave this room?* (turn off the lights, push in the chairs, clean the board, etc.) Say: *We use* supposed to *to talk about what we expect or about what we are expected to do.*

2. Have students uncover the grammar chart. Review the examples and explanations in both sections of the chart. Ask: *Can you tell me something that is supposed to happen soon? Can you tell us something that you are supposed to do next week?* Have several volunteers respond.

Grammar Variation

After students have reviewed the example sentences in the grammar chart, have them go back to the reading on page 162 and identify which explanation applies to each boldface instance of *be supposed to*.

1. Tell students that this exercise is about products and what they are supposed to do. Have students read the direction line.
2. Model the exercise. Review the example in the book.
3. Have students complete the exercise individually. Check answers as a class.

🎧 **CD 1, Track 29**

1. Tell students that this exercise is about products and their promises. Have students read the direction line.
2. Review the example in the book. Then have students complete the exercise individually and check their work in pairs. Circulate and observe the pair work.
3. Assess students' performance. If necessary, review grammar chart **4.9** on page 163.

🕐 To save class time, have students do half of the exercise in class and complete the other half for homework. Or assign the entire exercise for homework.

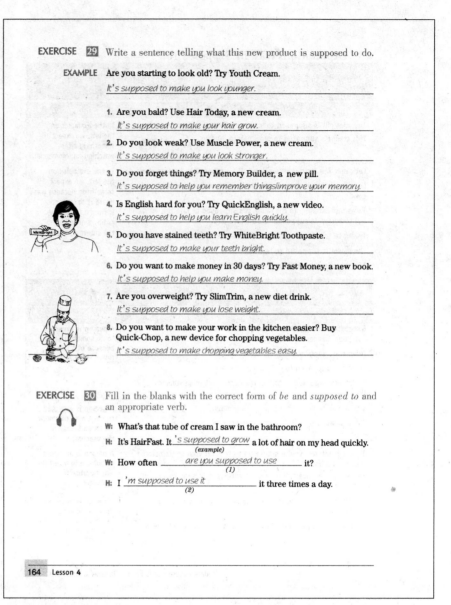

EXERCISE 29 Write a sentence telling what this new product is supposed to do.

EXAMPLE Are you starting to look old? Try Youth Cream.
It's supposed to make you look younger.

1. Are you bald? Use Hair Today, a new cream.
It's supposed to make your hair grow.

2. Do you look weak? Use Muscle Power, a new cream.
It's supposed to make you look stronger.

3. Do you forget things? Try Memory Builder, a new pill.
It's supposed to help you remember things/improve your memory.

4. Is English hard for you? Try QuickEnglish, a new video.
It's supposed to help you learn English quickly.

5. Do you have stained teeth? Try WhiteBright Toothpaste.
It's supposed to make your teeth bright.

6. Do you want to make money in 30 days? Try Fast Money, a new book.
It's supposed to help you make money.

7. Are you overweight? Try SlimTrim, a new diet drink.
It's supposed to make you lose weight.

8. Do you want to make your work in the kitchen easier? Buy Quick-Chop, a new device for chopping vegetables.
It's supposed to make chopping vegetables easy.

EXERCISE 30 Fill in the blanks with the correct form of *be* and *supposed to* and an appropriate verb.

W: What's that tube of cream I saw in the bathroom?
H: It's HairFast. It _'s supposed to grow_ a lot of hair on my head quickly.
(example)
W: How often _are you supposed to use_ it?
(1)
H: I _'m supposed to use it_ it three times a day.
(2)

Expansion

Exercise 29 After students complete the exercise, have groups work together to write a commercial or longer infomercial about one of the products in the exercise. Have groups write a script for their infomercial and then perform it for the class. If possible, have students vote after each performance on whether they would buy the product, and why or why not.

Exercise 30 Variation

To provide practice with listening skills, have students close their books and listen to the audio. Repeat the audio as needed. Ask comprehension questions, such as: *What is HairFast supposed to do?* (grow a lot of hair on the head quickly) *How much does it cost?* (about ten dollars for each tube) *How long does one tube last?* (a week) Then have students open their books and complete Exercise 30.

W: How much does it cost?

H: It's about ten dollars for each tube.

W: Ten dollars?

H: One tube ____is supposed to last____ for a week.
                    (3)

W: Just a week? How long will it take you to grow hair?

H: It __'s supposed to take__ about six months before I
                 (4)
start to see results.

W: Do you know how much money that's going to cost us?

H: I know it's expensive, but just imagine how much better I'll look with hair.

W: You know we want to buy a new house. We ___are supposed to___
                                                              (5)
___put/be putting___ our extra money into our house fund. But
you're wasting it on a product that may—or may not—bring results.

H: What about all the money you spend on skin products? All those
stupid creams that __are supposed to make__ you look younger?
                              (6)

W: Well, you want me to look young and beautiful, don't you?

H: Do you really think those products work?

W: This expensive cream I bought __is supposed to reduce__
                                              (7)
the wrinkles around my eyes.

H: You'll always be beautiful to me. I have an idea. Why don't you forget about the creams and I'll forget about the hair product. We can save our money, buy a house, and just get old together—in our new home.

EXERCISE **31** ABOUT YOU Work with a partner. Write a list of three things the teacher or this school expects from the students. Begin with *we*.

EXAMPLE   *We're supposed to come to class every day.*

1. _____Answers will vary._____

2. _____

3. _____

Modals—Present and Future; Related Expressions   165

EXERCISE   31

1. Tell students that this exercise is about things they are expected to do at school. Have students read the direction line. Ask: *How do we begin the sentences?* (with *We're supposed to*)

2. Model the exercise. Direct students to the example in the book. Elicit an additional response from the class.

3. Have students work in pairs. Have pairs report their lists back to the class.

4. Ask: *Do you always do the things you're supposed to do?*

Expansion

Exercise 30 Ask students if they think the people in the exercise are making the right choice. Ask if students have any other suggestions for the people; have students use *could* in their suggestions.

Exercise 30 Have students practice the conversation in pairs. Have volunteers act out the conversation for the class.

1. Tell students that this exercise is about things that they expect from you. Have students read the direction line. Ask: *How do we begin the sentences?* (with *He* or *She is supposed to*)
2. Model the exercise. Direct students to the example in the book. Elicit an additional response from the class.
3. Have students work in pairs and report their lists back to the class.

My Elderly Neighbor (Reading)

1. Have students look at the photo. Ask: *What's happening?* (an older woman is talking on the phone)
2. Have students look quickly at the reading. Ask: *What is the reading about? How do you know?* Have students make predictions.
3. Preteach any vocabulary words your students may not know, such as *elderly, in addition to,* and *take advantage of.*

BEFORE YOU READ

1. Activate students' prior knowledge about marketing to senior citizens. Ask: *Do you know any older people who live alone? Are older people more likely to enter a sweepstakes or listen to telemarketers than younger people? Why or why not?*
2. Have students discuss the questions in pairs. Try to pair students of different language backgrounds.
3. Ask a few volunteers to share their answers with the class.

To save class time, skip "Before You Read" or have students prepare answers for homework ahead of time.

Reading 🎧 CD 1, Track 30

1. Have students first read the text silently. Tell them to pay special attention to the use of *must.* Then play the audio and have students read along silently.
2. Check students' comprehension. Ask questions such as: *Why is person A worried about his or her neighbor?* (because she lives alone and enters a lot of sweepstakes) *What might person A do?* (suggest that she sign up for a do not call list; warn the neighbor)

To save class time, have students do the reading for homework ahead of time.

EXERCISE 32 Work with a partner. Write a list of three things that you expect from the teacher in this class. Begin with *he* or *she.*

EXAMPLE *She's supposed to correct us when we make a mistake.*

1. _____ Answers will vary. _____
2. _____
3. _____

MY ELDERLY NEIGHBOR

Before You Read
1. Why do you think elderly people enter so many sweepstakes?
2. What do you do when you get calls from telemarketers?

🎧 Read the following conversation. Pay special attention to *must.*

A: I'm worried about my elderly neighbor.
B: How old is she?
A: She **must be** about 80.
B: Why are you worried? Is her health bad?
A: No, she's fine. But she's all alone. Her children live far away. They don't call her very often.
B: She **must be** lonely.
A: I think she is. She enters sweepstakes and buys useless things all the time. She **must think** that if she buys things, she'll increase her chances of winning. I was in her garage yesterday, and she **must have** more than 50 boxes of things she doesn't use.
B: Doesn't she read the offers that are sent to her? Can't she see that her chances of winning are very small and that she doesn't have to buy anything to win?
A: She **must not read** those letters very carefully. In addition to these letters, she told me she gets about five or six calls from telemarketers every day. Her name **must be** on hundreds of lists.
B: Our family **must get** a lot of those calls too, but we're at work all day so we don't even know about them. Telemarketers don't usually leave a message.
A: Do you think I should warn my neighbor? I read an article that says that these companies take advantage of elderly people.
B: Why don't you talk to her about it? You can tell her to use Caller ID to see who's calling, or to put her name on a "Do Not Call" list.
A: I think I should.

166   Lesson 4

Expansion

Theme The topic for this lesson can be enhanced with the following ideas:

1. A flyer listing services at a local senior citizens center, especially one offering workshops, lectures, or financial planning
2. A copy of the federal government's consumer protection Web page for seniors, at: http://www.firstgov.gov/Topics/Seniors.shtml

---

Reading Variation

To practice listening skills, have students first listen to the audio alone. Ask a few comprehension questions. Repeat the audio if necessary. Then have students open their books and read along as they listen to the audio.

Reading Glossary

elderly: a polite word for *old*; a senior citizen
in addition to: also, plus
take advantage of: use a person or a situation unfairly for your own gain, or to make things better for yourself

---

4.10 | Logical Conclusions

Must has two completely different uses. In sections 4.3 and 4.4, we studied *must* as an expression of necessity. In the preceding reading and in the examples below, *must* shows a conclusion based on information we hear or observations we make.

Examples	Explanation
My elderly neighbor lives alone. Her children are far away. She **must be** lonely. She **must think** that if she buys things, her chances of winning will increase.	We make a conclusion based on information we have or observations we make.
How old is she? She **must be** about 80. How many boxes does she have? She **must have** more than 50 boxes.	We can use *must* to make an estimate.
She **must not read** the letters carefully. She **must not understand** the conditions of the contest.	For a negative conclusion, use *must not.* Do not use a contraction.

Language Note:
Must, in the above cases, talks about the presnt

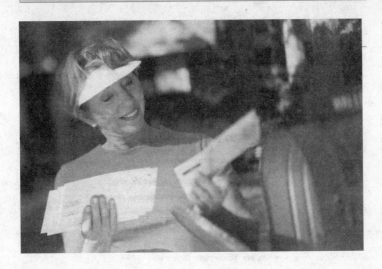

Modals—Present and Future; Related Expressions   167

Grammar Variation

After students have reviewed the example sentences in the grammar chart, have them go back to the reading on page 166 and identify which explanation applies to each boldface instance of *must*.

Culture Note

Elderly is usually used to describe a person who is over 75 or 80. *Older* or *senior* is much more polite than *old* in describing people. As people live longer and healthier lives, the age at which people become old continues to rise. To avoid offending someone, people frequently use *older* to refer to people in their 70s, 80s, or beyond.

4.10 | Logical Conclusions

1. Have students cover the grammar chart and look at the sentences with *must* in the reading on pages 166 and 167. Write several sentences about the neighbor on the board. For example, write: *She must be lonely. She must have 50 boxes of things in her garage.*

2. Ask: *What do you think* must *is used for in these sentences? Does it mean* have to*?* (No; it's used to show something we conclude or decide.) Ask: *Does person A know exactly how old his/her neighbor is?* (No; he/she is guessing.)

3. Have students review the examples and explanations in the grammar chart.

4. Draw students' attention to the Language Note. Be sure students understand that *must* for logical conclusions refers to the present time.

1. Tell students that this exercise is a series of conversations between different sets of people. Have students read the direction line. Tell students that more than one answer is possible.
2. Model the exercise. Review the example. Then complete the first conversation with the class.
3. Have students complete the exercise individually. Then have them check their answers by practicing the conversations in pairs. Circulate and observe the pair work. If necessary, check the answers as a class.

EXERCISE **33** In each of the conversations below, fill in the blanks with an appropriate verb to make a logical conclusion.

EXAMPLE
A: Have you ever visited Japan?

B: I lived there when I was a child.

A: Then you must ___*know how to speak*___ Japanese.

B: I used to, but I've forgotten it.

1. This is a conversation between two female students.

   A: Would you introduce me to Lee?

   B: Who's Lee?

   A: You must ___*know*___ who I'm talking about. He's in your speech class. He sits next to you.

   B: You mean Mr. Song?

   A: Yes, Lee Song. The tall handsome guy with glasses. He doesn't wear a wedding ring. He must ___*be*___ single.

   B: I'm not so sure about that. Not all married men wear a wedding ring.

2. This is a conversation between a married woman (M) and a single woman (S).

   M: My husband spends all his free time with our children.

   S: He must ___*love*___ kids very much.

   M: He does.

   S: How many kids do you have?

   M: We have four.

   S: Raising kids must ___*be*___ the hardest job in the world.

   M: It is, but it's also the most rewarding.

3. This is a conversation between a teacher (T) and a student (S).

   T: Take out the paper I gave you last Monday.

   S: I don't have it. Could you give me one, please?

   T: Were you in class last Monday?

   S: Yes, I was.

   T: Then you must ___*have*___ it.

   S: Oh, yes. You're right. Here it is.

Exercise 33 Variation

To provide practice with listening skills, have students close their books and listen to the audio. Repeat the audio as needed. Ask comprehension questions, such as: *In conversation 1, what does Lee Song look like?* (tall handsome guy with glasses) *Why does student A think Lee Song isn't married?* (He doesn't wear a wedding ring.) *Do all married men wear wedding rings?* (no) Then have students open their books and complete Exercise 33.

4. This is a conversation between an American (A) and an immigrant (I).

   A: It must ___be___ hard to start your life in a new country.

   I: Yes, it is.

   A: You must ___feel/be___ lonely at times.

   I: Yes. You must ___know___ how it feels. You went to live in Japan for a few years, didn't you?

   A: Yes, I did. It took me a long time to get used to it.

5. This is a conversation between two friends.

   A: I saw some experts on TV talking about a cure for baldness. They must ___know___ what they're talking about because they're experts.

   B: You must ___believe___ that if you see it on TV it's true. But don't believe everything you see.

6. This is a conversation between two friends.

   A: I saw your uncle yesterday at the gym. How old is he?

   B: I'm not sure. My mother is 69 and he's her older brother. So he must ___be___ in his seventies. He goes to the gym four days a week to work out.

   A: He must ___be___ in great health.

   B: He is.

7. This is a conversation between two students in the school cafeteria.

   A: I see you're not eating your apple. In fact, you never eat fruit. You must not ___like___ fruit very much.

   B: You're right. I don't like fruit. Do you want my apple?

   A: Thanks. You're always eating potato chips. They're so fattening. They must ___have___ a million calories in them.

   B: Probably, but I never think about it.

   A: You should.

   B: You're always talking about calories. You must ___worry___ about getting fat.

   A: I don't worry about it. I just try to eat well.

Culture Note

There are several old, commonly quoted expressions related to product claims and consumer awareness. One is "If it sounds too good to be true, it probably is." Another is *Caveat emptor*, Latin for "Buyer beware."

8. This is a conversation between two co-workers.

A: Do you want to see a picture of my new baby?

B: Yes.

A: Here she is. She's about two months old now.

B: She's so beautiful. You and your wife must _____be_____ very happy.

A: We are. But we don't get much sleep these days. You have a small baby. You must _____know_____ what I'm talking about.

B: I sure do.

9. This is a conversation between a young couple.

A: Do you see that beautiful ring in the window? I really love it. Don't you?

B: Yes, it's very beautiful. (*Thinking to himself*: This is an expensive jewelry shop. The ring must _____cost_____ over $5,000. She must _____think_____ that I'm rich.)

10. This is a conversation between two strangers on the street.

A: I see you're looking at a map. You must _____be_____ a tourist. Are you lost?

B: Please repeat.

A: Are you lost?

B: Speak slowly please.

A: ARE YOU LOST? (*To herself*: He must not _____speak_____ any English.)

B: (*To himself*: I asked her to speak more slowly and she's shouting instead. She must _____think_____ that I'm deaf.)

Expansion

Exercise 33 Have pairs of students choose one of the conversations in Exercise 33. Ask them to write two additional sentences to continue the dialogue. Ask volunteers to present their dialogues to the class.

4.11 | Probability vs. Possibility in the Present

Degrees of Certainty	Explanation
a. Who's calling? I have Caller ID. I see it **is** my sister.	a. We are certain that the information is true.
b. Who's calling? I don't know. I don't have Caller ID. It **might be** my sister. Or it **may be** my mother or it **could be** a telemarketer.	b. We have little or no evidence or information. There are many possibilities.
c. Who's calling? It **must be** my mother. It's 3 o'clock and she calls me every day at 3.	c. We conclude that something is true based on information we have or an estimate we make.
a. My elderly neighbor **has** no children.	
b. She **might have** nieces and nephews, but I'm not sure.	
c. She **must have** at least 50 boxes in her garage.	

EXERCISE **34** Decide if the situation is probable or possible. Fill in the blanks with *must* for probability or *may / might / could* for possibility.

EXAMPLES A: Where is Linda Ramirez from?

B: Ramirez is a Spanish name. She __*might*__ be from Mexico.

She __*may*__ be from Colombia. There are so many countries where Spanish is spoken that it's hard to know for sure.

A: She __*could*__ be from the Philippines. Filipinos have Spanish names, too.

B: Where is Tran Nguyen from?

A: I know that's a Vietnamese name. He __*must*__ be from Vietnam.

1. A: What time is it?

   B: I don't have a watch. The sun is directly overhead, so it
   _____*must*_____ be about noon.

2. A: Where's the teacher today?

   B: No one knows. She __*could / might / may*__ be sick.

3. A: Does Yoko speak Japanese?

   B: She __*must*__ speak Japanese. She's from Japan.

Modals—Present and Future; Related Expressions   171

4.11. | Probability vs. Possibility in the Present

1. On the board, write situations that contrast *could* (possibility) and *must* (probability). For example, write:
   1. A: Where's Ana?
   B: I don't know; she could be at work.
   2. A: Where's Ana?
   B: It's only 4:00. She must be at work.
   Ask: *Which one shows that Ana is probably at work? (#2) Which one shows that it's possible that Ana is at work? (#1)*
2. Have students look at grammar chart **4.11**. Review the example sentences and explanations.

EXERCISE   34

1. Tell students that this exercise is a series of conversations between friends. Have students read the direction line.
2. Model the exercise. Direct students to the examples in the book. Then complete #1 as a class.
3. Have students complete Exercise 34 individually. Then have them check their answers in pairs by practicing the dialogues. Circulate and observe the pair work. If necessary, check the answers as a class.
4. Assess students' performance. If necessary, review grammar chart **4.11**.

Expansion

Exercise 34 Bring in magazine pictures showing people whose situation or emotions students can conclude from the picture. Have students work in groups to write statements about the people and their conclusions (e.g., *She is holding her head. She must have a headache.*).

4.12 | Modals with Continuous Verbs

1. Have students look at the examples in the left column of the grammar chart. Ask: *How are these examples different from the examples we have been looking at?* (They use continuous verbs.)
2. Have students review the explanation in the grammar chart.
3. Give one or two examples of your own (e.g., *You shouldn't be looking at your book right now. You should be looking at the blackboard.*).

4. **A:** Where's Washington Avenue?
   B: I don't know. We're lost. There's a woman over there. Let's ask her. She _might / may_ know.

5. **A:** Why is that student sneezing so much?
   B: I don't know. She _might / may_ have a cold, or it _could_ be an allergy.

6. **A:** Is Susan married?
   B: She _must_ be married. She's wearing a wedding ring.

7. **A:** Why didn't Joe come to the party?
   B: Who knows? He _might / may_ not like parties.

8. **A:** I need to make some copies, but don't have change for the copy machine.
   B: I _might / could / may_ have some change. Let me look in my pocket.

9. **A:** I've never lived far from my parents before.
   B: You _must_ miss them very much.
   A: I do.

10. **A:** Look at that young couple. They're always holding hands, smiling at each other, and kissing.
    B: They _must_ be in love.

11. **A:** Linda never answers any questions in class.
    B: She _might / may / could_ be shy or she _might / may / could_ not know the answers to the questions.

12. **A:** I have a question about grammar.
    B: Let's ask the teacher. She _must_ know the answer.

13. **A:** I have a question about American history.
    B: Why don't you ask our grammar teacher? He _might / may / could_ know the answer.

4.12 | Modals with Continuous Verbs

Examples	Explanation
The child **should be sleeping**. She **shouldn't be watching** TV now.	Use modal + *be* + verb *-ing* for a present continuous meaning.
I can't reach my friend. His line is always busy. He **might be using** the Internet now.	
We **are supposed to be listening** to the teacher.	

172   Lesson 4

Grammar Variation

Ask: *What do you think your husband/child/roommate, etc., is doing right now? What is he/she supposed to be doing right now?* Say: *We can use modals with continuous verbs, too.* Then review the grammar chart in the book.

EXERCISE 35 A student is home sick today. She looks at her watch and knows that her English class is going on right now. She knows what usually happens is class. Read the following statements and tell what *may*, *must*, or *should* be happening now.

EXAMPLE The teacher usually asks questions. (must)
He must be asking questions now.

1. The teacher sometimes sits at the desk. (may)
He may be sitting at the desk now.
2. The teacher always does the exercises. (must)
He must be doing the exercises now.
3. The teacher explains the grammar. (should)
He should be explaining the grammar now.
4. The teacher always helps the students. (must)
He must be helping the students now.
5. The teacher sometimes reviews the lesson. (might)
He might be reviewing the lesson now.
6. Sometimes the students don't pay attention. (be supposed to)
They're supposed to be paying attention now.
7. The students are probably wondering where I am. (must)
They must be wondering where I am now.
8. The teacher sometimes passes back papers. (might)
He might be passing back papers now.

EXERCISE 36 *Combination Exercise.* Read this conversation. Choose the correct words in parentheses ( ) to complete the conversation. Sometimes both choices have the same meaning, so both answers are correct.

A: I received a letter about a sweepstakes. I think I
(may not, (am supposed to)) buy magazines in order to enter the contest.
(example)

B: You're wrong. You (must not, (don't have to)) buy anything.
(example)

A: But if I do, that (might not, (may)) increase my chances of winning.
(1)

B: That's not true. I've read several articles on the Internet about sweepstakes and scams recently.

A: Then you ((must,) might) know a lot about this topic.
(2)

B: I think I do. You ((shouldn't,) don't have to) believe everything you
(3)

read on the Internet either.

A: How do I know what to believe?

B: You (must, (should)) use common sense. If an ad tells you that you are
(4)

already a winner, you ((shouldn't,) must not) believe it.
(5)

A: But if a letter tells me I've won a million dollars, I'd be crazy not to look into it further.

B: You'd be crazy if you did. Do you think someone is going to give you a million dollars for nothing?

Modals—Present and Future; Related Expressions   173

EXERCISE 35

1. Tell students that this exercise is about a student's ideas of what may be happening while she is out of class. Have students read the direction line. Ask: *What words do we use (may, must, should) and what tenses?* (present continuous)
2. Direct students to the example in the book. Complete #1 with the class.
3. Have students complete the exercise in pairs. Check answers as a class.

EXERCISE 36

🎧 *CD 1, Track 32*

1. Tell students that this exercise is a conversation between friends about knowing what to believe. Have students read the direction line. Ask: *Is more than one answer possible?* (yes)
2. Direct students to the examples in the book. Then have volunteers answer items 1 and 2.
3. Have students complete the exercise individually, and then check their work by reading the conversation in pairs. Circulate and observe the pair work. If necessary, review the answers as a class.
4. Assess students' performance. If necessary, review the appropriate chart(s) from the lesson.

🕐 To save class time, have students do half of the exercise in class and complete the other half for homework. Or assign the entire exercise for homework.

Exercise 36 Variation

To provide practice with listening skills, have students close their books and listen to the audio. Repeat the audio as needed. Ask comprehension questions, such as: *What did person A receive in the mail?* (a letter about a sweepstakes) *Does buying something increase one's chances of winning a sweepstakes?* (no) *Should we believe everything we read on the Internet?* (no) Then have students open their books and complete Exercise 36.

A: No, but . . .

B: If you want to get rich, you (could, should) work hard and save your
(6)

money.

A: But it (could, might) take years to get rich that way.
(7)

B: That's the only way. Yes, you (could, can) buy lottery tickets and
(8)

enter sweepstakes, but you (should, might) lose a lot of money.
(9)

A: I get offers by e-mail too. There are offers for products that

(must, are supposed to) make me lose weight. I'm a bit overweight
(10)

and I (have to, have got to) lose 20 pounds.
(11)

B: If you want to lose weight, you (might, ought to) eat a healthy diet
(12)

and exercise every day.

A: But that takes time. It (could, might) take months before I see a
(13)

difference.

B: That's right. But it's the only way. All those ads tell you that problems

(can, must) be fixed with easy solutions. But life isn't like that.
(14)

A: You (must, should) think I'm stupid for believing all these things I
(15)

see and hear.

B: I don't think you're stupid. Some companies are very clever about
getting your interest. For example, infomercials often have celebrities
talking about a product. You (are expected to, are supposed to)
(16)

trust the celebrity and believe what he or she says is true.

A: Perhaps the government (should, could) do something to stop these
(17)

ads from appearing in our e-mail, in our postal mailboxes, and on TV.

B: There are already laws telling companies what they

(are allowed to, are permitted to) do or not. But it's up to you to be
(18)

informed, use your common sense, and protect yourself.

A: Well, thanks for your advice.

174 Lesson 4

Expansion

Exercise 36 Have students use what they have learned about the people in the conversation
to write logical conclusions about them, such as: *They must be good friends. Person A must
not read the newspaper very often.*

SUMMARY OF LESSON 4

Examples	Explanation
You **must** take a test to get a driver's license. You **must not** drive without a license.	Law or rule (official tone) Negative: Prohibition
You're **supposed to** wear your seat belt. You're **not supposed to** park here.	Law or rule (unofficial tone) Negative: Prohibition
I **have to** mail a letter. I've **got to** mail a letter. I **don't have to** go to the post office. I can put it in the mailbox.	Personal obligation Negative: Lack of necessity
You'd **better** study tonight, or you might fail the test. You'd **better not** stay up late tonight, or you won't be alert in the morning.	Warning; negative consequences statedor implied
You **should** exercise every day. You **ought to** exercise every day. You **shouldn't** eat so much ice cream.	Advice Negative: It's not advisable.
You **may / can** write the test with a pencil. You **cannot / may not** talk during a test.	Permission Negative: Prohibition
Students in the U.S. **can** wear jeans to class.	Social acceptability
I get annoying telemarketing calls. What **can** I do? You **could** be polite to the caller and listen, or you **can** say you're not interested and hang up.	Suggestions
You **may** win a prize. You **might** win a prize. You **could** win a prize.	Possibility about the future
It's **supposed to** rain tomorrow. This face cream **is supposed to** make you look younger. My brother **is supposed to** call me this weekend. We're **supposed to** write five compositions. You're **supposed to** take your hat off in church. The movie **is supposed to** begin at 8 p.m.	Expectation because of information we receive or because of a promise, requirement, custom, or schedule.
She won a lot of money. She **must** be happy. She's eating very little. She **must not** be very hungry.	Deduction or logical conclusion about the present
I can't find my keys. They **might be** in your pocket. Did you look there? They **could be** on the table. Or they **may be** in your car. She looks confused. She **may not** know the answer. She **might not** understand the question.	Possibility about the present

Modals—Present and Future; Related Expressions   175

Summary of Lesson 4

1. Write the first few words of six to eight sentences, using modals, on the board, such as: *You must, You can, You might, We're supposed to, We could, You'd better, You must not,* etc. Have students make sentences using the cues.

2. Have students cover the summary chart. Read sentences from the examples at random, for example, say: *You may not talk during the test.* Ask students to say what the modals mean in the sentence (It's not allowed; it's prohibited.).
If necessary, have students review: **Lesson 4.**

Summary Variation

1. Divide students into teams. Call out the beginnings of sentences with modals, as in the Summary of Lesson 4. The first team to complete a sentence correctly gets a point; the team with the most points wins.

2. Divide the class into Team A and Team B. Write a modal on the board. For example, write: *may.* Have one member of each team come to the board and write a sentence using *may.* Let team members help with the sentence. The first team to write a correct sentence gets a point.

Editing Advice

For each item, have students provide the grammar rule behind the Editing Advice. This can be done as an individual, a pair, a group, or a class activity.

1. Modals are usually followed by a verb; we don't use *to* before the verb.
2. Don't add an ending to the base form of a verb that follows a modal.
3. In informal speech, the *'d* ending on *supposed to, permitted to,* and *allowed to* may not be pronounced. It must be used in writing.
4. In informal speech, the *'d* ending on *had better* may not be pronounced. It must be used in writing.
5. In informal speech, the *have* or *has* in *have/has got to* may not be used. It must be used in writing.
6. We don't use two modals in a row.
7. The expressions *be supposed to, be able to, be permitted to,* and *be allowed to* are not complete without a form of *be* at the beginning and *to* at the end.
8. In *yes/no* and *wh-* (non-subject) questions with modals, the modal comes before the subject.

EDITING ADVICE

1. Don't use *to* after a modal. (Exception: *ought to*)

   You should to buy a new car.

2. Use the base form after a modal.

   She can't ~~goes~~ *go* with you.

   You should ~~studying~~ *study* every day.

3. Don't forget *d* in *supposed to, permitted to, allowed to.*

   He's not suppose*d* to drive. He's too young.

   You're not allow*ed* to talk during the test.

4. Don't forget *'d* to express *had better.*

   You*'d* better take the bus to work. Your car isn't working well.

5. Use *have / has* before *got to* in writing.

   We*'ve* got to leave now.

6. Don't put two modals together.

   You ~~must~~ *be able to* can drive well before you can get your license.

7. Don't forget *be* or *to* in these expressions: *be supposed to, be able to, be permitted to, be allowed to.*

   They *are* supposed to leave at 6 o'clock.

   I'm able *to* work on Saturday.

8. Use correct word order in a question with a modal.

   What ~~I should~~ *should I* do?

Lesson 4 Test/Review

LESSON 4 TEST/REVIEW

PART **1** Find the mistakes with the underlined words, and correct them. Not every sentence has a mistake. If the sentence is correct, write *C*.

EXAMPLES He got to talk to you.

You ought to come to class earlier. *C*

1. You must to leave the building immediately.
2. We not allowed to use our books during a test.
3. To become a U.S. citizen, you must be able to speak simple English. *C*
4. She can't find a job. *C*
5. You're almost out of gas. You better fill up your gas tank.
6. The boss expects everyone to be on time. You'd better don't come late to the meeting.
7. She cans type very fast.
8. Where I can find information about museums in this city?
9. You're not allowed to talk during a test. *C*
10. It's cold outside. You'd better take a sweater. *C*
11. We're supposed to write a composition about our parents. *C*
12. I got to buy a new car.
13. When is your brother supposed to arrive? *C*
14. It's suppose to rain tomorrow.

Modals—Present and Future; Related Expressions 177

Lesson 4 Test/Review

For additional practice, review, and assessment materials, see Assessment CD-ROM with *ExamView Pro*, *More Grammar Practice* Workbook 3, Interactive CD-ROM, and Web site http://elt.thomson.com/gic

PART 1

1. Part 1 may be used as an in-class test to assess student performance, in addition to the Assessment CD-ROM with *ExamView Pro*. Have students read the direction line. Ask: *Does every sentence have a mistake?* (no)
2. Collect for assessment.
3. If necessary, have students review: **Lesson 4.**

Lesson Review

To use Part 1 as a review, assign it as homework or use it as an in-class activity to be completed individually or in pairs. Check answers and review errors as a class. Reteach grammar points that students haven't mastered. Then student learning may be assessed using a test generated from the Assessment CD-ROM with *ExamView Pro*.

1. Part 2 may also be used as an in-class test to assess student performance, in addition to the Assessment CD-ROM with *ExamView Pro*. Tell students that this is a blank job application; the statements on page 179 are about the application. Make sure that students understand that the numbers on the left side of the application refer to the item numbers on page 179. Review the example. Then complete the first part of #1 on page 179 as a class. Ask: *What do we circle in the first sentence?* (have to)
2. Collect for assessment.
3. If necessary, have students review: **Lesson 4.**

PART 2 Look at the job application. Circle the best words to complete each sentence. The numbers on the application refer to each one of the sentences on the next page.

① Fill out the following form. Print in black ink or type. Bring it to the personnel office or mail it to:

Ms. Judy Lipton
P.O. Box 324
Tucson, Arizona 85744

Applications must be submitted by November 15.

② Name _____ _____ _____
        (last)   (first)   (middle initial)

Address _____

City _____ State _____ Zip Code _____

③ Telephone ( ) _____

④ Marital status (optional) _____ Sex _____ ⑤

⑥ Date of birth _____ _____ _____ (You must be at least 18.) ⑦
       (month) (day) (year)

⑧ Social Security number _____ _____ _____

⑨ Educational background

	Date graduated	Degree or major
High School		
College		
Graduate School		

⑩ Employment History (Please start with your present or last job.)

Company	Position	Dates	Supervisor	Reason for leaving

Do not write in the shaded box. For office use only.

⑪
Rec'd. by _____
Amer. cit. _____
Doc. checked _____
Transcripts received _____

⑫ The Immigration Act of 1986 requires all successful applicants to present documents to prove U.S. citizenship or permanent residence with permission to work in the U.S.

⑬ This company is an Equal Opportunity Employer. Race, religion, nationality, marital status, and physical disability will not influence our decision to hire.

⑭ I certify that these answers are true.

⑮ Signature: _____ Date: _____

EXAMPLE   You (aren't supposed to, couldn't) use a red pen to fill out the application.

1. You (have to, might) submit the application to Ms. Lipton. Ms. Lipton (must, should) be the person in charge of hiring. She wants the application by November 15. Today is November 14. You ('d better not, mustn't) send it by regular mail. If you use regular mail, it (must not, might not) arrive on time. You (could, are supposed to) send it by overnight express mail, or you (might, can) take it to Ms. Lipton's office.

2. You (could, are supposed to) write your last name before your first name.

3. You (are supposed to, could) include your phone number.

4. You (shouldn't, don't have to) include your marital status.

5. For sex, you (might, are supposed to) write M for male or F for female.

6. To write the date of your birth in the U.S., you (should, can) write the month before the day (June 7, for example). You have several choices in writing the date. You (must, could) write June 7 or 6/7 or 6-7. If you put the day before the month, an American (might, should) think you mean July 6 instead of June 7.

7. To apply for the job, you (might, must) be over 18.

8. People who work in the U.S. (may, must) have a Social Security number.

9. You (may, are supposed to) include the schools you attended.

10. In the employment history section, you are asked why you left your last job. The employer (might, should) want to know if you were fired or if you left on your own.

11. You (can't, aren't supposed to) write in the shaded box. "Amer. cit." (must, should) mean American citizen.

12. You (must not, don't have to) be an American citizen to apply for the job. You can be a permanent resident. You (have to, should) prove your citizenship or residency. If you don't have permission to work in the U.S., you (might not, cannot) apply for this job.

13. The company (might not, may not) choose a worker based on race, religion, or nationality.

14. You (don't have to, must not) lie on the application form.

15. You (may, must) sign the application and include the date.

Modals—Present and Future; Related Expressions   179

Lesson Review

To use Part 2 as a review, assign it as homework or use it as an in-class activity to be completed individually or in pairs. Check answers and review errors as a class. Reteach grammar points that students haven't mastered. Then student learning may be assessed using a test generated from the Assessment CD-ROM with *ExamView Pro*.

1. Part 3 may also be used as an in-class test to assess student performance, in addition to the Assessment CD-ROM with *ExamView Pro*. Have students read the direction line. Ask: *What do we write if the sentences have the same meaning? (S) If the sentences have different meanings? (D)*
2. Collect for assessment.
3. If necessary, have students review: **Lesson 4.**

PART **3** Read the pairs of sentences. If the sentences have the same meaning, write *S*. If the sentences have a different meaning, write *D*.

EXAMPLES   You have to wear your seat belt. / You must wear your seat belt. *S*
You must open the window. / You should open the window. *D*

1. She <u>can</u> drive a car. / She <u>is able to</u> drive a car. *S*
2. He <u>can't</u> speak Korean. / He <u>might not</u> speak Korean. *D*
3. I'm <u>supposed to</u> help my sister on Friday. / I <u>might</u> help my sister on Friday. *D*
4. You <u>don't have to</u> drive to work. / You <u>shouldn't</u> drive to work. *D*
5. You're <u>not supposed to</u> write the answer. / You <u>don't have to</u> write the answer. *D*
6. You're <u>not allowed to</u> use a pencil for the test. / You <u>may not</u> use a pencil for the test. *S*
7. We <u>should</u> visit our mother. / We <u>ought to</u> visit our mother. *S*
8. You <u>should</u> make a right turn here. / You <u>must</u> make a right turn here. *D*
9. If you need more help, you <u>could</u> go to a tutor. / If you need more help, you <u>can</u> go to a tutor. *S*
10. You <u>shouldn't</u> wear jeans. / You <u>must not</u> wear jeans. *D*
11. You <u>must not</u> come back after the final exam. / You <u>don't have to</u> come back after the final exam. *D*
12. I <u>have to</u> work tomorrow. / I've <u>got to</u> work tomorrow. *S*
13. You <u>can't</u> eat in the computer lab. / You <u>are not allowed to</u> eat in the computer lab. *S*
14. I <u>may</u> go to New York next week. / I <u>might</u> go to New York next week. *S*
15. The final exam <u>could</u> be hard. / The final exam <u>might</u> be hard. *S*
16. You <u>don't have to</u> call your teacher by her last name. / <u>It is not necessary to</u> call the teacher by her last name. *S*
17. You <u>don't have to</u> fill out the application with a red pen. / You <u>aren't supposed to</u> fill out the application with a red pen. *D*
18. <u>You'd better</u> wake up early tomorrow morning. / You <u>could</u> wake up early tomorrow morning. *D*

Lesson Review

To use Part 3 as a review, assign it as homework or use it as an in-class activity to be completed individually or in pairs. Check answers and review errors as a class. Reteach grammar points that students haven't mastered. Then student learning may be assessed using a test generated from the Assessment CD-ROM with *ExamView Pro*.

Classroom Activities

1. Form a small group. Take something from your purse or pocket that says something about you. Show it to your group. Your group will make deductions about you.

   EXAMPLE car keys
   You must have a car.

2. On the left are some American customs. On the right, tell if there is a comparable custom in your native culture. Write what that custom is.

In the U.S.	In my native culture
When someone sneezes, you're supposed to say, "Bless you."	
If you're invited to a party, in most cases you're not supposed to take your children.	
Americans sometimes have potluck parties. Guests are supposed to bring food to the party.	
There are some foods you can eat with your hands. Fried chicken and pizza are examples.	
Students are not supposed to talk to each other during an exam.	
When you're too sick to go to work, you're supposed to call your employer and say you're not coming in that day.	

3. Bring in two copies of an application. It can be an application for a job, driver's license, license plate, apartment rental, address change, check cashing card, rebate, etc. Work with a partner. One person will give instructions. The other person will fill the application out. Use modals to help the other person fill it out correctly.

4. Find a partner and write some sentences to give advice for each of the following problems.

   a. I got permission to come to the U.S. I have a dog. I've had this dog for six years, since she was a puppy, but I can't take her with me. What should I do?
   b. I got a D in my biology class. I think I deserve a C. What should I do?

Modals—Present and Future; Related Expressions 181

Classroom Activities Variation

Activity 1 Extend the activity. In a later class, have students bring in a more unusual object from home. Repeat the activity with the new objects.

Activity 2 Have students complete the chart at home and then collect the answers. In a later class, read some of the answers aloud. Have students guess which country each answer is from.

Activity 4 Have pairs of students choose one of the situations. Have them work together to add a few details to the situation. Then have pairs write a letter to an advice columnist asking for advice in that situation, and a response from the advice columnist. If possible, bring in several advice columns from a newspaper for students to look at. If appropriate, have students type their letters and responses and post them in the classroom.

Expansion Activities

These expansion activities provide opportunities for students to interact with one another and further develop their speaking and writing skills. Encourage students to use grammar from this lesson whenever possible.

🕐 To save class time, assign parts of the activities as homework. Then use class time for interaction and communication. If students do not need additional speaking practice, some of the activities may be assigned as writing activities for homework, or skipped altogether.

CLASSROOM ACTIVITIES

1. Tell students that this activity is about coming to logical conclusions. Ask students to choose an item and show it to the group without talking about it. When groups have finished the activity, ask: *Did everyone in the group come to the same conclusion?*

2. Have students complete the activity individually, or as homework. Then have students work in groups to compare answers. Have groups share interesting or unusual answers with the class.

3. Before beginning the activity, make sure each pair has two copies of the application. Ask: *What modals do we use to help someone do something correctly?* (should, could, have to, don't have to, can) Have students complete the activity in pairs; circulate to observe and assess conversations.

4. Tell students this activity is about giving advice. Have students work in pairs to brainstorm and write advice for each situation. When students have finished, ask groups to share their best or most interesting answer with the class. Then ask other groups if they had different advice for the same problem. Discuss and compare the advice as a class.

Have students work in groups. Either assign or have each group choose one or more of the topics to discuss. Review with students language for agreeing, checking for agreement, and disagreeing (e.g., *I think so too. Are you sure that's right? I'm not sure I agree.*). Set a time limit for discussion. Then have groups talk about their topics. If appropriate, have groups report back to the class; have each group appoint a spokesperson.

OUTSIDE ACTIVITIES

1. Have students report the information they get back to the class. Ask: *Do you already have Caller ID? Do you think everyone should have it?*

2. Have students report back to the class on the infomercial they watched. Ask: *Did you think the infomercial was persuasive? Did you want to buy the item? If so, how did the infomercial make you feel that way?*

3. Have students work in groups to compare the modals they find in their leases and have brought them. Pair students who have leases with those who don't.

INTERNET ACTIVITIES

1. As a review, brainstorm with students search terms they may want to use, e.g., *fraud*, *telemarketer*, and *sweepstakes*.

2. Have students share information they find. Ask: *Did you decide to add your name to the registry? Would you advise others to add their names? Why or why not?*

3. Have students report back to the class on what they've discovered about infomercials.

4. Have students share the advice they find in the articles with the class.

---

c. I need a new car, but I don't have enough money right now. What should I do?

d. I found an envelope with $100 in it in front of my apartment building. There is no name on it. What should I do?

e. My uncle came to live with us. He never cooks, cleans, or washes the dishes. I have to do everything. I'm very unhappy with the situation. What should I do?

Talk About it

1. Why do you think the elderly are often the victims of scams?

2. Have you ever seen a TV infomercial? For what kind of products? Do you believe the claims about the product?

3. How do you respond to telemarketing calls?

4. What do you think of TV commercials?

5. Did you ever win a prize in a contest, sweepstakes, or raffle? What did you win?

6. Did you ever buy a product that claims to do something but doesn't do it?

Outside Activities

1. Call your local phone company to find out how much it costs to order Caller ID service.

2. Watch an infomercial on TV. Write several sentences telling what the product is supposed to do.

3. If you have an apartment lease, make a copy of it and circle all the modals.

Internet Activities

1. Look for the Web sites of the Federal Trade Commission, the Better Business Bureau, or the National Fraud Information Center. Find some interesting consumer information to share with the class.

2. At a search engine, type in *do not call registry*. If you want to, add your phone number(s) to this registry.

3. At a search engine, type in *infomercial*. Find a report about TV infomercials. Print it and bring it to class.

4. At a search engine, type in *scam*. Print out an article about any type of scam you find and bring it to class. Circle all the modals in the article.

 Additional Activities at http://elt.thomson.com/gic

Talk About it Variation

Have students work in pairs. Have members of the pairs interview each other, using the questions in the activity, alternating interviewers. Have the interviewers take notes on their partners' responses.

Internet Activities Variation

Activities 1 and 4 Have learners use the information they find to write a list of "Dos and Don'ts for Consumers." Have students work in groups. If possible, have students type and post their lists in the classroom.

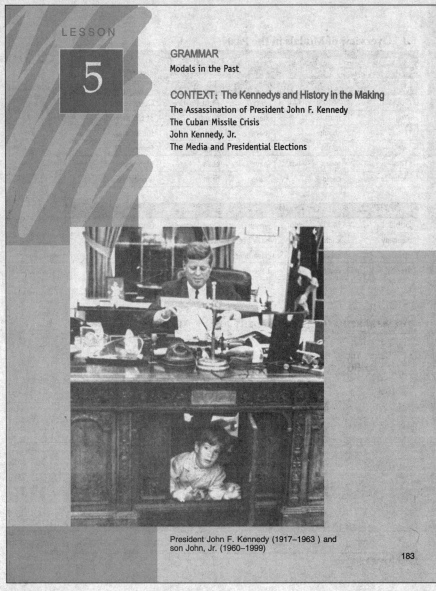

LESSON

5

GRAMMAR
Modals in the Past

CONTEXT: The Kennedys and History in the Making
The Assassination of President John F. Kennedy
The Cuban Missile Crisis
John Kennedy, Jr.
The Media and Presidential Elections

President John F. Kennedy (1917–1963) and
son John, Jr. (1960–1999)

183

Lesson Overview

GRAMMAR

1. Activate students' prior knowledge. Ask: *What did we study in lesson 4?* (modals in the present and future) Ask students to list as many modals as they can.
2. Ask: *What will we study in this lesson?* (modals in the past) Give several examples of your own of sentences using modals in the past (e.g., *I stayed up too late last night. I should have gone to bed earlier. This is a very famous picture; you must have seen it before.*).

CONTEXT

1. Elicit students' prior knowledge. Ask: *What will we learn about in this lesson?* (the assassination of President John F. Kennedy, the Cuban Missile Crisis, John Kennedy, Jr., and the media and presidential elections) *What do you know about John F. Kennedy? About his family?*
2. Have students share their knowledge and personal experiences.

Photo

1. Direct students' attention to the photo. Ask: *Who is this? Where is he?* (John F. Kennedy; in his office at the White House) *Who is under the desk?* (his son, John Kennedy, Jr.)
2. Have students share their knowledge about the Kennedys.

To save class time, have students do the Test/Review at the end of the lesson, or administer a lesson test generated from the Assessment CD-ROM with *ExamView® Pro*. Skip sections of the lesson that students have already mastered. You may also assign some sections for self-study for extra credit.

Expansion

Theme The topic for this lesson can be enhanced with the following ideas:

1. Photos of or articles about John F. Kennedy
2. Photos of or articles about the Kennedy family
3. Letters to a newspaper or online advice column with answers using *should, should have*, etc.

Culture Note

When John F. Kennedy was elected president, he was only 43 years old—the youngest person ever to be elected president. His children, John, Jr., and Caroline, were among the youngest children ever to live in the White House. The famous photograph on page 183 was taken by Stanley Tretick in October of 1963, when John, Jr., was almost 3 years old. John Kennedy was assassinated only a few weeks later.

5.1 | Overview of Modals in the Past

1. Have students cover grammar chart **5.1.** Ask: *What modals have we studied?* (*may, might, could, must, must not, be supposed to, have to, should, had better, ought to, can*) Say: *We have been using modals to express ideas about things that are happening now, or that could happen in the future. We can also use modals to express ideas about things that happened in the past.*

2. Have students uncover and review the example sentences in the grammar chart. Ask students to say what they observe about the rules for using modals in the past. If students have difficulty, say: *To use modals in the past, we add* have *or* have been *and the past participle.*

The Assassination of President John F. Kennedy (Reading)

1. Have students look at the photo on page 184. Ask: *Who are the man and woman in the car?* (President Kennedy and his wife, Jacqueline Kennedy) *Where are they?* (in Dallas, Texas) *Who are the other people?* (the governor of Texas, secret service agents) *Why is this picture famous?* (because it was taken just before Kennedy was shot)

2. Have students look briefly at the reading. Ask: *What is the reading about? How do you know?* Have students make predictions.

3. Preteach any essential vocabulary words your students may not know, such as *assassinated, suspect, evidence, investigation, concrete,* and *mysterious.*

BEFORE YOU READ

1. Have students discuss the questions in pairs. Try to pair students of different language backgrounds.

2. Ask for a few volunteers to share their answers with the class.

🕐 To save class time, skip "Before You Read" or have students prepare answers for homework ahead of time.

5.1 | Overview of Modals in the Past

You can express ideas about things that happened in the past by using a modal + *have* + past participle.

Active

Subject	Modal	*Not*	*Have*	Past Participle	Complement
You	must		have	heard	of the Kennedys.
I	should		have	read	the article.
We	might		have	seen	them on TV.
They	may	not	have	been	born yet.
John Junior	could		have	been	a politician.

Passive

Subject	Modal	*Not*	*Have Been*	Past Participle	Complement
Kennedy	might		have been	elected	again.
He	should		have been	protected	better.
He	could	not	have been	saved.	

THE ASSASSINATION OF PRESIDENT JOHN F. KENNEDY

Before You Read
1. Have you ever heard of President John F. Kennedy?
2. What political leaders have been assassinated?

Expansion

Theme The topic for this lesson can be enhanced with the following ideas:

1. An article about the Kennedy assassination
2. A list of U.S. presidents and the dates they held office
3. Copies of well-known photos of the days following the Kennedy assassination
4. An article or Web site about people's recollections of the day Kennedy was shot

---

Read the following article. Pay special attention to *must have*, *may have*, *might have*, and *could have*.

On November 22, 1963, Americans faced a great tragedy. President John F. Kennedy was assassinated in Dallas, Texas, while he was riding in an open car with the Governor of Texas. Who killed Kennedy, and why?

Immediately after the assassination, a suspect, Lee Harvey Oswald, 24 years old, was arrested. There was evidence showing that Oswald **must have shot** Kennedy from the sixth floor of a nearby building with a rifle. However, two days later, as Oswald was being transferred to a different jail, he was shot and killed by a man in the crowd. Why was he killed too? Because of Oswald's death, many questions remained unanswered.

An investigation took place to find out the truth behind the assassination. After examining a lot of evidence and questioning thousands of people, the investigating committee concluded that Oswald **must have been** the assassin and that he **must have acted** alone. But why did he do it? Some people think Oswald **might have been** an agent of the Soviet government. (In 1959, he gave up his American citizenship and moved to the Soviet Union.[1] He returned to the U.S. in 1962 with a Soviet wife.) Some think Oswald **may have been** a crazy man, just wanting to get attention. Others think the assassination **could have been ordered** by the Mafia.[2] Oswald's assassin, Jack Ruby, had connections with the Mafia. Did the Mafia want to prevent Oswald from talking?

Another question often asked is whether Oswald was the only gunman. Some witnesses report gunshots coming from two different directions. However, the investigating committee found no concrete evidence of this.

Even though the assassination occurred many years ago, people are still fascinated with this event. Books and movies have been made through the years offering new theories about this mysterious tragedy.

Did You Know?

John F. Kennedy was the fourth American president to be assassinated. The other three were Abraham Lincoln [1865], James Garfield [1881], and William McKinley [1901].

[1] In 1991, the country then called the Soviet Union broke up into 15 different countries, the largest of which is Russia. Other former Soviet countries are Ukraine, Belorus, Lithuania, Uzbekistan, and Georgia.
[2] The Mafia is a criminal organization.

Modals in the Past 185

Reading CD 2, Track 1

1. Have students first read the text silently. Tell them to pay special attention to *must have*, *may have*, *might have*, and *could have*. Then play the audio and have students read along silently.
2. Check students' comprehension. Ask questions such as: *When was Kennedy assassinated?* (in 1963) *Was a suspect found?* (yes; Lee Harvey Oswald) *What are some of the things people have wondered about over the years since the assassination?* (why Kennedy was shot, whether the Mafia was involved, whether there was another gunman)

To save class time, have students do the reading for homework ahead of time.

DID YOU KNOW?

Abraham Lincoln was shot in Washington, D.C., while he was at the theater. James Garfield was shot at a train station, also in Washington. William McKinley was shot in Buffalo, New York, where he was attending a fair.

Reading Variation

To practice listening skills, have students first listen to the audio alone. Ask a few comprehension questions. Repeat the audio if necessary. Then have students open their books and read along as they listen to the audio.

Reading Glossary

assassinate: kill intentionally, especially a public or political figure
concrete: real; solid
evidence: clues, proof
investigate: look at carefully; research; seek the truth about
mysterious: unknown; impossible to know or understand; unknowable
suspect: (as a noun) person who authorities think may have committed a crime

5.2 | Past Probability (Deduction, Conclusion)

1. Have students cover the grammar chart. Write an example in the present with *must* expressing probability on the board: *Presidents must worry a lot—they all have gray hair.* Then write a past sentence, e.g., *Kennedy's wife must have been heartbroken when her husband died.* Ask: *What is the difference between these two sentences?* (One is about present time; the other is about the past.) Say: *We don't know that Kennedy's wife was heartbroken, but we think that she probably was. We use must have to express probability in the past.*

2. Have students uncover and review the examples and explanations in the grammar chart.

3. Draw students' attention to the Language Note in the last section of the chart. Tell students that the pairs of sentences have the same meaning, but are formed differently.

EXERCISE 1

🎧 CD 2, Track 2

1. Tell students that this exercise is a series of conversations between friends and family members. Have students read the direction line. Ask: *Do we write verbs for probability in the present, the future, or the past?* (the past)

2. Model the exercise. Direct students to the example in the book. Then do several more lines with the class.

3. Have students complete the rest of Exercise 1 individually. Then have them check their answers in pairs by practicing the dialogues. Circulate and observe the pair work. If necessary, check the answers as a class.

4. Assess students' performance. If necessary, review grammar chart 5.2 on page 186.

5.2 | Past Probability (Deduction, Conclusion)

Examples	Explanation
After examining the evidence, the investigating committee concluded that Oswald **must have killed** Kennedy. Americans **must have felt** a great loss when their president died.	We use *must have* + past participle to make a statement of logical conclusion or deduction about a past event based on observations we make or information we have. We are saying that something is probably true.
When we were talking about Kennedy, Kim looked confused. She **must not have heard** of him.	For a negative probability, use *must not have* + past participle. Do not use a contraction for *must not* when it shows deduction or conclusion.

Language Note:
Compare:
> Oswald *probably killed* Kennedy.
> Oswald **must have killed** Kennedy.

> You *probably saw* a film about the assassination.
> You **must have seen** a film about the assassination.

EXERCISE **1**   Fill in the blanks with an appropriate verb for past probability. Answers may vary.

🎧

1. **A:** Kennedy's death was such a tragedy.

   B: Who's Kennedy?

   A: You don't know who Kennedy was? He was so famous. You must _____*have heard*_____ of him. Here's his picture in this book.
   (example)

   B: No, I've never heard of him. Wow. He was so handsome. He must _____*have been*_____ a movie star.

   A: No. He was an American president. He was assassinated in 1963 when he was only forty-six years old.

   B: That's terrible. It must _____*have been*_____ a hard time for Americans.

   A: Yes, it was. I remember my parents telling me about it. They were in high school when it happened. They must _____*have been*_____ about 15 or 16 years old. They really believed the Soviet government must _____*have ordered*_____ the assassination.

   B: Was Soviet involvement ever proven?

   A: No, but that's what my parents believed.

186   Lesson 5

Grammar Variation

After students have reviewed the example sentences in the grammar chart, have them go back to the reading on page 185 and locate the sentences with *must have*. Have them convert the sentences to statements in the past using *probably*; use the statements in the Language Note as models (e.g., *Oswald probably shot Kennedy from the sixth floor of a nearby building.*).

2. **A:** I followed your directions to go downtown yesterday. I took the number 60 bus, but it didn't take me downtown.

   B: You must ____*have misunderstood*____ me. I said, "16," not "60."

   A: Really? I thought you said, "60."

   B: It's hard to hear the difference between 16 and 60. Even native speakers misunderstand each other. Anyway, you must ____*have had*____ a terrible day.

   A: Yes, I had an awful day. When I got off the bus, I was totally lost, so I took a taxi downtown.

   B: A taxi must ____*have cost*____ you over $20!

   A: In fact, it cost me $30. So I wasted a lot of time and money yesterday.

3. **A:** I called you a couple of times yesterday, but you didn't answer the phone.

   B: You must ____*have called*____ a wrong number. I always keep my cell phone on. What time did you call?

   A: About 4 o'clock.

   B: Oh. I must ____*have been*____ at the hospital at that time visiting my sister. I had to turn off the phone when I was there. They don't allow cell phones in hospitals. Why did you call?

   A: I forgot already.

   B: Then it must not ____*have been*____ very important.

4. **A:** How did you like the party last Saturday, Terri?

   B: I wasn't there.

   A: What do you mean you weren't there? We talked for a few hours.

   B: You must ____*have talked*____ with my twin sister, Sherri. We look alike.

   A: She must ____*have thought*____ that I was crazy. I kept calling her Terri.

   B: I'm sure she didn't think anything of it. She's used to it.

5. **A:** How did you do on the last test?

   B: I didn't know about the test, so I didn't study. I failed it.

   A: The teacher announced it last Thursday.

   B: I must ____*have been*____ absent that day.

   A: I think Rona must ____*have failed*____ it too. When she got her paper, she started to cry.

Exercise 1 Variation

To provide practice with listening skills, have students close their books and listen to the audio. Repeat the audio as needed. Ask comprehension questions, such as: *In conversation 1, had person B ever heard of Kennedy?* (no) *How old was Kennedy when he was assassinated?* (forty-six years old) *How old were person A's parents when it happened?* (about 15 or 16 years old) Then have students open their books and complete Exercise 1.

B: Did you see Paula? She was so excited when she saw her exam. She must ___*have gotten*___ an A.

6. **A:** Maria's relatives just went back to Mexico. They were here for a month.

   B: She must ___*have had*___ a wonderful time with them.

   A: Yes, but she must ___*have been*___ sad when she took them to the airport. She didn't want them to leave. She took them everywhere—to museums, to fancy restaurants, to concerts.

   B: She must ___*have spent*___ a lot of money.

   A: She knew she was going to spend a lot of money, so she saved a lot before they came.

7. **A:** I thought I was driving east, but now I think I'm driving north.

   B: You must ___*have taken*___ a wrong turn somewhere. Let's take a look at the map. (*after looking in the glove compartment*). I can't find the map.

   A: I must ___*have left*___ it on the kitchen table. I was looking at it before we got in the car.

   B: No problem. Let's just call our friends. They'll tell us how to get to their house. Let me use your cell phone.

   A: Oh, no. The battery is dead. I must ___*have left*___ the phone on all night last night.

   B: I told you never to leave it on at night. Why don't we just stop at a gas station and get directions?

   A: You know I don't like to ask for directions.

8. **A:** I said, "How are you?" to one of my classmates, and she answered, "I'm 58 years old." What was she thinking?

   B: She must ___*have thought*___ that you said, "How *old* are you?"

   A: She gave me a strange look. She must ___*have thought*___ that I was impolite asking about her age.

   B: That's nothing. When I didn't speak much English, I went to a restaurant and asked the waitress for "soap" instead of "soup."

   A: So did she bring you soap or soup?

   B: Soup, of course.

   A: Then she must ___*have understood*___ you in spite of your mistake.

9. **A:** I haven't seen Peter this semester. Have you?

   B: He must ___*have dropped out*___.

Expansion

Exercise 1 Have students choose one of the conversations in the exercise. Have them write conclusions about the relationship between the people, based on the information in and tone of the conversations (e.g., *They must be classmates because they are talking about a test they both took.*).

Exercise 1 Have pairs of students choose one of the dialogues in Exercise 1. Ask them to write two additional sentences to continue the dialogue. Ask volunteers to present their extended dialogues to the class.

Culture Note

Cultures differ as to whether it is acceptable to ask adults about their age. In the U.S., it is generally not considered acceptable to ask adults their age. It is acceptable to ask children how old they are.

A: Why would he drop out? He was close to getting his degree.

B: He said that he wouldn't come back if he didn't get financial aid. He must not _____have gotten_____ financial aid this semester.

A: That's too bad.

10. A: You look tan. You must _____have been_____ out in the sun.

B: I was. I was in Florida for vacation.

A: That must _____have been_____ wonderful.

B: Actually, it was terrible. First, I lost our money and credit cards.

A: What did you do?

B: The credit card company cancelled our card and gave us a new one. We used the credit card to get cash.

A: So then the rest of your trip was fine, wasn't it?

B: Not really. We rented a car and it kept breaking down.

A: But it must _____have been_____ nice to get away from winter here and be in the sun.

B: We were there for two weeks. It must _____have rained_____ for all but the last few days. Finally when the rain stopped, I got some sun.

5.3 | Past Possibility

Examples	Explanation
Why did Oswald kill Kennedy? There are several theories: The Mafia **may have ordered** the assassination. Oswald **might have been** crazy. He **could have been** the agent of another government.	To express possibility about the past, use *may have*, *might have*, or *could have* + past participle. The sentences on the left give theories about the past.
Oswald **may not have acted** alone. He **might not have been** the only assassin.	To show negative possibility, use *may not have* and *might not have*. Don't use *could not have* because it has a different meaning. (See Section 5.9.)
Language Note: Compare: *Maybe* the Mafia ordered the assassination. The Mafia **may have ordered** the assassination. *Maybe* Oswald was a Soviet agent. Oswald **might have been** a Soviet agent.	

Modals in the Past   189

5.3 | Past Possibility

1. Have students cover the grammar chart. Ask: *Does everyone today agree about what happened on the day Kennedy was assassinated?* (no) Say: *Many people still think there might have been two gunmen.* Write the sentence on the board. Ask: *What does* might have been *show?* (a possibility in the past)

2. Have students uncover and review the examples and explanations in the grammar chart. Check that students understand that a theory is something we think may happen, or may have happened.

3. Draw students' attention to the Language Note in the last section of the chart. Tell students that the pairs of sentences have the same meaning, but are formed differently.

Grammar Variation

Have students look back at the reading on page 185. Ask them to underline the three sentences with *could have been*, *may have been*, and *might have been*. Ask: *Are we sure about these three things?* (No; they are theories.) Then review the grammar chart as a class.

1. Tell students that this exercise is about guesses about a student. Have students read the direction line. Ask: *What did the student do?* (He dropped out of the course after the first few weeks.)
2. Model the exercise. Direct students to the example in the book. Then do #1 with the class. Ask a volunteer to give the answer.
3. Have students complete Exercise 2 individually. Then have them check their answers in pairs. If necessary, check the answers as a class.

🎧 **CD 2, Track 3**

1. Tell students that this exercise is a series of conversations between friends and family members. Have students read the direction line. Ask: *Is more than one answer possible?* (yes)
2. Model the exercise. Direct students to the example in the book. Then finish the first conversation with the class.
3. Have students complete the rest of the exercise individually. Then have them check their answers in pairs by practicing the dialogues. Circulate and observe the pair work. If necessary, check the answers as a class.
4. Assess students' performance. If necessary, review grammar chart **5.3** on page 189.

🕐 To save class time, have students do half of the exercise in class and complete the other half for homework. Or assign the entire exercise for homework.

EXERCISE 2 Change these *maybe* statements to statements with *may have, might have,* or *could have.* Situation: A student dropped out of the course after the first few weeks. These are some guesses about why he did it.

EXAMPLE Maybe he registered for the wrong section. (may)
He may have registered for the wrong section.

1. Maybe he preferred an earlier class. (could)
   He could have preferred an earlier class.
2. Maybe he wanted to be in his friend's class. (might)
   He might have wanted to be in his friend's class.
3. Maybe the class was too hard for him. (may)
   The class may have been too hard for him.
4. Maybe he got sick. (could)
   He could have gotten sick.
5. Maybe he didn't like the teacher. (may)
   He may not have liked the teacher.
6. Maybe he found a full-time job. (might)
   He might have found a full-time job.
7. Maybe he had a lot of problems at home. (could)
   He could have had a lot of problems at home.
8. Maybe he left town. (might)
   He might have left town.

EXERCISE 3 Fill in the blanks with an appropriate verb for past possibility. Answers may vary.

1. A: I was trying to call you last night, but you didn't answer.
   B: What time did you call?
   A: After 8 p.m.
   B: Let's see. Where was I? I might ___*have been*___ at the
      (example)
      library at that time.
   A: But I tried calling your cell phone too.
   B: I may ___*have turned*___ it off. I often turn it off when I'm not expecting a call. Why didn't you leave a message?
   A: I did leave a message.
   B: Oh. I might ___*have deleted*___ it by mistake.
   A: You deleted my message?
   B: Sorry.

2. A: Have you seen my keys?
   B: You're always losing your keys. You may ___*have left*___ them in your pocket.
   A: No, they're not there. I already looked.

Expansion

Exercise 2 Have students work in groups to propose additional possible reasons the student dropped out.

Exercise 3 Have students choose item 4 or 5. In pairs, have students write follow-up conversations in which the person calls about the job (#4) or asks again about the raise (#5). Have pairs perform their conversations for the class.

B: Well, you could _have dropped_ them as you were getting out of the car.

A: When I drop keys, I can hear them hit the ground, so I'm sure that's not it.

B: Well, you might _have left_ them in the door when you came in last night.

A: Oh, you're right! They're in the door. Thanks.

3. **A:** I'm so upset. I left my dictionary in class yesterday. Now I'll have to buy a new one.

   B: Why don't you ask the teacher? She might _have picked_ it up.

   A: I already did. She didn't pick it up.

   B: Why don't you go to the "lost and found"? Somebody may _have found_ it and returned it there.

   A: Where's the "lost and found"?

   B: In front of the cafeteria.

4. **A:** I applied for a job three weeks ago, but so far I haven't heard anything. I probably didn't do well on the interview.

   B: You don't know that. They might _have interviewed_ hundreds of candidates for the job. Anyway, why don't you call and tell the company you're still interested?

   A: But they could _have hired_ someone else already.

   B: You won't know if they hired someone else unless you ask.

5. **A:** I asked my boss for a raise last week, and she said she'd get back to me. But so far she hasn't mentioned anything.

   B: She might _have forgotten_ about it. I'm sure she has a lot on her mind and can easily forget something. Why don't you ask her again?

6. **A:** I sent an e-mail to an old friend and I got a message saying it was undeliverable.

   B: You might _have written_ the address wrong.

   A: No. I checked. I wrote it correctly.

   B: Your friend may _have closed_ his old account and opened a new one.

Modals in the Past **191**

Exercise 3 Variation

To provide practice with listening skills, have students close their books and listen to the audio. Repeat the audio as needed. Ask comprehension questions, such as: *In conversation 1, what did person A do last night?* (tried to call person B) *Did person B answer?* (no) *Did person A call person B's home phone or cell phone?* (both) Then have students open their books and complete Exercise 3.

Expansion

Exercise 3 Have students practice the conversations in pairs. Have volunteers act out the conversations for the class.

The Cuban Missile Crisis (Reading)

1. Have students look at the photo. Ask: *What is this?* (a ship) *Where is it going?* (to Cuba) *What is the date in the picture?* (1962)
2. Have students look at the title, and look briefly at the reading. Ask: *What is the reading about? How do you know?* Have students make predictions.
3. Preteach any vocabulary words your students may not know, such as *nuclear war, missile, threat, national security, military base,* and *spy.*

BEFORE YOU READ

1. Activate students' prior knowledge about the Cuban Missile Crisis. Ask: *Where is Cuba?* (in the Caribbean, south of Florida) *In the early 1960s, what country supported Cuba?* (the Soviet Union) *Did the U.S. and the Soviet Union have a friendly relationship at that time?* (no)
2. Have students discuss the questions in pairs. Try to pair students of different language backgrounds.
3. Ask a few volunteers to share their answers with the class.

To save class time, skip "Before You Read" or have students prepare answers for homework ahead of time.

Reading 🎧 CD 2, Track 4

1. Have students first read the text silently. Tell them to pay special attention to *could have* in the reading. Then play the audio and have students read along silently.
2. Check students' comprehension. Ask questions such as: *What did the Soviet Union want to send to Cuba in 1962?* (nuclear missiles) *Why did President Kennedy consider the missiles a threat to the U.S.?* (because they could have been used to attack the U.S.) *What happened to the missiles? Were they delivered to Cuba?* (No; President Kennedy sent the U.S. Navy to block the Soviet ships, and after 13 days they were sent back to the Soviet Union.)

To save class time, have students do the reading for homework ahead of time.

THE CUBAN MISSILE CRISIS

Before You Read

1. Has your native country ever been at war with another country? What started the war?
2. Do you think a nuclear war is possible today?

🎧 Read the following article. Pay special attention to *could have* + past participle.

In October 1962, the United States and the Soviet Union came close to war. The U.S. discovered that the Soviet Union was beginning to send nuclear missiles to Cuba, which is only about 90 miles from Florida. President John Kennedy saw this as a direct threat to national security; these weapons **could have been** used to destroy cities and military bases in the U.S. On October 22, President Kennedy announced on TV that any attack from Cuba would be considered an attack from the Soviet Union, and he would respond with a full attack on the Soviets. He sent out the U.S. Navy to block Soviet ships from delivering weapons to Cuba. For 13 days, the world was at the edge of a major war. Finally, the Soviets agreed to send their missiles back and promised to stop building military bases in Cuba. In exchange, the U.S. promised to remove its missiles from Turkey.

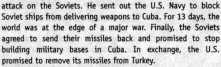

In October of 2002, there was a reunion of many of the surviving players in this crisis. Cuban President Fidel Castro met with former Secretary of Defense Robert McNamara and other Americans, Cubans, and Russians involved in the decisions made 40 years earlier. Remembering their experiences, they all agreed that this was indeed a major crisis that **could have changed** the world as we know it. Discussing the viewpoints and experiences of the Americans, McNamara explained that a nuclear attack on a U.S. ship **could** easily **have grown** into a full nuclear war between the U.S. and the Soviet Union. A former CIA[3] analyst who studied spy photos told the group that at least 16 intermediate-range missiles in Cuba **could have reached** any point in the continental United States[4] except the northwest corner. He said at the conference, "October 27 is a day I'll never forget. The planet **could have been destroyed**." A former Kennedy aide added, "It **could have been** the end of the world, but here we are, 40 years later."

Fortunately, diplomacy[5] won over war. What **could have been** a tragic event is now only a chapter in history.

---
[3] The *CIA* is the Central Intelligence Agency, the U.S. agency that protects American secrets from other countries and gathers information about the secrets of other nations.
[4] The *continental* United States refers to all states except Hawaii and Alaska, which are not part of the U.S. mainland.
[5] *Diplomacy* is skillful negotiation between countries to try to work out problems without fighting.

192　Lesson 5

Expansion

Theme The topic for this lesson can be enhanced with the following ideas:

1. Historical articles or pages from the Internet about the Cuban missile crisis
2. A map of North America and the Caribbean
3. A map of the world

Reading Variation

To practice listening skills, have students first listen to the audio alone. Ask a few comprehension questions. Repeat the audio if necessary. Then have students open their books and read along as they listen to the audio.

Reading Glossary

military base: center of operations for the army or other armed forces
missile: weapon thrown, dropped, or launched; rocket
national security: safety of a country
nuclear war: war involving nuclear weapons
spy: person who tries secretly to get information about an enemy or another country
threat: danger

5.4 | Past Direction Not Taken

We use *could have* + past participle to show that something did not happen.	
Examples	Explanation
The Cuban Missile Crisis **could have been** the end of the world. An attack on a U.S. ship **could have grown** into a full nuclear war. Missiles **could have reached** almost any place in the U.S.	Use *could have* + past participle to show that something was possible in the past, but it didn't happen.
Kennedy and his advisors looked at several possibilities. They **could have attacked** immediately. They **could have invaded** Cuba. But they decided to give the Soviets a chance to remove the missiles and turn the ships around.	Use *could have* + past participle to show that a past opportunity was not taken. Several options were possible, but all but one were rejected.
I heard you moved last weekend. Why didn't you tell me? I **could have helped** you.	Use *could have* + past participle to show missed opportunities.
I was so hungry I **could have eaten** the whole pie by myself. I was so tired I **could have slept** all day. I was so happy when I got an A on the test I **could have kissed** the teacher. When the missiles were moved, we **could have jumped** for joy.	Use *could have* + past participle to show a desire to do something. Often an exaggeration is made in showing the desire.
Driver to pedestrian: Watch out, you idiot! I **could have killed** you. Father to son: Don't play baseball so close to the house. Your ball came within inches of the window. You **could have broken** the window. The 1962 crisis **could have been** the end of the world, but here we are, 40 years later.	Use *could have* + past participle to show that something came close to happening, but didn't.

5.4 | Past Direction Not Taken

1. Ask students to cover the grammar chart. Tell students something about your past goals, such as: *I loved to draw when I was young. You've seen my drawings on the blackboard. I think I could have been a great artist. Do you agree?* Say: *It didn't happen. We use* could have *and the past participle to talk about something that was possible, but didn't happen.*
2. Have students uncover and look at the grammar chart. Review the examples and explanations.
3. Ask a few volunteers to give examples of their own about a time when something could have happened, but didn't.

Culture Note
People in the U.S. sometimes say, "I was so happy I could have cried." Ask students what they think this means. Ask if people use an expression like this one in their native countries.

1. Tell students that this exercise is a series of conversations between friends and family members. Have students read the direction line.
2. Direct students to the example. Ask: *Was it possible for the two superpowers to destroy the world?* (yes) *Did they destroy the world?* (no)
3. Complete #1 as a class. Have students complete the exercise individually. Then have them check their answers in pairs by practicing the dialogues. Circulate and observe the pair work. If necessary, check the answers as a class.
4. Assess students' performance. If necessary, review grammar chart **5.4** on page 193.

EXERCISE 4   Fill in the blanks with an appropriate verb for past direction not taken. Answers may vary.

🎧 EXAMPLE   A: Did you read about the Cuban Missile Crisis?
   B: Yes. The U.S. almost went to war with the Soviet Union.
   A: Those two big superpowers could _have destroyed_ the whole world!

Robert Kennedy

1.   A: Did you read about Robert Kennedy?
   B: You mean John Kennedy, don't you?
   A: No, Robert, John's brother. He was running for president in 1968 when he was assassinated. He could _have been_ president of the U.S., but he was assassinated. He was only 42 years old.

2.   A: I heard you bought a condo.
   B: We did.
   A: Why didn't you buy a house? Was it too expensive?
   B: We could _have bought_ a house, but we don't have enough time for maintenance. So we thought a condo would be better. There's someone to take care of the grass in the summer and the snow in the winter.

3.   A: What do you do for a living?
   B: I'm a waiter, but I could _have been_ a famous actor. Everyone says I've got a lot of talent. And my wife could _have had_ a career in modeling. She's so beautiful.
   A: It's not too late to follow your dream.
   B: We have small kids to support. So I think my acting days and her modeling days are over.

4.   A: Do you want to see our new apartment? We moved last Saturday.
   B: Why did you move? You had a lovely apartment. I'm surprised you didn't stay there.
   A: We could _have stayed_ there. The rent wasn't too bad and the landlord was nice. But it was too far from school and work.
   B: Who helped you move?

194   Lesson 5

Exercise 4 Variation

To provide practice with listening skills, have students close their books and listen to the audio. Repeat the audio as needed. Ask comprehension questions, such as: *In conversation 1, who is Robert Kennedy?* (John F. Kennedy's brother) *What happened to Robert Kennedy in 1968?* (He was running for president when he was assassinated.) *How old was Robert Kennedy when he was assassinated?* (forty-two years old) Then have students open their books and complete Exercise 4.

Culture Note

Robert (Bobby) Kennedy was John F. Kennedy's younger brother. He served as attorney general of the United States while his brother was president. In 1968, five years after the assassination, Bobby Kennedy decided to run for president. He was assassinated in Los Angeles five months before the presidential election.

A: We did it all ourselves.

B: Why didn't you let me know? I could _____have helped_____ you.

A: We didn't want to bother our friends.

B: What are friends for?

A: Anyway, you have a small car. We needed to rent a van.

B: I could _____have borrowed_____ my sister's van. She always lets me borrow it if I have to move stuff.

A: We appreciate your kindness, but everything worked out fine.

5. A: I can't believe you tried to fix the ceiling light without shutting off the electricity first. You could _____have killed_____ yourself.

B: But I didn't. I'm still alive and the light is fixed.

A: You shouldn't take chances. And you got up on that tall ladder when you were home alone. You could _____have fallen_____, and no one would have been here to help you.

B: But I didn't fall. You worry too much. Everything's okay. The light is fixed, and I didn't break a leg.

6. A: I bought stocks and sold them a few months later. Now they're worth four times as much as what I sold them for. I could _____have made_____ a lot of money.

B: You never know with the stock market. You could _____have lost_____ a lot of money too.

7. A: I'm so tired.

B: What happened?

A: I had to take three buses to get to a job interview in the suburbs. It took me almost two hours to get there.

B: Why didn't you tell me? I could _____have taken_____ you there in my car.

A: I didn't want to bother you.

B: You wasted a whole day today. You could _____have been_____ home hours ago.

A: That's not a problem. I'm home now. And I did my homework while I was on the bus on the way there. On the way home, I slept most of the way. It's a good thing the person sitting next to me woke me up. I could _____have missed_____ my bus stop.

Modals in the Past 195

Expansion

Exercise 4 Have students practice the conversations in pairs. Then have volunteers act out the conversations for the class.

Culture Note

Stocks are shares of the ownership of a company. Companies sell stocks to people who want to invest in the company. The value of the stocks goes up and down, and an investor who buys or sells stock at the right time can make, or lose, a lot of money. Stocks are bought and sold— or traded—on the stock market.

EXERCISE 5

1. Tell students that this exercise is about exaggerations. Have students read the direction line.
2. Model the exercise. Direct students to the example in the book. Ask: *What modal do we use?* (*could have*) Then do #1 with the class.
3. Have students complete Exercise 5 individually. Then have them compare their answers in pairs. If necessary, check the answers as a class.
4. Assess students' performance. If necessary, review grammar chart **5.4** on page 193.

🕐 To save class time, have students do half of the exercise in class and complete the other half for homework. Or assign the entire exercise for homework.

EXERCISE 6

1. Tell students that this exercise is about something they didn't do in the past. Have students read the direction line.
2. Review the example with the class. Ask: *What didn't this person do?* (go to Germany) *What did this person do?* (come to the U.S.) *Why?* (because it is easier to find a job in the U.S.)
3. Have students work in groups to discuss what they plan to write about. Circulate and observe the group work. Then have students complete the exercise individually. Have them share their final answers with the group, and then with the class.
4. Assess students' performance. If necessary, review grammar chart **5.4** on page 193.

🕐 To save class time, have students complete the exercise for homework.

EXERCISE **5** Fill in the blanks with the correct form of the verb in parentheses ( ) to show an exaggeration.

EXAMPLE The party was so wonderful that I could __have stayed__ all night.
(stay)

1. I was so tired that I could __have slept__ for 12 hours yesterday.
(sleep)

2. I was so embarrassed when I made a mistake in my speech that I could __have died__ of shame.
(die)

3. She was so happy when she fell in love that she could __have walked__ on air.
(walk)

4. I was so happy when my counselor told me about my scholarship that I could __have kissed__ him.
(kiss)

5. The movie was so good that I could __have watched__ it again and again.
(watch)

6. Your cookies were so good that I could __have eaten__ all of them.
(eat)

7. I enjoyed dancing so much last night that I could __have danced__ all night.
(dance)

8. It was so hot yesterday that we could __have fried__ an egg on the street.
(fry)

EXERCISE **6** ABOUT YOU Fill in the blanks to tell about a missed opportunity that you did not take. Share your answers in a small group or with the entire class.

EXAMPLE *I could have gone to Germany instead of coming to the U.S., but it's easier to find a job in my profession in the U.S.*

I could have __Answers will vary.__ instead of _____ but
(use verb + -ing)

_____

_____

_____

196   Lesson 5

Expansion

Exercise 5 Ask volunteers to give exaggerations of their own about a time when they were happy, tired, hungry, etc.

JOHN KENNEDY, JR.

Before You Read

1. Did you hear about the death of John Kennedy, Jr., in 1999? Where were you when you heard the news?

2. Do you know of any plane crashes in which someone famous died?

 Read the following article. Pay special attention to *was/were supposed to* and *should have* and other past modals.

The Kennedy family has seen more than its share of tragedies. President Kennedy was assassinated at the age of 46 in 1963. His brother, Robert, was assassinated at the age of 42 while he was running for president in 1968. Tragedy struck the Kennedy family again in 1999.

John Kennedy, Jr., could hardly remember his father. Born 17 days before his father was elected president of the U.S., he was three days short of his third birthday when his father was assassinated.

The president's son was handsome. Many people thought he could have been an actor, but his mother wanted him to be a lawyer. Some people expected him to follow in his father's and uncles' footsteps and go into politics. But after practicing law for a few years, he decided to publish a political magazine instead. Among the political leaders he interviewed was Fidel Castro, one of his father's political enemies.

Because he was so famous, Kennedy couldn't go out in public without being followed by photographers. He decided to learn to fly to avoid commercial airlines, where other passengers asked him questions, took his picture, and wanted his autograph.

On July 16, 1999, only 15 months after getting his pilot's license, he planned to fly to Massachusetts for his cousin's wedding. He took off with his wife and

(continued)

Modals in the Past 197

Expansion

Theme The topic for this lesson can be enhanced with the following ideas:

1. A timeline or family tree showing the Kennedy family members and history
2. An article or Web page about Kennedy's plane crash
3. An article about planes and safety

Reading Variation

To practice listening skills, have students first listen to the audio alone. Ask a few comprehension questions. Repeat the audio if necessary. Then have students open their books and read along as they listen to the audio.

Culture Note

Jr. (*junior*) is a title added to a boy's name (e.g., John Smith, Jr.) if he is given the same name his father has (e.g., John Smith). If John Smith, Jr., gives his son the same name, the child is named John Smith III, pronounced *John Smith the third.* The next generation would be John Smith IV, etc. There is no equivalent naming convention for girls.

John Kennedy, Jr. (Reading)

1. Have students look at the photos. Ask: *Who is this?* (John Kennedy, Jr.) *Do you know when the photo on the right was taken?* (when his father, President Kennedy, died)
2. Have students look briefly at the reading. Have students look at the title of the reading. Ask: *What is the reading about? How do you know?* Have students make predictions.
3. Preteach any vocabulary words your students may not know, such as: *short of, practicing law, deadly, visibility,* and *disoriented.*

BEFORE YOU READ

1. Activate students' prior knowledge about John Kennedy, Jr. Ask: *What do you know about John Kennedy, Jr.?*
2. Have students discuss the questions in pairs. Try to pair students of different language backgrounds.
3. Ask a few volunteers to share their answers with the class.

To save class time, skip "Before You Read" or have students prepare answers for homework ahead of time.

Reading 🎧 CD 2, Track 6

1. Have students first read the text silently. Tell them to pay special attention to *was/were supposed to, should have,* and other past modals. Then play the audio and have students read along silently.
2. Check students' comprehension. Ask questions such as: *What jobs did John Kennedy, Jr., have?* (He was a lawyer, and he published a political magazine.) *What happened to Kennedy and his wife and sister-in-law?* (They were killed when his plane went down.) *Why was Kennedy's death so tragic?* (because of the assassinations in his family, because he was young, etc.)

To save class time, have students do the reading for homework ahead of time.

5.5 | Past Mistakes

1. Have students cover the grammar chart. Ask students to look back at the reading on pages 197 and 198 and underline the instances of *should have* and *shouldn't have*. Ask: *What are two things the article says Kennedy should have done?* (stayed near the shoreline; left a flight plan) Write one sentence with an inference from the article on the board, e.g., *Kennedy should have waited for daylight.*

2. Have students uncover and look at grammar chart **5.5**. Review the examples and explanations in the chart. Point out that *ought to* has the same meaning as *should*, but is used less frequently with the past.

3. Draw students' attention to the Usage Note. Emphasize that *you shouldn't have* in this context does not mean that the person doesn't appreciate the gift, or thinks that the giver has made a mistake. If appropriate, role-play giving a gift and the polite use of *You shouldn't have. /But it is my pleasure.*

---

her sister as passengers at 8:30 p.m. They **were supposed to** arrive in Massachusetts a few hours later, but they never arrived. The next morning, searchers found their suitcases washed up on the shore. They concluded that Kennedy's plane must have crashed that night and that all three of them had died. The wedding that **was supposed to** take place was canceled as family members waited for more news. Six days later, the three bodies were found.

How or why did this accident occur? Experienced pilots believe that Kennedy made several deadly mistakes:

- He flew in darkness over water. As an inexperienced pilot, he **shouldn't have flown** in darkness.
- Because of the weather, visibility was very low that night, and he didn't have much experience using the instruments. He **shouldn't have flown** with such low visibility.
- He flew over water, where it is easy to become disoriented. He **should have stayed** close to the shoreline.
- He didn't leave a flight plan.[6] He **should have left** a flight plan.
- His plane was large and difficult to handle. He may not have been able to handle such a large plane in a difficult situation. As an inexperienced pilot, he **shouldn't have flown** such a big plane.
- He had broken his ankle a few months earlier and had to walk with a cane. Because of his injured ankle, he may not have been able to handle the foot pedals.

John Kennedy was only 39 years old when he died, seven years younger than his father was when he died. His wife was 33.

5.5 | Past Mistakes

Examples	Explanation
Kennedy **should have made** the trip in daylight. Kennedy **should have stayed** close to the shore. He **shouldn't have flown** in such bad weather conditions.	We use *should have* + past participle to comment on a mistake that was made. We are not really giving advice because it is impossible to change the past.
He **ought to have made** the trip in daylight.	Less frequently, we use *ought to have* + past participle. *Ought to* is not usually used for negatives.

Usage Note:
When a person receives an unexpected gift, he may be a little embarrassed. This person might say, *"You shouldn't have."* This means, "You shouldn't have gone to so much trouble or expense." or "You shouldn't have given me a gift. I don't deserve it." Saying this is considered polite, and an appropriate response might be, *"But it is my pleasure."*

[6] A *flight plan* gives information, such as the pilot's name, the speed of the airplane, the route, estimated flying time, fuel level, and registration of the airplane.

198   Lesson 5

Reading Glossary

deadly: extremely dangerous; life threatening
disoriented: confused; lost
practice law: work as a lawyer
short of: before; under
visibility: ability to see

EXERCISE **7** Fill in the blanks with *have* and an appropriate past participle.

EXAMPLE Kennedy should ___*have flown*___ before dark.

1. He didn't leave until after dark. He should ___*have left*___ earlier.

2. He bought a large plane that was difficult to handle. He shouldn't ___*have bought*___ such a large plane.

3. He chose to fly over water. He should ___*have chosen*___ a better route.

4. He didn't pay much attention to the weather conditions. He should ___*have paid*___ attention to the weather conditions.

5. He didn't have much experience with the instrument panel. He should ___*have had*___ more experience with the instrument panel if he wanted to fly at night.

6. When he realized it was getting dark, he should ___*have waited*___ until the next morning.

EXERCISE **8** Fill in the blanks with an appropriate verb for past mistakes.

EXAMPLES A: I didn't study for the last test, and I failed it.

B: You should ___*have studied*___.

A: I know, but there was a great party the night before, and I went with my friends.

B: You shouldn't ___*have gone*___ to a party the night before a test.

1. A: I'm so hungry. I didn't have time to eat breakfast this morning.

B: You should ___*have eaten*___ something before class.

A: I know, but I was late.

B: What time did you get up?

A: About 45 minutes before class.

B: You should ___*have gotten up*___ earlier. By the way, what topic did you use for your composition?

A: Oh, my gosh! I forgot about the composition.

B: You should ___*have written*___ down the assignment.

A: You're right. I'll get a calendar, and from now on, I'll write down all my assignments.

---

1. Tell students that this exercise is about experienced pilots' opinions about Kennedy's flight. Have students read the direction line. Ask: *How many words do we write?* (two: *have* and a past participle)

2. Direct students to the example in the book. Then do #1 with the class.

3. Have students complete Exercise 7 individually. Then have them compare their answers in pairs. Finally, check the answers as a class.

EXERCISE 8

🎧 *CD 2, Track 7*

1. Tell students that this exercise is about mistakes people have made. Have students read the direction line.

2. Direct students to the examples in the book. Have two students model the conversation. Then do #1 with the class.

3. Have students complete a part of Exercise 8 individually. Then have them check their answers by practicing the dialogues in pairs. Finally, check the answers as a class.

4. Assess students' performance. If necessary, review grammar chart **5.6** on page 198.

🕐 To save class time, have students do half of the exercise in class and complete the other half for homework. Or assign the entire exercise for homework.

Expansion

Exercise 7 Have students work in groups to make a list of all of the flight-related and airplane-related vocabulary they can find in Exercise 7 and in the reading on pages 197 and 198. Have groups use a dictionary to clarify the meanings of any terms they are not familiar with.

Exercise 8 Variation

To provide practice with listening skills, have students close their books and listen to the audio. Repeat the audio as needed. Ask comprehension questions, such as: *In conversation 1, why is person A hungry?* (Person A didn't have time to eat breakfast.) *What time did person A get up?* (about 45 minutes before class) *Did person A write a composition?* (no) Then have students open their books and complete Exercise 8.

2. (cell phone conversation)

A: Hi. I'm at the supermarket now. Did you ask me to buy cereal?

B: Yes. Don't you remember? You should _____ have taken _____ the list.

A: I know, but I thought I'd remember everything so I didn't take the list.

B: This is what we need: a gallon of milk, a bag of dog food, and a watermelon.

A: Those things are heavy. How do you expect me to carry all of those things home?

B: In the car, of course.

A: Oh. I came here by bike. I should _____ have driven / taken the car _____

B: Yes, you should have.

3. A: How was your trip during spring break?

B: It was great. You should _____ have come _____ with us.

A: I wanted to go with you, but I didn't have enough money.

B: You should _____ have saved _____ your money instead of spending it eating out in restaurants all the time.

A: You're right. And I shouldn't _____ have bought _____ so many CDs.

B: Did you get my postcard?

A: No. When did you send it?

B: Over two weeks ago. I should _____ have taken _____ it to the post office instead of putting it in the hotel mailbox.

4. (husband and wife)

A: I washed my blue pants with my new white shirt and now my shirt looks blue.

B: You should _____ have separated _____ the clothes by color before putting them in the washing machine. I always separate mine.

A: I should _____ have given _____ my clothes to you to wash.

B: I may be your wife, but I'm not your maid. So don't give me your dirty clothes.

5. (wife and husband)

A: This is a terrible trip. Why did you suggest going to the mountains? We should _____ have gone _____ to the coast. It's too cold here. I don't like cold weather.

B: You should _____ have told _____ me that before we left.

Culture Note

The phrase *second guessing* is sometimes used to refer to criticizing someone else's actions after they have happened (e.g., *I knew this would happen. You should have bought more pizza.*). Saying *I told you so* after someone makes a mistake is also second guessing. Second guessing is usually not socially appropriate, unless the people involved know each other well, or are not taking the conversation too seriously.

A: I *did* tell you that, but you didn't pay attention. We didn't take

B: jackets. We should ___have taken___ our jackets.

B: We can go and buy some.

A: I don't want to spend money on jackets when we've got perfectly good ones at home.

B: Maybe we should ___have stayed___ at home instead of taking a trip.

6. (*student and teacher*)

A: Can you tell me my midterm grade?

B: Didn't you receive it by mail?

A: No. I moved right after the semester began.

B: You should ___have reported___ a change of address in the school office when you moved.

A: I'll report it today. So can you tell me my grade?

B: It's a C.

A: Why C? I got B's and A's on the tests.

B: But you didn't do all your homework. You should ___have done___ all your homework.

A: But I had to work full time.

B: You should ___have thought___ about that before you registered for four courses.

A: You're right. I didn't think much about homework when I registered.

7. A: I took a young woman from class out for dinner last week, but I didn't have enough money.

B: You should ___have taken___ enough money with you.

A: I took about $30 with me. I thought we were going to go to a fast-food place, but she chose a fancy restaurant.

B: You should ___have chosen___ the restaurant.

A: I realized that later. She ordered appetizers, then dinner, then dessert and coffee. I thought she would pay for part of the dinner. But when the bill came, she just sat there.

B: You should ___have told___ her that you wanted to split the bill.

A: I couldn't tell her that. I was trying to impress her.

B: So what did you do?

Expansion

Exercise 8 Have students work in groups. Assign one of the conversations from Exercise 8 to each group. Ask groups to brainstorm ideas about the people in the conversation and their relationship, based on the way they address one another and the way they comment on one another's past mistakes. Ask groups to write a short description of the people and their relationship. Collect and redistribute the descriptions. Have each group guess which conversation matches the description they have been given.

5.6 | *Be Supposed To* in the Past

1. Have students cover grammar chart **5.6.** Give several examples of things you were supposed to do but didn't (e.g., *I was supposed to go to a meeting last night, but my children were sick. I was supposed to bring some pictures today, but I forgot.*). Elicit several examples from students.

2. Have students uncover and look at grammar chart **5.6.** Review the example sentences and explanations.

3. Remind students that the *d* in *supposed to* is not pronounced.

EXERCISE 9

1. Tell students that this exercise is about things people were supposed to do. Have students read the direction line. Ask: *Do we write about things people did or things people didn't do?* (things people didn't do)

2. Direct students to the example in the book. Then complete #1 with the class.

3. Have students complete the exercise individually. Have students compare their answers in pairs. If necessary, review answers as a class.

A: I went to the bathroom and called my brother on my cell phone. He rushed over to the restaurant and brought me some money. He pretended that our meeting there was an accident.

B: You should ___*have told*___ her the truth. Lying to her is no way to start a relationship.

A: I don't think I'm going to go out with her again.

8. A: What happened to your car?

B: I had an accident. Someone hit me from behind.

A: What did the police say?

B: We didn't call the police. The other driver gave me his phone number and told me he would pay for the damage. But when I called, it was a disconnected number.

A: You should ___*have called*___ the police.

B: And I should ___*have taken*___ information from his driver's license.

A: You mean you didn't even take information from his driver's license?

B: No. He looked honest.

A: You should ___*have gotten*___ information about his insurance too.

B: I know. It's too late to get it now.

5.6 | *Be Supposed To* in the Past

Examples	Explanation
Kennedy and his wife **were supposed to** arrive in Massachusetts on Friday night, but they didn't.	*Was/were supposed to* is used to show that an expected action did not happen.
His cousin's wedding **was supposed to** take place the next day, but it didn't.	
We **were supposed to** have a test today, but the teacher was absent.	
You **were supposed to** stop at the stop sign, but you didn't.	*Was/were supposed to* is used for rules or promises that have been broken.
I **was supposed to** call my parents last night, but I forgot.	

EXERCISE 9 Fill in the blanks with a verb.

EXAMPLE She was supposed to ___*finish*___ the report by Friday, but she didn't have enough time.

1. I was supposed to ___*print*___ my homework, but my printer wasn't working. So I wrote it by hand.

202 Lesson 5

Grammar Variation

Have students look back at the reading on pages 197 and 198. Have students locate the two sentences with *supposed to*. Ask: *Did Kennedy and his family arrive in Massachusetts?* (no) *Did the wedding take place that day?* (no) Then review the grammar chart.

2. You were supposed to _____ *call* _____ me this morning. I waited all morning for your call.

3. Our plane was supposed to _____ *leave / take off* _____ at 9:45, but it was late. We had to wait in the airport for two more hours to start our trip.

4. The teacher was supposed to _____ *return / collect* _____ our compositions yesterday, but he was sick and didn't do it.

5. It was supposed to _____ *rain* _____ last weekend, so we cancelled our picnic. But it never rained.

6. I got a parking ticket yesterday. I wasn't supposed to _____ *park* _____ on the east side of the street, but I didn't see the signs.

7. I couldn't get into the building. I was supposed to _____ *have / show* _____ my student ID, but I left it at home.

8. The kids weren't supposed to _____ *eat* _____ the cookies before they ate dinner, but they did.

9. The play was supposed to _____ *begin* _____ at 8 p.m., but it didn't begin until 8:10.

10. You were supposed to _____ *fill* _____ out the application with a black pen, but you used a red pen.

THE MEDIA AND PRESIDENTIAL ELECTIONS

Before You Read

1. Have you ever voted in an election?
2. What do you know about the election process in the U.S.?

Harry Truman, President 1945–1953

Modals in the Past | 203

The Media and Presidential Elections (Reading)

1. Have students look at the photo. Ask: *Have you seen this photo before? Who is this? Why is he smiling?* (Harry Truman; because he has been elected president and the newspaper's headline is wrong)

2. Have students look quickly at the reading on page 204. Ask: *What is the reading about? How do you know?* Have students make predictions.

3. Preteach any vocabulary words your students may not know, such as: *tirelessly, influence, body language, project,* and *victory.*

BEFORE YOU READ

1. Activate students' prior knowledge about the role of the media in politics in the U.S. Ask: *Do you pay attention to political news? Do you get news from TV? The radio? The Internet? The newspaper? Have you ever watched election results come in on television in the U.S.? In your country?*

2. Have students discuss the questions in pairs. Try to pair students of different language backgrounds.

3. Ask a few volunteers to share their answers with the class.

To save class time, skip "Before You Read" or have students prepare answers for homework ahead of time.

Expansion

Theme The topic for this lesson can be enhanced with the following ideas:

1. An article showing election results, national or local, or expected election results
2. An article about the 2000 U.S. presidential election
3. Campaign literature for a local political race or referendum
4. A local TV or radio schedule showing guest lists for political talk shows

Reading CD 2, Track 8

1. Have students first read the text silently. Tell them to pay special attention to *must have, had to, couldn't have,* and *couldn't.* Then play the audio and have students read along silently.

2. Check students' comprehension. Ask questions such as: *Who were the two major candidates for president in 1948?* (Thomas Dewey and Harry S. Truman) *Why did the newspapers report that Dewey had won?* (They had to prepare the election news. Early polls showed Dewey as stronger.) *Why do some people think that TV helped Kennedy win in 1960?* (His opponent looked nervous and uncomfortable; Kennedy was young and handsome.)

To save class time, have students do the reading for homework ahead of time.

Read the following article. Pay special attention to *must have* + past participle and *had to* + base form. Also pay attention to *couldn't have* + past participle and *couldn't* + base form.

Richard Nixon

John F. Kennedy

Did You Know?

Before 1951, a person **could be** president as many times as he wanted. Franklin Roosevelt was elected president four times (1932, 1936, 1940, and 1944). But in 1951, Congress passed a law limiting the presidency to two terms or a maximum of ten years. Truman **couldn't run** for re-election in 1952 because that would have given him 11 years as president.

The media—newspapers, magazines, radio, television, and now the Internet—play an important part in getting out information and often shaping public opinion. The media even played a historical role in two notable presidential elections.

When President Franklin Roosevelt died in 1945, Vice President Harry S. Truman became president. But in 1948, Truman **had to** campaign for re-election. He ran against Thomas Dewey. At that time, television was still new and most people did not own one. So candidates **had to** travel from city to city by train to meet the people. Truman traveled tirelessly, but Dewey was considered the stronger candidate.

Polls[7] were so sure of a Dewey victory that they stopped asking for public opinion a week before the election. The media, especially newspapers and the radio, thought that Truman **couldn't win.** When Truman went to bed the night of the election, he thought that he would lose.

The election results were coming in slowly and newspapers had to prepare the news of the election. On the basis of early opinion polls, the media concluded that Dewey **must have won** the election, and many newspapers showed Dewey's victory. However, they were wrong. Truman won by 2 million votes. When the votes were all counted, the newspapers **had to admit** their mistake.

Another example of how the media can influence results took place in the 1960 presidential race between John Kennedy and Richard Nixon. For the first time in history, the two candidates debated[8] each other on TV. They **had to** answer difficult questions. Many people who heard the Nixon-Kennedy debate on the radio thought that Nixon was the stronger candidate. But people who saw the debate on TV thought that the young, handsome Kennedy was the stronger candidate. Also Nixon was sweating under the hot lights, and people thought that he **must have been** nervous and uncomfortable with the questions. It was a close election, but Kennedy won. Many people think Kennedy **couldn't have won** without TV.

Today, presidential candidates know the power of television and other media in influencing public opinion. To enhance[9] their images, they wear clothes that make them look good on TV, practice their on-screen body language, and work hard to project a look that will result in victory.

[7] A *poll* is an analysis of public opinion on different matters compiled by special agencies. Statistics are made based on the answers to questions.

[8] In a debate, the candidates have to answer questions (on TV or radio) so that the public can judge who is the better candidate.

[9] *Enhance* means improve.

204   Lesson 5

Reading Variation

To practice listening skills, have students first listen to the audio alone. Ask a few comprehension questions. Repeat the audio if necessary. Then have students open their books and read along as they listen to the audio.

Reading Glossary

body language: gestures and motions we make with our hands, faces, and bodies that communicate our feelings

influence: (as a verb) change; affect

project: (as a verb) show; get across

tirelessly: without getting tired; without stopping

victory: winning

5.7 | Must Have vs. Had To

Must have + past participle and *had to* + base form have completely different meanings.	

Examples	Explanation
Truman became president in 1945 when Franklin Roosevelt died. But he **had to** campaign for re-election in 1948. Truman **had to** travel by train to meet the people. During the debate, the candidates **had to** answer difficult questions.	To show necessity (personal or legal) in the past, we use *had to* + base form. We cannot use *must* in the past with this meaning.
Based on opinion polls, the newspapers concluded that Dewey **must have won.** Truman **must have been** surprised when he woke up in the morning and saw the newspapers. People thought that Nixon **must have been** nervous and uncomfortable during the debate.	When *must* shows a conclusion or deduction in the past, use *must have* + past participle.

EXERCISE Below is a conversation between two American citizens about the 2000 presidential election. Write *had to* + base form for a past necessity. Write *must have* + past participle for a past deduction or conclusion.

A: The 2000 election between Al Gore, the Democratic candidate, and George W. Bush, the Republican candidate, was so strange.

B: It was?

A: Don't you remember? The election was close and they <u>had to count</u> *(example: count)* the votes again to see who won. It took them five weeks to figure out who won the election.

B: Bush and Gore <u>must have been</u> *(example: be)* nervous that whole time waiting to find out the results.

A: Yes, they probably were. And there were so many problems with the election that they <u>had to go</u> *(1 go)* to the Supreme Court to decide who won.

B: Did you vote in that election?

A: Of course.

B: You always vote for a Democrat, so you <u>must have voted</u> *(2 vote)* for Gore.

A: Yes, I did.

Modals in the Past   205

5.7 | Must Have vs. Had To

1. Have students cover grammar chart **5.7**. Review *must, have to, must not,* and *don't have to.* Say: *Tell me something voters must do; something you have to do every day; something you don't have to do anymore; something voters must not do.* Review the difference in meaning between *don't have to* (not necessary) and *must not* (prohibited). Tell students that in the past, *must have* and *had to* have completely different meanings. Give examples related to the reading, such as: *Kennedy must have been happy when he won. The newspapers had to admit their mistake.*

2. Have students look at grammar chart **5.7**. Review the example sentences and explanations carefully.

3. Provide several examples about yourself using *had to,* such as *The last time I voted, I had to wait in line for an hour.* Ask students to provide examples of their own.

EXERCISE 10

CD 2, Track 9

1. Tell students that this exercise is about the 2000 U.S. presidential election. Have students read the direction line.

2. Model the exercise. Direct students to the examples in the book. Then do #1 with the class.

3. Have students complete the rest of Exercise 10 individually. Then have them check their answers in pairs by practicing the conversation. Circulate and observe the pair work. If necessary, check the answers as a class.

Grammar Variation

Have students underline all of the sentences with *had to* or *must have* in the reading on page 204. Draw a chart on the board with two columns, headed: *necessity* and *conclusion.* Have students write the underlined sentences from the reading in the appropriate column.

Exercise 10 Variation

To provide practice with listening skills, have students close their books and listen to the audio. Repeat the audio as needed. Ask comprehension questions, such as: *Who was the Democratic candidate in the 2000 election?* (Al Gore) *How long did it take to figure out who won the election?* (five weeks) *Why did it take so long?* (The election was close, and they had to count the votes again.) Then have students open their books and complete Exercise 10.

1. Tell students that this exercise is about the John Kennedy, Jr.'s plane crash. Have students read the direction line. Ask: *What do we write?* (*had to* + base form or *must have* + past participle)

2. Direct students to the example in the book. Then complete #1 with the class.

3. Have students complete the exercise individually. Then have them check their answers in pairs by practicing the conversation. Circulate and observe the pair work. If necessary, check the answers as a class.

🕐 To save class time, have students do half of the exercise in class and complete the other half for homework. Or assign the entire exercise for homework.

B: You __must have been__ very disappointed when they finally
        (3 be)
announced that Gore lost.

A: Yes, I was. What about you? Who did you vote for?

B: I __had to work__ overtime that day so I didn't vote.
     (4 work)

A: That's no excuse for not voting. Besides your boss is required to give you time off to vote.

B: One person's vote doesn't matter much anyway.

A: It did in 2000. Every vote counted. The election was on November 7 and we __had to wait__ until December 13 to find out who
      (5 wait)
won the election because it was such a close race.

EXERCISE **11** Below is a conversation about John Kennedy, Jr.'s plane crash. 🎧 Write *had to* + base form for a past necessity. Write *must have* + past participle for a past deduction or conclusion.

A: The Kennedy family has had so many tragedies. It
__must have been__ very sad for them when John Junior died.
(example: be)

B: It __must have been__ especially hard for John's wife's family.
    (1 be)
They lost two family members: John's wife, Carolyn, and her sister.

A: They were going to a wedding, and the family
__had to cancel__ the wedding because of the tragedy.
(2 cancel)

B: I heard that John had injured his ankle and __had to walk__
         (3 walk)
with a cane. Maybe he couldn't control the plane because of it.

A: I don't think that was the problem. He didn't have enough
experience flying a big plane. It __must have been__ hard for
       (4 be)
him to control a plane that size.

B: At least they didn't suffer. When the plane hit the water, the three of
them __must have died__ immediately.
    (5 die)

A: John's poor uncle. He __had to go__ and identify the bodies.
      (6 go)

B: It __must have been__ very hard for him.
    (7 be)

206 Lesson 5

Expansion

Exercise 10 Have students practice the conversation in pairs. Then ask volunteers to act out the conversation for the class.

Exercise 11 Variation

To provide practice with listening skills, have students close their books and listen to the audio. Repeat the audio as needed. Ask comprehension questions, such as: *Which family members did John's wife's family lose?* (John's wife, Carolyn, and her sister) *Where were they going?* (to a wedding) *What did the family do because of the tragedy?* (canceled the wedding) Then have students open their books and complete Exercise 11.

Culture Note

Boys whose names include *Jr.* are sometimes known as "Junior" or John Junior, Mack Junior, etc.

5.8 | *Could* + **Base Form** vs. *Could Have* + **Past Participle**

There are several ways to express *can* in the past, depending on the meaning you want to convey.

Examples	Explanation
John Kennedy, Jr. was rich. He **could buy** anything he wanted. (He **was able to buy** anything he wanted.)	In affirmative statements, *could* + base form means *used to be able to*. The person had this ability over a period of time.
Now I can speak English well. A few years ago, I **could speak** only a few words of English. (I **was able to speak** only a few words of English.)	*Was / were able to* can also be used for ability over a past period of time.
President Kennedy **was able to prevent** a war. He **was able to convince** the Soviets to send back their missiles. I looked on the Internet and **was able to find** more information about President Kennedy.	Use *was / were able to* for success in doing a single action. Do not use *could* for a single action.
John Kennedy, Jr. was a small child when his father died. He **couldn't remember** much about his father. He **wasn't able to remember** his father. The newspapers **weren't able to predict** the outcome of the 1948 election. The newspapers **couldn't predict** the outcome of the 1948 election.	In negative statements, *couldn't* and *wasn't / weren't able to* are used interchangeably.
John Junior **could have been** a politician, but he decided to publish a political magazine. The Cuban Missile Crisis **could have destroyed** the world.	Use *could have* + past participle for an action that didn't happen.
Some people thought that Kennedy **couldn't have won** the election without TV. When Kennedy was shot, some people thought they heard shots coming from two directions. If this is true, Oswald **couldn't have acted** alone.	Use *couldn't have* + past participle to show that something was impossible in the past.

5.8 | *Could* + **Base Form** vs. *Could Have* + **Past Participle**

1. Have students cover page 193. Review *could have* + past participle. On the board, write: *Maybe without TV, Richard Nixon could have won the 1960 election.* Ask: *Did Nixon win the 1960 election?* (no) Say: *It was possible, but it didn't happen.* In the sentence on the board, underline *could have won.* Then write an example with *could* + base form, e.g., *Franklin Roosevelt could be president four times because there was no limit at that time.* Ask: *In this sentence, what does* could *mean?* (was able to) Say: *These two uses of* could *are very different.*

2. Have students uncover and review the examples and explanations in the grammar chart. In the first and second sections of the chart, draw students' attention to the difference between *could* and *was able to* in talking about a single action. Write on the board:
Correct: Kennedy was able to win the 1960 election.
Incorrect: Kennedy could win the 1960 election.

Grammar Variation

Ask students to write a few sentences about the history of their countries using *could have.* Provide an example, such as: *The Pilgrims couldn't have survived without the Native Americans' help.*

EXERCISE 12

1. Tell students that this exercise is about their personal histories. Have students read the direction line.
2. Direct students to the example in the book. Ask several volunteers to give an answer for #1.
3. Have students complete the exercise individually. Ask volunteers to share their answers with the class.
4. Assess students' performance. If necessary, review grammar chart **5.8** on page 207.

EXERCISE 13

1. Tell students that this exercise is about things John Kennedy, Jr., could have done. Have students read the direction line.
2. Direct students to the example in the book. Have students complete the exercise individually and then check their answers in pairs. Have pairs report their answers to the class.

To save class time, have students do half of the exercise in class and complete the other half for homework. Or assign the entire exercise for homework.

EXERCISE 12 **ABOUT YOU** Fill in the blanks and discuss your answers. Answers will vary.

EXAMPLE When I didn't know much English, I couldn't _talk to people on the phone._

1. When I was young, I could always count on
   _____ Answers will vary. _____.
2. When I was younger, I could _____ better than I can now.
3. When I was younger, I couldn't _____ as well as I can now.
4. One of my goals was to _____.
   I was / wasn't able (*choose one*) to achieve my goal.
5. I could never understand why _____.
6. When I didn't know much English, I couldn't
   _____.
7. I couldn't _____ because
   _____.
8. When I first came to the U.S., I was / wasn't (*choose one*) able to
   _____.
9. I could have _____, but I decided not to.

EXERCISE 13 John Kennedy, Jr., flew his own plane on the night of July 16, 1999. What are some other things he could have done that night? Write five sentences about opportunities he did not take.

EXAMPLE _He could have stayed in a hotel that night._

1. _____ Answers will vary. _____
   _____
2. _____
   _____
3. _____
   _____
4. _____
   _____
5. _____
   _____

Expansion

Exercise 12 Have students use *could, couldn't,* and *was/wasn't able to* to write statements contrasting a time in their past with their lives now. Possible formats include *When I was in my country, I could/couldn't/was able to/wasn't able to* _____ , *but now I can/can't.*

5.9 | More on *Couldn't Have*

Examples	Explanation
A: My parents voted for Kennedy in 1964. B: What? They **couldn't have voted** for him in 1964. He died in 1963. A: I think I saw your brother at the library yesterday. B: It **couldn't have been** him. He's in Europe on vacation.	*Couldn't have* + past participle is used to show disbelief or to show that someone's statement is absolutely impossible. We are saying that we can't believe this information because it is illogical.
Thanks so much for helping me paint my house. I **couldn't have done** it without you.	When we want to show gratitude or appreciation for someone's help, we often say, "I couldn't have done it without you."
Compare: a. I **couldn't vote** in the last election because I was out of town. b. You say you voted in the last election? You **couldn't have voted** because you weren't a citizen at that time. a. I **couldn't move** the refrigerator myself, so my brother helped me. b. You say you moved the piano by yourself? You **couldn't have moved** it by yourself. It's too heavy for one person.	In sentence (a), you know that something didn't happen in the past. In sentence (b), you are guessing that something didn't happen in the past. You are responding in disbelief to someone's statement.

EXERCISE 14 Fill in the blanks to make statements of disbelief.

EXAMPLE   A: When I was a child, I saw President Kennedy.

B: You *couldn't have seen him!* He died before you were born.

1. A: U.S. athletes won ten gold medals at the 1980 Olympics.
   B: They ____ *couldn't have won ten gold medals* ____ . The U.S. didn't participate in the 1980 Olympics.

2. A: We had an English test on December 25.
   B: You ____ *couldn't have had an English test on December 25* ____ The school was closed for Christmas Day.

3. A: President Kennedy ran for re-election in 1964.
   B: He ____ *couldn't have run for re-election in 1964* ____ . He died in 1963.

4. A: Oswald went to prison for many years for killing Kennedy.
   B: He ____ *couldn't have gone to prison for many years* ____ . He was killed before he went to trial.

Modals in the Past   209

Grammar Variation

Prepare a card with several statements about past events, such as: *I voted for Harry Truman. I remember when the Titanic went down.* Ask a volunteer to come to the front of the class. Have the volunteer read the statements aloud. Respond: *You couldn't have! You're only* (number) *years old!* Then review the grammar chart.

5.9 | More on *Couldn't Have*

1. Have students cover the grammar chart. Write *couldn't have* on the board; draw a line under the words dividing the space into two columns. In each column, write an example related to the class, one for past impossible and one for disbelief, such as: *Thank you for helping me carry in the books this morning. I couldn't have done it alone.* Or *Luz says she was here on November 6. She couldn't have been here! It was Election Day, and the schools were closed.*

2. Have students uncover the grammar chart. Review the examples and explanations.

3. Draw students' attention to the (a) and (b) sentences in the third section of the grammar chart. If possible, elicit two additional examples from students; write them on the board in the appropriate column. Then label one column *past impossible* and the other, *expressing disbelief.*

4. Demonstrate and have students practice the appropriate sentence intonation for expressing disbelief, with the sentence stress on *couldn't* (e.g., *You couldn't have moved it by yourself.*).

EXERCISE 14

1. Tell students that this exercise is a series of conversations between friends or family members. Have students read the direction line.

2. Model the exercise. Direct students to the example in the book. Then do #1 with the class.

3. Have students complete Exercise 14 individually. Then have them check their answers in pairs by practicing the dialogues. Circulate and observe the pair work. Encourage students to use appropriate intonation for expressing disbelief. If necessary, check the answers as a class.

4. Assess students' performance. If necessary, review grammar chart **5.9**.

🎧 *CD 2, Track 11*

1. Tell students that this exercise is an argument between a married couple. Have students read the direction line. Ask: *Why is this called a combination exercise?* (because it combines many of the past modals)

2. Have students complete Exercise 15 individually. Then have them check their answers in pairs by practicing the dialogues. Circulate and observe the pair work. Encourage students to use appropriate intonation for an argument. If appropriate, have pairs act out the conversation for the class.

🕐 To save class time, have students do half of the exercise in class and complete the other half for homework. Or assign the entire exercise for homework.

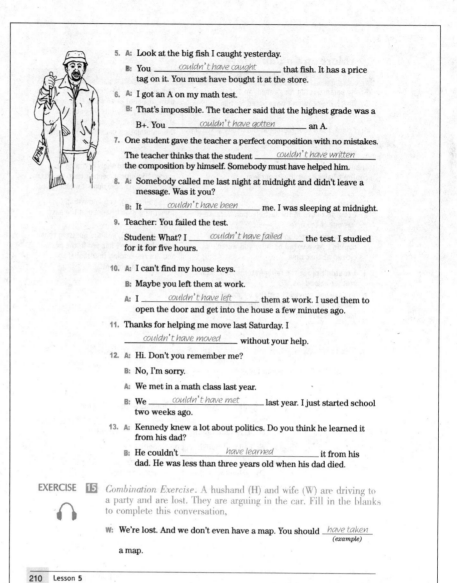

5. A: Look at the big fish I caught yesterday.

 B: You ___couldn't have caught___ that fish. It has a price tag on it. You must have bought it at the store.

6. A: I got an A on my math test.

 B: That's impossible. The teacher said that the highest grade was a B+. You ___couldn't have gotten___ an A.

7. One student gave the teacher a perfect composition with no mistakes. The teacher thinks that the student ___couldn't have written___ the composition by himself. Somebody must have helped him.

8. A: Somebody called me last night at midnight and didn't leave a message. Was it you?

 B: It ___couldn't have been___ me. I was sleeping at midnight.

9. Teacher: You failed the test.

 Student: What? I ___couldn't have failed___ the test. I studied for it for five hours.

10. A: I can't find my house keys.

 B: Maybe you left them at work.

 A: I ___couldn't have left___ them at work. I used them to open the door and get into the house a few minutes ago.

11. Thanks for helping me move last Saturday. I ___couldn't have moved___ without your help.

12. A: Hi. Don't you remember me?

 B: No, I'm sorry.

 A: We met in a math class last year.

 B: We ___couldn't have met___ last year. I just started school two weeks ago.

13. A: Kennedy knew a lot about politics. Do you think he learned it from his dad?

 B: He couldn't ___have learned___ it from his dad. He was less than three years old when his dad died.

EXERCISE **15** *Combination Exercise.* A husband (H) and wife (W) are driving to a party and are lost. They are arguing in the car. Fill in the blanks to complete this conversation.

 W: We're lost. And we don't even have a map. You should ___have taken___
 (example)

 a map.

Expansion

Exercise 14 Have students work in pairs to write conversations with expressions of disbelief similar to those in Exercise 14. Have pairs perform their conversations for the class.

Exercise 14 Have students write a paragraph about a time when someone told them something that they found difficult to believe.

Exercise 15 Variation

To provide practice with listening skills, have students close their books and listen to the audio. Repeat the audio as needed. Ask comprehension questions, such as: *Why didn't the husband take a map?* (He didn't think they were going to need one.) *How did they get lost?* (The husband made a wrong turn.) *Who does the wife want to call?* (the Allens) *Why?* (to ask them how to get to their house) Then have students open their books and complete Exercise 15.

H: I didn't think we were going to need one. I must _____have_____ (1)

_____made_____ a wrong turn.

W: I think you were supposed to make a right turn at the last

intersection, but you turned left. We should _____have_____ (2)

_____asked_____ for directions the last time we stopped for gas.

H: You know I don't like to ask for directions.

W: Let's use the cell phone and call the Allens and ask them how to get to their house.

H: Let's see. I thought I had the cell phone in my pocket. I can't find it.

I must _____have left_____ it at home. (3)

W: No, you didn't leave it at home. I've got the phone here in my purse. Oh, no. You forgot to recharge the battery. You should

_____have charged_____ it last night. (4)

H: Why is it my fault? You could _____have charged_____ it too. (5)

W: Well, we'll just have to look for a pay phone. Do you have any change?

H: I only have dollar bills.

W: You should _____have brought_____ some change with you. (6)

H: Again, it's my fault.

W: Watch out! You could _____have hit_____ that other car! (7)

H: I wasn't going to hit that car. I didn't come anywhere close to it.

W: I don't know why we're going in our car anyway. The Petersons

offered us a ride. We could _____have ridden_____ with them. (8)

H: You should _____have ridden_____ with the Petersons (9)

and I should _____have stayed_____ home. I could (10)

_____have watched_____ the football game today (11)

instead of listening to you complain!

Expansion

Exercise 15 Ask students to describe the relationship between the husband and wife in this exercise. Brainstorm adjectives to describe both partners and their relationship. Ask students how they feel around people who frequently say *You should have . . .* or *You shouldn't have . . . .*

5.10 | Continuous Forms of Past Modals

1. Have students look at the examples in the grammar chart. Ask: *How are these examples different from the examples we have been looking at?* (They use continuous verbs.)
2. Give one or two examples of your own (e.g., *I shouldn't have been talking on a cell phone while I was driving. My mom sounded tired. I think she might have been sleeping when I called.*).

EXERCISE 16

1. Tell students that this exercise is a series of conversations. Have students read the direction line. Ask: *What form do we use?* (the continuous form)
2. Review the example in the book.
3. Have students complete the exercise individually and then check their answers by practicing the conversations in pairs. Check answers as a class if necessary.
4. Assess students' performance. If necessary, review grammar chart **5.10**.

5.10 | Continuous Forms of Past Modals

We use continuous modals in the past to talk about a specific time in the past.

Subject	Modal	Not	Have Been	Present Participle	Complement
They	must		have been	waiting	at 8:30.
He	might		have been	sleeping	at 10:30 p.m.
You	could		have been	doing	your homework this morning.
I	should	not	have been	driving	so fast.

EXERCISE 16 Fill in the blanks with the continuous form of the modal.

EXAMPLE A: I was injured in a car accident. I wasn't wearing a seat belt.

B: You should _have been wearing_ your seat belt.

1. A: Why didn't you finish your homework?

   B: I was watching a movie on TV.

   A: You should _have been doing_ your homework instead.

2. A: I wasted so much time when I was young. I didn't take my studies seriously.

   B: But you had a good education.

   A: I know. But I could _have been studying_ English instead of playing soccer every day after school.

3. A: I tried to call you a few hours ago but there was no answer.

   B: I was home. I must _have been taking_ a shower when you called.

4. A: What do you think of last night's rainstorm?

   B: I didn't hear it. I must _have been sleeping_.

   A: How could you sleep through so much thunder?

   B: I'm a heavy sleeper.

5. A: I went to your house last Saturday, but you didn't answer the door. I thought you were going to be home.

   B: I often work on my car on Saturdays. I might _have been working_ on my car when you arrived. Did you look in the garage?

   A: No. I didn't think about it.

Expansion

Exercise 16 Have students work in pairs. Have pairs use the first sentence in items 1, 3, and 5 to write their own conversations. Have pairs perform their conversations for the class.

6. *(teacher to student)*

A: Peter, can you answer question number six?

B: I'm sorry. I wasn't listening. I was thinking of something else. What was the question?

A: You should *have been listening*.

SUMMARY OF LESSON 5

Must

Meaning	Present/Future	Past
Legal obligation	I **must go** to court next week.	I **had to go** to court last week.
Urgency	I **must talk** to the doctor right now!	
Strong necessity	I **must study** for the test next week.	I **had to study** for the test last month.
Prohibition	You **must not tell** a lie in court.	
Deduction; conclusion	He's wearing a coat inside. He **must be** cold.	I can't find my keys. There's a hole in my pocket. I **must have lost** them.

Should

Meaning	Present/Future	Past
Advice	You **should buy** a new car next year.	You **should have bought** a new car last year.
	You **shouldn't eat** fatty foods.	I **shouldn't have eaten** so many potato chips last night.

Summary of Lesson 5

1. ***Must, Should*** List the modals from this section on the board (*must, had to, should, shouldn't, should have* and *shouldn't have*). Have students make statements about themselves or someone else using the modals (e.g., *I had to pay a library fine last week. I should have returned my books on time.*).

If necessary, have students review:

Summary Variation

Have students look at the examples in each of the charts. In pairs, have students write examples of their own (in the present/future and past, when possible) for each of the meanings in the left column of the charts.

Summary of Lesson 5 (cont.)

2. Can/Could, May/Might, Ought To List the modals from this section on the board (*can, could, could have, couldn't have, may, might, may have had, might have had,* and *ought to*). Have students make statements about themselves or someone else using the modals from the list (e.g., *Alfredo didn't call me; he could have forgotten. I may need your help with this homework.*).

If necessary, have students review:

Can/Could

Meaning	Present/Future	Past
Ability	I **can speak** English now.	I **could speak** German when I was a child.
Acceptability	You **can wear** jeans to class every day.	You **could have worn** jeans to the party last week, but you didn't.
Permission/ prohibition	We **can use** a dictionary to write a composition. We **can't use** our books during a test.	We **could use** a dictionary to write the last composition. We **couldn't use** a dictionary during the last test.
Suggestion	How **can** I **learn** about computers? You **can take** a course, or you **could buy** a book and teach yourself.	
Possibility	Mary isn't here today. She **could be** sick.	Mary wasn't here yesterday. She **could have been** sick.
Direction not taken		I **could have gone** to Canada, but I decided to come to the U.S.
Impossibility; disbelief		A: I voted for President Clinton in 1996. B: You **couldn't have voted** for Clinton. You weren't a citizen in 1996.

May/ Might

Meaning	Present/Future	Past
Permission	You **may use** a dictionary during the test.	
Possibility	I **may have** a job interview next week. I'm still not sure. The teacher isn't here. She **might be** sick.	Simon is wearing a suit to class. He **may have had** a job interview this morning. The teacher wasn't here yesterday. She **might have been** sick.

Ought To

Meaning	Present/Future	Past
Advice	She **ought to buy** a new car soon.	She **ought to have bought** a new car last year. (*rare*)

214   Lesson 5

Summary Variation

Have students look at the examples in each of the charts. In pairs, have students write examples of their own (in the present/future and past, when possible) for each of the meanings in the left column of the charts.

Related Expressions

Have To

Meaning	Present/Future	Past
Necessity (personal or legal)	I **have to study** now. I **have to go** to court next week.	I **had to study** yesterday. I **had to go** to court last week.
Lack of necessity	My job is close to my home. I **don't have to drive.** I can walk.	My last job was close to my home. I **didn't have to drive.** I could walk.

Have Got To

Meaning	Present/Future	Past
Necessity	I**'ve got to go** to court next week.	

Be Able To

Meaning	Present/Future	Past
Ability	She **is able to play** chess now.	She **was able to play** chess when she was a child.

Be Allowed To / Be Permitted To

Meaning	Present/Future	Past
Permission	We **are not allowed to talk** during a test. You **are not permitted to park** at a bus stop.	We **were not allowed to talk** during the last test. You **were not permitted to park** on this street yesterday because the city was cleaning the streets.

Be Supposed To

Meaning	Present/Future	Past
Expectation	My brother **is supposed to arrive** at 10 p.m. The weatherman said it **is supposed to rain** tomorrow. I'm **supposed to help** my brother move on Saturday.	My brother **was supposed to arrive** at 10 p.m., but his plane was delayed. The weatherman said it **was supposed to rain** yesterday, but it didn't. I **was supposed to help** my brother move on Saturday, but I got sick.
Reporting rules and customs	You **are supposed to wear** your seat belt. You **are not supposed to talk** during a test.	He **was supposed to wear** his seat belt, but he didn't. They **weren't supposed to talk** during the test, but they did.

Modals in the Past 215

Summary Variation

Have students look at the examples in each of the charts. In pairs, have students write examples of their own (in the present/future and past, when possible) for each of the meanings in the left column of the charts.

Summary of Lesson 5 (*cont.*)

3. **Related Expressions** List the modals from this section on the board (*have to*, *have got to*, *able to*, *allowed/not allowed to*, and *supposed to*, *had better*). Have students make statements about themselves or someone else using the modals in the present/future, and, when appropriate, in the past (e.g., *I was supposed to take a dish to the party, but I forgot. We're not allowed to park in this section; you'd better move your car.*).

If necessary, have students review:

4.3 Necessity and Urgency with *Must, Have To, Have Got To* (p. 142)

4.4 Obligation with *Must* or *Be Supposed To* (p. 144)

4.5 Advice with *Should, Ought To,* and *Had Better* (p. 146)

4.6 Permission and Prohibition (p. 151)

4.7 Comparing Negative Modals (p. 154)

4.9 Expectations with *Be Supposed To* (p. 163)

5.6 *Be Supposed To* in the Past (p. 202)

5.7 *Must Have* vs. *Had To* (p. 205)

5.8 *Could* + Base Form vs. *Could Have* + Past Participle (p. 207).

Editing Advice

For each item, have students provide the grammar rule behind the Editing Advice. This can be done as an individual, a pair, a group, or a class activity.

1. Modals are followed by the base form of a verb.
2. The past of a modal is followed by *have* and the past participle.
3. *Must have* with the past participle is used for a conclusion; *had to* is used for a necessity or obligation.
4. *Couldn't have* with a past participle is used for a direction not taken or for disbelief; *couldn't* with a base form is used with inability or prohibition.
5. Don't confuse the past participle with the simple past form; they are sometimes, but not always, the same.
6. The *'d* in *supposed to* is not pronounced, but is necessary in writing. *Supposed to* requires a form of *be*.
7. *Can* cannot be used in the past.

Lesson 5 Test/Review

For additional practice, review, and assessment materials, see Assessment CD-ROM with *ExamView Pro, More Grammar Practice* Workbook 3, Interactive CD-ROM, and Web site http://elt.thomson.com/gic

PART 1

1. Part 1 may be used as an in-class test to assess student performance, in addition to the Assessment CD-ROM with *ExamView Pro*. Have students read the direction line. Ask: *Does every sentence have a mistake?* (no)
2. Collect for assessment.
3. If necessary, have students review: **Lesson 5.**

Had Better		
Meaning	Present/Future	Past
Warning	You'd **better take** an umbrella, or you'll get wet.	

EDITING ADVICE

1. After a modal, always use a base form.
   have
   He could has gone to the party.

2. To form the past of a modal, use *have* + past participle.
   have eaten
   I shouldn't ate so much before I went to bed last night.

3. Don't confuse *must have* + past participle and *had to* + base form.
   had to take
   I was absent last week and must have taken the test in the teacher's office.

4. Don't confuse *couldn't have* + past participle and *couldn't* + base form.
   find
   Last night when I got home I couldn't have found a parking space.

5. Use the correct form for the past participle.
   gone
   He should have went to the doctor when he felt the pain in his chest.

6. Don't forget the *d* in *supposed to*. Don't forget the verb *be*.
   d
   You were suppose to meet me after class yesterday.
   was
   I supposed to work last Saturday, but I got sick.

7. *Can* is never used for the past.
   couldn' t drive
   He can't drove his car this morning because the battery was dead.

LESSON 5 TEST/REVIEW

PART 1 Find the mistakes with the underlined words, and correct them. Not every sentence has a mistake. If the sentence is correct, write *C*.

216   Lesson 5

Lesson Review

To use Part 1 as a review, assign it as homework or use it as an in-class activity to be completed individually or in pairs. Check answers and review errors as a class. Reteach grammar points that students haven't mastered. Then student learning may be assessed using a test generated from the Assessment CD-ROM with *ExamView Pro*.

PART 2

1. Part 2 may also be used as an in-class test to assess student performance, in addition to the Assessment CD-ROM with *ExamView Pro*. Have students read the direction line.
2. Collect for assessment.
3. If necessary, have students review: **Lesson 5.**

EXAMPLES   When he heard the good news about his scholarship, he

must ~~has~~ *have* been excited.

I had to go to court last week. C

1. I was supposed to go on vacation last week, but I got sick. C

2. You should have seen the movie with us last week. We had a great time. C

3. When your son graduated from college last year, you must ~~be~~ *have been* proud.

4. Why did you take the bus to work this morning? You could have driven your car. C

5. He looked so tired when he got home from work. He must ~~had~~ *have* a hard day today.

6. I could have ~~went~~ *gone* to the University of Illinois, but I decided to go to Truman College instead.

7. My wife is angry because I was late. I should ~~had~~ *have* called her to tell her I was going to be late.

8. I didn't have time to call you yesterday because I had to ~~worked~~ all day yesterday.

9. Last week, he should ~~told~~ *have* told his mother the truth about his car accident, but he lied to her.

10. Thanks for helping me find a job. I couldn't have found it without your help. C

11. Her daughter was sick yesterday, so she had to leave work early. C

12. I should ~~studied~~ *have* studied English when I was a child.

13. I had to work last Saturday, so I couldn't go to the party. C

14. Everyone left the party early. They must not have had a very good time. C

15. There wasn't enough food at the party. The host should ~~has~~ *have* bought more food.

16. I ~~can't called~~ *couldn't call* you last night because I lost your phone number.

PART 2   Fill in the blanks with the correct appropriate verb. Answers may vary.

EXAMPLE   The report on President Kennedy's death said that Oswald

must _____ *have killed* _____ Kennedy.

1. President Kennedy might _____ *have been killed* _____ by the government of another country.

2. John Kennedy, Jr. grew up without a father. It must _____ *have been* _____ hard to grow up without a father.

Modals in the Past   217

Lesson Review

To use Part 2 as a review, assign it as homework or use it as an in-class activity to be completed individually or in pairs. Check answers and review errors as a class. Reteach grammar points that students haven't mastered. Then student learning may be assessed using a test generated from the Assessment CD-ROM with *ExamView Pro*.

1. Part 3 may also be used as an in-class test to assess student performance, in addition to the Assessment CD-ROM with *ExamView Pro*. Tell students that this is a completed job application; the statements in the activity are about the application. Review the example. Then complete #1 as a class.
2. Collect for assessment.
3. If necessary, have students review: **Lesson 5.**

---

3. John Kennedy, Jr. flew in the dark. He shouldn't _____ *have flown* _____ in the dark.

4. He got lost and couldn't _____ *find* _____ his way because he was flying over water.

5. He must _____ *have been* _____ confused because of poor visibility.

6. He went to the airport late that day. He should _____ *have gone* _____ to the airport earlier.

7. Carolyn Bessette's parents must _____ *have been* _____ very sad when they heard that two of their daughters had died.

8. Kennedy and his wife could _____ *have flown* _____ on a commercial airplane, but Kennedy decided to use his own airplane.

9. The search teams couldn't _____ *find* _____ the bodies for six days.

10. Some experts believe Kennedy didn't have enough experience flying. They think he should _____ *have had* _____ more experience.

11. A: I think Kennedy, his wife, and sister-in-law probably survived for a few days.

    B: They couldn't _____ *have survived* _____ at all. The airplane hit the water with great force. They must _____ *have died* _____ instantly.

12. Kennedy's cousin had to _____ *cancel* _____ her wedding because of the sad news.

PART **3** Look at the job application. Complete each sentence.

EXAMPLE His didn't print the application. He should _____ *have printed* _____ *or typed* _____ the application.

1. He wrote his application with a pencil. He was supposed to _____ *print / type it* _____ .

2. He didn't write his zip code. He should _____ *have written* _____ his zip code.

3. He forgot to include his area code. He should _____ *have included* _____ it.

4. He included his marital status. He didn't have to _____ *include* _____ it.

5. He wrote the day (18) before the month (2). He should _____ *have written the month first (before the day)* _____ .

Fill out the following form. Print in black ink or type. Bring it to the personnel office or mail it to:

Ms. Judy Lipton
P.O. Box 324
Tucson, Arizona 85744

Applications must be submitted by November 15.

Name ___Wilson___ ___Jack___ ___N___
     (last)   (first)   (middle initial)

Address ___3040 N. Albany Ave.___

City ___Chicago___ State ___ill___ Zip Code ___

Telephone ( ) ___539-2756___

Marital status (optional) ___divorced___ Sex ___M___

Date of birth ___18___ ___2___ ___69___ (You must be at least 18.)
            (month) (day) (year)

Social Security number ___549___ - ___62___ - ___7149___

Educational background:

		Date graduated	Degree or major
High School	Roosevelt	1897	
College			
Graduate School			

Employment History (Please start with your present or last job.)

Company	Position	Dates	Supervisor	Reason for leaving
Apex	Stockboy	5/83–3/90	R. Wilmot	personal
Smith, Inc.		5/90–12/94	M Smith	pay
Olson Co.	loading dock	1/95–present	B. Adams	

Do not write in the shaded box. For office use only.

Rec'd. by _J.W._
Amer. cit. _yes_
Doc. checked _?_
Transcripts received _yes_

The Immigration Act of 1986 requires all successful applicants to present documents to prove U.S. citizenship or permanent residence with permission to work in the U.S.

This company is an Equal Opportunity Employer. Race, religion, nationality, marital status, and physical disability will not influence our decision to hire.   *Catholic*
I certify that these answers are true.

Signature: _Jack N. Wilson_   Date: _13/11/04_

6. He wrote that he graduated from high school in 1897. He couldn't ___have graduated___ in 1897. That's more than 100 years ago! He must ___have meant___ 1987.

7. He didn't fill in any college attended. He might not _____ ___have attended___ college.

Lesson Review

To use Part 3 as a review, assign it as homework or use it as an in-class activity to be completed individually or in pairs. Check answers and review errors as a class. Reteach grammar points that students haven't mastered. Then student learning may be assessed using a test generated from the Assessment CD-ROM with *ExamView Pro*.

1. Part 4 may also be used as an in-class test to assess student performance, in addition to the Assessment CD-ROM with *ExamView Pro*. Tell students that this is a conversation between two friends. Words and phrases are missing. Review the example. Then do #1 as a class.
2. Collect for assessment.
3. If necessary, have students review: **Lesson 5.**

---

8. He said that he left his first job for personal reasons. He might _____ *have left* _____ because he didn't like his boss. Or he could _____ *have left* _____ because the salary wasn't high enough.

9. He didn't fill in his reason for leaving his last job. He should _____ *have filled it in* _____.

10. He wrote in the shaded box. He wasn't supposed to _____ *write in it* _____. He must not _____ *have* _____ _____ *read* _____ the directions very carefully.

11. He included his religion. He wasn't supposed to _____ *include* _____ it. He must not _____ *have read* _____ the sentence about religion.

12. He printed his name on the bottom line. He was supposed to _____ *sign it* _____.

13. He mailed the application by regular mail on November 14. He should *have brought it to the personnel office*. It might not *arrive* on time.

PART **4** Fill in the blanks with the past of the modal or expression in parentheses ( ).

After Alan (A) has waited for two hours for his friend Bill (B) to arrive for dinner, Bill finally arrives.

A: Why are you so late? You _____ *were supposed to* _____ be here two hours ago.
(example: be supposed to)

B: I'm sorry. I got lost and I _____ *couldn't find* _____ your house.
(1 can't/find)

A: You _____ *should have taken* _____ a road map.
(2 should/take)

B: I did, but I _____ *couldn't read* _____ it while I was driving. I
(3 can/not/read)

_____ *must have made* _____ a wrong turn.
(4 must/make)

A: Where did you get off the highway?

B: At Madison Street.

A: That's impossible. You _____ *couldn't have gotten* _____ off at Madison
(5 can/not/get)

Street. There's no exit there.

Lesson Review

To use Part 4 as a review, assign it as homework or use it as an in-class activity to be completed individually or in pairs. Check answers and review errors as a class. Reteach grammar points that students haven't mastered. Then student learning may be assessed using a test generated from the Assessment CD-ROM with *ExamView Pro*.

B: Oh. It _____ must have been _____ Adams Street, then.
                   (6 must/be)

A: But Adams Street is not so far from here.

B: I know. But I had a flat tire after I got off the highway.

A: Did you call for a tow truck?

B: I _____ could have called _____ for a tow truck because I'm a
             (7 can/call)
member of a motor club. But I thought it would take too long. So I
changed the tire myself.

A: But you're over two hours late. How long did it take you to change
the tire?

B: It _____ might have taken _____ about 15 minutes, but then I
          (8 might/take)
_____ had to go _____ home, take a shower, and change clothes.
    (9 have to/go)
I was so dirty.

A: You _____ should have called _____ me.
          (10 should/call)

B: I wanted to, but I _____ couldn't find _____ the paper where
         (11 can/not/find)
I had your phone number. I _____ must have lost _____ it while I was
           (12 must/lose)
changing the tire.

A: Well, thank goodness you're here now. But you'll have to eat dinner
alone. I got hungry and _____ couldn't wait _____ for you.
              (13 can/not/wait)

EXPANSION ACTIVITIES

Classroom Activities

1. A student will read one of the following problems out loud to the class. The student will pretend that this is his or her problem. Other students will ask for more information and give advice about the problem. Try to use past and present modals.

   Problem A My mother-in-law came to the U.S. last May. She stayed with us for three months. I told my husband that he had to find another apartment for her. He didn't want to. I finally said to my husband, "Tell her to leave, or I'm leaving." So he helped her move into her own apartment. Now my husband is mad at me. Do you think I did the right thing?

   Problem B I had a beautiful piano. I got if from my grandmother, who bought it many years ago. When I moved into my new apartment, I couldn't take the piano because it was too big for the entrance. So I sold it. Do you think I did the right thing?

Classroom Activities Variation

Activity 1 Have students write the advice for one or two of the problems. Have students treat the problems as letters to an advice column, and write answers in that style. Bring copies of newspaper advice columns to use as models.

Expansion Activities

These expansion activities provide opportunities for students to interact with one another and further develop their speaking and writing skills. Encourage students to use grammar from this lesson whenever possible.

🕐 To save class time, assign parts of the activities as homework. Then use class time for interaction and communication. If students do not need additional speaking practice, some of the activities may be assigned as writing activities for homework, or skipped altogether.

CLASSROOM ACTIVITIES

1. Tell students that this activity is about giving advice. Ask: *What modals do we use to give advice?* (*should, shouldn't, should/shouldn't have, ought to*) Review with students the difference between the use of the present/future forms (advice a person can take) and the past forms (advice about what the person should have done, but didn't; a past mistake). Have students who are listening cover page 221 during the activity.

CLASSROOM ACTIVITIES (cont.)

2. Have students complete the application on page 176 individually. Make sure that students are clear on the meaning of *on purpose* (intentionally). Remind students to make several mistakes. Then have students work in pairs to find and comment on mistakes. Have pairs switch roles and review each other's applications.

TALK ABOUT IT

Review with students language for agreeing, checking for agreement, and disagreeing (e.g., *I think so too. Are you sure that's right? I'm not sure I agree.*). Set a time limit for discussion. Then have groups share their ideas.

WRITE ABOUT IT

1. Review the use of modals to express past mistakes. Ask: *Which modals do we use to talk about past mistakes?* (*should have, shouldn't have*). Have students write a paragraph about a past mistake. Collect for assessment and/or have students review each other's work.

2. Have students make a few notes before they begin to write. Ask: *What modals do we use to show a direction not taken in the past?* (*could have*) Have students write a short composition on a path they didn't take.

3. Have students brainstorm people they might write about. If students have difficulty identifying a person to write about, suggest a person in fiction or poetry. Ask: *Which modal do we use to talk about a past action that didn't happen?* (*could have*)

INTERNET ACTIVITIES

1. Have students read and summarize the information they find.

2. Ask students to evaluate the theories they find. Ask: *Do you think this might have really happened? Or do you think this couldn't have happened?*

3. Ask students what they can conclude about the opinions of the writer of the article they find.

4. Brainstorm search terms to use to find information about the 2000 election.

Problem C My wife gave me a beautiful watch last Christmas. While I was on a business trip in New York last month, I left my watch in my hotel room. A few days later, I called the hotel, but they said that no one reported finding a watch. So far, I haven't told my wife that I lost the watch. What should I do?

Problem D A very nice American family invited me to dinner last night. The wife worked very hard to make a beautiful dinner. But I'm not used to eating American food and thought it tasted awful. But I ate it so I wouldn't hurt their feelings. They invited me to dinner again next week. What can I do about the food?

Problem E *Write your own problem, real or imaginary.*

2. Fill out the application on page 178 of Lesson Four. Make some mistakes on purpose. Find a partner and exchange books with him or her. Tell each other about the mistakes using modals.

EXAMPLE For "sex" you wrote *M*. You're a woman, so you should have written *F*.

Talk About it

The following excerpt from a poem by John Greenleaf Whittier is about regret. Discuss the meaning of the poem.

> For all sad words of tongue or pen,
> The saddest are these: "It might have been!"

Write About it

1. Write about a mistake you once made. Tell about what you should have done to avoid the problem.

2. Write a short composition about another direction your life could have taken. What made you decide not to go in that direction?

3. Write about a famous person who died tragically. What could this person have done differently to prevent his or her death?

Internet Activities

1. Look for information about President John F. Kennedy and his son, John Kennedy, Jr. Bring an article about one of these two men to class.

2. At a search engine, type in *Kennedy assassination*. Look at the different assassination theories. Summarize the theories.

3. Find an article about the Cuban Missile Crisis and bring it to class. Circle all the modals in the article.

4. Find out more information about the U.S. presidential election in 2000. What were some of the problems in counting the votes?

 Additional Activities at http://elt.thomson.com/gic

222   Lesson 5

Talk About it Variation

Ask students how the excerpt from the poem makes them feel. Discuss things people in general should do now to prevent regrets in the future. Ask students what they might do to avoid the kinds of regrets Whittier is talking about.

Write About it Variation

Have students exchange first drafts with a partner. Ask students to help their partners edit their drafts. Refer students to the Editing Advice on page 216.

Internet Activities Variation

If students don't have access to the Internet, they may find the information needed at a local public library.

GRAMMAR
Adjective Clauses
Descriptive Phrases

CONTEXT: Computers and the Internet
Spam
eBay
Handwritten Letters or E-mail?
Creating the World Wide Web

223

Lesson | 6

Lesson Overview

GRAMMAR

1. Activate students' prior knowledge. Ask: *What does an adjective do?* (describes something or someone) Ask volunteers to give some examples of adjectives. Ask: *What is a clause?* (a phrase with a subject and a verb)
2. Ask: *What will we study in this lesson?* (adjective clauses, descriptive phrases) Give several examples of sentences with adjective clauses (*I have a friend who has met Bill Gates.*) and descriptive phrases (*Bill Gates, the founder of Microsoft, is a very rich man.*). Have volunteers give examples. Write two or three examples on the board.

CONTEXT

1. Ask: *What will we learn about in this lesson?* (spam, eBay, handwritten letters or e-mail, and creating the World Wide Web) Elicit students' prior knowledge. Ask: *What do you know about eBay? About the history of the Web? Which do you use more often— e-mail or letters?*
2. Have students share their knowledge and personal experiences.

Photo

1. Direct students' attention to the photo. Ask: *What do you think this person is doing? How do you think he feels? Why do you think so?*
2. Have students share similar experiences.

To save class time, have students do the Test/Review at the end of the lesson, or administer a lesson test generated from the Assessment CD-ROM with *ExamView® Pro*. Skip sections of the lesson that students have already mastered. You may also assign some sections for self-study for extra credit.

Expansion

Theme The topic for this lesson can be enhanced with the following ideas:

1. Articles about the history of computers
2. Transcripts of a chat room or instant messaging conversation
3. Timelines showing the inventions of communication technologies
4. Articles, expressions, and opinions, both positive and negative, about technology and its uses

Culture Note

Early computers were really calculators; they were used to do basic math (addition, subtraction, multiplication, etc.). *Computer* comes from the verb *compute*, which means *figure out using math,* or *calculate.*

6.1 | Adjective Clauses— An Overview

1. Have students cover the explanations and look at the examples in grammar chart **6.1.** Ask: *What does the clause* who is a computer programmer *do?* (It tells you about *a friend.*) *What does the clause* that has a big memory *do?* (It tells you about *a computer.*)
2. Have students uncover the chart and review the examples and explanations.
3. Ask students to look at the sentences in the chart. Ask volunteers to identify the adjective clauses.
4. Draw students' attention to the definition of *adjective clause* in the top section of the grammar chart. Point out that adjective clauses do not necessarily include adjectives.

Spam (Reading)

1. Have students look at the photo. Ask: *What is this?* (a computer screen) *What is on the screen?* (an e-mail advertisement; spam)
2. Have students look briefly at the reading. Ask: *What is the reading about? How do you know?* Have students make predictions.
3. Preteach any essential vocabulary words your students may not know, such as *mortgage, junk mail, pollution, ecosystem, chat rooms, newsgroups, eliminate, retailers, primary, lawmakers,* and *enact.*

BEFORE YOU READ

1. Activate students' prior knowledge about spam and unwanted e-mail. Ask: *What is spam? Who sends it? Why do they send it?*
2. Have students discuss the questions in pairs. Try to pair students of different language backgrounds.
3. Ask for a few volunteers to share their answers with the class.

🕐 To save class time, skip "Before You Read" or have students prepare answers for homework ahead of time.

6.1 | Adjective Clauses—An Overview

An adjective clause is a group of words that describes or identifies the noun before it.

Examples	Explanation
I have a friend **who is a computer programmer.**	Here the adjective clause tells you about the friend.
You should buy a computer **that has a big memory.**	Here the adjective clause tells you about the computer.
People **who send e-mail** usually write letters **that are short.**	The adjective clause can describe any noun in the sentence. In the sentence to the left, an adjective clause describes both the subject (*people*) and the object (*letters*).

SPAM

Before You Read
1. Do you get unwanted e-mail asking you to buy products or order services?
2. What do you do with this e-mail?

Expansion

Theme The topic for this lesson can be enhanced with the following ideas:

1. Copies of spam e-mail messages
2. A copy of a Web page showing a checked box allowing the site to send more information, contact the user, etc.
3. Junk mail from advertisers, credit card companies, etc.

Culture Note

Commercial Web sites often have check boxes like the one in the picture. Some common phrases are *Add me to your mailing list, Send me special offers,* and *You may provide my contact information to other companies.* Frequently the default, or assumption, is for this box to already be checked. Tell learners to look carefully for these boxes when using the Web.

Read the following article. Pay special attention to adjective clauses.

Do you ever get e-mail **that promises to make you rich or thin?** Do you get e-mail **that tries to sell you a mortgage or a vacation package?** Do you ever receive an offer **that will give you a college diploma in a year?** This kind of advertising through e-mail is called "spam." Spam is e-mail **that you haven't asked for.** It is the electronic equivalent of junk mail or telemarketing calls. About half of the e-mail sent today is spam. In 2002, 260 billion spam e-mails were sent. A year later, in 2003, this number rose to 4.9 trillion. Bill Gates, the founder of Microsoft, calls spam "pollution of the e-mail ecosystem."

How do spammers get your e-mail address? They use several methods. When you buy something online, you are often asked for an e-mail address when you place an order. Spammers buy addresses from online companies. In addition, spammers search chat rooms, bulletin boards, and newsgroups for e-mail addresses. Spammers regularly sell lists of e-mail addresses to other spammers.

Where does spam come from? It comes from companies **that want your money.** Many of these companies try to take your money by making false claims ("Lose 50 pounds in 10 days!"). But most people delete this kind of e-mail without even reading it. So why do spammers send e-mail **that nobody wants to read?** The answer is simple: Some people *do* read this mail and a very small percentage even buy the product or order the service **that is offered.** And a small percentage of trillions of e-mails means money. One spammer **who lives in Florida** made so much money that he sold his business for $135 million dollars and retired at the age of 37.

What can you do to eliminate spam?

- You could simply delete it.
- You could get anti-spam software. (Some software is free, offered by the Internet service provider **you use.**)
- You can get a separate e-mail address to give to retailers **who require an e-mail address,** and use your primary e-mail address just for people **you know.**
- On a Web site, when you see a box **that asks you if you want more information,** make sure to uncheck the box.

Many people **who are unhappy with the amount of spam they receive** are asking their lawmakers to enact laws **that would stop spam.**

Adjective Clauses; Descriptive Phrases   225

Reading Variation

To practice listening skills, have students first listen to the audio alone. Ask a few comprehension questions. Repeat the audio if necessary. Then have students open their books and read along as they listen to the audio.

Reading Glossary

chat room: an online meeting room
ecosystem: environment
eliminate: stop; remove
enact: pass (a law)
junk mail: nonpersonal mail; usually advertising
lawmakers: members of Congress or another governing body; people who make laws
mortgage: a loan to help buy a home
newsgroup: an organized online area for people who share an interest
pollution: dirt; infection; contamination
primary: most important; first
retailer: seller; businessperson

6.2 | Relative Pronoun as Subject

1. Review relative pronouns. Ask students to name as many relative pronouns as they can (*who, which, that, whom, whose*).

2. Have students look at the examples in the first two sections of the grammar chart. Say: *The sentence with an adjective clause combines two sentences. The relative pronoun is the subject of the adjective clause.* Write two additional sets of sentences on the board, such as: *People have free e-mail addresses. Those people get a lot of spam.* With the class, write a sentence combining the two with an adjective clause (e.g., *People who have free e-mail addresses get a lot of spam.*).

3. Draw students' attention to the Language Notes. Ask: *Which relative pronouns do we use with people?* (*who, that*) *Which relative pronouns do we use with things?* (*that, which*) Point out the second note. Ask: *Why do we use* buy *in the first example?* (the subject, *people*, is plural) *Why do we use* buys *in the second example?* (the subject, *a person*, is singular)

EXERCISE 1

1. Tell students that this exercise is about online shopping and spam. Have students read the direction line. Ask: *What do we write?* (*who, that*, or *which* and a form of the verb)

2. Model the exercise. Direct students to the example in the book. Ask: *Why do we use* that *and not* who? (because *companies* are things, not people)

3. Have students complete the rest of Exercise 1 individually. Then have them check their answers in pairs. Circulate and observe the pair work. If necessary, check the answers as a class.

6.2 | Relative Pronoun as Subject

> The relative pronouns *who, that,* and *which* can be the subject or an adjective clause.

I received an e-mail. *The e-mail* promises to make me rich.

I received an e-mail [**that** / **which**] promises to make me rich.

People ....often give out their e-mail addresses.
  ┌─ *People* buy things online.
People → [**who** / **that**] buy things online often give out their e-mail addresses.

Language Notes:
1. Use the relative pronouns *who* and *that* for people. Use the relative pronouns *that* and *which* for things. (*Which* is less common than *that*.)
2. A present tense verb in the adjective clause must agree in number with its subject.
   People who **buy** things online should have a separate e-mail address.
   A person who **buys** things online should have a separate e-mail address.

EXERCISE 1 Fill in the blanks with *who, that,* or *which* + the correct form of the verb in parentheses ( ) to complete the adjective clause.

EXAMPLE Spam comes from companies ___*that want*___ to sell you something.
                                              (want)

1. Companies ___*that send*___ you spam want your money.
              (send)

2. People ___*who receive*___ spam are often annoyed.
          (receive)

3. People ___*who buy*___ products and services online give
          (buy)
   out their e-mail addresses.

✔ 4. Sometimes you see a box ___*that has*___ a check in it already.
                              (have)
   Don't forget to uncheck the box if you don't want more information.

5. I know a student ___*who buys*___ all her textbooks online.
                    (buy)
   She never goes to the bookstore anymore.

6. A spammer ___*who lives*___ in Florida became very rich
             (live)
   and retired young.

226   Lesson 6

Grammar Variation

On the board, write the first two examples with adjective clauses from the grammar chart, or similar sentences (*I have a friend who met Bill Gates.*). Have students try to make two sentences from each example (*I have a friend. My friend met Bill Gates.*).

7. You shouldn't believe an offer _____*that promises*_____ you that
   (promise)

   you will lose 50 pounds in a week.

EXERCISE 2   Use the phrase below to write a complete sentence.

EXAMPLES   **a computer that has a small memory**

A computer that has a small memory is not very useful today.

a company that promises to make me rich in three weeks

I wouldn't want to do business with a company that promises
to make me rich in three weeks.

1. **e-mail that comes from friends and relatives**

   _____Answers will vary._____

2. **companies that send spam**

   _____

3. **students who don't have a computer**

   _____

4. **children who spend all their time on the computer**

   _____

5. **people who have a high-speed Internet connection**

   _____

6. **Web sites that offer free music downloads**

   _____

7. **"colleges" that offer a four-year diploma in six months**

   _____

8. **people who don't know anything about computers**

   _____

EXERCISE 3   ABOUT YOU Fill in the blanks with an adjective clause.
Discuss your answers.

EXAMPLE   I don't like people _*who say one thing but do something else.*_

1. I don't like people _____Answers will vary._____
2. I don't like apartments _____ _____
3. I don't like movies _____

Adjective Clauses; Descriptive Phrases   **227**

EXERCISE 2

1. Tell students that this exercise is about computers and the ways we use them. Have students read the direction line. Ask: *What do we write?* (a complete sentence that includes the words given)

2. Direct students to the examples. Have volunteers read them aloud. Elicit several additional possible answers: *A computer that has a small memory could be upgraded. I don't trust a company that promises to make me rich in three weeks.*

3. Have students complete Exercise 2 individually. Then have them compare answers in pairs. Circulate and observe the pair work. Have pairs report interesting answers to the class.

4. Assess students' performance. If necessary, review grammar chart 6.2 on page 226.

EXERCISE 3

1. Tell students that this exercise is about their personal preferences. Have students read the direction line. Ask: *What do we write?* (adjective clauses)

2. Model the exercise. Direct students to the example. Provide an additional answer of your own. Ask a volunteer to give an answer.

3. Have students complete the exercise individually. Then have them work in groups to compare and check their answers. Circulate and observe the group work. Have groups report interesting answers to the class: *Eduardo likes to be around people who like to cook.*

🕐 To save class time, have students do half of the exercise in class and complete the other half for homework. Or assign the entire exercise for homework.

Expansion

Exercise 3 After students complete the exercise, have them work in pairs to ask each other about their statements with *why* or *why not:*

A: *I don't like movies with unhappy endings.*
B: *Why not?*
A: *Because they make me feel depressed.*

1. Tell students that this exercise is about their opinions about the best ways to learn English. Have students read the direction line.
2. Direct students to the examples. Ask: *Do you agree with the writer? Why or why not?*
3. Have students complete the exercise individually. Then have them compare their answers in pairs. Circulate and observe the pair work. If appropriate, participate in discussions. If necessary, check the answers as a class.
4. Assess students' performance. If necessary, review grammar chart **6.2** on page 226.

🕐 To save class time, have students do half of the exercise in class and complete the other half for homework. Or assign the entire exercise for homework.

---

4. I like movies _____
5. I don't like teachers _____
6. I like teachers _____
7. I don't like teenagers _____
8. I like to have neighbors _____
9. I don't like to have neighbors _____
10. I like to receive mail _____
11. I have never met a person _____
12. I can't understand people _____
13. I like classes _____
14. I like to be around people _____
15. I don't like to be around people _____
16. A good friend is a person _____
17. I have a good friend _____
18. I once had a car _____

EXERCISE 4 Work with a partner. Write a sentence with each of the words given to describe the ideal situation for learning English. You may use singular or plural.

EXAMPLES
class *Classes that have fewer than 20 sutdents are better than large classes.*

teacher *I prefer to have a teacher who doesn't explain things in my language.*

1. teacher _____ Answers will vary. _____
2. college / school _____
3. textbook _____
4. class _____
5. classroom _____
6. computer lab _____
7. school library _____
8. classmate _____
9. dictionary _____
10. study group _____

Expansion

Exercise 4 Have a student or group of students take responsibility for each question. Have students or groups move around the room and survey other students or groups on their preferences, write a conclusion, and present it to the class (e.g., *Most students would like to have a computer lab that has open hours before class.*).

6.3 | Relative Pronoun as Object

The relative pronouns *who(m)*, *that*, and *which* can be the object of an adjective clause.

Object

I don't read all the e-mail.   I receive *e-mail*.

I don't read all the e-mail | which / that / ø | I receive.

Object

I don't know *a person*.

A person .... sent me an e-mail with her picture.

A person | who(m) / that / ø | I don't know   sent me an e-mail with her picture.

Language Notes:

1. While all ways shown above are grammatically correct, the relative pronoun is usually omitted in conversation when it is the object of the adjective clause.

   I don't read all the e-mail that I receive.

   A person whom I don't know sent me an e-mail with her picture.

2. *Whom* is considered more correct than *who* when used as the object of the adjective clause. However, as seen in the above note, the relative pronoun is usually omitted altogether in conversation.

   A person whom I don't know sent me an e-mail. (Formal)

   A person who I don't know sent me an e-mail. (Less Formal)

   A person I don't know sent me an e-mail. (Informal)

3. In an adjective clause, omit the object pronoun.

   The computer that I bought it has a large memory.

EXERCISE 5   Fill in the blanks to make an appropriate adjective clause.

EXAMPLE My friend just bought a new dog. The last dog ___*he had*___ died a few weeks ago.

1. I have a hard teacher this semester. The teacher ___*I had*___ last semester was much easier.

2. I studied British English in my native country. The English ___*I'm studying*___ now is American English.

3. The teacher gave a test last week. Almost everyone failed the test ___*she / he gave*___.

Culture Note

There are many differences in English, as in most languages, between formal language—often used in writing, in speeches, or to show respect—and informal language, which is usually used in conversations between friends and family members and in comfortable settings. Students may be interested in giving some examples from their own languages and cultures of differences between formal and informal usages.

6.3 | Relative Pronoun as Object

1. Review objects. Write on the board: *I forwarded a funny e-mail to you.* Ask students to identify the object in the sentence (*funny e-mail*).

2. Have students look at the examples in the first two sections of the grammar chart. Say: *The sentence with an adjective clause combines two sentences. We saw this in grammar chart 6.2, too. Here the relative pronoun is the object of the adjective clause.* Write two examples of your own on the board, such as: *I saw the e-mail. You sent the e-mail.* With the class, write a sentence combining the two with an adjective clause (*I saw the e-mail that you sent.*). Make sure that students are familiar with the null symbol that means *nothing*.

3. Draw students' attention to the Language Notes. Ask: *Which relative pronouns do we use with people?* (who, whom, that, none) *Which relative pronouns do we use with things?* (that, which, none) Review the examples. Review the difference between formal settings (academic writing, an oral presentation) and informal settings (a conversation, a quick note to a friend). Point out item 3 and review the example.

EXERCISE 5

1. Tell students that this exercise is about identifying things and people. Have students read the direction line. Ask: *Do we have to use a relative pronoun when we're speaking informally?* (no)

2. Model the exercise. Direct students to the example in the book. Ask: *What is another possible answer?* (*that he/she had, which he/she had*) Then do #1 with the class. Ask a volunteer to give an answer.

3. Have students complete Exercise 5 individually. Then have them compare their answers in pairs. Finally, check the answers as a class.

4. Assess students' performance. If necessary, review grammar chart 6.3.

6.4 | Comparing Pronoun as Subject and Object

1. Have students review the examples and explanations in grammar chart **6.4.** Ask: *What difference do you see between the (a) sentences and the (b) sentences?* (The (a) sentences have a new subject after the relative pronoun.)

2. Draw students' attention to the second paragraph in the explanations. Say: *If you are not sure whether the relative pronoun is necessary, look to see if there is a new subject.* Provide several additional examples, such as: *I have a friend who forwards every joke e-mail she gets. Some of the jokes she forwards aren't very funny.* Ask: *Which one has the relative pronoun as the subject?* (the first) *As the object?* (the second)

4. When I read English, there are many new words for me. I use my dictionary to look up the words I _____ *don't know* _____.

5. I had a big apartment last year. The apartment _____ *I have* _____ now is very small.

6. Did you contact the owner of the wallet _____ *you found* _____ on the street?

7. I write poetry. One of the poems _____ *I wrote* _____ won a prize.

8. The last book _____ *I read* _____ was very sad. It made me cry.

9. She has met a lot of people at school, but she hasn't made any friends. The people _____ *she's met* _____ are all too busy to spend time with her.

6.4 | Comparing Pronoun as Subject and Object

Examples	Explanation
Compare: a. I receive a lot of e-mail **(that)** I delete without reading. b. I receive a lot of e-mail **that** promises to make me rich.	In sentences (a), the relative pronoun is the object of the adjective clause. It is often omitted, especially in conversation. The new subject introduced (*I*) indicates that the relative pronoun is an object and can be omitted.
a. A student **(whom)** I met in my math class doesn't want to own a computer. b. A student **who** has good grades can get a scholarship.	In sentences (b), the relative pronoun is the subject of the adjective clause. It cannot be omitted. The fact that there is no new subject after *that* or *who* indicates that the relative pronoun is the subject. *Wrong:* A student has good grades can get a scholarship.

Grammar Variation

Have students match the clauses in boldface in the reading on pages 224 to 225 to the appropriate explanation in the grammar chart.

EXERCISE **6**   Fill in the blanks with an adjective clause.

A: I'm so tired of all the spam ___I get___ .
(example)

B: Do you get a lot?

A: Of course, I do. Doesn't everyone?

B: I don't.

A: How is that possible?

B: I have an e-mail address ___I use___ just
(1)
for shopping online. I don't use it for anything else. The e-mail

address ___I give___ to my friends is private.
(2)
I don't give it to anyone else.

A: I never thought about having different e-mail addresses for different
things. Don't you have to pay for each e-mail account?

B: There are a lot of e-mail providers ___you can use___
(3)
___ for free.

For example, you can use Hotmail™ or Yahoo™ for free. But they have
limited space and aren't good for everything. I like to send a lot of

photos. The photos ___I send___ are often
(4)
too big for my free Hotmail account, but it's perfect for the shopping

___I do___ online.
(5)

A: Do you do a lot of shopping online?

B: Yes. For example, I buy a lot of textbooks online. The textbooks

___I buy___ online are often cheaper than
(6)
the ones in the bookstore.

Adjective Clauses; Descriptive Phrases   **231**

EXERCISE   6

🎧 *CD 2, Track 13*

1. Tell students that this exercise is a
conversation between friends about
e-mail. Have students read the
direction line.
2. Model the exercise. Direct students
to the first line in the interview.
Then complete items 1 and 2 as a
class.
3. Have students complete Exercise 6
individually. Then have them check
their answers in pairs by practicing
the conversation. Circulate and
observe the pair work. If necessary,
check the answers as a class.
4. Assess students' performance. If
necessary, review grammar chart **6.4.**

Exercise 6 Variation

To provide practice with listening skills, have students close their books and listen to the
audio. Repeat the audio as needed. Ask comprehension questions, such as: *Why doesn't
person B get a lot of spam?* (Person B has a separate e-mail address for shopping online.) *Are
some e-mail accounts free?* (yes) *Why does person B buy textbooks online?* (because they are
often cheaper than the ones in a bookstore) Then have students open their books and
complete Exercise 6.

A: How can I get one of these free accounts?

B: You just go to their Web site and sign up. Choose a username and password. If the username _____*you choose*_____ has
(7)
already been chosen by someone else, you can choose another one or simply add some numbers to it. For example, I chose SlyFox, but it was already taken, so I added the year of my birth, 1986. So I'm SlyFox1986.

B: Why did you choose that name?

A: That's the name _____*I had*_____ when I was a
(8)
child. My older brother was always giving people nicknames. After you choose a username, choose a password. Make sure it's a number or word _____*you can / will remember*_____ easily. If you forget your
(9)
password, you won't be able to use your account. The password _____*you choose*_____ should never be obvious.
(10)
Never, for example, use your birth date, address, phone number, or Social Security number.

B: What password did you choose?

A: The password _____*I chose*_____ is a secret.
(11)
I will never tell it to anyone.

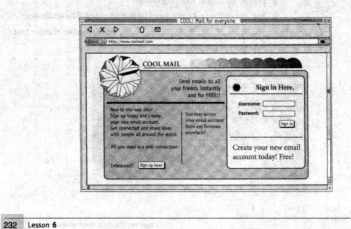

Expansion

Exercise 6 Have students work together to prepare a consumer's guide to e-mail services they are familiar with. Have groups research and report the costs, services, number of ads, and amount of spam for services they research. If possible, have them write their results and make copies for the class.

Culture Note

Use the picture at the bottom of page 232 to review or introduce language for the parts of a Web page, e.g., *user name*, *connection*, and *browser*.

6.5 | Relative Pronoun as Object of Preposition

The relative pronouns can be the object of a preposition (*to, about, with, of, for*, etc.).

	Prep.	*Object*
Spam is commercial e-mail.	You don't ask **for**	spam.

Spam is commercial e-mail **that / ø / which** ← you don't ask **for.**

Spam is commercial e-mail **for which** you don't ask. (*Very formal*)

	Prep.	*Object*
	I wrote **to**	a friend.

The friend..sent me a quick reply.

The friend **that / ø / who(m)** ← I wrote to   sent me a quick reply. (*Informal*)

The friend **to whom** I wrote sent me a quick reply. (*Very formal*)

Language Notes:

1. Informally, most native speakers put the preposition at the end of the adjective clause. The relative pronoun is usually omitted. The most common way to say the sentences in the above chart is:

    Spam is commercial e-mail you don't ask **for.**

    The friend I wrote **to** sent me a quick reply.

2. In very formal English, the preposition comes before the relative pronoun, and only *whom* and *which* may be used. *That* is not used directly after a preposition.

    The person **to whom** I spoke was very helpful.

    The college **to which** I applied is in California.

    Wrong: The college to *that* I applied is in California.

EXERCISE **1** ABOUT YOU Complete each statement.

EXAMPLE   The class I was in last semester _____ *was very crowded.* _____

1. The city I come from _____ *Answers will vary.* _____
2. The school I graduated from _____
3. The house / apartment I used to live in _____
4. The elementary school I went to _____

Culture Note

Students may be interested in additional examples of the differences between formal and informal English, and when each is used. If possible, bring in samples of written material showing the use and omission of the relative pronouns (especially *whom*) with prepositions, such as academic writing, junk mail, and newspaper articles.

6.5 | Relative Pronoun as Object of Preposition

1. Review prepositions. Have students cover the grammar chart. Ask students to name as many prepositions as they can. Write the list on the board. Elicit from students several examples of sentences with prepositions and objects (*Mia told me about a new e-mail service. I have a new picture of my nephew.*). Ask students to identify the objects of the prepositions (*a new e-mail service; my nephew*).

2. Have students look at the examples in the first two sections of the grammar chart. Copy the examples of the two sentences being combined on the board (*Spam is commercial e-mail. You don't ask for spam. I wrote to a friend. The friend sent me a quick reply.*). Demonstrate, as in the grammar chart, how the sentences are combined.

3. Write one or two examples of your own on the board, such as: *Here's the address for the free account. I told you about the free account.* With the class, write an informal sentence combining the two example sentences, using an adjective clause (*Here's the address for the free account I told you about.*).

4. Draw students' attention to the Language Notes. Review the examples of formal and informal English. Tell students that traditional formal grammar books frequently state that prepositions may not be used at the end of a sentence, but that they are commonly used today.

EXERCISE 7

1. Tell students that this exercise is about their personal experiences. Have students read the direction line.

2. Model the exercise. Direct students to the example in the book. Then ask several students to complete the example for themselves.

3. Have students complete Exercise 7 individually. Then have them compare their answers in pairs. Ask pairs to report interesting information about their partners to the class.

1. Tell students that this exercise is about speaking informally. Have students read the direction line. Ask: *What do we take out?* (the relative pronoun) *What do we move?* (the preposition)
2. Model the exercise. Direct students to the example in the book. Then do #1 with the class. Ask a volunteer to give the answer.
3. Have students complete Exercise 8 individually. Then have them compare their answers in pairs. Finally, check the answers as a class.

CD 2, Track 14

1. Tell students that this exercise is a conversation between friends. Have students read the direction line. Ask: *Where did one of the friends go?* (on vacation; to an island) Remind students that several answers may be possible.
2. Direct students to the example in the book. Complete #1 as a class.
3. Have students complete Exercise 9 individually. Then have them check their answers in pairs by practicing the conversation. Circulate and observe the pair work. If necessary, check the answers as a class.

To save class time, have students do half of the exercise in class and complete the other half for homework. Or assign the entire exercise for homework.

---

5. The teacher I studied beginning grammar with _____

_____

6. Most of the people I went to elementary school with _____

7. _____ is a subject I'm very interested in.

8. _____ is a topic I don't like to talk about.

EXERCISE 8 Make these sentences more informal by taking out the relative pronoun and putting the preposition at the end of the adjective clause.

EXAMPLE He applied to several colleges in which he was interested.
He applied to several colleges was interested in.

1. I don't understand a word about which you are talking.
   I don't understand a word you are talking about.

2. The gym to which I used to go raised its fee.
   The gym I used to go to raised its fee.

3. The pen for which you are looking is in your pocket.
   The pen you are looking for is in your pocket.

4. Those are the children for whom the babysitter is responsible.
   Those are the children the babysitter is responsible for.

5. There is very little of which I'm sure.
   There is very little I'm sure of.

6. That is the counselor with whom you need to speak.
   That is the counselor you need to speak with.

EXERCISE 9 This is a conversation between two friends. One just came back from an island vacation where he had a terrible time. Fill in each blank with an adjective clause. Answers may vary.

A: How was your trip?

B: Terrible.

A: What happened? Didn't your travel agent give you good advice?

B: I didn't use a travel agent. I asked some friends for cheap ways to take a vacation. One friend I ____talked to____ told me to look for
   (example)
   vacations online. So I did. There was a choice of hotels. The name of

234   Lesson **6**

Expansion

Exercise 7 Have students use the sentences in the exercise as models to write sentences of their own about places and topics with which they are familiar.

Exercise 9 Variation

To provide practice with listening skills, have students close their books and listen to the audio. Repeat the audio as needed. Ask comprehension questions, such as: *How was person A's trip?* (terrible) *What was the name of the hotel person A stayed at?* (Ocean View) *Did person A meet any interesting travelers?* (No; they weren't friendly) Then have students open their books and complete Exercise 9.

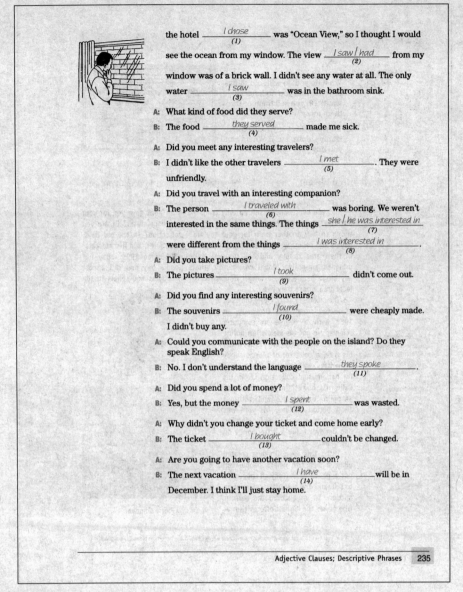

the hotel ___I chose___ was "Ocean View," so I thought I would
          (1)

see the ocean from my window. The view ___I saw / had___ from my
               (2)

window was of a brick wall. I didn't see any water at all. The only

water ___I saw___ was in the bathroom sink.
    (3)

A: What kind of food did they serve?

B: The food ___they served___ made me sick.
        (4)

A: Did you meet any interesting travelers?

B: I didn't like the other travelers ___I met___. They were
                (5)
unfriendly.

A: Did you travel with an interesting companion?

B: The person ___I traveled with___ was boring. We weren't
          (6)
interested in the same things. The things ___she / he was interested in___
                (7)
were different from the things ___I was interested in___.
             (8)

A: Did you take pictures?

B: The pictures ___I took___ didn't come out.
        (9)

A: Did you find any interesting souvenirs?

B: The souvenirs ___I found___ were cheaply made.
        (10)
I didn't buy any.

A: Could you communicate with the people on the island? Do they
speak English?

B: No. I don't understand the language ___they spoke___.
          (11)

A: Did you spend a lot of money?

B: Yes, but the money ___I spent___ was wasted.
        (12)

A: Why didn't you change your ticket and come home early?

B: The ticket ___I bought___ couldn't be changed.
      (13)

A: Are you going to have another vacation soon?

B: The next vacation ___I have___ will be in
        (14)
December. I think I'll just stay home.

Expansion

Exercise 9 Have students work individually or in groups to write a short paragraph about
person B's experience on vacation. Students should use sentences from the conversation as
models and add a conclusion about what person B should do or should have done.

eBay (Reading)

1. Have students look at the picture at the top of page 236. Ask: *What Web site is this? What is it for? Have you ever used it?*
2. Have students look briefly at the reading. Ask: *What is the reading about? How do you know?* Have students make predictions.
3. Preteach any vocabulary words your students may not know, such as *taking up space, garage sales, global, piece, merchandise, put up, changed hands,* and *collectibles.*

BEFORE YOU READ

1. Activate students' prior knowledge about online auctions. Ask: *Why do people use eBay?* (to sell items they don't want; to buy items they want or need) *Do you know of any sites like eBay?*
2. Have students discuss the questions in pairs. Try to pair students of different language backgrounds.
3. Ask a few volunteers to share their answers with the class.

🕐 To save class time, skip "Before You Read" or have students prepare answers for homework ahead of time.

Reading 🎧 *CD 2, Track 15*

1. Have students first read the text silently. Tell them to pay special attention to *when* and *where* in the reading. Then play the audio and have students read along silently.
2. Check students' comprehension. Ask questions such as: *How did the founder of eBay get the idea?* (from trying to help his wife find an unusual item she wanted to buy) *What can you do on eBay?* (buy or sell items; talk to other people; exchange information; find friends)

🕐 To save class time, have students do the reading for homework ahead of time.

The owner of a Web auction site may make money by collecting a small percentage of each sale or trade, called a *commission.* Real estate agents and some salespeople also make part of their pay from commissions.

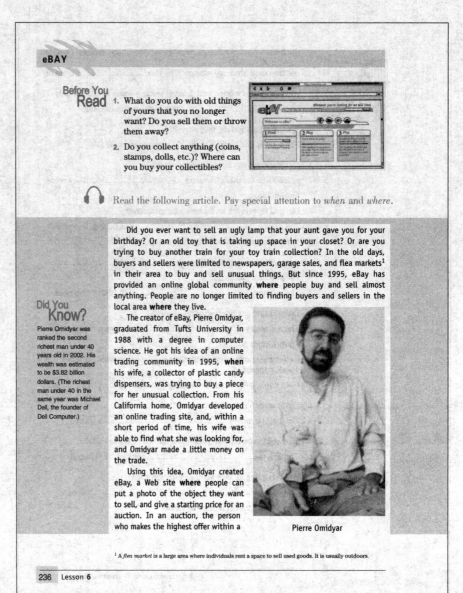

eBAY

Before You Read

1. What do you do with old things of yours that you no longer want? Do you sell them or throw them away?
2. Do you collect anything (coins, stamps, dolls, etc.)? Where can you buy your collectibles?

🎧 Read the following article. Pay special attention to *when* and *where*.

Did you ever want to sell an ugly lamp that your aunt gave you for your birthday? Or an old toy that is taking up space in your closet? Or are you trying to buy another train for your toy train collection? In the old days, buyers and sellers were limited to newspapers, garage sales, and flea markets[1] in their area to buy and sell unusual things. But since 1995, eBay has provided an online global community **where** people buy and sell almost anything. People are no longer limited to finding buyers and sellers in the local area **where** they live.

Did You Know?

Pierre Omidyar was ranked the second richest man under 40 years old in 2002. His wealth was estimated to be $3.82 billion dollars. (The richest man under 40 in the same year was Michael Dell, the founder of Dell Computer.)

The creator of eBay, Pierre Omidyar, graduated from Tufts University in 1988 with a degree in computer science. He got his idea of an online trading community in 1995, **when** his wife, a collector of plastic candy dispensers, was trying to buy a piece for her unusual collection. From his California home, Omidyar developed an online trading site, and, within a short period of time, his wife was able to find what she was looking for, and Omidyar made a little money on the trade.

Using this idea, Omidyar created eBay, a Web site **where** people can put a photo of the object they want to sell, and give a starting price for an auction. In an auction, the person who makes the highest offer within a

Pierre Omidyar

[1] A *flea market* is a large area where individuals rent a space to sell used goods. It is usually outdoors.

236   Lesson **6**

Expansion

Theme The topic for this lesson can be enhanced with the following ideas:

1. A plastic candy dispenser
2. A page from eBay showing articles for sale
3. A message from a trading or recycling listserv showing available items

Reading Variation

To practice listening skills, have students first listen to the audio alone. Ask a few comprehension questions. Repeat the audio if necessary. Then have students open their books and read along as they listen to the audio.

certain period of time gets to buy the item. Not everything on eBay is sold by auction. Some items have fixed prices too. eBay makes its money by charging the seller a small percentage of the final price.

Meg Whitman

By 1998, eBay had become so big that Omidyar and his partner could no longer handle it without expert help. They brought in Meg Whitman, whose knowledge of business helped make eBay the success it is today. She changed eBay from a company that sold several categories of used things to a large marketplace of 11 million items in 18,000 categories of both new and used merchandise. Every day more than half a million items are sold. In the year 2001 alone, over $9 billion worth of merchandise changed hands on eBay, including cars, jewelry, toys, computers—and anything else you can imagine.

Not only can you buy and sell on eBay, you can also meet people whose interests you share. Whitman is proud of the online communities she has created. For example, doll collectors all over the world can "meet" each other and exchange information on bulletin boards and in chat rooms. Friendships are formed on eBay among people who share an interest in the same collectibles.

eBay is now among the top 10 Web sites visited.

6.6 | *Where* and *When* in Adjective Clauses

Examples	Explanation
eBay is a Web site **where people can buy and sell things.** eBay is a community **where you can meet people who share your hobby.**	*Where* means "in that place." *Where* cannot be omitted.
There was a time **(when)** collectors were limited to their local areas. Do you remember the day **(when)** you saw a computer for the first time?	*When* means "at that time." *When* can be omitted.

Adjective Clauses; Descriptive Phrases 237

6.6 | *Where* and *When* in Adjective Clauses

1. Have students look back at the reading on pages 236 and 237 and underline clauses with *when* and *where*. Write information from one of the sentences on the board, such as: *eBay provides a community where people buy and sell almost anything.* Ask: *What does where mean?* (in that place) Write: *He got the idea in 1995, when his wife wanted to buy something.* Ask: *What does when mean?* (at that time)

2. Have students review the examples in grammar chart **6.6.** Draw students' attention to the explanations. Ask: *Which one can be omitted?* (when)

3. Elicit several examples from students. Provide a cue (*Our city is a place where . . . ; There was a time when . . .*) and have students complete sentences.

Reading Glossary

change hands: move from one owner to another

collectible: piece, item, or part of a set of items that people collect, e.g., antique or small decorative or household items

garage sale: a sale held by an individual or neighborhood, usually outside their home, to sell items they don't want

global: around the world

merchandise: items, usually for sale

piece: item

put up: post, publish on a Web site (on the Internet)

take up space: use or occupy a place without providing much benefit

Culture Note

The World Wide Web has inspired creative, catchy names like *eBay* that people remember and can type easily. *eBay* is not capitalized, even as the first word in a sentence, as in the reading.

EXERCISE 10

1. Tell students that this exercise is about Web sites. Have students read the direction line.
2. Direct students to the example in the book.
3. Have students complete the exercise individually. Tell students to complete the items using information about Web sites they are familiar with. Ask volunteers to share their answers with the class.

EXERCISE 11

1. Tell students that this exercise is about their opinions. Have students read the direction line.
2. Direct students to the example in the book. Ask for volunteers to provide additional answers.
3. Have students read the prompts silently and think about their answers for a few minutes. Encourage students to take notes. Then have them complete the exercise. Ask volunteers to share their answers with the class.

🕐 To save class time, have students do half of the exercise in class and complete the other half for homework. Or assign the entire exercise for homework.

EXERCISE 12

1. Tell students that this exercise is about their thoughts and interests. Have students read the direction line.
2. Direct students to the examples in the book. Ask several volunteers to complete the sentence for themselves.
3. Have students complete the exercise individually. Then have them share their answers with a partner. Ask volunteers to share their partners' answers with the class. Model: *The park is a place where Jeanne can relax.*
4. Assess students' performance. If necessary, review grammar chart **6.6**.

🕐 To save class time, have students do half of the exercise in class and complete the other half for homework. Or assign the entire exercise for homework.

EXERCISE **10** Tell what information you can find on certain Web sites. If you're not sure, go to the Web site. Or you can take a guess and check it out later.

EXAMPLE WhiteHouse.gov is a Web site ___*where you can read about*___ *the White House and the president.*

1. Weather.com is a Web site ___*where you can check the weather.*___
2. Mapquest.com is a Web site ___*where you can find maps.*___
3. CNN.com is a Web site ___*where you can read the news.*___
4. USPS.gov is a Web site ___*where you can buy stamps.*___
5. Hotmail.com is a Web site ___*where you can get free e-mail*___
6. Travelocity.com is a Web site ___*where you can make travel plans.*___
7. Newsweek.com is a Web site ___*where you can read the news.*___
8. IRS.gov is a Web site ___*where you can get information about taxes.*___
9. Redcross.org is a Web site ___*where you can donate money.*___
10. Harvard.edu is a Web site *where you can get information about Harvard.*

EXERCISE **11** Fill in the blanks.

EXAMPLE I like to use the computer lab at a time ___*when it isn't crowded.*___

1. The teacher shouldn't give a test on a day when ___*Answers will vary.*___
2. I like to study at a time when _____
3. Saturday is the day when _____
4. _____ is the season when _____
5. Between 7 and 9 a.m. is the time when _____
6. _____ was the year when _____

EXERCISE **12** ABOUT YOU Fill in the blanks to tell about yourself.

EXAMPLE ___*June*___ is the month when I was born.

1. ___*Answers will vary.*___ is a place where I can relax.
2. _____ is a place where I can have fun.
3. _____ is a place where I can be alone and think.
4. _____ is a place where I can meet my friends.
5. _____ is a place where I can study undisturbed.

238 Lesson **6**

Expansion

Exercise 10 As homework, have students who have Internet access research sites they were not familiar with. Have them write a sentence about each site they research using the model in the exercise.

Exercise 10 Have students add their favorite Web sites to the list in the exercise.

6. _____ is a time when I can relax.

7. _____ is a time when I like to watch TV.

8. _____ is a day when I have almost no free time.

9. _____ is a time when I like to use the Internet.

6.7 | *Where, When, That,* or *Which* in Adjective Clauses

Examples	Explanation
a. In 2002, Pierre gave the graduation speech at the college **where** he had gotten his degree.	Instead of *where* (a), the adjective clause can have preposition + *which* (b) or *that* + preposition (c). If you use *where*, don't use a preposition (in this case, *from*).
b. In 2002, Pierre gave the graduation speech at the college *from* **which** he had gotten his degree.	
c. In 2002, Pierre gave the graduation speech at the college **(that)** he had gotten his degree *from*.	The meaning of (a), (b), and (c) is essentially the same.
a. 1995 is the year **when** eBay got its start.	Instead of *when* (a), the adjective clause can have preposition + *which* (b) or *that* + preposition (c). If you use *when*, don't use a preposition.
b. 1995 is the year *in* **which** eBay got its start.	
c. 1995 is the year **(that)** eBay got started *in*.	The meaning of (a), (b), and (c) is essentially the same.
Compare:	In sentence (a), *where* means *there* or *in that place*.
a. She lives in a home **where** people use the computer a lot.	People use the computer a lot *there*.
b. She lives in a home **that** has three computers.	In sentence (b), *that* means *home*.
	The *home* has three computers.
a. February is the month **when** I was born.	In sentence (a), *when* means *then* or *in that month*.
b. February is the month **that** has only 28 days.	I was born *then*.
	In sentence (b), *that* means *the month*.
	The *month* has only 28 days.

6.7 | *Where, When, That,* or *Which* in Adjective Clauses

1. Have students cover grammar chart **6.7**. On the board, write:
   1. *eBay is a site where you can buy almost anything.*
   2. *eBay is a site on which you can buy almost anything.*
   3. *eBay is a site you can buy almost anything on.*
   Say: *These three sentences mean the same thing. Which one is the most formal?* (#2) *Which one doesn't have a preposition?* (#1)

2. Have students uncover and review grammar chart **6.7**. Review the example sentences and explanations in the first two sections carefully.

3. Draw students' attention to the last two sections of the chart. Point out that in the (a) sentences, *where* and *when* are followed by a subject, and that in the (b) sentences, *where* and *when* are followed by a verb.

4. Ask students to use the examples in the last two sections to provide information about themselves, such as *I live in a home where . . .* or *(year) is the year when . . . .*

Expansion

Exercise 12 Have students work in teams to use the information in Exercise 12 to plan a game show. Have each team write five quiz sentences about places in the community, e.g., _____ *is a place where you can borrow books and movies.* (Answer: the library) Then have teams take turns asking each other to fill in the blanks. Award points for each correct answer; the team with the most points wins.

EXERCISE 13

1. Tell students that this exercise is about places. Have students read the direction line.
2. Model the exercise. Direct students to the example in the book. Then complete #1 as a class.
3. Have students complete Exercise 13 individually. Then have them compare their answers in pairs. If necessary, check the answers as a class.

EXERCISE 13

1. Tell students that this exercise is about times. Have students read the direction line.
2. Model the exercise. Direct students to the example in the book. Then do #1 with the class.
3. Have students complete Exercise 14 individually. Then have them compare their answers in pairs. If necessary, check the answers as a class.

To save class time, have students do half of the exercise in class and complete the other half for homework. Or assign the entire exercise for homework.

EXERCISE 13 Fill in the blanks with *where, that,* or *which*.

EXAMPLE The home ____*where*____ I grew up had a beautiful fireplace.

1. The store ____*where*____ I bought my computer is having a sale now.
2. Do you bookmark the Web sites ____*that / which*____ you visit often?
3. The box at the top of your browser is the place in ____*which*____ you write the Web address.
4. There are Web sites ____*where*____ you can compare prices of electronics.
5. The city ____*where*____ I was born has a lot of parks.
6. I don't like cities ____*that*____ have a lot of factories.
7. I like to shop at stores ____*that*____ have products from different countries.
8. I like to shop at stores ____*where*____ I can find products from different countries.
9. A department store is a store in ____*which*____ you can find all kinds of goods—clothing, furniture, toys, etc.
10. I have a photograph of the home ____*where*____ I grew up.
11. The office ____*where*____ you can get your transcripts is closed now.
12. She wants to rent the apartment ____*that / which*____ she saw last Sunday.
13. I would like to visit the city ____*where*____ I grew up.
14. The town in ____*which*____ she grew up was destroyed by the war.

EXERCISE 14 Fill in the blanks with *when* or *that* or nothing.

EXAMPLE December 31, 1999 was a time ____*when*____ people celebrated the beginning of the new century.

1. Six o'clock is the time ____*when / that / ø*____ the auction stops.
2. Do you remember the year ____*when / that / ø*____ Meg Whitman started to work for eBay?
3. 2004 was a year ____*that*____ had 366 days.
4. New Year's Eve is a time ____*that / ø*____ I love.
5. February is the only month ____*that*____ has fewer than 30 days.

Expansion

Exercise 13 After students complete the exercise, write on the board: *I like to shop at stores that . . . and I like to shop at store sites where . . .* Have students complete the sentences to make true statements about themselves. Then have them work in pairs to ask each other about their statements using *why* or *why not*:

A: I like to shop at stores that are clean and organized.
B: Why?
A: Because it's easy to find what I need.

---

6. My birthday is a day _when/that/ø_ I think about my past.

7. December is a time _when/that/ø_ a lot of Americans buy gifts.

8. My parents' anniversary is a date _____ _that_ _____ has a lot of meaning for them.

9. Do you give yourself the time _____ _that/ø_ you need to write a good composition?

10. She wrote about a time _____ _when/that/ø_ she couldn't speak English well.

11. Our vacation to Paris was the best time _____ _that/ø_ we had ever had.

HANKWRITTEN LETTERS OR E-MAIL?

Before You Read

1. What are some differences between a handwritten letter and an e-mail?

2. Do you ever use instant messages?

🎧 Rart 1: Read the following handwritten letter, instant message, and e-mail.

> _May 14, 2005_
>
> Dear Fran,
>   I was so happy to receive the letter you sent me with the photos of your adorable children. They've grown so big since the last time I saw them. How do they like their new school?
>   As you know, our wedding is planned for September 12. We hope you'll be able to come. I've been so busy planning for the wedding, working, and studying that I haven't had much time to write lately. I hope you can understand.
>   I'm enclosing a picture of my fiancé. He has a sister **whose daughter goes to the same school as your son in Oakland**. I wonder if they know each other. Her name is Wanda Chen. Ask your son if he knows her.
>   I'm working now as a babysitter. The family **whose daughter I take care of** is from Japan. I'm even learning a few words in Japanese.
>   I'm also taking math classes at City College. The teacher **whose class I'm taking this semester** is very young. She just graduated from college, but she teaches very well.

(continued)

Adjective Clauses; Descriptive Phrases **241**

Expansion

Theme The topic for this lesson can be enhanced with the following ideas:

1. Personal letters from friends or family, especially old letters
2. Copies of holiday letters
3. Printouts of brief, informal e-mails from friends or acquaintances
4. Mailing information and postal rates from the post office

Reading Variation

To practice listening skills, have students first listen to the audio alone. Ask a few comprehension questions. Repeat the audio if necessary. Then have students open their books and read along as they listen to the audio.

Reading Glossary, Part 1

adorable: cute; loveable
enclose: include; add to a message or to an envelope

Handwritten Letters or E-mail? (Reading)

1. Have students look at the photo on page 241. Ask: *What is she doing? How do you think she feels?* Then have students look at the photo on page 242. Ask: *What is this person doing?* (text messaging)

2. Have students look briefly at the reading. Have students look at the title of the reading. Ask: *What is the reading about? How do you know?* Have students make predictions.

3. Preteach any vocabulary words your students may not know, such as: *adorable, enclosing, distant, exposes, viruses, shut down, intimate,* and *regardless.*

BEFORE YOU READ

1. Activate students' prior knowledge about e-mail and instant messaging. Ask: *How often do you write handwritten letters? E-mail? Instant messages?*

2. Have students discuss the questions in pairs. Try to pair students of different language backgrounds.

3. Ask a few volunteers to share their answers with the class.

🕐 To save class time, skip "Before You Read" or have students prepare answers for homework ahead of time.

Reading 🎧 CD 2, Track 16

1. Have students read Part 1 of the text silently. Then play the audio and have students read along silently.

2. Check students' comprehension. Ask questions such as: *What are some things the letter writer talks about?* (her wedding, her job, her class) *Where is Joe P?* (at his job) *What is Jill sending to Fran?* (pictures)

3. Have students make a list of abbreviations and nonstandard expressions in the instant message and the e-mail. Write them on the board. With the class, figure out what each one stands for, e.g., *wanna = want to; do you want to pics = pictures.*

Reading (*cont.*)

4. Have students read Part 2 of the text silently. Tell them to pay special attention to adjective clauses beginning with *whose*. Then play the audio and have students read along silently.

5. Check students' comprehension. Ask questions such as: *What are some reasons people like e-mail?* (It's fast; it's a good way to keep in touch.) *What are some reasons people like handwritten letters?* (They are more personal; the paper can be attractive.)

🕐 To save class time, have students do the reading for homework ahead of time.

DID YOU KNOW ?

Point out the drawing of a snail. Make sure that students recognize its slow pace.

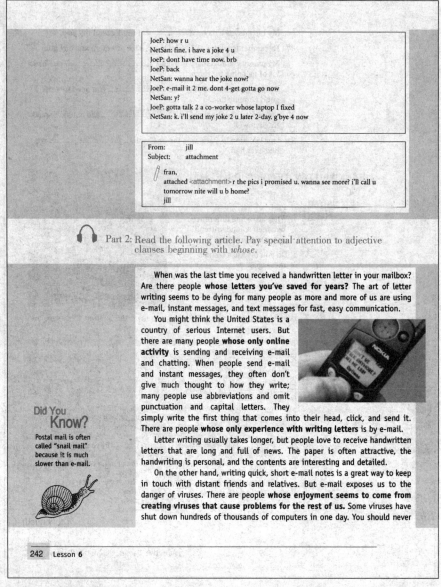

JoeP: how r u
NetSan: fine. i have a joke 4 u
JoeP: dont have time now. brb
JoeP: back
NetSan: wanna hear the joke now?
JoeP: e-mail it 2 me. dont 4-get gotta go now
NetSan: y?
JoeP: gotta talk 2 a co-worker whose laptop I fixed
NetSan: k. i'll send my joke 2 u later 2-day. g'bye 4 now

From: jill
Subject: attachment

fran,
attached <attachment> r the pics i promised u. wanna see more? i'll call u tomorrow nite will u b home?
jill

🎧 Part 2: Read the following article. Pay special attention to adjective clauses beginning with *whose*.

When was the last time you received a handwritten letter in your mailbox? Are there people **whose letters you've saved for years?** The art of letter writing seems to be dying for many people as more and more of us are using e-mail, instant messages, and text messages for fast, easy communication.

You might think the United States is a country of serious Internet users. But there are many people **whose only online activity** is sending and receiving e-mail and chatting. When people send e-mail and instant messages, they often don't give much thought to how they write; many people use abbreviations and omit punctuation and capital letters. They simply write the first thing that comes into their head, click, and send it. There are people **whose only experience with writing letters** is by e-mail.

Letter writing usually takes longer, but people love to receive handwritten letters that are long and full of news. The paper is often attractive, the handwriting is personal, and the contents are interesting and detailed.

On the other hand, writing quick, short e-mail notes is a great way to keep in touch with distant friends and relatives. But e-mail exposes us to the danger of viruses. There are people **whose enjoyment seems to come from creating viruses that cause problems for the rest of us.** Some viruses have shut down hundreds of thousands of computers in one day. You should never

Did You Know?
Postal mail is often called "snail mail" because it is much slower than e-mail.

242   Lesson **6**

Reading Glossary, Part 2

distant: far away
expose: leave open
intimate: very personal; from someone who knows you well
regardless of: no matter; not important
shut down: cause to stop working
virus: 'contagious' program that can harm or take control of your computer

open an attachment from a sender **whose name you don't recognize.** Postal letters never contain viruses. And they provide a personal, intimate connection with a friend or relative.

Regardless of whether you prefer to send and receive handwritten letters or e-mails, it is important and fun to stay connected with friends and family.

6.8 | *Whose* + Noun in an Adjective Clause

Whose is the possessive form of *who*. It stands for *his, her, its, their,* or the possessive form of the noun.

Whose + noun can be the subject of the adjective clause

Subject
There are people. *Their enjoyment* comes from creating viruses.
↓
There are people **whose enjoyment comes from creating viruses.**

Subject
Companies can lose a lot of money. *Their computers* are infected with a virus.

Companies **whose computers are infected with a virus** can lose a lot of money.

Whose + noun can be the object of the adjective clause

Object
Don't open an attachment from a sender. You don't recognize *the sender's name.*

Don't open an attachment from a sender **whose name you don't recognize.**

Object
I've saved *my friends' letters* for years. They are amazed that I still have their mail.

Friends **whose** letters I've saved for years are amazed that I still have their mail.

Adjective Clauses; Descriptive Phrases   243

6.8 | *Whose* + Noun in an Adjective Clause

1. Review *whose.* Write on the board: *Whose e-mail address is this?* Ask: *What does* whose *ask here?* (*Who does this belong to?*) Review the difference between *whose* and *who's* (*who is*).
2. Have students review the examples in the grammar chart carefully. Say: *The sentence with an adjective clause combines two sentences here, too.* Whose *can be the subject or the object of an adjective clause.* Write an example of your own on the board, such as: *I have intelligent friends. Their e-mails are full of mistakes.* With the class, write a sentence combining the two with an adjective clause (*I have intelligent friends whose e-mails are full of mistakes.*).

Expansion

Reading Have students prepare a chart with columns headed *letters, e-mail,* and *instant messaging,* and rows labeled *advantages* and *disadvantages.*

	letters	e-mail	instant messaging
advantages			
disadvantages			

Have students make as many notes as they can about each method of communication in the appropriate box. Compare answers as a class.

1. Tell students that this exercise is about using electronic communication. Have students read the direction line. Ask: *What do we underline?* (the adjective clause)
2. Direct students to the example in the book. Review the example, and then ask a volunteer to answer #1.
3. Have students complete the exercise individually. Check answers as a class.

1. Tell students that this exercise is about identifying people. Have students read the direction line.
2. Direct students to the example in the book. Review the example, and then ask a volunteer to answer #1.
3. Have students complete the exercise individually, and compare answers in pairs. Circulate and observe the pair work. If necessary, check answers as a class.
4. Assess students' performance. If necessary, review grammar chart **6.8** on page 243.

🕐 To save class time, have students do half of the exercise in class and complete the other half for homework. Or assign the entire exercise for homework.

EXERCISE 15 Underline the adjective clause in each sentence.

EXAMPLE Companies whose sites you visit may sell your e-mail address to spammers.

1. Spammers send e-mail to all the people whose names are on their lists.
2. On eBay you can meet people whose interests you share.
3. I sent an e-mail to all the people whose e-mail addresses are in my address book.
4. I only open attachments of senders whose names I recognize.
5. The person whose e-mail I forwarded to you got angry at me for not asking her permission first.
6. A company whose Web site I visit often sends me coupons by e-mail.
7. Companies whose computers are infected with a virus can lose all their data.
8. I have to talk to a co-worker whose laptop I borrowed.

EXERCISE 16 Use the sentence in parentheses to form an adjective clause.

EXAMPLE eBay is a company _whose customers buy and sell thousands of items a day_. (Its customers buy and sell thousands of items a day.)

1. Pierre Omidyar is a creative person _whose idea for eBay made him a very wealthy man_. (His idea for eBay made him a very wealthy man.)
2. My friend has a sister _whose daughter is studying to be a computer programmer_. (Her daughter is studying to be a computer programmer.)
3. The teacher _whose class I'm taking_ uses a computer in the classroom. (I'm taking his class.)
4. There are some people _whose idea of fun is to infect other people's computers with a virus_. (Their idea of fun is to infect other people's computers with a virus.)
5. The police have arrested people _whose viruses have infected thousands of computers_. (Their viruses have infected thousands of computers.)
6. The person _whose letter I forwarded to everyone in my address book_ got angry with me. (I forwarded her letter to everyone in my address book.)
7. I received a letter with an attachment from a sender _whose name I didn't recognize_. (I don't recognize his or her name.)
8. The family _whose daughter I babysit for_ has three computers in their house. (I babysit for their daughter).

Expansion

Exercise 16 Have students use items 2, 4, and 6 as models to write statements of their own, e.g., *My friend has a sister whose teenagers have a successful Web site.*

6.9 | Adjective Clauses After Indefinite Pronouns

An adjective clause can follow an indefinite pronoun: *someone, something, everyone, everything, no one, nothing, anything.*

Examples	Explanation
IP RP Everyone **who received my e-mail** knows about the party. IP RP I don't know anyone **who has never used e-mail.**	The relative pronoun (RP) after an indefinite pronoun (IP) can be the subject of the adjective clause. The relative pronoun cannot be omitted.
IP RP Something **(that) he wrote** made me angry. IP RP I didn't read anything **(that) I received** today.	The relative pronoun (RP) after an indefinite pronoun (IP) can be the object of the adjective clause. In this case, it is usually omitted.

Language Notes:
1. An indefinite pronoun takes a singular verb (the *-s* form).
   Everyone who **uses** e-mail has an e-mail address.
   I don't know anyone who **doesn't** have a computer.
2. An adjective clause does not usually follow a personal pronoun, except in very formal language and in some proverbs.
   He **who** laughs last laughs best.
   He **who** hesitates is lost.

EXERCISE 17   Fill in the blanks with an adjective clause. Use information from nearby sentences to help you. Answers may vary.

A woman (W) is trying to break up with a man (M).

M: I heard you want to talk to me.

W: Yes. There's something _____ *I want to tell you* _____.
                                 (example)

M: What do you want to tell me?

W: I want to break up.

M: Are you angry at me? What did I say?

W: Nothing _____ *(that) you said* _____ made me angry.
                        (1)

M: Did I do something wrong?

W: Nothing _____ *(that) you did* _____ made me mad.
                       (2)

M: Then what's the problem?

W: I just don't love you anymore.

6.9 | Adjective Clauses After Indefinite Pronouns

1. Draw students' attention to the list of indefinite pronouns in the top section of the grammar chart. Ask: *Why are these called indefinite pronouns?* (because they don't name a specific person)
2. Have students review the examples and explanations in the grammar chart.
3. Draw students' attention to the Language Notes. Point out #1. Provide some examples of your own (e.g., *Everyone I know hates spam. No one who uses the lab likes those old computers.*).

EXERCISE 17

🎧 *CD 2, Track 17*

1. Tell students that this exercise is about an unhappy couple. Have students read the direction line. Ask: *What does* break up with *mean?* (stop dating; stop being in love)
2. Direct students to the example in the book. Then do #1 with the class.
3. Have students complete the exercise in writing individually. Then have them check their answers in pairs by practicing the dialogue. Circulate and observe the pair work. If necessary, check the answers as a class.

Culture Note

Students may be interested in the proverbs in the Language Notes. Have students work in groups to try to figure out the meanings of the proverbs. Ask students whether they know of proverbs with similar meanings in their languages.

Exercise 17 Variation

To provide practice with listening skills, have students close their books and listen to the audio. Repeat the audio as needed. Ask comprehension questions, such as: *What does the woman want to tell the man?* (that she wants to break up) *Does the woman love the man?* (no, not anymore) *What did the man send the woman by e-mail?* (love letters) Then have students open their books and complete Exercise 17.

1. Tell students that this exercise is about e-mail. Have students read the direction line.
2. Model the exercise. Direct students to the example in the book; point out that different answers are possible.
3. Have students complete Exercise 18 individually. Then have them compare their answers in pairs. Circulate and observe the pair work. If necessary, check the answers as a class.
4. Assess students' performance. If necessary, review grammar chart **6.9** on page 245.

To save class time, have students do half of the exercise in class and complete the other half for homework. Or assign the entire exercise for homework.

M: But I can buy you anything ___(that) you want___
(3)

W: I don't want anything from you. In fact, I'm going to return everything ___(that) you gave me___.
(4)

M: But I can take you anywhere ___(that) you want to go___
(5)

W: I don't want to go anywhere with you.

M: What about all the love letters I sent you by e-mail?

W: I deleted everything ___(that) you sent me___.
(6)

M: Didn't you believe anything ___(that) I said to you___?
(7)

W: I found out that you said the same thing to three other women.

M: That's not true. Everything ___(that) I wrote___ was sincere.
(8)

W: How can it be sincere? You wrote the same thing to my cousin's best friend, my neighbor, and my classmate. The only thing you changed was the name after "Dear." Everything else ___(that) you wrote___
(9)

was the same. So goodbye!

EXERCISE 18 Fill in the blanks with an adjective clause. Answers may vary.

EXAMPLE   I don't send e-mail to everyone ___I know___.

1. You should read everything ___you wrote___ in an e-mail before sending it.

2. When sending an e-mail, you shouldn't write anything ___you might regret later___.

3. I received 20 e-mails today. Nothing ___I received___ was important. It was all spam.

4. Some people delete everything ___they get___ after they read it.

5. If you have a buddy list, you can send an instant message to someone ___you know___

6. People you don't know may send you attachments. You shouldn't open an attachment from anyone ___you don't know___. It may contain a virus.

246   Lesson **6**

Expansion

Exercise 17 Have volunteer pairs of students perform the conversation for the class. Have the class vote on the most dramatic, funniest, or most emotional performance.

Culture Note

Internet matchmaking, in which couples meet online before they meet in person, is increasingly popular. If appropriate, students may be interested in ways that couples meet, date, and break up.

EXERCISE **19** Fill in the blanks with an adjective clause.

EXAMPLE I know someone _who can help you with your car problem_.

1. I don't know anyone ___Answers will vary.___.

2. I know someone _____.

3. Everyone _____ can go to the next level.

4. Anyone _____ should ask the teacher.

5. Everything _____ is useful.

EXERCISE **20** *Combination Exercise.* Circle the correct word in parentheses ( ) to complete the sentences. Ø means no word is necessary.

EXAMPLE What is a computer virus? A virus is a computer code (what, (that,) who, whose) attaches itself to other programs and causes harm to programs, data, or hardware.

1. Viruses are written by people (they, who, whom, whose) enjoy causing problems for the rest of us.

2. What is spam? Spam is commercial e-mail (who, where, what, (Ø)) you haven't asked for.

3. Who is Bill Gates? Bill Gates is the man ((who,) whom, which, what) created Microsoft.

4. Bill Gates was born at a time ((when,) that, which, then) personal computers were not even in people's imaginations.

5. Who is Meg Whitman? She is the woman (to who, whom, (to whom,) to which) Pierre Omidyar turned over the operation of eBay in 1998.

6. Omidyar needed to bring in someone (who, (whose,) who's, who his) knowledge of business was greater than his own.

7. A computer is a tool ((Ø), whom, about which, whose) most of us use today for fast access to information.

8. The Internet is a tool ((that,) what, when, Ø) has been around since the 1970s.

9. What is eBay? eBay is a Web site (that, (where,) there, which) you can buy and sell items.

10. The Internet can be slow at times (where, (when,) that, which) there is a lot of traffic.

Adjective Clauses; Descriptive Phrases 247

EXERCISE 19

1. Tell students that this exercise is on adjective clauses. Have students read the direction line.
2. Direct students to the example in the book. Have several volunteers provide their own statements.
3. Have students complete the exercise individually. Ask for volunteers to share their answers with the class.

⏱ To save class time, have students do the exercise for homework.

EXERCISE 20

1. Tell students that this exercise is a combination exercise on the clauses they have been studying. Have students read the direction line.
2. Direct students to the example. Review the example with the class. Then complete items 1 and 2 as a class.
3. Have students complete the first ten items and then check their work in pairs or as a class. Then have students complete the exercise.
4. Assess students' performance. If necessary, review the applicable grammar charts.

⏱ To save class time, have students do half of the exercise in class and complete the other half for homework. Or assign the entire exercise for homework.

Expansion

Exercise 19 Have each student prepare a statement beginning with *I know someone who . . .* about a member of the class. Then have students read their sentences aloud. Have the class guess which person is being described.

🎧 *CD 2, Track 18*

1. Tell students that this exercise is a conversation between two friends about moving. Have students read the direction line. Ask: *What does* context *mean?* (information around a word; situation)
2. Model the exercise. Direct students to the example in the book. Then complete #1 and #2 with the class.
3. Have students complete Exercise 21 individually. Check the answers as a class; have pairs of students perform parts of the dialogue.
4. Assess students' performance. If necessary, review the appropriate grammar charts.

🕐 To save class time, have students do half of the exercise in class and complete the other half for homework. Or assign the entire exercise for homework.

11. The people (Ø, which, whose, where) you meet in chat rooms are sometimes very rude.
12. I have all the letters (that, what, where, whose) my parents have sent to me.
13. The computer lab is never open at a time (which, then, where, when) I need it.
14. I always delete the spam (who, that, when, whose) I receive.
15. On eBay, you can meet people (who, whom, who they, they) have the same interests as you do.
16. You can create an address book (when, that, where, whose) you can keep the e-mail addresses of all your friends.
17. You can create an address book (which, in which, there, in that) you can keep the e-mail addresses of all your friends.
18. There are chat rooms (there, where, which, that) people with the same interests can meet each other.
19. A virus writer is a person (his, whose, who, whom) enjoyment comes from creating problems for computer users.
20. Do you know anyone (Ø, who, whom, which) doesn't own a computer?
21. A man (who, whom, whose, who's) in my math class doesn't own a computer.
22. Don't believe everything (what, who, whom, Ø) you read on the Internet.

EXERCISE 21 🎧 *Combination Exercise.* Fill in the blanks with an adjective clause by using the sentences in parentheses in parentheses or the context to give you clues.

A: How was your move last month?

B: It was terrible.

A: Didn't you use the moving company ___I recommended___? *(example)*

(I recommended a company.)

B: The company ___you recommended___ was not available on *(1)*

the day ___I had to move___. *(I had to move on *(2)*

this day.)* I used a company ___whose name I found on the Internet___. *(3)*

(I found the name on the Internet.)

A: What happened?

Exercise 21 Variation

To provide practice with listening skills, have students close their books and listen to the audio. Repeat the audio as needed. Ask comprehension questions, such as: *What did person A recommend to person B?* (a moving company) *Did person B use that moving company?* (no) *Why not?* (The moving company wasn't available on the day person B had to move.) Then have students open their books and complete Exercise 21.

B: First of all, it was raining on the day _____*I moved*_____ .
(4)

That made the move take longer, so it was more expensive than I thought it would be.

A: It's not the company's fault that it rained.

B: I know. But there are many other things _____*that were their fault*_____ .
(5)

(Things were their fault.) The movers broke the mirror
_____*I had just bought*_____ . *(I had just bought the mirror.)* And
(6)

they left muddy footprints on the carpet _____*I had just cleaned*_____ .
(7)

(I had just cleaned the carpet.) I thought I was getting professional

movers. But the men *(They sent these men to my home.)* _____

_____*they sent to my home*_____ were college students. They
(8)

didn't have much experience moving. Because the move took them so long, they charged me much more than I expected to pay. The

information *(They have information.)* _____*they had*_____
(9)

on their Web site says $100 an hour. But they charged me $800 for six hours of work.

A: You should talk to the owner of the company.

B: I called the company several times. The woman *(I talked to a*

woman.) _____*I talked to*_____ said that the owner would
(10)

call me back, but he never has.

A: You should keep trying. Make a list of everything _____*they*_____

_____*broke or ruined*_____ . *(They broke or ruined things.)*
(11)

Their insurance will probably pay for these things.

B: I don't know if they have insurance.

A: You should never use a company _____*that doesn't have insurance*_____ .
(12)

B: Everyone _____*I've talked to*_____ *(I've talked to people.)*
(13)

tells me the same thing.

A: Don't feel so bad. Everyone makes mistakes. We learn from the

mistakes _____*we make*_____ . Why didn't you ask
(14)

your friends to help you move?

Adjective Clauses; Descriptive Phrases   **249**

Expansion

Exercise 21 Ask students what kind of experience person B had when she or he moved (terrible). Ask students to write a list of reasons that the experience was terrible (*It was raining on the day she moved. The company charged too much money*.).

Creating the World Wide Web (Reading)

1. Have students look at the photos. Ask: *What kind of work do you think this man does?*
2. Have students look quickly at the reading on page 251. Ask: *What is the reading about? How do you know?* Have students make predictions.
3. Preteach any vocabulary words your students may not know, such as: *printing, commercially available, poor, keep track of, devised,* and *weaving.*

BEFORE YOU READ

1. Activate students' prior knowledge about the invention and development of the World Wide Web, and about the difference between the Web and the Internet. Ask: *What do you know about the invention of the Internet? Is the person who invented the World Wide Web famous? How much do you use the Internet?*
2. Have students discuss the questions in pairs. Try to pair students of different language backgrounds.
3. Ask a few volunteers to share their answers with the class.

🕐 To save class time, skip "Before You Read" or have students prepare answers for homework ahead of time.

B: Everyone _____*I know*_____ (*I know people.*) is so
  ⁽¹⁵⁾
  busy. I didn't want to bother anyone.

A: By the way, why did you move? You had a lovely apartment.

B: It wasn't mine. The person (*I was renting her apartment.*)
  ____*whose apartment I was renting*____ spent a year in China,
    ⁽¹⁶⁾
  but when she came back last month, I had to leave.

A: How do you like your new place?

B: It's fine. It's across the street from the building
  ____*where my sister lives*____. (*My sister lives in that*
      ⁽¹⁷⁾
  building.) So now we get to see each other more often. Why don't
  you come over sometime and see my new place?

A: I'd love to. How about Saturday after 4 p.m.? That's the only time
  ___*when I don't have too much to do.*___ (*I don't have too much to do at*
    ⁽¹⁸⁾
  that time.)

B: Saturday would be great.

CREATING THE WORLD WIDE WEB

Before You Read

1. Besides computers, what other inventions have changed the way people communicate with each other?
2. When you think about computers and the Internet, what famous names come to mind?

Tim Berners-Lee

Expansion

Theme The topic for this lesson can be enhanced with the following ideas:

1. An article on the development of the Internet
2. An article on the invention of the printing press
3. Statistics on the numbers of people using the Internet or World Wide Web over time
4. A timeline of communication inventions, including the telephone, telegraph, television, Internet, etc.

Read the following article. Notice that some adjective clauses are separated from the main clause with a comma.

Most people have never heard of Tim Berners-Lee. He is not rich or famous like Bill Gates.

Berners-Lee, who works in a small office at the Massachusetts Institute of Technology, is the creator of the World Wide Web. The creation of the Web is so important that some people compare Berners-Lee to Johann Gutenberg, who invented printing by moveable type in the fifteenth century.

Berners-Lee was born in England in 1955. His parents, who helped design the world's first commercially available computer, gave him a great love of mathematics and learning.

In 1980, Berners-Lee went to work at CERN, a physics laboratory in Geneva, Switzerland, where he had a lot of material to learn quickly. He had a poor memory for facts and wanted to find a way to keep track of things he couldn't remember. He devised a software program that allowed him to create a document that had links to other documents. He continued to develop his idea through the 1980s. He wanted to find a way to connect the knowledge and creativity of people all over the world.

In 1991, his project became known as the World Wide Web. The number of Internet users started to grow quickly. However, Berners-Lee is not completely happy with the way the Web has developed. He thinks it has become a passive tool for so many people, not the tool for creativity that he had imagined.

In 1999, Berners-Lee published a book called *Weaving the Web,* in which he answers questions he is often asked: "What were you thinking when you invented the Web?" "What do you think of it now?" "Where is the Web going to take us in the future?"

Did You Know?

What is the difference between the Web and the Internet? In 1989, Berners-Lee created a system of hyperlinks (words or pictures you can click on to take you to other information), making the 15-year-old Internet easy for everyone to use. This system of hyperlinks is known as the (World Wide) Web.

Adjective Clauses; Descriptive Phrases 251

Reading CD 2, Track 19

1. Have students first read the text silently. Tell them to pay special attention to adjective clauses, and especially to adjective clauses that follow a comma. Then play the audio and have students read along silently.

2. Check students' comprehension. Ask questions such as: *What famous person in history is Berners-Lee compared to and what did he do?* (Johann Gutenberg; he invented printing by moveable type) *What was Berners-Lee trying to find?* (a way to link documents) *How does he feel about the World Wide Web now?* (He is not completely happy about it.)

To save class time, have students do the reading for homework ahead of time.

DID YOU KNOW ?

The Internet developed from an earlier network called ARPAnet, which first went online in 1969.

Reading Variation

To practice listening skills, have students first listen to the audio alone. Ask a few comprehension questions. Repeat the audio if necessary. Then have students open their books and read along as they listen to the audio.

Reading Glossary

commercially available: available to buy
devise: invent; develop
keep track of: remember; keep in mind
poor: bad; not effective
printing: putting words or symbols on paper
weave: combine threads to make cloth

6.10 | Nonessential Adjective Clauses

1. Have students cover the grammar chart. Review the meaning of *essential* (necessary; needed). Write on the board: *Berners-Lee needed a way to keep track of material.* Ask: *Is this sentence a complete idea?* (yes) Then write: *Berners-Lee, who had a poor memory, needed a way to keep track of material.* Say: *The adjective clause is nonessential information; the sentence is complete without it. We use commas to separate it from the rest of the sentence.*

2. Have students uncover and review the example sentences and explanation in the grammar chart. Ask: *Do sentences with nonessential adjective clauses always have two commas?* (no)

3. Ask volunteers to give sentences about their classmates using nonessential adjective clauses (e.g., *Maria, who is from El Salvador, is a teacher's aide.*).

EXERCISE 22

1. Tell students that this exercise is about the development of technology over time. Have students read the direction line. Ask: *Do we add commas in every sentence?* (yes)

2. Model the exercise. Direct students to the example in the book. Ask: *Where do we put the commas?* (before and after the adjective clause) Then do #1 with the class. Point out the picture of the abacus.

3. Have students complete the rest of the exercise individually. Then have them check their answers in pairs. Circulate and observe the pair work. If necessary, check answers as a class.

6.10 | Nonessential Adjective Clauses

Examples	Explanation
Berners-Lee, **who was born in England**, now lives in the U.S.	Some adjective clauses are not essential to the meaning of the sentence. A nonessential adjective clause adds extra information. The sentence is complete without it.
Berners-Lee's parents, **who helped design the first computer**, gave their son a love of learning.	
Berners-Lee went to work at CERN, **which is a physics laboratory in Geneva.**	A nonessential adjective clause is separated by commas from the main part of the sentence.
Berners-Lee was born in 1955, **when personal computers were beyond people's imagination.**	
Pierre Omidyar, **who created eBay,** was born in France.	A nonessential adjective clause begins with *who, whom, which, where, when,* or *whose. That* is not used in a nonessential adjective clause.
Pierre Omidyar, **whose wife is a collector,** got his idea for eBay in 1995.	
Pierre brought in Meg Whitman, **whose knowledge of business helped make eBay the success it is today.**	

EXERCISE 22 Put commas in the following sentences to separate the adjective clause from the main part of the sentence.

EXAMPLE The abacus, which is a wooden rack with beads, was probably the first computer.

1. The abacus, which was created about 2,000 years ago, helped people solve arithmetic problems.

2. The first modern computer, which was called ENIAC, took up a lot of space (1,800 square feet).

3. ENIAC was created in 1942, when the U.S. was involved in World War II.

4. ENIAC, which helped the government store important data, was built at the University of Pennsylvania.

5. Personal computers, which were introduced in the 1970s, are much smaller and faster than previous computers.

6. Bill Gates went to Harvard University, where he developed the programming language BASIC.

252 Lesson 6

Grammar Variation

Have students underline all of the adjective clauses they can find in the reading on page 251 before they look at the grammar chart.

7. Bill Gates dropped out of Harvard to work with Paul Allen, who was his old high school friend.

8. Together Gates and Allen founded Microsoft, which has made both of them very rich.

9. In 1984, Apple produced the first Macintosh computer, which was easier to use than earlier computers.

10. In 1990, Bill Gates introduced Windows, which was Microsoft's version of the popular Macintosh operating system.

11. Berners-Lee, whose name is not widely recognized, made a great contribution to the world.

12. The Internet, which has been around since the 1970s, was not available to most people until the Web was created.

Bill Gates

Expansion

Exercise 22 Have students work in groups. Have groups use the information in Exercise 22, in the reading on page 251, and in other parts of the lesson to make a timeline of the development of technology.

6.11 | Essential vs. Nonessential Adjective Clauses

1. Have students cover the explanations column in grammar chart **6.11.** In pairs, ask students to look at the sentences in the first two rows of the chart, and to decide which row includes nonessential adjective clauses (the first row) and which row includes essential adjective clauses (the second row). Then have students uncover and review the explanations. Have volunteers read each sentence in the first two rows aloud without the adjective clause, as suggested in the chart, as an aide to distinguishing between the two.

2. Have students compare the (a) and (b) sentences in the remaining three rows of the chart on page 254.

6.11 | Essential vs. Nonessential Adjective Clauses[2]

Examples	Explanation
Bill Gates, **who created Microsoft,** never finished college. Berners-Lee, **whose parents helped design the first computer,** loved mathematics. Berners-Lee works at MIT, **where he has a small office.** eBay was in Omidyar's hands until 1998, **when he turned over the operation of the company to Meg Whitman.**	In the examples to the left, the adjective clause is **nonessential** because, without it, we can still identify the noun in the main clause. Try reading the sentences without the adjective clause. The sentences are complete. The adjective clause adds extra information to the sentence. A nonessential adjective clause is set off from the rest of the sentence by commas.
The people **who built the first computers** worked at the engineering department of the University of Pennsylvania. There are many people **whose only online activity is sending and receiving e-mail.**	In the examples to the left, the adjective clause is **essential** because, without it, we can't identify the noun. Try reading the sentences without the adjective clause. If we take it out, the noun isn't properly identified and the idea isn't complete.
Compare: a. The computer, **which was invented in the 1940s,** has become part of our everyday lives. (Nonessential)	Example (a) refers to the whole class of computers as an invention.
b. The computer **(that, which) I bought two years ago** is slow compared to today's computers. (Essential)	Example (b) refers to only one computer, which is identified by the adjective clause.
Compare: a. A person who invents something is very creative and intelligent. (Essential)	In sentence (a), the adjective clause is essential in order to explain which person is creative and intelligent.
b. Berners-Lee, who invented the Web, is not rich. (Nonessential)	In sentence (b), the adjective clause is nonessential because it provides extra information. Berners-Lee is unique and does not need to be identified. The adjective clause is nonessential.
Compare: a. The computer **(which or that)** she just bought has a big memory. (Essential)	In an essential adjective clause (a), the relative pronouns *which* or *that* can be used or omitted.
b. Microsoft, **which** Bill Gates helped create, is a billion-dollar company. (Nonessential)	In a nonessential adjective clause (b), only the relative pronoun *which* can be used. It cannot be omitted.

[2] Nonessential adjective clauses are often called nonrestrictive adjective clauses.

254 Lesson 6

Grammar Variation

Model a short sentence of your own; write it on the board. Then have students write short sentences about themselves (e.g., *My family gets together at holidays. Our apartment is not big enough.*). Then add a nonessential clause (e.g., *My family, which is quite large, gets together at holidays. Our apartment, which costs $950 a month, is not big enough.*). Encourage students to add clauses that add to the description of the subject.

- Can I put the adjective clause in parentheses?
  Bill Gates **(who created Microsoft)** never finished college.
- Can I write the adjective clause as a separate sentence?
  Bill Gates created Microsoft. **He never finished college.**
- If the adjective clause is deleted, does the sentence still make sense?
  Bill Gates never finished college.
- Is the noun a unique person or place?
  Berners-Lee, who works at MIT, invented the Web.
- If the noun is plural, am I including all members of a group (all my cousins, all my friends, all Americans, all computers)?
  My friends, who are wonderful people, always help me. (All of my friends are wonderful people.)

Compare:

I send e-mail to my friends **who have home computers and Internet service.**
(Not all of my friends have home computers and Internet service.)

EXERCISE 23 Decide which of the following sentences contains a nonessential adjective clause. Put commas in those sentences. If the sentence doesn't need commas, write *NC.*

EXAMPLES   People who send e-mail often use abbreviations.   *NC*

My father, who sent me an e-mail yesterday, is sick.

1. Kids who spend a lot of time on the computer don't get much exercise.   *NC*

2. My grammar teacher, who has been teaching here for 20 years, knows a lot about computers.

3. Viruses, which can be sent in attachments, can destroy your hard drive.

4. People who get spam every day can get very annoyed.   *NC*

5. My best friend, who gets at least 30 pieces of spam a day, wrote a letter to his senator to complain.

6. Berners-Lee, whose parents were very educated, loves learning new things.

7. Marc Andreesseon created Netscape, which is a popular Web browser.

8. Berners-Lee worked in Switzerland, where the CERN physics laboratory is located.

9. The Instant Message, which was a creation of America Online, is available to many e-mail users.

Adjective Clauses; Descriptive Phrases   255

6.11 Essential vs. Nonessential Adjective Clauses (*cont.*)

3. Draw students' attention to the Language Note. Point out the use of commas with subjects that are unique, e.g., *My mother* (I have only one mother); *Our city* (We have only one city); *Bill Gates.*

EXERCISE 23

1. Tell students that this exercise is about essential and nonessential adjective clauses. Have students read the direction line. Ask: *When do we write NC?* (when no commas are necessary)

2. Model the exercise. Direct students to the examples in the book. Then complete #1 with the class.

3. Have students complete the rest of the exercise individually. Then have them check their answers in pairs and as a class.

Expansion

Exercise 23 Have students work in pairs to decide which items in Exercise 23 require commas because a noun is a unique person or place.

1. Tell students that this exercise is about some of the people they have been reading about in this lesson. Have students read the direction line.
2. Direct students to the example in the book. Then complete #1 with the class.
3. Have students complete the exercise individually, and then compare their answers in pairs. Check answers as a class.
4. Assess students' performance. If necessary, review grammar chart **6.11** on pages 254 and 255.

🕐 To save class time, have students do half of the exercise in class and complete the other half for homework. Or assign the entire exercise for homework.

10. Did you like the story that we read about Berners-Lee? *NC*

11. The computer you bought three years ago doesn't have enough memory. *NC*

12. The computer, which is one of the most important inventions of the twentieth century, has changed the way people process information.

13. Bill Gates, who created Microsoft with his friend, became a billionaire.

14. My best friend, whose name is on my buddy list, contacts me every day through an instant message.

EXERCISE 24 Combine the two sentences into one. The sentence in parentheses ( ) is not essential to the main idea of the sentence. It is extra information.

EXAMPLE eBay is now a large corporation. (It was started in Pierre Omidyar's house.)

eBay, which was started in Pierre Omidyar's house, is now a large corporation.

1. Marc Andreessen was only 24 when he became rich. (He founded Netscape.)

Marc Andreessen, who founded Netscape, was only 24 when he became rich.

2. The World Wide Web is used by millions of people around the world. (It was created by Tim Berners-Lee.)

The World Wide Web, which was created by Tim Berners-Lee, is used by millions of people around the world.

3. Tim Berners-Lee was born in England. (We saw his picture on page 250 and 251.)

Tim Berners-Lee, whose picture we saw on page 250 and 251, was born in England.

4. The book *Weaving the Web* answers a lot of questions about the creation of the Web. (It was written by Berners-Lee in 1999.)

The book Weaving the Web, which was written by Berners-Lee, in 1999, answers a lot of questions about the creation of the Web.

5. Berners-Lee knew about computers from an early age. (His parents helped design one of the first computers.)

Berners-Lee, whose parents helped design one of the first computers, knew about computers from an early age.

6. Tim Berners-Lee works at MIT. (He has a small office there.)

Tim Berners-Lee works at MIT, where he has a small office.

7. Pierre Omidyar got his idea for eBay in 1995. (His wife couldn't find one of her favorite collectibles at that time.)

Pierre Omidyar got his idea for eBay in 1995, when his wife couldn't find one of her favorite collectibles.

8. eBay hired Meg Whitman in 1998. (More expert business knowledge was needed at that time to run the company.)

eBay hired Meg Whitman in 1998, when more expert business knowledge was needed to run the company.

9. E-mail did not become popular until the 1990s. (It was first created in 1972.)

E-mail, which was first created in 1972, did not become popular until the 1990s.

10. Bill Gates often gets spam asking him if he wants to become rich. (He's the richest man in the U.S.)

Bill Gates, who is the richest man in the U.S., often gets spam asking him if he wants to become rich.

11. Pierre Omidyar came to the U.S. when he was a child. (His father was a professor of medicine.)

Pierre Omidyar, whose father was a professor of medicine, came to the U.S. when he was a child.

Expansion

Exercise 24 Have students write simple sentences about their schools, classes, teachers, or classmates without adjective clauses. Collect the sentences. Read the sentences aloud; ask students to add a nonessential adjective clause to each sentence.

6.12 | Descriptive Phrases

1. Have students cover the grammar chart. Write an example of a sentence that can be shortened on the board, such as *My Uncle George, who is my mother's brother, lives in Cleveland.* Then cross out *who is* to get: *My Uncle George, my mother's brother, lives in Cleveland.* Say: *In some sentences, we can shorten the adjective clauses to get a descriptive phrase.*

2. Have students uncover and review the example sentences and explanations in the grammar chart. In each pair of sentences, have students say what words have been removed.

3. Point out to students that not all adjective clauses can be shortened. *Shoppers who use eBay can locate hard-to-find items,* for example, cannot be shortened to *Shoppers use eBay can . . . .*

6.12 | Descriptive Phrases

Some adjective clauses can be shortened to descriptive phrases. We can shorten an adjective clause in which the relative pronoun is followed by the verb *be*.

Examples	Explanation
Compare:	
a. People **who are unhappy with the amount of spam they receive** should write to their lawmakers.	Sentences (a) have an adjective clause.
b. People **unhappy with the amount of spam they receive** should write to their lawmakers.	Sentences (b) have a descriptive phrase.
a. Pierre Omidyar, **who is the founder of eBay,** is one of the richest men in the world.	
b. Pierre Omidyar, **the founder of eBay,** is one of the richest men in the world.	
a. One-half of all of the e-mail **that is sent today** is spam.	A descriptive phrase can begin with a **past participle.**
b. One-half of all the e-mail *sent* today is spam.	Compare sentences (a) with an adjective clause to sentences (b) with a descriptive phrase.
a. There are about 11 million items **that are listed on eBay.**	
b. There are about 11 million items *listed* on eBay.	
a. A man **who is living in Florida** retired at the age of 37 after making millions in the spam business.	A descriptive phrase can begin with a **present participle** (verb *-ing*).
b. A man *living* in Florida retired at the age of 37 after making millions in the spam business.	Compare sentences (a) with an adjective clause to sentences (b) with a descriptive phrase.
a. Shoppers **who are using eBay** can locate a hard-to-find item.	
b. Shoppers *using* eBay can locate a hard-to-find item.	
a. Spam, **which is unwanted commercial e-mail,** is an annoying problem.	A descriptive phrase can give a definition or more information about the noun it follows. This kind of descriptive phrase is called an **appositive.**
b. Spam, **unwanted commercial e-mail,** is an annoying problem.	
a. eBay, **which is an auction Web site,** is very popular.	Compare sentences (a) with an adjective clause to sentences (b) with an appositive.
b. eBay, **an auction Web site,** is very popular.	
a. A man **who is in Florida** retired at the age of 37.	A descriptive phrase can begin with a preposition (*with, in, from, of,* etc.)
b. A man *in* Florida retired at the age of 37.	
a. Pierre, **who is from France,** created eBay.	Compare sentences (a) with an adjective clause to sentences (b) with a prepositional phrase.
b. Pierre, *from France,* created eBay.	

Grammar Variation

Have students cover the explanation column in the grammar chart. Have them compare the (a) and (b) sentences in the examples. Ask students what they can figure out about descriptive phrases from the examples. Then review the explanations in the chart.

Language Notes:
1. A descriptive phrase can be essential or nonessential. A nonessential phrase is set off by commas.

People **unhappy** with the amount of spam they receive should write to their lawmakers. (*Essential*)

Pierre Omidyar, **the founder of eBay,** is one of the richest men in the world. (*Nonessential*)

2. An appositive is always nonessential.

Amazon.com, **an online store,** is a very popular Web site.

EXERCISE Shorten the adjective clauses by crossing out the unnecessary words.

EXAMPLE On eBay, people who are living in California can sell to people who are living in New York.

1. Netscape is a popular Web browser which is used by millions.

2. Bill Gates, who is one of the richest people in the world, gets spam asking him if he wants to become rich.

3. There are a lot of dishonest companies which are trying to take your money.

4. eBay takes a percentage of each sale that is made on its Web site.

5. A virus is a harmful program which is passed from computer to computer.

6. Tim Berners-Lee, who was born in England, now works at M.I.T.

7. M.I.T., which is located in Cambridge, Massachusetts, is an excellent university.

8. Berners-Lee developed the idea for the Web when he was working at CERN, which is a physics lab in Switzerland.

9. Berners-Lee's parents worked on the first computer that was sold commercially.

10. People who are using the Web can shop from their homes.

11. People who are interested in reading newspapers from other cities can find them on the Web.

12. The World Wide Web, which is abbreviated WWW, was first introduced on the Internet in 1991.

13. Computers which are sold today have much more memory and speed than computers which were sold 10 years ago.

14. Marc Andreessen, who was the creator of Netscape, quickly became a billionaire.

15. You can download Netscape, which is a popular Internet browser.

Adjective Clauses; Descriptive Phrases   259

6.12 | Descriptive Phrases (*cont.*)

4. Draw students' attention to the Language Notes. Point out that shortening the adjective clause has no effect on the need for commas.

EXERCISE   25

1. Tell students that this exercise is about identifying words we don't need in sentences. Have students read the direction line.
2. Direct students to the example in the book; then complete items 1 and 2 with the class.
3. Have students complete the rest of Exercise 25 individually. Then have them check their answers in pairs. Circulate and observe the pair work. If necessary, check the answers as a class.

Culture Note

A millionaire is a person who has more than a million (1,000,000) dollars. Sometimes very rich people are referred to as multimillionaires. A billionaire is a person who has more than a billion (1,000,000,000) dollars.

EXERCISE 26 Combine the two sentences. Use a phrase for the sentence in parentheses ( ).

EXAMPLE Microsoft Windows made personal computers easy to use. (Windows was created by Bill Gates.)

Microsoft Windows, created by Bill Gates, made personal computers easy to use.

1. Google is very easy to use. (It is a popular search engine.)
   Google, a popular search engine, is very easy to use.

2. Have you ever used Mapquest? (It is a Web site that gives maps and driving directions.)
   Have you ever used Mapquest, a Web site that gives maps and driving directions?

3. "Melissa" infected a lot of computers in 1999. (It is a virus.)
   "Melissa," a virus, infected a lot of computers in 1999.

4. Tim Berners-Lee was born in 1955. (This is the same year Bill Gates was born.)
   Tim Berners-Lee was born in 1955, the same year Bill Gates was born.

5. Marc Andreessen quickly became a billionaire. (He is the creator of Netscape.)
   Marc Andreessen, the creator of Netscape, quickly became a billionaire.

Marc Andreessen

260   Lesson 6

Expansion

Exercise 26 Have students use information about famous people they know to make sentences similar to those in Exercise 26, using descriptive phrases. Have students share their examples with the class.

EXERCISE **27** *Combination Exercise.* Combine these short sentences into longer sentences using adjective clauses or descriptive phrases.

EXAMPLE Pierre Omidyar came to the U.S. when he was a child. His father was a professor of medicine.

Pierre Omidyar, whose father was a professor of medicine, came to

the U.S. when he was a child.

1. Pierre Omidyar was born in France. He wrote his first computer program at age 14.

   Pierre Omidyar, who wrote his first computer program at age 14, was born in

   France.

2. *Business Week* named Meg Whitman among the 25 most powerful business managers. *Business Week* is a popular business magazine.

   Business Week, a popular business magazine, named Meg Whitman among

   the 25 most powerful business managers.

3. Bill Gates was born in 1955. His father was a lawyer.

   Bill Gates, whose father was a lawyer, was born in 1955.

4. Bill Gates wrote his first computer program in 1967. He was only 12 years old at that time.

   Bill Gates, wrote his first computer program in 1967, when he was only

   12 years old.

5. Bill Gates has three children. His wife was a marketing executive at Microsoft.

   Bill Gates, whose wife was a marketing executive at Microsoft, has three

   children.

6. Marc Andreessen is the co-founder of Netscape. He taught himself BASIC programming at the age of nine.

   Marc Andreessen, the co-founder of Netscape, taught himself BASIC

   programming at the age of nine.

1. Tell students that this exercise is about people who have been important in the development of technology. Have students read the direction line. Ask: *What do we write?* (longer sentences with adjective clauses or descriptive phrases)
2. Direct students to the example in the book. Complete items 1 and 2 with the class.
3. Have students complete the exercise individually. Have them compare their answers in pairs. If necessary, check answers as a class.
4. Assess students' performance. If necessary, review grammar chart **6.12**.

To save class time, have students do half of the exercise in class and complete the other half for homework. Or assign the entire exercise for homework.

7. Andreessen and James Clark created Netscape. It was originally called "Mosaic."

Andreessen and James Clark created Netscape, which was originally called "Mosaic."

8. Netscape went public in 1995. Andreessen was only 24 years old.

Netscape went public in 1995, when Andreessen was only 24 years old.

9. Michael Dell created Dell computers. He dropped out of college after his first year.

Michael Dill, who created Dell computers, dropped out of college after his first year.

10. Dell's parents were worried about Michael. His grades were dropping.

Dell's parents were worried about Michael, whose grades were dropping.

11. Dell's business started to perform well at the end of his first year of college. At that time, his business was making over $50,000 a month.

Dell's business started to perform well at the end of his first year of college, when his business was making over $50,000 a month.

12. Dell Computers was one of the first companies to sell computers online. It was selling about $18 million of computers a day by the late 1990s.

Dell Computers, which was one of the first companies to sell computers online, was selling about $18 million of computers a day by the late1990s.

13. In 2000, *Forbes* named Dell Computers the third most admired company in the U.S. *Forbes* is a business magazine.

In 2000, Forbes, a business magazine, named Dell Computers the third most admired company in the U.S.

Expansion

Exercise 27 After students complete the exercise, have them write sentences about people or institutions they admire. Ask them to combine facts and opinions in their statements, such as: *I admire Tim Berners-Lee, who invented the World Wide Web.* Or *I admire the Red Cross, which helps people after disasters.*

SUMMARY OF LESSON 6

	Essential	Nonessential
Pronoun as subject	People (**who** or **that**) **write e-mail** aren't careful about spelling. I just bought a computer **that** (or **which**) **has a very big memory.**	Bill Gates, **who created Microsoft,** is one of the richest people in the world. eBay was created in San Jose, **which is a city near San Francisco.**
Pronoun as object	The first computer (**that** or **which**) **I bought** didn't have a mouse. The people (**who, whom, that**) **you meet in chat rooms** are sometimes very silly.	My first computer, **which I bought in 1996,** is much slower than my new computer. My father, **whom you met at the party,** is a programmer.
Pronoun as object of preposition	The person **to whom I sent an e-mail** never answered me. (Formal) The person (**whom, who, that**) **I sent an e-mail to** didn't answer me. (Informal)	Berners-Lee, **about whom we read,** is an interesting person. (Formal) Berners-Lee, **whom we read about,** is an interesting person. (Informal)
Where	The store **where I bought my computer** has good prices.	Berners-Lee works at the Massachusetts Institute of Technology, **where he has a small office.**
When	I'll never forget the day (**when**) **I saw a personal computer for the first time.**	The Web was created in 1991, **when most people did not have home computers.**
Whose + noun as subject	Children **whose parents are poor** often don't have a home computer.	Berners-Lee, **whose parents worked on computers,** learned a lot in his home.
Whose + noun as object	There are friends **whose letters I've saved for years.**	My mother, **whose letters I've saved,** died two years ago.
Adjective clause after indefinite compound	I don't know anyone **who has a Macintosh computer.** Everything **I learned about computers** is useful.	_____
Descriptive phrase	Home computers **made 20 years ago** didn't have a big memory.	Bill Gates, **the founder of Microsoft,** became a billionaire.

Adjective Clauses and Descriptive Phrases Have students use the first few words of the sentences in the chart to make new statements about themselves (e.g., *People who write e-mail save a lot of time. Bill Gates, who is very rich, gives a lot of money away.*).

If necessary, have students review: **Lesson 6.**

Summary Variation

Write cues with partial adjective clauses or descriptive phrases on the board (e.g., *The first computer I had . . .* , *The people I know . . .* , *My brother, who . . .* , etc.). In pairs, have students talk about themselves using the phrases in statements.

Editing Advice

For each item, have students provide the grammar rule behind the Editing Advice. This can be done as an individual, a pair, a group, or a class activity.

1. Relative pronouns *who*, *that*, and *which* can be the subject of an adjective clause; *who(m)*, *that*, and *which* can be the object of an adjective clause.
2. When a relative pronoun is the subject of an adjective clause, it can't be omitted.
3. In an adjective clause, omit the object pronoun.
4. A verb in an adjective clause must agree in number with its subject.
5. An adjective clause must be preceded by a noun or a pronoun. The adjective clause describes or identifies the noun or pronoun before it.
6. An adjective clause should not be separated from the noun it describes.
7. *Whose* means *belonging to whom*; *who's* means *who is*.
8. The subject goes before the verb in an adjective clause.
9. *Whose* is the possessive form of *who*. It stands for *his*, *her*, *its*, *their*, or the possessive form of the noun.

EDITING ADVICE

1. Never use *what* as a relative pronoun.
   She married a man ~~what~~ *who* has a lot of money.
   Everything ~~what~~ *that* you did was unnecessary.

2. You can't omit a relative pronoun that is the subject of the adjective clause.
   I know a man *who* speaks five languages.

3. If the relative pronoun is the object of the adjective clause, don't put an object after the verb.

   The car that I bought ~~it~~ has a stick shift.

4. Make sure you use subject-verb agreement.

   I know several English teachers who speaks Spanish.
   A car that ~~have~~ *has* a big engine is not economical.

5. Put a noun before an adjective clause.
   The student w
   ~~Who~~ wants to leave early should sit in the back.

6. Put the adjective clause near the noun it describes.

   The teacher speaks Spanish (whose class I am taking).

7. Don't confuse *whose* with *who's*.
   whose
   A student ~~who's~~ grades are good may get a scholarship.

8. Put the subject before the verb in an adjective clause.
   my cousin bought
   The house that ~~bought my cousin~~ is very beautiful.

9. Use *whose*, not *his*, *her*, or *their*, to show possession in an adjective clause.
   whose
   I have a friend ~~who his~~ knowledge of computers is very great.

264 Lesson 6

PART 1 Find the mistakes with the underlined words, and correct them. Not every sentence has a mistake. If the sentence is correct, write C.

EXAMPLES The students should correct the mistakes <u>that they make them</u>.

The students <u>about whom we were speaking</u> entered the room. C

1. The teacher <u>what we have</u> is from Canada.

2. Five students were absent on the day when <u>was given</u> the final test.

3. The room <u>where we took the test</u> was not air-conditioned. C

    Students who
4. <u>Who</u> missed the test can take it next Friday.

5. Students <u>who knows</u> a lot of English grammar can take a composition course.

6. The teacher <u>whose class I'm taking</u> speaks English clearly. C

7. A tutor is a person <u>whom helps students</u> individually.

8. Everyone wants to have a teacher <u>whose pronunciation is clear</u>. C

9. The student <u>whose sitting</u> next to me is trying to copy my answers.

10. A teacher <u>helped me at registration</u> who speaks my native language.

    that
11. The teacher gave a test <u>had 25 questions</u>.

    who
12. The student <u>which sits</u> near the door always leaves early.

    whose
13. I have a neighbor <u>who his son</u> plays with my son.

14. Do you know <u>anyone who has</u> a German car? C

15. The textbook <u>we are using</u> has a lot of exercises. C

16. The people <u>who lives</u> upstairs make a lot of noise in the morning.

PART 2 Fill in the blanks to complete the adjective clause. Answers may vary.

EXAMPLES A: Do you like your new roommate?

B: Not really. The roommate _I had last year_ was much nicer.

A: Are there any teachers at this school _who speak Spanish_?

B: Yes. Ms. Lopez speaks Spanish.

Adjective Clauses; Descriptive Phrases   **265**

Lesson 6 Test/Review

For additional practice, review, and assessment materials, see Assessment CD-ROM with *ExamView Pro, More Grammar Practice* Workbook 3, Interactive CD-ROM, and Web site http://elt.thomson.com/gic

PART 1

1. Part 1 may be used as an in-class test to assess student performance, in addition to the Assessment CD-ROM with *ExamView Pro*. Have students read the direction line. Ask: *Does every sentence have a mistake?* (no) Then have students complete the test.

2. Collect for assessment.

3. If necessary, have students review: **Lesson 6.**

PART 2

1. Part 2 may also be used as an in-class test to assess student performance, in addition to the Assessment CD-ROM with *ExamView Pro*. Tell students that this is a series of conversations. Phrases are missing. Review the examples. Then have students complete the test.

2. Collect for assessment.

3. If necessary, have students review: **Lesson 6.**

Lesson Review

To use Parts 1 and 2 as a review, assign them as homework or use them as in-class activities to be completed individually or in pairs. Check answers and review errors as a class. Reteach grammar points that students haven't mastered. Then student learning may be assessed using a test generated from the Assessment CD-ROM with *ExamView Pro*.

1. Part 3 may also be used as an in-class test to assess student performance, in addition to the Assessment CD-ROM with *ExamView Pro*. Review the example. Complete #1 as a class. Then have students complete the test.
2. Collect for assessment.
3. If necessary, have students review: **Lesson 6.**

1. **A:** I heard you had a car accident. You hit another car.
   B: Yes. The woman whose _____ *car I hit* _____ wants me to pay her $700.

2. **A:** I bought a laptop for $1,500.
   B: That's a lot of money. The laptop _____ *I bought* _____ only cost $1,000.

3. **A:** Did you buy your textbooks at Berk's Bookstore?
   B: No. The store _____ *where I bought my books* _____ is about ten blocks from school. Books are cheaper there.

4. **A:** My husband's mother always interferes in our married life.
   B: That's terrible. I wouldn't want to be married to a man whose _____ *mother interferes* _____.

5. **A:** What did the teacher say about registration?
   B: I don't know. She spoke very fast. I didn't understand everything _____ *she said* _____.

6. **A:** Do you remember your first day in the U.S.?
   B: Of course. I'll always remember the day _____ *I arrived* _____ in my new country.

7. **A:** The teacher is talking about a very famous American, but I didn't hear his name.
   B: The man _____ *she / he is talking about* _____ is John Kennedy.

8. **A:** Did you buy the dictionary I recommended to you?
   B: No. The dictionary _____ *I bought* _____ is just as good as the one you recommended.

9. **A:** Do you remember the names of all the students?
   B: No. There are some students _____ *whose names I don' t remember* _____.

PART 3 Complete each statement. Every sentence should have an adjective clause.

EXAMPLE   The library is a place _____ *where you can read* _____.

1. The teacher _____ *Answers will vary.* _____ doesn't teach here anymore.

2. Everything _____ is important to me.

3. Teachers _____ aren't good for foreign students.

4. The teacher will not pass a student whose _____.

Lesson Review

To use Part 3 as a review, assign it as homework or use it as an in-class activity to be completed individually or in pairs. Check answers and review errors as a class. Reteach grammar points that students haven't mastered. Then student learning may be assessed using a test generated from the Assessment CD-ROM with *ExamView Pro*.

5. I would like to live in a house _____.

6. The classroom _____ is clean and pleasant.

7. I will never forget the day _____.

8. I never got an answer to the question _____ about the test.

9. Everyone _____ had a great time.

10. I don't like the dictionary _____, so I'm going to buy a better one.

11. Computers _____ ten years ago are slow compared to today's computers.

12. A laboratory is a place where _____.

13. There's so much noise in my house. I need to find a place

_____.

14. Small children whose _____ learn to read faster than children who sit in front of the TV all day.

PART 4 Combine each pair of sentences into one sentence. Use the words in parentheses ( ) to add a nonessential adjective clause to the first sentence.

EXAMPLE Pierre Omidyar got the idea for eBay in 1995. (His wife is a collector.)

Pierre Omidyar, whose wife is a collector, got the idea

for eBay in 1995.

1. Berners-Lee was born in 1955. (Most people knew nothing about computers in 1955.)

Berners-Lee was born in 1955, when most people knew nothing about computers.

2. The Internet changed the way people get their information. (It became popular in the 1990s.)

The Internet, which became popular in the 1990s, changed the way people get their information.

3. Berners-Lee studied physics in college. (His parents were programmers.)

Berners-Lee, whose parents were programmers, studied physics in college.

4. Berners-Lee is not a well-known person. (We read about him in this lesson.)

Berners-Lee, whom we read about in this lesson, is not a well-known person.

5. Berners-Lee works at MIT. (He has a small office there.)

Berners-Lee, works at MIT, where he has a small office.

Adjective Clauses; Descriptive Phrases 267

PART 4

1. Part 4 may also be used as an in-class test to assess student performance, in addition to the Assessment CD-ROM with *ExamView Pro*. Review the example. Then complete #1 as a class. Have students complete the test individually.

2. Collect for assessment.

3. If necessary, have students review:

6.11 Essential vs. Nonessential Adjective Clauses (pp. 254–255).

Lesson Review

To use Part 4 as a review, assign it as homework or use it as an in-class activity to be completed individually or in pairs. Check answers and review errors as a class. Reteach grammar points that students haven't mastered. Then student learning may be assessed using a test generated from the Assessment CD-ROM with *ExamView Pro*.

1. Part 5 may also be used as an in-class test to assess student performance, in addition to the Assessment CD-ROM with *ExamView Pro.* Ask: *Can every sentence be changed?* (no) Review the examples. Then complete #1 as a class. Have students complete the test individually.
2. Collect for assessment.
3. If necessary, have students review:
   6.12 Descriptive Phrases (pp. 258–259).

PART 6

1. Part 6 may also be used as an in-class test to assess student performance, in addition to the Assessment CD-ROM with *ExamView Pro.* Ask: *Does every sentence need commas?* (no) Review the examples. Then complete #1 as a class. Have students complete the test individually.
2. Collect for assessment.
3. If necessary, have students review:
   6.11 Essential vs. Nonessential Adjective Clauses (pp. 254–255).

PART 5 Some of these adjective clauses can be shortened. Shorten them by crossing out unnecessary words. Some of the adjective clauses cannot be shortened. Do not change them. Write "no change" *(NC)*.

EXAMPLES Thanksgiving, ~~which is~~ an American holiday, is in November.

Everyone who came to dinner enjoyed the food. *NC*

1. The English ~~that is~~ spoken in the U.S. is different from British English.
2. A lot of people like to shop on eBay, ~~which is~~ an auction Web site.
3. Do not disturb the students ~~who are~~ studying in the library.
4. In the U.S. there are many immigrants ~~who are~~ from Mexico.
5. The computer ~~that~~ you bought has a very big memory.
6. She doesn't like the music ~~that~~ her daughter listens to.
7. Everyone who saw the movie liked it a lot. *NC*
8. Everyone whom I met at the party was very interesting.
9. Children who watch TV all day don't get enough exercise. *NC*
10. Parents whose children are small should control the TV programs that their kids watch. *NC*
11. The teacher with whom I studied beginning grammar comes from Canada. *NC*
12. The Web, ~~which was~~ introduced in 1991, has changed the way many companies do business.

PART 6 Some of the following sentences need commas. Put them in. If the sentence doesn't need commas, write "no commas."

EXAMPLES The last article we read was about the Internet.

no commas

Alaska, which is the largest state, has a very small population.

1. Ms. Thomson, who was my English teacher last semester, will retire next year.
2. I don't like teachers who give a lot of homework. *no commas*
3. I studied engineering at the University of Michigan, which is located in Ann Arbor, Michigan.
4. The computer I bought last month has a very big memory. *no commas*
5. The computer, which is one of the most important inventions of the twentieth century, can be found in many American homes.

Lesson Review

To use Parts 5 and 6 as a review, assign them as homework or use them as in-class activities to be completed individually or in pairs. Check answers and review errors as a class. Reteach grammar points that students haven't mastered. Then student learning may be assessed using a test generated from the Assessment CD-ROM with *ExamView Pro.*

6. eBay is a Web site where people can buy and sell items. *on commas*

7. My mother, who lives in Miami, has a degree in engineering.

8. I have two sisters. My sister who lives in New Jersey has three children. *on commas*

9. Our parents, who live with us now, are beginning to study English.

10. The American flag, which has 13 stripes and 50 stars, is red, white, and blue.

11. The city where I was born has beautiful museums. *on commas*

12. St. Petersburg, where I was born, has beautiful museums.

EXPANSION ACTIVITIES

Classroom Activities

1. **Game. Yes, but . . .** Work with a partner. One person will finish the sentence giving a point of view. The other person will contradict the first person by saying, "Yes, but . . ." and giving a different point of view.

   EXAMPLE   People who get married when they are young . . .
   A: People who get married when they are young have a lot of energy to raise their children.
   B: Yes, but people who get married when they are young are not very responsible.

   a. Couples who have a lot of children . . .

   b. People who immigrate to the U.S. . . .

   c. English books that have the answers in the back . . .

   d. People who have a lot of money . . .

   e. People who have a car . . .

   f. People who live in the same place all their lives . . .

   g. Teachers who speak fast . . .

   h. People who use credit cards . . .

   i. Cities that have a lot of factories . . .

   j. Movies that have a lot of violence . . .

   k. Parents who do everything for their children . . .

   l. Couples who have children when they're in their 40s . . .

   m. People who use the Internet a lot . . .

Expansion Activities

These expansion activities provide opportunities for students to interact with one another and further develop their speaking and writing skills. Encourage students to use grammar from this lesson whenever possible.

🕐 To save class time, assign parts of the activities as homework. Then use class time for interaction and communication. If students do not need additional speaking practice, some of the activities may be assigned as writing activities for homework or skipped altogether.

CLASSROOM ACTIVITIES

1. Tell students that this activity is about their opinions. Ask: *When do we say* Yes, but . . . *?* (when we want to disagree politely) Have students complete the activity in pairs. When students have finished, have volunteers present their sentences to the class.

Classroom Activities Variation

Activity 1 Have students make notes about their ideas before they begin the conversations. Have students listen as their partners present the first sentence. If they do not disagree, have students begin the second sentence with *Yes, and . . .* rather than *Yes, but . . . .*

2. Have students complete the sentences individually, in class, or as homework. Have students discuss their opinions in groups.
3. Ask: *Have you every played the Dictionary Game?* Have students read the directions in the book. Encourage students to choose interesting-sounding words that they are sure their teammates will not know. Tell students to be creative in writing their "false" definitions.

TALK ABOUT IT

Have students work in groups. Either assign or have each group choose one or both of the topics to discuss. Review with students language for agreeing, checking for agreement, and disagreeing (e.g., *I think so too. Are you sure that's right? I'm not sure I agree.*). Set a time limit for discussion. Then have groups talk about their topics. If appropriate, have groups report back to the class; have each group appoint a spokesperson.

WRITE ABOUT IT

1. Before students begin, have them think of three ways they use computers and write a sentence or two about each one. Then have students write an introductory and a concluding sentence for their paragraphs. Then have them combine the sentences into a paragraph. Collect for assessment and/or have students review each other's work.
2. Have students brainstorm people they might like to write about. Ask them why they think the person they chose didn't receive much attention or money. Then have them write one or two paragraphs. Collect for assessment and/or have students present their writing to a group.
3. Have students work independently to write about an invention. Encourage them to make notes before they begin to write. Have students write a paragraph about the invention they chose. Collect for assessment and/or have students review each other's work.

---

2. Fill in the blanks and discuss your answers in a small group.

a. People _____ have an easy life.

b. No one likes or respects people _____

c. People who _____ want to come to the U.S.

d. There are a lot of people who _____

3. **Dictionary Game.** Form a small group. One student in the group will look for a hard word in the dictionary. (Choose a noun. Find a word that you think no one will know.) Other students will write definitions of the word. Students can think of funny definitions or serious ones. The student with the dictionary will write the real definition. Students put all the definitions in a box. The student with the dictionary will read the definitions. The others have to guess which is the real definition.

EXAMPLE   nonagenarian
Sample definition: A nonagenarian is a person who has none of the characteristics of his generation.
Real definition: A nonagenarian is a person who is between 90 and 99 years old.

(**Alternate:** The teacher can provide a list of words and definitions beforehand, writing them on small pieces of paper. A student can choose one of the papers that the teacher has prepared.)

Talk About it
1. In what ways does the computer make life better? In what ways does it make life worse?
2. Discuss the differences between using e-mail and postal mail. In what cases is it better to use e-mail? In what cases is it better to write a letter, put it in an envelope, and mail it?

Write About it
1. Write a paragraph telling the different ways you use your computer (or the computers at this school).
2. Write about an important person you know about who didn't receive much attention or money for his or her work.
3. Write about an important invention. How did this invention change society?

Classroom Activities Variation

Activity 3 Prepare lists of nouns that students probably do not know and their definitions. Write one word and its definition on an index card or piece of paper. Have students take turns choosing a card and asking his or her teammates to write definitions of the word. Then play the game as in #3 above.

Talk About it Variation

Have students work in pairs. Have members of the pairs interview each other using the questions in the activity, alternating interviewers. Have the interviewers take notes on their partners' responses.

Item 1 Have students debate item 1. Divide the class into two teams. Each team should represent one point of view. Tell each team to list five reasons supporting its view. Have each team present its arguments. Then give each team an opportunity to respond to the other team's arguments. After the debate, survey the class—which opinion is more popular?

Write About it Variation

Have students exchange first drafts with a partner. Ask students to help their partners edit their drafts. Refer students to the Editing Advice on page 264.

Internet Activities

1. Find Tim Berners-Lee's Web site. What kind of information can you get from his Web site?

2. Go to a Web site that sells books. Find Berners-Lee's book, *Weaving the Web*. How much is it? Find a review of his book and print it out.

3. If you don't use AOL, type in *AOL Instant Messenger* at a search engine. Find out how to use this service.

4. Bring in a copy of a spam e-mail you received. Talk about the offers. Are they believable?

5. Go to eBay and find an item you might be interested in buying. Find the starting price.

6. At a search engine, type in *How Stuff Works*. Look up an article about spam. Circle all the adjective clauses in the article.

 Additional Activities at http://elt.thomson.com/gic

INTERNET ACTIVITIES

1. Before students begin the activity, brainstorm search terms students might use to find the Web site.

2. Ask students to name Web sites that sell books. Make a class list of sites and Web addresses. Have students compare the prices they find. Review the difference between new and used books.

3. Have students report back to the class on information they find.

4. Before students begin, review the types of spam e-mail that are appropriate to bring into class. If appropriate, review the types of e-mails students should not bring to class. Review methods e-mail service providers have for reporting or blocking spam e-mail.

5. Have students tell the class why they chose the items they did and whether there were a lot of choices for their items.

6. Have students bring in their articles. Discuss the information in the articles.

Internet Activities Variation

Activity 2 Divide the class in half. Have one half locate a new copy of the book and the other half locate a used copy. Compare prices.

Activity 4 If students don't have access to the Internet, they may bring in junk mail as an alternative.

7

GRAMMAR
Infinitives
Gerunds

CONTEXT : Helping Others
Andrew Carnegie, Philanthropist
Charity and Volunteering
Bicycling to Raise Money for AIDS
Helping Others Get an Education
Mimi's Bike Ride
Global Volunteers

273

Lesson 7

Lesson Overview

GRAMMAR

1. Activate students' prior knowledge. Write *infinitive* and *gerund* on the board. Ask students what they know about each one.
2. Give several examples of sentences using infinitives and gerunds: *I want to learn Spanish. I learn best by trying. Practicing is the best way to learn.* Have volunteers give examples. Write one or two examples of each on the board.

CONTEXT

1. Ask: *What will we learn about in this lesson?* (helping others; volunteering) Elicit students' prior knowledge. Ask: *What do you know about volunteering? Have you ever volunteered for an organization or an event? Why do people volunteer?*
2. Have students share their knowledge and personal experiences.

Photo

1. Direct students' attention to the photo. Ask: *Where are the people? What are they doing? Do you think this is a restaurant? Why/Why not?*
2. Have students share their ideas about the photo.

🕐 To save class time, have students do the Test/Review at the end of the lesson, or administer a lesson test generated from the Assessment CD-ROM with *ExamView® Pro*. Skip sections of the lesson that students have already mastered. You may also assign some sections for self-study for extra credit.

Expansion

Theme The topic for this lesson can be enhanced with the following ideas:

1. A Web article that compares charities by the percent of donations that go directly to recipients
2. Charitable solicitations received in the mail
3. Articles about people who have donated time or money to a cause
4. Articles about children volunteering their time
5. Nomination forms for Volunteer of the Year or similar programs for children or adults

7.1 | Infinitives—An Overview

1. Have students look at grammar chart **7.1**. Ask: *What is an infinitive?* (*to* + the base form of the verb)
2. Have students look at the examples and explanations in the chart.
3. Have students make their own examples beginning with *It's important* and an infinitive.

Andrew Carnegie, Philanthropist (Reading)

1. Have students look at the photo on page 274. Ask: *Who is this? How long did he live?* (Andrew Carnegie; 84 years)
2. Have students look briefly at the reading. Ask: *What is the reading about? How do you know?* Have students make predictions.
3. Preteach any essential vocabulary words your students may not know, such as *fortune, access, key to, contribution, gospel, moral, set an example,* and *spirit.*

BEFORE YOU READ

1. Activate students' prior knowledge of public libraries and charitable donations. Ask: *Do you use the public library? Are there public libraries in your native country? Do you know of rich people who give their money away? Why do you think they do?*
2. Have students discuss the questions in pairs. Try to pair students of different language backgrounds.
3. Ask for a few volunteers to share their answers with the class.

To save class time, skip "Before You Read" or have students prepare answers for homework ahead of time.

Reading 🎧 *CD 3, Track 1*

1. Have students first read the text silently. Tell them to pay special attention to the infinitives in the reading. Then play the audio and have students read along silently.

7.1 | Infinitives—An Overview

An infinitive is *to* + base form: *to go, to be, to see.*

Examples	Explanation
I want **to help.**	An infinitive is used after certain verbs.
I want him **to help.**	An object can be added before an infinitive.
I'm happy **to help.**	An infinitive can follow certain adjectives.
It's important **to help** others.	An infinitive follows certain expressions with *it.*
Do you volunteer your time in order **to help** others?	An infinitive is used to show purpose.
He's old enough **to help.** She's too young **to help.**	An infinitive is used after expressions with *too* and *enough.*

ANDREW CARNEGIE, PHILANTHROPIST[1]

 Before You Read

1. Who are some of the richest people today?
2. Should rich people help others?

Andrew Carnegie, 1835–1919

Read the following article. Pay special attention to infinitives.

Andrew Carnegie was one of the world's richest men. He made a fortune in the oil and steel industries but spent most of his life giving his money away.

Carnegie was born in Scotland in 1835. When he was 13 years old, his family immigrated to the United States. A year later, he started **to work** for $1.20 a week. He was intelligent and hardworking, and it didn't take him long **to become** rich. But he always remembered the day he wanted **to use** a library in Pittsburgh but was not permitted **to enter.** He was disappointed **to learn** that the library was for members only.

[1] A *philanthropist* is a person who gives away money to help other people.

274   Lesson **7**

Expansion

Theme The topic for this lesson can be enhanced with the following ideas:

1. Article or Web article showing donations by wealthy individuals
2. Information from the local public library showing services, policies, and fees

---

Reading Variation

To practice listening skills, have students first listen to the audio alone. Ask a few comprehension questions. Repeat the audio if necessary. Then have students open their books and read along as they listen to the audio.

As Carnegie's fortunes grew, he started **to give** his money away. One of his biggest desires was **to build** free public libraries. He wanted everyone **to have** access to libraries and education. He believed that education was the key to a successful life. In 1881, there were only a few public libraries. Carnegie started to build free libraries for the people. Over the doors of the Carnegie Library of Pittsburgh, carved in stone, are his own words, "Free to the People." By the time Carnegie died, there were more than 2,500 public libraries in the English-speaking world.

But building libraries was not his only contribution. In his book, *The Gospel of Wealth*, he tried **to persuade** other wealthy people **to give** away their money. These are some of the ideas he wrote about in his book:

- **To give** away money is the best thing rich people can do.
- It is the moral obligation of the wealthy **to help** others.
- It is important for a rich person **to set** an example for others.
- It is not good **to have** money if your spirit is poor.
- It is the mind that makes the body rich.
- It is a disgrace[2] **to die** rich.

By the time he died in 1919, Carnegie had given away more than $350 million.

[2] A *disgrace* is something that brings shame or dishonor.

Infinitives; Gerunds   275

Reading (cont.)
2. Check students' comprehension. Ask questions such as: *When did Andrew Carnegie come to the U.S.?* (when he was 13) *When Carnegie was a child, who could use libraries?* (only members) *What did libraries represent for Andrew Carnegie?* (education; the key to a successful life) *What did Carnegie believe rich people should do?* (give money away; set an example for others)

To save class time, have students do the reading for homework ahead of time.

DID YOU KUOW ?

Money loses its buying power during periods of economic inflation. *Inflate* means *blow up* or *get bigger*.

Reading Glossary

access: entrance; ability to get in or use
contribution: gift; personal help
fortune: a large amount of money
gospel: a moral or religious message
key to: way to get to; secret to
moral: related to right or good behavior
set an example: show other people how to help, or how to do something well
spirit: essence; soul; guiding force

Culture Note

Andrew Carnegie is credited with founding more than 2,500 libraries in English-speaking countries, including more than 1,600 in the U.S. Some of these libraries are still called Carnegie Libraries, or Carnegie Free Libraries, today. Carnegie also founded Carnegie Hall in New York City and contributed to other well-known cultural and educational organizations. The Carnegie Foundation still gives grants, including donations to *Sesame Street* on public television.

7.2 | Verbs Followed by an Infinitive

1. Have students cover grammar chart **7.2**. Say: *Tell me something you know how to do; something you like to do; something you refuse to do.* Elicit several examples from volunteers. Say: Know how, like, *and* refuse *are verbs that can be followed by an infinitive.* Ask students if they can name other verbs that can be followed by an infinitive.

2. Have students review the examples and explanations in the grammar chart.

3. Draw students' attention to the Language Note. Provide several examples of your own using verbs in the list: *I hope to take a vacation in Latin America some day. I've managed to save some money, but I need to save more.* Clarify any vocabulary students are unfamiliar with. Ask volunteers to give sentences about themselves using the verbs and infinitives.

EXERCISE 1

1. Tell students that this exercise is about Andrew Carnegie. Have students read the direction line. Ask: *What do we write?* (an infinitive)

2. Model the exercise. Direct students to the example. Complete #1 with the class.

3. Have students complete Exercise 1 individually. Then have them check their answers in pairs. If necessary, check the answers as a class.

4. Assess students' performance. If necessary, review grammar chart **7.2** on page 276.

7.1 | Verbs Followed by an Infinitive

Examples	Explanation
Carnegie wanted **to build** libraries. He started **to work** when he was 14. He decided **to give** away money. Everyone deserves **to have** an education.	Some verbs are followed by an infinitive.
I want **to make** money and **help** others.	In a sentence with two infinitives connected by *and*, the second *to* is usually omitted.
Everyone wants **to be given** an opportunity to succeed.	To make an infinitive passive, use *to be* + past participle.

Language Note:
The verbs below can be followed by an infinitive.

agree	deserve	love*	seem
appear	expect	manage	start*
attempt	forget	need	try*
begin*	hate*	offer	want
can('t) afford	hope	plan	wish
can't stand*	intend	prefer*	would like
choose	know how	prepare	refuse
continue*	learn	pretend	
decide	like*	promise	

* These verbs can also be followed by a gerund with little or no change in meaning. See Section 7.14.

EXERCISE   1   Fill in the blanks with an infinitive based on the story you just read.

EXAMPLE   Andrew Carnegie started _____ *to work* _____ when he was very young.

1. He tried _____ *to use* _____ a library when he was young, but he wasn't allowed inside.

2. He wanted _____ *to build* _____ free public libraries.

3. He thought it was important for rich people _____ *to help* _____ poor people.

4. He thought it was better _____ *to have* _____ a rich spirit than a big bank account.

5. He thought that rich people needed _____ *to set* _____ an example for others.

6. He decided _____ *to give away* _____ a lot of money to help others.

7. He thought it was a terrible thing _____ *to die* _____ rich.

Grammar Variation

Brainstorm with students methods for memorizing verbs that can be followed by an infinitive. Possibilities include quizzing one another, using flashcards, filling in worksheets on paper or on grammar quiz Web sites, or using computer software.

EXERCISE **2** ABOUT YOU Fill in the blanks with an infinitive. Share your
answers with the class.

EXAMPLE I like _____to eat Chinese food_____ .

1. I don't like _____Answers will vary._____ , but I have to do it anyway.
2. I can't afford _____ .
3. I've decided _____ .
4. I want _____ , but I don't have enough time.
5. I don't want _____ , but I have to do it.
6. I sometimes forget _____ .
7. I love _____ .
8. I need _____ and _____ every day.
9. I don't know how _____ , but I'd like to learn.
10. I would like _____ .

Infinitives; Gerunds 277

Expansion

Exercise 2 Put students in groups. Ask students to make true or false statements about
themselves, using the prompts in the exercise. The other students guess if the statements are
true or false. Model an example. Say: *I don't like to clean my house, but I have to do it
anyway. True or false?* Students guess if you're telling the truth.

1. Tell students that this exercise is
   about their interests and feelings.
   Have students read the direction
   line.
2. Model the exercise. Direct students
   to the example in the book. Ask
   several volunteers to complete the
   statement for themselves.
3. Have students complete Exercise 2
   individually. Then have them check
   their answers by reading their
   statements to each other in pairs.
   Circulate and observe the pair work;
   if appropriate, participate in
   discussions. Ask students to share
   interesting answers with the class.

🕐 To save class time, have
   students do half of the exercise
in class and complete the other half for
homework. Or assign the entire
exercise for homework.

EXERCISE 3

1. Tell students that this exercise is about their ideas and plans. Have students read the direction line.
2. Model the exercise. Direct students to the example. Ask several volunteers to answer the question.
3. Have students look at the questions in the exercise; encourage students to make notes in their notebooks. Then have them work in pairs, taking turns asking and answering the questions. Have the student who is answering questions cover the exercise in his or her book. For items 6 and 7, remind students to ask the questions one at a time. Circulate and observe the pair work; if appropriate, participate in discussions. Have pairs share interesting answers with the class.

🕐 To save class time, have students do half of the exercise in class and complete the other half in writing for homework. Or if students do not need speaking practice, the entire exercise may be skipped or done in writing.

EXERCISE 4

1. Tell students that this exercise is about ways that people help each other. Have students read the direction line.
2. Direct students to the example. Complete #1 with the class.
3. Have students complete the exercise individually. Check answers as a class.
4. Assess students' performance. If necessary, review grammar chart **7.2** on page 276.

🕐 To save class time, have students do half of the exercise in class and complete the other half for homework. Or assign the entire exercise for homework.

EXERCISE 3 ABOUT YOU Answer these questions. You may discuss your answers.

EXAMPLE Why did you decide to come to this city?
I decided to come here because I wanted to go to this school.

Answers will vary.
1. Why did you decide to come to this school?
2. What did you need to do to get into this school?
3. When did you start to study English?
4. What do you expect to have five years from now (that you don't have now)?
5. What do you hope to accomplish in your lifetime?
6. Do you want to learn any other languages? Which ones? Why?
7. Do you plan to get a college degree? In what field?
8. Do you plan to transfer to a different school?
9. What do you plan to do after you graduate?

EXERCISE 4 Fill in the blanks with the passive form of the verb in parentheses ( ).

EXAMPLE Children like ___to be given___ toys.
(give)

1. Children have ___to be taught___ about giving, not just taking.
(teach)

2. My elderly neighbor needs ___to be driven___ to the hospital
(drive)
because he can't drive. I'm going to offer to drive him.

3. Some people who make donations don't want their names
___to be known___.
(know)

4. Money for a charity needs ___to be collected___.
(collect)

5. There are many ways to help. Parks need ___to be cleaned___.
(clean)

6. There are many ways of helping children. Children need
___to be loved___ and ___to be respected___.
(love)   (respect)

7. Carnegie thought that libraries needed ___to be built___ for
(build)
the public.

8. Everyone wants ___to be given___ a chance to succeed in life.
(give)

278 Lesson 7

Expansion

Exercise 3 Have students work in pairs to extend the conversations in the exercise:

A: *When did you start to study English?*
B: *I started to study English when I came to the U.S.*
A: *When was that?*
B: *In 2002.*

7.3 | Object Before Infinitive

After the verb, we can use an object + an infinitive.

Examples	Explanation
a. Carnegie wanted *everyone* **to have** educational opportunities. b. He encouraged *rich people* **to help** others. c. He wanted *them* **to donate** money. d. Our parents want *us* **to help** others.	The object can be a noun (a and b) or a pronoun (c and d).
Carnegie encouraged people *not* **to be** selfish. The teacher advised us *not* **to talk** during an exam.	Put *not* before an infinitive to make a negative.

Language Note:
The verbs below can be followed by a noun or object pronoun + an infinitive.

advise	expect	persuade
allow	forbid	remind
appoint	force	teach*
ask	invite	tell
beg	need	urge
convince	order	want
encourage	permit	would like

*After *teach*, *how* is sometimes used: He taught me *how to ski*.

EXERCISE **5** ABOUT YOU Tell if you want or don't want the teacher to do the following.

EXAMPLES speak fast
I don't want the teacher to speak fast.

answer my questions
I want him to answer my questions.

Answers will vary.
1. explain the grammar
2. review modals
3. give us a lot of homework
4. give us a test on gerunds and infinitives
5. give a lot of examples
6. speak slowly
7. correct my pronunciation
8. teach us idioms

Expansion

Grammar Have students work in groups to classify the verbs in the Language Note into categories by strength or urgency, e.g., gentle (*ask, would like, invite*) and strong (*order, forbid, beg*).

Expansion

Exercise 5 After students complete the exercise, have them work in pairs to ask each other about their statements with *why* or *why not*:

A: *I want her to explain the grammar.*
B: *Why?*
A: *Because I have never studied grammar before.*

7.3 | Object Before Infinitive

1. Have students cover the grammar chart. Draw a four-column chart on the board. Elicit several sentences with objects before an infinitive: *What did Andrew Carnegie want rich people to do?* (He wanted rich people to donate money.) *What did he want everyone to have?* (He wanted everyone to have access to libraries.) Write the answers on the board with the subjects in the first column, the verbs in the second column, the objects in the third column, and the infinitive and remainder in the fourth column.
2. Ask students to say what they observe about objects and infinitives. If students have difficulty, say: *The infinitive follows the object.*
3. Have students look at grammar chart **7.3**. Point out the placement of *not*.
4. Draw students' attention to the Language Note. Provide several examples of your own using verbs from the list: *The library encourages people to donate books. My friends asked me to help.* Clarify any vocabulary students are unfamiliar with. Ask volunteers to give sentences about themselves using the verbs, objects, and infinitives.

EXERCISE 5

1. Tell students that this exercise is about their expectations for their teacher. Have students read the direction line.
2. Model the exercise. Direct students to the examples. Say: *One student said: I don't want the teacher to speak fast. Do you agree with that?* For the second example, ask a volunteer to give an answer; be sure students use the appropriate pronoun (*him* or *her*).
3. Have students complete the rest of Exercise 5 in pairs, taking turns completing the statements. Ask volunteers to share their statements with the class.

EXERCISE 6

1. Tell students that this exercise is about their teacher's expectations of them. Have students read the direction line.
2. Model the exercise. Direct students to the examples. Say: *One student said: The teacher expects us to come on time. Do you agree with that?* Repeat for the second example.
3. Have students complete Exercise 6 in pairs, taking turns completing the statements. Ask volunteers to share their statements with the class.

EXERCISE 7

1. Tell students that this exercise is about what parents teach their children. Have students read the direction line.
2. Model the exercise. Direct students to the example in the book. Then do #1 with the class.
3. Have students complete Exercise 7 individually. Then have them compare their answers in pairs. Finally, check the answers as a class.
4. Assess students' performance. If necessary, review grammar chart **7.3**.

🕐 To save class time, have students do half of the exercise in class and complete the other half for homework. Or assign the entire exercise for homework.

EXERCISE **6** Tell if the teacher expects or doesn't expect you to do the following.

EXAMPLES come on time
The teacher expects us to come on time.

wear a suit to class
The teacher doesn't expect us to wear a suit to class.

Answers will vary.
1. write perfect compositions
2. learn English in six months
3. do the homework
4. stand up to answer a question
5. raise our hands to answer a question
6. ask questions
7. study on Saturdays
8. practice English every day
9. speak English without an accent
10. use the Internet

EXERCISE **7** Change the following imperative statements to statements with an object pronoun plus an infinitive.

EXAMPLE A woman says to her husband, "Teach the children good values."
She wants him to teach the children good values.

1. My parents always said to me, "Help others."
My parents expected _____ *me to help others.*

2. A mother says to her children, "Be kind to others."
She wants _____ *them to be kind to others.*

3. The father said to his children, "Give to charity."
The father advised _____ *them to give to charity.*

4. Parents say to their children, "Study hard."
Parents want _____ *them to study hard.*

5. I said to you, "Work hard."
I would like _____ *you to work hard.*

6. My parents said to us, "Give money to the poor."
My parents reminded _____ *us to give money to the poor.*

7. A father says to his daughter, "Be generous."
He wants _____ *her to be generous.*

8. My parents said to me, "Don't be selfish."
My parents encouraged _____ *me not to be selfish.*

9. Parents say to their children, "Be polite."
They expect _____ *them to be polite.*

280   Lesson 7

Expansion

Exercises 5 and 6 Have students work in groups to survey the class using the items in Exercises 5 and 6. If possible, have each group take responsibility for one or two items. Have groups prepare questions (e.g., *Do you want the teacher to give us a lot of homework? Does the teacher expect us to study on Saturdays?*). Have groups use their results to make graphs showing how students answered each question.

EXERCISE 8 ABOUT YOU Use the words given to tell what your family wanted from you when you were growing up.

EXAMPLES want / move away
My parents didn't want me to move away.

expect / get married
My mother expected me to get married when I graduated from college.

Answers will vary.
1. expect / respect older people
2. allow / stay out late at night
3. want / help them financially
4. expect / get good grades in school
5. encourage / have a lot of friends
6. want / be obedient

7. want / be independent
8. permit / choose my own friends
9. expect / get married
10. encourage / save money
11. advise / be honest
12. encourage / go to college

CHARITY AND VOLUNTEERING

Before You Read
1. Do you ever receive address labels in the mail with your name and address printed on them?
2. Do you ever watch a TV channel that asks you to send money to support it?

American Red Cross Disaster Relief

Infinitives; Gerunds 281

Expansion

Theme The topic for this lesson can be enhanced with the following ideas:

1. Mail solicitations from charities, especially with address labels or greeting cards enclosed
2. Flyers or announcements of payroll deduction opportunities for charity
3. A newspaper article about community volunteers or volunteer programs
4. A newspaper or Web list of volunteer opportunities

EXERCISE 8

1. Tell students that this exercise is about their families' expectations of them when they were young. Have students read the direction line.
2. Model the exercise. Direct students to the examples. Then do #1 with the class. Ask a volunteer to give a response. Encourage students to personalize their statements with *usually*, *generally*, and *always*.
3. Have students complete Exercise 8 individually. Then have them compare their responses in pairs. Finally, ask volunteers to share their responses with the class.
4. Assess students' performance. If necessary, review grammar chart **7.3**.

⏱ To save class time, have students do half of the exercise in class and complete the other half in writing for homework. Or if students do not need speaking practice, the entire exercise may be skipped or done in writing.

Charity and Volunteering (Reading)

1. Have students look at the photos on page 281 and page 282. Ask: *What do you think the people are doing?* (volunteering at a disaster site; volunteering in a soup kitchen) *Why?*
2. Have students look briefly at the reading. Have students look at the title of the reading. Ask: *What is the reading about? How do you know?* Have students make predictions.
3. Preteach any vocabulary words your students may not know, such as *charity*, *willingly*, *keep in mind*, *guilty*, and *fundraisers*.

BEFORE YOU READ

1. Activate students' prior knowledge about charities, fund drives, solicitation of donations, etc. Ask: *What kinds of organizations ask people to donate money? Why? How do you feel when an organization asks you to donate money?*
2. Have students discuss the questions in pairs. Try to pair students of different language backgrounds.
3. Ask a few volunteers to share their answers with the class.

⏱ To save class time, skip "Before You Read" or have students prepare answers for homework ahead of time.

1. Have students first read the text silently. Tell them to pay special attention to verbs followed by infinitives and base forms. Then play the audio and have students read along silently.
2. Check students' comprehension. Ask questions such as: *What are four ways to ask for or donate money?* (payroll deductions; volunteers at intersections; free items in the mail; fundraisers) *What else can people donate besides money?* (time) *What are two reasons to give or volunteer?* (It makes us feel good; we can deduct contributions from our taxes.)

To save class time, have students do the reading for homework ahead of time.

Read the following article. Pay special attention to verbs followed by infinitives and base forms.

There are more than 600,000 charities in the U.S. that you can give to. In addition, there are thousands of volunteer organizations. But it isn't always easy to **get** people **to give** willingly.

One way charities **get** people **to contribute** is by offering a payroll deduction at work. An employee can have a certain amount of each paycheck deducted, so the money goes to charity before the employee even sees it. If you are asked to give at your job, keep in mind that it is voluntary; no one can **make** you **give.**

Another way to **get** you **to give** is to send you something free in the mail, such as address labels with your name and address printed on them. Some people feel guilty about accepting the gift without giving something. Also some charities **have** volunteers **stand** at intersections with a can or box, asking passing drivers for donations. Often they give you something, such as candy, for your donation.

Public TV and radio stations have fundraisers. Several days out of the year, they ask for your money to support the programs you like. The station **has** volunteers **answer** phones to take your credit card number.

Besides giving money, people can volunteer their time. Some volunteers **help** kids **learn** to read; others help feed the homeless; others **help** elderly people **get** meals.

Helping others **makes** us **feel** good. To encourage us to give, the government **lets** us **deduct** our contribution, which lowers our taxes.

282   Lesson **7**

Reading Variation

To practice listening skills, have students first listen to the audio alone. Ask a few comprehension questions. Repeat the audio if necessary. Then have students open their books and read along as they listen to the audio.

Reading Glossary

charity: an organization that helps people (or animals), usually by asking for donations and volunteers
fundraiser: event that raises money by asking for donations
(feel) guilty: feel wrong, feel bad
keep in mind: remember
willingly: by choice

Culture Note

Charity is used in the article to mean an organization that uses donations and/or volunteers to help others. *Charity* also means the feeling or act of caring about and helping others. Volunteer organizations usually use donated time and money to support causes, especially helping people or animals, protecting the environment, and political or social causes.

7.4 | Causative Verbs

Some verbs are often called *causative* verbs because one person causes, enables, or allows another to do something.

Examples	Explanation
Carnegie **persuaded** wealthy people **to give** away their money. You **convinced** me **to help** the poor. They **got** us **to contribute** to charity.	*Get, persuade, convince* are followed by an object + infinitive. *Get*, in the example on the left, means persuade.
Carnegie **helped** people **to get** an education. Volunteers **help** kids **learn** to read.	After *help* + object, either the infinitive or the base form can be used. The base form is more common.
The government **lets** you **deduct** your contribution to charity. The teacher doesn't **let** us **talk** during a test.	*Let* means permit. *Let* is followed by an object + base form. (*Permit* and *allow* are followed by an infinitive.) Compare: The teacher doesn't **let** us **talk.** The teacher doesn't **permit** us **to talk.**
a. No one can **make** you **give** to charity. b. Volunteering my time **makes** me **feel** good. c. A sad movie **makes** me **cry.**	*Make* is followed by an object + base form. In sentence (a), *make* means force. In sentences (b) and (c), *make* means to cause something to happen.
Public TV stations **have** volunteers **answer** the phones and take donations. The teacher **had** us **write** a composition about charity.	*Have* means to give a job or task to someone. *Have*, in this case, is followed by an object + base form.

EXERCISE 9 Fill in the blanks with the base form or the complete infinitive of the verb in parentheses ( ).

I volunteer for my local public radio station. Several times a year the

station tries to persuade listeners _____*to give*_____ money to the station.
                                         (example: give)

Without listener support, the radio station could not exist. The station

managers have us _____*answer*_____ the phones when listeners
                        (1 answer)

call to contribute. We let callers _____*pay*_____ by check or
                                        (2 pay)

credit card. To get listeners _____*to contribute*_____, the station offers
                                    (3 contribute)

_____

Infinitives; Gerunds   283

7.4 | Causative Verbs

1. Have students cover the grammar chart. Say: *Tell me about something that someone convinced you to do. About something that makes you happy. About something that someone helped you do.* Then say: Convince, make, *and* help *are called causative verbs because they show that something or someone causes us to do something.*
2. Have students look at the grammar chart. Review the examples and explanations in the chart.
3. Point out the verbs in the chart that take the base form instead of the infinitive.

EXERCISE 9

🎧 *CD 3, Track 3*

1. Tell students that this exercise is about volunteering at a public radio station. Have students read the direction line.
2. Direct students to the example.
3. Have students complete the exercise individually and then compare answers in pairs. Check answers as a class.

Grammar Variation

After students have reviewed the example sentences in the grammar chart, have them go back to the reading on page 282 and identify causative verbs followed by the infinitive and causative verbs followed by the base form.

Exercise 9 Variation

To provide practice with listening skills, have students close their books and listen to the audio. Repeat the audio as needed. Ask comprehension questions, such as: *What do the radio and TV stations do several times a year?* (try to persuade listeners to give money to the stations) *Why?* (because without listener support, the stations could not exist) *How can callers pay?* (by check or credit card) Then have students open their books and complete Exercise 9.

1. Tell students that this exercise is about parents and teachers. Have students read the direction line.
2. Direct students to the example. Ask volunteers to provide their own statements using the prompt.
3. Have students complete the exercise individually. Ask volunteers to share their answers with the class.

🕐 To save class time, have students do half of the exercise in class and complete the other half for homework. Or assign the entire exercise for homework.

some prizes. For example, for a $60 contribution, you can get a coffee mug. For a $100 contribution, you can get a book. Everyone can listen to public radio for free. No one makes you ___*pay*___ for it.
(4 pay)

But listeners should pay for this service, if they can. They should help the station ___*pay / to pay*___ for its excellent programming.
(5 pay)

EXERCISE **10** ABOUT YOU Fill in the blanks with the base form and finish the sentence.

EXAMPLE The teacher lets us ___*talk in groups when we work on a problem.*___

Answers will vary.

1. When I was a child, my parents didn't let me _____
_____

2. When I was a child, my parents made me _____
_____

3. During a test, the teacher doesn't let us _____

4. The teacher often has us _____

5. My parents helped me _____

Expansion

Exercise 10 Have students make similar statements about things teachers in their native countries let them do.

Culture Note

Many communities have public radio and television stations. Many public stations specialize in educational programming. Ask students if they can identify a public station in their area, or name a public radio or television show they are familiar with.

7.5 | Adjective Plus Infinitive

Certain adjectives can be followed by an infinitive.	
Examples	**Explanation**
Some people are happy **to help** others. Are you willing **to donate** your time? I am proud **to be** a volunteer. I am sad **to see** so many needy people in the world. We are pleased to be able **to help**.	Certain adjectives can be followed by an infinitive. Many of these adjectives describe a person's emotional or mental state.

Language Note:
The following adjectives can be followed by an infinitive.

afraid	eager	pleased*	sad
ashamed*	glad	prepared*	sorry
delighted*	happy	proud	surprised*
disappointed*	lucky	ready	willing

*Note: Many *-ed* words are adjectives.

EXERCISE 11 **ABOUT YOU** Fill in the blanks with an infinitive (phrase).

EXAMPLE Before I came here, I was afraid _____*to speak English.*_____

Answers will vary.
1. When I left my parents' house, I was eager _____
   _____

2. When I started college or high school, I was surprised (to see, learn, find out) _____

3. When I was a child, I was afraid _____
   _____

4. Now I'm afraid _____

5. I'm happy _____

6. I'm lucky _____

7. When I left my hometown, I was sorry _____
   _____

8. When I was _____ years old, I was ready _____
   _____

7.5 | Adjective Plus Infinitive

1. Ask students to cover the grammar chart. Write on the board: *I'm proud to be . . .* and *I'm happy to be able to . . . .* Ask students to complete the statements for themselves and then ask volunteers to share. Point out that in each case an adjective is followed by an infinitive.
2. Have students look at the grammar chart. Review the examples and explanations in the chart.
3. Point out the adjective list in the Language Note. Clarify the meaning of any words students are not familiar with.

EXERCISE 11

1. Tell students that this exercise is about their own experiences. Have students read the direction line.
2. Direct students to the example in the book. Ask several volunteers to complete the statement for themselves.
3. Have students read the prompts silently and think about their answers for a few minutes. Encourage students to take notes. Then have them complete the exercise in writing. Ask volunteers to share their statements with the class.

Expansion

Exercise 11 Have students write questions about the items in the exercise, such as: *What were you eager to do when you left your parents' house?* Have pairs of students use the questions to interview each other. Then have each student write sentences about his or her partner based on his or her answers (*Nikolai was eager to travel when he left his parents' house.*).

1. Tell students that this exercise is a conversation between a nephew and his uncle. Have students read the direction line. If necessary, clarify the meaning of *uncle* and *nephew*. Ask: *What do we write?* (an infinitive or a base form)
2. Direct students to the example. Complete items 1 and 2 with the class.
3. Have students complete the exercise individually. Then have them check their answers in pairs by practicing the conversation. Check answers as a class.
4. Assess students' performance. If necessary, review grammar chart **7.5**.

🕐 To save class time, have students do half of the exercise in class and complete the other half for homework. Or assign the entire exercise for homework.

EXERCISE 🔢 *Combination Exercise.* Fill in the blanks with an infinitive or a base form in this conversation between an uncle (U) and his nephew (N). Answers may vary.

🎧

U: What do you plan ___to do___ this summer?
     (example)

N: I wanted ___to get___ a summer job, but I couldn't find
          (1)
   one. It's going to be boring. I'm ready ___to work___, but
                                            (2)
   no one wants ___to hire___ me. And my parents expect me
                   (3)
   ___to get___ a job. My mom won't let me
      (4)
   ___stay___ home all day and watch TV or hang out with
      (5)
   my friends at the swimming pool.

U: Are you trying ___to earn___ money for your college
                      (6)
   education?

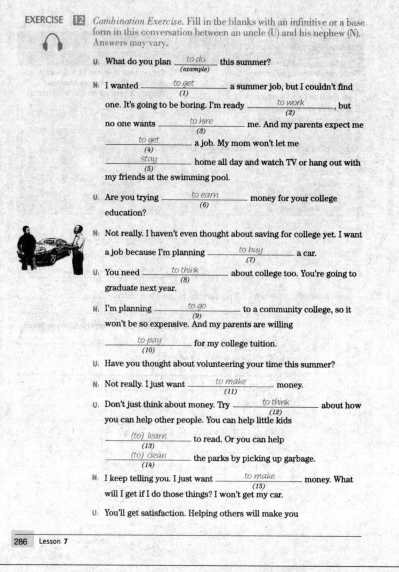

N: Not really. I haven't even thought about saving for college yet. I want
   a job because I'm planning ___to buy___ a car.
                                 (7)

U: You need ___to think___ about college too. You're going to
               (8)
   graduate next year.

N: I'm planning ___to go___ to a community college, so it
                   (9)
   won't be so expensive. And my parents are willing
   ___to pay___ for my college tuition.
      (10)

U: Have you thought about volunteering your time this summer?

N: Not really. I just want ___to make___ money.
                              (11)

U: Don't just think about money. Try ___to think___ about how
                                        (12)
   you can help other people. You can help little kids
   ___(to) learn___ to read. Or you can help
      (13)
   ___(to) clean___ the parks by picking up garbage.
      (14)

N: I keep telling you. I just want ___to make___ money. What
                                      (15)
   will I get if I do those things? I won't get my car.

U: You'll get satisfaction. Helping others will make you

Exercise 12 Variation

To provide practice with listening skills, have students close their books and listen to the audio. Repeat the audio as needed. Ask comprehension questions, such as: *What do the nephew's parents expect him to do this summer?* (find a job) *Why does the nephew want a job?* (because he's planning on buying a car) *When is the nephew going to graduate?* (next year) Then have students open their books and complete Exercise 12.

Expansion

Exercise 12 Have students work in groups to brainstorm adjectives they think describe the uncle and nephew. Ask them to explain their choices using the items in the exercise. If appropriate, have students write a paragraph describing the uncle or the nephew as homework.

feel (16) good. And you will learn

_to be_ (17) responsible. After you finish community college and go to a four-year college, it will look good on your application if you say you volunteered. It will help you

get (18) into a good college.

A: Why are you trying so hard to get me _to be_ (19) a volunteer?

B: I volunteered when I was your age, and I found that it was more valuable than money.

A: OK. I'll volunteer if you're willing _to give / to lend_ (20) me the money for the car.

BICYCLING TO RAISE MONEY FOR AIDS

Before You Read

1. How can one person help solve a big problem like AIDS or cancer?
2. Can you imagine riding a bike over 500 miles?

 Read the following article. *Pay special attention to *in order to* and *to*.

San Francisco
Los Angeles
California

Since the early 1980s, more than 25 million people have died of AIDS worldwide and more than 40 million people are now infected. How can one person do his or her part **to help** fight this deadly disease? Dan Pallotta decided to try. In 1994, at the age of 32, he organized a bike ride from San Francisco to Los Angeles **in order to call** attention to the AIDS epidemic. He found 471 people willing to bike the 525 miles (845 km) in seven days. **To raise** money, each rider asked friends and relatives to give donations in support of the ride. Since 1994, more than 124,000 people have taken part in the rides and more than $222 million have been raised for AIDS research.

*Statistics are as of May 2003.

(continued)

Expansion

Theme The topic for this lesson can be enhanced with the following ideas:

1. A flyer, Web page, or newspaper ad soliciting participants for a walk or bicycle ride for a charity or cause
2. An article from the newspaper or a Web site about the results of a walk or bicycle ride to support a health, social service, or other cause

Reading Variation

To practice listening skills, have students first listen to the audio alone. Ask a few comprehension questions. Repeat the audio if necessary. Then have students open their books and read along as they listen to the audio.

Bicycling to Raise Money for AIDS (Reading)

1. Have students look at the photo. Ask: *What are the people in the picture doing? How do they feel? Why do you think they feel that way? How many people do you think there are in the picture?*
2. Have students look briefly at the reading. Have students look at the title of the reading. Ask: *What is the reading about? How do you know?* Have students make predictions.
3. Preteach any vocabulary words your students may not know, such as *bike, infected, do one's part, call attention to, epidemic, take part in, take place in,* and *in good shape.*

BEFORE YOU READ

1. Activate students' prior knowledge about bicycle rides or walks for a charity or cause. Ask: *Have you ever seen signs for or heard of a charity walk or bicycle (bike) ride? What kinds of causes do you know of that sponsor walks or bicycle rides?* (breast cancer, AIDS, homelessness, etc.) *Have you, or do you know someone who has, participated in a walk or bicycle ride for charity?*
2. Have students discuss the questions in pairs. Try to pair students of different language backgrounds.
3. Ask a few volunteers to share their answers with the class.

To save class time, skip "Before You Read" or have students prepare answers for homework ahead of time.

Reading CD 3, Track 5

1. Have students first read the text silently. Tell them to pay special attention to *in order to* and *to*. Then play the audio and have students read along silently.
2. Check students' comprehension. Ask questions such as: *How far is it from San Francisco to Los Angeles?* (525 miles) *How much money did the ride that Dan Pallotta organized raise for AIDS research?* (more than $222 million) *What do the riders get from finishing a long ride for a charity?* (the satisfaction of having finished the ride; the satisfaction of having raised money to help fight AIDS)

To save class time, have students do the reading for homework ahead of time.

7.6 | Using the Infinitive to Show Purpose

1. Have students cover the grammar chart. Elicit from students two sentences with *in order to* from the reading, such as: *Dan Pallotta organized a ride in order to call attention to AIDS* and *Riders prepare for months in order to be ready for the ride.* Write the sentences on the board. Elicit the help of volunteers to write questions about the statements using *why* (e.g., *Why did Dan Pallotta organize a ride? Why do riders prepare for months?*). Ask: *What does* in order to *show?* (purpose)

2. Have students look at grammar chart **7.6**. Review the examples and explanations. Draw students' attention to *to* in the second row.

3. Provide several examples of your own (e.g., *I left my last job in order to come here. He went to college to study art.*). Ask volunteers to provide examples about themselves.

EXERCISE 13

1. Tell students that this exercise is about volunteering. Have students read the direction line. Ask: *Are different answers possible?* (yes)

2. Model the exercise. Direct students to the example.

3. Have students complete the exercise individually. Then have students compare their answers in pairs. If necessary, check answers as a class.

These rides take place in many locations in the U.S. (Alaska, Minneapolis to Chicago, Boston to New York, San Francisco to Los Angeles). Of course, **to ride** such a long distance, a rider has to be in good shape. Many riders prepare for months ahead **in order to be** ready for the ride. But even riders in good shape sometimes need a break. Vans ride along with the cyclists **in order to pick up** anyone who needs to rest for a while.

At the end of the ride, cyclists are tired, but they have the satisfaction of having finished the ride and of raising money **to fight** the problem of AIDS.

7.6 | Using the Infinitive to Show Purpose

Examples	Explanation
Dan organized the bike ride **in order to** raise money for AIDS.	*In order to* shows purpose. It answers the question "Why?" or "What for?"
Vans ride along with the cyclists **in order to** pick up tired riders.	
In order to ride a long distance, you have to be in good shape.	
Dan organized the bike ride **to** raise money for AIDS.	*In order to* can be shortened. We can simply use *to*.
Vans ride along with the cyclists **to** pick up tired riders.	
To ride a long distance, you have to be in good shape.	
a. **In order to help others,** Carnegie gave away his money.	a. The purpose clause can precede the main clause. Use a comma to separate the two clauses.
b. Carnegie gave away his money **in order to help others.**	b. The purpose clause can follow the main clause. Don't use a comma.

EXERCISE **13** Fill in the blanks to complete the sentences. Answers may vary.

EXAMPLE In order to _learn more about volunteering_, you can use the Internet. You can find lots of information there.

1. Carnegie donated his money to _____*build*_____ libraries.

2. You can volunteer in order to _____*get*_____ job experience. But in order to _____*make*_____ money, you need a paying job.

3. To _____*get*_____ a job, you need experience. To _____*get*_____ experience, you need a job.

4. You can volunteer your time in order to _____*help*_____ people. There are many people who need help.

5. Dan Pallotta organized bike rides in order to _call attention to AIDS_.

Reading Glossary

bike: bicycle
call attention to: make other people aware of; let other people know about
do one's part: contribute; help take responsibility for
epidemic: a condition in which large numbers of people are infected with a disease
infected: affected by a disease; having caught a disease
in good shape: in good physical condition; fit; healthy
take part in: participate in
take place in: happen in or at

EXERCISE **14** Complete each sentence. Answers may vary.

EXAMPLE   Many students have jobs in order ___*to pay for their education*___.

1. I want to learn English in order to ___*Answers will vary.*___
2. I came to this school to _____.
3. We're studying this lesson to _____.
4. I use my dictionary to _____.
5. Many people use spell-check in order to _____.
6. Many people use Caller ID to _____.
7. I _____ in order to relax.
8. I _____ to learn new words.
9. You should register early to _____.
10. Many students apply for financial aid to _____.
11. If you aren't satisfied with your score on the TOEFL test, you can
    take it a second time in order to _____
    your score.
12. If you're absent, you can call a classmate to _____.
13. You need a password in order to _____.
14. You can use the Web site "weather.com" to _____.
15. Many people use e-mail to _____.

1. Tell students that this exercise is about purposes and reasons. Have students read the direction line.
2. Model the exercise. Direct students to the example in the book. Ask several volunteers to provide their own statements.
3. Have students complete the rest of Exercise 14 individually. Then have them compare answers in pairs. Circulate and observe the pair work. Have volunteers share interesting answers with the class.

To save class time, have students do half of the exercise in class and complete the other half for homework. Or assign the entire exercise for homework.

Expansion

Exercise 14 Have students work in pairs or groups to write questions about the items in the exercise, such as: *Why do you want to learn English? What do you use your dictionary for?* Then have students use the questions to interview each other in pairs.

Exercise 14 Have students work in pairs to write short conversations using *What for*, such as:

A: *I need a dollar.*
B: *What for?*
A: *To buy a soda.*

7.7 | Infinitive as Subject

1. Have students cover grammar chart **7.7.** Write on the board: *It is important for people to . . .* Ask volunteers to complete the statement.
2. Have students look at the grammar chart. Review the example sentences and explanations carefully.
3. Point out the use of indirect objects with *take* and *cost* in the third row of the chart. Provide several examples about yourself, such as: *It didn't take me long to get here today. The traffic was light.*

EXERCISE 15

1. Tell students that this exercise is about their opinions. Have students read the direction line. Ask: *What do we write?* (an infinitive phrase)
2. Direct students to the example in the book. Ask: *Do you agree with the statement?* Ask several volunteers to complete the statement with their ideas.
3. Have students complete the exercise in writing individually. Ask volunteers to share their answers with the class.

7.7 | Infinitive as Subject

Examples	Explanation
It's good **to help** other people. **It** was Carnegie's dream **to build** libraries. **It's** hard **to ride** a bike 500 miles.	An infinitive phrase can be the subject of a sentence. We usually begin the sentence with *it* and put the infinitive phrase at the end of the sentence.
It is important **for rich people** to set an example. It is necessary **for bike riders** to train for the long ride.	*For* + an object can give the infinitive a specific subject.
It costs a lot of money **to build** a library. **It takes** many days **to ride** from Los Angeles to San Francisco.	An infinitive is often used after *cost* + money and *take* + time.
Carnegie was a poor immigrant, but it didn't take **him** long **to become** rich. How much did it cost **him** to build a library?	An indirect object can follow *take* and *cost*.
To build libraries was Carnegie's dream. **To give** money away is the best thing rich people can do. **To help** others gives a person satisfaction.	Sometimes we begin a sentence with an infinitive phrase. A sentence that begins with an infinitive is very formal.

EXERCISE 15 Complete each statement with an infinitive phrase.

EXAMPLE It isn't polite _____ *to interrupt a conversation.* _____

1. It's dangerous _____ Answers will vary. _____
2. It isn't healthy _____
3. It isn't polite _____
4. It's illegal _____
5. It's a good idea _____
6. It's the teacher's responsibility _____
7. It costs a lot of money _____
8. It's important for me _____
9. It's boring for the students _____

Expansion

Exercise 15 In groups or as a class, have individuals take turns stating their opinions for each item. Have other students respond with *I agree because . . .*, *I agree, but . . .*, or *I disagree because . . . .*

Culture Note

A polite way to lessen the strength of an opinion, and to ask for agreement, is to add *don't you think?* at the end of a positive sentence (a sentence without *not*), as in: *It's a good idea to give to public radio, don't you think?*

---

10. It's fun for children _____

11. It's easy for Americans _____

12. It took me a long time _____

13. It cost me a lot of money _____

14. It will probably take me a long time _____

EXERCISE **15** Make sentences with the words given.

EXAMPLE   dangerous / children
It's dangerous for children to play with matches.
_____

1. fun / children
_____ Answers will vary. _____

2. necessary / children
_____

3. important / a family
_____

4. difficult / a large family
_____

5. necessary / working parents
_____

6. difficult / women in my native culture
_____

7. hard / single parents
_____

8. difficult / the teacher
_____

1. Tell students that this exercise is also about their opinions. Have students read the direction line.

2. Direct students to the example in the book. Ask: _Do you agree with the statement?_ Ask several volunteers to complete the statement with their ideas.

3. Have students complete the exercise in writing individually. Ask volunteers to share their answers with the class.

4. Assess students' performance. If necessary, review grammar chart **7.7** on page 290.

To save class time, have students do half of the exercise in class and complete the other half for homework. Or assign the entire exercise for homework.

Expansion

Exercise 16 Have students make new statements by adding _not_ to each item in Exercise 16, e.g., _It's not fun for children to have to work when they are young._

EXERCISE 17

1. Tell students that this exercise is about effort and costs. Have students read the direction line.
2. Model the exercise. Direct students to the examples in the book. Ask volunteers to complete the statements about themselves.
3. Have students complete the exercise in writing individually. Ask volunteers to share their answers with the class.

🕐 To save class time, have students do half of the exercise in class and complete the other half for homework. Or assign the entire exercise for homework.

EXERCISE 18

1. Tell students that this exercise is about helping others. Have students read the direction line.
2. Model the exercise. Direct students to the example in the book.
3. Have students complete the exercise individually. Then have them check their answers in pairs. If necessary, check answers as a class.

EXERCISE 17 Complete each statement. Begin with *it*.

EXAMPLES   *It's impossible* _____ to be perfect.

It costs me 30¢ a minute _____ to make a long-distance phone call to my hometown.

1. _____ Answers will vary. _____ to work hard.
2. _____ to fall in love.
3. _____ to get married.
4. _____ to make a mistake in English.
5. _____ to be lonely.
6. _____ to help other people.
7. _____ to take a taxi from this school to my house.
8. _____ to eat lunch in a restaurant.
9. _____ to go to college.
10. _____ to buy my textbooks.
11. _____ to learn English.
12. _____ to give away money.
13. _____ to have a lot of friends.
14. _____ to travel.
15. _____ to ride your bike from New York to Boston.

EXERCISE 18 Complete each statement to make them less formal by staring them with *it*.

EXAMPLE   To raise money for charity is a good thing.
It's a good thing to raise money for charity.

1. To ride a bike 500 miles is not easy.
   It's not easy to ride a bike 500 miles.

2. To fight disease takes a lot of money.
   It takes a lot of money to fight disease.

3. To give away money is the responsibility of the rich.
   It's the responsibility of the rich to give away money.

4. To produce high quality public radio takes a lot of money.
   It takes a lot of money to produce high quality public radio.

Expansion

Exercise 17 Have students extend items in the exercise by providing more detail to support their statements, or by contrasting them with other ideas. For example: *It's important to work hard. But it's important to have some fun, too. It doesn't take a lot of time to help other people. You can volunteer an hour or two a week.*

5. To build libraries was Carnegie's dream.

It was Carnegie's dream to build libraries.

6. To raise money for AIDS was Dan Pallotta's goal.

It was Dan Pallotta's goal to raise money for AIDS.

7.8 | Infinitive with *Too* and *Enough*

Too shows that the adjective or adverb is excessive for a specific purpose. *Enough* shows that an adjective, adverb, or noun is sufficient for a specific purpose.

Examples	Explanation
Young Carnegie was **too poor to enter** the library. You drive **too slowly to drive** on the highway. She's **too old to cook** for herself. A volunteer delivers her meals.	Word Order: *too* + adjective / adverb + infinitive
I have **too much work to do,** so I have no time to volunteer. There are **too many problems** in the world **to solve** in one day.	Word Order: *too much* + noncount noun + infinitive *too many* + plural count noun + infinitive
Are you **strong enough to ride** a bike for 500 miles? She trained **hard enough to finish** the AIDS ride.	Word Order: Adjective / adverb + *enough* + infinitive
Carnegie had **enough money to build** libraries. I don't have **enough time to volunteer** this summer.	Word Order: *enough* + noun + infinitive
There is enough volunteer work **for everyone** to do. The bike ride is too hard **for me** to do.	The infinitive phrase can be preceded by *for* + object.
a. I can't volunteer this summer because I'm **too busy.** b. Carnegie could build libraries because he had **enough money.**	Sometimes the infinitive phrase can be omitted. It is understood from the context. a. too busy to volunteer b. enough money to build libraries

7.8 | Infinitive with *Too* and *Enough*

1. Have students cover the grammar chart. Review *too* and *enough*. Say: *My shoes are size 7. Size 8 is too big, and size 6 isn't big enough.* If necessary, tell students that *too* is generally more than necessary or not possible, *enough* is just right, and *not enough* is less than necessary or not possible.

2. Have students review the examples and explanations in the grammar chart.

3. Provide several examples of your own: *I don't have enough time to . . ., I'm not old enough to . . . .* Ask students to provide examples of their own.

Grammar Variation

Have students cover the explanation column in the grammar chart. Ask students to identify the parts of each sentence in the examples (*poor* is an adjective; *to enter* is an infinitive). Then review the explanations.

EXERCISE 19

1. Tell students that this exercise is about using *too*. Have students read the direction line.
2. Direct students to the example in the book. Then have a volunteer complete #1.
3. Have students complete the exercise individually. Check answers as a class.
4. Assess students' performance. If necessary, review grammar chart **7.8** on page 293.

EXERCISE 20

1. Tell students that this exercise is about using *enough*. Have students read the direction line.
2. Direct students to the example in the book. Then have a volunteer complete #1.
3. Have students complete the exercise individually. Check answers as a class.
4. Assess students' performance. If necessary, review grammar chart **7.8** on page 293.

To save class time, have students do half of the exercise in class and complete the other half for homework. Or assign the entire exercise for homework.

EXERCISE 19 Fill in the blanks with *too* + adjective or adverb, or *too many / much* + noun. Answers may vary.

EXAMPLE It's ___too late___ for a student to register for this semester.

1. This lesson is ___too long___ to finish in one class period.
2. The cafeteria is ___too noisy___ for me to study there.
3. Some Americans speak English ___too fast___ for me to understand.
4. The bus is sometimes ___too crowded___ for me to get a seat.
5. It's ___too cold___ to go swimming today.
6. It's ___too hard___ to predict next week's weather.
7. She earns ___too much money___ to qualify for a scholarship.
8. I can't go out with you. I have ___too many things/too much___ to do this afternoon.

EXERCISE 20 Fill in the blanks with *enough* + noun, or adjective / adverb + *enough*. Answers may vary.

EXAMPLE I don't speak English ___well enough___ to be in a college-credit writing course.

1. This exercise is ___easy / short enough___ to finish in a few minutes.
2. I don't type ___well enough___ to write my compositions by computer.
3. He doesn't have ___enough time___ to do all the things he wants to do.
4. She's only 16 years old. She's not ___old enough___ to get married.
5. You didn't run ___fast enough___ to win the race.
6. He doesn't have ___enough money___ to buy a new computer.

Expansion

Exercises 19 and 20 Ask students to discuss ages at which they think people are old enough, or too old/too young, to have various responsibilities and rights. If necessary, provide several prompts: *People who are 18 aren't old enough to . . .* , *People who are over 70 are still young enough to . . . .*

7.9 | Gerunds—An Overview

To form a gerund, put an *-ing* ending on a verb. A gerund is used as a noun (subject or object).

Examples	Explanation
Subject a. **Tennis** is fun. b. **Swimming** is fun. *Object* a. I enjoy **summer.** b. I enjoy **helping** people.	You can use a gerund in the same place you use any subject or object.
Contributing money is one way to help. **Volunteering** can give you a lot of satisfaction.	A gerund (phrase) can be used as the subject of a sentence.
I enjoy **volunteering my time.** I can't imagine **riding a bike** for 500 miles.	A gerund (phrase) can be used as the object of a sentence.
I'm excited *about* **going on a bike trip.** Let's volunteer this summer instead *of* **wasting our time at the beach.**	A gerund (phrase) can be used as the object of a preposition.
Carnegie accused rich people of **not helping** others. **Not being** able to enter a library made Carnegie feel bad.	To make a gerund negative, put *not* before the gerund.
I appreciate **being corrected** when I make a mistake. She enjoys **being treated** like a queen.	A gerund can be passive: *being* + past participle.

HELPING OTHERS GET AN EDUCATION

Before You Read
1. Do you think that all rich people like to live in luxury?
2. Do you know anyone who is very generous?

7.9 | Gerunds—An Overview

1. Have students look at grammar chart 7.9. Ask: *What is a gerund?* (a verb with the *-ing* ending)
2. Have students look at the examples and explanations in the chart.
3. Have students make their own examples beginning with *I enjoy* and a gerund.

Helping Others Get an Education (Reading)

1. Have students look at the photo on page 296. Ask: *Who is this?* (Matel Dawson) *How long did he live?* (81 years)
2. Have students look quickly at the reading on page 296. Ask: *What is the reading about? How do you know?* Have students make predictions.
3. Preteach any vocabulary words your students may not know, such as *philanthropist, investing, fancy, drop out, grateful, lifestyle,* and *shortly.*

BEFORE YOU READ

1. Activate students' prior knowledge about philanthropists. Ask: *What do philanthropists do? Can you name someone who is a philanthropist?*
2. Have students discuss the questions in pairs. Try to pair students of different language backgrounds.
3. Ask a few volunteers to share their answers with the class.

To save class time, skip "Before You Read" or have students prepare answers for homework ahead of time.

Expansion

Theme The topic for this lesson can be enhanced with the following ideas:

1. A Web site about philanthropy or a philanthropist.
2. A Web or magazine article about different types of financial investments, such as: http://www.atg.wa.gov/teenconsumer/finances/investing101.htm
3. Flyer from a local bank or credit union showing investment services

1. Have students first read the text silently. Tell them to pay special attention to gerunds. Then play the audio and have students read along silently.
2. Check students' comprehension. Ask questions such as: *What did Matel Dawson care about? What didn't he care about?* (education and helping others; fancy cars or houses, expensive vacations)

⏱ To save class time, have students do the reading for homework ahead of time.

7.10 | Gerund as Subject

1. Have students review the examples and explanations in the grammar chart.
2. Point out the use of the singular verb with gerunds as subjects, and the placement of *not* (before the gerund).

🎧 Read the following article. Pay special attention to gerunds.

When we think of philanthropists, we usually think of the very rich and famous, like Andrew Carnegie. However, Matel Dawson, who was a forklift driver in Michigan, was an ordinary man who did extraordinary things.

Dawson started **working** at Ford Motor Company in 1940 for $1.15 an hour. By **working** hard, **saving** carefully, and **investing** his money wisely, he became rich. But he didn't care about **owning** expensive cars or **taking** fancy vacations. Instead of **spending** his money on himself, he enjoyed **giving** it away. Since 1995, he donated more than $1 million for college scholarships to help poor students who want to get an education.

Matel Dawson, 1921–2002

Why did Dawson insist on **giving** his money away to college students? One reason was that he did not have the opportunity to finish school. He had to drop out of school after the seventh grade to help support his poor family. He realized the importance of **having** an education and regretted not **having** the opportunity. Also, he learned about **giving** from his parents. He watched them work hard, save their money, and help others less fortunate. His mother made Dawson promise to always give something back. He was grateful to his parents for **teaching** him the importance of **helping** others.

When he became rich, he didn't change his lifestyle. He continued **driving** his old car and **living** in a one-bedroom apartment. And he didn't stop **working** until shortly before he died at the age of 81. When asked why he worked long past the time when most people retire, he replied, "It keeps me **going**, **knowing** I'm helping somebody."

7.10 | Gerund as Subject

Examples	Explanation
Working gave Dawson satisfaction. **Giving away money** made Dawson feel good.	A gerund or a gerund phrase can be the subject of the sentence.
Helping others *gives* a person pleasure.	A gerund subject takes a singular verb.
Not finishing school can affect your whole life.	To make a gerund negative, put *not* before the gerund.

296   Lesson 7

Reading Variation

To practice listening skills, have students first listen to the audio alone. Ask a few comprehension questions. Repeat the audio if necessary. Then have students open their books and read along as they listen to the audio.

Reading Glossary

drop out: leave school permanently
fancy: very nice; very expensive; very decorative
grateful: thankful; appreciative
invest (money): use money to earn money; buy stocks or bonds
lifestyle: way of living; style of living
philanthropist: a person who gives large amounts of money to charity
shortly (before): just; a short time

Grammar Variation

Before looking at the grammar chart, have students write one or two sentences about Matel Dawson beginning with gerunds (e.g., *Giving money away made Mr. Dawson happy. Having a fancy car wasn't important to him.*).

EXERCISE **21** Fill in the blanks with a gerund.

EXAMPLE ___Helping___ others made Dawson feel good.

1. ___Working___ in a factory was not an easy job.
2. Not ___having___ an education always bothered Dawson.
3. ___Getting___ an education is expensive in the U.S.
4. ___Spending___ money didn't give Dawson satisfaction.
5. ___Owning___ an old car was not a problem for Dawson.
6. ___Taking___ a vacation wasn't important for Dawson.
7. ___Knowing___ that he was helping people was very important to Dawson.

EXERCISE **22** Complete each statement.

EXAMPLE Leaving home ___was the most difficult decision I have ever made.___

1. Making new friends ___Answers will vary.___
2. Changing old habits _____
3. Finding an apartment _____
4. Thinking about my future _____
5. Getting a job _____

EXERCISE **23** Complete each statement with a gerund (phrase) as the subject.

EXAMPLE ___Taking a warm bath___ relaxes me at the end of the day.

1. ___Answers will vary.___ is difficult for people who don't speak English.
2. _____ is an important decision in a person's life.
3. _____ is a healthy activity.
4. _____ isn't good for you (is an unhealthy activity).
5. _____ makes me feel proud.

Expansion

Exercise 23 Have students extend the statements in the exercise orally or in writing (e.g., *Walking is a healthy activity because it burns calories and exercises your muscles.*).

7.11 | Gerund After Prepositions and Nouns

1. Have students cover the grammar chart. Brainstorm a list of prepositions. Write the list on the board.

2. Have students review the examples and explanations in the grammar chart. Have students identify the preposition in each example sentence in the first three rows of the chart.

3. Draw students' attention to the list of phrases followed directly by a noun in the last row of the chart.

4. Have students provide examples of their own using *I don't care about . . .* and *I don't spend money . . .* with gerunds. Provide examples of your own.

EXERCISE 24

1. Tell students that this exercise is a chance to ask their classmates questions. Have students read the direction line.

2. Direct students to the example in the book. Ask volunteers to provide other possible questions.

3. Have students complete the questions in writing individually. Then have them work in pairs to alternate asking and answering their questions. Have the student who is answering questions cover the exercise in his or her book.

EXERCISE 25

1. Tell students that this exercise is about their experiences. Have students read the direction line.

2. Direct students to the example in the book. Provide a statement of your own; ask several volunteers to complete the statement for themselves.

3. Have students complete the statements in writing individually. Then have them work in pairs to share their statements. Ask volunteers to share their partners' statements with the class.

4. Assess students' performance. If necessary, review grammar chart **7.11**.

To save class time, have students do half of the exercise in class and complete the other half for homework. Or assign the entire exercise for homework.

7.11 | Gerund After Prepositions and Nouns

Examples	Pattern
Dawson **didn't care about owning** fancy things. He **believed in helping** others.	Verb + preposition + gerund
Carnegie was **famous for building** libraries. Dawson was **concerned about helping** poor college students. Dan Pallotta was **successful at raising** money for AIDS.	Adjective + preposition + gerund
Dawson **thanked his parents for teaching** him to save money.	Verb + object + preposition + gerund
Dawson didn't **spend money going** on vacations or **eating** in expensive restaurants. He didn't **have a hard time saving** money.	A gerund is used directly after the noun in the following expressions: *have a difficult time, have difficulty, have experience, have fun, have a good time, have a hard time, have a problem, have trouble, spend time, spend money*

EXERCISE **24**   Complete the questions with a gerund (phrase). Then ask another student these questions.

EXAMPLE   Are you lazy about _____ *writing compositions?* _____

1. Are you worried about _____ Answers will vary. _____
2. Are you interested in _____
3. Do you ever think about _____
4. Were you excited about _____
5. Do you ever dream about _____

EXERCISE **25**   ABOUT YOU Fill in the blanks with a gerund phrase.

EXAMPLE   I had problems _____ *getting a student loan.* _____

1. I had a hard time _____ Answers will vary. _____
2. I have a lot of experience _____
3. I don't have much experience _____
4. I spent a lot of money _____
5. I don't like to spend my time _____

Expansion

Exercise 24 Have pairs of volunteers ask and answer their questions for the class, or have students work in pairs to extend one of the question and answer sets in the exercise by adding an additional question and answering it.

---

6. I have a lot of fun _____

7. I don't have a good time _____

8. I don't have a problem _____

7.12 | Using the Correct Preposition

It is important to choose the correct preposition after a verb, adjective, or noun.

Preposition Combinations		Common Phrases	Examples
Verb + Preposition	verb + *about*	care about complain about dream about forget about talk about think about worry about	I **care about helping** people. Carnegie **dreamed about opening** public libraries.
	verb + *to*	adjust to look forward to object to	I am **looking forward to volunteering.**
	verb + *on*	depend on insist on plan on	I **insist on helping** my grandmother.
	verb + *in*	believe in succeed in	Does he **believe in giving** to those in need?
Verb + Object + Preposition	verb + object + *of*	accuse . . . of suspect . . . of	He **accused me of leaving** work early.
	verb + object + *for*	apologize to . . . for blame . . . for forgive . . . for thank . . . for	They **thanked me for taking** care of their children.
	verb + object + *from*	keep . . . from prevent . . . from prohibit . . . from stop . . . from	Don't let him **keep you from getting** to your job.
	verb + object + *about*	warn . . . about	The teacher **warned the students about talking** in the library.

(continued)

Infinitives; Gerunds   299

Culture Note

A common, polite way to end a conversation is "I don't want to keep you from getting where you're going" or "Don't let me keep you from finishing your work."

7.12 | Using the Correct Preposition

1. Have students look briefly at the grammar chart. Tell students not to spend too much time on each section of the chart. Ask: *What are the four categories of combinations in the chart?* (verb and preposition, verb and object and preposition, adjective and preposition, noun and preposition)

2. Divide students into four groups. Have each group review a section of the chart. Have groups present some examples from their section to the class.

3. Ask volunteers to give sentences about themselves using one of the phrases in the chart; give one or two examples of your own (e.g., *I have taught this class three times. My parents have visited me twice this year.*).

7.12 | Using the Correct Preposition (*cont.*)

4. Tell students that the phrases in the chart and their uses are best learned by practice; brainstorm ideas for memorizing the phrases and combinations.
5. Draw students' attention to the Language Notes. Review the examples carefully.

Preposition Combinations		Common Phrases	Examples
Adjective + Preposition	adjective + *of*	afraid of capable of guilty of proud of tired of	I'm **afraid of going** out at night.
	adjective + *about*	concerned about excited about upset about worried about	The students are **worried about passing** the exam.
	adjective + *for*	responsible for famous for grateful . . . to . . . for	The victims are **grateful to the** volunteers **for helping.**
	adjective + *at*	good at successful at	Bill Gates is very **good at giving** a lot of money away.
	adjective + *to*	accustomed to used to	I'm not **accustomed to wearing** glasses.
	adjective + *in*	interested in	Are you **interested in getting** a volunteer job?
Noun + Preposition	noun + *of*	in danger of in favor of the purpose of	The students are all **in favor of having** class outside.
	noun + *for*	a need for a reason for an excuse for technique for	What is your **reason for going** home early?

Language Notes:
1. *Plan, afraid,* and *proud* can be followed by an infinitive too.
   I plan **on buying** a laptop. / I plan **to buy** a laptop.
   I'm afraid **of going** out at night. / I'm afraid **to go** out at night.
   He's proud **of being** a volunteer. / He's proud **to be** a volunteer.
2. Notice that in some expressions, *to* is a preposition followed by a gerund, not part of an infinitive.
   Compare:
   I need *to wear* glasses. (infinitive)
   I'm not accustomed *to wearing* glasses. (*to* + gerund)

300   Lesson 7

Grammar Variation

Before presenting the grammar chart, have students underline phrases with prepositions and a gerund in the reading on page 296.

EXERCISE 26 Fill in the blanks with a preposition (if necessary) and the gerund of the verb in parentheses ( ). In some cases, no preposition is necessary.

A: My father's going to retire next month. He's worried _about having_
(example: have)
nothing to do.

B: I don't blame him _for being_ worried. For a lot of people,
(1 be)
their self-worth depends _on working_, and when they
(2 work)
retire, they feel worthless.

A: My mother is afraid that he'll spend all his time _watching_
(3 watch)
TV. Besides, she's not accustomed _to having_ him home
(4 have)
all day.

B: Doesn't he have any interests?

A: Well, he's interested _in gardening_, but he lives in an apartment
(5 garden)
now so he doesn't have a garden. When he had a house, he was always
proud _of having_ the nicest garden on the block.
(6 have)

B: Has he thought _about volunteering_ at the Botanical Gardens?
(7 volunteer)

A: Do they use volunteers?

B: I think so. He would have a great time _working_ there.
(8 work)

A: You're right. He would be good _at giving_ tours because
(9 give)
he knows so much about flowers. This would give him a reason
for getting up in the morning. I'm grateful to you
(10 get)
for giving me this idea. I can't wait to tell him.
(11 give)

B: I'm sure your mother will be grateful too.

EXERCISE 27 ABOUT YOU Ask a question with the words given. Use the correct preposition (if necessary) and a gerund. Another student will answer.

EXAMPLES fond / read
A: Are you fond of reading?
B: Yes, I am.

Infinitives; Gerunds 301

Exercise 26 Variation

To provide practice with listening skills, have students close their books and listen to the audio. Repeat the audio as needed. Ask comprehension questions, such as: *What is person A's father going to do next month?* (retire) *What is he worried about?* (having nothing to do) *How do a lot of people feel when they retire?* (worthless) Then have students open their books and complete Exercise 26.

Expansion

Exercise 26 Have students practice the conversation in pairs. Then ask volunteers to act out the conversation for the class.

Culture Note

Many older people who have retired from their jobs volunteer in their communities. Some programs pair older adults with children who need extra help with schoolwork or children who aren't able to spend time with their own grandparents.

🎧 CD 3, Track 7

1. Tell students that this exercise is a conversation between friends. Have students read the direction line. Ask: *Does every sentence require a preposition?* (no)
2. Direct students to the example in the first sentence. Complete #1 as a class.
3. Have students complete the exercise individually. Have them check their answers by practicing the conversation. If necessary, check the answers as a class.
4. Assess students' performance. If necessary, review grammar chart **7.12** on pages 299 and 300.

1. Tell students that this exercise is a chance to find out more about their partners. Have students read the direction line. Ask: *Does every question require a preposition?* (no)
2. Direct students to the example in the book. Ask several students the question.
3. Have students complete the exercise orally in pairs, alternating asking and answering questions. Have the student who is answering questions cover the exercise in his or her book.
4. Assess students' performance. If necessary, review grammar chart **7.12** on pages 299 and 300.

🕐 To save class time, have students do half of the exercise in class and complete the other half in writing for homework. Or if students do not need speaking practice, the entire exercise may be skipped or done in writing.

7.13 | Verbs Followed by Gerunds

1. Have students cover grammar chart **7.13**. Say: *Tell me something you enjoy doing; something you avoid doing; something you recommend doing.* Elicit several examples from volunteers. Say: *Enjoy, avoid, and* recommend *are verbs that can be followed by a gerund.* Ask students if they can name other verbs that can be followed by a gerund.

2. Have students review the examples, explanations, and word lists in the grammar chart. Clarify any vocabulary students are unfamiliar with. Provide examples of your own using verbs in the list: *I dislike having the radio on while I'm eating. I don't mind helping my children with their homework.* Ask volunteers to give sentences about themselves using the verbs in the list.

3. Draw students' attention to the Language Notes. Go over the explanations and examples.

---

care / get a good grade

A: Do you care about getting a good grade?
B: Of course I do.

1. **have trouble / understand spoken English**
   Do you have trouble understanding spoken English?
2. **lazy / do the homework**
   Are you lazy about doing the homework?
3. **have a technique / learn new words**
   Do you have a technique for learning new words?
4. **afraid / fail this course**
   Are you afraid of failing this course?
5. **good / spell English words**
   Are you good at spelling English words?
6. **interested / study computer programming**
   Are you interested in studying computer programming?
7. **have experience / work with computers**
   Do you have experience working with computers?
8. **think / buy a house some day**
   Are you thinking about buying a house some day?

7.13 | Verbs Followed by Gerunds

Examples	Explanation
Dawson enjoyed **giving** money away. He couldn't imagine not **helping** others. Students appreciate **receiving** financial aid.	Many verbs are followed by a gerund.

The following verbs take a gerund.

admit	delay	finish	permit	recommend
advise	deny	imagine	postpone	resent
appreciate	discuss	keep (on)	practice	risk
avoid	dislike	mind[2]	put off[3]	stop
can't help[1]	enjoy	miss	quit	suggest
consider				

Do you **go shopping** every day? Do you like to **go fishing**?	*Go* + gerund is used in many idiomatic expressions of sport and recreation.

Below are expressions with *go* + gerund.

go boating	go fishing	go sailing	go skiing
go bowling	go hiking	go shopping	go swimming
go camping	go hunting	go sightseeing	
go dancing	go jogging	go skating	

Language Notes:
[1] *Can't help* means to have no control: When I see a sad movie, I *can't help* crying.
[2] I *mind* means that something bothers me. I *don't mind* means that something is OK with me; it doesn't bother me: Do you *mind* living with your parents? No, I don't *mind*.
[3] *Put off* means postpone: I can't *put off* buying a car. I need one now.

302   Lesson 7

Grammar Variation

Have students use the expressions with *go* in the chart to talk about themselves using the present perfect and simple past tenses (e.g., *I've never gone hunting; I went sightseeing when I was in New York last year.*).

EXERCISE **28** Fill in the blanks to complete these statements about the reading on Matel Dawson. Answers may vary.

EXAMPLE Matel Dawson liked ___*helping students.*___

1. He regretted not ___*finishing school.*___

2. Students appreciated ___*receiving money*___ from Dawson.

3. He didn't mind ___*driving*___ an old car.

4. He couldn't imagine not ___*working*___, so he didn't retire.

5. He didn't mind ___*living*___ in a small apartment.

6. He kept on ___*working*___ until shortly before he died at the age of 81.

EXERCISE **29** ABOUT YOU Complete the sentences with a gerund (phrase).

EXAMPLE I avoid ___*walking alone at night.*___

1. The teacher doesn't permit ___Answers will vary.___

2. I don't mind _____

3. It's difficult to quit _____

4. I enjoy _____

5. I don't enjoy _____

6. I can't imagine _____

7. I don't like to go _____

8. I avoid _____

9. I appreciate _____

10. I often put off _____

Expansion

Exercise 29 Have students create new statements making a contrast from the prompts (except for #2). Model an example: *I avoid eating fried foods, but I don't avoid spicy foods.*

1. Tell students that this exercise is about Matel Dawson. Have students read the direction line.
2. Direct students to the example in the book.
3. Have students complete the exercise individually. Have students compare their answers in pairs. Check answers as a class.

EXERCISE 29

1. Tell students that this exercise is about their feelings and thoughts. Have students read the direction line. Ask: *What do we use in the sentences?* (a gerund or gerund phrase)
2. Review the example. Ask several volunteers to complete the example for themselves.
3. Have students complete the exercise individually in writing. Have students compare answers in pairs. Have pairs share interesting answers with the class.

To save class time, have students do half of the exercise in class and complete the other half for homework. Or assign the entire exercise for homework.

7.14 | Verbs Followed by Gerund or Infinitive

1. Have students look at the grammar chart. Review the examples and explanations.
2. Draw students' attention to the Language Note. Review the list of verbs that can be followed by a gerund or an infinitive.
3. Have students make their own sentences with the verbs in the list and either a gerund or an infinitive (e.g., *I started to volunteer at the animal shelter a few years ago; I want to continue helping there after I retire.*).

EXERCISE 30

1. Tell students that this exercise is about gerunds and infinitives. Have students read the direction line.
2. Have students complete the exercise individually and check their work in pairs. If necessary, check answers as a class.
3. Assess students' performance. If necessary, review grammar chart **7.14**.

EXERCISE 31

🎧 *CD 3, Track 8*

1. Tell students that this exercise is about a teenager's plans for the summer. Have students read the direction line. Ask: *Who is talking?* (a teenager and his older brother)
2. Model the exercise. Direct students to the example in the book.
3. Have students complete the exercise individually and then check their answers by practicing the conversation. If necessary, check answers as a class.

🕐 To save class time, have students do half of the exercise in class and complete the other half for homework. Or assign the entire exercise for homework.

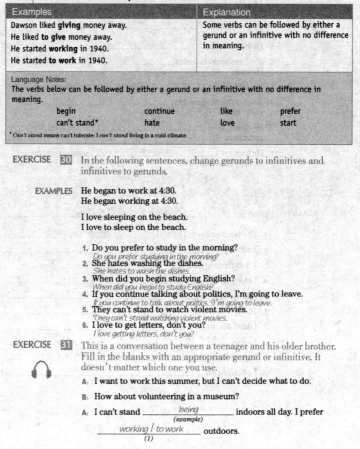

Grammar Variation

Have students cover the grammar chart. Write the eight verbs in the Language Note on the board. Ask students to write examples using the verbs on the board. Then convert each gerund to an infinitive and each infinitive to a gerund and write the new sentences. Say: *These verbs can be followed by an infinitive or a gerund.*

Exercise 31 Variation

To provide practice with listening skills, have students close their books and listen to the audio. Repeat the audio as needed. Ask comprehension questions, such as: *What does the teenager want to do this summer?* (work) *Why doesn't he want to volunteer in a museum?* (He can't stand being indoors all day.) *Why does the older brother suggest volunteering to teach kids how to swim?* (because the teenager is a great swimmer) Then have students open their books and complete Exercise 31.

B: Well, what do you like?

A: I love _____ being / to be _____ at the beach.
            (3)

B: Maybe you should get a job as a lifeguard.

A: Great idea! I'll start _____ looking / to look _____ for a job tomorrow.
                         (4)

B: That's what you said yesterday.

A: I guess I'm lazy. I just don't like _____ looking / to look for a job _____.
                                        (5)

7.15 | Infinitive and Gerund as Subject

Examples	Explanation
It is expensive **to go** to college. **It** is important **to have** a college education. **It** makes me feel good **to give** money to poor people.	An infinitive phrase can be the subject of a sentence. We usually begin the sentence with *it* and put the infinitive phrase at the end of the sentence.
Going to college is expensive. **Having** a college education is important. **Giving** money to poor people makes me feel good.	A gerund phrase can be used as the subject.
To pay for college is difficult for most families. **To build** libraries was Carnegie's dream. **To give** money away is the best thing rich people can do, according to Carnegie.	Sometimes we begin a sentence with an infinitive phrase. A sentence that begins with an infinitive is very formal.

EXERCISE 32   Change these statements. Change the subject to a gerund form.

EXAMPLE   It is wonderful to help others.
           Helping others is wonderful.

1. It costs a lot of money to go to college.
   Going to college costs a lot of money.

2. It is hard to work and study at the same time.
   Working and studying at the same time is hard.

3. It is important to invest your money wisely.
   Investing your money wisely is important.

4. It is difficult to work in a factory.
   Working in a factory is difficult.

5. It can be boring to do the same thing every day.
   Doing the same thing every day can be boring.

Infinitives; Gerunds   305

7.15 Infinitive and Gerund as Subject

1. Have students cover grammar chart **7.15.** Ask students to provide examples of their own of sentences with a gerund or infinitive as subject; remind students that they looked at these in grammar chart **7.7** on page 290 and grammar chart **7.10** on page 296. If necessary, provide several examples of your own (e.g., *Driving is an important skill. It's wonderful to have friends you can count on.*).

2. Have students review the grammar chart.

EXERCISE 32

1. Tell students that this exercise is about earning and giving money. Have students read the direction line. Ask: *What do we write?* (a gerund form)

2. Direct students to the example in the book. Complete #1 as a class.

3. Have students complete the exercise individually and compare their answers in pairs. If necessary, check answers with the class.

Expansion

Exercise 31 Have students practice the conversation in pairs. Then ask volunteers to act out the conversation for the class.

Expansion

Exercise 32 Have students look back at Exercise 15 on page 290. Have them convert the sentences they wrote in the exercise to sentences with gerunds.

7.16 | Gerund or Infinitive After a Verb: Differences in Meaning

1. Have students cover the grammar chart. Ask: *What did we learn about in grammar chart 7.14?* (verbs that can be followed by a gerund or an infinitive with no difference in meaning) Say: *Three verbs that do have a difference in meaning between a gerund and an infinitive are* stop, remember, *and* try. On the board, write:
A: I tried to call my sister, but she wasn't home.
B: Try calling her cell phone.
Tell students that *try* in the first sentence means *make an effort* and *try* in the second sentence means *experiment*.

2. Have students look at the grammar chart. Review the example sentences and explanations carefully.

EXERCISE 33

1. Tell students that this exercise is about learning and trying. Have students read the direction line. Ask: *What do we write?* (a gerund or infinitive)

2. Model the exercise using the examples in the book. Complete items 1 and 2 with the class.

3. Have students complete the exercise individually. Then have them compare their answers in pairs. Finally, check the answers as a class.

4. Assess students' performance. If necessary, review grammar chart **7.16**.

---

6. It is satisfying to help others.
   Helping others is satisfying.

7. It is a challenge to ride a bike for 500 miles.
   Riding a bike 500 miles is a challenge.

8. It is necessary to ask viewers to contribute to public TV.
   Asking viewers to contribute to public TV is necessary.

7.16 | Gerund or Infinitive After a Verb: Differences in Meaning

After *stop, remember,* and *try,* the meaning of the sentence depends on whether you follow the verb with a gerund or an infinitive.

Examples	Explanation
a. Dawson loved to work. He didn't **stop working** until he was 80.	a. *Stop* + gerund = Quit or discontinue an activity
b. Dawson wanted to finish school, but he **stopped to get** a job.	b. *Stop* + infinitive = Quit one activity in order to start another activity
a. Do you **remember reading** about Carnegie?	a. *Remember* + gerund = Remember that something happened earlier
b. Dawson's mother said, "Always **remember to help** other people."	b. *Remember* + infinitive = Remember something and then do it
a. Dawson has always had a simple lifestyle. When he became rich, he **tried living** a fancier lifestyle, but it didn't bring him satisfaction. a. I always write my compositions by hand. I **tried writing** them on a computer, but I don't type fast enough. b. Carnegie **tried to enter** a library when he was young, but he was told it was for members only. b. Mary **tried to ride** her bike 500 miles, but she couldn't.	a. *Try* + gerund = Experiment with something new. You do something one way, and then, if that doesn't work, you try a different method. b. *Try* + infinitive = Make an effort or an attempt

EXERCISE **33** Fill in the blanks with the gerund or infinitive of the verb in parentheses ( ).

EXAMPLES Stop ___*bothering*___ me. I'm trying to study.
(bother)

The teacher always says, "Remember ___*to do*___ your homework."
(do)

1. When the teacher came in, the students stopped ___*talking*___ .
(talk)

2. When you learn more English, you will stop ___*using*___ your
(use)
dictionary so much.

3. When you're tired of studying, stop ___*to take*___ a break.
(take)

Grammar Variation

Have students cover the explanation column of the grammar chart. Review the examples with students. Ask students to try to figure out the difference between the examples with gerunds and the examples with infinitives.

4. I saw my friend in the hall, and I stopped _to speak_ to her.
   (speak)

5. My sister and I had a fight, and we stopped _speaking_
   (speak)

   to each other. We haven't spoken to each other for two weeks.

6. Cyclists in the AIDS ride often stop _to rest_ .
   (rest)

7. If they are tired, they can stop _riding_ their bicycles.
   (ride)

8. There's a van that will stop _to pick_ up tired cyclists.
   (pick)

9. The teacher usually remembers _to return_ the homework papers.
   (return)

10. You should remember _to use_ an infinitive after certain verbs.
    (use)

11. Will you remember _to do_ the homework during spring break?
    (do)

12. Do you remember _learning_ the passive voice last month?
    (learn)

13. Remember _to use_ the passive voice when the subject does
    (use)

    not perform the action of the verb.

14. I remember not _understanding_ much English a few years ago.
    (understand)

15. I remember _studying_ the present perfect tense even
    (study)

    though I don't always use it correctly.

16. I always try _to learn_ a few new words every day.
    (learn)

17. I need more money. I'm going to try _to find_ a part-time job.
    (find)

18. Susan tried _to ride_ her bike 100 miles, but she couldn't
    (ride)

    because she was out of shape.

19. I need to find out information about a new bike. I went to the
    company's Web site, but I couldn't find the information I needed. I

    tried _e-mailing_ the Webmaster, but I got no answer. I tried
    (e-mail)

    calling the phone number on the Web site, but I didn't get a
    (call)

    person to talk to. I tried _sending_ a letter by postal mail. I'm
    (send)

    still waiting for an answer.

Culture Note

The person in item 5 says *we stopped speaking to each other*. When people say that they are
not speaking to someone, it usually means that they are very angry with that person
temporarily. People say: *I'm not speaking to my brother.* Or *My sister and I aren't speaking.*
People usually don't say: *I'm not talking to my sister.*

🎧 *CD 3, Track 9*

1. Tell students that this exercise is a conversation between a mother and her son. Have students read the direction line.
2. Model the exercise. Direct students to the example in the book.
3. Have students complete Exercise 34 individually. Then have them check their answers in pairs by practicing the conversation. Circulate and observe the pair work. If necessary, check the answers as a class.
4. Assess students' performance. If necessary, review grammar chart **7.16** on page 306.

🕐 To save class time, have students do half of the exercise in class and complete the other half for homework. Or assign the entire exercise for homework.

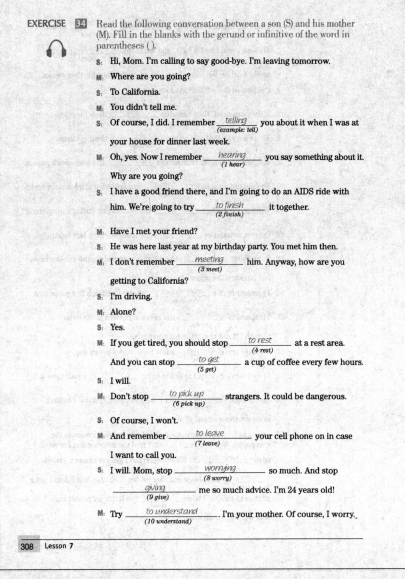

EXERCISE **34** Read the following conversation between a son (S) and his mother (M). Fill in the blanks with the gerund or infinitive of the word in parentheses ( ).

S: Hi, Mom. I'm calling to say good-bye. I'm leaving tomorrow.

M: Where are you going?

S: To California.

M: You didn't tell me.

S: Of course, I did. I remember ___*telling*___ you about it when I was at
   (example: tell)
   your house for dinner last week.

M: Oh, yes. Now I remember ___*hearing*___ you say something about it.
   (1 hear)
   Why are you going?

S: I have a good friend there, and I'm going to do an AIDS ride with
   him. We're going to try ___*to finish*___ it together.
   (2 finish)

M: Have I met your friend?

S: He was here last year at my birthday party. You met him then.

M: I don't remember ___*meeting*___ him. Anyway, how are you
   (3 meet)
   getting to California?

S: I'm driving.

M: Alone?

S: Yes.

M: If you get tired, you should stop ___*to rest*___ at a rest area.
   (4 rest)
   And you can stop ___*to get*___ a cup of coffee every few hours.
   (5 get)

S: I will.

M: Don't stop ___*to pick up*___ strangers. It could be dangerous.
   (6 pick up)

S: Of course, I won't.

M: And remember ___*to leave*___ your cell phone on in case
   (7 leave)
   I want to call you.

S: I will. Mom, stop ___*worrying*___ so much. And stop
   (8 worry)
   ___*giving*___ me so much advice. I'm 24 years old!
   (9 give)

M: Try ___*to understand*___. I'm your mother. Of course, I worry.
   (10 understand)

Exercise 34 Variation

To provide practice with listening skills, have students close their books and listen to the audio. Repeat the audio as needed. Ask comprehension questions, such as: *Why did the son call his mother?* (to say good-bye) *What is he doing tomorrow?* (leaving for California) *When did the son tell his mother about the trip?* (when he was at her house for dinner last week) Then have students open their books and complete Exercise 34.

Expansion

Exercise 34 Tell students that the mother in this conversation has a lot of advice for her son. Have students work in groups to make a list of the advice she gives him, and then add advice they think a person traveling a long distance should follow. Have groups share their advice with the class.

MIMI'S BIKE RIDE

Before You Read

1. After reading the articles in this lesson, can you think of ways you'd like to volunteer to help others?
2. What do you think motivates people to volunteer?

 Read the following personal account of Mimi, a woman who went on several AIDS rides. Pay special attention to *used to*, *be used to*, and *get used to*.

Before I went on my AIDS ride, I **used to think** that one person's contribution is not very important. But I was wrong. In 1998, I went on my first AIDS ride in California, from San Francisco to Los Angeles.

Even though I bike to and from work every day (20 miles round trip), I **wasn't used to riding** long distances. Also, I live in Chicago, where the land is flat, so I **wasn't used to riding** in hills and mountains. I trained for about six months before the ride, riding at least 150 miles a week.

I **used to own** a ten-speed road bike, but I realized that I would need something better for the long, hilly ride. I bought a new 24-speed mountain bike. This new bicycle helped me a lot in the California trip. It was so satisfying to complete the ride. I raised almost $5,000 for AIDS research. I felt so good about it that I started looking for more rides to do.

In 2001, I did the Alaska ride, which was especially difficult. It was much colder than expected. Some of the riders **couldn't get used to** the cold and had to quit. But I'm proud to say that I finished it and went on to do four more AIDS rides.

Infinitives; Gerunds   309

Expansion

Theme The topic for this lesson can be enhanced with the following ideas:

1. A flyer or newspaper article listing volunteer opportunities
2. Newspaper or Web articles about bicycle rides, walks, or other charity fund raisers
3. Articles about other fundraising trends, such as ribbons for breast cancer awareness or bracelets for cancer research

Reading Variation

To practice listening skills, have students first listen to the audio alone. Ask a few comprehension questions. Repeat the audio if necessary. Then have students open their books and read along as they listen to the audio.

Reading Glossary

bike: ride a bicycle
round trip: travel from one place to another and then back again
ten-speed road bike: a bicycle with a choice of ten gears, for riding on roads
24-speed mountain bike: a heavier bicycle with a choice of 24 gears, for riding on dirt, rocky trails, etc.

Mimi's Bike Ride (Reading)

1. Have students look at the photo. Ask: *What are the people in the photo doing?* (riding bicycles) *Are they riding in the city or in the country?* (in the country)
2. Have students look quickly at the reading. Ask: *What is the reading about? How do you know?* Have students make predictions.
3. Preteach any vocabulary words your students may not know, such as *bike, round trip, ten-speed road bike,* and *24-speed mountain bike.*

BEFORE YOU READ

1. Activate students' prior knowledge about bicycle rides for charity. Ask: *Where was the AIDS ride we read about earlier in this lesson?* (from San Francisco to Los Angeles) *How many miles was it?* (525 miles)
2. Have students discuss the questions in pairs. Try to pair students of different language backgrounds.
3. Ask a few volunteers to share their answers with the class.

To save class time, skip "Before You Read" or have students prepare answers for homework ahead of time.

Reading CD 3, Track 10

1. Have students first read the text silently. Tell them to pay special attention to *used to, be used to,* and *get used to.* Then play the audio and have students read along silently.
2. Check students' comprehension. Ask questions such as: *What did Mimi do to get ready for the ride?* (She bought a new bike; she trained for six months; she rode 150 miles a week.) *How many AIDS rides has Mimi done?* (six)

To save class time, have students do the reading for homework ahead of time.

7.17 | Used To / Be Used To / Get Used To

1. Have students cover the grammar chart. Say: *Ten years ago, I rode my bike a lot. Now I don't ride it very often. I used to ride my bike a lot. I moved here six years ago. I didn't like the weather at first, but now I'm used to it. In my hometown, there wasn't a lot of traffic. I had to get used to driving in traffic when I came here.* Write the sentences with *used to* on the board; underline *used to* and *get used to.* Ask: *Are all of these the same?* (no)

2. Have students review the examples and explanations in the grammar chart carefully. Point out the different meanings of *used to.* Point out the negative *didn't use to* in the first row of the grammar chart.

3. Ask students to provide examples of their own. Say: *Tell me something you used to do that you don't do now. Tell me something you are used to doing now. Tell me something you had to get used to when you came to the U.S.* Write several examples on the board (e.g., *Natalia had to get used to living in an apartment.*).

4. Draw students' attention to the Pronunciation Note. Have students practice pronouncing *used to* correctly.

EXERCISE 35

1. Tell students that this exercise is about things people used to do. Have students read the direction line.

2. Direct students to the example in the book.

3. Have students complete the rest of the exercise individually, and then compare answers in pairs. If necessary, check answers as a class.

7.17 | *Used To / Be Used To / Get Used To*

Used to + base form and *be used to* + gerund have completely different meanings.

Examples	Explanation
Mimi **used to** own a ten-speed bike. Now she owns a 24-speed bike. She **used to** think that one person couldn't make a difference. Now she knows that every person's contribution counts. Libraries **used to be** for rich people only. Now anyone can use the library. I didn't **use to** speak English at all. Now I speak it fairly well.	*Used to* + base form shows that an activity was repeated or habitual in the past. This activity has been discontinued. For the negative, use *didn't use to.* Note: Omit the *d* in the negative.
Mimi **is used to riding** her bike in Chicago, which is flat. She **is used to riding** in nice weather. She **isn't used to** cold wind in August.	*Be used to* + gerund or noun means "be accustomed to." The sentences to the left describe a person's habits. They show what is normal and comfortable. For the negative, use *be + not + used to.*
Some of the riders **couldn't get used to** the cold and wind and had to quit. Dawson **couldn't get used to spending** money on himself. I'm from Arizona. I **can't get used to** the cold Chicago winters. My friend comes from India, where they drive on the left side of the street. He had to **get used to driving** on the right side in the U.S.	*Get used to* + gerund or noun means "become accustomed to." Often we use *can, can't, could,* or *couldn't* before *get used to.* For the negative, use *can't* or *couldn't get used to.* Do not omit the *d* in the negative.

Pronunciation Note:
The **d** in *used to* is not pronounced.

EXERCISE 35 Finish these statements. Answers may vary.

EXAMPLE I used to _____*go everywhere by bus*_____, but now I have a car and drive everywhere.

1. My uncle used to _____Answers will vary._____, but now he's rich.

2. I used to _____ a stick shift car, but now I drive an automatic.

3. They used to _____ an apartment, but now they have a house.

4. When she was younger, she used to _____, but now she stays home on Saturday nights.

Grammar Variation

After students have reviewed the example sentences in the grammar chart, have them go back to the reading on page 309 and identify which explanation applies to each boldfaced phrase in the reading.

5. He used to _____ money on foolish things, but now he saves his money.

6. My college used to _____ Northeast College, but they changed the name. Now it's called Kennedy College.

EXERCISE 36 ABOUT YOU Write sentences comparing the way you used to live with the way you live now.

EXAMPLES *I used to live with my whole family. Now I live alone.*

I used to work in a restaurant. Now I'm a full-time student.

I didn't use to speak English at all. Now I speak English pretty well.

Ideas for sentences:

| school | job | hobbies | fashions |
| apartment / house | family life | friends | |

1. _____ Answers will vary. _____

2. _____

3. _____

4. _____

5. _____

EXERCISE 37 A student wrote about things that are new for her in the U.S. Fill in the blanks with a gerund or a noun.

EXAMPLE I'm not used to _shopping in large supermarkets_. In my native country, I shopped in small stores.

1. I'm not used to _____ *living in* _____ a small apartment. In my native country, we lived in a big house.

2. I'm not used to _____ *being cold/cold weather* _____. In my native country, it's warm all year round.

3. I'm not used to _____ *being* _____ a student. I'm 35 years old, and I've been out of school for 15 years.

4. I'm not used to _____ *speaking American English* _____. I studied British English in my native country.

5. I'm not used to _____ *shopping/working* _____ on Sundays. In my native country, Sunday is a day when people rest, not shop and do laundry.

6. I'm not used to _____ *talking* _____ in class. In my native country, the teacher talks and the students only listen and write.

7. I'm not used to _____ *driving* _____ on the right side of the road. In my native country, we drive on the left side of the road.

Infinitives; Gerunds   311

EXERCISE 36

1. Tell students that this exercise is about comparing their lives before and their lives now. Have students read the direction line.
2. Direct students to the examples in the book.
3. Have students complete the exercise individually. Ask volunteers to share their statements with the class.

EXERCISE 37

1. Tell students that this exercise is about a student getting used to a new country. Have students read the direction line. Ask: *What do we write?* (a gerund or a noun)
2. Direct students to the example in the book.
3. Have students complete the exercise individually and compare their answers in pairs. If necessary, check answers as a class.
4. Assess students' performance. If necessary, review grammar chart **7.17** on page 310.

⊙ To save class time, have students do half of the exercise in class and complete the other half for homework. Or assign the entire exercise for homework.

Expansion

Exercise 36 Have students take turns interviewing each other in pairs about their answers to the exercise using *prefer.* Here's an example:

A: I used to have a full-time job. Now I work part-time.

B: Which one do you prefer?

A: I prefer working part-time.

B: Why?

A: Because I can spend more time with my children.

EXERCISE 38

1. Tell students that this exercise is about things they aren't used to. Have students read the direction line.
2. Review the example in the book. Ask: *Is this true for you?*
3. Have students complete the exercise individually. Have students read their sentences to a partner. Then have partners report interesting answers to the class.
4. Assess students' performance. If necessary, review grammar chart **7.17** on page 310.

EXERCISE 39

1. Tell students that this exercise is about things that it was hard for them to get used to. Have students read the direction line.
2. Direct students to the examples in the book. Have volunteers read the examples. Ask: *Is this true for you?*
3. Have students complete the exercise. Ask volunteers to share their answers with the class.
4. Assess students' performance. If necessary, review grammar chart **7.17** on page 310.

To save class time, have students do the exercise for homework.

EXERCISE 40

∩ *CD 3, Track 11*

1. Tell students that this exercise is about a woman who did the Alaska AIDS ride. Have students read the direction line.
2. Have students complete the exercise and check their answers in pairs.
3. Assess students' performance. If necessary, review grammar chart **7.17** on page 310.

To save class time, have students do half of the exercise in class and complete the other half for homework. Or assign the entire exercise for homework.

EXERCISE 38 ABOUT YOU Fill in the blanks to make three different sentences beginning with "I'm not used to . . ."

EXAMPLE *I'm not used to wearing a coat in the winter.*

1. _____ Answers will vary. _____
2. _____
3. _____

EXERCISE 39 ABOUT YOU Fill in the blanks with three different answers.

EXAMPLES When I came to this city, it was hard for me to get used to:

living in a small apartment.

American pronunciation.

When I came to this city, it was hard for me to get used to:

1. _____ Answers will vary. _____
2. _____
3. _____

EXERCISE 40 Here is a story of a San Francisco woman who did the Alaska AIDS ride. Circle the correct words in parentheses ( ) to complete the story.

In 2000 I went on the AIDS bike ride in Alaska. My friends told me about it and asked me to join them. At first I was afraid. My friends are good bike riders. They (used to / *are used to*) (ride / *riding*) long distances because they do it all the time. They persuaded me to try it because it was for such a good cause.

To get ready for the ride, I had to make some lifestyle changes. (*I'm* / *I*) used to be a little overweight, so I had to slim down and get in shape. First, I went on a diet. (*I* / *I'm*) used to a lot of meat, but now I try to eat mostly vegetables and fish. Also, I decided to get more exercise. I used to (*take* / taking) the bus to work every day, but I decided to start riding my bike to work. I work ten miles from home, so it was hard for me at first. But little by little, I (*got used to* / used to) it.

On the weekends, I started to take longer rides. Eventually I got used to (ride / *riding*) about 45–50 miles a day.

312 Lesson 7

Expansion

Exercises 38 and 39 Have students work in pairs to tell each other about things they aren't used to and had a hard time getting used to. Ask students to write information they don't mind sharing. Then have students write a paragraph about their partners using the information in the exercises. Collect the paragraphs and read them to the class. Have students guess which student is being described.

Exercise 40 Variation

To provide practice with listening skills, have students close their books and listen to the audio. Repeat the audio as needed. Ask comprehension questions, such as: *What did the woman do in 2000?* (She went on the AIDS bike ride in Alaska.) *How did she feel when her friends first asked her to join the bike ride?* (afraid) *How often do her friends ride long distances?* (all the time) Then have students open their books and complete Exercise 40.

When the time came for the AIDS ride, I thought I was prepared. I live in San Francisco, which is hilly, so I was used to (*ride* / *riding*) up and down hills. But it's not cold in San Francisco. On some days the temperature in Alaska was only 25 degrees (F) with strong winds. At first I (*wasn't* / *couldn't*) get used to the cold and sometimes had to ride in the van. It was especially hard to (*used* / *get used*) to the strong winds. But little by little, I got (*use* / *used*) to it.

I am proud to say I was one of the 1,600 riders who finished the ride. I didn't (*use* / *used*) to think that one person could make a difference, but I raised close to $4,000. As a group we raised $4 million. And I've become a much healthier person because of this experience.

GLOBAL VOLUNTEERS

Before You Read
1. Do you ever think about all the poor people in the world?
2. How can we help poor people in other countries?

 Read the following article. Pay special attention to base forms and -*ing* forms after sense-perception verbs (*see, listen, hear*. etc.).

When Michele Gran and Bud Philbrook were planning to get married in 1979, they were planning to take a relaxing honeymoon cruise. But whenever Michele turned on the news, she **saw** people **living** in poverty. She **saw** children **go** without proper nutrition and education. Instead of their planned honeymoon, Michele suggested that they spend a week helping poor people in Guatemala.

When their friends and relatives **listened** to them **tell** about their unusual honeymoon, they became interested in how they could also help. In 1984, Bud and Michele established Global Volunteers, an organization that helps people throughout the world. Since then, they have sent almost 13,000 volunteers to 25 countries. Volunteers work together with the local people on projects, such as building schools in Ghana or taking care of orphans in Romania.

Bud used to practice law and Michele used to work in state government, but in the early '90s, they quit their jobs to spend all their time with Global Volunteers.

Infinitives; Gerunds   313

Expansion

Theme The topic for this lesson can be enhanced with the following ideas:

1. An article or copy of a Web page about Global Volunteers or other short-term or longer-term international volunteer organizations (e.g., the Peace Corps)
2. A mail solicitation from an international organization showing the cost of feeding or immunizing children, providing health or school supplies, etc.

Reading Variation

To practice listening skills, have students first listen to the audio alone. Ask a few comprehension questions. Repeat the audio if necessary. Then have students open their books and read along as they listen to the audio.

Reading Glossary

cruise: a vacation on a large, luxurious ship
honeymoon: trip people take after they get married
nutrition: healthy food to eat
orphan: a child whose parents have died

Global Volunteers (Reading)

1. Have students look at the photo. Ask: *Where do you think these people are? What do you think the man is doing?*
2. Have students look quickly at the reading. Ask: *What is the reading about? How do you know?* Have students make predictions.
3. Preteach any vocabulary words your students may not know, such as *cruise, nutrition, honeymoon,* and *orphans.*

BEFORE YOU READ

1. Activate students' prior knowledge about international volunteers. Ask: *Can you name any international volunteer agencies? What kind of work do they do?*
2. Have students discuss the questions in pairs. Try to pair students of different language backgrounds.
3. Ask a few volunteers to share their answers with the class.

🕐 To save class time, skip "Before You Read" or have students prepare answers for homework ahead of time.

Reading 🎧 CD 3, Track 12

1. Have students first read the text silently. Tell them to pay special attention to base forms and -*ing* forms after *see, listen,* and *hear.* Then play the audio and have students read along silently.
2. Check students' comprehension. Ask questions such as: *How did Michele Gran and Bud Philbrook spend their honeymoon?* (helping poor people in Guatemala) *What did Bud and Michele do before they started Global Volunteers?* (Bud used to practice law; Michele used to work in state government.)

🕐 To save class time, have students do the reading for homework ahead of time.

7.18 | Sense-Perception Verbs

1. Have students cover the grammar chart. Brainstorm with the class a list of sense-perception verbs. Say: *Tell me all the verbs you can think of that we use to talk about our senses.* Write the verbs on the board.
2. Have students review the examples and explanations in the grammar chart. Point out the meaning of *slight difference* (a very small difference). Ask: *What did you notice or see people doing on your way to school today? What did you see your parents do when you were young?*

 CD 3, Track 13

1. Tell students that this exercise is about one person's parents and the lessons they taught him or her about charity. Have students read the direction line.
2. Direct students to the example in the book. Have a volunteer complete #1.
3. Have students complete the exercise individually. Check answers as a class.
4. Assess students' performance. If necessary, review grammar chart **7.18** on page 314.

7.18 | Sense-Perception Verbs

After sense-perception verbs (*hear, listen to, feel, smell, see, watch, observe*), we can use either the *-ing* form or the base form with only a slight difference in meaning.

a. Their friends **listened to** them **tell** about their unusual honeymoon. b. Matel Dawson **saw** his mother **work** hard.	The base form shows that a person sensed (*saw, heard,* etc.) something from start to finish. a. They listened to Bud and Michele tell the whole story. b. All his life, Dawson saw his mother's work habits.
a. Michele **saw** people **living** in poverty. b. When I entered the classroom, I **heard** the teacher **talking** about volunteer programs.	The *-ing* form shows that something is sensed while it is in progress. a. Michele saw people while they were living in poverty. b. I heard the teacher while she was talking about volunteer programs.

EXERCISE **41** Fill in the blanks with the base form of *-ing* form of the verb in parentheses ( ). In many cases, both forms are possible.

By their example, my parents always taught me to help others. One time when I was a child going to a birthday party with my father, we saw a small boy ___walking___ alone on the street. As we approached him, we
(example: walk)

heard him ___crying___. My father went up to him and asked him
(1 cry)

what was wrong. The boy said that he was lost. I saw my father ___take___ his hand and heard him ___tell / telling___ the boy
(2 take) (3 tell)

that he would help him find his parents. My father called the police on his cell phone. Even though we were in a hurry to go to the party, my father insisted on staying with the boy until the police arrived. I really wanted to go to the party and started to cry. I felt my father ___take___ my hand and talk to me softly. He said, "We
(4 take)

can't enjoy the party while this little boy is alone and helpless." Before the police arrived, I saw a woman ___running / run___ frantically in
(5 run)

our direction. It was the boy's mother. She was so grateful to my father for helping her son that she offered to give him money. I heard my father ___tell / telling___ her, "I can't take money from you. I'm happy to
(6 tell)

be of help to your son."

Grammar Variation

Have students match the verbs in boldface in the reading on page 313 to the appropriate explanation in the grammar chart.

Exercise 41 Variation

To provide practice with listening skills, have students close their books and listen to the audio. Repeat the audio as needed. Ask comprehension questions, such as: *Why was the small boy crying?* (because he was lost) *What did the father do to the boy?* (He took his hand and told the boy that he would help him find his parents.) *How long did the father stay with the boy?* (until the police arrived) Then have students open their books and complete Exercise 41.

Another time we saw new neighbors ___move / moving___ into
(7 move)
the house next door. We saw them ___struggling___ to move a piano
(8 struggle)
into the apartment. We had planned a picnic that day, but my parents
suggested that we help them. I heard my mother ___tell / telling___
(9 tell)
my father, "We can have a picnic another day. But these people need to
move in today. Let's offer them a hand." There are many other cases
where I saw my parents ___sacrifice / sacrificing___ their own pleasure to
(10 sacrifice)
help others.

I hear so many children today ___say / saying___, "I want" or
(11 say)
"Buy me" or "Give me." I think it's important to teach children to think
of others before they think of themselves. If they see their parents

___help / helping___ others, they will probably grow up to be
(12 help)

charitable people.

EXERCISE 42 *Combination Exercise.* Read the true story of a young woman,
Charity Bell, who became a foster mother (a person who gives
temporary care to a child in her home). Fill in the blanks with the
correct form of the verb in parentheses ( ) and add prepositions
to complete the story.

It's difficult ___for___ a college student ___to have___ time for
(example)   (example: have)
anything else but studying. But Charity Bell, a student at Harvard, made
time in her busy schedule ___to help___ babies in need. Bell, a single
(1 help)
woman, became a foster mother.

Bell became interested in ___helping___ needy babies when she was 23
(2 help)
years old. At that time, she volunteered at a hospital for very sick
children. The volunteer organization wanted her ___to read___ to the kids
(3 read)
and ___to play___ games with them. The parents of these very sick
(4 play)
children were there too, but they were often too tired ___to read___ or
(5 read)
___to play___ with their kids. They were grateful to her ___for helping___
(6 play)   (7 help)
them. One day she went to the hospital and heard a baby ___crying___
(8 cry)
so loudly in the next room. She went into that room and picked up the
baby; the baby immediately stopped ___crying___. She stayed with the
(9 cry)

Infinitives; Gerunds   315

EXERCISE   42

🎧 *CD 3, Track 14*

1. Tell students that this exercise is
   about one person's commitment to
   helping those who need help. Have
   students read the direction line.
   Ask: *What do we write?* (the correct
   form of the verb; prepositions)
2. Direct students to the examples in
   the book. Then have a volunteer
   complete #1.
3. Have students complete the
   exercise individually and then check
   their work in pairs. If necessary,
   review the answers as a class.

   🕐 To save class time, have
   students do half of the exercise
   in class and complete the other half for
   homework. Or assign the entire
   exercise for homework.

Expansion

Exercise 41 Ask students to share stories from their childhoods about parents teaching their
children by example.

Exercise 42 Variation

To provide practice with listening skills, have students close their books and listen to the
audio. Repeat the audio as needed. Ask comprehension questions, such as: *Why did Bell make
time in her busy schedule?* (to help babies in need; to become a foster mother) *How old was
Bell when she became interested in helping needy babies?* (23 years old) *Where was she
volunteering at that time?* (at a hospital for very sick children) Then have students open their
books and complete Exercise 42.

baby for a few hours. When she began _to leave/leaving_, the baby started
(10 leave)

to cry / crying again. Bell asked the nurse about this baby, and the nurse
(11 cry)

told her that the baby was taken away from her parents and they couldn't
find a temporary home for her.

The next day, Bell made some phone calls and started _to learn / learning_
(12 learn)

about how to be a foster parent. She made herself available to help on

nights and weekends. Her phone started _to ring / ringing_ immediately.
(13 ring)

She got used to _picking_ up the phone in the middle of the night.
(14 pick)

She became accustomed _____ _to taking_ _____ in children that
(15 take)

no one else wanted. Before she started taking care of babies, she used

to sleep seven or eight hours a night. Now she sometimes gets as
(16 sleep)

little as three or four hours of sleep a night.

By the time she was 28 years old and in graduate school, Bell had

been foster mother to 50 children. ___ _In_ ___ order ___ _to_ ___
(17)   (18)

complete her studies, she had ___ _to_ ___ take "her" babies to class
(19)

with her. Her professors let her ___ _do_ ___ this. They understood that it
(20 do)

was necessary ___ _for_ ___ her ___ _to study_ ___ and ___ _to take_ ___ care
(21)   (22 study)   (23 take)

of the babies at the same time. And her classmates didn't complain

_____ _about having_ _____ a baby crying in the back of the class.
(24 have)

Everyone understood how important it was _____ _for_ ___ her
(25)

___ _to help_ ___ these babies.
(26 help)

Usually, she takes in babies for a few days, but one time she had a
baby for six months. Even though she is sometimes tired, she is never

too tired ___ _to take_ ___ in a child that needs her. Incredibly, she only
(27 take)

gets $12 a day for _____ _taking_ _____ care of these children. However, she
(28 take)

gets great satisfaction watching a baby _____ _grow_ _____. Bell has had
(29 grow)

Culture Note

Babies and children whose parents are unable to care for them are usually put into foster care.
A foster parent takes care of the child until his or her parents are able to resume care. The
foster parent receives a small stipend, or payment, for taking care of the child. Social services
agencies are always looking for good foster families for children in need.

as many as eight children at a time. It is hard ___for___ her
(30)

___to see___ "her babies" ___leave___, but there are more babies
(31 see)   (32 leave)

waiting for her. ___Bringing___ love to an unwanted child is her
(33 bring)

greatest joy.

SUMMARY OF LESSON 7

Infinitives and Base Forms	
Examples	Explanation
Dawson wanted **to help** others.	An infinitive is used after certain verbs.
His mother wanted him **to help** others.	An object can be added before an infinitive.
He was happy **to give** away his money.	An infinitive can follow certain adjectives.
Public TV stations have fundraisers **in order to get** money. Matel Dawson gave his money **to help** students get an education.	An infinitive is used to show purpose.
It's important **to help** others. **To help** others is our moral obligation.	*It* can introduce an infinitive subject. (INFORMAL) The infinitive can be in the subject position. (FORMAL)
It's important **for rich people to help** others. It's fun **for me to volunteer**.	*For* + noun or object pronoun is used to give the infinitive a subject.
Carnegie had enough money **to build** libraries. Dawson was too poor **to finish** school.	An infinitive can be used with *too* and *enough*.
Dawson heard his mother **talk** about helping others. I hear a baby **crying**.	After sense perception verbs, a base form or an *-ing* form is used.
It is important **to be loved**.	An infinitive can be used in the passive voice.
She let me **work**. She made me **work**. She had me **work**.	After causative verbs *let, make,* and *have,* use the base form.
She got me **to work**. She convinced me **to work**. She persuaded me **to work**.	After causative verbs *get, convince,* and *persuade,* use the infinitive.
Dawson helped students **to get** an education. He helped them **pay** their tuition.	After *help,* either the infinitive or the base form can be used.

Infinitives; Gerunds **317**

Summary Variation

1. Write phrases from the chart on the board (e.g., *My parents wanted me to . . .* , *It's important to . . .* , *My friend convinced me to . . .* , etc.). In pairs, have students talk about themselves using the phrases in statements.

Summary of Lesson 7

1. **Infinitives and Base Forms** Have students work in pairs to write a question for each example in the chart, e.g., *What did Dawson want? What did his mother want?* Have pairs ask and answer their questions using the examples.
   If necessary, have students review:

   7.2 Verbs Followed by an Infinitive (p. 276)
   7.3 Object Before Infinitive (p. 279)
   7.4 Causative Verbs (p. 283)
   7.5 Adjective Plus Infinitive (p. 285)
   7.6 Using the Infinitive to Show Purpose (p. 288)
   7.7 Infinitive as Subject (p. 290)
   7.8 Infinitive with *Too* and *Enough* (p. 293)
   7.18 Sense-Perception Verbs (p. 314).

Summary of Lesson 7 (*cont.*)

2. Gerunds In pairs, have students make statements about things they enjoy doing, don't like doing, or have a hard time doing.

If necessary, have students review:

7.10 Gerund as Subject (p. 296)

7.11 Gerund After Prepositions and Nouns (p. 298)

7.12 Using the Correct Preposition (pp. 299–300)

7.13 Verbs Followed by Gerunds (p. 302).

3. Gerund or Infinitive— Differences in Meaning Have students make statements about themselves based on the examples in the chart, such as: *I used to be a nurse, but now I work at home. I stopped to get some coffee on the way to school today.* Have students look at Appendix D for a list of words followed by gerunds or infinitives.

If necessary, have students review:

7.16 Gerund or Infinitive After a Verb: Differences in Meaning (p. 306)

7.17 *Used To / Be Used To / Get Used To* (p. 310).

Gerunds

Examples	Explanation
Going to college is expensive in the U.S.	A gerund can be the subject of the sentence.
Dawson enjoyed **giving** money away.	A gerund follows certain verbs.
Dawson learned about **giving** from his parents.	A gerund is used after a preposition.
He had a hard time **supporting** his family.	A gerund is used after certain nouns.
He doesn't like to **go shopping**.	A gerund is used in many idiomatic expressions with *go*.
I dislike **being told** a lie.	A gerund can be used in the passive voice.

Gerund or Infinitive—Differences in meaning

Examples	Explanation
My father **used to be** a lawyer. Now he is retired. I **used to be** overweight. Now I'm in great shape.	Discontinued past habit
She has six children. She **is used to being** around kids. I ride my bike to work every day. I **am used to riding** my bike in all kinds of weather.	Present custom
I have never lived alone before and it's hard for me. I can't **get used to living** alone.	Change of custom
I met a friend at the library, and I **stopped to talk** to her.	Stop one activity in order to do something else
I had a fight with my neighbor, and we **stopped talking** to each other.	Stop something completely
I **try to give** a little money to charity each year. Mimi **tries to ride** her bike to work a few times a week.	*Try* = make an attempt or effort
I put 85¢ in the soda machine and nothing came out. I **tried hitting** the machine, but still nothing happened.	*Try* = experiment with a different method
You must **remember to turn off** the stove before you leave the house.	Remember and then do
My grandmother repeats herself a lot. She didn't **remember telling** the story, so she told it again.	Remember something about the past

For a list of words followed by gerunds or infinitives, see Appendix D.

Summary Variation

2. Have students use gerunds to make statements about things that have been easy and things that have been hard in the U.S. (*Learning English has been easy. Making friends has been hard.*).

3. Have students work in pairs to make sentences contrasting *remember, stop,* and *try* followed by a gerund and by an infinitive, using the models in the chart.

1. Don't forget *to* when introducing an infinitive.

          to
   He needs ^ leave.

             to
   It's necessary ^ have a job.

2. Don't omit *it* when introducing an infinitive.

   It's
   Is important to know a second language.

   It c
   Costs a lot of money to get a college education.

3. With a compound infinitive, use the base form after *and*.

                                 go
   He needed to finish the letter and ~~went~~ to the post office.

4. After *want*, *need*, and *expect*, use the object pronoun, not the subject pronoun, before the infinitive.

              me to
   She wants ~~that I~~ speak English all the time.

5. Don't use *to* between *cost* or *take* and the indirect object.

   It cost ~~to~~ me $500 to fly to Puerto Rico.

   It took ~~to~~ him three months to find a job.

6. Use *for*, not *to*, when you give a subject to the infinitive.

            for
   It is easy ~~to~~ me to speak Spanish.

7. Use *to* + base form, not *for*, to show purpose.

                          to
   He exercises every day ~~for~~ improve his health.

8. Use a gerund or an infinitive, not a base form as a subject.

         ing
   Find ^ a good job takes time. OR *It takes time to find a good job.*

Editing Advice

For each item, have students provide the grammar rule behind the Editing Advice. This can be done as an individual, a pair, a group, or a class activity.

1. An infinitive is *to* plus the base form of the verb.
2. An infinitive phrase can be the subject of a sentence. We usually begin the sentence with *it* and put the infinitive phrase at the end of the sentence.
3. In a sentence with two infinitives connected by *and*, the second *to* is usually omitted.
4. After some verbs, an object can be added before the infinitive.
5. An indirect object can follow *take* and *cost*.
6. *For* + an object can give the infinitive a specific subject.
7. *In order to* or *to* + the base form is used to show purpose.
8. Infinitive phrases and gerund phrases can both be used as subjects, but the base form cannot.

Editing Advice (cont.)

9. *Used to* shows that an activity was repeated or habitual in the past. *Be used to* means *be accustomed to*.

10. After *stop, remember,* and *try,* using a gerund or an infinitive gives the statement different meanings.

11. Gerunds are used after prepositions.

12. Some verbs can be followed by either a gerund or an infinitive with no difference in meaning. Other verbs can only be followed by a gerund or an infinitive.

13. To make a gerund negative, put *not* before the gerund.

14. After sense-perception verbs we can use either the *-ing* form or the base form. The *-ing* form shows that something is sensed while it is in progress. The base form shows that a person sensed something from start to finish.

15. Many recreational activities are expressed with *go* and a gerund.

16. *Let, make,* and *have* are causative verbs followed by an object and the base form.

---

9. Be careful with *used to* and *be used to*.

  My brother is used to live in New York. Now he lives in Boston.

  I've lived alone all my life and I love it. I used to live alone.
  ^{'m} ^{living}

10. Be careful to use the correct form after *stop*.

  She told her son to stop to watch TV and go to bed.
  ^{ing}

11. Use a gerund, not an infinitive, after a preposition.

  I thought about to return to my hometown.
  ^{ing}

12. Make sure to choose a gerund after certain verbs and an infinitive after others.

  I enjoy to walk in the park.
  ^{ing}

  I like to walk in the park. *Correct*

13. Use *not* to make the negative of a gerund.

  He's worried about don't finding a job.
  ^{not}

14. Use a base form or an *-ing* form after a sense-perception verb.

  I saw the accident to happen.

  I can smell the soup to cook.
  ^{ing}

15. Use a gerund, not the infinitive, with *go* + a recreational activity.

  I like to go to fish at the river.
  ^{ing}

16. Use the base form, not the infinitive, after causative verbs *let, make,* and *have*.

  He let me to borrow his car.

  The teacher made me to rewrite my composition.

PART 1 Find the mistakes with the underlined words, and correct them. Not every sentence has a mistake. If the sentence is correct, write C.

EXAMPLES   He was surprised ~~get~~ *to* get the job.

To help other people is our moral obligation. C

1. She let me to use her cell phone.
2. My daughter is out of town. I want ~~that she call~~ *her to call* me.
3. Do you like to watch TV? C
4. She's old enough ~~get~~ *to* get married.
5. She wanted me to help her with her homework. C
6. He decided to rent a car and ~~drove~~ *drive* to San Francisco.
7. It took me five minutes *to* finish the job.
8. My friend helped me move the piano. C
9. ~~Live~~ *Living* in a foreign country is difficult.
10. The teacher had us come to her office to discuss our grades. C
11. It will cost to me a lot of money to replace my old computer.
12. She needs *to* speak with you.
13. She got me to tell her the secret. C
14. The teacher made the student take the test a second time. C
15. It was hard ~~to~~ *for* me to find a job.
16. She persuaded her son to wash the dishes. C
17. *It costs* ~~Costs~~ a lot of money to buy a house.
18. He turned on the TV ~~for~~ *to* watch the news.
19. He stopped ~~to work~~ *working* at 4:30 and went home.
20. I met my friend in the cafeteria, and I stopped to talk to her for a few minutes. C
21. I like to cook, but I dislike ~~to wash~~ *washing* the dishes.
22. I had a good time talking with my friends. C
23. Do you go ~~shop~~ *shopping* for groceries every week?
24. I used to ~~living~~ *live* with my parents, but now I live alone.
25. My sister couldn't get used to ~~live~~ *living* in the U.S., so she went back to our native country.

Lesson 7 Test/Review

For additional practice, review, and assessment materials, see Assessment CD-ROM with *ExamView Pro*, *More Grammar Practice* Workbook 3, Interactive CD-ROM, and Web site http://elt.thomson.com/gic

PART 1

1. Part 1 may be used as an in-class test to assess student performance, in addition to the Assessment CD-ROM with *ExamView Pro*. Have students read the direction line. Ask: *Does every sentence have a mistake?* (no) Review the examples. Then have students complete Part 1 individually.
2. Collect for assessment.
3. If necessary, have students review: **Lesson 7.**

Lesson Review

To use Part 1 as a review, assign it as homework or use it as an in-class activity to be completed individually or in pairs. Check answers and review errors as a class. Reteach grammar points that students haven't mastered. Then student learning may be assessed using a test generated from the Assessment CD-ROM with *ExamView Pro*.

1. Part 2 may also be used as an in-class test to assess student performance, in addition to the Assessment CD-ROM with *ExamView Pro*. Tell students that this is one person's thoughts about unwanted phone calls. Words and phrases are missing. Review the example. Complete the next sentence as a class. Then have students complete Part 2 individually.
2. Collect for assessment.
3. If necessary, have students review: **Lesson 7.**

---

26. When I came into the room, I heard the teacher <u>talking</u> about the final exam. C

27. The walls of my apartment are thin, and I can hear my neighbors <s>to fight.</s> *fighting / fight*

28. I can smell my neighbors' dinner <u>cooking</u>. C

29. She thanked me for <s>take</s> *taking* care of her dog while she was on vacation.

30. Did you have trouble <s>to find</s> *finding* my apartment?

31. Please remember <u>to turn</u> off the lights before you go to bed. C

32. I started <u>learning</u> English when I was a child. C

33. I thought about <s>don't</s> *not* coming back to this school next semester.

34. She complained about <u>being disturbed</u> while she was trying to study. C

35. Your dress needs <u>to be cleaned</u> before you can use it again. C

36. He tried <u>to repair</u> the car by himself, but he couldn't. C

37. Did you see the boy <s>fell</s> *fall* from the tree?

PART **2**   Fill in the blanks with the gerund, the infinitive, or the base form of the verb in parentheses ( ). In some cases, more than one answer is possible.

EXAMPLE   ___Answering___ the phone during dinner really bothers me.
              (answer)

1. I started ___to eat / eating___ dinner last night and the phone rang.
              (eat)

2. Someone was trying ___to sell___ me something.
              (sell)

3. I don't enjoy ___being interrupted___ during dinner.
              (passive: interrupt)

4. Sometimes they want me ___to donate___ money to charity, but I
              (donate)
   don't like ___giving / to give___ my credit card number to strangers on
              (give)
   the phone.

5. I tell them I'm not interested in ___buying___ their product.
              (buy)

6. ___Telling___ them you're not interested doesn't stop them.
    (tell)
   They don't let you ___interrupt___ their sales pitch.
              (interrupt)

7. I used to ___listen___ to the caller politely, but I don't do it
              (listen)
   anymore.

322   Lesson 7

Lesson Review

To use Part 2 as a review, assign it as homework or use it as an in-class activity to be completed individually or in pairs. Check answers and review errors as a class. Reteach grammar points that students haven't mastered. Then student learning may be assessed using a test generated from the Assessment CD-ROM with *ExamView Pro*.

8. I've told them politely that I don't want to ___be bothered___ ,
   (passive: *bother*)

   but they don't listen.

9. I keep ___getting___ these phone calls.
   (*get*)

10. I've thought about ___changing___ my phone number, but I
    (*change*)

    heard that they'll get my new number.

11. ___Changing___ my phone number is not the answer to the
    (*change*)

    problem.

12. It's impossible ___to stop___ them from ___calling___ you.
    (*stop*)   (*call*)

13. I finally decided ___to get___ Caller ID.
    (*get*)

14. It's better ___to see___ who's calling before you pick up the
    (*see*)

    phone.

15. Now I have the choice of ___picking___ up or
    (*pick*)

    ___not picking___ up the phone when it rings.
    (*not pick*)

PART **3** Fill in the blanks with the correct preposition.

EXAMPLE We must concentrate ___on___ learning English.

1. What is the reason ___for___ doing this exercise?

2. Your grade in this course depends ___on___ passing the tests and
   doing the homework.

3. I dreamed ___of___ climbing a mountain.

4. The teacher insists ___on___ giving tests.

5. The Wright brothers are famous ___for___ inventing the airplane.

6. I hope I succeed ___in___ passing this course.

7. Most students care ___about___ getting good grades.

8. I'm not accustomed ___to___ wearing jeans to school.

9. Students are interested ___in___ improving their pronunciation.

10. Are you afraid ___of___ getting a bad grade?

11. Are you worried ___about___ getting a bad grade?

12. I'm not used ___to___ speaking English all the time.

Infinitives; Gerunds 323

PART 3

1. Part 3 may also be used as an in-class test to assess student performance, in addition to the Assessment CD-ROM with *ExamView Pro*. Review the example and do #1 as a class. Then have students complete Part 3 individually.
2. Collect for assessment.
3. If necessary, have students review: **Lesson 7.**

Lesson Review

To use Part 3 as a review, assign it as homework or use it as an in-class activity to be completed individually or in pairs. Check answers and review errors as a class. Reteach grammar points that students haven't mastered. Then student learning may be assessed using a test generated from the Assessment CD-ROM with *ExamView Pro*.

1. Part 4 may also be used as an in-class test to assess student performance, in addition to the Assessment CD-ROM with *ExamView Pro*. Tell students that this is an exercise on meaning. Review the examples. Then have students complete Part 4 individually.
2. Collect for assessment.
3. If necessary, have students review: **Lesson 7.**

Expansion Activities

These expansion activities provide opportunities for students to interact with one another and further develop their speaking and writing skills. Encourage students to use grammar from this lesson whenever possible.

🕐 To save class time, assign parts of the activities as homework. Then use class time for interaction and communication. If students do not need additional speaking practice, some of the activities may be assigned as writing activities for homework or skipped altogether.

CLASSROOM ACTIVITIES

1. Tell students that this activity is about expectations at your school. Ask: *What do you expect your teacher(s) to do? What do the teachers here expect you to do?* Brainstorm several answers. Then have students fill in the chart individually. When students have filled in the chart, have them compare answers in pairs. Have pairs share interesting answers with the class.

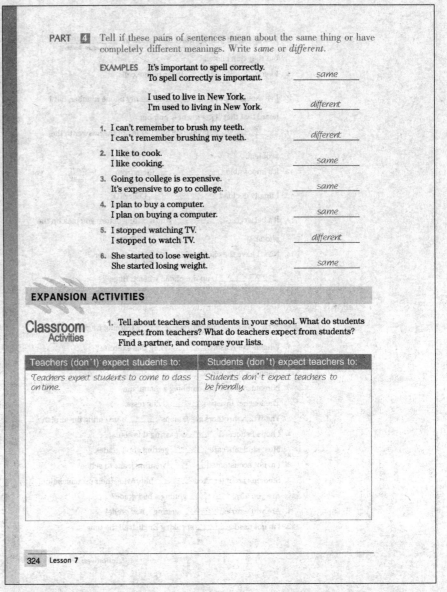

PART **4**   Tell if these pairs of sentences mean about the same thing or have completely different meanings. Write *same* or *different*.

EXAMPLES   It's important to spell correctly.
To spell correctly is important.   *same*

I used to live in New York.
I'm used to living in New York.   *different*

1. I can't remember to brush my teeth.
I can't remember brushing my teeth.   *different*

2. I like to cook.
I like cooking.   *same*

3. Going to college is expensive.
It's expensive to go to college.   *same*

4. I plan to buy a computer.
I plan on buying a computer.   *same*

5. I stopped watching TV.
I stopped to watch TV.   *different*

6. She started to lose weight.
She started losing weight.   *same*

EXPANSION ACTIVITIES

Classroom Activities

1. Tell about teachers and students in your school. What do students expect from teachers? What do teachers expect from students? Find a partner, and compare your lists.

Teachers (don't) expect students to:	Students (don't) expect teachers to:
Teachers expect students to come to class on time.	Students don't expect teachers to be friendly.

324   Lesson 7

Lesson Review

To use Part 4 as a review, assign it as homework or use it as an in-class activity to be completed individually or in pairs. Check answers and review errors as a class. Reteach grammar points that students haven't mastered. Then student learning may be assessed using a test generated from the Assessment CD-ROM with *ExamView Pro*.

Classroom Activities Variation

Activity 1 After pairs have finished the activity, ask students to talk about what they know about teachers' expectations of children in schools in the U.S. Ask students if teachers in the U.S. have different expectations from teachers in their native countries.

2. Fill in the blanks. Discuss your answers in a small group.

a. I used to worry about _____

b. Now I worry about _____

c. I used to have difficulty _____

d. Now I have difficulty _____

e. People in my family are not used to _____

f. Americans are not used to _____

g. I'm used to _____ because I've done it all my life.

h. I'm not used to _____

because _____

i. I often used to _____,

but I don't do it anymore. (OR I rarely do it.)

Talk About it

R.I.P.

Here Lies
Jon Doe
1774-1822

1. These words are written on Andrew Carnegie's tombstone: "Here lies a man who was able to surround himself with men far cleverer than himself." What do you think this means?

2. In your native culture, do rich people help poor people?

3. Do you ever give money to people on the street who collect money for charity? Why or why not?

4. If a homeless person asks you for money, do you help this person? Why or why not? Are there a lot of homeless people or beggars in your hometown? Do other people help them?

5. Would you like to volunteer your time to help a cause? What would you like to do?

Write About it

1. Write a paragraph telling if you agree or disagree with the following statements by Andrew Carnegie:

- It is not good to have money if your spirit is poor.
- It is the mind that makes the body rich.
- It is a disgrace to die rich.

2. Write about a belief you used to have that you no longer have. What made you change your belief?

3. Write a paragraph or short essay telling how your lifestyle or habits have changed over the last ten years.

4. Write about an expectation that your parents had for you that you did not meet. Explain why you did not do what they expected.

5. Write about an expectation you have for your children (or future children).

Infinitives; Gerunds 325

Refer students to the Editing Advice on pages 319–320.

Talk About it Variation

Have students work in pairs. Have members of the pairs interview each other using the questions in the activity, alternating interviewers. Have the interviewers take notes on their partners' responses.

Item 4 Have students debate item 4. Divide the class into two teams. Ask: *Should you give money to a homeless person who asks for money on the street?* Tell each team to list five reasons supporting its view. Have each team present its arguments. Then give each team an opportunity to respond to the other team's arguments. At the end of the debate, survey the class to see which opinion is more popular.

Write About it Variation

Have students exchange first drafts with a partner. Ask students to help their partners edit their drafts. Refer students to the Editing Advice on pages 319–320.

2. Have students complete the statements for themselves, and then share their answers with a group. Encourage group members to ask each other questions about their statements (e.g., *Why do you worry about getting sick? Why don't you go swimming anymore?*).

TALK ABOUT IT

Have students work in groups. Either assign or have each group choose one or more of the topics to discuss. Review with students the language for agreeing, checking for agreement, disagreeing, etc. (e.g., *I think you're right. I agree with you. Actually, I think . . . . I don't really agree.*). Set a time limit for discussion. Then have groups talk about their topics. If appropriate, have groups report back to the class. Have each group appoint a spokesperson.

WRITE ABOUT IT

1. Review Andrew Carnegie's statements with the class. Make sure that the meaning of each statement is clear. Have students write a paragraph about their opinions. Collect for assessment and/or have students review each other's work.

2. Have students give a few examples of beliefs they used to have, and why they changed them. Have students choose one belief to write about. Collect for assessment and/or have students present their paragraphs to a group.

3. Have students make notes about ways that their lifestyles or habits have changed, and then brainstorm an outline. Have students write a paragraph or short essay on the changes. Collect for assessment and/or have students review each other's work.

4. Review language for talking about expectations (e.g., *My mother expected me to . . . ; She didn't expect me to . . .*). Encourage students to make a few notes. Have students write about their parents' expectations. Collect for assessment and/or have students present their writing to a partner or group.

5. Have students think about their expectations for their children and make a few notes. Then have students write a short paragraph about their expectations. Collect for assessment and/or have students present their paragraphs or essays to a partner or group.

1. Instruct students to ask a friend, neighbor, or acquaintance outside of class to complete the statements. In class, have students tell who completed the statements, and then report his or her answers to the class.

2. If some students are unable to rent and see the movie, ask students who did to present a short summary of the movie.

INTERNET ACITIVITIES

1. Check that students are familiar with *.org* for noncommercial organizations. Point out that *.com* is usually for commercial sites.

2. Help students decide whether to look for local, national, or international volunteer organizations. Have students share information they find. Ask: *Which organizations do you think are good organizations? Why?*

3. Brainstorm search terms to use to find volunteer organizations' Web sites and terms for types of organizations (e.g., social services, tutoring, environmental, political action, etc.).

4. Have students tell the class why they chose the article they did and whether or not it was easy to find.

Outside Activities

1. Ask a friend or neighbor to fill in the blanks in these statements. Report this person's answers to the class.

- I'm worried about _____
- I'm grateful to my parents for _____.
- I have a good time _____.
- I used to _____, but I don't do it anymore.

2. Rent the movie *Pay It Forward*. Write a summary of the movie.

Internet Activities

1. At a search engine, type in *charity*. Find the names of charitable organizations. What do these organizations do to help people?

2. Type in *volunteer*. Find the names of volunteer organizations. Write down three ways people can volunteer to help others.

3. Find the name of a volunteer organization near you. What kind of volunteers are needed?

4. At a search engine, type in *AIDS bike ride*. Print an article about someone's personal account of a specific ride.

Additional Activities at http://elt.thomson.com/gic

326   Lesson 7

Internet Activities Variation

Activity 3 Have learners use the information they find to write a paragraph about the organization, the services it provides, the kinds of volunteers it is looking for, the number of hours a week help is needed, special skills needed, etc. Have students present their organizations to the class.

If students don't have access to the Internet, they may find the information needed in a local phone book, at a local public library, etc.

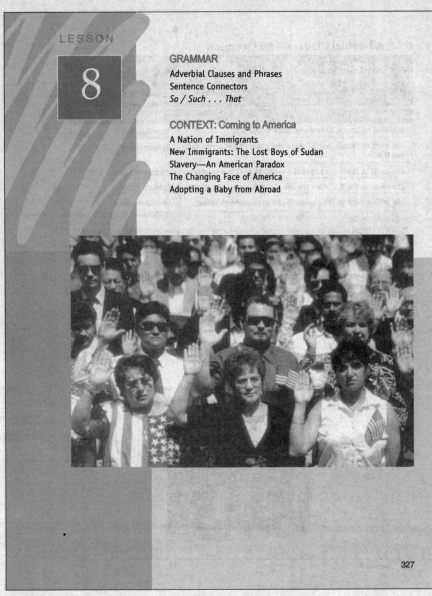

GRAMMAR

Adverbial Clauses and Phrases
Sentence Connectors
So / Such . . . That

CONTEXT: Coming to America

A Nation of Immigrants
New Immigrants: The Lost Boys of Sudan
Slavery—An American Paradox
The Changing Face of America
Adopting a Baby from Abroad

327

Lesson 8

Lesson Overview

GRAMMAR

1. Activate students' prior knowledge. Ask students if they can name words that combine phrases to make longer sentences; elicit as many as possible (*and, but, so, since, before, after, although,* etc.).

2. Ask: *What will we study in this lesson?* (adverbial clauses and phrases, sentence connectors, *so* and *such that*) Give several examples of your own of sentences using adverbial clauses (e.g., *My grandparents came here because of problems in their native country. They worked hard so that they could help their families back home.*). Have volunteers give examples using *because* and *so that.* Write two or three examples on the board.

CONTEXT

1. Ask: *What will we learn about in this lesson?* (coming to America, immigrants, slavery, adopting a baby from abroad) Elicit students' prior knowledge. Ask: *What do you know about immigration in the U.S.? About refugees? About the history of slavery in the U.S.?*

2. Point out that *immigrate* means to come to a new country, and *emigrate* means to leave one's own country.

3. Have students who are comfortable with the topic share their knowledge and personal experiences.

Photo

1. Direct students' attention to the photo. Ask: *What do you think these people are doing? How do you think they feel?*

2. Have students who are comfortable with the subjects share stories about immigration or naturalization.

🕐 To save class time, have students do the Test/Review at the end of the lesson, or administer a lesson test generated from the Assessment CD-ROM with *ExamView® Pro.* Skip sections of the lesson that students have already mastered. You may also assign some sections for self-study for extra credit.

Expansion

Theme The topic for this lesson can be enhanced with the following ideas:

1. Census data showing foreign-born population data over time
2. Magazine, newspaper, or Web articles about refugees around the world
3. An editorial from a local newspaper about immigration issues
4. Online U.S. and world population clocks,
   e.g., http://www.census.gov/main/www/popclock.html

Culture Note

In some parts of the U.S., the local USCIS (U.S. Citizenship and Immigration Services; formerly the INS) office holds naturalization ceremonies for large groups of new citizens. People raise their right hands and take the oath of citizenship. People are frequently given small U.S. flags to hold and wave.

8.1 | Adverbial Clauses—An Overview

1. Have students review the top part of the grammar chart. Ask: *Which one is the adverbial clause?* (*even though I miss my country*)
2. Have students review the examples in the chart. Ask, at random: *Which word(s) begins a contrast clause?* (*even though*) *A time clause?* (*before*) etc. Clarify any vocabulary students are unfamiliar with.
3. Draw students' attention to the Language Notes. Review the notes carefully. Point out the use of a comma when the dependent clause comes before the main clause.

A Nation of Immigrants (Reading)

1. Have students look at the photo. Ask: *Where are the people? Why are they standing in line? How do you think they feel?*
2. Have students look at the title of the reading and look briefly at the reading. Ask: *What is the reading about? How do you know?* Have students make predictions.
3. Preteach any essential vocabulary words your students may not know, such as *unique, takes in, diverse, unrest, persecution, restricting, reunited,* and *estimate.*

BEFORE YOU READ

1. Activate students' prior knowledge about the history and current state of immigration to the U.S. Ask: *How long do you think immigrants have been coming to this country? What countries have immigrants come from? What policies does the U.S. have for immigration?*
2. Have students discuss the questions in pairs. Try to pair students of different language backgrounds.
3. Ask for a few volunteers to share their answers with the class.

To save class time, skip "Before You Read" or have students prepare answers for homework ahead of time.

8.1 | Adverbial Clauses—An Overview

An adverbial clause gives more information about the main clause. It is also called a *dependent clause*.

Main clause	*Dependent clause*
I like living in the U.S.	even though I miss my country.

Example	Type of Clause
She went to Canada **before she came to the U.S.**	Time clause
She went to Canada first **because she couldn't get a visa for the U.S.**	Reason clause
She came to the U.S. **so that she could be with her relatives.**	Purpose clause
She came to the U.S. **even though she didn't know English.**	Contrast clause
She will go back to her country **if she saves enough money.**	Condition clause

Language Notes:
1. An adverbial clause is dependent on the main clause for its meaning. It must be attached to the main clause.
   Wrong: She came to America. Because she wanted to study English.
   Right: She came to America because she wanted to study English.
2. The dependent clause can come before or after the main clause. If it comes before, it is usually separated from the main clause with a comma.
   Compare:
   I went to Canada before I came to the United States. (No comma)
   Before I came to the United States, I went to Canada. (Comma)

A NATION OF IMMIGRANTS

Before You Read
1. Why do many people leave one country and move to another?
2. What do immigrants have to give up? What do they gain?

328   Lesson **8**

Expansion

Theme The topic for this lesson can be enhanced with the following ideas:

1. Information on immigration and/or naturalization from the USCIS Web site at http://uscis.gov/graphics/index.htm
2. Newspaper, magazine, or Web articles showing numbers and/or proportions of areas of origin for immigrants settling in the local area
3. A timeline showing the history of U.S. immigration

Read the following article. Pay special attention to different ways of giving reasons.

The United States is unique in that it is a nation of immigrants, old and new. The U.S. takes in more immigrants than the rest of the world combined, about 1.3 million a year. In 2003, 32.5 million people, or 11.5 percent of the population, was foreign born. Between 1995 and 1998, three million immigrants entered the U.S. legally. Why have so many people from other countries left family and friends, jobs, and traditions to start life in a new country? The answer to that question is as diverse as the people who have come to America.

Between 1820 and 1840, many Germans came **because of** political unrest and economic problems. Between 1840 and 1860, many Irish people came **because of** famine.[1] The potato crop, which they depended on, had failed. Between 1850 and 1882, many Chinese people came to America **because of** famine.

The early group of immigrants came from Northern and Western Europe. In 1881, a large group started arriving from Eastern and Southern Europe. Jews from Eastern Europe came **to** escape religious persecution; Italians came **for** work. Most came **to** find freedom and a better life. The number of immigrants grew; between 1881 and 1920, more than 23.4 million immigrants came. In 1910, 15 percent of the population was foreign born.

In 1924, Congress passed a law restricting the number of immigrants, and immigration slowed. In 1965, Congress opened the doors again and immigration started to rise. In the 1960s and 1970s, Cubans and Vietnamese people came **to** escape communism. In the 1980s, Jews from the former Soviet Union came **because of** anti-Semitism,[2] and in the 1990s, Bosnians came **because of** war. Many people came **so that** they could be reunited with their families who had come before.

In addition to legal immigration, about 300,000 come to the U.S. each year illegally. **Since** the U.S. Census cannot count these people, this number is only an estimate.

[1] *Famine* means extreme hunger because of a shortage of food.
[2] *Anti-Semitism* means prejudice or discrimination against Jews.

Adverbial Clauses and Phrases; Sentence Connectors; *So/Such . . . That*   329

Reading 🎧 *CD 3, Track 15*

1. Have students first read the text silently. Tell them to pay special attention to different ways of giving reasons. Then play the audio and have students read along silently.
2. Check students' comprehension. Ask questions such as: *Approximately what percent of the U.S. population was foreign-born in 2003?* (11.5%) *What are some reasons that immigrants have come to the U.S.?* (famine, political unrest, economic problems, to escape persecution, work, freedom, a better life)

🕐 To save class time, have students do the reading for homework ahead of time.

DID YOU KNOW ?

The U.S. Census Bureau makes statistics available on the population of the U.S., including information on immigrants and the foreign-born population in general. *Foreign-born* means anyone born in another country. The Census Bureau's Web site is at http://www.census.gov.

Reading Variation

To practice listening skills, have students first listen to the audio alone. Ask a few comprehension questions. Repeat the audio if necessary. Then have students open their books and read along as they listen to the audio.

Reading Glossary

diverse: different; varied
estimate: guess; approximation
persecution: bad treatment because of race, social class, religion, etc.
restrict: limit
reunited: back together after a separation
take in: accept; allow in
unique: one-of-a-kind; the only one
unrest: disturbance; fighting

8.2 | Reason and Purpose

1. Have students cover the grammar chart. On the board, write *because, because of, since, in order to, so that,* and *for.* Ask: *Which two show reason?* (*because* and *since*) Say: *The others are used to show purpose.*
2. Have students uncover the explanation column of the grammar chart. Have students locate and underline the words that show reason and purpose (*because, because of, since, in order to, so that,* and *for*). Then have students review the example sentences.
3. Ask volunteers to give sentences about themselves using *because, because of, since, in order to, so that,* and *for.* Provide several examples of your own: *I moved here so that I could be near my family. I'm saving money for retirement.*

8.2 | Reason and Purpose

There are several ways to show reason and purpose.

Examples	Explanation
We came to the U.S. **because our relatives are here.** **Because** he couldn't find a job in his country, he came to the U.S.	*Because* introduces a clause of reason.
Many Irish immigrants came to the U.S. **because of hunger.** **Because of** war in their country, many people left Ethiopia.	*Because of* introduces a noun (phrase).
Since the U.S. Census cannot count illegal immigrants, their number is only an estimate. **Since** the U.S. limits the number of immigrants it will accept, many people cannot get an immigrant visa.	*Since* means *because*. It is used to introduce a fact. The main clause is the result of this fact. Remember: *Since* can also be used to show time. **Example:** He has been in the U.S. *since* 2003. The context tells you the meaning of *since*.
In order to make money, my family came to the U.S. Many people come to America **to escape economic hardship.**	*In order to* shows purpose. The short form is *to*. We follow *to* with the base form of the verb.
Many people come to the U.S. **so that they can be reunited with family members.** Many people come to the U.S. **so they can be reunited with family members.** **So that** I **would** learn English, I came to the U.S. **So** I **would** learn English, I came to the U.S.	*So that* shows purpose. The short form is *so*. The purpose clause usually contains a modal: *can, will,* or *may* for future; *could, would,* or *might* for past.
People come to America **for freedom.** Some people come to America **for better jobs.**	*For* + noun or noun phrase shows purpose.
Compare: a. She came here **to** be with her family. b. They came here **for** a better life.	a. Use *to* before a verb. b. Use *for* before a noun.
Compare: a. He came to the U.S. **because he wanted to be** reunited with his brother. b. He came to the U.S. **so that he could be** reunited with his brother.	a. **Because** can be followed with **want.** b. Do not follow *so that* with **want.** *Wrong:* He came to the U.S. *so that he wanted to be* reunited with his brother.

330   Lesson **8**

Grammar Variation

Write sentences with *because, because of, since, in order to, so that,* and *for* on the board (e.g., *I checked the TV in order to see the weather forecast. Since the weather was bad, class was cancelled. I called my students to tell them.*). Ask students whether each sentence shows reason or purpose. Then review the grammar chart.

Language Note:

So is also used to show result.

Compare:

Purpose: I came to the U.S. alone **so** I could get an education.

Result: I came to the U.S. alone, **so** I miss my family.

Notice that in the above sentences, a comma is used for result but not for purpose.

EXERCISE **1** Fill in the blanks with *because, because of, since, for, (in order) to,* or *so (that).*

EXAMPLE Many immigrants came to America ___*to*___ escape famine.

1. Many immigrants came ___*because*___ they didn't have enough to eat.

2. Many immigrants came ___*so (that)*___ they could feed their families.

3. Many immigrants came ___*so (that)*___ they could escape religious persecution.

4. Many immigrants came ___*because*___ the political situation was unstable in their countries.

5. Many immigrants came ___*because of*___ the poor economy in their countries.

6. Many immigrants came ___*(in order) to*___ be reunited with their relatives.

7. ___*Because / Since*___ war destroyed many of their homes and towns, many people had to leave their countries.

8. Many immigrants came ___*(in order) to*___ escape poverty.

9. Many immigrants came ___*for*___ freedom.

10. Often immigrants come ___*so (that)*___ they can make more money.

11. Often immigrants come ___*(in order) to*___ make more money.

12. Often immigrants come ___*because*___ they see a better future for their children here.

13. Most immigrants come to America ___*for*___ a better life.

Adverbial Clauses and Phrases; Sentence Connectors; *So/Such . . . That* | 331

8.2 | Reason and Purpose (*cont.*)

4. Direct students' attention to the Language Note. Review the use of the comma for *so* meaning result.

EXERCISE 1

1. Tell students that this exercise is about immigrants and immigration. Have students read the direction line.

2. Model the exercise. Direct students to the example in the book. Ask: *What does* to *show?* (purpose) Complete #1 with the class.

3. Have students complete Exercise 1 individually. Then have them check their answers in pairs. Circulate and observe the pair work. If necessary, check the answers as a class.

Expansion

Exercise 1 After students complete the exercise, have them match each item with an explanation in grammar chart **8.2** on pages 330 and 331.

EXERCISE 2

1. Tell students that this exercise is about reasons and purposes. Have students read the direction line. Ask: *Is more than one answer possible?* (yes)
2. Model the exercise. Direct students to the example in the book. Ask: *Is this sentence about a reason or a purpose?* (a reason)
3. Have students complete Exercise 2 individually. Then have them compare answers in pairs. Circulate and observe the pair work. Have volunteers share their answers with the class.
4. Assess students' performance. If necessary, review grammar chart **8.2** on pages 330 and 331.

EXERCISE 3

🎧 *CD 3, Track 16*

1. Tell students that this exercise is a conversation between two women about parents and children. Have students read the direction line.
2. Model the exercise. Direct students to the example. Then do #1 with the class.
3. Have students complete the exercise individually. Then have them check their answers by practicing the conversation. If necessary, check the answers as a class.
4. Assess students' performance. If necessary, review grammar chart **8.2** on pages 330 and 331.

🕐 To save class time, have students do half of the exercise in class and complete the other half for homework. Or assign the entire exercise for homework.

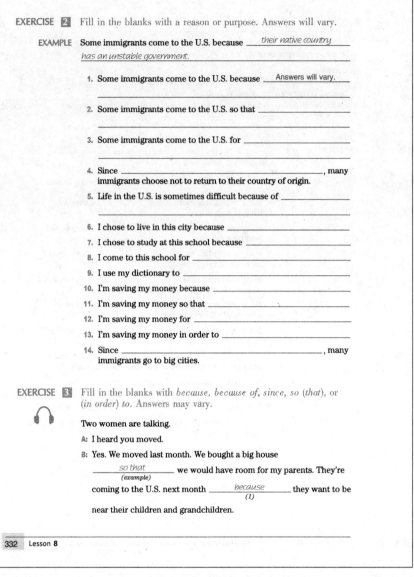

EXERCISE **2** Fill in the blanks with a reason or purpose. Answers will vary.

EXAMPLE Some immigrants come to the U.S. because ____*their native country*____
*has an unstable government.*____

1. Some immigrants come to the U.S. because ___Answers will vary.___

2. Some immigrants come to the U.S. so that _____

3. Some immigrants come to the U.S. for _____

4. Since _____, many immigrants choose not to return to their country of origin.

5. Life in the U.S. is sometimes difficult because of _____

6. I chose to live in this city because _____
7. I chose to study at this school because _____
8. I come to this school for _____
9. I use my dictionary to _____
10. I'm saving my money because _____
11. I'm saving my money so that _____
12. I'm saving my money for _____
13. I'm saving my money in order to _____
14. Since _____, many immigrants go to big cities.

EXERCISE **3** Fill in the blanks with *because, because of, since, so (that),* or *(in order) to.* Answers may vary.

Two women are talking.

A: I heard you moved.

B: Yes. We moved last month. We bought a big house
___*so that*___ we would have room for my parents. They're
_____*(example)*_____
coming to the U.S. next month ___*because*___ they want to be
_____*(1)*_____
near their children and grandchildren.

332 Lesson **8**

Expansion

Exercise 2 Have students work in pairs to write questions for items 6 through 12. For items 6, 7, 10, and 11, have students write questions with *why*. For items 8, 9, and 12, have students write questions with *What . . . for.*

Exercise 3 Variation

To provide practice with listening skills, have students close their books and listen to the audio. Repeat the audio as needed. Ask comprehension questions, such as: *Why did person B move into a big house?* (so they would have room for her parents) *When are her parents coming to the U.S.?* (next month) *Why are they coming?* (because they want to be near their children and grandchildren) Then have students open their books and complete Exercise 3.

A: Don't you mind having your parents live with you?

B: Not at all. It'll be good for them and good for us.
_____*Because of*_____ our jobs, we don't get home until after 6 p.m.
        (2)

A: Aren't your parents going to work?

B: No. They're not coming here _____*for*_____ jobs. They're in
                                    (3)
their late 60s and are both retired. They just want to be grandparents.

A: It's great for kids to be near their grandparents.

B: I agree. Grandparents are the best babysitters. We want the kids
to stay with their grandparents _____*so (that)*_____ they won't
                                       (4)
forget our language. Also, we want them to learn about our native
culture _____*since*_____ they have never been to our country.
            (5)
Our son, who's five, is already starting to speak more English than
Spanish. He prefers English _____*because*_____ all his friends in
                                   (6)
kindergarten speak English.

A: That's how kids are in America. They don't want to speak their
native language _____*because*_____ they want to be just like
                       (7)
their friends. Do your parents speak English?

B: Just a little. When we get home after work, we hope they'll take
classes at a nearby college _____*(in order) to*_____ improve their
                                    (8)
English. What about your parents? Where do they live?

A: They live a few blocks away from me.

B: That's great! You can see them any time.

A: Yes, but we almost never see each other _____*because*_____ we
                                                  (9)
don't have time. _____*Since*_____ they work in the
                       (10)
day and I work in the evening, it's hard for us to get together.

Expansion

Exercise 3 Have students discuss their opinions about the issues raised in the exercise, including raising bilingual children, multigenerational families, maintaining ties to a culture, etc. On the board, write students' ideas using the reason and purpose expressions from grammar chart **8.2.**

Exercise 3 Have students work in groups to list the issues raised in the article, e.g., for person A: *She almost never gets to see her parents because she's busy.* For person B: *She wants her parents to take classes to improve their English.*

New Immigrants: The Lost Boys of Sudan (Reading)

1. Have students look at the photos. Ask: *Where do you think the people are in the picture on the left? Where do you think the boy is in the picture on the right? What do you think the reading will be about?*
2. Have students look at the title of the reading and look briefly at the reading. Ask: *What is the reading about? How do you know?* Have students make predictions.
3. Preteach any vocabulary words your students may not know, such as *cattle, starvation, refugee camp, resettle, uncertain, appliances, surroundings, amazed, palace,* and *homeland.*

BEFORE YOU READ

1. Activate students' prior knowledge about refugees, refugee resettlement, and the Lost Boys of Sudan. Ask: *What is a refugee?* (a person who has had to leave his or her country against his or her will) *Where do refugees live while they wait for another country to help them?* (in refugee camps)
2. Have students discuss the questions in pairs. Try to pair students of different language backgrounds.
3. Ask a few volunteers to share their answers with the class.

🕐 To save class time, skip "Before You Read" or have students prepare answers for homework ahead of time.

Reading 🎧 CD 3, Track 17

1. Have students first read the text silently. Tell them to pay special attention to the time words *when, while, until, during, for,* and *whenever.* Then play the audio and have students read along silently.
2. Check students' comprehension. Ask questions such as: *Where did the Lost Boys go when they left their homes?* (to Ethiopia, then back to Sudan and Kenya) *How many of the Lost Boys were brought to the U.S.?* (3,700) *What are the Lost Boys in the U.S. doing today?* (working and studying English)

🕐 To save class time, have students do the reading for homework ahead of time.

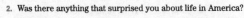

Before You Read
1. Was your trip to America difficult? In what ways?
2. Was there anything that surprised you about life in America?

 Read the following article. Pay special attention to time words: *when, while, until, during, for,* and *whenever.*

Africa

The Lost Boys of Sudan are new immigrants in America, eager to start a new life. They are called "the Lost Boys" because, after their families were killed in war, they went from country to country until some of them found a home in America.

The Lost Boys were just children living in southern Sudan **when** their long journey to America began in the late 1980s. **While** these young boys were in the field taking care of their cattle, their villages were bombed. These boys, mostly between the ages of 4 and 12 years old, ran for their lives. **For** three months, they walked hundreds of miles **until** they reached Ethiopia. They survived by eating leaves, roots, and wild fruit. **During** that time, many died of starvation and disease or were eaten by lions. They finally reached Ethiopia, where they stayed in refugee camps **until** 1991, **when** a war started in Ethiopia and the camps were closed. They ran again, back to Sudan and then to Kenya, where they stayed in a refugee camp **for** almost ten years. Of the approximately 27,000 boys who left Sudan, only 11,000 of them survived.

During their time in the refugee camp, they got some schooling and learned basic English. In 1999, the United Nations and the U.S. government agreed to resettle 3,700 lost boys in the U.S. **As** they were coming to America, they were thinking about the new and uncertain life ahead. Things in the U.S. would certainly be different.

Now in their twenties and early thirties, the Lost Boys living in America have had to learn a completely new way of life. **When** they moved to their

334　Lesson **8**

Expansion

Theme The topic for this lesson can be enhanced with the following ideas:

1. Newsletter or donation solicitation from a refugee resettlement agency
2. Newspaper, magazine, or Web articles on a recent refugee situation in the news
3. A flyer or brochure from a local refugee service or refugee resettlement agency
4. A page from the Web site of the Office of the United Nations High Commissioner for Refugees at http://www.unhcr.ch
5. A web article on U.S. refugee resettlement or refugee assistance from the U.S. Department of State's Bureau of Population, Refugees, and Migration at http://www.state.gov/g/prm/

Reading Variation

To practice listening skills, have students first listen to the audio alone. Ask a few comprehension questions. Repeat the audio if necessary. Then have students open their books and read along as they listen to the audio.

Culture Note

People's ages are frequently referred to by decades (periods of ten years). For example, the Lost Boys are now in their twenties and thirties, or between 20 and 39 years old. People from 13 to 19 years old are teenagers or adolescents. Ten- to 12-year olds are frequently called preteens.

---

new homes, they had to learn about new foods, different appliances, and new technologies. They had not even seen a refrigerator or stove or telephone **until** they came to America. In addition to their home surroundings, their world around them was completely different. **When** John Bol of Chicago saw an American supermarket for the first time, he was amazed at the amount of food. He asked if it was the palace of a king.

Agencies helped them with money for food and rent for a short time **until** they found jobs. Most of them have been studying English and working full time **since** they arrived. Although their future in the U.S. looks bright, **whenever** they think about their homeland, they are sad because so many of their family members and friends have died.

Reading Glossary

amazed: astonished, very surprised
appliance: large kitchen or household item (refrigerator, stove, washing machine, etc.)
cattle: cows; livestock
homeland: native country
palace: home of a king or dictator; very luxurious home
refugee camp: settlement where refugees stay, outside of their homeland, while waiting for a permanent place to live
resettle: settle in a new country or a new place
starvation: not having enough, or not having anything, to eat
surroundings: environment; area around a person
uncertain: not sure; unknown

Culture Note

According to the United Nations, a refugee is a person who cannot return to his or her own country because of a "well-founded fear" of persecution based on race, religion, nationality, membership in a social group, or political opinion. There are at least 17 million refugees waiting for help in the world today.

8.3 | Time Expressions

1. Have students cover the grammar chart. Ask students what time words they found in the reading on pages 334 and 335. Elicit and write on the board: *when, while, until, during, for,* and *whenever.* Ask students to name other time words; write them on the board (*before, after, since, ever since, as*).

2. Provide several examples of your own using the time words on the board (e.g., *When I was young, a family in my neighborhood sponsored a refugee family. Ever since I met them, I have been interested in refugee issues.*). Ask: *Which clause is the time clause in each example?* (*when I was young; ever since I met them*)

3. Have students review the grammar chart. Review the time expressions carefully. If appropriate, have students underline or highlight the usage information for each time expression in the right column, e.g., *at that time, amount of time,* or *a named period of time.*

8.3 | Time Expressions

Examples	Explanation
When their villages were bombed, the Lost Boys ran. Some Sudanese boys think they will go home **when** their country *is* at peace.	*When* means "at that time" or "immediately after that time." In a future sentence, use the present tense in the time clause.
Whenever they think about their country, they are sad. **Whenever** they tell their story, Americans are amazed.	*Whenever* means "any time" or "every time."
They walked **until** they reached Ethiopia. They received money for a short time **until** they got jobs.	*Until* means "up to that time."
Some of them have had no news of their families **since** they left Sudan. They have been studying English **ever since** they came to the U.S.	*Since* or *ever since* means "from that time in the past to the present." Use the present perfect or present perfect continuous in the main clause.
They walked **for** three months. They stayed in a refugee camp **for** many years.	Use *for* with the amount of time.
During the day, they walked. **During** their time in the refugee camp, they studied English.	Use *during* with a time such as *day, night, summer* or a specific time period (*the time they were in Ethiopia, the month of August, the week of March 2*) or an event (*the class, the trip, the movie, the meeting*).
While they were taking care of their cattle, their villages were bombed. **As** they were coming to America, they were thinking about their new life ahead.	Use *while* or *as* with a continuous action.
Compare: a. They walked **for** three months. b. They walked **during** the day. They lived in refugee camps **during** their childhood.	a. Use *for* with the amount of time. b. Use *during* with a named period of time (such as *the day, their childhood, the class, the month of May*).
Compare: a. They were taking care of their cattle **when** their villages were bombed. b. **While** they were taking care of their cattle, their villages were bombed.	a. Use *when* with a simple past action. b. Use *while* with a continuous action.

336   Lesson 8

Grammar Variation

After students have reviewed the example sentences in the grammar chart, have them go back to the reading on pages 334 and 335 and identify which explanation applies to each boldface time word in the reading.

EXERCISE **4** Fill in the blanks with *since, until, while, when, as during, for,* or *whenever.* In some cases, more than one answer is possible.

EXAMPLE The Lost Boys were very young _____ *when* _____ they left Sudan.

1. They had never seen a gas stove _____ *until / when* _____ they came to the U.S.

2. Some of them have not heard anything about their families _____ *since* _____ they left Sudan.

3. _____ *While / As* _____ they were traveling to the U.S., they were wondering about their future.

4. _____ *During* _____ their march to Ethiopia, many of them died.

5. _____ *When* _____ they came to the U.S., they saw modern appliances for the first time.

6. They walked _____ *for* _____ many months.

7. They crossed the river _____ *during* _____ the rainy season.

8. Some died _____ *while / as* _____ they were marching to Ethiopia.

9. They studied English _____ *while* _____ they were living in Kenya.

10. _____ *Since* _____ they came to the U.S., they have been studying English.

11. _____ *Whenever* _____ they think about their families, they feel sad.

12. In the U.S. many of them work _____ *while* _____ they are going to school.

13. They lived in Ethiopia _____ *for* _____ about four years.

14. They had very little to eat _____ *until* _____ they came to America.

EXERCISE **5** Fill in the blanks with an appropriate time word. In some cases, more than one answer is possible.

_____ *When* _____ I was a child, I had heard many stories about life in
    (example)

America. _____ *Whenever* _____ I saw American movies, I imagined that
    (1)

one day I would be in a place like the one I saw. My uncle had lived in

the U.S. _____ *for* _____ many years, and he often came back to
    (2)

Adverbial Clauses and Phrases; Sentence Connectors; *So/Such . . . That* | 337

---

1. Tell students that this exercise is about the Lost Boys. Have students read the direction line. Ask: *Are different answers possible?* (yes)
2. Model the exercise. Direct students to the example. Complete #1 with the class.
3. Have students complete the exercise individually. Then have them compare their answers in pairs. Circulate and observe the pair work. If necessary, check the answers as a class.

CD 3, Track 18

1. Tell students that this exercise is about one person's experience coming to the U.S. Have students read the direction line.
2. Model the exercise. Direct students to the example in the book. Then do #1 with the class.
3. Have students complete Exercise 5 individually. Then have them compare their answers in pairs. Finally, check the answers as a class.
4. Assess students' performance. If necessary, review grammar chart **8.3** on page 336.

To save class time, have students do half of the exercise in class and complete the other half for homework. Or assign the entire exercise for homework.

Expansion

Exercise 4 Have students use the information about the Lost Boys in the exercise, in the reading on pages 334 and 335, and the explanations in grammar chart **8.3,** to make a timeline of the lives of the Lost Boys.

Exercise 5 Variation

To provide practice with listening skills, have students close their books and listen to the audio. Repeat the audio as needed. Ask comprehension questions, such as: *What kind of stories did the speaker hear as a child?* (stories about life in America) *Who showed the speaker pictures of the U.S.?* (the speaker's uncle) Then have students open their books and complete Exercise 5.

EXERCISE 6

1. Tell students that this exercise is about an immigrant from Poland. Have students read the direction line.
2. Model the exercise. Direct students to the examples. Discuss the reasons for each answer.
3. Have students complete Exercise 6 individually. Have them compare their answers in pairs. Finally, check the answers as a class.

---

visit. ___Whenever___ he came back, he used to tell me stories and
(3)

show me pictures of the U.S. ___When___ I was a teenager, I
(4)

asked my mother if she would let me visit my uncle ___during___
(5)

my summer vacation, but she said I was too young and the trip was too

expensive. ___When___ I was 20, I finally decided to come to the
(6)

U.S. ___While / As___ I was traveling to the U.S., I thought about all
(7)

the stories my uncle had told me. But I really knew nothing about the

U.S. ___until___ I came here.
(8)

___Since___ I came to the U.S., I've been working hard and
(9)

trying to learn English. I haven't had time to meet Americans or have

much fun ___since___ I started my job. I've been here
(10)

___for___ five months now, and I just work and go to
(11)

school. ___When / While___ I'm at school, I talk to my classmates
(12)

___during___ our break, but on the weekends I'm alone most of
(13)

the time. I won't be able to make American friends ___until___
(14)

I learn more English.

The American movies I had seen showed me beautiful places, but I never imagined how much I would miss my family and friends.

EXERCISE **6**   Fill in the blanks with an appropriate expression.

EXAMPLES   For ___many years___, she has been living in the U.S.

Since ___1997___, she has been living in the U.S.

1. During ___Answers will vary.___, she lived in Poland.
2. For _____, she lived in Poland.
3. Since _____, she has been working in the U.S.
4. While _____, she met her future husband.
5. When _____, she was living in Poland.

Expansion

Exercise 5 Have students use Exercise 5 as a model to write a short paragraph about either their ideas about the U.S. before they came here or the experiences they have had since they came here. Collect for assessment, or have pairs review each others' paragraphs.

6. Until _____, she lived with her parents.

7. Whenever _____, she visits her parents.

EXERCISE **7** ABOUT YOU Complete the statements that apply to you. If the time expression is at the beginning of the sentence, add a comma before the main clause.

EXAMPLES Whenever I have a job interview *I feel nervous.*

Ever since I found a job *I haven't had much time to study.*

1. Ever since I was a child _____ Answers will vary. _____

2. When I was a child _____

3. _____ ever since I started attending this school.

4. _____ when I started attending this school.

5. _____ until I started attending this school.

6. When the semester began _____

7. Since the semester began _____

8. _____ when I was ____ years old.

9. _____ until I was ____ years old.

10. _____ ever since I was ____ years old.

11. When I graduated _____

12. Since I graduated _____

13. Until I graduated _____

14. _____ when I found a job.

15. _____ since I found a job.

16. _____ until I found a job.

17. When I bought my car _____

18. Until I bought my car _____

19. Since I bought my car _____

20. Whenever I drive _____

1. Tell students that this exercise is about their lives and experiences. Have students read the direction line. Ask: *When do we add a comma?* (when the time expression is at the beginning of the sentence)

2. Model the exercise. Direct students to the examples. Ask: *Does this statement describe you?* Then do items 1 and 2 with the class. Ask a volunteer to give an answer.

3. Have students complete Exercise 7 individually. Then have them compare their answers in pairs. Ask volunteers to share interesting statements about their partners with the class.

4. Assess students' performance. If necessary, review grammar chart **8.3**.

To save class time, have students do half of the exercise in class and complete the other half for homework. Or assign the entire exercise for homework.

Expansion

Exercise 7 Have students work in pairs. Ask students to write several statements about their partners (e.g., *Dawit's English has been improving since he found a job.*).

8.4 | Using the *-ing* Form After Time Words

1. Ask students to cover the grammar chart. On the board, write: *The boys have been telling their story since they came to the U.S.* Ask: *What are the two clauses?* (*The boys have been telling their story; since they came to the U.S.*) Ask: *Do the two clauses have the same subject?* (yes; the boys) Point to the sentence on the board. Say: *When the subject of the main clause and the subject of the time clause are the same, we can use the -ing form of the verb in the time clause and omit the subject in the time clause.*

2. Have students look at grammar chart **8.4.** Review the examples. Ask: *Why is a phrase with -ing called a participial phrase?* (because the *-ing* form is the present participle) Point out that the use of commas does not change when the *-ing* form is used.

EXERCISE 8

1. Tell students that this exercise is about using time clauses. Have students read the direction line.
2. Model the exercise. Direct students to the example in the book.
3. Have students complete Exercise 8 individually. Check answers as a class.
4. Assess students' performance. If necessary, review grammar chart **8.4.**

8.4 | Using the *-ing* Form After Time Words

If the subject of a time clause and the subject of the main clause are the same, the time clause can be changed to a participle phrase. The subject is omitted, and the present participle (*-ing* form) is used.

Examples

    Subject   *Subject*

a. The Lost Boys went to Ethiopia after **they left** Sudan.

b. The Lost Boys went to Ethiopia after **leaving** Sudan.

    Subject   *Subject*

a. While **they were crossing** the river, some of the Lost Boys drowned.

b. While **crossing** the river, some of the Lost Boys drowned.

In sentences (a), the subject of the main clause and the subject of the time clause are the same.

In sentences (b), we delete the subject after the time word (*after, while*) and use a present participle (*-ing*).

EXERCISE 8   Change the time clause to a participle phrase.

EXAMPLE   While they were crossing a river, many boys drowned.
                  While crossing a river, many boys drowned.

1. The Lost Boys went to Kenya before they came to America.
    The Lost Boys went to Kenya before coming to America.

2. While they were living in Kenya, they studied English.
    While living in Kenya, they studied English.

3. Before they came to America, the Lost Boys had never used electricity.
    Before coming to America, the Lost Boys had never used electricity.

4. Santino learned how to use a computer after he came to America.
    Santino learned how to use a computer after coming to America.

5. Until he found a job, Daniel got help from the U.S. government.
    Until finding a job, Daniel got help from the U.S. government.

6. Peter wants to go back to Sudan after he graduates from college.
    Peter wants to go back to Sudan after graduating from college.

Grammar Variation

Have students cover the first row of the grammar chart giving the grammar rule. Have students review the examples and notes. Ask volunteers to say what they observe about the difference between the (a) sentences and the (b) sentences. Then review the rule and examples as a class.

SLAVERY—AN AMERICAN PARADOX[3]

Before You Read
1. What do you know about the history of slavery in the U.S.?
2. Do you think everyone is equal in the U.S. today?

 Read the following article. Pay special attention to *even though, although,* and *in spite of (the fact that).*

Did You Know?
African-Americans make up about 12.3 percent of the U.S. population today.

For the first three centuries after Columbus came to America in 1492, the largest group of immigrants arrived in America—unwillingly. Ten to twelve million Africans were brought to work as slaves in the rice, sugar, tobacco, and cotton fields of the agricultural south.

In 1776, when America declared its independence from England, Thomas Jefferson, one of the founding fathers of the United States, wrote, "All men are created equal" and that every person has a right to "life, liberty, and the pursuit of happiness." **In spite of** these great words, Jefferson owned 200 slaves at that time.

Even though the importation of slaves finally ended in 1808, the slave population continued to grow as children were born to slave mothers. The country became divided over the issue of slavery. The North wanted to end slavery; the South wanted to continue it. In 1861, civil war broke out between the North and the South. In 1865, when the North won, slavery was ended. **In spite of the fact that** African-Americans were freed, it took another 100 years for Congress to pass a law prohibiting discrimination because of race, color, religion, sex, or national origin.

Although many new arrivals see the U.S. as the land of equality, it is important to remember this dark period of American history.

[3] A *paradox* is a situation that has contradictory aspects.

Adverbial Clauses and Phrases; Sentence Connectors; So/Such . . . That   341

Expansion

Theme The topic for this lesson can be enhanced with the following ideas:

1. A timeline of the history of slavery in the U.S. and the Civil War
2. A copy of the text of the Declaration of Independence

Reading Variation

To practice listening skills, have students first listen to the audio alone. Ask a few comprehension questions. Repeat the audio if necessary. Then have students open their books and read along as they listen to the audio.

Reading Glossary

agricultural: related to growing crops
civil war: war between parts of a country; war within a country
discrimination: bad treatment of people because of their race, sex, national origin, etc.
founding fathers: the people who declared independence from Britain for the U.S. and started the United States of America
importation: bringing in
slavery: keeping people as involuntary servants
the South: In the U.S., the southern states that formed a union before and during the Civil War

Slavery—An American Paradox (Reading)

1. Have students look at the photo. Ask: *Who do you think these people are? Where do you think the photo was taken?*
2. Have students look briefly at the reading. Have students look at the title of the reading. Ask: *What is the reading about? How do you know?* Have students make predictions.
3. Preteach any vocabulary words your students may not know, such as *slavery, agricultural, the South, founding fathers, importation, civil war,* and *discrimination.*

BEFORE YOU READ

1. Activate students' prior knowledge about the history of slavery in the U.S. Ask: *Where were slaves brought to America from?* (Africa) *What ended the period of slavery in the U.S.?* (the Civil War)
2. Have students discuss the questions in pairs. Try to pair students of different language backgrounds.
3. Ask a few volunteers to share their answers with the class.

To save class time, skip "Before You Read" or have students prepare answers for homework ahead of time.

Reading CD 3, Track 19

1. Have students first read the text silently. Tell them to pay special attention to *even though, although,* and *in spite of.* Then play the audio and have students read along silently.
2. Check students' comprehension. Ask questions such as: *What kind of work were many slaves brought to the U.S. to do?* (agricultural work) *Why did the Civil War break out?* (because the South wanted to keep slavery and the North wanted to end it) *When did the Civil War end?* (in 1865)

To save class time, have students do the reading for homework ahead of time.

DID YOU KNOW ?

U.S. population estimates are available from the U.S. Census Bureau at http://www.census.gov/popest/estimates.php

8.5 | Contrast

1. Have students cover the grammar chart. On the board, write *contrast*. Discuss the meaning of *contrast* with the class. Then list words and phrases that show contrast (*even though, although, in spite of the fact that, in spite of, still, anyway*). Write several examples with contrast (e.g., *I like my neighborhood even though I don't know many people there. In spite of the long commute, I love my job.*). Elicit examples from students. Write them on the board.

2. Have students look at grammar chart **8.5**. Review the examples and explanations in the chart. Clarify any vocabulary students are unfamiliar with.

3. Draw students' attention to the last row in the chart. Point out that *still* and *anyway* can be added to the main clause when contrast terms are used in the dependent clause to emphasize or strengthen the contrast.

<table>
<tr><td colspan="2">EXERCISE 9</td></tr>
</table>

1. Tell students that this exercise is about contrasts in life. Have students read the direction line.

2. Model the exercise. Direct students to the examples in the book.

3. Have students complete the exercise individually. Check answers as a class.

8.5 | Contrast

Examples	Explanation
Even though slavery ended, African-Americans did not get equality.	For an unexpected result or contrast of ideas, use a clause beginning with *even though, although,* and *in spite of the fact that.*
Although life in the refugee camps was hard, the Lost Boys learned English.	
In spite of the fact that Jefferson wrote about equality for everyone, he owned 200 slaves.	A clause has a subject and a verb.
In spite of Jefferson's declaration of liberty for all, he owned slaves.	Use *in spite of* + noun or noun phrase to show contrast.
In spite of their hard lives, the Lost Boys are hopeful about their future.	A clause doesn't follow *in spite of.*
Even though the Lost Boys are happy in the U.S., they **still** miss their families in Sudan.	*Still* and *anyway* can be used in the main clause to emphasize the contrast.
Even though it's hard for an immigrant to work and go to school, they have to do it **anyway.**	

EXERCISE 9 Fill in the blanks with *in spite of* or *in spite of the fact that.*

EXAMPLES ___In spite of the fact that___ the law says everyone has equal rights, some people are still suffering.

The Sudanese boys have not lost their hopes for a bright future, ___in spite of their hard lives___.

1. ___In spite of the fact that___, slavery ended in 1865, African-Americans did not receive equal treatment under the law.

2. The slave population continued to grow ___in spite of the fact that___ Americans stopped importing slaves from Africa.

3. ___In spite of___ Thomas Jefferson's belief in equality for all, he owned slaves.

4. Many immigrants come to America ___in spite of___ the difficulty of starting a new life.

5. ___In spite of___ their busy work schedules, the Sudanese boys go to school.

6. ___In spite of the fact that___ everything in America is new for them, the Sudanese boys are adapting to American life.

7. ___In spite of the fact that___ life is not perfect in the U.S., many immigrants want to come here.

Grammar Variation

Have students match the phrases in boldface in the reading on page 341 to the appropriate explanation in the grammar chart.

Expansion

Exercise 9 Tell students that *in spite of* and *in spite of the fact that* always occur as phrases, although *spite* as a noun on its own means *hate* or *bad feeling.* Something done 'out of spite' means done because of hatred or just to be mean. *Despite* is a synonym for *in spite of.*

Culture Note

Today, Americans celebrate African-American History (or Black History) month every February. Events commemorate the history and accomplishments of African-Americans in the U.S.

EXERCISE 10 Complete each statement with an unexpected result.

EXAMPLE I like the teacher even though _____ *he gives a lot of homework.* _____

1. I like my apartment even though _____ Answers will vary. _____
_____

2. I like this city even though _____
_____

3. I like this country even though _____
_____

4. I like this school even though _____
_____

5. I have to study even though _____
_____

6. I like my job in spite of (the fact that) _____
_____

7. Some students fail tests in spite of (the fact that) _____
_____

8. My uncle passed the citizenship test even though _____
_____

9. The U.S. is a great country in spite of (the fact that) _____
_____

10. Many people want to come to the U.S. even though _____
_____

11. There are many poor people in the U.S. in spite of (the fact that) _____
_____

1. Tell students that this exercise is about unexpected results. Have students read the direction line.
2. Direct students to the example in the book. Ask: *Is this true for you?* Have volunteers complete the sentence for themselves.
3. Have students read the prompts silently and think about their answers for a few minutes. Encourage students to take notes. Then have students complete the exercise. Have students work in pairs to compare answers. Circulate and observe the pair work. If possible, participate with pairs to provide statements of your own. Ask volunteers to share interesting information about their partners with the class.
4. Assess students' performance. If necessary, review the appropriate sections of grammar chart **8.5.**

To save class time, have students do half of the exercise in class and complete the other half for homework. Or assign the entire exercise for homework.

Expansion

Exercise 10 Have students interview each other in pairs about the information in items 1 through 6. Encourage students to use positive or negative statements as appropriate, e.g.,

A: Do you like your apartment?
B: Yes, I do, even though it's very small.
         or
B: No, I don't, even though it's in a great location.

Exercise 10 Have students work in pairs to write statements about each other based on items 1 through 6 (e.g., *Petra likes this school even though it's a long way from where she lives.*). Collect for assessment.

EXERCISE 11

1. Tell students that this exercise is about contrasts. Have students read the direction line.
2. Model the exercise. Direct students to the example in the book. Ask a few volunteers to provide additional answers.
3. Have students complete the exercise individually. Then have students compare their answers in pairs. Ask volunteers to share their answers with the class.
4. Assess students' performance. If necessary, review grammar chart **8.5**.

To save class time, have students do half of the exercise in class and complete the other half for homework. Or assign the entire exercise for homework.

The Changing Face of America (Reading)

1. Have students look at the photo. Ask: *Where do you think these people are from? Where do you think they live?*
2. Have students look quickly at the reading. Ask: *What is the reading about? How do you know?* Have students make predictions.
3. Preteach any vocabulary words your students may not know, such as *patterns, majority, trend, dramatically, minority, birth rate,* and *influence.*

BEFORE YOU READ

1. Activate students' prior knowledge about Hispanic immigration into the U.S. Ask: *How do you think immigration to the U.S. has changed over the last 100 years?* (from mostly Europeans to mostly Hispanics) *Which states have a lot of Hispanic residents?* (California, Texas, Florida, New York)
2. Have students discuss the questions in pairs. Try to pair students of different language backgrounds.
3. Ask a few volunteers to share their answers with the class.

To save class time, skip "Before You Read" or have students prepare answers for homework ahead of time.

EXERCISE **11** Complete each statement by making a contrast.

EXAMPLE Even though many students have jobs, *they manage to come to class and do their homework.*

1. Even though the U.S. is a rich country, _____ Answers will vary. _____

2. In spite of the fact that Thomas Jefferson wrote "All men are created equal," _____

3. Even though I don't speak English perfectly, _____

4. In spite of the fact that my teacher doesn't speak my language, _____

5. Even though I miss my friends and family, _____

6. In spite of my accent, _____

THE CHANGING FACE OF AMERICA

Before You Read
1. What do you think is the largest ethnic minority in the U.S.?
2. Do you ever see signs in public places in Spanish or any other language?

Expansion
Theme The topic for this lesson can be enhanced with the following ideas:

1. A flyer or newspaper article about a community event sponsored by a Hispanic or other cultural or ethnic group or organization
2. Bilingual or multilingual government or commercial publications or notices
3. Information from the U.S. Census on population trends, projections, and numbers from the Census Web site at http://www.census.gov/index.html

Read the following article. Pay special attention to condition clauses beginning with *if, even if,* and *unless.*

The U.S. population is over 295 million. This number is expected to rise to more than 400 million by 2050. **Unless** there are changes in immigration patterns, 80 million new immigrants will enter the U.S. in the next 50 years.

For most of the nineteenth and twentieth centuries, the majority of immigrants to the U.S. were Europeans. However, since 1970, this trend has changed dramatically. Today most immigrants are Hispanics.[4] In 2003, Hispanics passed African-Americans as the largest minority. The Hispanic population increased more than 50% between 1990 and 2000. **If** current patterns of immigration continue and **if** the birth rate remains the same, Hispanics, who are now 13% of the total population, will be 24% of the population by 2050. Hispanics are already about 32% of the population of California and Texas. More than 50% of the people who have arrived since 1970 are Spanish speakers. The largest group of Hispanic immigrants comes from Mexico.

Because of their large numbers, Hispanic voters will have political power. **If** they vote as a group, they will have a great influence on the choice of our nation's leaders.

There are many questions about the future of America. One thing is certain: the face of America is changing and will continue to change.

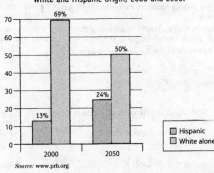

Estimated and Projected U.S. Population, White and Hispanic Origin, 2000 and 2050.

Source: www.prb.org

[4] A *Hispanic* is an American whose origin is a Spanish-speaking country, such as Mexico or Cuba.

Adverbial Clauses and Phrases; Sentence Connectors; *So/Such . . . That*   345

Reading 🎧 *CD 3, Track 20*

1. Have students first read the text silently. Tell them to pay special attention to condition clauses beginning with *if, even if,* and *unless.* Then play the audio and have students read along silently.

2. Check students' comprehension. Ask questions such as: *How many new immigrants are expected to enter the U.S. in the next 50 years?* (80 million) *What is one kind of change a large number of Hispanics could make? How?* (political change; by voting)

🕐 To save class time, have students do the reading for homework ahead of time.

DID YOU KNOW ?

Loretta and Linda Sanchez were the first sisters ever elected to the U.S. Congress at the same time. They are two of the seven children of Mexican immigrants; all seven of whom graduated from college. Linda Sanchez worked as an ESL teacher while she was in college.

Reading Variation

To practice listening skills, have students first listen to the audio alone. Ask a few comprehension questions. Repeat the audio if necessary. Then have students open their books and read along as they listen to the audio.

Reading Glossary

birth rate: number of babies born per woman, or per population
dramatically: very noticeably
influence: effect
majority: most; largest number
minority: population group that is not the largest population group in a society or country
pattern: arrangement or sequence of events; trend
trend: general direction; a change or development

8.6 | Condition

1. Have students cover the grammar chart. On the board, make two columns. In the left column, write:
   1. *If you register,*
   2. *Even if you are going to be away on Election Day,*
   3. *Unless you register,*
   In the right column, write:
   a. *you can't vote.*
   b. *you can vote.*
   c. *you can vote by absentee ballot.*
   Have students combine the phrases to make three statements (1b, 2c, 3a). Review each sentence with the class. Say: *In #1, the condition affects the result. In #2, the condition doesn't affect the result.* Ask: *What does* unless *mean in #3?* (if not) Write: *Unless you register = If you don't register.*

2. Have students look at grammar chart **8.6.** Review the examples and explanations carefully. Draw students' attention to the future tense meaning of the examples in the first three rows, and to the present tense meaning in the fourth row.

3. Write prompts on the board, such as: *If I . . . , I will; Even if I . . . , I won't*; and *Unless I . . . , I won't.* Ask volunteers to provide examples about themselves from the prompts.

EXERCISE 12

1. Tell students that this exercise is about immigration and population. Have students read the direction line.

2. Direct students to the example. Ask: *Why are these answers correct?* (because the condition in the present [*continues to grow*] affects the result in the future [*will be*]) Complete #1 with the class.

3. Have students complete the exercise individually, and check their answers in pairs. If necessary, check answers as a class.

4. Assess students' performance. If necessary, review grammar chart **8.6.**

8.6 | Condition

If, even if, and *unless* are used to show that a condition is needed for something to happen.

If current immigration patterns and birth rates **remain** the same, Hispanics **will be** 25 percent of the population by 2050. **If** Hispanics **vote** together, they **will have** a lot of political power. **If** my brother **comes** to the U.S., he **will live** with me.	Use *if* to show that the condition affects the result. In a future sentence, use the simple present tense in the condition clause.
Even if the immigration of Hispanics **slows** down, their number **will increase** because of their present birth rate. **Even if** the economy of my country **improves**, I **won't go** back.	Use *even if* to show that the condition doesn't affect the result.
Unless immigration laws **change**, 80 million new immigrants **will come** here in the next 50 years. My brother **won't come** to the U.S. *unless* he **gets** a scholarship at an American university. I **won't go** back to my country *unless* my parents **need** me.	Use *unless* to mean *if not.* Compare: I won't go **unless** you **go.** I won't go **if** you **don't go.**
a. *If* I **think** about my native country, I **get** homesick. b. *Whenever* I **think** about my native country, I **get** homesick. c. Children in America **learn** English *even if* their parents **speak** another language at home. d. You **can't come** to the U.S. *unless* you **have** a visa.	Sentences with *if, even if,* and *unless* can also be about the general **present.** In that case, the present tense is used in both clauses. Note: Sentences (a) and (b) have the same meaning.

EXERCISE 12   Fill in the blanks with the correct form of the verb in parentheses ( ).

EXAMPLE   If the Hispanic population _____*continues*_____ to grow, 24% of the
                                              (continue)
U.S. population _____*will be*_____ Hispanic by the year 2050.
                              (be)

1. If the U.S. _____*adds*_____ almost 80 million people
                           (add)
to the population in the next 50 years, it _____*will have to*_____
                                                        (have to)
build 30 million more housing units.

Grammar Variation

Have students cover grammar chart **8.6.** Write sentences from the chart or similar to those in the chart on the board, without *if, even if,* or *unless* (e.g., _____ *my brother comes to the U.S., he will live with me.* _____ *the economy of my country improves, I won't go back. I won't go back to my country* _____ *my parents need me.*). Ask students whether they would use *if, even if,* or *unless* in the sentences, and why. Then have students uncover and review the chart.

---

2. Even if the number of immigrants _____goes_____ down,
   (go)
   the population ___will increase___ because of the high birth
   (increase)
   rates of immigrants.

3. If more children _____are_____ born in the next 50 years,
   (be)
   more schools ___will be needed___.
   (passive: need)

4. The class size ___will increase___ if the number of school-age
   (increase)
   children _____grows_____.
   (grow)

5. The U.S. population ___will be___ over 400 million by
   (be)
   2050 if immigration ___continues___ at the same rate.
   (continue)

6. Immigrants ___will continue___ to come to the U.S. unless
   (continue)
   there _____is_____ a change in immigration policy.
   (be)

7. Children of immigrants ___will forget___ their native
   (forget)
   language unless their parents ___encourage___ them to
   (encourage)
   speak, read, and write it.

8. If immigrant parents ___don't educate___ their children about
   (not/educate)
   their former country, their children ___won't know___ about
   (not/know)
   their family history.

EXERCISE 13 ABOUT YOU Complete each statement.

EXAMPLE If I speak my native language all the time, ___I won't learn English.___

1. If I make a lot of long distance calls, ___Answers will vary.___

2. I'll get a good grade if _____

3. If I don't pass this course, _____

4. My English will improve if _____

5. I'll go back to my native country if _____

Adverbial Clauses and Phrases; Sentence Connectors; *So/Such . . . That*   347

1. Tell students that this exercise is about conditions that affect them. Have students read the direction line.
2. Model the exercise. Direct students to the example in the book. Ask one or two volunteers to complete the example for themselves.
3. Have students complete the exercise individually, and then compare answers in pairs. Have pairs share interesting answers with the class.

⊘ To save class time, have students do half of the exercise in class and complete the other half for homework. Or assign the entire exercise for homework.

Expansion

Exercise 12 Have students brainstorm and write a list of ways immigrant children can learn about or remember their parents' cultures and languages. Have students use *if* and *even if* in their statements.

1. Tell students that this exercise is about immigration. Have students read the direction line. Ask: *What do we write?* (an *unless* clause)
2. Model the exercise. Direct students to the example in the book.
3. Have students complete Exercise 14 individually. Check answers as a class.

🕐 To save class time, have students do half of the exercise in class and complete the other half for homework.

1. Tell students that this exercise is about their habits and plans. Have students read the direction line.
2. Direct students to the example in the book. Review the example, and then ask several volunteers to complete the example for themselves.
3. Have students complete the exercise in writing individually and compare answers in pairs. Have students report interesting information about their partners to the class.

🕐 To save class time, have students do the exercise for homework.

---

6. I will become a citizen if _____
7. If I can't come to class next week, _____

EXERCISE 14 Change the *if* clause in the sentences below to an *unless* chause.

EXAMPLE You can't get on an airplane if you don't have a photo ID. *You can't get on an airplane unless you have a photo ID.*

1. You can't enter the U.S. if you don't have a passport. _____
   You can't enter the U.S. unless you have a passport.

2. Children of immigrants will forget their language if they don't use it.
   Children of immigrants will forget their language unless they use it.

3. Immigrants will continue to come to the U.S. if conditions in their native countries don't improve. *Immigrants will continue to come to the U.S. unless condition in their native country improve.*

4. An American citizen can't be president of the U.S. if he or she was not born in the U.S. *An American citizen can't be president of the U.S. unless he or she was born in the U.S.*

5. If the increase in the Hispanic population doesn't change, Hispanics will be 24% of the U.S. population by the middle of the century. _____
   Hispanics will be 24% of the U.S. population by the middle of the century unless the increase in the Hispanic population changes.

EXERCISE 15 ABOUT YOU Complete each statement.

EXAMPLE I don't usually eat fast food _____ *unless I'm in a hurry.*

1. I work / study every day unless _____ Answers will vary.
2. I'm usually in a good mood unless _____
3. I usually answer the phone unless _____
4. I'm going to stay in this city unless _____
5. I will continue to study at this school unless _____
   _____
6. I can't afford to go to college / school unless _____
   _____
   _____

348   Lesson 8

Expansion

Exercises 13 and 15 Have students choose one or two statements from Exercises 13 and 15 and write each one on a slip of paper. Students can use their statements from the exercises or a new statement. Collect the papers and read them at random to the class. Have the class guess which student wrote each statement. Alternatively, divide students into teams and have teams take turns guessing; award points for correct guesses. The team with the most points wins.

7. I won't be able to take the next course unless _____

_____

EXERCISE **16** Complete each statement. Answers will vary.

EXAMPLE   Coffee doesn't affect me. I can sleep even if _____I drink a cup of coffee_____
at night.

1. Cold weather doesn't bother me. I go out even if __Answers will vary.__

_____

2. Making grammar mistakes is OK. People will understand you even if

_____

3. A lot of people in the U.S. have a foreign accent. People will

understand you even if _____

4. Will they call off the football game for bad weather? No. They will

play football even if _____

5. He will fail the course because he never does his homework and he's

absent a lot. Even if _____, he will

fail the course.

6. I always do my homework. I may be absent next week, but I'll do my

homework even if _____

7. I may move to a suburb. I will continue to study in the city even if

_____

8. Children of immigrants learn English even if _____

_____

EXERCISE **17** Fill in the blanks in this conversation between two Hispanic
mothers.

A: My youngest daughter is seven years old, and she doesn't speak

Spanish anymore. _____*If*_____ I say something to
(example)

her in Spanish, she understands, but she answers in English.

B: _____*If*_____ all her friends speak English, of course she's
(1)

going to speak English.

Adverbial Clauses and Phrases; Sentence Connectors; *So/Such . . . That*   **349**

EXERCISE 16

1. Tell students that this exercise is about results. Have students read the direction line.
2. Direct students to the example in the book. Review the example. Ask: *Is this true for you?*
3. Have students complete the exercise individually. Have volunteers report their answers to the class.
4. Assess students' performance. If necessary, review grammar chart **8.6** on page 346.

To save class time, have students do half of the exercise in class and complete the other half for homework. Or assign the entire exercise for homework.

EXERCISE 17

CD 3, Track 21

1. Tell students that this exercise is a conversation between two mothers. Have students read the direction line.
2. Direct students to the example.
3. Have students complete the exercise individually, and check answers in pairs by practicing the conversation.

To save class time, have students do half of the exercise in class and complete the other half for homework. Or assign the entire exercise for homework.

Exercise 17 Variation

To provide practice with listening skills, have students close their books and listen to the audio. Repeat the audio as needed. Ask comprehension questions, such as: *How old is person A's youngest daughter?* (seven years old) *What language(s) does she speak?* (English) *What language(s) does she understand?* (English and Spanish) Then have students open their books and complete Exercise 17.

Expansion

Exercise 17 Ask students to discuss the situation the mothers are talking about in the exercise. If appropriate, ask students to share their experiences with children who are at home in two cultures.

Adopting a Baby From Abroad (Reading)

1. Have students look at the photos on pages 350 and 351. Ask: *How do these people feel? Why?*
2. Have students look at the title of the reading and look briefly at the reading. Ask: *What is the reading about? How do you know?* Have students make predictions.
3. Preteach any vocabulary words your students may not know, such as *adopt, waiting list, turning to,* and *tiny.*

BEFORE YOU READ

1. Activate students' prior knowledge about adoption in the U.S. Ask: *What are some reasons that people adopt children?* (for humanitarian reasons; because a family member is ill or dies; because they cannot have biological children) *Why do you think people in the U.S. adopt babies from other countries?*
2. Have students discuss the questions in pairs. Try to pair students of different language backgrounds.
3. Ask a few volunteers to share their answers with the class.

To save class time, skip "Before You Read" or have students prepare answers for homework ahead of time.

A: My mother lives with us. She doesn't speak English. She can't understand what my daughter is saying _____*unless*_____
(2)

I translate it for her.

B: I have the same problem. My son is 14 and he won't speak Spanish _____*unless*_____ he has to. Last month he had to because
(3)

my parents came to visit from Guatemala. But he mixes Spanish with English. My parents had a hard time understanding him. There are a lot of Spanish words he doesn't remember _____*unless*_____
(4)

I remind him.

A: We can't fight it. Our kids won't speak Spanish well _____*unless*_____
(5)

we go back to live in our native countries. And we're not going to do that. We came to the U.S. as immigrants.

ADOPTING A BABY FROM ABROAD

Before You Read
1. Do you know anyone who has adopted a baby?
2. Is it important for parents to teach their children about their ancestors?

Expansion

Theme The topic for this lesson can be enhanced with the following ideas:

1. Web sites about domestic or international adoption
2. Sections of the U.S. Citizenship and Immigration Services Web site on international adoption, such as: http://uscis.gov/graphics/howdoi/fororphan.htm

Read the following article. Pay special attention to sentence connectors: *however, in addition, furthermore,* and *as a result.*

Many American couples want to adopt children. **However,** there is such a long waiting list and there are so few babies available that people often have to wait years for a child. **In addition,** the process has become so complicated and slow that people often get discouraged with American adoptions. **As a result,** many Americans are turning to foreign countries for adoption. Americans bring home babies from countries such as China, Russia, Ukraine, South Korea, Guatemala, and the Philippines. In 2002, 20,000 foreign babies were adopted by American families.

However, the process of foreign adoption is not easy or cheap. First, it can cost from $10,000 to $25,000. **In addition,** the Immigration and Naturalization Service (INS) often takes six weeks to four months to process the paperwork. **Furthermore,** parents usually have to travel to the country for a one- to four-week stay.

In spite of all these difficulties, these tiny immigrants bring joy to many American families.

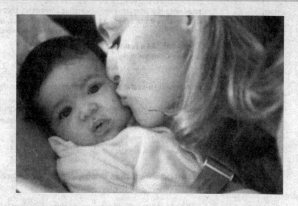

Adverbial Clauses and Phrases; Sentence Connectors; *So/Such . . . That*   351

Reading CD 3, Track 22

1. Have students first read the text silently. Tell them to pay special attention to the sentence connectors *however, in addition, furthermore,* and *as a result.* Then play the audio and have students read along silently.
2. Check students' comprehension. Ask questions such as: *What are some reasons people in the U.S. adopt children from other countries?* (long waiting lists and few babies available in the U.S.; a complicated and slow adoption process) *What are some difficulties U.S. families have to overcome to adopt a child from another country?* (expenses from $10,000 to $25,000; paperwork delays, traveling to another country for one to four weeks)

To save class time, have students do the reading for homework ahead of time.

Reading Variation

To practice listening skills, have students first listen to the audio alone. Ask a few comprehension questions. Repeat the audio if necessary. Then have students open their books and read along as they listen to the audio.

Culture Note

Adopted children sometimes refer to the women who gave birth to them as their biological mothers or birth mothers. Generally adopted children refer to their adoptive parents as their parents.

Reading Glossary

adopt: to take a child into a family; to make something your own (an animal, an idea, a plan, etc.)
tiny: very small
turn to: decide to try
waiting list: a list of names of people who are waiting until a service or an action becomes available

8.7 | Sentence Connectors

1. Have students cover the left column in grammar chart **8.7.** Have students scan the right column and underline sentence connectors. Have a volunteer list the connectors on the board.
2. Have students review the example sentences in the grammar chart. Ask: *How are these sentence connectors different from the clauses we have been looking at?* (Sentence connectors can connect two separate sentences.)
3. Draw students' attention to the Punctuation Note. Point out that connectors can be used to combine two sentences into one if a semicolon is used.

EXERCISE 18

1. Tell students that this exercise is about immigrants and refugees. Have students read the direction line.
2. Model the exercise. Direct students to the example in the book. Complete #1 with the class.
3. Have students complete Exercise 18 individually. Then have them compare answers in pairs. Circulate and observe the pair work. If necessary, check the answers as a class.
4. Assess students' performance. If necessary, review grammar chart **8.7** on page 352.

8.7 | Sentence Connectors

Ideas can be connected by sentence connectors. These connectors show the relationship between ideas.

Examples	Explanation
Many couples want to adopt American children. **However,** there are very few babies available. The U.S. is not a perfect country. **Nevertheless,** many people want to immigrate to this country.	Sentence connectors that show contrast are *however* and *nevertheless*. These words are similar in meaning to *but*.
Foreign adoption is not for everyone. It can be expensive. **In addition,** it can take a long time. My sister came to the U.S. to earn more money. **Furthermore,** she wanted to be reunited with our family. The Hispanic population is growing for several reasons. **First,** immigration brings in a large number. **In addition,** the birth rate among Hispanics is high.	Sentence connectors that add more information to the same idea are *in addition, furthermore,* and *moreover*. These words are similar in meaning to *and*. Sometimes people order their thoughts using *first, second, third,* etc. These ordinal numbers can be replaced with *in addition, furthermore,* and *moreover*.
Many couples are frustrated with the adoption process in the U.S. **Therefore,** they go to other countries to adopt. Many couples in China prefer sons. **As a result,** the majority of adoptions from China are girls.	Sentence connectors that show result or conclusion are *therefore, as a result,* and *for this reason*. These words are similar in meaning to *so*.

Punctuation Note:
Use either a period or a semicolon (;) before a sentence connector. Use a comma after a sentence connector.
My friends couldn't adopt a baby here. **Therefore,** they went to another country to adopt.
My friends couldn't adopt a baby here; **therefore,** they went to another country to adopt.

EXERCISE **18** Fill in the blanks with an appropriate connecting word.

EXAMPLE The Lost Boys were happy living with their families in Sudan. _However_, a war forced them to leave.

1. The Lost Boys faced many problems when they left Sudan. They didn't know where to go. _In addition / Furthermore_, they didn't have enough to eat.
2. Some of them couldn't swim. _Therefore / As a result_, some drowned when they had to cross a river in their escape.
3. Finally they found safety in a refugee camp in Kenya. _However_, conditions in the camp were very poor.

Culture Note

The sentence connectors in the grammar chart are usually used in more formal or written English. In informal spoken English, *and* is common for more information, *but* is common for contrast, and *so* is common to show a result or conclusion.

4. Many of the boys had never seen a gas stove before they came to the U.S. _Therefore / As a result_, they did not understand how to cook at first.

5. They faced problems in the U.S. They had to find jobs quickly. _In addition / Furthermore_, they had to go to school to improve their English.

6. They are happy that they came to the U.S. _However / Nevertheless_, they still miss their family and friends back home.

7. Many immigrants came to America at the beginning of the twentieth century. _____However_____, immigration slowed down during World War I.

8. Jews had a hard life in Russia and Poland. Many lived in poor conditions. _In addition / Furthermore_, they were the victims of anti-Semitism.

9. My grandfather immigrated to the U.S. to find a job and make more money. _____However_____, he wanted to be reunited with his relatives.

10. There was a big famine in Ireland. _____As a result_____, many Irish people left and came to America.

11. In 1924, Congress passed a law restricting the number of immigrants. _Therefore / As a result_, many people who wanted to come here couldn't.

12. Many Cubans wanted to escape communism in the 1960s. _____However_____, many of them couldn't get permission to leave Cuba.

13. Many Cubans tried to get permission to leave Cuba legally but couldn't. _Nevertheless / However_, many people found other ways of leaving. Some built or bought small boats and tried to reach Florida by sea.

14. More than a million legal immigrants came to the U.S. in 2001. _____in addition_____, about 400,000 illegal immigrants came that year.

15. A war broke out in Yugoslavia in 1992. _____As a result_____, many people died or lost their homes.

16. Most immigrants came to the U.S. because they wanted to. _____However_____, Africans were brought here against their will to work as slaves.

Adverbial Clauses and Phrases; Sentence Connectors; _So/Such . . . That_   353

Culture Note

Cuba is only 90 miles from Florida by sea. Some Cubans have reached Florida by boat. People who must leave their countries and arrive in the U.S. can apply for political asylum if they have a "well-founded fear" of being returned to their own countries. Asylum applicants must explain their cases to a court. Applicants who are granted asylum are called _asylees_.

1. Tell students that this exercise is about connecting ideas. Have students read the direction line.
2. Direct students to the example in the book. Then have a volunteer complete #1.
3. Have students complete the exercise individually. Have students compare their answers in pairs. Ask volunteers to share their answers with the class.
4. Assess students' performance. If necessary, review grammar chart **8.7** on page 352.

To save class time, have students do half of the exercise in class and complete the other half for homework. Or assign the entire exercise for homework.

17. In 1776, Thomas Jefferson wrote, "All men are created equal." _However / Nevertheless_, Jefferson had 200 slaves at the time he wrote these words.

18. Africans were brought to the U.S. to work as slaves in different areas of the U.S. _____As a result_____, many African families were destroyed.

19. Slavery officially ended in 1865. _However / Nevertheless_, many African-Americans continued to suffer.

20. African-Americans had been the largest minority for many years. _____However_____, this changed in 2003 when the Hispanic population became the largest minority.

21. Adopting a foreign baby is complicated. People have to pay a lot of money. _in addition / Furthermore_, they have to travel to the foreign country to fill out forms and pick up the baby.

EXERCISE 19 Complete each statement. Answers will vary.

EXAMPLE The U.S. is a rich country. However, _____it has many poor people._____

1. It is important for me to learn English. Therefore, Answers will vary.
_____

2. It is important for me to learn English. However, _____
_____

3. Living in another country is difficult. Immigrants have to adjust to a new language. In addition, _____
_____

4. Some children speak one language at home and another at school. As a result, _____
_____

5. To learn a new language, you must master the grammar. In addition,
_____

6. No one wants to leave friends and family. However, _____
_____

7. If someone wants to come to the U.S. to visit, he or she must have a passport. In addition, _____
_____

8. It's important for a new immigrant to know English. Therefore,
_____
_____

354   Lesson **8**

Expansion

Exercise 19 After students complete the exercise, have them use the items in the exercise as models to write statements of their own using *It is important for . . . . Therefore, . . .* and *It is important for . . . . However, ...* Collect for assessment or have students share their answers with the class.

9. I wanted to study English when I was young. However, _____

_____

10. I may not speak English perfectly. However, _____

_____

EXERCISE 20 *Combination Exercise.* Circle the correct words to complete this story.

Many people have come to America (*because* / *for*) freedom. But Africans lost their freedom and were brought to America against their will (*for* / *to*) work in the fields. Africans were taken from their homes
(1)
and put on slave ships (*for* / *to*) cross the Atlantic. (*Because of* / *Since*)
(2)   (3)
hard conditions, many died along the way.

(*In spite of* / *In spite of the fact that*) they worked hard from morning
(4)
till night, they received no money. In fact, they were often beaten if they didn't obey. They were forced to work hard (*so that* / *in order to*) white
(5)
plantation owners could become rich. (*Although* / *Unless*) many people
(6)
in the North were against slavery, slavery continued in the South

(*because of* / *since*) Southern slave owners did not want to give up their
(7)
cheap labor supply.

(*Even though* / *However*,) the law prohibited the importation of slaves,
(8)
slavery continued to increase. (*In spite of* / *In spite of the fact that*) the
(9)
difficulties of living under slavery, slaves formed strong communities. They tried to keep their African cultural practices, which included music and dance. (*Because* / *For*) people from the same regions in Africa
(10)
were separated from each other, they lost their native languages, used English, and were given biblical names rather than African names.

Most of the African-Americans in the North were free. (*In addition* / *However*), they didn't have an easy life. They couldn't
(11)
attend public schools. (*Furthermore* / *However*), they weren't allowed
(12)
to vote. Many slaves from the South tried to run away to the North. (*However*, / *Although*) some were caught and sent back to their "owners."
(13)

Adverbial Clauses and Phrases; Sentence Connectors; *So/Such . . . That*   355

EXERCISE 20

CD 3, Track 23

1. Tell students that this exercise is a review of what they have learned so far in this lesson. Have students read the direction line.
2. Direct students to the example. Review the example with the class; then complete items 1 and 2 as a class.
3. Have students complete the exercise individually and then check their work in pairs. Review the answers as a class.

To save class time, have students do half of the exercise in class and complete the other half for homework. Or assign the entire exercise for homework.

Exercise 20 Variation

To provide practice with listening skills, have students close their books and listen to the audio. Repeat the audio as needed. Ask comprehension questions, such as: *Why were Africans brought to America?* (to work in the fields) *Did they want to come?* (No; they came against their will.) *What happened on the trip from Africa to America?* (Many Africans died.) Then have students open their books and complete Exercise 20.

Culture Note

From the late 1700s through the 1800s, some slaves were able to escape from southern states to northern states by using the Underground Railroad. The railroad was not a train; it was a system of people who were willing to help escaped slaves move from one place to another, and to hide them in their homes between stops. The railroad used secret codes and signs to help the slaves move from stop to stop, until they reached safety and freedom in the North. One of the most famous "conductors" on the railroad was Harriet Tubman.

8.8 | So . . . That / Such . . . That

1. Have students cover the explanation column of the grammar chart. Ask students to scan the examples quickly and tell the class what is covered in this chart (*such . . . that, so . . . that, so many/few . . . that, so much/little . . . that*). Ask the class what they can figure out about the rules for *so* and *such . . . that*.
2. Have students review the explanations in the grammar chart. If necessary for the third and fourth rows, review count nouns (nouns for items that can be counted and take a plural ending such as *-s* or *-es*) and noncount or mass nouns (nouns for items that cannot be counted individually and do not take a plural ending).
3. Draw students' attention to the Language Note. If necessary, review contexts for informal speech (among friends and family; in everyday public interactions; in informal work situations) and formal speech (among colleagues or to a supervisor in a formal work situation; speaking before a group).
4. Remind students that *so that* and *so* used with purpose clauses have a different usage; if necessary, review the appropriate sections of grammar chart **8.2** on page 330.

(*Unless /Until*) the slaves were finally freed in 1865, they
(14)

faced many difficulties. (*In spite of the fact that / In spite of*) the
(15)

majority of Africans by that time were born in America, they suffered
discrimination (*because / because of*) the color of their skin.
(16)

Discrimination was still legal (*when /until*) 1965, when Congress
(17)

passed a law prohibiting discrimination in jobs and education.
(*Although / In spite of*) there has been progress toward equality for
(18)

all, there are still many inequalities in American life.

8.8 | So . . . That / Such . . . That

We can show result with *so . . . that* and *such (a) . . . that.*

Examples	Explanation
Americans have to wait **such a long time** to adopt an American baby **that** many are turning to foreign adoptions. The Sudanese Boys had **such an awful trip that** many of them died along the way.	We use: *Such* + adjective + noun + *that* Note: Use *a* or *an* before a singular count noun.
Foreign adoption is **so expensive that** many people cannot afford it. Small children learn English **so easily that** they become fluent in a short time.	We use: *So* + adjective + *that* *So* + adverb + *that*
There are **so many** Spanish-speaking people in Miami **that** you can hear Spanish wherever you go. There are **so few** babies available for adoption in the U.S. **that** many Americans adopt foreign babies.	We use: *So many* + plural count noun + *that* *So few* + plural count noun + *that*
There was **so much** poverty in Ireland in the 1800s **that** Irish people were forced to leave. The Sudanese Boys had **so little** to eat **that** many of them died.	We use: *So much* + noncount noun + *that* *So little* + noncount noun + *that*

Language Note:
That is often omitted in informal speech.
John works **so hard** (*that*) he doesn't have time to rest.
American life is **so strange** for him (*that*) it will take him time to understand it.

356   Lesson **8**

Grammar Variation

Have students look back at the reading on page 351 and underline the examples of *so . . . that* in the reading.

EXERCISE **21** Fill in the blanks with *so, so much, so many, so few, so little,* or *such (a / an).*

EXAMPLE We had _so many_ problems in our country that we decided to leave.

1. I waited _____ such a _____ long time that I thought I would never get permission.

2. When I got to the Miami airport, the security lines were _____ so _____ long that I had to wait for almost two hours. There were _____ so many _____ people arriving at the same time.

3. I came to the U.S. by winning the Green Card Lottery. I was _____ so _____ happy when I got my letter that I started to cry.

4. The U.S. is _____ such a _____ rich and powerful country that people from all over the world want to come here.

5. I come from Mexico. There is _____ so much _____ unemployment in Mexico that many people try to come to the U.S. for jobs.

6. Before I got my visa, I had to fill out _____ so many _____ papers and answer _____ so many _____ questions that I thought I would never be able to do it.

7. Our family has been in the U.S. for _____ such a _____ long time that we hardly even speak our native language anymore.

8. My neighbor's baby was _____ so _____ young when she arrived from China that she doesn't remember anything about China at all.

9. There are _____ so few _____ American babies to adopt that many families adopt babies from China, Russia, and other countries.

10. My uncle earned _____ so little _____ money in Guatemala that he couldn't support his family, so he came to the U.S.

Adverbial Clauses and Phrases; Sentence Connectors; *So/Such . . . That*   357

EXERCISE   21

1. Tell students that this exercise is about showing results. Have students read the direction line. Ask: *What do we write?* (*so, so much, so many, so few, so little,* or *such a/an*)
2. Model the exercise. Direct students to the example in the book. Then complete #1 with the class.
3. Have students complete the exercise individually. Then have them check their answers in pairs. Circulate and observe the pair work. If necessary, check the answers as a class.
4. Assess students' performance. If necessary, review grammar chart **8.8** on page 356.

Expansion

Exercise 21 Have students use the sentences in the exercise (particularly items 1, 2, 5, and 6) to write sentences using *so . . . that* or *such . . . that* about their native countries or about their experiences coming to the U.S. Collect for assessment or review in class.

EXERCISE 22

1. Tell students that this exercise is about schools and classes. Have students read the direction line.
2. Model the exercise. Direct students to the examples in the book. Ask volunteers to provide their own answers for the second example.
3. Have students complete the exercise individually. Then have them compare answers in pairs. Circulate and observe the pair work. Ask volunteers to share interesting answers with the class.

🕐 To save class time, have students do half of the exercise in class and complete the other half for homework. Or assign the entire exercise for homework.

EXERCISE 22 Fill in the blanks with *so, so much / many / little / few,* or *such (a / an).* Then complete each statement with a result.

EXAMPLES Michael is _such a_ good student _that he gets 100% on all his tests._

Learning another language is _so_ hard _it can take a lifetime to do it._

1. My math class is _Answers will vary._ easy _____

2. Peter is taking _____ classes this semester _____

3. The teacher gives _____ homework _____

4. Sometimes the teacher talks _____ fast _____

5. My roommate is from India. She speaks English _____ well _____

6. My biology class is _____ boring _____

7. Ms. Stevens is _____ good teacher _____

8. English has _____ irregular verbs _____

9. We had _____ long test _____

10. I had _____ mistakes on my test _____

11. The teacher gave _____ confusing explanation _____

12. I was _____ tired in class yesterday _____

358   Lesson 8

Expansion

Exercise 22 Have pairs of students write their own conversations using an item from the exercise as the first line and continuing with their own words. Have volunteers perform their conversations for the class.

SUMMARY OF LESSON 8

Abbreviations: C = Clause
NP = Noun Phrase
VP = Verb Phrase

1.

Words that connect a dependent clause or phrase to an independent clause:		
Function	Connectors	Examples
Reason	*because* + C *since* + C *because of* + NP	**Because** he doesn't understand English, he can't find a job. **Since** he doesn't understand English, he can't find a job. **Because of** his poor English, he can't find a job.
Time	*when* *whenever* *until* *while* *for* *during* *since*	**When** I find a job, I'll buy a car. **Whenever** I work overtime, I make extra money. I worked **until** 8 p.m. I worked **until** the store closed. **While** I was slicing the bread, I cut my finger. I've been working **for** three hours. I worked **during** my summer vacation. I've been working **since** 9 a.m. I've been working **since** I woke up this morning.
Purpose	*(in order) to* + VP *so (that)* + C *for* + NP	He exercises **(in order) to** lose weight. He exercises **so (that)** he can lose weight. He exercises **for** his health.
Contrast	*even though* + C *although* + C *in spite of the fact that* + C *in spite of* + NP	**Even though** he's rich, he's not happy. **Although** he's rich, he's not happy. **In spite of the fact that** he's rich, he's not happy. **In spite of** his wealth, he's not happy.
Condition	*if* *even if* *unless*	**If** it snows, we won't drive. We'll drive **even if** it rains. I won't go **unless** you go with me. I don't want to go alone.

Adverbial Clauses and Phrases; Sentence Connectors; *So/Such . . . That*   359

Summary of Lesson 8

1. **Words that connect a dependent clause or phrase to an independent clause** Draw students' attention to the abbreviations at the top of the page. Have students cover page 359. Read cues based on the examples in the chart (e.g., *Because my mother-in-law doesn't understand English, . . .* Or *I exercise in order to . . .*). Have students complete the statements orally or in writing.

If necessary, have students review:
8.2   Reason and Purpose (pp. 330–331)
8.3   Time Expressions (p. 336)
8.5   Contrast (p. 342)
8.6   Condition (p. 346).

Summary Variation

Write phrases with connectors from the chart on the board. In pairs, have students talk about themselves using the connectors in statements.

Summary of Lesson 8 (cont.)

2. **Words that connect two independent clauses** Have students write pairs of connected sentences about one of the issues they have studied in this lesson (immigration, refugees, adoption, diversity) using connectors from the chart.

   If necessary, have students review:
   8.7   Sentence Connectors (p. 352).

3. **Words that introduce result clauses** Have students work in pairs to ask each other questions about the examples in the chart. Model the activity: *Why do we use so many in the third example?* (*letters* is a plural count noun)
   If necessary, have students review:
   8.8   *So ... That / Such ... That* (p. 356).

2.

Words that connect two independent clauses:

Function	Connectors	Examples
To add more to the same idea	*in addition* *furthermore* *moreover*	Adopting a baby from another country is not easy. Parents have to pay a lot of money. **In addition,** they have to get permission from the INS.
To add a contrasting idea	*however* *nevertheless*	The law says that everyone is equal. **However,** inequalities still exist.
To show a result	*therefore* *as a result* *for this reason*	It is difficult for an uneducated person to find a job that pays well. **Therefore,** I've decided to educate myself and get a degree. There was a war in Sudan. **For this reason,** many people left.

3.

Words that introduce result clauses:

Function	Connectors	Examples
Result with adjectives and adverbs	*so* + adjective + *that* *so* + adverb + *that*	I was **so tired that** I fell asleep in front of the TV. She speaks English **so fluently that** everyone thinks it's her first language.
Result with quantity words	*so many* + plural noun + *that* *so much* + noncount noun + *that* *so few* + plural noun + *that* *so little* + noncount noun + *that*	I received **so many letters that** I didn't have time to read them all. I received **so much mail that** I didn't have time to read it all. He has **so few friends that** he's lonely. She has **so little time that** she rarely takes a vacation.
Result with nouns	*such (a)* + adjective + noun + *that*	It was **such a good movie that** I watched it three times. These are **such good grapes that** I can't stop eating them.

Punctuation Note:
Compare:

He went home from work early because he was sick. (No comma)

Because he was sick, he went home from work early. (Comma)

He was sick. Therefore, he went home from work early. (Period before the connecting word, comma after *therefore*)

He had such a bad headache that he had to go to bed. (No comma)

EDITING ADVICE

1. Use *to*, not *for*, with a verb when showing purpose.

   She went to the doctor ~~for~~ get a checkup.

   to

2. Don't combine *so* with *because*, or *but* with *even though*.

   ~~Because~~ he was late, so he didn't hear the explanation.

   ~~Even though~~ she speaks English well, but she can't write it.

3. Use *because of* when a noun phrase follows.

   He came late because ^*of* bad traffic.

4. Don't use *even* without *though* or *if* to introduce a clause.

   though
   Even ^ he's a poor man, he's happy.

   if
   I won't call you even ^ I need your help.

5. Use the *-ing* form, not the base form, after a time word if the subject is deleted.

   going
   Before ~~go~~ home, he bought some groceries.

6. Don't confuse *so that* with *because*.

   because
   He came to the U.S. ~~so that~~ he wanted freedom.

7. After *so that*, use a modal before the verb.

   could
   I bought a DVD player so that I ^ watch all my favorite movies at home.

8. Always follow a sentence connector with a complete sentence.

   He came to the U.S. because he wanted more freedom. In
   he wanted to get a better
   addition, education.

9. In a future sentence, use the simple present tense in the *if* clause or time clause.

   If I ~~will~~ go back to my hometown, I will visit my best friend.

Editing Advice

For each item, have students provide the grammar rule behind the Editing Advice. This can be done as an individual, a pair, a group, or a class activity.

1. *In order to* shows purpose. The short form is *to*. We follow *to* with the base form of the verb.
2. *Because* and *so* both introduce a clause of reason. Use only one in a sentence. *Even though* and *but* both show contrast. Use only one in a sentence.
3. *Because of* introduces a noun phrase.
4. For an unexpected result of contrast of ideas use a clause beginning with *even though*. Use *even if* to show that a condition doesn't affect a result.
5. If the subject of a time clause and the subject of the main clause are the same, the time clause can be changed to a participle phrase. The subject is omitted, and the *-ing* form is used.
6. *Because* can be followed by *want*. Do not follow *so that* with *want*.
7. *So that* (or *so*) shows purpose. The purpose clause usually contains a modal: *can*, *will*, or *may* for future; *could*, *would*, or *might* for past.
8. Sentence connectors connect two independent and complete clauses or sentences.
9. Use *if* to show that the condition affects the result in the future. Use the simple present tense in the condition clause.

Editing Advice (*cont.*)

10. *Although* shows an unexpected result or contrast of ideas and is followed by a clause with a subject and verb. *However* is a sentence connector.

11. Use *so* + adjective or adverb + *that*; use *such* + adjective + noun + *that*.

Lesson 8 Test/Review

For additional practice, review, and assessment materials, see Assessment CD-ROM with *ExamView Pro*, *More Grammar Practice* Workbook 3, Interactive CD-ROM, and Web site http://elt.thomson.com/gic

PART 1

1. Part 1 may be used as an in-class test to assess student performance, in addition to the Assessment CD-ROM with *ExamView Pro*. Have students read the direction line. Ask: *Does every sentence have a mistake?* (no) Have students complete the exercise.

2. Collect for assessment.

3. If necessary, have students review: **Lesson 8.**

---

10. *However* connects two sentences. *Although* connects two parts of the same sentence.

> However,
> She was absent for three weeks. Although she did all the homework.

11. Use *so* + adjective / adverb. Use *such* when you include a noun.

> such a
> My grandfather is so wise person that everyone goes to him for advice.

LESSON 8 TEST / REVIEW

PART 1   Find the mistakes with the underlined words, and correct them. Not every sentence has a mistake. If the sentence is correct, write C. Do not look for punctuation mistakes.

EXAMPLES   I came here so that I <u>am</u> with my family. *(could be)*

After leaving Greece, I went to Turkey.   *C*

1. <u>Even</u> he is a rich man, he isn't very happy. *(though)*
2. <u>Since</u> she came to the U.S., she has been living with her sister.   *C*
3. She can't go to the party <u>unless</u> she gets a babysitter for her baby.   *C*
4. Because he can't find a job, <u>so</u> he doesn't have much money.
5. If I <u>will go</u> to the library today, I'll return your books for you.
6. Even though she has good qualifications and speaks English well, <u>but</u> she can't find a job.
7. I'm saving my money <u>for</u> buy a new car. *(to)*
8. <u>Because</u> her health is bad, she is going to quit her job.   *C*
9. The children couldn't go out and play <u>because</u> the rain. *(of)*
10. <u>In spite of</u> she has a big family, she feels lonely. *(In spite of the fact that)*
11. The weather won't stop me. I'll drive to New York <u>even</u> it rains. *(if)*
12. Before <u>prepare</u> dinner, she washed her hands. *(preparing)*
13. <u>Since</u> the stores are very crowded on the weekends, I like to shop during the week.   *C*
14. He's going to buy a digital camera <u>so that</u> he can take pictures of his children.   *C*
15. He sent his mother a picture of his children <u>so that she sees</u> her grandchildren. *(can see)*

Lesson Review

To use Part 1 as a review, assign it as homework or use it as an in-class activity to be completed individually or in pairs. Check answers and review errors as a class. Reteach grammar points that students haven't mastered. Then student learning may be assessed using a test generated from the Assessment CD-ROM with *ExamView Pro*.

16. Alex left his country ~~so that~~ *because* he didn't like the political situation there.

17. You shouldn't open the door <u>unless</u> you know who's there. *C*

18. He uses spell-check <u>to</u> check the spelling on his compositions. *C*

19. She is <u>so a bad cook</u> *such* that no one wants to eat dinner at her house.

20. I have <u>so much</u> homework that I don't have time for my family and friends. *C*

21. I use e-mail <u>for stay</u> *to* in touch with my friends.

22. I need to get some credits before I enter the university. In addition, *I have to take* the TOEFL test.

PART 2 Punctuate the following sentences. Some sentences are already complete and need no more punctuation. If the sentence is correct, write *C*.

EXAMPLES   When he met her, he fell in love with her immediately.

I'll help you if you need me. *C*

1. The teacher will help you if you go to her office. *C*

2. She always gets good grades because she studies hard. *C*

3. Even though owning a dog has some disadvantages, there are more advantages.

4. Because he didn't study, he failed the test.

5. Before he got married, his friends had a party for him.

6. She did all the homework and wrote all the compositions; however, she didn't pass the course.

7. Although I didn't do the homework, I understood everything that the teacher said.

8. Even though he worked hard all weekend, he wasn't tired.

9. I stayed home last night so that I wouldn't miss a call from my parents. *C*

10. I am unhappy with my job because I don't get paid enough; furthermore, my boss is an unpleasant person.

11. She was so emotional at her daughter's wedding that she started to cry. *C*

12. My boss never showed any respect for the workers; as a result, many people quit.

Lesson Review

To use Part 2 as a review, assign it as homework or use it as an in-class activity to be completed individually or in pairs. Check answers and review errors as a class. Reteach grammar points that students haven't mastered. Then student learning may be assessed using a test generated from the Assessment CD-ROM with *ExamView Pro*.

PART 2

1. Part 2 may also be used as an in-class test to assess student performance, in addition to the Assessment CD-ROM with *ExamView Pro*. Tell students that this is an exercise on punctuation. Review the types of punctuation covered in the lesson (comma, semicolon). Review the examples. Complete #1 as a class. Have students complete the exercise.
2. Collect for assessment.
3. If necessary, have students review: **Lesson 8.**

1. Part 3 may also be used as an in-class test to assess student performance, in addition to the Assessment CD-ROM with *ExamView Pro*. Tell students that this exercise is about time words; point out the list of time words in the direction line. Review the example. Have students complete the exercise.
2. Collect for assessment.
3. If necessary, have students review:
   8.3   Time Expressions (p. 336).

1. Part 4 may also be used as an in-class test to assess student performance, in addition to the Assessment CD-ROM with *ExamView Pro*. Tell students that this exercise is about reason and purpose words; point out the list of words in the direction line. Review the example. Have students complete the exercise.
2. Collect for assessment.
3. If necessary, have students review:
   8.2   Reason and Purpose (pp. 330–331)
   8.7   Sentence Connectors (p. 352).

PART 3 Fill in the blanks with an appropriate thim word: *when, whenever, while, for; during, since,* or *until*.

EXAMPLE My friends were talking __during__ the whole movie. Everyone around them was annoyed.

1. They talk ___whenever___ they go to the movies. This happens every time.
2. They were talking ___while___ everyone else was trying to watch the movie.
3. They started talking ___when___ they sat down at the beginning of the movie.
4. They talked ___for___ two hours.
5. They didn't stop talking ___until___ they left.
6. ___When___ the movie was over, they left and went their separate ways.
7. I haven't seen them ___since___ we went to the movies last week.
8. I hate it when people talk to each other ___during___ a movie.

PART 4 Fill in the blanks with *because, because of, since, for, so that, in order to,* or *therefore*. In some cases, more than one answer is possible.

EXAMPLE I came to this school ___in order to___ learn English.

1. He came to the U.S. ___so that___ he could learn English.
2. He came to the U.S. ___in order to___ find a better job.
3. He came to the U.S. ___because of___ economic problems in his country.
4. He came to the U.S. ___in order to___ be with his family.
5. He came to the U.S. ___for___ a better future.
6. ___Because / Since___ the U.S. is a land of opportunity, many immigrants want to come here.
7. The U.S. is a land of opportunity. ___Therefore___, many people from other countries want to immigrate here.
8. Irish people came to America in the 1800s ___because___ they didn't have enough to eat.

Lesson Review

To use Parts 3 and 4 as a review, assign them as homework or use them as in-class activities to be completed individually or in pairs. Check answers and review errors as a class. Reteach grammar points that students haven't mastered. Then student learning may be assessed using a test generated from the Assessment CD-ROM with *ExamView Pro*.

PART 5 Fill in the blanks with *even though, in spite of the fact that, in spite of,* or *however.* In some cases, more than one answer is possible.

EXAMPLE ___Even though___ there are many opportunities in the U.S., my cousin can't find a job.

1. ___In spite of___ his fluency in English, he can't find a job.

2. He's fluent in English. ___However___, he can't find a job.

3. ___In spite of the fact that / Even though___ he has lived here all his life, he can't find a job.

4. He can't find a job ___even though / in spite of the fact that___ he has good job skills.

PART 6 Fill in the blanks with *if, unless,* or *even if.*

EXAMPLE ___If___ you're absent, you should call the teacher to let him know.

1. You must do the homework ___even if___ you're absent. Absence is no excuse for not doing the homework.

2. You should come to every class ___unless___ you're sick. If you're sick, stay home.

3. ___If___ you can't come to class, you need to call the teacher.

4. Some people go to work ___even if___ they have a cold. They don't want to lose a day's pay.

PART 7 Fill in the blanks with *so, so many, so much,* or *such.*

EXAMPLE I was ___so___ late that I missed the meeting.

1. There were ___so many___ people at the party that there wasn't anywhere to sit down.

2. The food was ___so___ delicious that I didn't want to stop eating.

3. I had ___such___ a hard day at work yesterday that I didn't have time for lunch.

4. My son is ___so___ intelligent that he graduated from high school at the age of 15.

5. She spent ___such___ a long time on her composition that she didn't have time to do the grammar exercises.

Adverbial Clauses and Phrases; Sentence Connectors; *So/Such . . . That* 365

Lesson Review

To use Parts 5, 6, and 7 as a review, assign them as homework or use them as in-class activities to be completed individually or in pairs. Check answers and review errors as a class. Reteach grammar points that students haven't mastered. Then student learning may be assessed using a test generated from the Assessment CD-ROM with *ExamView Pro.*

1. Part 5 may also be used as an in-class test to assess student performance, in addition to the Assessment CD-ROM with *ExamView Pro.* Tell students that this exercise is about contrast words; point out the list of words in the direction line. Review the example. Have students complete the exercise.
2. Collect for assessment.
3. If necessary, have students review:
   8.5 Contrast (p. 342)
   8.7 Sentence Connectors (p. 352).

1. Part 6 may also be used as an in-class test to assess student performance, in addition to the Assessment CD-ROM with *ExamView Pro.* Tell students that this exercise is about condition words; point out the list of words in the direction line. Review the example. Have students complete the exercise.
2. Collect for assessment.
3. If necessary, have students review:
   8.6 Condition (p. 346).

1. Part 7 may also be used as an in-class test to assess student performance, in addition to the Assessment CD-ROM with *ExamView Pro.* Tell students that this exercise is about result words; point out the list of words in the direction line. Review the example. Have students complete the exercise.
2. Collect for assessment.
3. If necessary, have students review:
   8.8 *So . . . That / Such . . . That* (p. 356).

1. Part 8 may also be used as an in-class test to assess student performance, in addition to the Assessment CD-ROM with *ExamView Pro.* Tell students that this exercise is a combined review of Lesson 8. Review the example. Have students complete the exercise.
2. Collect for assessment.
3. If necessary, have students review: **Lesson 8.**

PART 8 Complete each sentence.

EXAMPLE I didn't learn to drive until _____ I was 25 years old. _____

1. I come to this school for _____ Answers will vary. _____
2. I come to this school so that _____
3. People sometimes don't understand me because of _____
   _____
4. Since _____, it is necessary for immigrants to learn it.
5. She came to the U.S. to _____
6. I don't watch much TV because _____
7. I like to watch movies even though _____
8. Many people like to live in big cities in spite of the fact that _____
   _____
9. Please don't call me after midnight unless _____
10. I can usually understand the general meaning of a movie even if _____
    _____
11. I didn't speak much English until _____
12. I fell asleep during _____
13. Some students didn't study for the last test. As a result, _____
    _____
14. The teacher expects us to study before a test. However, _____
    _____
15. When applying for a job, you need to write a good résumé. In addition, _____
16. My mother has such a hard job that _____
17. There are so many opportunities in the U.S. that _____
    _____
18. It was so cold outside last night that _____
    _____

366   Lesson **8**

Lesson Review

To use Part 8 as a review, assign it as homework or use it as an in-class activity to be completed individually or in pairs. Check answers and review errors as a class. Reteach grammar points that students haven't mastered. Then student learning may be assessed using a test generated from the Assessment CD-ROM with *ExamView Pro.*

EXPANSION ACTIVITIES

Classroom Activities

1. Write the following sentence on a card, filling in the blank with one of your good qualities. The teacher will collect the cards and read them one by one. Other students will guess who wrote the card.

   My friends like me because _____

2. Form a small group. Tell which one of each pair you think is better and why. Practice reason and contrast words.

   - owning a dog or owning a cat
   - driving a big car or driving a small sports car
   - sending an e-mail or writing a letter by hand
   - watching a movie at home on a DVD player or watching a movie in a theater
   - writing your compositions by hand or writing them on a computer
   - studying at a small community college or studying at a large university
   - living in the city or living in a suburb

3. For each of the categories listed below, write a sentence with *even though* in the following pattern:

   I like _____ even though _____.

   Categories: food, exercise, movies, people, places, restaurants, hobbies, or animals

   EXAMPLES I like to travel even though it's expensive.
   I like to eat fast food even though I know it's not good for me.

   Find a partner and compare your answers to your partner's answers.

4. Write three sentences to complain about this city. Work with a small group. Practice *so / such . . . that*.

   EXAMPLE There is so much traffic in the morning that in takes me over an hour to get to work.

5. Write three sentences about this school. Try to convince someone that this is a good school.

   EXAMPLE The teachers are so friendly that you can go to them whenever you need help.

Talk About it

1. Frederick Douglass was an ex-slave who became a leader against slavery. In 1852, at a celebration of American Independence Day, Frederick Douglass gave a speech. He said, "This Fourth of July is yours, not mine. You may rejoice, I must mourn." Look up the words *rejoice* and *mourn*. Then tell what you think he meant by this.

CLASSROOM ACTIVITIES

1. To start the activity, brainstorm several good qualities (e.g., *I'm honest; I'm loyal; I'm funny.*). Tell students to be creative in writing their good qualities.
2. Review reason and contrast words before beginning the activity (*because, because of, since, even though, although, in spite of the fact that, in spite of, still, anyway*).
3. Have students work individually and then share their sentences with a group or with the class.
4. Have groups brainstorm their ideas before they begin to write. Have groups share interesting answers with the class.
5. Tell students to make their statements as convincing as possible. Encourage students to be creative.

TALK ABOUT IT

Have students work in groups. Either assign or have each group choose one or more of the topics to discuss. Review with students language for agreeing, checking for agreement and disagreeing. (e.g., *I think so too. Are you sure that's right? I'm not sure I agree.*). Set a time limit for discussion. Then have groups talk about their topics. If appropriate, have groups report back to the class. Have each group appoint a spokesperson.

Expansion Activities

These expansion activities provide opportunities for students to interact with one another and further develop their speaking and writing skills. Encourage students to use grammar from this lesson whenever possible.

To save class time, assign parts of the activities as homework. Then use class time for interaction and communication. If students do not need additional speaking practice, some of the activities may be assigned as writing activities for homework, or skipped altogether.

Classroom Activities Variation

Activity 2 After groups finish their work, have students survey the class by voice vote to see which option most students preferred. Model the question: *How many said owning a dog is better? How many said owning a cat is better?*

Activity 3 Have students repeat the activity with *I don't like _____ even though _____* using the same categories.

Activity 5 After students complete the activity, have the class vote on the most convincing sentences. If possible, post students' reasons in the classroom or hallway.

Talk About it Variation

Have students work in pairs. Have students interview each other using the questions in the activity, alternating interviewers. Have the interviewers take notes on their partners' responses.

Items 4 and 6 Have students debate item 4 or item 6. Divide the class into two teams. Tell each team to list five reasons supporting its view. Have each team present its arguments. Then give each team an opportunity to respond to the other team's arguments. At the end of the debate, survey the class to see which opinion is more popular.

WRITE ABOUT IT

1. Before students begin to write, have the class brainstorm types of assistance they have received and the people or agencies who provided it. List people and agencies on the board; list types of assistance in the appropriate column. Have students write a paragraph about their experiences. Collect for assessment and/or have students review each other's work.

2. To help students activate their ideas, work as a class to list possible arguments on both sides of the board. List phrases, such as: *People can learn about different cultures; social services agencies may be overworked,* etc. Have students choose the point of view they will write from. Collect for assessment and/or have students present their paragraphs to a group.

OUTSIDE ACTIVITIES

Instruct students to identify and interview someone in each of the categories listed. Work as a class to write out the questions to ask in each case.

INTERNET ACTIVITIES

1. Try to have students research all of the people on the list. Have students choose the person they want to research or assign names so that the entire list is covered.

---

2. In what ways will the U.S. be different when Hispanics make up 25 percent of the population?

3. What are the major reasons people immigrate to the U.S. from your native country?

4. Do you think the U.S. is richer or poorer because of its immigrant population?

5. Besides the U.S., what other countries have large numbers of immigrants? Is the immigrant population accepted by the native population?

6. When American parents adopt babies from other countries, should they try to teach them about their native countries? Why or why not?

Write About it

1. Write about how an agency or people have helped you and your family since you came to the U.S.

2. Do you think a country is richer or poorer if it has a large number of immigrants? Write a short composition to explain your point of view.

Outside Activities

1. Interview an African-American. Ask him to tell you how slavery has affected his life today. Ask him to tell you about discrimination in America today. Tell the class what you learned about this person.

2. Interview a Hispanic who has been in the U.S. for a long time. Ask him to tell you if Spanish is still used in the home. Ask him if he feels discrimination as a Hispanic-American. Tell the class what you learned about this person.

3. Interview an American-born person. Tell him or her some of the facts you learned in this lesson about immigration. Ask this person to tell you his or her opinion about immigration.

4. Ask an American-born person where his ancestors were originally from. How many generations of his family have lived in the U.S.? Does he have any desire to visit his family's country of origin?

Internet Activities

1. The following people came to America as immigrants. Find information about one of them on the Internet. Who is this person? What country did he / she come from? Print out a page about one of these people.

Madeleine Albright	David Ho	Carlos Santana
Mario Andretti	Henry Kissinger	Sammy Sosa
Liz Claiborne	Yo-Yo Ma	Arnold Schwarzenegger
Gloria Estefan	Zubin Mehta	Elizabeth Taylor
Andy Garcia	Martina Navratilova	Elie Wiesel

Write About it Variation

Have students exchange first drafts with a partner. Ask students to help their partners edit their drafts. Refer students to the Editing Advice on pages 361 and 362.

Outside Activities Variation

For one or more of the categories, have students as a group or class interview you or other members of school staff who fit the categories listed.

2. Type in *Ellis Island* at a search engine. What is Ellis Island and why is it important in the history of immigration? Where is it?

3. Find information about one of the following African-Americans: Frederick Douglass, Harriet Tubman, John Brown, Martin Luther King, Jr. Write a summary of an article you found on the Internet.

4. Find the Declaration of Independence on the Internet. Print it out and read it.

5. Type in *Lost Boys of Sudan* at a search engine. Print an article and bring it to class. Write a short summary of the article.

6. Type in *Foreign Adoption* or *International Adoption* at a search engine. Find a Web site that gives information about adopting a baby abroad. Find out the costs, where the babies come from, how long a family has to wait to get a baby, or any other interesting information. Report your information to the class.

7. Go to About.com. Type in *Immigration Policies* or *Immigration Affairs* or *Immigration 9/11*. Find an article about pre- and post-9/11 immigration guidelines. Did the events of September 11, 2001, change immigration policies? If so, how?

 Additional Activities at http://elt.thomson.com/gic

CLASSROOM ACTIVITIES (*cont.*)

2. Have students bring the information they find back to share with the class.

3. Have students include in their summaries the time period in which each person lived and his or her major accomplishments.

4. Have students talk about the form of English used in the Declaration of Independence. If appropriate, review some of the more well-known parts of the document and restate them in today's English.

5. Have students share the information they find on where the Lost Boys are now living, what kinds of work they have found, whether they are attending school, etc.

6. If students are interested, also have them research domestic U.S. adoption, "hard-to-place" adoptions, foster care, or adoption scams.

7. Have students share their information with the class. Ask students which source they found most useful and why.

Internet Activities Variation

Activity 3 Have students research how each person is remembered or celebrated today (Martin Luther King, Jr. holiday, national park sites, etc.).

Activity 5 Have students research other refugee or asylee groups who have been resettled in the U.S. (e.g., Cubans, Somali Bantu, Kosovars, Haitians, etc.).

Activity 7 Have students give their opinions about changes in U.S. immigration policy after 9/11.

If students don't have access to the Internet, they may find the information needed using the resources available at a local public library.

LESSON

9

GRAMMAR: Noun Clauses

Noun Clauses After Verbs and Adjectives
Noun Clauses as Included Questions
Noun Clauses as Direct Quotes
Noun Clauses in Reported Speech

CONTEXT: Caring for Children

Bringing Up Baby
Pediatricians' Recommendations
Day Care
Dr. Benjamin Spock
A Folk Tale
Being an Au Pair

371

Lesson Overview

GRAMMAR

1. Activate students' prior knowledge. Write *noun clauses, reported speech,* and *direct quotes* on the board. Ask students what they can say about each one.
2. Ask: *What will we study in this lesson?* (noun clauses after verbs and adjectives, noun clauses as included questions, noun clauses as direct quotes, noun clauses in reported speech) Give several examples of your own of sentences using the passive voice (e.g., *I'm sure that this lesson is going to be easy. The students said that the last lesson was easy.*). Write two or three similar examples on the board.

CONTEXT

1. Ask: *What will we learn about in this lesson?* (babies and children, pediatricians' recommendations, day care, a folk tale, au pairs) Elicit students' prior knowledge. Ask: *What do you know about taking care of babies and children? Do you think it's an important job? An easy job?*
2. Have students share their knowledge and personal experiences.

Photo

1. Direct students' attention to the photo. Ask: *What do you think the person who took this picture was trying to make us think?*
2. Have students share their impressions.

🕐 To save class time, have students do the Test/Review at the end of the lesson, or administer a lesson test generated from the Assessment CD-ROM with *ExamView® Pro.* Skip sections of the lesson that students have already mastered. You may also assign some sections for self-study for extra credit.

Expansion

Theme The topic for this lesson can be enhanced with the following ideas:

1. Brochures or Web articles showing laws governing in-home day care, babysitting, licensed day-care providers, preschools, etc.
2. A community college catalog showing classes to prepare to work in or run a child-care center
3. A brochure or handbook from local or state agencies showing requirements to become an in-home day-care provider
4. Booklets or brochures for parents listing day-care options and suggestions for evaluating them

9.1 | Noun Clauses—An Overview

1. Have students look at grammar chart **9.1**. Ask: *What is a clause?* (a group of words that has a subject and a verb) *How does a noun clause function in a sentence?* (as a noun)

2. Have students review the example sentences and explanations in the grammar chart. Ask: *What are four things we use a noun clause to do?* (include a statement within a statement, include a question within a statement, repeat someone's exact words, report what someone has said or asked) Clarify any vocabulary students are unfamiliar with.

Bringing Up Baby (Reading)

1. Have students look at the drawing on page 372 and the photo on page 373. Ask: *What are these parents doing?* (playing with and reading to their children) *How do you think the parents and the children feel?*

2. Have students look briefly at the reading. Ask: *What is the reading about? How do you know?* Have students make predictions.

3. Preteach any essential vocabulary words your students may not know, such as *bringing up, development, emotional, evidence, raised, poverty, disadvantage,* and *stimulating.*

BEFORE YOU READ

1. Have students discuss the questions in pairs. Try to pair students of different language backgrounds.

2. Ask for a few volunteers to share their answers with the class.

🕐 To save class time, skip "Before You Read" or have students prepare answers for homework ahead of time.

9.1 | Noun Clauses—An Overview

A **clause** is a group of words that has a subject and verb. A **noun clause** function as a noun in a sentence.

Compare:

    noun
He said hello.

       noun clause
He said that he wanted to see the baby.

Examples	Explanation
I think **that babies are cute.** It's important **that children get a good education.** She didn't realize **that the baby was sick.**	We use a noun clause to include a *statement* within a statement.
I don't know **how old the child is.** I don't remember **if I had a babysitter when I was a child.**	We use a noun clause to include a *question* within a statement.
She said, **"I will pick up my son at 4:30."** I asked, **"Where will you pick him up?"**	We use a noun clause to *repeat* someone's exact words.
She said **that she would pick up her son at 4:30.** I asked her **where she would pick him up.**	We use a noun clause to *report* what someone has said or asked.

BRINGING UP BABY

Before You Read

1. Should employers provide maternity leave for new mothers? Why or why not?

2. Do you think grandparents should have a big part in raising children? Why or why not?

Expansion

Theme The topic for this lesson can be enhanced with the following ideas:

1. Newspaper, magazine, or Web articles on early childhood development
2. Enrollment information for a program such as Head Start or Even Start
3. Family or newspaper photos of preschool children in a classroom or at an event
4. A flyer or brochure for a local nursery school, preschool, or early learning center

Reading Variation

To practice listening skills, have students first listen to the audio alone. Ask a few comprehension questions. Repeat the audio if necessary. Then have students open their books and read along as they listen to the audio.

Read the following article. Pay special attention to noun clauses.

Research shows **that a baby's early experiences influence his brain development.** What happens in the first three years of a baby's life affects his emotional development and learning abilities for the rest of his life. It is a well-known fact **that talking to infants increases their language ability** and **that reading to them is the most important thing parents can do to raise a good reader.** Some parents even think **that it's important to play Mozart to babies and show them famous works of art.** However, there is no scientific evidence to support this. It is known, however, **that babies whose parents rarely talk to them or hold them can be damaged for life.** One study shows **that kids who hardly play or who aren't touched very much develop brains 20 to 50 percent smaller than normal.**

Educators have known for a long time **that kids raised in poverty enter school at a disadvantage.** To prevent a gap[1] between the rich and the poor, they recommend early childhood education. A recent study at the University of North Carolina followed children from preschool to young adulthood. The results showed **that children who got high quality preschool education from the time they were infants benefited in later life.** In this study, 35 percent of children who had preschool education graduated from college, compared with only 14 percent of children who did not have preschool education.

While it is important to give babies stimulating activities, experts warn **that parents shouldn't overstimulate them.**

[1]A gap, in this case, means a difference.

Noun Clauses   373

Reading CD 4, Track 1

1. Have students first read the text silently. Tell them to pay special attention to noun clauses in the reading. Then play the audio and have students read along silently.
2. Check students' comprehension. Ask questions such as: *What are some things that the reading says are good for young children?* (reading to them, holding them, talking to them, a good preschool, stimulating activities) *What was the connection between preschool and college in one study?* (children who had preschool education were more likely to go to college)

🕐 To save class time, have students do the reading for homework ahead of time.

DID YOU KNOW?

In France and Italy, nearly 100% of children ages three to five attend preschool.

Reading Glossary

bring up: raise; take care of a child while he or she is growing up
development: growth; maturing
disadvantage: less than equal, less than average; without an advantage
emotional: related to feelings or mental stability
evidence: proof
poverty: environment in which a person or family has very little money
raise (a child): bring up; take care of while he or she is growing up
stimulating: enriching; interesting

Culture Note

Preschool usually means a school for children who are two to four years old. Some preschools are full day programs; others are half a day or three mornings a week. In most preschools, children learn to play together and develop social skills, do projects and artwork, play outside, and take a nap. At age five, most children begin kindergarten.

9.2 | Noun Clauses After Verbs and Adjectives

1. Have students cover grammar chart **9.2.** Say: *I know that learning a language can be difficult. Tell me something that you know or think.* Elicit several examples with *I know* from volunteers. Then provide an example with *be* (*I'm sure that practice is a good way to learn; I'm glad that you are in my class.*). Elicit several additional examples from students; write the examples on the board. Say: *After think, know, be sure, be glad, and other verbs and adjectives, we can use a noun clause.*

2. Have students review the examples and explanations in the grammar chart.

3. Direct students' attention to the two lists in the chart. Clarify any vocabulary students are unfamiliar with. Ask volunteers to give sentences about themselves using verbs and *be* phrases in the chart.

9.2 | Noun Clauses After Verbs and Adjectives

Examples	Explanation
Parents know **(that) kids need a lot of attention.** Some parents think **(that) babies should listen to Mozart.** Studies show **(that) early childhood education is important.**	A noun clause can follow certain **verbs.** *That* introduces a noun clause. *That* is often omitted, especially in conversation.

A noun clause often follows one of these verbs:

believe	find out	notice	remember
complain	forget	predict	show
decide	hope	pretend	suppose
dream	know	realize	think
expect	learn	regret	understand
feel*			

Feel followed by a noun clause means "believe" or "think." I *feel* that it's important for a mother to stay home with her baby. = I *believe / think* that it's important for a mother to stay home with her baby.

Examples	Explanation
I am sure **(that) children need a lot of attention.** Are you surprised **(that) some parents read to babies?** Parents are worried **(that) they don't spend enough time with their kids.**	A noun clause can be the complement of the sentence after certain **adjectives.**

A noun clause often follows *be* + an adjective:

be afraid	be clear	be obvious
be amazed	be disappointed	be sure
be aware	be glad	be surprised
be certain	be happy	be worried

Examples	Explanation
It has been said **that it takes a village to raise a child.**	A noun clause can be used after certain verbs in the passive voice.
A: I hope **that our children will be successful.** B: I hope **so** too. A: Do you think **that the children are learning something?** B: Yes, I think **so.**	Noun clauses can be replaced by *so* after *think, hope, believe, suppose, expect,* and *know.* Do not include *so* if you include the noun clause. *Wrong:* I think **so** the children are learning something.
I realize that the child is tired **and that** he hasn't eaten lunch. I know that you are a loving parent **but that** you can't spend much time with your child.	Connect two noun clauses in the same sentence with *and that* or *but that.*

374   Lesson **9**

Grammar Variation

Before students review the grammar chart, have them look back at the reading on page 373 and underline clauses with *that*. Then review the chart. Tell students that not every clause with *that* in the reading is included in the grammar chart.

EXERCISE **1**   Underline the noun clauses in the conversation below between two mothers.

EXAMPLE   **A:** Do you know <u>that it's good to read to children when they're very young</u>?

B: Yes, I do. But I didn't realize <u>that playing music was important too.</u>

A: I'm not so sure <u>that music is beneficial</u>, but I suppose <u>it can't hurt.</u>

B: I think <u>that it's good to give kids as much education as possible before they go to school.</u>

A: I'm sure <u>that's a good idea</u>. But don't forget <u>that they're just kids.</u> They need to play too.

B: Of course they do. I hope <u>my children will be successful one day.</u>

A: I predict <u>they will be very successful and happy.</u>

EXERCISE **2**   Fill in the blanks to complete the noun clause. Answers may vary.

EXAMPLE   Research shows that _____*a baby's early experiences*_____ influence his brain development.

1. Educators know that _____Answers will vary._____ enter school at a disadvantage.

2. Some parents think that _____ classical music for babies.

3. We all know that _____ to babies increases their language ability.

4. A study shows that _____ have smaller brains.

EXERCISE **3**   Respond to each statistic about American families by beginning with "*I'm surprised that . . .*" or "*I'm not surprised that . . .*"

EXAMPLE   Fifty percent of marriages in the U.S. end in divorce. I'm not surprised that 50 percent of marriages end in divorce.

Answers will vary.

1. Only 26 percent of American households are made up of a mother, a father, and children.

2. About 7 million American children are home alone after school.

3. About 12 percent of American children don't have health insurance.

4. About 20 percent of American children live in poverty.

5. Sixty-eight percent of married mothers work outside the home.

Noun Clauses   375

Exercise 1 Variation

To provide practice with listening skills, have students close their books and listen to the audio. Repeat the audio as needed. Ask comprehension questions, such as: *When is it good to read to children?* (when they're very young) Then have students open their books and complete Exercise 1.

Expansion

Exercise 2 Have students work in groups to write several statements about what their group thinks is good for babies and young children. Model sentences with *We think that . . .* , *We believe that . . .* , and *We feel that . . . .* Have groups share their ideas with the class.

 CD 4, Track 2

1. Tell students that this exercise is a conversation between two mothers. Have students read the direction line. Ask: *What do we underline?* (noun clauses)

2. Model the exercise. Direct students to the example in the book.

3. Have students complete Exercise 1 individually. Check answers as a class.

EXERCISE   2

1. Tell students that this exercise is about early childhood development. Have students read the direction line. Ask: *Are different answers possible?* (yes)

2. Direct students to the example. Tell students to refer to the reading on page 373 as they complete the exercise.

3. Have students complete Exercise 2 individually. Then have them compare their answers in pairs. Circulate and observe the pair work. Check the answers as a class.

4. Assess students' performance. If necessary, review grammar chart **9.2** on page 374.

EXERCISE   3

1. Tell students that this exercise is about statistics on American families. Have students read the direction line.

2. Model the exercise. Direct students to the example. Ask: *Do you agree with the second statement?* Ask several volunteers to give answers.

3. Have students complete the exercise in pairs. Have students take turns reading the statements and responding. Circulate and observe the pair work; participate in pair work by providing your own responses. Ask volunteers to share their responses with the class.

To save class time, have students do half of the exercise in class and complete the other half in writing for homework. Or if students do not need speaking practice, the entire exercise may be skipped or done in writing.

EXERCISE 4

1. Tell students that this exercise is about their knowledge and impressions of the U.S. Have students read the direction line.
2. Direct students to the examples. Ask several volunteers to complete the examples for themselves.
3. Have students complete the exercise individually. Then have them share their answers in groups. Circulate and observe the groups; if appropriate, add statements of your own. Have groups report interesting answers to the class.
4. Assess students' performance. If necessary, review grammar chart **9.2** on page 374.

To save class time, have students do half of the exercise in class and complete the other half for homework. Or assign the entire exercise for homework.

EXERCISE 5

1. Tell students that this exercise is about their opinions on child rearing. Have students read the direction line.
2. Model the exercise. Direct students to the example in the book. Ask: *Do you agree with this statement? What's your opinion?*
3. Have students review the questions and think about their answers; encourage students to take notes. Then have students discuss their opinions in groups.
4. Assess students' performance. If necessary, review grammar chart **9.2.**

To save class time, have students do half of the exercise in class and complete the other half in writing for homework. Or if students do not need speaking practice, the entire exercise may be skipped or done in writing.

---

6. In families where both parents work, women do most of the housework and child care.
7. Thirty-two percent of working wives with full-time jobs earn more than their husbands.
8. Fifty-six percent of adults are married.
9. About ten percent of adults live alone.
10. Sixty-five percent of families own their homes.
11. The average size of new American homes has increased as the size of the American family has decreased.
12. Twenty-five percent of households have only one person.
13. Twenty-seven percent of kids live in single-parent families.

EXERCISE 4 ABOUT YOU Fill in the blanks with a noun clause to talk about your knowledge and impressions of the U.S.

EXAMPLES   I know _that there are fifty states in the U.S._

I'm surprised that _so many people live alone._

1. I think _____ Answers will vary. _____
2. I'm disappointed _____
3. I know _____
4. I'm afraid _____
5. It's unfortunate _____
6. I'm surprised _____
7. I've noticed _____
8. Many people think _____

EXERCISE 5 What's your opinion? Answer the questions using *I think* and a noun clause. Discuss your answres.

EXAMPLE   Should mothers of small kids stay home to raise them?

I think mothers of small kids should stay home if their husbands can make enough money. But if they need the money, I think they should work.

Answers will vary.   1. Should the government pay for child care for all children?
2. Can children get the care and attention they need in day care?
3. Should fathers take a greater part in raising their kids?
4. Should grandparents help more in raising their grandchildren?

376   Lesson **9**

Expansion

Exercise 3 Have students use the models in the exercise to write additional statements about things that surprise, or don't surprise them. Suggest topics, or allow students to choose topics to write about.

Exercise 5 Have students write a short paragraph stating their opinions about one of the questions in the exercise. Collect for assessment or have students review each other's work.

5. Should the government give new mothers maternity leave? For how long?

6. Should parents read books to babies before they learn to talk?

7. Should parents buy a lot of toys for their children?

PEDIATRICIANS' RECOMMENDATIONS

Before You Read

1. What are some good habits that children should develop? How can their parents encourage these habits?

2. Is television a bad influence on children? Why or why not?

 Read the following article. Pay special attention to noun clauses.

Did You Know?

The average American child spends an average of 5.5 hours a day using some form of media (TV, compute, CD player, radio, etc.). More than nine out of ten food ads on Saturday morning TV are for unhealthy foods, such as candy and fast food.

The American Academy of Pediatrics (AAP) is worried that American children spend too much time in front of the TV. The AAP suggests **that pediatricians help parents evaluate their children's entertainment habits.** Doctors are concerned that children who spend too much time in front of the TV don't get enough exercise. At least one in five children is overweight. In the last 20 years, this number has increased more than 50 percent.

The AAP recommends **that children under two not watch any TV at all.** It is essential **that small children have direct interactions with parents for healthy brain growth.** The AAP advises **that parents offer children stimulating activities.**

The AAP recommends **that pediatricians be good role models** by not having TVs in their waiting rooms.

Noun Clauses 377

Expansion

Theme The topic for this lesson can be enhanced with the following ideas:

1. Local television schedule showing Saturday morning programming and afternoon programming for children
2. Newspaper, magazine, or Web articles on increases in the number of overweight children
3. Schedule of children's activities from a local community center, after school program, or recreational center

Reading Variation

To practice listening skills, have students first listen to the audio alone. Ask a few comprehension questions. Repeat the audio if necessary. Then have students open their books and read along as they listen to the audio.

Reading Glossary

ad: advertisement; commercial message
interactions: time spent with; conversations or activities with
pediatrics: children's medicine
role model: model to follow in life; someone whose example a person follows

Pediatricians' Recommendations (Reading)

1. Have students look at the photo. Ask: *How would you describe this child?* (overweight) *What is he doing?* (watching television; using a remote control)
2. Have students look at the title of the reading, and look briefly at the reading. Ask: *What is the reading about? How do you know?* Have students make predictions.
3. Preteach any essential vocabulary words your students may not know, such as *pediatrics, interactions, role models,* and *ads.*

BEFORE YOU READ

1. Activate students' prior knowledge about children's health and TV. Ask: *How much TV do you think children should watch? Why?*
2. Have students discuss the questions in pairs. Try to pair students of different language backgrounds.
3. Ask for a few volunteers to share their answers with the class.

To save class time, skip "Before You Read" or have students prepare answers for homework ahead of time.

Reading CD 4, Track 3

1. Have students first read the text silently. Tell them to pay special attention to noun clauses in the reading. Then play the audio and have students read along silently.
2. Check students' comprehension. Ask questions such as: *What is the AAP?* (The American Academy of Pediatrics) *What percent of children are overweight?* (at least 20%) *What does the AAP recommend children under two do instead of watching TV?* (have direct interaction with their parents) *What does the AAP say that children's doctors should do?* (not have TVs in their waiting rooms)

To save class time, have students do the reading for homework ahead of time.

DID YOU KNOW?

Traditionally, many Saturday morning TV shows are cartoons and other entertaining shows intended for young children who do not go to school on Saturday.

9.3 | Noun Clauses After Expressions of Importance

1. Have students work in groups to look at the list of verbs in the second row of the grammar chart. Have groups look up verbs that are unfamiliar. Ask: *What do these verbs have in common?* (They all express importance or urgency.) Say: *We can use a noun clause with these verbs. We use the base form of the verb and a subject pronoun.*

2. Have students review the rest of the grammar chart. Draw students' attention to the list of expressions and examples.

3. Have students use the examples in the chart to make statements of their own expressing importance with: *It is important that; I insist that; My doctor recommended that*, etc.

EXERCISE 6

1. Tell students that this exercise is about doctors' recommendations for raising healthy children. Have students read the direction line.

2. Model the exercise. Direct students to the example. Ask: *Do you agree with this statement?*

3. Have students complete Exercise 6 individually. Have them compare their answers in pairs. Finally, check the answers as a class.

4. Assess students' performance. If necessary, review grammar chart **9.3**.

9.3 | Noun Clauses After Expressions of Importance

Examples	Explanation
The AAP *recommends* **that pediatricians be good role models.** The pediatrician *suggested* **that she read to her kids.**	A noun clause is used after verbs that show importance or urgency. The base form is used in the noun clause. The subject pronoun is used before the base form. Compare Pronouns: He wants *her* to read. He suggested that *she* read.

Some verbs that express importance or urgency are:

advise*	forbid*	request
ask*	insist	require*
beg*	order*	suggest
demand	recommend	urge*

*The starred verbs can also be followed by an object + infinitive.
I advise *that she stay* home with her small children.
I advise *her to stay* home with her small children.

It is essential **that a baby have stimulation.** *It is important* **that parents spend time with their children.**	A noun clause is used after expressions of importance beginning with *it*. The base form is used in the noun clause.

Some expressions that show importance or urgency are:

It is advisable	It is important
It is essential	It is necessary
It is imperative	It is urgent

The above expressions can also be followed by *for* + object + infinitive.
It is essential *that they play* with their children. =
It is essential *for them to play* with their children.

The AAP advises that children under two **not watch** any TV at all.	For negatives, put *not* before the base form.

EXERCISE **6**   Rewrite these sentences as noun clauses.

EXAMPLE   Kids should see a doctor regularly.
It is important that *Kids see a doctor regularly.*

1. Kids should eat a healthy diet.
   It is essential that *Kids eat a healthy diet.*

2. A child should exercise regularly.
   It is important that *a child exercises regularly.*

Grammar Variation

Have students match the clauses in boldface in the reading on page 377 to the appropriate explanation in the grammar chart.

3. A child must receive love.

It is essential that *a child receive love.*

4. Children shouldn't watch a lot of TV.

Doctors recommend that *children not watch a lot of TV.*

5. Doctors want parents to give their children a healthy diet.

Doctors suggest that *parents give their children a healthy diet.*

6. Parents should talk to their babies and hold them.

It is essential that *parents talk to their babies and hold them.*

7. Some parents tell their children to turn off the TV.

Some parents insist that *their children turn off the TV.*

8. Children shouldn't eat a lot of candy.

Dentists recommend that *children not eat a lot of candy.*

9. Parents should be good role models.

It is essential that *parents be good role models.*

DAY CARE

Before You Read

1. Do you think it's OK for mothers of small babies to work outside the home?

2. In your native culture, do women with babies work outside the home? Who takes care of the children?

Noun Clauses   379

Day Care (Reading)

1. Have students look at the photo on page 379. Ask: *Where are these children? Who is the adult? What is she doing?*

2. Have students look briefly at the reading. Ask: *What is the reading about? How do you know?* Have students make predictions.

3. Preteach any vocabulary words your students may not know, such as *observations, loving, first aid, per,* and *preschoolers.*

BEFORE YOU READ

1. Activate students' prior knowledge about day care for children. Ask: *Do you know any children who are in day care? What do they do there? Do you think sending young children to day care is a good idea? What is good day care like?*

2. Have students discuss the questions in pairs. Try to pair students of different language and native country backgrounds.

3. Ask a few volunteers to share their answers with the class.

To save class time, skip "Before You Read" or have students prepare answers for homework ahead of time.

Expansion

Theme The topic for this lesson can be enhanced with the following ideas:

1. Ads from the newspaper or telephone book for day care providers
2. Brochure or Web page on regulations for day care providers
3. Magazine, newspaper or Web articles on how to choose a day care provider

Culture Note

People frequently use the phrase *work outside the home* to mean be employed for a salary. Using this phrase recognizes that homemakers and parents who take care of children and homes do work, even if the work is not paid.

Reading CD 4, Track 4

1. Have students first read the text silently. Tell them to pay special attention to noun clauses in the reading. Then play the audio and have students read along silently.
2. Check students' comprehension. Ask questions such as: *What are some ways a good day care provider interacts with children?* (hug them, talk to them, smile at them, play with them) *How many babies per caregiver is considered OK?* (three) *How many older children?* (eight)

🕐 To save class time, have students do the reading for homework ahead of time.

DID YOU KNOW?

Before the 1960s, married women in the U.S. frequently did not work outside of the home; many stayed at home and cared for their children and homes. During the 1960s and 1970s, more women began to have careers outside of the home, and day care for young children became much more common. *Working parents* are parents who have jobs outside the home. A parent who does not work outside the home is frequently called an *at-home mom* or a *stay-at-home dad*.

🎧 Read the following article. Pay special attention to noun clauses.

Working parents often put their children in day care. While most parents interviewed say they are satisfied with the day care they use, experts believe that only about 12 percent of children receive high quality care. Many parents really don't know **how good their day care service is.**

When choosing a day care center, of course parents want to know **how much it costs.** But there are many other questions parents should ask and observations they should make. Parents need to know **if the caregiver is loving and responds to the child's needs.** Does the caregiver hug the child, talk to the child, smile at the child, play with the child?

It is also important to know **if the day care center is clean and safe.** A parent should find out **how the caregiver takes care of sick children.** Is there a nurse or doctor available to help with medical care? Do caregivers know first aid?

Parents should ask **how many children there are per caregiver.** One caregiver for a group of eight four- or five-year-olds may be enough, but babies need much more attention; one caregiver for three babies is recommended.

Experts believe that parents should not put their babies in child care for the first four months. During this time, it is important for babies to form an attachment to their mothers.

Did You Know?

Twenty percent of preschoolers in married families are cared for by fathers, up from 17 percent in 1997.

380   Lesson **9**

Reading Variation

To practice listening skills, have students first listen to the audio alone. Ask a few comprehension questions. Repeat the audio if necessary. Then have students open their books and read along as they listen to the audio.

Reading Glossary

first aid: emergency medical care
loving: (as an adjective) caring, affectionate
observation: watching; observing; paying attention
per: for each
preschooler: a young child aged two to five years

9.4 | Noun Clauses as Included Questions

A noun clause is used to include a question in a statement or another question.

Examples	Explanation
Wh-Questions with auxiliaries or be	
Where is the mother? I don't know **where the mother is.** What should she do? I'm not sure **what she should do.** When will the children go home? Do you know **when the children will go home?**	Use statement word order in an included question—put the subject before the verb.
Wh-Questions with do / does / did	
When do the children go home? I don't know **when the children go home.** What does the child want? Do you know **what the child wants?** Where did the child go? I wonder **where the child went.**	Remove *do / does / did* in the noun clause. The verb will show the *-s* ending or the past tense.
Wh-Questions About the subject	
Who takes care of the kids? I'd like to know **who takes care of the kids.** How many teachers work there? Please tell me **how many teachers work there.**	There is no change in word order in questions about the subject.
Yes / No Questions with auxiliaries or be	
Will the children be safe? I don't know **if the children will be safe.** Is the center clean? I'd like to know **if the center is clean or not.** Can the child play outside? I'm not sure **whether the child can play outside or not.**	Add the word *if* or *whether* before including a *yes / no* question. You can add *or not* at the end. Use statement word order—put the subject before the verb.
Yes / No Questions with do / does / did	
Do the kids like their teacher? Can you tell me **whether the kids like their teacher?** Does the child want to go home? I don't know **if the child wants to go home.** Did your parents give you toys? I can't remember **if my parents gave me toys or not.**	Remove *do / does / did* in the included question. Add *if* or *whether* (. . . *or not*). The verb in the included question will show the *-s* ending or the past tense.

(continued)

Noun Clauses **381**

9.4 | Noun Clauses as Included Questions

1. Ask students to cover page 381. On the board, write: *What is her name? Where is she from? Who is she? Is she a student? Does she work here?* Say: *If we don't know the answers to these questions, we can say that by including them in a longer sentence.* Elicit students' help, if possible, to write: *I don't know what her name is. I don't know where she is from. I don't know who she is. I don't know if she is a student. I don't know if she works here.* Ask students if they can figure out the rules for including the questions in longer sentences. Elicit students' ideas.

2. Have students look at the grammar chart. Review the examples and explanations in the chart carefully. Help students identify the patterns in each section of the chart on page 381.

Grammar Variation

After students have reviewed the example sentences in the grammar chart on page 381, have them go back to the reading on page 380 and identify the explanation that applies to each boldface noun clause in the reading.

9.4 | Noun Clauses as Included Questions (cont.)

3. Review with students the list of phrases used before included questions. Provide a few examples of your own (*I'm not sure whose pen this is. Can you tell me if there is day care available here?*). If possible, have volunteers provide examples.

4. Draw students' attention to the Punctuation and Usage Notes. Point out the use of included questions, especially with people we don't know, to sound more polite.

EXERCISE 7

1. Tell students that this exercise is about finding out about a day care center. Have students read the direction line. Ask: *What do we write?* (a question word or phrase)

2. Model the exercise. Direct students to the examples in the book. Then do #1 with the class.

3. Have students complete Exercise 7 individually. Then have them compare their answers in pairs. Finally, check the answers as a class.

An included question is used after phrases such as these:

I don't know	Do you remember
Please tell me	Do you know
I have no idea	Can you tell me
I wonder	Are you sure
I don't remember	Do you understand
You need to decide	Would you like to know
It's important to ask	Does anyone know
I'm not sure	
Nobody knows	
I can't understand	
I'd like to know	
I can't tell you	

Punctuation Note: Use a period at the end of the included question if the sentence is a statement. Use a question mark if the sentence begins with a question.

   I don't know what time it is.
   Do you know what time it is?

Usage Note: When asking for information, especially from a stranger, an included question sounds more polite than a direct question.

  Direct Question: Who is the director of the day care center?
  More Polite: Can you tell me who the director of the day care center is?

EXERCISE 7   Fill in the blanks with an appropriate question word or phrase *(who, what, where, when, why, how, how many, or how much)* or *if* or *whether*.

EXAMPLE   Can you tell me _how much_ time the children spend watching TV?

    I'd like to know _if_ the day care center is expensive.

1. I don't know _what_ my child's teacher's name is.

2. I can't remember _whether / if_ the class begins at seven o'clock or eight o'clock.

3. You should ask _how many_ people take care of the children. It's good to have a lot of teachers.

4. I would like to know _whether / if_ the day care center is clean or not.

5. I would like to know _whether / if_ the day care center is expensive.

Expansion

Grammar Have students write a simple question about a service (a school, a children's program, a bus or train schedule, the location of an office or facility, etc.). Collect the questions and read them to the class one at a time. Have students convert them to more polite questions using an included question, as in the Usage Note.

6. I would like to know _____ what _____ the caregivers do if the child gets sick.

7. Can you tell me _____ who _____ the director of the program is? I've never met her.

8. I have no idea _____ how much _____ the day care center costs.

9. Please tell me _____ where _____ the day care center is located.

EXERCISE 8 Circle the correct words to complete the statement or question.

EXAMPLE Please tell me how old (*is your child* / *your child is*).

1. I'd like to know when (*I have to* / *do I have to*) pick my child up.

2. Do you know what (*is the teacher's name* / *the teacher's name is*)?

3. Do you know (*is the center open* / *if the center is open*) on Saturday?

4. Can you tell me how much (*you paid* / *did you pay*) for the service?

5. I don't know where (*the day care center is located* / *is located the day care center*).

6. I want to know how old (*your son is* / *is your son*).

7. I'd like to know how much (*the service costs* / *does the service cost* / *costs the service*).

8. Can you tell me when (*the center closes* / *closes the center*)?

9. I'd like to know (*the children watch TV* / *do the children watch TV* / *if the children watch TV*) at the center.

10. Please tell me (*if works a nurse* / *whether a nurse works* / *does a nurse work*) at the center.

11. I'd like to know (*the center has* / *has the center* / *whether the center has*) an outdoor playground or not.

12. I wonder (*if the teacher loves* / *does the teacher love* / *if loves the teacher*) small children.

Noun Clauses **383**

EXERCISE 8

1. Tell students that this exercise is about asking polite questions about a day care center. Have students read the direction line.
2. Model the exercise. Direct students to the example in the book.
3. Have students complete Exercise 8 individually. Then have them compare their answers in pairs. If necessary, check answers as a class.
4. Assesss students' performance. If necessary, review grammar chart **9.4**.

To save class time, have students do half of the exercise in class and complete the other half for homework. Or assign the entire exercise for homework.

Expansion

Exercise 8 After students finish Exercise 8, have them locate the explanation for each item in Grammar Chart **9.4** on pages 381 and 382.

1. Tell students that this exercise is about asking included questions. Have students read the direction line. Ask: *What kind of questions are these?* (questions about the subject)
2. Direct students to the example in the book.
3. Have students complete the exercise individually and compare answers in pairs. If necessary, check answers as a class.
4. Assess students' performance. If necessary, review the appropriate sections of grammar chart **9.4**.

To save class time, have students do half of the exercise in class and complete the other half for homework.

1. Tell students that this exercise is about asking included questions. Have students read the direction line. Ask: *What kind of questions are these?* (*wh-* questions with *be* or an auxiliary verb)
2. Direct students to the example in the book.
3. Have students complete the exercise individually and compare answers in pairs. If necessary, check answers as a class.
4. Assess students' performance. If necessary, review the appropriate sections of grammar chart **9.4**.

To save class time, have students do half of the exercise in class and complete the other half for homework.

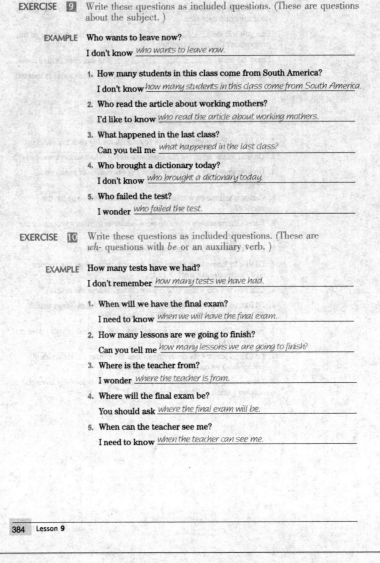

EXERCISE 9 Write these questions as included questions. (These are questions about the subject.)

EXAMPLE Who wants to leave now?
I don't know *who wants to leave now.*

1. How many students in this class come from South America?
I don't know *how many students in this class come from South America.*

2. Who read the article about working mothers?
I'd like to know *who read the article about working mothers.*

3. What happened in the last class?
Can you tell me *what happened in the last class?*

4. Who brought a dictionary today?
I don't know *who brought a dictionary today.*

5. Who failed the test?
I wonder *who failed the test.*

EXERCISE 10 Write these questions as included questions. (These are *wh-* questions with *be* or an auxiliary verb.)

EXAMPLE How many tests have we had?
I don't remember *how many tests we have had.*

1. When will we have the final exam?
I need to know *when we will have the final exam.*

2. How many lessons are we going to finish?
Can you tell me *how many lessons we are going to finish?*

3. Where is the teacher from?
I wonder *where the teacher is from.*

4. Where will the final exam be?
You should ask *where the final exam will be.*

5. When can the teacher see me?
I need to know *when the teacher can see me.*

384   Lesson **9**

Expansion

Exercises 9 and 10 Have students work in groups. Have each student write a simple question about the subject (using the questions in Exercise 9 as a model) and a *wh-* question with *be* or an auxiliary verb (using the questions in Exercise 10 as a model). Then have students pass their questions to other students. Refer students to the list of phrases in the grammar chart on page 382. Have each student use the phrases to convert the questions he or she is given to included questions using the first student's name: *Juan needs to know where the post office is. Mariama would like to know who brought the cookies.*

EXERCISE **11** Write these questions as included questions. (These are *wh*-questions with *do, does,* or *did.*)

EXAMPLE Where did you buy your books?

Can you tell me *where you bought your books?*

1. When does the class begin?

Can you tell me *when the class begins?*

2. What grade did I get on the last test?

Can you tell me *what grade I got on the last test?*

3. How many mistakes did I make?

I'd like to know *how many mistakes I made.*

4. How many questions does the test have?

It's not important to know *how many questions the test has.*

5. How many compositions does the teacher want?

You should ask the teacher *how many compositions he/she wants.*

EXERCISE **12** Write these questions as included questions. (These are *yes / no* questions with an auxiliary verb or *be.*)

EXAMPLE Is the teacher American?

I'd like to know *if the teacher is American.*

1. Is the test going to be hard?

I don't know *if/whether the test is going to be hard (or not).*

2. Will you be our teacher next semester?

I'd like to know *if/whether you will be our teacher next semester (or not).*

3. Can you help us with registration?

I'd like to know *if/whether you can help us with registration (or not).*

4. Have you been teaching here for a long time?

Can you tell me *if/whether you have been teaching here for a long time?*

5. Are the students confused?

I have no idea *if/whether the students are confused (or not).*

Noun Clauses **385**

EXERCISE 11

1. Tell students that this exercise is about asking included questions. Have students read the direction line. Ask: *What kind of questions are these?* (*wh*- questions with *do, does,* or *did*)
2. Direct students to the example in the book.
3. Have students complete the exercise individually and compare answers in pairs. If necessary, check answers as a class.
4. Assess students' performance. If necessary, review the appropriate sections of grammar chart **9.4.**

To save class time, have students do half of the exercise in class and complete the other half for homework.

EXERCISE 12

1. Tell students that this exercise is about asking included questions. Have students read the direction line. Ask: *What kind of questions are these?* (*yes/no* questions with an auxiliary verb or *be*)
2. Direct students to the example in the book.
3. Have students complete the exercise individually and compare answers in pairs. If necessary, check answers as a class.
4. Assess students' performance. If necessary, review the appropriate sections of grammar chart **9.4.**

To save class time, have students do half of the exercise in class and complete the other half for homework. Or assign the entire exercise for homework.

Expansion

Exercises 11 and 12 Have students work in groups. Have each student write a simple *wh*-question with *do, does,* or *did* (using the questions in Exercise 11 as a model) and a *yes/no* question with an auxiliary verb or *be* (using the questions in Exercise 12 as a model). Then have students pass their questions to another student. Refer students to the list of phrases in the grammar chart on page 382. Have each student convert the questions he or she is given to included questions using the first student's name: *Josef wants to know when the semester ends. Luisa wonders if there is going to be a class party.*

1. Tell students that this exercise is about asking included questions. Have students read the direction line. Ask: *What kind of questions are these?* (yes/no questions with *do, does,* or *did*)
2. Direct students to the example in the book.
3. Have students complete the exercise individually and compare answers in pairs. If necessary, check answers as a class.
4. Assess students' performance. If necessary, review the appropriate sections of grammar chart 9.4.

🕐 To save class time, have students do half of the exercise in class and complete the other half for homework. Or assign the entire exercise for homework.

1. Tell students that this exercise is a series of questions parents can ask about day care providers. Have students read the direction line.
2. Model the exercise. Direct students to the example in the book.
3. Have students complete Exercise 14 individually. Have them compare answers in pairs. Check answers as a class.

🕐 To save class time, have students do half of the exercise in class and complete the other half for homework. Or assign the entire exercise for homework.

EXERCISE 13 Write these questions as included questions. (These are *yes / no* questions with *do, does,* or *did.*)

EXAMPLE Does your teacher give a lot of homework?

Can you tell me *if your teacher gives a lot of homework?*

1. Does the school have a cafeteria?
   You should ask *if/whether the school has a cafeteria (or not).*

2. Did everyone pass the last test?
   I don't know *if/whether everyone passed the last test (or not).*

3. Did you buy a used book?
   Please tell me *if/whether you bought a used book (or not).*

4. Does the teacher speak Spanish?
   I'm not sure *if/whether the teacher speaks Spanish (or not).*

5. Do I need to write a composition?
   Can you tell me *if/whether I need to write a composition (or not)?*

EXERCISE 14 These are some questions parents can ask before choosing day care for their children. Include each question after "I'd like to know."

EXAMPLE How much does it cost?

I'd like to know *how much it costs.*

1. Do the caregivers have a lot of experience?
   I'd like to know *if/whether the caregivers have a lot of experience (or not).*

2. How does the caregiver discipline the children?
   I'd like to know *how the caregivers discipline the children.*

3. Can the caregiver handle problems without getting angry or impatient?
   I'd like to know *if/whether the caregiver can handle problems without getting angry or impatient (or not).*

4. Am I welcome to drop in and visit?
   I'd like to know *if/whether I'm welcome to drop in and visit (or not).*

5. How does the caregiver take care of sick children?
   I'd like to know *how the caregiver takes care of sick children.*

6. Is there a nurse or doctor to help with medical care?
   I'd like to know *if/whether there is a nurse or doctor to help with medical care (or not).*

Expansion

Exercises 9 through 13 Provide additional oral practice with included questions using role-plays. Have students work in threes. Have students B and C in each group close their books. Have student A (playing a shy student, a new student, or a student on the telephone) direct questions from the exercises to student B. Have student B convert the question to an included question and student C (playing an informed student) answer the question, e.g.:

A (to B): *Where is the teacher from?*
B (to C): *She'd like to know where the teacher is from.*
C (to B): *He's from Los Angeles.*
Have students switch roles several times during the activity.

7. Are there smoke alarms in the building?

I'd like to know _if/whether there are smoke alarms in the building (or not)._

8. How many caregivers are there?

I'd like to know _how many caregivers there are._

9. Does the caregiver hug the children?

I'd like to know _if/whether the caregiver hugs the children (or not)._

10. How many children are there for each caregiver?

I'd like to know _how many children there are for each caregiver._

11. Are the toys clean?

I'd like to know _if/whether the toys are clean (or not)._

12. Is the day care center licensed by the state?

I'd like to know _if/whether the day care center is licensed by the state (or not)._

13. Do the children have stimulating activities?

I'd like to know _if/whether the children have stimulating activities (or not)._

9.5 | Question Words Followed by an Infinitive

Examples	Explanation
What should I do? a. I don't know **what I should do.** b. I don't know **what to do.** Where can I find information? a. Please tell me **where I can find information.** b. Please tell me **where to find information.**	Some noun clauses with *can, could,* and *should* can be shortened to an infinitive phrase. Sentences (a) use a noun clause. Sentences (b) use an infinitive.
Should she work or stay home with her children? a. She can't decide **if she should work or stay home with her children.** b. She can't decide **whether to work or stay home with her children.**	Sentence (a) uses a noun clause. Sentence (b) uses an infinitive. Use *whether,* not *if,* to introduce an infinitive. *Wrong:* She can't decide *if* to work or stay home with her children.
How can I find a good day care center? I don't know **how to find a good day care center.**	An infinitive is used after *know how.*

9.5 | Question Words Followed by an Infinitive

1. Have students cover the grammar chart. Tell the students about a problem you are having or have had. For example, write on the board: *Which computer should I buy?* Have a volunteer convert the question to an included question with *I don't know* (e.g., *I don't know which computer I should buy.*). Say: *I can also say* I don't know which computer to buy. Ask: *What does this sentence use?* (an infinitive phrase)

2. Have students look at grammar chart **9.5.** Review the examples and explanations in the chart.

3. Have students provide several examples with *I can't decide whether to* and *I don't know how to.*

Expansion

Exercise 14 Use role-plays as in the Expansion on page 386. Have students work in threes. Have students B and C in each group cover pages 386 and 387. Have student A (playing a shy parent) whisper each question in Exercise 14 to student B. Have student B (playing a second parent) convert the question to an included question and student C (playing a day care employee) answer, e.g.:

A (to B): *How much does it cost?*
B (to C): *We'd like to know how much it costs.*
C (to B): *It costs $150 a week.*

Have students switch roles partway through the exercise.

EXERCISE 15

1. Tell students that this exercise is about asking for help or advice. Have students read the direction line. Ask: *What do we write?* (an infinitive phrase)
2. Direct students to the example.
3. Have students complete the exercise individually. Check answers as a class.

EXERCISE 16

1. Tell students that this exercise is about their decisions and information. Have students read the direction line.
2. Direct students to the example in the book. Review the example, and then ask several volunteers to complete the example with information about themselves.
3. Have students complete the exercise individually and then share their statements in pairs. Circulate and observe the pair work. If possible, participate in the exercise. Have pairs report interesting information to the class.
4. Assess students' performance. If necessary, review grammar chart **9.5** on page 387.

To save class time, have students do half of the exercise in class and complete the other half for homework. Or assign the entire exercise for homework.

EXERCISE **15** Complete these sentences with an infinitive phrase.

EXAMPLE   What should I do about my problem?
I don't know *what to do about my problem.*

1. Where can I buy textbooks?
I don't know *where to buy textbooks.*

2. What classes should I register for?
I can't decide *what classes to register for.*

3. Should I take morning classes or evening classes?
I don't know *whether to take morning classes or evening classes.*

4. What else should I do?
I don't know *what else to do.*

5. How can I use the computer in the library?
I don't know *how to use the computer in the library.*

6. What can I do about cancelled classes?
I don't know *what to do about cancelled classes.*

7. Should I take biology or physics?
I can't decide *whether to take biology or physics.*

8. Should I buy new textbooks or used books?
I'm not sure *whether to buy new textbooks or used books.*

EXERCISE **16** ABOUT YOU Complete each statement with an infinitive phrase. Discuss your answers in a small group or with the entire class.

EXAMPLE   I can't decide *whether to stay in this city or move to another city.*

1. When I came to this school, I didn't know _____ Answers will vary.

2. I can't decide _____

3. When I came to this city, I had to decide _____

4. A new student at this college needs to know _____

5. There are so many choices of products in the stores. Sometimes I can't decide _____

Expansion

Exercise 16 Have students write additional statements about decisions they have made or will make. Provide prompts, such as: *In the next few years, I'm going to have to decide . . .* and *When I was young, I couldn't decide . . . .* Collect for assessment, or have students share their statements with the class.

EXERCISE 🎧 Two students are talking. Fill in the blanks to complete the included questions. Answers may vary.

A: Hi. Where are you going in such a hurry?

B: I need to get to the library before it closes. What time does it close?

A: I'm not sure what time _____ it closes _____.
                                    (example)

B: What time is it now?

A: I don't have my watch, so I don't know what time _____ it is _____
                                                           (1)
But I'm sure it must be after six. Why do you need to use the library?

B: The teacher told us to write a paper. She told us to choose a topic.
I don't know what topic _____ to choose _____.
                                (2)

A: You have small children. Why don't you write about child development?

B: That's a good topic. But I have to start somewhere. I don't even
know where _____ to start _____.
                  (3)

A: Try going to the Internet. Use a search engine and type in *child development.*

B: I don't know how _____ to use _____ the Internet.
                           (4)
And I don't have a computer at home.

A: You don't? Let's go to the library and use the computers there.

B: I don't know where _____ they are _____.
                              (5)

A: They're in the back. Come. I'll show you.

(Later)

B: Uh-oh. The library is closed. I wonder what time
_____ it opens _____ tomorrow.
         (6)

A: The sign says, "Open 9 a.m. to 6 p.m."

B: Can you meet me at the library at 10 o'clock tomorrow and help me?

A: I'm not sure _____ if/whether I can _____ or not. I have an appointment
                        (7)
at 8:30, and I don't know _____ if/whether I'll be finished _____
                                     (8)
by 10 o'clock or not. But don't worry; the librarian can show you how to do a search.

Noun Clauses   389

EXERCISE 17

🎧 *CD 4, Track 5*

1. Tell students that this exercise is a conversation between two students. Have students read the direction line. Ask: *Are different answers possible?* (yes)
2. Direct students to the example. Then complete #1 with the class.
3. Have students complete the exercise individually. Have students check their answers by practicing the conversation in pairs. If necessary, check answers with the class.

🕐 To save class time, have students do half of the exercise in class and complete the other half for homework. Or assign the entire exercise for homework.

Exercise 17 Variation

To provide practice with listening skills, have students close their books and listen to the audio. Repeat the audio as needed. Ask comprehension questions, such as: *Why is person B in such a hurry?* (because person B needs to get to the library before it closes) *Does person B know what time the library closes?* (no) *Does person A?* (no) Then have students open their books and complete Exercise 17.

Expansion

Exercise 17 Have students make lists for person *A* and person *B* of the things each one doesn't know or isn't sure about (*Person A isn't sure what time the library closes.*).

Dr. Benjamin Spock (Reading)

1. Have students look at the photo. Ask: *What kind of person do you think this man is? Why?*
2. Have students look at the title of the reading and the caption under the photo, and look briefly at the reading. Ask: *What is the reading about? How do you know?* Have students make predictions.
3. Preteach any essential vocabulary words your students may not know, such as *leading, rigid, strict, supportive, scold, common-sense,* and *deserve.*

BEFORE YOU READ

1. Have students discuss the questions in pairs. Try to pair students of different language backgrounds.
2. Ask for a few volunteers to share their answers with the class.

To save class time, skip "Before You Read" or have students prepare answers for homework ahead of time.

Reading ∩ CD 4, Track 6

1. Have students first read the text silently. Tell them to pay special attention to the words in quotation marks and other noun clauses. If necessary, clarify the meaning of *quotation marks* on the board (" "). Then play the audio and have students read along silently.
2. Check students' comprehension. Ask questions such as: *What is Dr. Spock famous for?* (his book about baby and child care) *What two adverbs describe the way Dr. Spock thought babies should be treated?* (gently and lovingly) *Before Dr. Spock, who was the best-known "expert" on child care in the U.S.?* (John Watson) *Did Dr. Spock agree with John Watson?* (no)

To save class time, have students do the reading for homework ahead of time.

DID YOU KNOW ?

Ask students if they have seen Dr. Spock's book in their language. Have them discuss child-rearing philosophies in their cultures. Ask: *Where do people in your culture get information about raising children? From books? Relatives?*

DR. BENJAMIN SPOCK

Before You Read

1. Have you ever heard of Dr. Benjamin Spock? What do you know about him?
2. What are some differences in the ways that children are raised in different cultures?

Dr. Benjamin Spock, 1903–1998

 Read the following article. Pay special attention to the words in quotation marks (". . .") and other noun clauses.

Did You Know?

Dr. Spock's book has been translated into 40 different languages.

New parents are always worried that they might be making a mistake with their new baby. The baby cries, and they don't know if they should let him cry or pick him up. The baby is sick, and they don't know what to do. **"Trust yourself. You know more than you think you do,"** wrote Benjamin Spock in his famous book *Dr. Spock's Baby and Child Care,* which first appeared in 1946. This book has sold over 50 million copies, making it the biggest-selling book after the Bible. In fact, many parents say **that it is the parents' bible for raising children.**

Before Dr. Spock's book appeared, John Watson was the leading child-care expert in the 1920s and 1930s. He wrote, **"Never hug or kiss your children; never let them sit in your lap."** He continued, **"If you must, kiss them once on the forehead when they say good night. Shake hands with them in the morning."** Also, he told parents **that it was necessary to feed children on a rigid schedule.** Dr. Spock disagreed with this strict manner of raising children and decided **that he would write a book.** "I wanted to be supportive of parents rather than scold them," Dr. Spock said. "Every baby needs to be smiled at, talked to, played with . . . gently and lovingly. Be natural and enjoy your baby."

Dr. Spock never imagined **that his book would become so popular.** The last edition came out in 1998, a few months after his death at age 94. He will be remembered for his common-sense advice. **"Respect children because they deserve respect, and they'll grow up to be better people."**

390   Lesson **9**

Expansion

Theme The topic for this lesson can be enhanced with the following ideas:

1. A copy of Dr. Spock's book, *Dr. Spock's Baby and Child Care*
2. An advice column on caring for young children from a newspaper, magazine, or Web site

Reading Glossary

common-sense: instinctively logical
deserve: show that you should be given or have something
leading: most popular; best-known
rigid: unbending; unchanging
scold: speak to angrily; blame
strict: demanding regarding rules
supportive: helpful

Culture Note

The Bible (with a capital *B*) is the holy book of Christian religions; it is sometimes called the Holy Bible. The word *bible*, with a small *b*, is used for an authoritative book on a subject.

9.6 | Noun Clauses as Exact Quotes of Notable Words

Examples	Explanation
Dr. Spock said, "Trust yourself." John Watson said, "**Never hug or kiss your children.**" Parents ask, "**What is the right way to take care of a baby?**"	An exact quote is used when the exact words are worth repeating and they are remembered because: • they have been recorded on video or audio. • they are a quote from a book, newspaper, or magazine.
a. **Dr. Spock said,** "Every baby needs to be smiled at." b. "Every baby needs to be smiled at," **Dr. Spock said.** c. "Every baby needs to be smiled at," **said Dr. Spock.**	The *said* or *asked* phrase can come at the beginning (a) or the end of a quote (b and c). If it comes at the end, the subject and the verb can be inverted (c).
"More than anything else," **said Dr. Spock,** "children want to help."	An exact quote can be split, with the *said* or *asked* phrase in the middle, separated from the quote by commas.

Language Note:

Study the punctuation of sentences that contain an exact quote. Note that the first letter of an exact quote is a capital.

Dr. Spock said, "Trust yourself."

The mother asked, "Why is the baby crying?"

"Why is he crying?" asked the father.

"I'm going to feed him," said the mother.

"More than anything else," said Spock, "children want love."

EXERCISE 18 Read these quotes by Dr. Spock and Dr. Watson. Add quotation marks and capital letters where they are needed.

EXAMPLE Watson said, never kiss your child.

1. Spock said you know more than you think you do.

2. Spock said what good mothers and fathers instinctively feel like doing for their babies is usually best.

3. I wanted to be supportive of parents said Spock.

4. Watson said treat your children like small adults.

5. Too much love will harm your baby said Watson.

9.6 | Noun Clauses as Exact Quotes of Notable Words

1. Have students cover up grammar chart **9.6.** Ask the class: *What do you think about Dr. Spock's ideas? What about Dr. Watson's ideas?* Elicit from students two short sentences, such as: *Dr. Spock had good ideas. I don't agree with Dr. Watson.* Write the sentences on the board; then add the name of the student who said each one, with a comma and quotation marks (*Victoria said, "Dr. Spock had good ideas."*). Elicit the help of volunteers to write several more sentences with exact quotes from the class.

2. Have students look at grammar chart **9.6.** Review the example sentences and explanations. If necessary, go over the meanings of: *quote, notable, invert, split, comma,* and *capital.*

3. Direct students' attention to the Language Note. Review the rules for punctuation in sentences that contain an exact quote.

EXERCISE 18

1. Tell students that this exercise is about two different pediatricians' advice. Have students read the direction line. Ask: *What do we add?* (quotation marks and capital letters)

2. Model the exercise. Direct students to the example in the book. *Complete #1 with the class.*

3. Have students complete Exercise 18 individually. Then have them check their answers in pairs. If necessary, check the answers as a class.

Grammar Variation

Have students underline sentences that include quotation marks in the reading on page 390 before they look at the grammar chart. Ask students what they can figure out about the rules for reporting a speaker's exact words.

A Folk Tale (Reading)

1. Have students look at the drawing. Ask: *Where do you think these men are?* (a small village; in the country) *What kind of story do you think this picture is from?* (a folk tale; a children's story) *Do you know who the man with the white beard is?* (Nasreddin, a well-known folk tale character) *What is a folk tale?* (a famous or well-known story in a country or culture)

2. Have students look briefly at the reading. *What is the reading about? How do you know?* Have students make predictions.

3. Preteach any vocabulary words your students may not know, such as *barn, milking,* and *fool.*

BEFORE YOU READ

1. Activate students' prior knowledge about folk tales. Ask: *Does your native country or culture have a character who appears in a lot of folk tales? Have you ever heard of Nasreddin?*

2. Have students discuss the questions in pairs. Try to pair students of different language backgrounds.

3. Ask a few volunteers to share their answers with the class.

⏱ To save class time, skip "Before You Read" or have students prepare answers for homework ahead of time.

Reading 🎧 *CD 4, Track 7*

1. Have students first read the text silently. Tell them to pay special attention to exact quotes. Then play the audio and have students read along silently.

2. Check students' comprehension. Ask questions such as: *What was Nasreddin looking for?* (his ring) *Where did he lose it?* (in the barn) *Why was he looking for it outside?* (because it was too dark to see in the barn) *What kind of person does Nasreddin's neighbor probably think he is?* (a fool)

⏱ To save class time, have students do the reading for homework ahead of time.

---

6. The most important value is to bring up children to help others, first in their family, and then other people, said Spock.

7. To reduce violence in our society, said Spock, we must eliminate violence in the home and on television.

8. If children worship material success rather than truth or compassion, Spock said, it is because they have absorbed those values from others.

A FOLK TALE

Before You Read

1. What kinds of stories or folk tales are popular for children in your native culture?

2. What stories do you remember your parents telling you when you were a child?

🎧 Nasreddin is a character in many folk tales throughout the world. Read this story about Nasreddin. Pay special attention to exact quotes.

392   Lesson **9**

Expansion

Theme The topic for this lesson can be enhanced with the following ideas:

1. Text of folk tales from other cultures (e.g., Grimm's Fairy Tales)
2. Children's book of folk tales
3. Additional Nasreddin folk tales

Reading Variation

To practice listening skills, have students first listen to the audio alone. Ask a few comprehension questions. Repeat the audio if necessary. Then have students open their books and read along as they listen to the audio.

Culture Note

Nasreddin stories and folk tales are famous throughout the Middle East, Turkey, and Central Asia.

One day a neighbor passed Nasreddin's house and saw him outside his barn on his hands and knees. He appeared to be looking for something.

"What are you doing?" the neighbor asked.

"I'm looking for something," answered Nasreddin.

"What are you looking for?" the neighbor asked.

"I'm looking for my ring. It's very valuable," Nasreddin replied.

"I'll help you," said his neighbor. The neighbor got down on his hands and knees and started to help Nasreddin look for his ring. After searching for several hours, the neighbor finally asked, "Do you remember where you were when you lost it?"

"Of course," replied Nasreddin. "I was in the barn milking my cow."

"If you lost your ring inside the barn, then why are we looking for it outside the barn?" asked the neighbor.

"Don't be a fool," said Nasreddin. "It's too dark in the barn. But out here we have light."

9.6 | Exact Quotes in Telling a Story

Examples	Explanation
"What are you doing?" the neighbor asked. **"I'm looking for my ring,"** said Nasreddin.	Exact quotes are used in story telling to give words to the characters. Follow the same punctuation and word order rules as in Section 9.6.
"I will help you," said the neighbor, **"as soon as I can."**	An exact quote can be split, with the *said / asked* phrase in the middle.

EXERCISE 19 Read the following fable[2] by Aesop. Insert quotation marks and correct punctuation.

A hungry wolf was looking for food when he met a house dog that was passing by. Cousin said the dog. Your life is much harder than mine. Why don't you come to work with me and get your food given to you regularly?

I would like that said the wolf. Do you know where I can find such a job?

I will easily arrange that for you said the dog. Come with me to my master's house and we will share my work.

So the wolf and the dog went towards the town together. On the way there, the wolf noticed that the hair on a certain part of the dog's neck was very much worn away, so he asked him how that had come about.

Oh, it is nothing said the dog. That is only the place where the collar is put on me every night to keep me chained up. It hurts a bit at first, but you will soon get used to it.

Then good-bye to you said the wolf. I would rather starve than be a fat slave.

[2] A *fable* is a short story that teaches a lesson. Usually the characters of a fable are animals.

9.7 | Exact Quotes in Telling a Story

1. Have students review the grammar chart.
2. Point out the split quote in the second row of the grammar chart. Tell students that split quotes are very common in stories and longer fiction books.

EXERCISE 19

1. Tell students that this exercise is a folk tale, or fable, by Aesop. Have students read the direction line. Ask: *What do we add?* (quotation marks and correct punctuation)
2. Go over the first paragraph with the class.
3. Have students complete the exercise individually, and compare their work in pairs. If necessary, check answers as a class.
4. Assess students' performance. If necessary, review grammar chart **9.7**.

Reading Glossary

barn: building on a farm for housing cows, horses, or other farm animals

fool: unwise person; unintelligent person

milk (a cow): to take milk from a cow

Grammar Variation

Have students review the reading on page 393 before looking at the grammar chart. Elicit their observations about the use of exact quotes in telling a story.

9.8 | Noun Clauses as Reported Speech

1. Have students review the grammar rule in the top row of the grammar chart. Clarify any unfamiliar vocabulary. Ask: *When do we use reported speech?* (when the idea is more important than the exact words)
2. Review the exact and reported speech in the grammar chart carefully. Draw students' attention to the paraphrased ideas in the reported speech examples.

EXERCISE 20

1. Tell students that this exercise is a woman's story about what happened to her one day last week. Have students read the direction line. Ask: *What do we underline?* (noun clauses that show reported speech) *What do we circle?* (the verbs in the noun clauses)
2. Have students complete the exercise individually and then check their work in pairs. Review the answers as a class.
3. Ask students to identify the verb tenses used in the paragraph. List the verb tenses on the board.

9.8 | Noun Clauses as Reported Speech

We use an **exact quote** when we want to write exactly what someone has said. The exact words are important. We use **reported speech** when we want to paraphrase what someone has said. The exact words are not important or not remembered. The idea is more important than the exact words.

Exact Quote	Reported Speech
Dr. Spock said, "You know more than you think you do."	Dr. Spock told parents that they should trust their own instincts.
The dog said to the wolf, "I will take you to my master's house."	The dog told the wolf that he **would** show him his way of life.
John Watson said, "It is necessary to feed children on a rigid schedule."	John Watson told parents that it **was** necessary to control their children's eating.
Nasreddin said, "I lost my ring."	Nasreddin told his neighbor that he **couldn't find** his ring.

EXERCISE 20 In the paragraph below, underline the noun clauses that show reported speech. Circle the verbs in the noun clauses. What tenses are used?

simple past; past continuous
simple past
simple modal
past perfect continuous
past perfect continuous
simple past; simple past
simple past; simple past
past perfect; past perfect continuous
past modal; modal
simple past

Last week my daughter's day care teacher called me at work and told me that my daughter (had) a fever and (was resting) in the nurse's office. I told my boss that I (needed) to leave work immediately. He said that it (would be) fine. As I was driving my car on the expressway to the school, a police officer stopped me. She said that I (had been driving) too fast. She said that I (had been driving) 10 miles per hour over the limit. I told her that I (was) in a hurry because my daughter (was) sick. I said I (needed) to get to her school quickly. I told the police officer that I (was) sorry, that I (hadn't realized) I (had been driving) so fast. She said she (wouldn't give) me a ticket that time, but that I (should be) more careful in the future, whether my daughter (was) sick or not.

394   Lesson **9**

Expansion

Grammar After students have reviewed the grammar chart, have them look back at the reading on page 390 and write several sentences from the cue: *Dr. Watson told parents that they should . . . .*

9.9 | The Rule of Sequence of Tenses

After a past tense verb in the main clause (such as *said, told, reported,* etc.), the tense of the verb in the noun clause moves back one tense. This change in tense is called the **rule of sequence of tenses.** Observe the difference in verb tenses in the exact quotse on the left and the reported speech on the right.

Exact Quote	Reported Speech
He said, "I **know** you." (present)	He said (that) he **knew** me. (simple past)
He said, "I **am studying**." (present continuous)	He said (that) he **was studying.** (past continuous)
He said, "She **saw** me yesterday." (simple past)	He said (that) she **had seen** him the day before. (past perfect)
He said, "She **was helping** me." (past continuous)	He said (that) she **had been helping** him. (past perfect continuous)
He said, "I **have taken** the test." (present perfect)	He said (that) he **had taken** the test. (past perfect)
He said, "I **had** never **done** that." (past perfect)	He said (that) he **had** never **done** that. (past perfect)
	Note: There is no change for the past perfect.

Modals	
He said, "I **can** help you tomorrow."	He said (that) he **could** help me the next day.
He said, "She **may** leave early." (*may* = possibility)	He said (that) she **might** leave early.
He said, "You **may** go." (*may* = permission)	He said (that) I **could** go.
He said, "I **must** go."	He said (that) he **had to** go.
He said, "I **will** stay."	He said (that) he **would** stay.

Modals That Do Not Change Their Forms in Reported Speech	
He said, "You **should** leave."	He said (that) I **should** leave.
He said, "You **should have** left this morning."	He said (that) I **should have** left that morning.
He said, "You **could have** come."	He said (that) I **could have** come.
He said, "You **must have** known."	He said (that) I **must have** known.

Language Note:
We even change the tense in the following sentence:
  The teacher asked me what my name **was.**
Even though your name is still the same, the tense shows that the conversation took place at a different time and place.

(continued)

Grammar Variation

Have students begin with Exercise 20 on page 394. With the class, convert several of the reported speech clauses with *said* to exact quotes (e.g., *I said, "I need to get to her school quickly."*). Ask students to give their observations on the rules for verb tenses in reported speech.

9.9 | The Rule of Sequence of Tenses

1. Have students cover the grammar chart. Review the list of verb tenses on the board from Exercise 20, or brainstorm with the class and list all of the verb tenses students can name. Be sure that the list includes all of the tenses listed in the first row of reported speech examples in the grammar chart.
2. Draw a timeline on the board. Write: *present* in the center of the timeline, and *present perfect* and *present perfect continuous* in a vertical column below it. To the left, write: *simple past* and *past continuous* below it. To the far left, write *past perfect* and *past perfect continuous* below it. Say, and demonstrate on the timeline: *When we move to the left along a timeline, we say that we are moving back. Each time we move back, we are moving back one tense.*
3. Have students look at the grammar rule in the top row of the chart. Clarify any unfamiliar vocabulary.
4. With the class, review the exact quote and reported speech examples in the first section of the chart one at a time. Point out that in each example the verb in the noun clause in the reported speech moves back one tense. Refer to the timeline on the board as necessary.
5. Review the modals that change form and the modals that do not change form in the second and third sections of the chart.
6. Draw students' attention to the Language Note. Have students practice by providing examples with *The teacher asked me what my* _____ (address, native country, date of birth, etc.) *was.*

9.9 | The Rule of Sequence of Tenses (*cont.*)

7. As a class, review the list of differences between exact quotes and reported speech carefully.
8. Review the Language Note. Have students identify examples of changes in time words in the sections of the grammar chart on page 395.

EXERCISE 21

1. Tell students that this exercise is about things one woman's parents and grandparents used to tell her. Have students read the direction line.
2. Model the exercise. Direct students to the example in the book. Then complete #1 with the class.
3. Have students complete Exercise 21 individually. Then have them check their answers in pairs. Circulate and observe the pair work. If necessary, check the answers as a class.
4. Assess students' performance. If necessary, review grammar chart **9.9**.

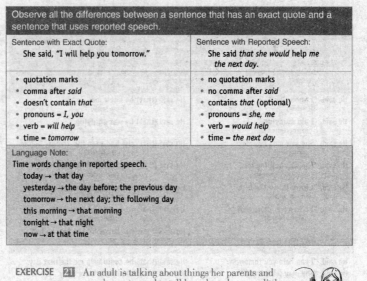

Observe all the differences between a sentence that has an exact quote and a sentence that uses reported speech.

Sentence with Exact Quote:	Sentence with Reported Speech:
She said, "I will help you tomorrow."	She said *that she would help me the next day.*
• quotation marks	• no quotation marks
• comma after *said*	• no comma after *said*
• doesn't contain *that*	• contains *that* (optional)
• pronouns = *I, you*	• pronouns = *she, me*
• verb = *will help*	• verb = *would help*
• time = *tomorrow*	• time = *the next day*

Language Note:
Time words change in reported speech.
today → that day
yesterday → the day before; the previous day
tomorrow → the next day; the following day
this morning → that morning
tonight → that night
now → at that time

EXERCISE 21   An adult is talking about things her parents and grandparents used to tell her when she was a little girl. Change to reported speech. Follow the rule of sequence of tenses.

EXAMPLE   You are the love of my life.
My grandmother told me that *I was the love of her life.*

1. You will always be my baby.
   My mother told me that *I would always be her baby.*
2. You have an easy life compared to mine.
   My father told me that *I had an easy life compared to his.*
3. We had a much harder life.
   My grandparents told me that *they had had a much harder life.*
4. We want you to be happy.
   My parents told me that *they wanted me to be happy.*
5. You don't understand life.
   My mother told me that *I didn't understand life.*

396   Lesson 9

Expansion

Grammar Have students use the list of differences in the grammar chart on this page to talk about the examples in earlier sections of the chart on page 395 (e.g., *I* changes to *he*; *may* changes to *could*.).

6. You have to listen to your teacher.

My father told me that _I had to listen to my teacher._

7. You can be anything you want if you study hard.

My parents told me that _I could be anything I wanted if I studied hard._

8. We don't like to punish you, but sometimes it's necessary.

My parents told me that _they didn't like to punish me, but sometimes it was necessary._

9. Punishing you hurts me more than it hurts you.

My father told me that _punishing me hurt him more than it hurt me._

10. We will always love you.

My grandparents told me that _they would always love me._

11. You should wash your hands before meals.

My mother told me that _I should wash my hands before meals._

12. We will take you to the circus if your grades are good.

My grandparents promised me that _they would take me to the circus if my grades were good._

9.10 | *Say* vs. *Tell*

Examples	Explanation
a. She **said that** the children were happy.	a. In reported speech, we **say that** . . . .
b. She **told me that** the children were happy.	b. In reported speech, we **tell** *someone* **that** . . . . *Tell* is followed by an indirect object, but *said* is not.
c. She **added that** the day care had 15 staff members.	c. Other common verbs used in reported speech that *do not* have an indirect object are: add / answer / explain / reply } *that*
d. She **informed the parents that** the day care center would be closed for the holiday.	d. Other common verbs used in reported speech that have an indirect object are: inform / notify / remind / promise } *someone that* . . .
Compare: She **said,** "I love you." She **said to her daughter,** "I love you."	In an exact quote, we use *say* or *say to someone*. We do not usually use *tell* in an exact quote. *Wrong:* She *told,* "I love you."

Noun Clauses 397

9.10 | *Say* vs. *Tell*

1. Have students cover the grammar chart. Ask a volunteer: *Do you have children?* Then ask another volunteer to report the first student's answer with say: *She said that she has one child./He said that he doesn't have any children.* Write the reported speech sentence with *said* on the board. Then write the reported speech sentence with *told*: *She told me that she has one child./He told me that he doesn't have any children.*

2. Have students review the examples and explanations in the grammar chart. Ask: *How is reported speech with say different from reported speech with tell?* (*tell* is followed by an indirect object; *say* is not)

3. Ask: *Do we use tell with an exact quote?* (not usually)

4. Ask volunteers to give sentences about things someone has said using *say* and *tell*.

Grammar Variation

Have students look back at Exercise 20 on page 394. Have them underline *said* and *told*. Ask students what they observe about the differences in usage between *say* and *tell* (*Tell* is followed by an indirect object, but *say* is not.).

EXERCISE 22

1. Tell students that this exercise is about parents and children. Have students read the direction line.
2. Model the exercise. Direct students to the examples in the book. Then do #1 with the class.
3. Have students complete the rest of the exercise individually, and check their answers in pairs. If necessary, check the answers as a class.

EXERCISE 23

1. Tell students that this exercise is about a family. Have students read the direction line. Ask: *What do we do?* (change each sentence to reported speech)
2. Model the exercise. Direct students to the example. Then do #1 with the class.
3. Have students complete the rest of the exercise individually. Then have them check their answers in pairs. Circulate and observe the pair work.

🕐 To save class time, have students do half of the exercise in class and complete the other half for homework. Or assign the entire exercise for homework.

EXERCISE **22** Fill in the blanks with *said* or *told*.

EXAMPLES   He _____told_____ his children that they should study hard.

I _____said_____ that I was a very happy child.

1. I _____said_____ that I wanted to learn more about raising children.

2. Dr. Spock _____told_____ parents that they should trust their instincts.

3. John Watson _____said_____ that parents should not hug their children.

4. Dr. Spock _____said_____, "You know more than you think you do."

5. The mother _____said_____ to her son, "Eat your vegetables."

6. The mother _____told_____ her son that she would pick him up after school.

7. My parents _____told_____ me that they wanted me to get a good education.

8. I called my parents last week and _____told_____ them about my new roommate.

9. The little girl _____said_____ to her mother, "I want to grow up to be just like you."

10. My parents _____told_____ us to be honest.

EXERCISE **23** Change each sentence to reported speech. Follow the rule of sequence of tenses.

EXAMPLE   Lisa said, "I need to put the kids to bed."

Lisa said that she needed to put the kids to bed.

1. Lisa said, "I have never read Dr. Spock's books."

   Lisa said that she had never read Dr. Spock's books.

2. Lisa said to her friend, "I want to take my children to the zoo."

   Lisa told her friend that she wanted to take her children to the zoo.

3. Lisa said, "My children need to get exercise."

   Lisa said that her children needed to get exercise.

4. Lisa and Paul said, "We will take our kids to the park tomorrow."

   Lisa and Paul said that they would take their kids to the park tomorrow.

Expansion

Exercise 22 Have students convert the sentences with exact quotes in the exercise to reported speech, and the sentences in reported speech to exact quotes.

5. Lisa said, "I forgot to give the kids their vitamins this morning."
   Lisa said that she had forgotten to give the kids their vitamins that morning.

6. Lisa said, "The children went to bed early last night."
   Lisa said that the children had gone to bed early the night before.

7. Lisa said to her neighbor, "My son is in kindergarten."
   Lisa told her neighbor that her son was in kindergarten.

8. Lisa and Paul said, "Our son wants us to read him a story."
   Lisa and Paul said that their son wanted them to read him a story.

9. Lisa said to Paul, "It's your turn to put the kids to bed."
   Lisa told Paul that it was his turn to put the kids to bed.

10. Lisa said to the teacher, "Our son's name is Tod."
    Lisa told the teacher that their son's name was Tod.

11. Tod said to his mother, "I don't want to go to bed."
    Tod told his mother that he didn't want to go to bed.

12. Tod said to his father, "I'm thirsty."
    Tod told his father that he was thirsty.

13. Tod said to his friend, "I love my new bicycle."
    Tod told his friend that he loved his new bicycle.

14. Tod said to his teacher, "I can write my name."
    Tod told his teacher that he could write his name.

15. Tod said to his friend, "My grandmother will buy me a toy."
    Tod told his friend that his grandmother would buy him a toy.

16. Lisa said to Tod, "You must go to bed."
    Lisa told Tod that he had to go to bed.

17. Tod said to his father, "I can't sleep."
    Tod told his father that he couldn't sleep.

18. Tod said to his father, "I want to watch my favorite program on TV."
    Tod told his father that he wanted to watch his favorite program on TV.

19. Paul said to Tod, "You will not get enough sleep."
    Paul told Tod that he wouldn't get enough sleep.

20. Paul said to Tod, "I don't want to argue with you."
    Paul told Tod that he didn't want to argue with him.

Expansion

Exercise 23 Ask students what they can conclude about Lisa and Paul's family from Exercise 23, such as: *Lisa wants her children to get more exercise. Tod has a new bicycle.*

Exercise 23 Have students work in pairs to tell a partner something new or surprising about themselves. Then have partners report the information to the class, or to a group, using reported speech with *said* or *told* (e.g., *Ella told me that she used to be a dancer. Gustavo said that he loves to cook.*).

9.11 | Exceptions to the Rule of Sequence of Tenses

1. Have students cover grammar chart **9.11**. Ask the class to say as much as they can about the rule of sequence of tenses. Make notes on the board about the rule. When students have said all they can, say: *There are some exceptions to the rule of sequence of tenses.* Write examples from the chart on the board. Elicit the exceptions to the rule of sequence of tenses.

2. Have students look at grammar chart **9.11**. Review the example sentences and explanations carefully.

3. Have the class help you make a timeline for the examples in the last row in the grammar chart. In the timeline for example (a), show a vertical line for *present* and another vertical line for *She said*, with a block of time around it for *I am angry*:

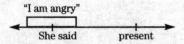

In the timeline for example (b), show a vertical line for *present*, another vertical line for *She said*, and a block of time to its left for *I was angry*:

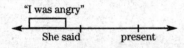

9.11 | Exceptions to the Rule of Sequence of Tenses

Examples	Explanation
Parents **say** that Dr. Spock's book **is** their bible for raising children.	When the main verb is in the **present** tense, we do not change tenses.
Dr. Spock said that children **deserve** respect. Dr. Spock told parents that children **need** love.	In reporting a general truth, it is not necessary to follow the rule of sequence of tenses.
My brother has five children. He said that he **loves** (or **loved**) children. He said that he **wants** (or **wanted**) to have more children.	In reporting something that is still present, you can leave the tenses with no change or follow the rule of sequence of tenses.
Compare: a. Our teacher said that the test on Lesson 9 **will** (or **would**) be next week. b. My kindergarten teacher said that she **would** always remember me.	a. When the action has not happened yet, you can use *will* or *would*. b. When the action is past, use *would*.
A: I can't find my wallet. B: I didn't hear you. What did you say? A: I said I **can't** find my wallet.	When repeating speech immediately after it was said for someone who did not hear it, we do not usually follow the rule of sequence of tenses.
a. My mother said that she **was** born in 1948. b. My mother said that she **had** (or **had had**) a difficult childhood. c. She said that she lived (or had lived) in Poland when she was a child.	In reporting a statement about the past, it is not necessary to follow the rule of sequence of tenses if it is clear that the original verb was past. In sentence (a), it is clear that she said, "I **was** born in 1948" and not "I **am** born in 1948." It is rare to change *be* to past perfect if there is no confusion of time. In sentence (b), it is clear that she said, "I **had** a difficult childhood" not "I **have** a difficult childhood." In sentence (c), it is clear that she said, "I **lived** in Poland when I was a child."
Compare: a. She said that she **was** angry. b. She said that she **had been** angry, but that later she calmed down.	In sentence (a), she said, "I **am** angry." In sentence (b), she said, "I **was** angry." We change to past perfect in sentence (b) to show that the anger was gone by the time she said something about it.

EXERCISE **24** Circle the correct verb to complete these sentences. In a few cases, both answers are possible.

1. She said that she *will* / *would* come to the U.S. in 2001.
2. The teacher said that we *will* / *would* finish this lesson next week.
3. I always say that money *isn't* / *wasn't* as important as health.
4. She said that she *can't* / *couldn't* come to my party last week.
5. Pediatricians say that children *watch* / *watched* too much TV.
6. My little brother said that he *wants* / *wanted* to be president when he grows up.
7. Last semester our teacher said that we *will* / *would* have our final exam on Saturday, so all the students were unhappy. But they came anyway.
8. Our teacher last semester said that her name *is* / *was* Sandy and that she *wants* / *wanted* us to call her by her first name.
9. My doctor said that fatty food *is* / *was* bad for your health.
10. My boss said that he *lost* / *had lost* his keys.
11. Last Saturday, he said that he *needed* / *had needed* my help because he was moving that day.

9.12 | Reporting an Imperative

Examples	Explanation
"Trust yourself." Spock **told** parents **to trust** themselves. "Sit down, please." She **asked** me **to sit** down.	To report an imperative, an infinitive is used. Use *ask* for an invitation or request. Use *tell* for a command or instruction. Don't use *say* to report an imperative. *Wrong:* She *said me to sit* down. Use an object after *tell* or *ask*. *Wrong:* He *told to close* the door.
"Don't hit your children." The doctor told us **not to hit** our children.	For a negative, put *not* before the infinitive.

Language Notes:
Don't forget to change the pronouns and possessive forms in the infinitive phrase.
"Show **your** children love."
He told us to show **our** children love.

"Give **me** your book."
He asked me to give **him my** book.

Culture Note

Review with students interactions in which they might tell someone to do something (their children, a good friend, a subordinate at work) and ask someone to do something (an acquaintance, a co-worker, a store or office employee, etc.).

---

1. Tell students that this exercise is about reporting information. Have students read the direction line.
2. Model the exercise. Complete #1 with the class.
3. Have students complete the exercise individually. Check answers as a class.
4. Assess students' performance. If necessary, review grammar chart **9.11** on page 400.

9.12 | Reporting an Imperative

1. Have students cover the grammar chart. Ask: *What did Dr. Spock tell parents to do? What did Dr. Watson tell parents not to do?* Elicit several answers; write them on the board using the infinitive (e.g., *Dr. Spock told parents to be natural. Dr. Watson told parents not to kiss their children.*). Say: *We use an infinitive to report something that someone invited, requested, commanded, or instructed us to do.*
2. Have students review the examples and explanations in the grammar chart. Point out the placement of *not* for a negative.
3. Give several examples of your own (e.g., *My mother told me not to get married too young. My parents told me to save money for a rainy day.*).

1. Tell students that this exercise is about parents and children. Have students read the direction line. Ask: What verbs do we use? (*asked* and *told*)
2. Model the exercise. Direct students to the example in the book. Complete #1 with the class.
3. Have students complete the rest of the exercise individually. Then have them check their answers in pairs. Circulate and observe the pair work. If necessary, check the answers as a class.
4. Assess students' performance. If necessary, review grammar chart **9.12**.

EXERCISE 25   Change these imperatives to reported speech. Use *asked* or *told* + an object pronoun.

EXAMPLE   The mother told her children, "Study for your test."
The mother told them to study for their test.

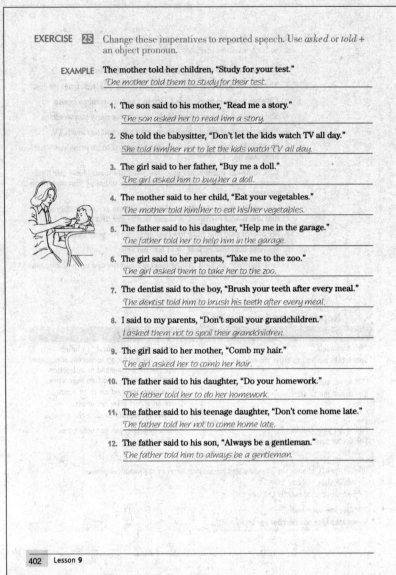

1. The son said to his mother, "Read me a story."
The son asked her to read him a story.

2. She told the babysitter, "Don't let the kids watch TV all day."
She told him/her not to let the kids watch TV all day.

3. The girl said to her father, "Buy me a doll."
The girl asked him to buy her a doll.

4. The mother said to her child, "Eat your vegetables."
The mother told him/her to eat his/her vegetables.

5. The father said to his daughter, "Help me in the garage."
The father told her to help him in the garage.

6. The girl said to her parents, "Take me to the zoo."
The girl asked them to take her to the zoo.

7. The dentist said to the boy, "Brush your teeth after every meal."
The dentist told him to brush his teeth after every meal.

8. I said to my parents, "Don't spoil your grandchildren."
I asked them not to spoil their grandchildren.

9. The girl said to her mother, "Comb my hair."
The girl asked her to comb her hair.

10. The father said to his daughter, "Do your homework."
The father told her to do her homework.

11. The father said to his teenage daughter, "Don't come home late."
The father told her not to come home late.

12. The father said to his son, "Always be a gentleman."
The father told him to always be a gentleman.

402   Lesson **9**

Expansion

Exercise 25 Have students write examples of their own about things their parents told or asked them to do, or told or asked them not to do.

EXERCISE **26** Circle the correct word to complete this story about a babysitter.

Last month I babysat for a family that lives near me. It was my first

babysitting job. They (*said* / *told*) that the children (*would* / *will*) sleep
          (example)   (1)

through the night and not cause any problems. But Danielle, the three-

year-old girl, woke up at 9 and (*said* / *told*) that (*I* / *she*) (*can't* / *couldn't*)
                   (2)   (3)   (4)

sleep. I (*said* / *told*) her that I (*will* / *would*) read (*her* / *you*) a story. Every
      (5)   (6)   (7)

time I finished the story, she (*said* / *told*) me (*read* / *to read*) (*her* / *me*)
                  (8)   (9)   (10)

another one. She finally fell asleep at 10. Then Estelle, the five-year-old,

started crying. When I went to her room, she told me that (*I* / *she*)
                             (11)

(*has seen* / *had seen*) a monster in the closet. I tried to (*tell* / *say*) her that
  (12)   (13)

there (*aren't* / *weren't*) any monsters in her closet, but she didn't stop
      (14)

crying. I wanted to call the parents and tell them that Estelle (*is* / *was*)
                                  (15)

upset and that she (*is* / *was*) crying. They had given me their cell phone
          (16)

number and told me (*call* / *to call*) (*us* / *them*) in case of any problem,
            (17)   (18)

but when I called, there was no answer. Later they told me that they

(*must* / *had to*) turn off their cell phone because they were at a concert.
  (19)

They said (*we* / *they*) (*would* / *will*) be home by 11. But they
        (20)   (21)

didn't come home till 1 a.m. They called and told me that the concert

(*has started* / *had started*) an hour late. I called my mother and told
        (22)

her that I (*can't* / *couldn't*) leave because the parents hadn't come home.
      (23)

Noun Clauses   **403**

 CD 4, Track 8

1. Tell students that this exercise is about a young babysitter. Have students read the direction line.
2. Model the exercise. Direct students to the example. Then complete #1 as a class.
3. Have students complete the exercise individually. Then have them compare their answers in pairs. Circulate and observe the pair work. Check the answers as a class.
4. Assess students' performance. If necessary, review grammar charts **9.9, 9.10, 9.11,** and **9.12.**

🕐 To save class time, have students do half of the exercise in class and complete the other half for homework. Or assign the entire exercise for homework.

Exercise 26 Variation

To provide practice with listening skills, have students close their books and listen to the audio. Repeat the audio as needed. Ask comprehension questions, such as: *Who did the babysitter babysit for last month?* (a family that lives near her) *Had the babysitter babysat before?* (no) *Who is Danielle?* (the three-year-old girl) Then have students open their books and complete Exercise 26.

Culture Note

Teenagers in the U.S. often babysit for their neighbors. Babysitters stay with children while the parents are out for the evening, or during the day while parents are at work (when school is not in session). The parents usually pay babysitters by the hour. Laws about the age at which children may babysit are different in each area, and families should check the law before using a teenage or preteen babysitter.

Being an Au Pair
(Reading)

1. Have students look at the photos on pages 404 and 405. Ask: *Who do you think these young adults are? What are they doing? How do you think they feel?*

2. Have students look at the title of the reading, and look briefly at the reading. Ask: *What is the reading about? How do you know?* Have students make predictions.

3. Preteach any vocabulary words your students may not know, such as *in the process, join, far from perfect, talk it over, play dates,* and *outings*.

BEFORE YOU READ

1. Activate students' prior knowledge about au pairs. Ask: *Do you know anyone who has come to the U.S. as an au pair? Do you know any families who have had an au pair living with them?*

2. Have students discuss the questions in pairs. Try to pair students of different language backgrounds.

3. Ask a few volunteers to share their answers with the class.

🕐 To save class time, skip "Before You Read" or have students prepare answers for homework ahead of time.

She told me (*don't /* *not to*) worry. She said that it (*is /* *was*) my respon-

(24)   (25)

sibility to stay with the kids until the parents came home. When they

finally got home, they told me that (*we / they*) (*don't / didn't*) have any

          (26)   (27)

money to pay (*you / me*) because they (*have forgotten / had forgotten*)

       (28)   (29)

to stop at a cash machine. They said that (*they / we*) (*would / will*)

          (30)   (31)

pay (*you / me*) (*next / the following*) week.

   (32)   (33)

    When I got home, my mother was waiting up for me. I told her that I

(*don't / didn't*) ever want to have children. She laughed and told me that

(34)

the children's behavior (*wasn't / isn't*) unusual. She told me that (*you / I*)

          (35)   (36)

(*will / would*) change (*my / your*) mind some day. I (*said / told*) her

  (37)   (38)   (39)

that I (*don't / didn't*) want to babysit ever again. She told me that I

   (40)

(*will / would*) get used to it.

  (41)

BEING AN AU PAIR

Before You Read
1. Have you ever taken care of small children?
2. Do you know anyone who works in child care?

Expansion

Theme The topic for this lesson can be enhanced with the following ideas:

1. Information on becoming or hiring an au pair from the U.S. Department of State's au pair Web page at: http://exchanges.state.gov/education/jexchanges/private/aupair_brochure.htm or http://exchanges.state.gov/education/jexchanges/private/aupair.htm

2. Ads offering and seeking babysitting services from a local or community newspaper or Web site

3. Flyers or brochures listing local rules or laws governing babysitting and child care

Read the following article. Pay special attention to reported questions.

Five years ago, when I was 18 years old and living in my native Estonia, I read an article about an "au pair" program in the U.S. This is a program where young people, mostly women between the ages of 18 and 25, go to live in the U.S. with an American family for a year to take care of their small children. In the process, these young people can improve their English, learn about American culture, and travel in the U.S.

When I heard about it, I became very excited and asked my mother **if I could join.** At first she said, "Absolutely not." She asked me **why I wanted to leave our family for a year.** I told her that it would be an opportunity for me to improve my English. I have always wanted to be an English teacher in Estonia, but my English was far from perfect. My mother said she would talk it over with Dad, and they finally agreed to let me go.

After filling out the application, I had an interview. The interviewer asked **why I wanted to be an au pair.** She also asked me **whether I knew how to drive.** Sometimes an au pair has to drive kids to school and to play dates. I told her that I had just gotten my license. I asked her **how many hours a week I would have to work,** and she said 45. I wanted to know **if I would get paid,** and she said I would be paid about $200 a week. I also wanted to know **if I would have the opportunity to go to school in the U.S.,** and she said, "Yes." She told me that the family would have to help pay for my schooling. I asked her **if I had to do housework,** and she said no, that my job was only to take care of the kids: wake them up, get them dressed, give them breakfast, take them to school, and help them with homework.

I was so excited when I was accepted.

My year in the U.S. (in Lansing, Michigan) was wonderful. The family treated me like a member of their family, taking me with them on trips and other family outings. I met other au pairs from around the world and have made many new friends. My English is 100 percent better now.

Friends often ask me **if I am happy that I spent a year in the U.S.,** and I say, "This was the opportunity of a lifetime."

Did You Know?

Parents today spend 22 hours a week less with their kids than parents did in 1969.

Noun Clauses 405

1. Have students first read the text silently. Tell them to pay special attention to reported questions in the reading. Then play the audio and have students read along silently.
2. Check students' comprehension. Ask questions such as: *Who are most au pairs?* (young women from 18–25 who are from countries outside the U.S.) *What are some advantages of the program for au pairs?* (They can improve their English, learn about U.S. culture, and travel in the U.S.) *Do you think being an au pair is a good job experience? Why/Why not?*

🕐 To save class time, have students do the reading for homework ahead of time.

DID YOU KNOW?

In 2001, 61% of babies and children not yet in kindergarten were in day care for at least part of the day.

Reading Variation

To practice listening skills, have students first listen to the audio alone. Ask a few comprehension questions. Repeat the audio if necessary. Then have students open their books and read along as they listen to the audio.

Reading Glossary

far from (perfect): the opposite of (perfect); not (perfect) at all
in the process: at the same time; in the meantime
join: become a participant
outing: trip; visit to a local attraction, restaurant, or event; vacation
play date: (for young children) appointment or agreement parents make for children to play together at one child's home or a playground, park, etc.
talk it over: discuss it

9.13 | Noun Clauses as Reported Questions

1. Have students cover the grammar chart. Ask students to suggest several questions the au pair in the reading on pages 404 and 405 probably asked before she took the job. Write the question on the board as exact quotes (*How many children do you have? Will I have to do housework?*). Ask: *How do you think we report these questions?* Elicit students' ideas; write the reported questions on the board (*She asked them how many children they had. She asked them if she would have to do housework.*).

2. Tell students that the grammar rules for reported questions are similar to the grammar rules for included questions, which they studied earlier in the lesson.

3. Have students look at the grammar chart. Review the examples and explanations in the chart carefully. Help students identify the patterns in each of the sections of the chart.

4. Ask volunteers to give sentences about a question someone asked them in the recent past; give one or two examples of your own: (*Yesterday evening, my husband asked me if I had paid the electricity bill.*).

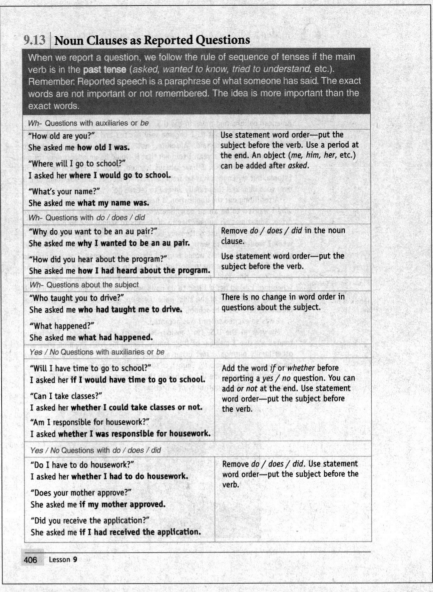

9.13 | Noun Clauses as Reported Questions

When we report a question, we follow the rule of sequence of tenses if the main verb is in the **past tense** (*asked, wanted to know, tried to understand*, etc.). Remember: Reported speech is a paraphrase of what someone has said. The exact words are not important or not remembered. The idea is more important than the exact words.

Wh- Questions with auxiliaries or *be*	
"How old are you?" She asked me **how old I was.** "Where will I go to school?" I asked her **where I would go to school.** "What's your name?" She asked me **what my name was.**	Use statement word order—put the subject before the verb. Use a period at the end. An object (*me, him, her*, etc.) can be added after *asked*.
Wh- Questions with *do / does / did*	
"Why do you want to be an au pair?" She asked me **why I wanted to be an au pair.** "How did you hear about the program?" She asked me **how I had heard about the program.**	Remove *do / does / did* in the noun clause. Use statement word order—put the subject before the verb.
Wh- Questions about the subject	
"Who taught you to drive?" She asked me **who had taught me to drive.** "What happened?" She asked me **what had happened.**	There is no change in word order in questions about the subject.
Yes / No Questions with auxiliaries or *be*	
"Will I have time to go to school?" I asked her **if I would have time to go to school.** "Can I take classes?" I asked her **whether I could take classes or not.** "Am I responsible for housework?" I asked **whether I was responsible for housework.**	Add the word *if* or *whether* before reporting a *yes / no* question. You can add *or not* at the end. Use statement word order—put the subject before the verb.
Yes / No Questions with *do / does / did*	
"Do I have to do housework?" I asked her **whether I had to do housework.** "Does your mother approve?" She asked me **if my mother approved.** "Did you receive the application?" She asked me **if I had received the application.**	Remove *do / does / did.* Use statement word order—put the subject before the verb.

406 Lesson 9

Grammar Variation

After students have reviewed the example sentences in grammar chart **9.4** on page 381, have them go back to the reading on pages 404 and 405 and identify the explanation that applies to each boldface clause in the reading.

EXERCISE 27   These are some questions the interviewer asked the au pair candidate. Change these questions to reported speech.

EXAMPLE   How old are you?

She asked me _how old I was._

1. Have you discussed this with your parents?

   She asked me _if/whether I had discussed this with my parents (or not)._

2. Do you have experience with small children?

   She asked me _if/whether I had experience with small children (or not)._

3. When did you graduate from high school?

   She asked me _when I had graduated from high school._

4. Do you have younger sisters and brothers?

   She asked me _if/whether I had younger sisters and brothers (or not)._

5. Do you speak English?

   She asked me _if/whether I spoke English (or not)._

6. Have you ever traveled to another country?

   She asked me _if/whether I had ever traveled to another country (or not)._

7. Do you have a driver's license?

   She asked me _if/whether I had a driver's license (or not)._

8. How long have you had your driver's license?

   She asked me _how long I had had my driver's license._

9. Did you receive our brochure?

   She asked me _if/whether I had received their brochure (or not)._

10. What are your plans for the future?

    She asked me _what my plans for the future were._

11. Have you ever left your parents before?

    She asked me _if/whether I had ever left my parents before (or not)._

Noun Clauses   407

9.13 | Noun Clauses as Reported Questions (*cont.*)

5. Draw students' attention to the Language Notes. Point out that the exceptions to the rule of sequence of tenses apply to reported questions as well.

EXERCISE 27

1. Tell students that this exercise is about interview questions a person applying for an au pair position was asked. Have students read the direction line. Ask: *What do we do?* (change the questions to reported speech)
2. Model the exercise. Direct students to the example in the book. Then complete #1 with the class.
3. Have students complete the exercise individually and compare their answers in pairs. If necessary, check answers as a class.
4. Assess students' performance. If necessary, review grammar chart **9.13** on pages 406 and 407.

Expansion

Exercise 27   Have students write several additional questions they think the interviewer should ask the candidate. Provide the cue: *The interviewer should ask the candidate . . . .*

EXERCISE 28

1. Tell students that this exercise is about questions an au pair candidate asked the interviewer. Have students read the direction line.
2. Model the exercise. Direct students to the example in the book. Then complete #1 with the class.
3. Have students complete the exercise individually. Collect for assessment, or have students compare their answers in pairs. If necessary, check answers as a class.
4. Assess students' performance. If necessary, review grammar chart 9.13 on pages 406 and 407.

🕐 To save class time, have students do half of the exercise in class and complete the other half for homework. Or assign the entire exercise for homework.

EXERCISE 28 These are some questions the au pair candidate asked the interviewer. Change these questions to reported speech.

EXAMPLE How much will I get paid?
She asked her _how much she would get paid._

1. Will I have my own room?
   She asked her _if/whether she would have her own room (or not)._

2. How many children does the family have?
   She asked her _how many children the family had._

3. How old are the children?
   She asked her _how old the children were._

4. Are the children in school?
   She asked her _if/whether the children were in school (or not)._

5. Should I get an international driver's license?
   She asked her _if/whether she should get an international driver's license (or not)._

6. What is the climate like in Michigan?
   She asked her _what the climate is/was like in Michigan._

7. Does the family have a computer?
   She asked her _if/whether the family had a computer (or not)._

8. Can I e-mail my own family every day?
   She asked her _if/whether she could e-mail her own family every day (or not)._

9. When will I get a vacation?
   She asked her _if/whether she would get a vacation (or not)._

10. How much is the airfare?
    She asked her _how much the airfare was._

11. Who will pay for the airfare?
    She asked her _who would pay for the airfare._

12. Where can I study English?
    She asked her _where she could study English._

Expansion

Exercise 28 Have students write several additional questions they think the candidate should ask the interviewer. Provide the cue: *The candidate should ask the interviewer* . . . .

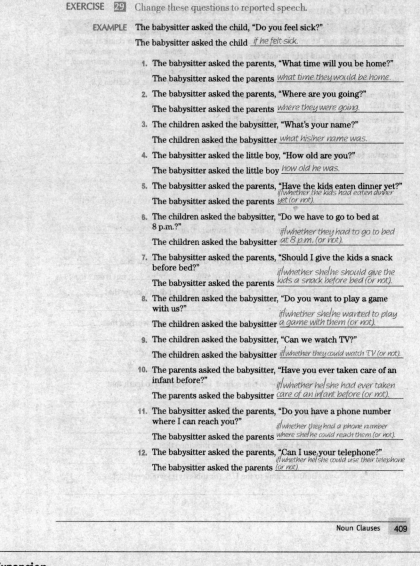

EXERCISE 29

1. Tell students that this exercise is about a babysitter. Have students read the direction line.
2. Model the exercise. Direct students to the example. Ask a volunteer to complete #1.
3. Have students complete the exercise individually. Have students check their answers in pairs. Circulate to observe pair work. If necessary, check answers as a class.
4. Assess students' performance. If necessary, review grammar chart 9.13 on pages 406 and 407.

To save class time, have students do half of the exercise in class and complete the other half for homework. Or assign the entire exercise for homework.

EXERCISE 29 Change these questions to reported speech.

EXAMPLE The babysitter asked the child, "Do you feel sick?"

The babysitter asked the child _if he felt sick._

1. The babysitter asked the parents, "What time will you be home?"
The babysitter asked the parents _what time they would be home._

2. The babysitter asked the parents, "Where are you going?"
The babysitter asked the parents _where they were going._

3. The children asked the babysitter, "What's your name?"
The children asked the babysitter _what his/her name was._

4. The babysitter asked the little boy, "How old are you?"
The babysitter asked the little boy _how old he was._

5. The babysitter asked the parents, "Have the kids eaten dinner yet?"
The babysitter asked the parents _if/whether the kids had eaten dinner yet (or not)._

6. The children asked the babysitter, "Do we have to go to bed at 8 p.m.?"
The children asked the babysitter _if/whether they had to go to bed at 8 p.m. (or not)._

7. The babysitter asked the parents, "Should I give the kids a snack before bed?"
The babysitter asked the parents _if/whether she/he should give the kids a snack before bed (or not)._

8. The children asked the babysitter, "Do you want to play a game with us?"
The children asked the babysitter _if/whether she/he wanted to play a game with them (or not)._

9. The children asked the babysitter, "Can we watch TV?"
The children asked the babysitter _if/whether they could watch TV (or not)._

10. The parents asked the babysitter, "Have you ever taken care of an infant before?"
The parents asked the babysitter _if/whether he/she had ever taken care of an infant before (or not)._

11. The babysitter asked the parents, "Do you have a phone number where I can reach you?"
The babysitter asked the parents _if/whether they had a phone number where she/he could reach them (or not)._

12. The babysitter asked the parents, "Can I use your telephone?"
The babysitter asked the parents _if/whether he/she could use their telephone (or not)._

Noun Clauses 409

Expansion

Exercise 29 Have students write sentences reporting questions they were asked recently in a job interview, in a social situation, or by a family member. Have students share their reported questions in groups. Encourage group members to ask follow-up questions: *How did you answer that question? What did you tell her?*

Culture Notes

The word *babysitting* applies to taking care of children of all ages, not just babies. The word has been expanded to include *housesitting* (taking care of someone's house while they are away) and *pet-*, *cat-* or *dogsitting* (taking care of someone's pets).

Au pairs and babysitters are usually child-care providers who come to the parents' home. Babysitters are usually used for a few hours a week and are often teenagers. Au pairs work full time, and, under the U.S. Department of State programs, are generally limited to one year. A *nanny* is also a full-time, in-home child-care provider, but without the crosscultural and educational components of the au pair program.

9.14 | Noun Clauses After Other Past Tense Verbs

1. Have students review the example sentences and explanation in the grammar chart.

2. Provide several examples of your own with one of the main clause verbs listed in the grammar chart in the past tense (e.g., *I was sure that my daughter would like this babysitter. When they were 13 or 14, my kids realized that they could make money by babysitting.*).

EXERCISE 30

1. Tell students that this exercise is about things they have thought and learned. Have students read the direction line. Ask: *Do we follow the rule of sequence of tenses?* (yes)

2. Model the exercise. Direct students to the example. Ask: *Was this true for you?* Ask volunteers to provide their own statements using the example.

3. Have students complete the exercise individually. Have students compare their answers in pairs. Circulate and observe the pair work; provide your own answers as appropriate. Ask pairs to share interesting answers with the class.

4. Assess students' performance. If necessary, review grammar chart **9.14**.

9.14 | Noun Clauses After Other Past Tense Verbs

Examples	Explanation
Dr. Spock *decided* that **he would write a book.**	If the verb in the main clause is past tense (*thought, knew, believed, wondered, realized, decided, imagined, understood, was sure*, etc.), follow the rule of sequence of tenses in Section 9.9.
He *thought* that **he could help parents feel more comfortable with their kids.**	
He *knew* that **he wanted to help parents.**	
The au pair *didn't know* **if she would be happy in the U.S.**	
She *wondered* **what her life would be like in the U.S.**	
Her mother *wasn't sure* **whether she should let her daughter to go the U.S. or not.**	

EXERCISE 30 ABOUT YOU Fill in the blanks and discuss your answers. Follow the rule of sequence of tenses.

EXAMPLE Before I came to this city, I thought that *everybody here was unfriendly.* but it isn't true.

1. Before I came to this city (or the U.S.), I thought that _____
   _____ Answers will vary. _____, but it isn't true.

2. Before I came to this city (or the U.S.), I didn't know that _____
   _____

3. Before I came to this city (or the U.S.), I was worried that _____
   _____

4. When I lived in my hometown, I was afraid that
   _____

5. When I came to this school, I was surprised to learn that
   _____

6. When I came to this school, I realized that _____
   _____

7. When I was younger, I never imagined that _____
   _____

8. Before I came to the U.S. (or this city), I wondered _____
   _____

EXERCISE **31** ABOUT YOU Fill in the blanks to tell about you and your parents when you were a child.

EXAMPLE When I was a child, I dreamed that _____*I would be a movie star.*_____

1. My parents told me that _____*Answers will vary.*_____
2. My parents hoped that _____
3. My parents thought that _____
4. When I was a child, I dreamed that _____
5. When I was a child, I thought that _____
6. When I was a child, I didn't understand _____
7. When I was younger, I never imagined that _____
8. When I was younger, I wondered _____
9. When I was younger, I didn't know _____
10. When I was younger, I couldn't decide _____

EXERCISE **32** *Combination Exercise.* The author of this book remembers this true story from her childhood. Change the words in parentheses to reported speech.

When I was about 6 years old, I had the measles.[3] My mother told me

_____*to stay in the bedroom*_____ because it was dark in there. She said
(example: "Stay in the bedroom.")

_____*that she didn't want the bright light to hurt my eyes*_____. My bedroom was
(1 "I don't want the bright light to hurt your eyes.")

near the dining room of the house. My mother told me ___*that I could*___

_____*go into the dining room*_____ because it was dark in
(2 "You can go into the dining room.")

there. She told me _____*not to go into the living room*_____ because
(3 "Don't go into the living room.")

it was too light there. The TV was in the living room and she thought

_____*that the brightness of the TV could hurt my eyes*_____
(4 "The brightness of the TV can hurt your eyes.")

My sister Micki was three years older than I and liked to bully[4] me.
She had already had the measles, so she wasn't afraid of getting

sick. She came to the door of my bedroom and asked me ___*if I knew*___

_____*why I couldn't go into the living room*_____ I told her
(5 "Do you know why you can't go into the living room?")

[3] *Measles* is an illness that children often get. The medical name is rubeola.
[4] To *bully* means to act cruel to someone who is smaller and more helpless.

Noun Clauses **411**

EXERCISE 31

1. Tell students that this exercise is about them and their parents when they were young. Have students read the direction line.
2. Model the exercise. Direct students to the example in the book. Ask several volunteers to complete the example for themselves.
3. Have students complete the exercise individually. Then have them compare answers in groups. Have groups share interesting answers with the class.
4. Assess students' performance. If necessary, review grammar chart **9.14** on page 410.

To save class time, have students do half of the exercise in class and complete the other half for homework.

EXERCISE 32

CD 4, Track 10

1. Tell students that this exercise is a true story from the childhood of the author of this book. Have students read the direction line.
2. Model the exercise. Direct students to the example. Complete #1 with the class.
3. Have students complete the exercise individually. Have students check answers in pairs. If necessary, check answers with the class.

To save class time, have students do half of the exercise in class and complete the other half for homework.

Expansion

Exercises 30 and 31 Have students work in pairs to practice conversations about things they have learned or thought in the past. In each pair, have a student begin a conversation with *I learned that . . . , I didn't realize that . . . , I didn't know that . . . , I hoped that . . . ,* or *I decided that . . . .* If appropriate, have each student write one or two statements before beginning the activity. Have the second student ask a question with *when: When did you learn/realize/find out, hope, decide that/to . . . .* Have the first student answer with a time clause (e.g., *when I came here, when I started school, when I lived at home*). Have several pairs perform their conversations for the class.

Exercise 32 Variation

To provide practice with listening skills, have students close their books and listen to the audio. Repeat the audio as needed. Ask comprehension questions, such as: *How old was the author when this story happened?* (about 6 years old) *What did her mother tell her?* (to stay in the bedroom) *Why?* (because it was dark in there) Then have students open their books and complete Exercise 32.

1. Tell students that this exercise is an essay written by a former au pair about her experiences. Have students read the direction line.
2. Model the exercise using the example in the book. Complete #1 with the class.
3. Have students complete the exercise individually; to collect for assessment, have students write their answers on a separate piece of paper. To check in class, have students compare their answers in pairs, and check answers as a class.

🕐 To save class time, have students do half of the exercise in class and complete the other half for homework. Or assign the entire exercise for homework.

_____ that I didn't understand _____. She said, "The living room is
(6 "I don't understand.")

for living people. The dining room is for dying people, and you're gonna die." Of course, I believed her because she was 9 years old and knew

much more than I did. I didn't understand that _____ 'dining' meant

_____ 'eating,' not 'dying' _____.
(7 " 'Dining' means 'eating,' not 'dying'.")

Today we can laugh about this story, but when I had the measles, I was

afraid that _____ I would die _____.
(8 "I will die.")

EXERCISE 33 🎧 *Combination Exercise.* This is a composition written by a former au pair. Change the words in parentheses ( ) to reported speech.

Two years ago, when I was 18 and living in my native Poland, I didn't

know exactly _____ what I should do _____ with my life. I had just graduated
(example: "What should I do?")

from high school and I couldn't decide _____ whether to go to college or not _____
(1 "Should I go to college or not?")

I was not sure _____ what I wanted to do with my life _____. A neighbor of mine
(2 "What do I want to do with my life?")

told me _____ that she had had the same problem when she was my age _____ and
(3 "I had the same problem when I was your age.")

decided to go to the U.S. for a year to work as an "au pair." She asked me

_____ whether I had ever heard of the au pair program in America _____. I told
(4 "Have you ever heard of the au pair program in America?")

her that _____ I hadn't _____. She told me that
(5 "I haven't.")

_____ she had lived with an American family for a year _____, helping them take care
(6 "I lived with an American family for a year.")

of their two small children. I asked her _____ how much that program would cost me _____
(7 "How much will this program cost me?")

She laughed and told me _____ that I would earn about $200 a week, get my
(8 "You will earn about $200 a week, get your own room, and

own room, and get three meals a day _____. She also told me _____ that I would have a chance to travel
get three meals a day.") (9 "You will have a chance to travel in the U.S.")

_____ in the U.S. _____. I asked her _____ if it had been a good experience for her _____,
(10 "Was it a good experience for you?")

and she said _____ that it had changed her life _____. She said _____
(11 "It has changed my life.")

Expansion

Exercise 32 Ask students if they have a family story to share from childhood that they can laugh about now, but that wasn't funny at the time.

Exercise 33 Variation

To provide practice with listening skills, have students close their books and listen to the audio. Repeat the audio as needed. Ask comprehension questions, such as: *How old was the person two years ago?* (18 years old) *Where was the person living?* (in Poland) *What did the person just do?* (graduate from high school) Then have students open their books and complete Exercise 33.

that she had gained a new understanding of people and _____ that her
(12 "I have gained a new understanding of people.")

English had improved a lot . I asked her if the work was very hard
(13 "My English has improved a lot.")   (14 "Is the work very hard?")

and she said _____ that it was but that it was very rewarding .
(15 "It is.")   (16 "It is very rewarding.")

I looked up *au pair* on the Internet and found out how to apply. I
told my parents that _____ I was thinking about going to America for a year
(17 "I am thinking about going to America for a year.")

At first they told me _____ not to go . They thought that
(18 "Don't go.")

_____ I was too young and that I didn't have any experience
(19 "You are too young.")   (20 "You don't have any experience.")

I reminded them that I had babysat many times for our neighbors' kids
(21 "I have babysat many times for our neighbors' kids.")

and that by working in America _____ I would get even more experience
(22 "I will get even more experience.")

I also told them that _____ my English would improve if I lived with an
(23 "My English will improve if I live with an American family.")

American family . My parents finally agreed to let me go. I filled out the
application, had an interview, and was accepted.

I told my parents _____ not to worry . I promised them
(24 "Don't worry.")

_____ that I would keep in touch with them by e-mail almost every day
(25 "I will keep in touch with you by e-mail almost every day.")

When I arrived, my American family explained to me _____ what I
_____ had to do . They had two small kids, and I had to wake them
(26 "What do I have to do?")

up, make them breakfast, and take them to school in the morning. I asked
them _____ if I had to wait for them at school , and they laughed. They told
(27 "Do I have to wait for them at school?")

me _____ that while the kids were in school, I could take English classes at a
(28 "While the kids are in school, you can take English classes at a local college.")

local college . I told them _____ that I didn't have enough money to pay for
(29 "I don't have enough money to pay for school.")

school , but they told me _____ that they would pay for my classes . So that's
(30 "We will pay for your classes.")

what I did. I met students from all over the world. I also had a chance to
travel to many American cities with other au pairs. When the year was

Noun Clauses   413

Culture Note

In addition to au pair programs that bring au pairs to the U.S. through the U.S. Department of
State, many domestic and other international au pair programs advertise on the Internet. As
with any online service, potential participants should investigate au pair programs thoroughly.

Summary of Lesson 9

Have students work in pairs. In each pair, have student A say a simple sentence about himself or herself, ask a simple question, and give a simple imperative. Have student B write student A's exact words on separate cards or slips of paper, and add: Speaker: (*student A's name*) and Writer: (*student B's name*). Then have students reverse roles. Collect all of the slips and put them into a bag or container. Then have students take three slips at random from the container. Have students take turns making a sentence with an included statement, question, or direction, using the original speaker's name (e.g., *Isabella said that her son is available to babysit. Hashim asked if Trung could recommend a good dentist.*). If necessary, have students review: **Lesson 9.**

---

over, I was very sad to leave my new family, but we promised _____

_____ *that we would stay in touch* _____ . They told me
  (31 "We will stay in touch.")

that I would always be welcome in their house .
  (32 "You will always be welcome in our house.")

   Now I am back home and in college, majoring in early childhood

education. My parents told me *that they were happy they had let me go to*
  (33 "We are happy we let you go to America.")

   America . They can see that I've become much more confident
and mature. Becoming an au pair in America was one of the best
experiences of my life.

SUMMARY OF LESSON 9

Direct statement or question	Sentence with included statement or question	Use of noun clause or infinitive
She loves kids. She is patient.	I know **that she loves kids.** I'm sure **that she is patient.**	A noun clause is used after verbs and adjectives.
Talk to your children. Don't be so strict.	It is essential **that you talk to your children.** He recommends **that we not be so strict.**	A noun clause is used after expressions of importance. The base form is used in the noun clause.
Is the baby sick? What does the baby need?	If don't know **if the baby is sick or not.** I'm not sure **what the baby needs.**	A noun clause is used as an included question.
What should I do with the crying baby? Where can I get information about the "au pair" program?	I don't know **what to do with the crying baby.** Can you tell me **where to get information about the "au pair" program?**	An infinitive can replace *should* or *can.*
You know more than you think you do. Do you have children?	Dr. Spock said, **"You know more than you think you do."** **"Do you have children?"** asked the doctor.	A noun clause is used in an exact quote to report what someone has said.
I will read a book about child care. Do you have experience with children?	She said **that she would read a book about child care.** She asked me **if I had experience** with children.	A noun clause is used in reported speech to paraphrase what someone has said.
Trust yourself. Don't give the child candy.	He told us **to trust ourselves.** He told me **not to give the child candy.**	An infinitive is used to report an imperative.

414   Lesson 9

Summary Variation

Have students prepare sentences and questions as above. Encourage students to be creative. After students take slips or cards from the container, have them write a sentence with an included statement or question for each slip or card, mentioning the writer's name as above. Collect for assessment.

Editing Advice

EDITING ADVICE

1. Use *that* or nothing to introduce an included statement. Don't use *what*.

        that
   I know ~~what~~ she likes to swim.

2. Use statement word order in an included question.

        it is
   I don't know what time ~~is it~~.

   I don't know where ⟨lives⟩ your brother.

3. We *say* something. We *tell* someone something.

     told
   He ~~said~~ me that he wanted to go home.

     said
   He ~~told~~, "I want to go home."

4. Use *tell* or *ask*, not *say*, to report an imperative. Follow *tell* and *ask* with an object.

      told
   I ~~said~~ you to wash your hands.

         me
   She asked ˄ to show her my ID card.

5. Don't use *to* after *tell*.

   He told ~~to~~ me that he wanted to go home.

6. Use *if* or *whether* to introduce an included *yes/no* question.

         if
   I can't decide ˄ I should buy a car or not.

       whether
   I don't know ˄ it's going to rain or not.

7. Use *would*, not *will*, to report something that is past.

          would
   My father said that he ~~will~~ come to the U.S. in 1995.

8. Follow the rule of sequence of tenses when the main verb is in the past.

                 wanted
   When I was a child, my grandmother told me that she ~~wants~~ to travel.

9. Don't use *so* before a noun clause.

   He thinks ~~so~~ the U.S. is a beautiful country.

Noun Clauses   **415**

Editing Advice

For each item, have students provide the grammar rule behind the editing advice. This can be done as an individual, a pair, a group, or a class activity.

1. *That* introduces a noun clause. *That* is often omitted, especially in conversations.
2. Use statement word order in an included question—put the subject before the verb.
3. In reported speech, we **say** that . . . , but we **tell** *someone* that . . . .
4. To report an imperative, an infinitive is used. Use *ask* for an invitation or request. Use *tell* for a command or instruction. Don't use *say* to report an imperative. Use an object after *tell* or *ask*.
5. *Tell* is followed by an indirect object.
6. Add the word *if* or *whether* before including a *yes/no* question. You can add *or not* at the end. Use statement word order—put the subject before the verb.
7. To report an action with *will* that is past, use *would*.
8. If the verb in the main clause is in past tense, follow the rule of sequence of tenses.
9. Noun clauses can be replaced by *so* after *think, hope, believe, suppose, expect*, and *know*. Do not include *so* if you include the noun clause.

Editing Advice (*cont.*)

10. A noun clause is used after verbs that show importance or urgency. The base form is used in the noun clause.
11. For negatives after verbs that show importance of urgency, put *not* before the base form.
12. Use a period at the end of the included question if the sentence is a statement. Use a question mark if the sentence begins with a question.
13. Use a comma before an exact quote and quotation marks around the quote. The first letter of an exact quote is a capital.
14. In a sentence with reported speech, there is no comma after the main verb.
15. For a negative imperative, put *not* before the infinitive.

Lesson 9 Test/Review

For additional practice, review, and assessment materials, see Assessment CD-ROM with *ExamView Pro*, *More Grammar Practice* Workbook 3, Interactive CD-ROM, and Web site http://elt.thomson.com/gic

PART 1

1. Part 1 may be used as an in-class test to assess student performance, in addition to the Assessment CD-ROM with *ExamView Pro*. Have students read the direction line. Ask: *Does every sentence have a mistake?* (no) Have students complete the exercise.
2. Collect for assessment.
3. If necessary, have students review: **Lesson 9**.

---

10. Use the base form after expressions showing importance or urgency.

    It is urgent that you ~~are~~ on time for the meeting. *(be)*

    I suggested that the teacher ~~reviewed~~ the last lesson. *(review)*

11. Use *not* + base form to form the negative after expressions showing importance or urgency.

    Doctors recommend that small children ~~don't~~ watch TV. *(not)*

12. Use a period, not a question mark, if a question is included in a statement.

    I don't know what time it is?

13. Use correct punctuation in an exact quote.

    He said "I love you."

14. Don't use a comma before a noun clause (EXCEPTION: an exact quote).

    He knows, that you like him.

15. *Don't* isn't used in reporting a negative imperative.

    He told me don't open the door. *(not to)*

LESSON 9 TEST/REVIEW

PART 1 Find the mistakes with the underlined words and correct them. Not every sentence has a mistake. If the sentence is correct, write *C*.

EXAMPLES I don't know <u>where does your brother live</u>. *(s)*

"What do you want?" asked the man.   C

1. I'd like to know <u>what I need to study</u> for the final exam.   *C*
2. She is happy <u>what</u> her daughter got married. *(that)*
3. I don't know <u>what you want</u>.   *C*
4. He <u>said</u> me that he wanted my help. *(told)*
5. I don't know <u>what time is it</u>. *(it is)*
6. The president said, "There <u>will be</u> no new taxes."   *C*
7. I don't know <u>what to do</u>.   *C*

Lesson Review

To use Part 1 as a review, assign it as homework or use it as an in-class activity to be completed individually or in pairs. Check answers and review errors as a class. Reteach grammar points that students haven't mastered. Then student learning may be assessed using a test generated from the Assessment CD-ROM with *ExamView Pro*.

8. I don't know where ~~should I~~ *I should* go for registration.

9. I told you not to leave the room.   C

10. The weatherman said that it ~~will~~ *would* rain on Sunday, but it didn't.

11. Do you think *that* ~~so~~ New Yorkers are friendly people?

12. Do you think I'm intelligent?   C

13. I don't know ~~whether/if~~ *whether/if* she understands English or not.

14. He asked me how ~~do I~~ *I felt* feel.

15. He told *me* that he wanted to speak with me.

16. He said to his father, "I'm an adult now."   C

17. I didn't know that learning English would be so hard.   C

18. Before I started looking for a job, I thought that I ~~will~~ *would* find a job right away, but I didn't.

19. He told ~~to~~ me that he wanted to buy a car.

20. He ~~said~~ *told* me to open the window.

21. She told me ~~don't use~~ *not to* use her computer.

22. I didn't understand what ~~did I need~~ *I needed* to do.

23. It is important that you be here before 9 o'clock.

24. I recommend that you not give the answers to anyone.

25. I suggest that my friend visits me during vacation.

26. My counselor advised ~~that I didn't take~~ *that I not take/me not to take* so many credit hours.

PART 2 Find the mistakes with **punctuation** in the following sentences. Not every sentence has a mistake. If the sentence is correct, write C.

EXAMPLES He said, "I can't help you."

He said, "I have to leave now."   C

1. I don't know what time it is?

2. Do you know what time it is?   C

3. I'm sure, that you'll find a job soon.

4. The teacher said "I will return your tests on Monday."

5. I didn't realize, that you had seen the movie already.

6. He asked me, "What are you doing here?"   C

7. "What do you want?," he asked.

8. "I want to help you," I said.   C

Lesson Review

To use Part 2 as a review, assign it as homework or use it as an in-class activity to be completed individually or in pairs. Check answers and review errors as a class. Reteach grammar points that students haven't mastered. Then student learning may be assessed using a test generated from the Assessment CD-ROM with *ExamView Pro*.

1. Part 2 may also be used as an in-class test to assess student performance, in addition to the Assessment CD-ROM with *ExamView Pro*. Have students read the direction line. Ask: *What do we correct?* (punctuation) *Does every sentence have a mistake?* (no) Have students complete the exercise.

2. Collect for assessment.

3. If necessary, have students review: **Lesson 9.**

1. Part 3 may also be used as an in-class test to assess student performance, in addition to the Assessment CD-ROM with *ExamView Pro*. Have students read the direction line. Review the example. Then do #1 as a class. Have students complete the exercise.
2. Collect for assessment.
3. If necessary, have students review:

   9.4 Noun Clauses as Included Questions (pp. 381–382)

   9.5 Question Words Followed by an Infinitive (p. 387).

1. Part 4 may also be used as an in-class test to assess student performance, in addition to the Assessment CD-ROM with *ExamView Pro*. Have students read the direction line. Review the example. Then do #1 as a class. Have students complete the exercise.
2. Collect for assessment.
3. If necessary, have students review: **Lesson 9.**

---

9. I told him that I didn't need his help. C

10. Can you tell me where I can find the bookstore?

PART 3 Fill in the blanks with an included question.

EXAMPLE How old is the president?

Do you know _____ *how old the president is?*

1. Where does Jack live?

   I don't know _____ *where Jack lives.*

2. Did she go home?

   I don't know _____ *whether she went home or not.*

3. Why were they late?

   Nobody knows _____ *why they were late.*

4. Who ate the cake?

   I don't know _____ *who ate the cake.*

5. What does "liberty" mean?

   I don't know _____ *what "liberty" means.*

6. Are they working now?

   Can you tell me _____ *if they are working now?*

7. Should I buy the car?

   I don't know _____ *whether I should buy the car or not.*

8. Has she ever gone to Paris?

   I'm not sure _____ *if she has ever gone to Paris.*

9. Can we use our books during the test?

   Do you know _____ *if we can use our books during the test?*

10. What should I do?

    I don't know _____ *what to do/what I should do.*

PART 4 Change the following sentences to reported speech. Follow the rule of sequence of tenses or use the infinitive where necessary.

EXAMPLE He said, "She is late."

He said that she was late.

1. She said, "I can help you."

   She said that she could help me.

Lesson Review

To use Part 3 as a review, assign it as homework or use it as an in-class activity to be completed individually or in pairs. Check answers and review errors as a class. Reteach grammar points that students haven't mastered. Then student learning may be assessed using a test generated from the Assessment CD-ROM with *ExamView Pro*.

2. He said, "Don't go away."
   He asked me not to go away.

3. He said, "My mother left yesterday."
   He said that his mother had left the day before.

4. She said, "I'm learning a lot."
   She said that she was learning a lot.

5. He said, "I've never heard of Dr. Spock."
   He said that he had never heard of Dr. Spock.

6. He said, "Give me the money."
   He asked me to give him the money.

7. They said to me, "We finished the job."
   They told me that they had finished the job.

8. He said to us, "You may need some help."
   He told us that we might need some help.

9. He said to her, "We were studying."
   He told her that we had been studying.

10. He said to her, "I have your book."
    He told her that he had her book.

11. He said to us, "You should have called me."
    He told us that we should have called him.

12. He said to his wife, "I will call you."
    He told his wife that he would call her.

13. He asked me, "Do you have any children?"
    He asked me whether I had any children.

14. He asked me, "Where are you from?"
    He asked me where I was from.

15. He asked me, "What time is it?"
    He asked me what time it was.

16. He asked me, "Did your father come home?"
    He asked me if my father had come home.

17. He asked me, "Where have you been?"
    He asked me where I had been.

Lesson Review

To use Part 4 as a review, assign it as homework or use it as an in-class activity to be completed individually or in pairs. Check answers and review errors as a class. Reteach grammar points that students haven't mastered. Then student learning may be assessed using a test generated from the Assessment CD-ROM with *ExamView Pro*.

Expansion Activities

These expansion activities provide opportunities for students to interact with one another and further develop their speaking and writing skills. Encourage students to use grammar from this lesson whenever possible.

🕐 To save class time, assign parts of the activities as homework. Then use class time for interaction and communication. If students do not need additional speaking practice, some of the activities may be assigned as writing activities for homework, or skipped altogether.

CLASSROOM ACTIVITIES

1. Tell students that this activity is about the topics they have read about in this lesson. Ask: *What topics did we read about?* (raising children, pediatricians' ideas, finding out about and using day care, Dr. Spock, folk tales, au pairs) Write, or have a volunteer write, the list of topics on the board. Have students look at the examples in the book, and then write questions of their own. When students have finished, have them compare their questions in small groups.

2. Tell students that this activity is about advice their families gave them. Have students look at the examples in the book, and then write sentences of their own. When students have finished, have them compare their sentences in small groups.

TALK ABOUT IT

Items 1 through 6 Have students work in groups. Either assign or have each group choose one or more of the topics to discuss. Review with students language for agreeing, checking for agreement, and disagreeing (e.g., *I think so too. Are you sure that's right? I'm not sure I agree.*). Set a time limit for discussion. Then have groups talk about their topics. If appropriate, have groups report back to the class; have each group appoint a spokesperson.

---

18. He asked me, "Will you leave tomorrow?"
    He asked me if I would leave the next day.

19. He asked me, "What do you need?"
    He asked me what I needed.

20. He asked me, "Are you a student?"
    He asked me whether I was a student.

21. He asked us, "Can you help me today?"
    He asked us to help him that day.

22. He asked us, "Who needs my help?"
    He asked us who needed his help.

EXPANSION ACTIVITIES

Classroom Activities

1. Write questions you have about the topics in the readings of this lesson. Express your questions with "*I wonder . . .*" Compare your questions in a small group.

    EXAMPLES I wonder why parents spend so much less time with their children than they used to.
    I wonder why it is so hard to raise a child.

2. What advice did your parents, teachers, or other adults give you when you were younger? Write three sentences. Share them in a small group.

    EXAMPLES My mother told me to be honest.
    My grandfather told me that I should always respect older people.

Talk About it

1. How is your philosophy of raising children different from your parents' philosophy or methods?

2. Do you think parents should or shouldn't hit children when they misbehave?

3. Did your parents read to you when you were a child?

4. Did you have a lot of toys when you were a child?

420   Lesson 9

Classroom Activities Variation

Activity 2 After groups have compared sentences, have each group choose several sentences to read to the class. Have students in other groups guess which student wrote each sentence.

Activity 2 Ask volunteers to talk about whether or not they have followed the advice that their families gave them.

Talk About it Variation

Items 1 through 6 Have students work in pairs. Have members of the pairs interview each other using the questions in items 1 to 6, alternating interviewers. Have the interviewers take notes on their partners' responses.

Items 2 and 6 Have students debate item 2 or item 6. Divide the class into two teams. Tell each team to list five reasons supporting its view. Have each team present its arguments. Then give each team an opportunity to respond to the other team's arguments. At the end of the debate, survey the class to see which opinion is more popular.

WRITE ABOUT IT

Have students use the lesson summary on page 414 to check the noun clauses in their paragraphs. Collect students' work for assessment and/or have students review each other's work.

5. Do you think children today behave differently from when you were a child?

6. Is it hard to raise children? Why?

7. Read the following poem. Discuss the meaning.

Your children are not your children.
They are the sons and daughters of Life's longing for itself.
They come through you but not from you,
And though they are with you, yet they belong not to you.
You may give them your love but not your thoughts.
For they have their own thoughts.
You may house their bodies but not their souls,
For their souls dwell in the house of tomorrow, which you cannot visit, not even in your dreams.
You may strive to be like them, but seek not to make them like you.
For life goes not backward nor tarries with yesterday.
You are the bows from which your children as living arrows are sent forth.
. . .
Let your bending in the archer's hand be for gladness;
For even as he loves the arrow that flies, so he loves also the bow that is stable.

Kahlil Gibran (From *The Prophet*)

Write About it

1. Write a paragraph about an interesting conversation or argument that you had or that you heard recently.

EXAMPLE   Last week I had a conversation with my best friend about having children. I told her that I didn't want to have children. She asked me why I was against having kids. . . .

2. Write about an unpopular belief that you have. Explain why you have this belief and why it is unpopular.

EXAMPLES   I believe that there is life on other planets.
I believe that schools shouldn't have tests.

3. Write about a belief you used to have that you no longer have. Explain what this belief was and why you no longer believe it to be true.

EXAMPLES   I used to believe that communism was the best form of government.
I used to believe that marriage made people happy.

Noun Clauses   421

Culture Note

Khalil Gibran is a well-known poet, artist, and essayist. His most famous work, *The Prophet*, is loved by many readers around the world and frequently quoted. Khalil (also spelled Kahlil, possibly 'Americanized' by an English teacher in Boston) Gibran was born in Lebanon in 1883. His family immigrated to Boston when he was 12. *The Prophet* was published in 1923. Gibran died in 1931.

Write About it Variation

Have students exchange first drafts with a partner. Ask students to help their partners edit their drafts. Refer students to the Editing Advice on pages 415–416.

OUTSIDE ACTIVITIES

Instruct students to interview a friend, family member, or acquaintance outside the class, using the questions in the book and others, if possible. For Activity 1, encourage students to write out their questions before the interview.

INTERNET ACTIVITIES

1. When students bring their Web sites to class, have them tell the class why they chose the Web sites they did and whether they agree with the parenting information on the Web sites.
2. Ask students to also bring in the name and Web address of the Web site they found. Have students find out what the requirements are for au pairs.
3. Have students report the information that surprised them to the class. Ask: *Why did this information surprise you? Do you think the information is helpful/true/useful for parents or teachers?*
4. Have students say what the day care facilities they found have in common and what, if anything, is unusual about each one.

---

4. Write about a general belief that people in your native culture have. Explain what this belief means. Do you agree with it?

   EXAMPLES In my native country, it is said that it takes a village to raise a child.

   In my native culture, it is believed that wisdom comes with age.

5. Write a short fable or fairy tale that you remember. Include the characters' words in quotation marks. See the folk tale on page 393 for an example.

6. Write about an incident from your childhood, like the one in Exercise 32.

Outside Activities

1. Interview a classmate, coworker, or neighbor about his or her childhood. Find out about this person's family, school, house, activities, and toys. Tell the class what this person said, using reported speech.

2. Interview a friend, coworker, or neighbor who has a child or children. Ask him or her these questions:

   What's the hardest thing about raising a child?
   What's the best thing about raising a child?

   Report this person's answers to the class.

Internet Activities

1. At a search engine, type in *parents*, *parenting*, or *family*. What kind of information can parents get about raising children from a Web site? Bring this information to class.

2. At a search engine, type in *au pair*. Find out how to apply for an au pair program. Bring an application to class.

3. For information about parenting and children, find these Web sites by typing in their names at a search engine:

   Zero to Three
   I am your child

   Find some information about children that surprises you. Bring this information to class.

4. At a search engine, type in *day care center* and the name of the city where you live. Find out five facts about a specific day care center. Bring this information to class.

 Additional Activities at http://elt.thomson.com/gic

422   Lesson **9**

Outside Activities Variation

As an alternative, you may invite a guest to your classroom (e.g., an administrator, a librarian, or a service worker at your school) and have students do a class interview. Students should prepare their interview questions ahead of time.

Internet Activities Variation

Activities 1 and 3 Have students use the information they find in activities 1 and 3 to write an information sheet about parenting and child care for newly arrived immigrant parents in their area. Have them include information they think will be new or surprising to newly arrived parents.

Activity 4 Have students use the information they find to make a list of day care providers in your area. If appropriate, have students use the information they have learned in the lesson to write a list of questions parents should ask a potential day care or child care provider.

LESSON

10

GRAMMAR
Unreal Conditions—Present
Real Conditions vs. Unreal Conditions
Unreal Conditions—Past
Wishes

CONTEXT: Science or Science Fiction?
Time Travel
Traveling to Mars
Life 100 Years Ago
Science or Wishful Thinking?

Lesson | 10

Lesson Overview

GRAMMAR

1. **Activate students' prior knowledge.** Write *unreal conditions* and *wishes* on the board. Ask students what they can say about each one.
2. Ask: *What will we study in this lesson?* (unreal conditions in the present, real vs. unreal conditions, unreal conditions in the past, wishes) Give several examples of your own of sentences using conditions (e.g., *If I lived closer to school, I'd ride my bike here. If I hadn't studied Latin, I wouldn't have learned French so easily. I wish that I were in better shape.*). Have volunteers give examples. Write two or three examples on the board.

CONTEXT

1. **Elicit students' prior knowledge.** Ask: *What will we learn about in this lesson?* (time travel, traveling to Mars, life 100 years ago, science or wishful thinking) *Do you think life has changed a lot in the last 100 years? What changes do you think the next 100 years will bring?*
2. Have students share their knowledge and opinions.

Picture

1. **Direct students' attention to the picture.** Ask: *Where do you think this man is? What does the picture make you think about?*
2. Have students share their thoughts about the picture.

🕐 To save class time, have students do the Test/Review at the end of the lesson, or administer a lesson test generated from the Assessment CD-ROM with *ExamView® Pro*. Skip sections of the lesson that students have already mastered. You may also assign some sections for self-study for extra credit.

Expansion

Theme The topic for this lesson can be enhanced with the following ideas:

1. Science fiction books, magazines, movie synopses, or comic books
2. Brochure from a historical reenactment site or event in the area
3. Articles or Web pages about the history of the space program
4. Television program listing summarizing episodes of science fiction programs

Culture Note

Science fiction is fiction that imagines the future or another world. Science fiction novels (books), movies, and television shows are often very popular.

Time Travel (Reading)

1. Have students look at the photo. Ask: *Who is this? What is he famous for?* (Albert Einstein; for his theory of relativity)
2. Have students look briefly at the reading. Ask: *What is the reading about? How do you know?* Have students make predictions.
3. Preteach any essential vocabulary words your students may not know, such as *physicists, dimensions, ticks, theoretically, light years, evolving, pace, fantasy, roots, universe, shortcomings, means,* and *patents.*

BEFORE YOU READ

1. Have students discuss the questions in pairs. Try to pair students of different language backgrounds.
2. Ask for a few volunteers to share their answers with the class.

To save class time, skip "Before You Read" or have students prepare answers for homework ahead of time.

Reading 🎧 *CD 4, Track 12*

1. Have students first read the text silently. Tell them to pay special attention to unreal conditions in the reading. Then play the audio and have students read along silently.
2. Check students' comprehension. Ask questions such as: *What is time travel?* (travel into the future or the past) *Did Albert Einstein think that travel to the future was possible?* (yes) *What do some other physicists think?* (Time travel to the future is possible, but time travel to the past is not.)
3. Review the quotations in the box on page 425 with the class. Ask: *Why do we laugh at these predictions today?* (because all of the inventions mentioned are an integral part of society today)

To save class time, have students do the reading for homework ahead of time.

TIME TRAVEL

Before You Read

1. Do you think time travel is a possibility for the future?
2. Can you name some changes in technology or medicine that have happened since you were a child?

🎧 Read the following article. Pay special attention to unreal conditions.

> If you **could travel** to the past or the future, which time period **would** you **visit?** What would you like to see? **Would** you **want** to come back to the present? If you **could travel** to the past and prevent your grandfather from meeting your grandmother, then you **wouldn't be** here, right? These ideas may seem the subject of science fiction movies and novels now, but believe it or not, physicists are studying the possibility of time travel seriously.
>
> About 100 years ago, Albert Einstein proved that the universe has not three dimensions but four—three of space and one of time. He proved that time changes with motion. A moving clock ticks more slowly than one that does not move. Einstein believed that, theoretically, time travel is possible. If

Albert Einstein 1879-1955

Expansion

Theme The topic for this lesson can be enhanced with the following ideas:

1. Biography of Albert Einstein from a Web site or encyclopedia
2. An article on the development of Einstein's theory of relativity
3. Copy of a synopsis of *The Time Machine*, by H. G. Wells

Reading Variation

To practice listening skills, have students first listen to the audio alone. Ask a few comprehension questions. Repeat the audio if necessary. Then have students open their books and read along as they listen to the audio.

Did You Know? In 1955, Albert Einstein died at the age of 76. He had requested that his body be cremated but that his brain be saved and studied for research.

you **wanted** to visit the Earth in the year 3000, you **would have to** get on a rocket ship going at almost of the speed of light,[1] go to a star 500 light years away, turn around and come back at that speed. When you got back, the Earth **would be** 1,000 years older, but you **would** only **be** ten years older. You **would** be in the future.

However, using today's technologies, if you **wanted** to travel to the nearest star, it **would take** 85,000 years to arrive. (This assumes the speed of today's rockets, which is 35,000 miles per hour.) According to Einstein, you can't travel faster than the speed of light. While most physicists believe that travel to the future is possible, many believe that travel to the past will never happen.

Science and technology are evolving at a rapid pace. **Would** you **want** to travel to the future to see all the changes that will occur? **Would** you **be** able to come back to the present and warn people of future earthquakes or accidents? These ideas, first presented in a novel called *The Time Machine*, written by H.G. Wells over 100 years ago, are the subject not only of fantasy but of serious scientific exploration. In fact, many of today's scientific discoveries and explorations, such as traveling to the moon, had their roots in science fiction novels and movies.

Read what people have said in the past about the future.

"Heavier-than-air flying machines are impossible."
(Lord Kelvin, president, Royal Society, 1895)

"There is no reason for any individual to have a computer in their home."
(Ken Olsen, president, chairman, and founder of Digital Equipment Corp., 1977)

"The telephone has too many shortcomings to be seriously considered as a means of communication. The device is inherently of no value to us."
(Western Union internal memo, 1876)

"Airplanes are interesting toys but of no military value."
(Marshal Ferdinand Foch, French commander of Allied forces during the closing months of World War I, 1918)

"Who . . . wants to hear actors talk?"
(Harry M. Warner, Warner Brothers, 1927)

"Everything that can be invented has been invented."
(Charles H. Duell, commissioner, U.S. Office of Patents, 1899)

---

[1] The *speed of light* is 299,792,458 meters per second (or 186,000 miles per second).

Unreal Conditions; Real Conditions; Wishes   425

Reading Glossary

dimension: measure of size (width, height, and length)
evolve: change over time
fantasy: unreal story; imagined story
light year: the distance light travels in a year
means: method, way
pace: speed
patent: a document from the government saying that a person invented something
physicist: scientist who studies physics, the science of matter and motion
roots: beginnings
shortcomings: problems; deficiencies
theoretically: thought to be true; possible according to scientific analysis (but not yet actualized)
tick: sound a clock makes as it marks the passing of time moving ahead or counting seconds
universe: everything that exists, including earth and everything around it

10.1 | Unreal Conditions—Present

1. Have students cover the grammar chart. On the board, write: *unreal conditions.* Ask: *What do you think this means?* (situations or events that are not real, or imagined)
2. Give several examples of your own; write them on the board (*I don't have much time, and I don't get much exercise. If I had more time, I'd get more exercise. If I got more exercise, I'd be in better shape.*).
3. Have students review the examples and explanations in the grammar chart carefully. Draw students' attention to the use of a past form with *if,* the use of *were* in unreal *if* clauses, and the use of *What if* to propose an unreal idea. Say: *The verb in the if clause has a past form, but not a past meaning.* Tell students that it is important not to confuse the past form with a past meaning; the examples are about an unreal condition in present, not past, time.
4. Draw students' attention to the Punctuation Note. Point out the use of a comma when the *if* clause comes before the main clause.

10.1 | Unreal Conditions—Present

An unreal condition is used to talk about a hypothetical or imagined situation.

Examples	Explanation
If we **had** a time machine, we **could travel** to the future or past. (Reality: We **don't have** a time machine.) If I **could travel** to the past, I **would visit** my ancestors. (Reality: I **can't travel** to the past.) If we **didn't have** computers, our lives **would be** different. (Reality: We **have** computers.)	An unreal condition in the **present** describes a situation that is not real now. Use a past form in the *if* clause and *would* or *could* + base form in the main clause.
If we **could travel** at the speed of light, we'd **be able to** visit the future. If I **visited** my great-great-great-grandparents, they'd **be** very surprised to meet me.	All pronouns except *it* can contract with *would*: *I'd, you'd, he'd, she'd, we'd, they'd.*
If time travel **were** possible, many people **would do** it. If we **were** time travelers, we'd **see** the future.	*Were* is the correct form in the condition clause for all subjects, singular and plural. However, you will often hear native speakers use *was* with *I, he, she,* and *it.*
If I **were** you, I'd **study** more science.	We often give advice with the expression "*If I were you . . .*"
What if you could travel to the future? **What if** you had the brain of Einstein?	We use *what if* to propose a hypothetical situation.
If you **had** Einstein's brain, what **would** you **do**? If you **could** fly to another planet, **would** you **go**?	When we make a question with conditionals, the *if* clause uses statement word order. The main clause uses question word order.

Punctuation Note:
When the *if* clause precedes the main clause, a comma is used to separate the two clauses. When the main clause precedes the *if* clause, a comma is not used.
> If I had Einstein's brain, I would be smarter. (Comma)
> I would be smarter if I had Einstein's brain. (No comma)

426   Lesson **10**

Grammar Variation

Have students underline *if* clauses with unreal conditions in the reading on pages 424 and 425 before they look at the grammar chart. Ask students for their observations on the rules for unreal conditions with *if* clauses.

EXERCISE **1** ABOUT YOU Answer the following questions with *I would*. Give
an explanation for your answers.

EXAMPLE If you could meet any famous person, who would you meet?

I would meet Einstein. I would ask him how he discovered his theory

of relativity.

1. If you could travel to the past or the future, which direction would
   you go?

   <u>Answers will vary.</u>

2. If you could make a clone of yourself, would you do it? Why or
   why not?

3. If you could travel to another planet, would you want to go?

4. If you could change one thing about today's world, what would
   it be?

5. If you could find a cure for only one disease, what would it be?

6. If you could know the day of your death, would you want to know it?

7. If you could have the brain of another person, whose brain would
   you want?

8. If you could be a child again, what age would you be?

9. If you could change one thing about yourself, what would it be?

10. If you could meet any famous person, who would it be?

11. If you could be any animal, what animal would you be?

Unreal Conditions; Real Conditions; Wishes 427

EXERCISE 1

1. Tell students that this exercise is
   about things they would do if they
   could. Have students read the
   direction line.
2. Model the exercise. Direct students
   to the example in the book. Ask
   several volunteers to complete the
   example for themselves.
3. Have students complete Exercise 1
   individually. Then have them
   compare their answers in pairs.
   Circulate and observe the pair work.
   If possible, participate in
   conversations with pairs. Have
   volunteers share interesting
   answers with the class.
4. Assess students' performance. If
   necessary, review grammar
   chart **10.1** on page 426.

Expansion

Exercise 1 After students complete the exercise, have them work in pairs to ask each other
about their statements with *why* or *why not*:

A: *If I could travel to the past or the future, I would travel to the past.*
B: *Why would you travel to the past?*
A: *Because I would like to meet my grandmother.*

EXERCISE 2

1. Tell students that this exercise is a series of conversations between friends and acquaintances. Have students read the direction line; review the directions with the class.
2. Model the exercise. Direct students to the examples. Then complete #1 with the class.
3. Have students complete Exercise 2 individually. Then have them check their answers in pairs by practicing the conversations. Circulate and observe the pair work. If necessary, check the answers as a class.
4. Assess students' performance. If necessary, review grammar chart **10.1** on page 426.

🕐 To save class time, have students do half of the exercise in class and complete the other half for homework. Or assign the entire exercise for homework.

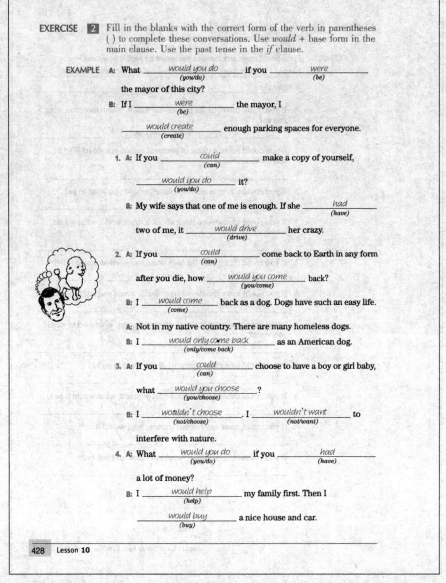

EXERCISE 2 Fill in the blanks with the correct form of the verb in parentheses ( ) to complete these conversations. Use *would* + base form in the main clause. Use the past tense in the *if* clause.

EXAMPLE A: What ___would you do___ if you ___were___ the mayor of this city?
(you/do)   (be)

B: If I ___were___ the mayor, I
(be)

___would create___ enough parking spaces for everyone.
(create)

1. A: If you ___could___ make a copy of yourself,
(can)

___would you do___ it?
(you/do)

B: My wife says that one of me is enough. If she ___had___
(have)

two of me, it ___would drive___ her crazy.
(drive)

2. A: If you ___could___ come back to Earth in any form
(can)

after you die, how ___would you come___ back?
(you/come)

B: I ___would come___ back as a dog. Dogs have such an easy life.
(come)

A: Not in my native country. There are many homeless dogs.

B: I ___would only come back___ as an American dog.
(only/come back)

3. A: If you ___could___ choose to have a boy or girl baby,
(can)

what ___would you choose___ ?
(you/choose)

B: I ___wouldn't choose___ . I ___wouldn't want___ to
(not/choose)   (not/want)

interfere with nature.

4. A: What ___would you do___ if you ___had___
(you/do)   (have)

a lot of money?

B: I ___would help___ my family first. Then I
(help)

___would buy___ a nice house and car.
(buy)

428 Lesson **10**

Culture Note

People in the U.S. sometimes talk about coming back as an animal or as another person after death. Usually these comments are meant as jokes. Some religions believe that humans can be *reincarnated*, or return to life as different people or animals, after death. An entertainer or other public figure is said to be "making a comeback" if he or she returns to public life after an absence, or after losing popularity for a period of time.

5. **A:** If you _____ _could_ _____ look like any movie star,
(can)

   who _____ _would you look like_ _____?
(you/look like)

   B: I _____ _would look like_ _____ a young Harrison Ford.
(look like)

6. **A:** If I _____ _could_ _____ find a way to teach a person a
(can)

   foreign language in a week, I _____ _would make_ _____ a million
(make)

   dollars.

   B: And I _____ _would be_ _____ your first customer.
(be)

7. **A:** If you _____ _could_ _____ be invisible for a day,
(can)

   what _____ _would you do_ _____?
(you/do)

   B: I _____ _would go_ _____ to my teacher's house the day she
(go)

   writes the final exam.

8. **A:** What _____ _would you do_ _____ if you _____ _didn't have_ _____
(you/do)   (not/have)

   a TV?

   B: I think I _____ _would go_ _____ crazy if
(go)

   I _____ _didn't have_ _____ a TV.
(not/have)

9. **A:** Why are you writing your composition by hand?

   B: I don't know how to type. I _____ _would type_ _____ my
(type)

   compositions on the computer if I _____ _could_ _____ type fast.
(can)

   A: If I _____ _were_ _____ you, I _____ _would take_ _____ a
(be)   (take)

   keyboarding class to learn to type.

10. **A:** What _____ _would you do_ _____ if you _____ _could travel_ _____
(you/do)   (can/travel)

    to the past or future?

    B: I _____ _would go_ _____ to the past.
(go)

    A: How far back _____ _would you go_ _____?
(you/go)

Unreal Conditions; Real Conditions; Wishes | 429

Expansion

Exercise 2 Have pairs of students choose one of the conversations in Exercise 2. Ask them to write two additional sentences to continue the conversation. Ask volunteers to present their conversations for the class.

Exercise 2 Have students work in pairs to write conversations with *if* clauses and unreal conditions. Pairs should use one or more of the conversations in Exercise 2 as a model. Have pairs perform their conversations for the class. Have the class vote on the most original or funniest conversation.

1. Tell students that this exercise is a conversation between friends about trying to get in shape. Have students read the direction line. Ask: *What do we write?* (the correct form of the verb)

2. Model the exercise. Direct students to the example. Complete #1 with the class.

3. Have students complete the exercise individually. Then have them check their answers by practicing the conversation. Circulate and observe the pair work. If necessary, check the answers as a class.

4. Assess students' performance. If necessary, review grammar chart 10.1 on page 426.

🕐 To save class time, have students do half of the exercise in class and complete the other half for homework. Or assign the entire exercise for homework.

B: I _____would go_____ to the nineteenth century and stay there.
    (go)

A: Why?

B: If I _____lived_____ in the nineteenth century, I
    (live)

    __would not have to__ work. My life ____would be____ easy.
    (not/have to)   (be)

A: Yes, but if you _____lived_____ in the nineteenth
    (live)

    century, you __would not be able to__ vote.
                  (not/be able to)

11. A: It _____would be_____ nice if people _____could_____
         (be)   (can)

       live forever.

    B: If people ____didn't die____, the world
                  (not/die)

       _____would be_____ overpopulated. There
                (be)

       ____wouldn't be____ enough resources for everybody.
          (not/be)

    A: I didn't think of that. If the world _____were_____
                                               (be)

       overpopulated, I ____would never find____ a parking space!
                        (never/find)

EXERCISE ③ Fill in the blanks with the correct form of the verb in parentheses ( ) to complete this conversation.

🎧

A: If you _____could_____ change one thing about yourself,
         (example: can)

   what ____would it be____ ?
        (1 it/be)

B: I _____would be_____ thinner. If I _____lost_____
         (2 be)   (3 lose)

   about 30 pounds, I ____would be____ much happier—
                      (4 be)

   and healthier. If I ____didn't eat____ so much, I
                       (5 not/eat)

   ____would lose____ weight.
      (6 lose)

A: Diet is not enough. You need to get exercise too. You can start right now with exercise. Let's go jogging every day after work.

Exercise 3 Variation

To provide practice with listening skills, have students close their books and listen to the audio. Repeat the audio as needed. Ask comprehension questions, such as: *How many pounds does person B want to lose?* (30 pounds) *Is dieting enough to lose weight?* (no) *What kind of exercise does person A suggest?* (jogging) Then have students open their books and complete Exercise 3.

B: If I _____ weren't _____ so tired after work,
      (7 be/not)

   I _____ would go _____ jogging with you. But I work
      (8 go)

   nine hours a day and it takes me two hours to commute². So I'm too
   tired at the end of the day.

A: Can't you get any exercise at your job?

B: If I _____ had _____ a different kind of job,
      (9 have)

   I _____ would get _____ more exercise. But I sit at a desk all day.
      (10 get)

A: How about going swimming with me on Saturdays? I go every
   Saturday. Swimming is great exercise.

B: If I _____ knew _____ how to swim, I _____ would go _____
      (11 know)   (12 go)

   with you. The problem is I don't know how to swim.

A: You can take lessons. My gym has a pool and they give lessons on
   the weekends. Why don't you sign up for lessons?

B: I'm too busy with the kids on the weekends. If I

   _____ didn't have _____ kids, I _____ would have _____ much
      (13 not/have)   (14 have)

   more free time.

A: If I _____ were _____ you, I _____ would try _____ to
      (15 be)   (16 try)

   simplify my life.

EXERCISE 4 ABOUT YOU Make a list of things you would do if you had more
              time. You may share your sentences in a small group or with the
              entire class.

EXAMPLES   If I had more free time, I'd read more novels.

           I'd visit my grandmother more often if I had more free time.

1. _____ Answers will vary. _____

2. _____

3. _____

4. _____

² To *commute* means to travel from home to work and back.

Unreal Conditions; Real Conditions; Wishes   431

1. Tell students that this exercise is
   about what they would do if they
   had more time. Have students read
   the direction line.

2. Model the exercise. Direct students
   to the example. Ask: *Is either of
   these examples true for you? Which
   one? Why?* Have several volunteers
   provide examples of their own.

3. Have students complete the
   exercise individually. Tell students
   that they should write information
   they are comfortable with sharing.
   Then have them share their
   sentences in groups. Circulate and
   observe the group work; participate
   in conversations if possible. Have
   volunteers share their sentences
   with the class.

4. Assess students' performance. If
   necessary, review grammar
   chart **10.1** on page 426.

⏱ To save class time, have
   students do the exercise for
homework.

Expansion

Exercise 3 Tell students that people who give a lot of reasons they are not doing something
they think they should be doing is sometimes considered making excuses, or inventing
reasons. Ask: *Do you think that person B's reasons for not losing weight are good reasons,
or do you think that he or she is making excuses? Why?*

Culture Note

"Simplifying your life" is a popular concept that means reducing the number of activities and
responsibilities a person is involved in, to allow time to slow down and enjoy life more.
Magazines, television shows, and numerous Web sites are available for people who want
information on simplifying their lives.

1. Tell students that this exercise is about what they would do if their English were better. Have students read the direction line.
2. Model the exercise. Direct students to the examples. Ask: *Is either of these examples true for you? Which one? Why?* Have several volunteers provide examples of their own.
3. Have students complete the exercise individually. Tell students that they should write information they are comfortable sharing. Then have them share their sentences in groups. Circulate and observe the group work. Have volunteers share their sentences with the class.
4. Assess students' performance. If necessary, review grammar chart **10.1** on page 426.

🕐 To save class time, have students do the exercise for homework.

EXERCISE 6

1. Tell students that this exercise is about what different people are thinking. Have students read the direction line.
2. Model the exercise. Direct students to the example. Ask: *Do you think this is what a one-year-old is thinking?*
3. Have students complete the rest of Exercise 6 individually. Have them compare their answers in pairs. Finally, check the answers as a class.
4. Assess students' performance. If necessary, review grammar chart **10.1** on page 426.

🕐 To save class time, have students do half of the exercise in class and complete the other half for homework. Or assign the entire exercise for homework.

EXERCISE 5 ABOUT YOU Make a list of things you would do differently if you spoke or understood English better. You may share your sentences in a small group or with the entire class.

EXAMPLES If I spoke English fluently, I wouldn't come to this class.

I wouldn't be so nervous when I talk on the telephone if I understood English better.

1. _____ Answers will vary. _____
2. _____
3. _____

EXERCISE 6 Fill in the blanks to tell what the following people are thinking.

EXAMPLE One-year-old: If I ___could___ walk, I ___would walk___ into the kitchen
         (can)   (walk)
and take a cookie out of the cookie jar.

1. Two-year-old: If I ___could___ talk,
                        (can)

   I ___would tell___ my mother that I hate peas.
       (tell)

2. 14-year-old: I ___would be___ happier if
                    (be)

   I ___could___ drive.
       (can)

3. 16-year-old: If I ___had___ a car, my friends and
                       (have)

   I ___would go___ out every night.
       (go)

4. 19-year-old: I ___would attend___ a private university if
                    (attend)

   I ___had___ a lot of money.
       (have)

5. 25-year-old: If I ___were___ married, my parents
                       (be)

   ___wouldn't worry___ about me so much.
       (not/worry)

6. 35-year-old mother: I ___would have___ more time for
                            (have)

   myself if my kids ___were___ older.
                         (be)

Expansion

Exercise 6 Have students use the sentences in the exercise as models to write the thoughts (using *if* clauses) of a famous person (*If I weren't president, I could go outside by myself.*). Then have them read their sentences to the class. Have the class guess the identity of the "famous person."

7. 60-year-old grandmother: If I _____didn't have_____
   (not/have)

   grandchildren, my life _____wouldn't be_____ so interesting.
   (not/be)

8. 90-year-old: If I _____were_____ young today,
   (be)

   I _____would have to_____ learn all about computers and other
   (have to)

   high-tech stuff.

9. 100-year-old: If I _____told_____ you the story of
   (tell)

   my life, you _____wouldn't believe_____ it.
   (not/believe)

10. The dog: If I _____could_____ talk, I
    (can)

    _____would say_____, "Feed me a steak."
    (say)

EXERCISE **7** ABOUT YOU Complete each statement.

EXAMPLES   If I studied harder, _I would get better grades._

If I were the president, _I would lower taxes._

1. If I were the English teacher, _____Answers will vary._____

2. If I could live to be 200 years old, _____

3. If I could predict the future, _____

4. If I were rich, _____

5. If I could be a child again, _____

6. If I could change places with any other person in the world, _____
   _____

7. My life would be better if _____

8. I'd be learning English much faster if _____

9. I'd study more if _____

10. I'd travel a lot if _____

11. I'd be very unhappy if _____

12. I wouldn't borrow money from a friend unless _____
    _____

1. Tell students that this exercise is about their thoughts and ideas. Have students read the direction line.
2. Model the exercise. Direct students to the examples. Ask: *Is either of these answers true for you? Which one?* Ask several volunteers to complete the examples for themselves.
3. Have students complete Exercise 7 individually. Then have them compare their answers in pairs. Ask volunteers to share their sentences with the class.

   To save class time, have students do half of the exercise in class and complete the other half for homework. Or assign the entire exercise for homework.

Exercise 7 Variation

After students complete their own sentences, have them extend their answers by interviewing one another about their ideas:

A: *If you were the English teacher, what would you do?*
B: *I would invite all the students to a party at my house.*
A: *Why would you do that?*
B: *Because it would be good for them to get to know an American family.*

EXERCISE 8

1. Tell students that this exercise is about their lives. Have students read the direction line. Ask: *What do we write?* (an answer and a statement with an unreal condition)
2. Model the exercise. Direct students to the examples in the book. Then do #1 with the class. Ask a volunteer to give an answer.
3. Have students complete the rest of Exercise 8 individually. Then have them check their answers in pairs by asking a partner the question. Have pairs take turns asking and answering the question. Have pairs share interesting answers with the class.

To save class time, have students do half of the exercise in class and complete the other half for homework. Or assign the entire exercise for homework.

EXERCISE 8 ABOUT YOU Answer each question with *yes* or *no*. Then make a statement with an unreal condition.

EXAMPLES Do you have the textbook?

Yes. If I didn't have the textbook, I wouldn't be able to do this exercise.

Is this lesson easy?

No. If it were easy, we wouldn't have to spend so much time on it.

1. Are you an American?

Answers will vary.

2. Do you know how to use the Internet?

3. Do you work on Sundays?

4. Do all the students in this class speak the same language?

5. Does the teacher speak your native language?

6. Are you taking other courses this semester?

7. Do you have a high school diploma?

8. Do you have a car?

9. Do you live far from school?

10. Do you have a job?

11. Do you speak English perfectly?

12. Do you have a computer?

434 Lesson 10

Expansion

Exercise 8 After pairs have interviewed each other, have them close their books and recall and write one or two sentences about their partners' answers: *If Toya didn't know how to use the Internet, she wouldn't be able to help her children with their homework.*

10.2 | Implied Conditions

Examples	Explanation
I **would** never lie to a friend. **Would** you jump in a river to save a drowning person? She **would** never leave her children with a babysitter.	Sometimes the condition (the *if* clause) is implied, not stated. In the examples on the left, the implication is "if you had the opportunity" or "if the possibility presented itself."
Would you **want** to live without today's technologies? **Would** you **want** to travel to another planet? **Would** you **want** to have Einstein's brain? I **wouldn't want** to live for 500 years, **would** you?	*Would want* is used to present hypothetical situations. The *if* clause is implied.

EXERCISE 9 ABOUT YOU Answer these questions and discuss your answers.

Answers will vary.

1. Would you give money to a beggar?
2. Would you marry someone from another country?
3. Would you buy a used computer?
4. Would you lend a large amount of money to a friend?
5. Would you open someone else's mail?
6. Would you lie to protect a friend?
7. Would you tell a dying relative that he or she is dying?
8. Would you want to travel to the past or the future?
9. Would you want to live more than 100 years?
10. Would you want to visit another planet?
11. Would you want to live on the top floor of a hundred-story building?
12. Would you want to go on an African safari?

EXERCISE 10 ABOUT YOU Answer these questions.

EXAMPLE What would you do if a stranger on the street asked you for money?
I would say, "I'm sorry, I can't give you any."

1. What would you do if you found a wallet in the street with a name and phone number in it?

Answers will vary.

2. What would you do if you lost your money and didn't have enough money to get home by public transportation?

Unreal Conditions; Real Conditions; Wishes **435**

Grammar Variation

After students have reviewed the example sentences in the grammar chart, have them go back to the reading on pages 424 and 425 and identify sentences with implied conditions.

10.2 | Implied Conditions

1. Have students cover the grammar chart. On the board, write: *implied conditions*. Ask: *What does* implied *mean?* (giving information without exactly saying it) Write: *imply, implied, implication.* Review the meaning of each if necessary.
2. Have students look at the examples and explanations in the grammar chart. Ask: *What is missing in each of the examples?* (the *if* clause) Say: *In each example, the* if *clause is implied, not stated (said).*
3. Provide several examples of your own (e.g., *I would never ask my parents for money. Would you?*). Ask volunteers to provide examples of their own.

EXERCISE 9

1. Tell students that this exercise is about what they would and would not do in different situations. Have students read the direction line.
2. Have students read the prompts silently and think about their answers for a few minutes. Encourage students to make notes. Then have students interview each other in pairs. Say: *Ask your partner the question, and then ask for more details about his or her answer.* When students have finished the conversation, ask volunteers to share their partners' information with the class, as appropriate.
3. Assess students' performance. If necessary, review grammar chart **10.2**.

EXERCISE 10

1. Tell students that this exercise is about making choices in difficult situations. Have students read the direction line.
2. Model the exercise. Go over to the example.
3. Have students complete the exercise individually. Ask volunteers to share their answers in small groups. Encourage groups to ask each other about their answers. Then have groups report their opinions to the class: *In our group, Jamila and Alfredo would call the person. Priti and I would take the wallet to the closest police station.*
4. Assess students' performance. If necessary, review grammar chart **10.2**.

Traveling to Mars
(Reading)

1. Have students look at the graphic on page 436. Ask *What are these?* (the planets in our solar system) *Where are they?* (in space; in the universe; rotating around our sun) Have students look at the photo on page 437. Ask: *What is this?* (NASA's Spirit Rover)

2. Have students look briefly at the reading. Have students look at the title of the reading. Ask: *What is the reading about? How do you know?* Have students make predictions.

3. Preteach any vocabulary words your students may not know, such as *planetary, climate, geology, not-so-distant, astronauts, miss their chance,* and *rely on.*

BEFORE YOU READ

1. Activate students' prior knowledge about space travel and Mars and other unmanned space exploration. Ask: *When did humans first land on the moon?* (in 1969) *Has anyone landed on Mars?* (no) *What do you think we can learn from space travel?*

2. Have students discuss the questions in pairs. Try to pair students of different language backgrounds.

3. Ask a few volunteers to share their answers with the class.

To save class time, skip "Before You Read" or have students prepare answers for homework ahead of time.

---

3. What would you do if you saw a person in a public park picking flowers?

_____

4. What would you do if a cashier in a supermarket gave you a ten-dollar bill in change instead of a one-dollar bill?

_____

5. What would you do if you hit a car in a parking lot and no one saw you?

_____

6. What would you do if you saw another student cheating on a test?

_____

7. What would you do if your doctor told you that you had six months left to live?

_____

8. What would you do if you lost your job and couldn't pay your rent?

_____

9. What would you do if your best friend borrowed money from you and didn't pay you back?

_____

10. What would you do if your best friend told your secret to another person?

_____

TRAVELING TO MARS

Before You Read
1. Are you interested in exploration of different planets?
2. Do you think there is life on other planets?

Expansion

Theme The topic for this lesson can be enhanced with the following ideas:

1. Magazine, newspaper, or Web articles about the Mars rovers
2. Pictures, timelines, and other information on lunar and planetary exploration from NASA at http://nssdc.gsfc.nasa.gov/planetary/
3. Web pages on Mars exploration, space in general, and research from NASA at http://www.nasa.gov

---

Expansion

Exercise 10 After students have finished discussing their answers, have students write a paragraph about the opinions in their groups. Have them compare or contrast their opinions with those of others in their group. Collect the paragraphs for assessment, or have students check each other's work.

Read the following article. Pay special attention to conditions beginning with *if*.

Exploration on Mars, our closest planetary neighbor, has already begun. In 2004, Spirit Rover landed on Mars to gather information about possible life-forms there, to study the climate and geology of the planet, and to prepare for human exploration in the not-so-distant future of our neighbor. Before anyone goes to Mars, however, more needs to be learned.

Going to Mars is more difficult than going to the moon. **If** astronauts go to Mars, they **will be have** to return within a given time period. If they **don't come** back within this period of time, they **will miss** their chance. **If** astronauts have a problem with their equipment, they **will not be able** to rely on a message from Earth to help them. Because of the distance from Earth, it can take about 40 minutes from the time a message goes out from Earth until it is received on Mars. Also, a visitor to Mars will have to be gone for at least three years because of the distance and time necessary to travel.

If you **had** the chance to go to Mars, **would** you go?

Spirit Rover

Reading CD 4, Track 14

1. Have students first read the text silently. Tell them to pay special attention to conditions beginning with *if* in the reading. Then play the audio and have students read along silently.
2. Check students' comprehension. Ask questions such as: *Which planet is Mars?* (our closest planetary neighbor) *Why was Spirit Rover sent to Mars?* (to gather information about possible lifeforms, study the climate and geology, and prepare for human exploration) *Will it be easy to travel to and explore Mars?* (no)

To save class time, have students do the reading for homework ahead of time.

Reading Variation

To practice listening skills, have students first listen to the audio alone. Ask a few comprehension questions. Repeat the audio if necessary. Then have students open their books and read along as they listen to the audio.

Reading Glossary

astronauts: space travelers
climate: usual weather conditions
geology: physical features of the earth or another planet
miss their chance: miss or lose an opportunity
not-so-distant: not very far away
planetary: related to a planet or the planets
rely on: count on; be sure of

Culture Note

Travel to Mars and invasion of Earth by Martians, or creatures from Mars, are popular subjects for science fiction books and movies. In 1938, a famous radio broadcast of the story "War of the Worlds," written by H. G. Wells and broadcast by Orson Welles, convinced millions of listeners that creatures from Mars had attacked Earth.

10.3 | Real Conditions vs. Unreal Conditions

1. Have students cover the grammar chart. Ask: *What kind of conditions have we been looking at with* if? (unreal conditions) *Do you remember another kind of* if *clause that we have studied?* (if clauses to show that a condition affects a result) Ask students to locate the grammar chart on *if* with conditions (grammar chart 8.6 on page 346).

2. On the board, write: *If I get a new e-mail address, . . .* and *If I had several e-mail addresses, . . .* Ask: *Which one of these shows a possibility?* (If I get . . .) *Which one is unreal right now?* (If I had . . .) Ask volunteers to complete the two sentences using information about themselves.

3. Have students look at grammar chart 10.3. Review the examples and explanations with the class. If necessary, have students go back and review grammar chart 8.6 on page 346.

EXERCISE 11

1. Tell students that this exercise is about real versus unreal conditions. Have students read the direction line. Ask: *What kinds of conditions are used?* (real and unreal)

2. Model the exercise. Direct students to the examples in the book. Then complete #1 with the class.

3. Have students complete the exercise individually and check their answers in pairs. Circulate and observe the pair work. Check answers as a class.

4. Assess students' performance. If necessary, review grammar charts 8.6 on page 346, 10.2 on page 436, and/or 10.3 on page 438.

10.3 | Real Conditions vs. Unreal Conditions

Examples	Explanation
If astronauts **go** to Mars, they **will have** to return within a given time period. **If** they **have** problems, they **will have** to solve them by themselves. **If** a person goes to Mars, he **will be** gone for three years.	The sentences on the left describe a real possibility for the **future**. Notice that for real possibilities, we use the present tense in the *if* clause and the future tense in the main clause.

If you **were** on Mars, you **would weigh** about one-third of what you weigh on Earth.
If you **could** go to Mars, **would** you go?
If you **met** a Martian, what **would** you **do** or **say**?
	The statements to the left are about hypothetical or imaginary situations in the **present**. They are not plans for the future.
	  Reality: You are not on Mars now.
	  Reality: You can't go to Mars now.
	Notice that we use the past tense in the *if* clause and *would* or *could* in the main clause.

EXERCISE 11 Fill in the blanks with the correct form of the verb in parentheses ( ). Both real conditions and unreal conditions are used.

EXAMPLES The government is planning to send astronauts to Mars in the near future. If an astronaut ___decides___ to go to Mars, he or she
　　　　　(decide)

___will be___ away from family for at least three years.
　(be)

If I ___saw___ a Martian, I ___would shake___ his hand.
　　　(see)　　　　　　　　(shake)

1. I'm thinking of going to California next month. If I
___go___, I ___'ll bring___ back
　(go)　　　　　　(bring)
a souvenir for you.

2. If I ___could___ go to Mars, I ___would bring___
　　　(can)　　　　　　　　　(bring)
back a rock as a souvenir.

3. If the weather ___were___ nice today,
　　　　　　　(be)
I ___would go___ out. But it's raining now.
　　(go)

4. If the weather ___is___ nice this weekend,
　　　　　　　(be)
we ___will go___ for a walk in the forest.
　　(go)

438　Lesson 10

Grammar Variation

Have students match the *if* clauses in boldface in the reading on page 437 to the appropriate explanations in the grammar chart.

5. The temperature on Mars is very cold. If it _____weren't_____
   (not/be)

   so cold, maybe it _____could_____ sustain life.
   (can)

6. My sister is thinking about getting married soon. If she

   _____gets_____ married in the summer, she
   (get)

   _____will have_____ an outdoor wedding.
   (have)

7. My brother hates the woman next door. He _____wouldn't marry_____
   (not/marry)

   her if she _____were_____ the last woman on Earth.
   (be)

8. My mother may visit me next week. If she _____comes_____
   (come)

   here, I _____will take_____ her to an art museum.
   (take)

9. Sue's father died when she was a child. If her father

   _____were_____ here, he _____would be_____
   (be)   (be)

   so proud of her.

10. Our cat just had six kittens. If you _____want_____ a kitten,
    (want)

    we _____will give_____ you one.
    (give)

11. We love our dog. She's like a member of the family. We

    _____wouldn't sell_____ our dog if you _____paid_____
    (not/sell)   (pay)

    us a million dollars.

12. She may get some money from her parents. If her parents

    _____send_____ her some money, she
    (send)

    _____will buy_____ some new clothes.
    (buy)

13. She's always dreaming about winning the lottery. If she

    _____wins_____ the lottery, she _____will quit_____
    (win)   (quit)

    her job.

14. If I _____were_____ a child, I _____would play_____
        (be)   (play)

    video games all day.

Unreal Conditions; Real Conditions; Wishes **439**

Expansion

Exercise 11 Have students write pairs of sentences of their own using real and unreal conditions. Have students use the models:

I'm hoping to . . . soon.
If I . . . , I'll . . . .
I'm not . . . .
If I were . . . , I would . . . .

Culture Note

Several phrases with *if* or implied *if* are commonly used to show a strong opinion, such as: *I wouldn't _____ if you/he/she were the last man/woman/person on Earth; I wouldn't trade _____ for a million dollars; If they could see me now . . . .* and *I'll _____ if it's the last thing I do!*

🎧 *CD 4, Track 15*

1. Tell students that this exercise is a conversation between friends. Have students read the direction line.
2. Direct students to the example. Complete the first sentence as a class.
3. Have students complete the exercise individually. Have them check their answers by practicing the conversation in pairs. If necessary, check answers as a class.
4. Assess students' performance. If necessary, review grammar chart **10.3**.

🕐 To save class time, have students do half of the exercise in class and complete the other half for homework. Or assign the entire exercise for homework.

---

15. My son is thinking about a career in medicine. If my son ___*becomes*___ a doctor when he grows up, we
    (become)
    ___*will be*___ so happy.
    (be)

16. I study a lot. If I ___*don't study*___ , I ___*won't pass*___
    (not/study)   (not/pass)
    this course.

17. My brother is a great student and will probably get a scholarship.
    If he ___*gets*___ a scholarship, he ___*will go*___
    (get)   (go)
    to the University of Wisconsin.

EXERCISE 12 *Combination Exercise.* Fill in the blanks with the correct form of the verb in parentheses ( ).
🎧

A: If you ___*could*___ change one thing in your life,
   (example: can)

   what ___*would you change*___ ?
   (1 you/change)

B: I ___*would be*___ younger.
   (2 be)

A: You're not very old now. You're just in your 30s.

B: But if I ___*were*___ younger,
   (3 be)

   I ___*wouldn't have*___ so many responsibilities.
   (4 not/have)
   Now I have two small children who need all my attention.

A: What ___*would you do*___ if you ___*didn't have*___ kids?
   (5 you/do)   (6 not/have)

B: I ___*would play*___ golf all day on Saturday. And I
   (7 play)

   ___*would sleep*___ late on Sunday mornings.
   (8 sleep)

A: Are you sorry you had kids?

B: Of course not. I love them very much. If I ___*didn't have*___
   (9 not/have)

   them, I ___*would be*___ very unhappy. But I'm just
   (10 be)

   dreaming about a simpler, easier time.

A: It ___*would be*___ nice if we ___*could*___
   (11 be)   (12 can)

   go back in time and make some changes.

Exercise 12 Variation

To provide practice with listening skills, have students close their books and listen to the audio. Repeat the audio as needed. Ask comprehension questions, such as: *Does person B want to be younger or older?* (younger) *Is person B very old now?* (no) *Why does person B want to be younger?* (then person B would have fewer responsibilities) Then have students open their books and complete Exercise 12.

Expansion

Exercise 12 Have students role-play conversations about unreal conditions with a famous person. Have student A play an interviewer and student B play a famous person. Have student A ask student B what he or she would change about his or her life if he or she could, and why. Then have students reverse roles.

Exercise 12 Students have done several exercises in which people talked about things they would do if they could change one thing in their lives. Have students discuss whether there is anything they would change in their lives if they could.

LIFE 100 YEARS AGO

Before You Read

1. Can you imagine what life was like 100 years ago? 1,000 years ago?

2. Would you want to live at a different time in history? Would you want to visit a different time in history? What period in history would you want to visit?

 Read the following article. Pay special attention to unreal conditions in the past.

Did You Know?

The average life expectancy for someone born in the U.S. in the year 1900 was 47 years. For someone born in the year 2000 it was 75. Today the leading cause of death is heart disease.

Most of us are amazed by the rapid pace of technology at the beginning of the twenty-first century. We often wonder what life will be like 20 or 50 or 100 years from now. But do you ever wonder what your life **would have been** like if you **had been** alive 100 years ago?

If you **had lived** around 1900 in the U.S., you **would have earned** about $200-$400 a year. You probably **wouldn't have graduated** from high school. Only 6 percent of Americans had a high school diploma at that time. If you **had been** a dentist or an accountant, you **would have made** $2,500 a year. If you **had been** a child living in a city, you **might have had** to work in a factory for 12-16 hours a day.

If you **had gone** to a doctor, he probably **would not have had** a college education. Only 10 percent of doctors at that time had a college degree. And if you **had had** a baby at that time, it **would have been** born at home. If you **had gotten** an infection at that time, you probably **would have died** because antibiotics had not yet been discovered. The leading causes of death at that time were pneumonia, influenza, and tuberculosis.

What about your home? If you **had been living** 100 years ago, you probably **wouldn't have had** a bathtub or a telephone. You **would have washed** your hair about once a month.

Do you think you **would have been** happy with life 100 years ago?

Unreal Conditions; Real Conditions; Wishes   441

Expansion

Theme The topic for this lesson can be enhanced with the following ideas:

1. A timeline of major inventions in the early 1900s
2. Magazine, newspaper, or Web articles about life in the early 1900s

Reading Variation

To practice listening skills, have students first listen to the audio alone. Ask a few comprehension questions. Repeat the audio if necessary. Then have students open their books and read along as they listen to the audio.

Reading Glossary

infection: the growth of harmful bacteria in a person's body
influenza: a contagious respiratory (related to breathing) disease caused by a virus
pneumonia: a respiratory disease; an infection of the lungs
tuberculosis: a bacterial infection, usually of the lungs; often called *TB*

Life 100 Years Ago (Reading)

1. Have students look at the photos. Ask: *What are these people doing?* (working in a tailor shop; building a railroad) *When do you think these pictures were taken?* (around 100 years ago)
2. Have students look at the title and photos. Ask: *What is the reading about? How do you know?* Have students make predictions.
3. Preteach any vocabulary words your students may not know, such as *infection, pneumonia, influenza,* and *tuberculosis.*

BEFORE YOU READ

1. Activate students' prior knowledge about life in the U.S. around 1900. Ask: *What kinds of work did most people do then?* (manual labor) *How many hours a day did people work?* (10–12 or more) *What are some things we have today that most people probably didn't have?* (telephones, cars, vacations)
2. Have students discuss the questions in pairs. Ask a few volunteers to share their answers with the class.

To save class time, skip "Before You Read" or have students prepare answers for homework ahead of time.

Reading ◯ *CD 4, Track 16*

1. Have students first read the text silently. Tell them to pay special attention to unreal conditions in the past in the reading. Then play the audio and have students read along silently.
2. Check students' comprehension. Ask questions such as: *About how much money did people earn per year in the early 1900s?* ($200 to $400, or $2,500 for a dentist or accountant) *What percent of Americans had a high school diploma?* (6%) *What were some of the most dangerous diseases?* (pneumonia, influenza, tuberculosis)

To save class time, have students do the reading for homework ahead of time.

DID YOU KNOW ?

The leading (or #1) cause of death in the U.S. in 2001 was heart disease, followed by cancer, stroke, chronic respiratory diseases, and accidents.

10.4 | Unreal Conditions—Past

1. Ask students to cover page 442. On the board, write: *If we had been alive 100 years ago, we wouldn't have had telephones.* Ask volunteers what they can say about life 100 years ago, using the model on the board.

2. Have students look at the grammar chart. Review the examples and explanations. Point out the reference to the rule of sequence of tenses in the third row of the grammar chart.

3. Draw students' attention to the Language Notes. Pronounce each of the examples in the chart using fast, informal pronunciation (*would've, woulda*). For #2, tell students that the very informal use of *would have known* instead of *had known* is often heard, but not considered correct and not appropriate for formal conversation or in writing.

4. Have a few volunteers provide examples of their own about things that would have, wouldn't have, might have, or could have happened in the past, but didn't.

5. If necessary, have students review the list of irregular verbs in Appendix M.

EXERCISE 13

1. Tell students that this exercise is about life in the U.S. 100 years ago. Have students read the direction line.

2. Model the exercise. Direct students to the example in the book. Then complete #1 with the class.

3. Have students complete the rest of Exercise 13 individually. Then have them check their answers in pairs. If necessary, check the answers as a class.

10.4 | Unreal Conditions—Past

Examples	Explanation
If you **had been** alive 100 years ago, you **would have made** about $200 a year. If you **had lived** 100 years ago, you probably **wouldn't have graduated** from high school.	An unreal condition can describe a situation that is not real in the **past**. Use the past perfect in the *if* clause and *would have* + past participle in the main clause.
If you **had gotten** an infection, you **could have died**. If you **had had** a baby, it **might have died** young.	*Could* or *might* can be used in the main clause instead of *would*.
If I **had known** that learning English *was going* to be so hard, I **would have studied** it in my country. If I **had realized** how hard I *would have to* work as a waitperson, I **would have gone** to college.	A noun clause can be used within an *if* clause (after *know, realize*, etc.). Follow the rule of sequence of tenses in the noun clause. (See Section 9.9.)
If my great-grandparents **had been able to** come to the U.S. 100 years ago, our lives **would have been** easier.	In the *if* clause, use *had been able to* for the past perfect of *could*.
a. If you **were** born 100 years ago, your life **would have been** different. OR b. If you **had been** born 100 years ago, your life **would have been** different.	Sometimes we don't change to the past perfect, especially with the verb *be*, if it is clear that the action is past. It is clear that you *were* born in the past. Sentences (a) and (b) have the same meaning.

Language Notes:

1. In informal speech, *have* after *could, would*, or *might* is pronounced like *of* or /ə/. Listen to your teacher pronounce the sentences above with fast, informal pronunciation.

2. In very informal conversational English, you often hear *would have* in both clauses.

    If I *would have known* about the problem, I *would have told* you. (Informal)

    If I *had known* about the problem, I *would have told* you. (Formal)

EXERCISE **13** Fill in the blanks with the correct form of the verb about life in the U.S. 100 years ago.

EXAMPLE   If you _____*had been*_____ a doctor 100 years ago, you
                                     (be)

_____*wouldn't have been*_____ rich.
                    (not/be)

1. If you _____*had (had)*_____ a baby 100 years ago, it probably
                        (have)

_____*would have been born*_____ at home.
                    (be/born)

Grammar Variation

Have students review the example sentences and explanations first. Then have students write statements about themselves using *If I had lived in my country 100 years ago, ...*

2. If you _____had gotten_____ an infection, you
      (get)

   probably _____would have died_____ .
      (die)

3. If you _____(had) lived_____ around 1900,
      (live)

   you probably ___would not have finished___ high school.
      (not/finish)

4. You ___would not have had___ a car if you
      (not/have)

   _____(had) lived_____ in the U.S. 100 years ago.
      (live)

5. Your president ___would have been___ Theodore Roosevelt if you
      (be)

   _____(had) lived_____ in the U.S. 100 years ago.
      (live)

6. If you _____had needed_____ to travel to another city,
      (need)

   you ___would have traveled___ by train.
      (travel)

7. You probably ___would have worked___ if you
      (work)

   ___had been/were___ child 100 years ago.
      (be)

EXERCISE **14** A middle-aged women is telling her daughter how the young
lady's life would have been different if she had grown up in the
late fifties. Fill in the blanks with the correct form of the verb in
parentheses ( ) to complete the story.

   It's great that you're thinking about becoming a doctor or astronaut.
When I was your age, I didn't have the opportunity you have today.
You can be anything you want, but if you ___had been___ a woman
                                          (example: be)
growing up in the fifties, your opportunities ___would have been___ limited.
                                                    (1 be)
If you _____had gone_____ to college, you probably
            (2 go)

___would have majored___ in nursing or education, or you
      (3 major)

___would have taken___ a secretarial course.
      (4 take)

You probably ___would have gotten___ married in your
                  (5 get)
early twenties.

Unreal Conditions; Real Conditions; Wishes **443**

1. Tell students that this exercise is
about what it was like to grow up in
the late 50s in the U.S. Have
students read the direction line.
Ask: *What do we write?* (the correct
form of the verb in parentheses)
2. Model the exercise. Direct students
to the example. Then do items 1 and
2 with the class.
3. Have students complete Exercise 14
individually. Then have them check
their answers in pairs. Circulate and
observe the pair work. If necessary,
check the answers as a class.

🕐 To save class time, have
students do half of the exercise
in class and complete the other half for
homework. Or assign the entire
exercise for homework.

Exercise 14 Variation

To provide practice with listening skills, have students close their books and listen to the
audio. Repeat the audio as needed. Ask comprehension questions, such as: *What is the
daughter thinking about becoming?* (doctor, astronaut) *What did most women in the fifties
major in?* (nursing, education) *When did they usually get married?* (in their early twenties)
Then have students open their books and complete Exercise 14.

Culture Note

Theodore Roosevelt became president of the U.S. in 1901, when President William McKinley
was assassinated. He was 42 years old and the youngest president in U.S. history. Roosevelt
had been a cowboy and a war hero, and he was a popular president. He is remembered for his
conservation and national forest projects, and for making famous the proverb, "Speak softly
and carry a big stick."

10.5 | Mixed Tenses in Condition Statements

1. Have students cover the grammar chart. On the board, write several examples of your own of condition statements with mixed tenses (*1. If I had learned to swim when I was young, I wouldn't be afraid of the water now. 2. If I were better at remembering dates, I wouldn't have forgotten my niece's birthday.*). For each sentence, ask: *When is the condition?* (1. in the past; 2. in the present) *When is the result?* (1. in the present; 2. in the past) Say: *We can make sentences with the condition and the result in different times.*

2. Have students look at grammar chart **10.5**. Review the examples. For each example, ask: *When is the condition?* (in the present in the first section; in the past in the second section) *When is the result?* (in the past in the first section; in the present in the second section) Remind students that the past form does not necessarily show a condition or result in past time.

EXERCISE 15

1. Tell students that this exercise is about unreal conditions and results. Have students read the direction line. Ask: *Will every sentence have the same tense?* (no; the tenses are mixed)

2. Direct students to the example in the book. Review the example, and then do #1 with the class.

3. Have students complete the exercise in writing individually and then check answers in pairs. If necessary, check answers with the class.

4. Assess students' performance. If necessary, review grammar chart **10.5**.

If you _____had gotten_____ pregnant, you probably
(6 get)

_____would have quit_____ your job. You probably
(7 quit)

_____would have had_____ two or more children. Your husband
(8 have)

_____would have worked_____ to support you and the children. But today,
(9 work)

you have the opportunity to continue working after you have children.

Technology _____would have been_____ different too. Your house
(10 be)

_____would have had_____ one TV and one phone. Because we had only
(11 have)

one TV, the family spent more time together. You _____wouldn't have had_____
(12 not/have)

a computer or a cell phone.

If you _____had grown_____ up in the fifties, your life
(13 grow)

_____would have been_____ completely different.
(14 be)

10.3 | Mixed Tenses in Condition Statements

We can mix a present condition with a past result, or a past condition with a present result.	
Present Condition (Use simple past)	**Past Result (Use *would have* + past participle)**
If I **were** you,	I **wouldn't have bought** that old computer.
If I **had** a car,	I **would have taken** you to the airport last week.
If I **were** rich,	I **would have bought** a big house when I came to the U.S.
Past Condition (Use past perfect)	**Present Result (Use *would* + base form)**
If you **had lived** during the fifties,	you **would have** a different way of looking at the world now.
If I **hadn't come** to the U.S.,	I **would be living** with my parents now.
If she **hadn't lost** her job last month,	she **would be able** to take a vacation now.

EXERCISE **15** Fill in the blanks with the correct form of an appropriate verb. These sentences have mixed tenses.

EXAMPLE She just came to the U.S., so she doesn't speak English perfectly. If she _____had come_____ here a long time ago, she _____would speak_____ English much better.

Expansion

Exercise 14 Have students use Exercise 14 as a model to write sentences or a paragraph directed to an American, beginning: *If you had been a boy/girl growing up in my country 50 years ago, ...*

1. He invested a lot of money in a good stock, and now he's rich. If he _hadn't invested_ in that stock, he _wouldn't be_ rich today.

2. Luckily she didn't marry her high school boyfriend. If she _had married_ him, she _wouldn't be_ happy now.

3. I passed the last course, and now I'm in this course. I _wouldn't be_ in this course if I _hadn't passed_ the last course.

4. The car you bought is terrible. If I _were_ you, I _wouldn't have bought_ that car.

5. She didn't see the accident, so she can't tell you what happened. She _could tell_ you what happened if she _had seen_ the accident.

6. You didn't come to class yesterday, so you don't understand the teacher's explanation today. You _would understand_ the teacher's explanation today if you _had come_ to class yesterday.

7. She has a lot of work to do, so she got up early. If she _didn't have_ so much work, she _would have stayed_ in bed all morning.

8. She doesn't have a car, so she didn't drive you to the hospital. If she _had_ a car, she _would have driven_ you to the hospital yesterday.

9. I didn't learn English as a child. If I _had learned_ English as a child, I _wouldn't have_ so many problems with it now.

EXERCISE **16** ABOUT YOU Complete each statement with a past or present result.

EXAMPLES If I had taken the TOEFL test last year, _I wouldn't have passed it._

If I hadn't brought my book to class today, _I wouldn't be able to do this exercise._

1. If I hadn't taken this course, _Answers will vary._

EXERCISE   16

1. Tell students that this exercise is about conditions and results in their lives. Have students read the direction line.
2. Model the exercise. Direct students to the examples in the book. Review the examples, and then ask several volunteers to complete them for themselves.
3. Have students complete the exercise individually, and then compare answers in pairs. Circulate and observe the pair work. Have pairs share interesting answers with the class.
4. Assess students' performance. If necessary, review grammar chart **10.5** on page 444.

To save class time, have students do half of the exercise in class and complete the other half for homework. Or assign the entire exercise for homework.

Expansion

Exercise 15 Ask students to write a sentence about a past condition that would have changed their lives today (e.g., *If I had learned to drive when I was young, I wouldn't be studying for the driving test now.*). Collect the sentences and read them to the class. Have students guess who wrote each sentence.

1. Tell students that this exercise is about unreal conditions in their lives. Have students read the direction line.
2. Model the exercise. Direct students to the examples in the book. Ask several volunteers to complete the sentences for themselves.
3. Have students complete the exercise in writing individually. Ask volunteers to share their answers with the class.
4. Assess students' performance. If necessary, review grammar chart **10.5** on page 444.

🕐 To save class time, have students do half of the exercise in class and complete the other half for homework. Or assign the entire exercise for homework.

1. Tell students that this exercise is about unreal conditions and results. Have students read the direction line.
2. Model the exercise. Direct students to the examples in the book. Then do #1 with the class.
3. Have students complete the exercise individually. Then have them check their answers in pairs. If necessary, check the answers as a class.

🕐 To save class time, have students do half of the exercise in class and complete the other half for homework. Or assign the entire exercise for homework.

---

2. If I hadn't taken beginning English, _____
3. If I hadn't come to class today, _____
4. If I hadn't studied for the last test, _____
5. If I hadn't paid last month's rent, _____
6. If I had been born 200 years ago, _____

EXERCISE 17 ABOUT YOU Complete each statement with a past or present condition.

EXAMPLES I would have saved money if *I had bought a used book.*
I would have studied last night if *we were having a test today.*

1. I would have stayed after class yesterday if _____ Answers will vary. _____

2. I would have stayed home today if _____

3. I would have done better on the last test if _____

4. The teacher would have explained the last lesson again if _____

5. I would have taken an easier course if _____

6. I would have studied English when I was a child if _____

7. My parents would have been disappointed in me if _____

EXERCISE 18 Fill in the blanks with the correct form of an appropriate verb. Some sentences have mixed tenses.

EXAMPLES I took a wrong turn on the highway. I arrived at the meeting one hour late.
If I _____ *hadn't taken* _____ a wrong turn on the highway, I
_____ *would have arrived* _____ at the meeting on time.

1. I forgot to set my alarm clock, so I didn't wake up on time.
I _____ *would have woken up* _____ on time if I
_____ *hadn't forgotten to set* _____ my alarm clock.

446 Lesson 10

Expansion

Exercise 17 Ask students to write several sentences about something that they didn't learn when they were young, and the result. Provide a model of your own: *When I was young, I didn't learn to work on cars. If I had learned to work on cars, I wouldn't have to pay the garage to get my car fixed.*

2. She didn't pass the final exam, so she didn't pass the course. If she
_____ *had passed* _____ the final exam, she
_____ *would have passed* _____ the course.

3. I didn't see the movie, so I can't give you any information about it.
If I _____ *had seen* _____ the movie, I
_____ *could give* _____ you some information about it.

4. He loves her, so he married her. If he _____ *didn't love* _____
her, he _____ *wouldn't have married* _____ her.

5. She didn't hear the phone ring, so she didn't answer it. She
_____ *would have answered* _____ the phone
if she _____ *had heard* _____ it ring.

6. He left his keys at the office, so he couldn't get into the house. If he
_____ *hadn't left* _____ his keys at the office,
he _____ *could have gotten* _____ into the house.

7. I don't have much money, so I didn't buy a new coat. I
_____ *would have bought* _____ a new coat if I
_____ *had* _____ more money.

8. He didn't take the medicine, so his condition didn't improve. If he
_____ *had taken* _____ the medicine, his
condition _____ *would have improved* _____ .

9. I didn't have my credit card with me, so I didn't buy the computer I
saw last week. I _____ *would have bought* _____ the computer
if I _____ *had had* _____ my credit card with me.

EXERCISE 19   Complete each statement.

EXAMPLES   If I had a million dollars, *I would travel around the world.*
If I had a computer, *I would have typed my last composition.*

1. People would live longer if _____ *Answers will vary.* _____
_____

2. I wouldn't have to work if _____
_____

3. If we had had a test on this lesson last week, _____
_____

Unreal Conditions; Real Conditions; Wishes   **447**

EXERCISE   19

1. Tell students that this exercise is additional practice in unreal conditions. Have students read the direction line.
2. Direct students to the examples in the book. Ask: *Are these sentences true for you? Why/why not?*
3. Have students complete the exercise individually. Have students compare their answers in pairs. Circulate and observe the pair work. Ask volunteers to share their answers with the class.

To save class time, have students do half of the exercise in class and complete the other half for homework. Or assign the entire exercise for homework.

Expansion

Exercise 19 After students compare answers in pairs, have them form new pairs and ask each other about items 2, 4, and 6. Tell students not to show their new partners their written answers. Then have each student use reported speech to write a sentence about what his or her partner said.

Science or Wishful Thinking? (Reading)

1. Have students look at the photo. Ask: *How old are most women when their children are born?*
2. Have students look at the title, and look briefly at the reading. Ask: *What is the reading about? How do you know?* Have students make predictions.
3. Preteach any vocabulary words your students may not know, such as *clone, extend,* and *long dead.*

BEFORE YOU READ

1. Activate students' prior knowledge about the use of new technologies to extend life, allow older women to have babies, and clone animals. Ask: *What are some things medical technology allows us to do today that weren't possible 100 years ago?* (medical tests; new treatments; live longer, healthier lives)
2. Have students discuss the questions in pairs. Try to pair students of different language backgrounds.
3. Ask a few volunteers to share their answers with the class.

🕐 To save class time, skip "Before You Read" or have students prepare answers for homework ahead of time.

Reading 🎧 CD 4, Track 18

1. Have students read the text on page 448 silently. Tell them to pay special attention to *wish* and the verbs that follow it in the reading. Then play the first part of the audio and have students read along silently.
2. Check students' comprehension of this section. Ask questions such as: *Have the scientists at the University of Connecticut doubled the life span of humans?* (no; only of fruit flies) *How much money does the U.S. company charge to clone a cat?* ($50,000)

🕐 To save class time, have students do the reading for homework ahead of time.

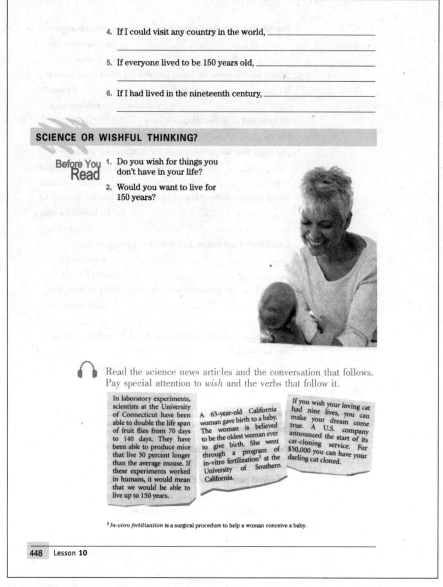

4. If I could visit any country in the world, _____

5. If everyone lived to be 150 years old, _____

6. If I had lived in the nineteenth century, _____

SCIENCE OR WISHFUL THINKING?

Before You Read
1. Do you wish for things you don't have in your life?
2. Would you want to live for 150 years?

🎧 Read the science news articles and the conversation that follows. Pay special attention to *wish* and the verbs that follow it.

In laboratory experiments, scientists at the University of Connecticut have been able to double the life span of fruit flies from 70 days to 140 days. They have been able to produce mice that live 30 percent longer than the average mouse. If these experiments worked in humans, it would mean that we would be able to live up to 150 years.

A 63-year-old California woman gave birth to a baby. The woman is believed to be the oldest woman ever to give birth. She went through a program of in-vitro fertilization[3] at the University of Southern California.

If you wish your loving cat had nine lives, you can make your dream come true. A U.S. company announced the start of its cat-cloning service. For $50,000 you can have your darling cat cloned.

[3] *In-vitro fertilization* is a surgical procedure to help a woman conceive a baby.

448   Lesson **10**

Expansion

Theme The topic for this lesson can be enhanced with the following ideas:

1. Magazine, newspaper, or Web articles about medical technologies that have led to better health, longer lives, or other breakthroughs
2. An article about a medical controversy involving the use of a new technology, such as life support machines for patients in a coma
3. An article about the cloning of an animal

Reading Variation

To practice listening skills, have students first listen to the audio alone. Ask a few comprehension questions. Repeat the audio if necessary. Then have students open their books and read along as they listen to the audio.

A: I **wish** I **were** younger. I **wish** I **didn't have to** get old and sick. Science can do so much these days. I **wish** they **could find** a way to keep us young.

B: I read an article about how scientists are working to extend our lives. It's possible that soon people will be able to live 150 years.

A: I wouldn't want to be 150 years old and sick. I **wish** I **could be** 21 forever.

B: I don't think scientists will ever find a way to make us any younger than we are now. The best they can do is extend our lives and keep us healthier longer. What would you do differently if you were 21?

A: I would be going to parties on weekends. I wouldn't have so many responsibilities. I **wouldn't have to** take care of children. I started to have my children when I was in my early twenties. I **wish** I **had waited** until I was older.

B: My aunt is 55 and just got married for the first time a few years ago. She **wishes** she **had gotten** married when she was young and she **wishes** she **had had** children. But now she's too old.

A: I'm not so sure about that. I read an article about a 63-year-old woman who gave birth to a baby with the help of science.

B: That's amazing! What will science do for us next?

A: Scientists have started to clone animals.

B: I used to have a wonderful dog. I miss her. I **wish** I **could have** cloned her. But it's too late. She died 10 years ago.

A: Technology in the twenty-first century is moving so fast, isn't it? Don't you **wish** you **could come** back in 1,000 years and see all the changes in the world after that period of time?

B: I read an article that says that if we could travel at almost the speed of light, we could leave the Earth and come back a thousand years from now.

A: I wouldn't want to live in the future. I just **wish** I **could visit** the future. All our friends and relatives would be long dead if we left the present.

Unreal Conditions; Real Conditions; Wishes   449

Reading Glossary

clone: make an exact copy of a human or an animal
extend: lengthen
long dead/long gone: already dead/gone for a long time

3. Have students read the text on page 449 silently. Tell them to pay special attention to *wish* and the verbs that follow it in the reading. Then play the second part of the audio and have students read along silently.

4. Check students' comprehension of this section. Ask questions such as: *How old does person A want to be?* (21 forever) *Could person B have her dog cloned? Why/why not?* (No; her dog died 10 years ago and scientists are just starting to clone animals now.)

10.6 | Wishes

1. Have students cover grammar chart **10.6** and look at the reading on pages 448 and 449. Ask: *What do the people in the conversation we just read wish?* Elicit several wishes from the reading: *She wishes she could have cloned her dog; she wishes she were younger.* Write the sentences on the board.

2. Demonstrate the forms for wishes. Write a present tense and a past tense sentence on the board, such as: *I don't speak Chinese. I didn't study physics.* Say: *These are things that didn't happen or aren't true. A wish says that I'd like them to be true.* Write: *I wish I spoke Chinese. I wish I had studied physics.* Say: *We use a past tense form verb to talk about a wish about the present and a past perfect form verb to talk about a wish about the past.*

3. Have students look at grammar chart **10.6**. Review the example sentences and explanations. Draw students' attention to the verb tense forms and use of *could*.

4. Point out the use of *was* instead of *were* in informal usage in the chart. Draw students' attention to the Usage Note. Tell students that the very informal use of *would have told* instead of *had told* is often heard, but not considered correct and not appropriate for formal conversation or in writing.

10.6 | Wishes

We often wish for things that are not real or true.	
Examples	**Explanation**
Present	Use a **past** tense verb to wish for something in the **present**.
Reality: I **don't have** a dog.	
Wish: I wish (that) I **had** a dog.	After *wish*, you can use *that* to introduce the clause, but it is usually omitted.
Reality: We **have** to get old.	
Wish: I wish (that) we **didn't have** to get old.	
Reality: I **can't live** 150 years.	
Wish: I wish I **could live** 150 years.	
Past	Use a **past perfect** verb to wish for something in the **past**.
Reality: I **didn't know** my grandparents.	
Wish: I wish I **had known** them.	If the real situation uses *could*, use *could have* + past participle after *wish*.
Reality: My aunt **didn't have** kids when she was young.	
Wish: She wishes she **had had** kids when she was young.	
Reality: My favorite dog died years ago. I **couldn't clone** my dog.	
Wish: I wish I **could have cloned** her.	
Formal: I wish I **were** younger. Informal: I wish I **was** younger.[4]	With *be*, *were* is the correct form for all subjects. In conversation, however, you will often hear native speakers use *was* with *I, he, she,* and *it.*
Formal: I wish it **were** Sunday. Informal: I wish it **was** Sunday.	
I'm not young, but I wish I were. I don't have a car, but I wish I **did.** I didn't bring my photo album to the U.S., but I wish I **had.** I couldn't go to the party last week, but I wish I **could have.**	We can use an auxiliary verb (*were, did, had,* etc.) to shorten the *wish* clause.
Wish you were here! John Smith 123 Busy Road Anytown NY 11235	When people on vacation send postcards to friends and relatives, they sometimes write these words.

Usage Note:
 In conversation, you often hear Americans use *would have* + past participle for past wishes.
  Formal: I wish you *had told* me the truth.
  Informal: I wish you *would have told* me the truth.	

[4]Many native speakers consider *was*, in this case, to be incorrect.

Grammar Variation

Have students match the phrases with *wish* in boldface in the reading on pages 448 and 449 to the appropriate explanations in the grammar chart.

Culture Note

Traditions related to wishing (usually wishing for something, not wishing that something will happen) include wishing when you see the first star of the evening, wishing when you see a falling star, and making a wish before you blow out the candles on your birthday cake.

Students may be interested in the old saying, "If wishes were horses, beggars would ride."

EXERCISE 20 Fill in the blanks to make a wish about the present.

EXAMPLE Today isn't Friday. I wish it _____ were _____ Friday.

1. You're not here with me. I wish you _____ were _____ here.

2. I have to work 60 hours a week. I wish I _____ didn't have to _____ work so much.

3. I can't speak English perfectly. I wish I _____ could speak _____ English perfectly.

4. I don't have a car. I wish I _____ had _____ a car.

5. You're going on vacation to Hawaii, but I can't go with you. I wish I _____ could go _____ with you.

6. I'm not rich. I wish I _____ were _____ rich.

7. I have a lot of responsibilities. I wish I _____ didn't have _____ so many responsibilities.

8. I don't have time to read much. I wish I _____ had _____ more time to read.

9. I'm not 18 years old. I wish I _____ were 18 years old _____.

10. Do you wish you _____ could live _____ to be 150 years old?

11. I can't speak French. I wish I _____ could speak _____ French.

EXERCISE 21 ABOUT YOU Fill in the blanks to complete each statement.

EXAMPLE I wish I had _more time to spend with my family._

1. I wish I were _____ Answers will vary. _____

2. I wish I knew how to _____

3. I wish I didn't have to _____

4. I wish I had _____

5. I wish I could _____

EXERCISE 22 Fill in the blanks to make a wish about the past.

EXAMPLE You didn't see the movie. I wish you _had seen it._

1. I didn't know it was your birthday. I wish I _____ had known _____. I would have baked you a cake.

2. I didn't go to the concert. Everyone said it was wonderful. I wish I _____ had gone _____.

Unreal Conditions; Real Conditions; Wishes 451

Expansion

Exercise 21 Have students write a short paragraph about someone from the past whom they wish they could have met, and why.

EXERCISE 20

1. Tell students that this exercise is about wishes about the present. Have students read the direction line.
2. Model the exercise. Review the example; then do #1 with the class.
3. Have students complete the exercise individually and then check their work in pairs. Review the answers as a class.

EXERCISE 21

1. Tell students that this exercise is about their wishes. Have students read the direction line.
2. Model the exercise. Direct students to the example in the book. Provide an answer of your own; ask several volunteers to provide answers of their own.
3. Have students complete the rest of the exercise individually. Then have them share their answers with a partner. Circulate and observe the pair work; participate if possible. Have volunteers share their answers with the class.

To save class time, have students do half of the exercise in class and complete the other half for homework. Or assign the entire exercise for homework.

EXERCISE 22

1. Tell students that this exercise is about wishes about the past. Have students read the direction line.
2. Model the exercise. Review the example; then do #1 with the class.
3. Have students complete the exercise individually and then check their work in pairs. Review the answers as a class.
4. Assess students' performance. If necessary, review grammar chart 10.6 on page 450.

To save class time, have students do half of the exercise in class and complete the other half for homework. Or assign the entire exercise for homework.

1. Tell students that this exercise is a series of conversations about wishes. Have students read the direction line. Ask: *What do we write?* (the correct form of the verb in parentheses)
2. Model the exercise. Direct students to the examples in the book.
3. Have students complete the exercise individually. Then have them check their answers in pairs by practicing the conversations. If necessary, check answers as a class.
4. Assess students' performance. If necessary, review grammar chart **10.6** on page 450.

🕐 To save class time, have students do half of the exercise in class and complete the other half for homework. Or assign the entire exercise for homework.

3. I didn't see the parade. I wish I ____had seen____ it.
4. I studied German in high school. I wish I ____had studied____ _____ English instead.
5. I didn't see his face when he opened the present. I wish I ____had seen____ his face.
6. I lost my favorite ring. I was wearing it at the party. I wish I ____had left____ it at home.
7. I told Larry my secret, and he told all his friends. I wish I ____hadn't told____ him my secret.
8. I forgot to bring my photo album when I moved to this city. I wish I ____had brought____ it.

EXERCISE 23 🎧 EXAMPLE

Combination Exercise. Fill in the blanks with the correct form of the verb in parentheses ( ) in each of the conversations below. Some wishes are about the present, some are about the past.

A: I wish I ____had____ good vision.
(have)

You *can* have perfect or near perfect vision. Why don't you try laser surgery?

A: What can that do for me?

A lot. I had it two years ago, and I don't need glasses anymore. I wore glasses since I was a child. I wish they ____had had____ this surgery
(have)

years ago. Now I can see first thing in the morning, read, drive, and play sports without wondering where my glasses are.

1. A: I wish I ____were____ thin.
(be)

B: Why don't you try a diet?

A: I've tried every diet. Nothing works.

B: You need to exercise every day.

A: I'm too tired when I get home from work. I wish scientists
____could____ find a pill that would make me thin
(can)
with no effort on my part.

2. A: I've been bald since I was 25 years old. I wish I
____weren't____ bald.
(be/not)

B: They say bald men are very manly.

Expansion

Exercise 22 Have students look back at Exercise 17 in Lesson 9, on page 389. Have students work in groups to write a list of wishes the student in Exercise 17 might have. Compare lists as a class.

Exercise 23 Variation

To provide practice with listening skills, have students close their books and listen to the audio. Repeat the audio as needed. Ask comprehension questions, such as: *In conversation 1, what does person A wish?* (to be thin) *What does person B suggest?* (a diet and exercise) Then have students open their books and complete Exercise 23.

A: I don't care what they say. I wish I ___*had*___ hair.
   ___(have)___

   I wish someone ___*could*___ find a cure for
   ___(can)___
   baldness.

3. A: It's so expensive to call my country. I wish I

   ___*could*___ talk to my family every day.
   ___(can)___

   B: You can. Just get a microphone for your computer and you can
   chat with them online for free.

   A: I wish I ___*knew*___ how to do that.
   ___(know)___

   B: Don't worry. I'll show you.

4. A: I wish I ___*were*___ older.
   ___(be)___

   B: Why? No one wants to get old.

   A: I didn't say old. I just said "older." Older people have more
   experience and wisdom.

   B: I wish we ___*could*___ have the wisdom of old
   ___(can)___
   people and the bodies of young people.

   A: If everyone stayed young and no one died, where would we find
   space on the Earth for all the new babies born every day?

   B: We could colonize Mars.

5. A: I wish I ___*could*___ travel to the future.
   ___(can)___

   B: Why?

   A: I would be able to see future problems and then come back and
   warn people about them.

   B: I wish I ___*could*___ go to the past.
   ___(can)___

   A: Why?

   B: I would like to meet my grandparents. I never knew them. I wish
   I ___*had known*___ them, but they died before I was born.
   ___(knew)___

6. A: We saw a great movie last night about time travel.

   B: I wish I ___*could have gone*___ with you, but I had to study
   ___(can/go)___
   for my biology test.

Expansion

Exercise 23 Have pairs of students choose one of the dialogues in Exercise 23. Ask them to
write two additional sentences to continue the dialogue. Ask volunteers to present their
dialogues to the class.

10.7 | Wishing for a Desired Change

1. Have students cover grammar chart **10.7**. On the board, write: *I wish our classroom were larger. I wish the janitor would fix the lights.* Ask: *Which one of these things could change?* Say: *The janitor could fix the lights, but he doesn't. The room can't change size. When we wish for a change that could really happen, we use would.*

2. Have students look at grammar chart **10.7**. Review the example sentences and explanations carefully.

3. Provide several examples about yourself, similar to those in the grammar chart, such as *I wish our dog would stop chewing on things. I wish my daughter would find a better part-time job.* Ask volunteers to provide examples of wishes for a desired change.

---

7. **A:** I studied Italian when I was a child. I wish I _____had studied_____ English.
   (study)

   B: I wish I _____had been_____ born in the U.S. Then English
   (be)
   would be easy.

8. **A:** I wish I _____had finished_____ college before getting married.
   (finish)

   B: But you have a great husband.

   A: I know. But I wish I _____had waited_____ a few years. Now
   (wait)
   I have no education and a lot of responsibilities.

   B: You can finish college now.

   A: I wish I _____could_____, but with my two kids, there's no
   (can)
   time.

9. **A:** I'm an only child. I wish I _____had_____ a sister or brother.
   (have)

   B: Maybe you will someday.

   A: I don't think so. My mom is in her fifties already.

   B: With today's biological technologies, older women can still have kids.

   A: Maybe so. But she doesn't have the energy to raise a small child.

10.7 | Wishing for a Desired Change

Examples	Explanation
I wish you **wouldn't watch** so many science fiction movies. I wish you **would take** a science course. Your hair is too long. I wish you **would cut** it.	*Would* + base form is used after *wish* to show that a person wants something different to happen in the future. It shows a desire for change.
Compare: a. I wish I **could** travel to the past. (I can't travel to the past.) a. I wish I **were** young. (I'm not young.) b. I wish my parents **would come** to the U.S. (I want them to come to the U.S.) b. I wish you **wouldn't talk** so much about the past. (I want you to stop talking about the past.)	a. *Wish* without *would* is not a desire for change but an expression of discontent with the present situation. b. *Wish* with *would* shows a desire for change.

Grammar Variation

Have students cover the explanation column of the chart. Review the examples as a class. Ask students what they can figure out about the difference between the (a) sentences and the (b) sentences in the second row of the chart.

EXERCISE **24** Fill in the blanks to show a desire that someone do something differently. Answers may vary.

EXAMPLE   My parents are going back to my country. I wish they _would stay here._

1. Are you leaving so soon? I wish you _____ _would stay_ for a few more hours.

2. My son doesn't want to clean his room. I wish he _____ _would clean_ _____ his room.

3. My daughter wants to use the Internet all day. I wish she _would_ _____ _play_____ with her friends instead of sitting in front of the computer all day.

4. Some students are talking so loudly in the library that I can't think. I wish they _would stop talking so loudly_ .

5. My son's hair is so long. I don't like long hair on a boy. I wish he _____ _would cut_ _____ his hair.

6. The teacher gives a lot of homework. I wish she _wouldn't give_ _____ so much homework.

7. My friend doesn't want to go to the party with me. I wish he _____ _____ _would go_ _____ to the party with me.

EXERCISE **25** A man is complaining about his apartment situation. Fill in the blanks with the correct form of the verb in parentheses ( ). Include *would* if you think he is hoping for a change. Don't include *would* if you think there is no possibility of change.

EXAMPLES   I wish my neighbors _would be_ more quiet.
                        (be)

I wish the walls _were_ thicker.
                    (be)

1. I wish my landlord _would give_ more heat.
                           (give)

2. I wish the people upstairs from me _wouldn't walk_
                                            (not/walk)
around so much at night.

3. I wish the landlord _would clean_ the hallways more often.
                           (clean)

4. I wish the building _had_ an elevator.
                          (have)

5. I wish there _were_ more trees and flowers around
                   (be)
the building.

Unreal Conditions; Real Conditions; Wishes   455

Expansion

Exercise 24 Have students make sentences of their own about things they wish a friend or family member would do to change something (using *would*).

Exercise 24 Have students write a list of things they wish their school or teacher(s) would do to change something (using *would*).

1. Tell students that this exercise is about wishing for a difference. Have students read the direction line. Ask: *Are different answers possible?* (yes)
2. Direct students to the example. Then complete #1 with the class.
3. Have students complete the exercise individually, and check their answers in pairs. If necessary, check answers as a class.
4. Assess students' performance. If necessary, review grammar chart **10.7** on page 454.

EXERCISE 25

1. Tell students that this exercise is about one person's complaints about his apartment building. Have students read the direction line. Ask: *Does every sentence use would?* (no)
2. Direct students to the examples in the book. For each example, ask: *Why is this answer correct?* (Example 1: He is hoping for a change. Example 2: He is wishing, but a change isn't possible.) Then complete #1 with the class.
3. Have students complete Exercise 25 individually. Then have them check their answers in pairs. If necessary, check the answers as a class.
4. Assess students' performance. If necessary, review grammar chart **10.7** on page 454.

To save class time, have students do half of the exercise in class and complete the other half for homework. Or assign the entire exercise for homework.

EXERCISE 26

1. Tell students that this exercise is about their wishes and wishes for a change. Have students read the direction line. Ask: *Do all of the answers have to be wishes for a change?* (no)
2. Direct students to the examples. Ask: *Are these wishes true for you? Why/Why not?*
3. Have students complete the exercise individually and compare answers in pairs. Have volunteers share interesting answers with the class.
4. Assess students' performance. If necessary, review grammar chart **10.7** on page 454.

🕐 To save class time, have students do half of the exercise in class and complete the other half for homework. Or assign the entire exercise for homework.

EXERCISE 27

1. Tell students that this exercise is about one student's complaints about her class. Have students read the direction line.
2. Direct students to the examples in the book. For each example, ask: *What does this answer mean?* (Example 1: She thinks the teacher won't change. Example 2: She thinks a change is possible.) Then complete #1 with the class.
3. Have students complete the exercise individually. Then have them check their answers in pairs. If necessary, check the answers as a class.

🕐 To save class time, have students do half of the exercise in class and complete the other half for homework. Or assign the entire exercise for homework.

---

6. I wish the landlord ___wouldn't raise___ my rent every year.
   (not/raise)

7. I wish my kitchen ___were___ larger.
   (be)

8. I wish I ___had___ a gas stove, not an electric stove.
   (have)

9. I wish the apartment ___were___ sunnier.
   (be)

10. I wish I ___were___ rich enough to buy a house.
    (be)

11. I wish I ___had___ air-conditioning.
    (have)

12. I wish I ___could___ move, but I can't.
    (can)

EXERCISE 26   ABOUT YOU Fill in the blanks to complete these statements. Your wish can include a desire for a change (by using *would*) or it can simply state that you're unhappy with the way things are right now.

EXAMPLES   I wish the class _didn't have so many students._

I wish my parents _would let me go out with my friends._

1. I wish my family _____ Answers will vary. _____
2. I wish the teacher _____
3. I wish my neighbors _____
4. I wish the government _____
5. I wish more people _____
6. I wish my apartment _____

EXERCISE 27   A student is complaining about her class. Fill in the blanks with the correct form of the verb. Include *would* if you think she hopes for a change. Don't include *would* if you think there is no possibility of change. Both present and past wishes are included.

EXAMPLES   I wish the teacher ___didn't give___ so much homework.
            (not/give)

I wish the teacher ___would spend___ more time on conditionals.
            (spend)

1. I wish I ___could___ skip ESL and go into regular
   (can)
   English.

Expansion

Exercise 26 Have pairs of students write their own conversations using one of the items in Exercise 26 as a first line, and continuing with their own words. Have volunteers perform their conversations for the class.

2. I wish the book _____ had _____ the answers in the back.
   (have)

3. I wish I _____ had paid _____ more attention to learning
   (pay)
   English when I was in my native country.

4. I wish I _____ had bought _____ a dictionary in my native country.
   (buy)
   Dictionaries are much cheaper there.

5. I wish I _____ had taken _____ my counselor's advice and
   (take)
   registered early. I couldn't get into the biology class I wanted.

6. I wish I _____ had brought _____ my dictionary to class today.
   (bring)
   We're going to write a composition, and I need to check my
   spelling.

7. I wish the teacher _____ would let _____ us use our books
   (let)
   during a test.

8. I wish we _____ didn't have to _____ write so many compositions.
   (not/have to)

9. I wish the students in the back _____ would be _____ quiet.
   (be)
   They're always making so much noise.

10. I wish I _____ had _____ the teacher's brain. Then I would
    (have)
    know English perfectly.

EXERCISE 28 *Combination Exercise.* A mother (M) is complaining to her son (S).
Fill in the blanks with the correct form of the words in parentheses
( ) to express their wishes.

M: You never visit. I wish you _____ would visit _____ me more
   (example: visit)
   often. I'm not going to live forever, you know.

S: I *do* visit you often. Isn't once a week often enough?

M: Some day I won't be here, and you'll say to yourself, "I wish I
   _____ had visited _____ my mom more often."
   (1 visit)

S: Mom, you're only 48 years old.

M: Who knows how long I'll be here? There are no guarantees in life.
   My own mother died when I was a teenager. I wish she
   _____ had lived _____ to see you and your sister.
   (2 live)

Unreal Conditions; Real Conditions; Wishes 457

EXERCISE 28

🎧 *CD 4, Track 20*

1. Tell students that this exercise is a
   conversation between an unhappy
   mother and her son. Have students
   read the direction line.
2. Direct students to the example in
   the book.
3. Have students complete the
   exercise individually, and check
   their answers in pairs by practicing
   the conversation. Check answers as
   a class.
4. Assess students' performance. If
   necessary, review grammar
   chart **10.7** on page 454.

🕐 To save class time, have
students do half of the exercise
in class and complete the other half for
homework. Or assign the entire
exercise for homework.

Expansion

Exercise 27 Have students write sentences with wishes and hopes for a change about a
supervisor, a co-worker, a neighbor, or an acquaintance. Collect students' sentences for
assessment, or have volunteers share their sentences with the class.

Exercise 28 Variation

To provide practice with listening skills, have students close their books and listen to the
audio. Repeat the audio as needed. Ask comprehension questions, such as: *How often does the
son visit?* (once a week) *Does the mother think this is enough?* (no) *How old is the mother?*
(48 years old) Then have students open their books and complete Exercise 28.

S: I do too. But what can we do?

M: I wish you _____were_____ married already.
       (3 be)

S: Mom, I'm only 25 years old. There's plenty of time to get married.

M: Well, your sister's only 23, and she's already married.

S: I wish you ____would stop____ comparing me to my sister.
       (4 stop)
   She has different goals in life. Besides you don't like Shari's husband.

M: You're right. I wish she ____had married____ a better man.
       (5 marry)

S: There's nothing wrong with Paul. He's a good husband to her.

M: We'll see. You know, I wish you ____would cut____ your hair.
       (6 cut)
   It's too long.

S: Mom. I'm old enough to decide how long to wear my hair.

M: You're too thin. I wish you ____would eat____ more.
       (7 eat)

S: I eat enough. When I was a teenager, you said I was too fat.

M: I'm still your mother. I wish you ____would listen____ to me.
       (8 listen)

S: I *do* listen to you. But I've got to live my own life.

M: Sometimes you act like a child and tell me you're old enough to make
   your own decisions. Then you tell me you're too young to get married.

S: I'm not too young to get married. I just don't want to now. I want to
   be a rock musician.

M: I wish you ____would find____ a real job.
       (9 find)

S: It *is* a real job.

M: You didn't finish college. I wish you ____would get____ your
       (10 get)
   degree. How are you ever going to find a real job?

S: You don't need a college degree to be a rock musician.

M: Well, I hope I live long enough to see you married, with a good job.

S: With today's technologies, you'll probably live to be 150 years old
   and not only see me married, but also see your great-great-great-
   grandchildren married.

M: I wouldn't want to live so long.

S: You wouldn't? Just think, you'll be 150 years old and I'll be 127.
   You'll still be telling me how to live my life. That would make you
   happy, wouldn't it?

Expansion

Exercise 28 Tell students that the mother and son in this exercise disagree about a lot of
things. Ask students what they think each one could do to make their relationship better. Ask:
If you were the mother/the son/the daughter, what would you do? Have volunteers share their
ideas with the class, or have students write their ideas and collect for assessment.

SUMMARY OF LESSON 10

1.

Unreal Conditions—Present	
Verb → Past	Verb → *Would / Might / Could* + Base Form
If I **were** an astronaut,	I **would go** to Mars.
If I **could** live to be 150 years old,	I **would know** my great-great-grandchildren.
If I **spoke** English perfectly,	I **might have** more opportunities.
If I **could** travel to the past,	I **could meet** my ancestors.
If she **didn't have** children,	she **would have** more free time.
If I **were** in Hawaii,	I **would be** on a beach right now.
If we **didn't have** advanced technology,	we **wouldn't be** able to explore space.

2.

Unreal Conditions—Past	
Verb → Past Perfect	Verb → *Would / Might / Could* + Have + Past Participle
If you **had lived** 100 years ago,	you **wouldn't have had** a computer.
If a doctor **had lived** 100 years ago,	he **could have practiced** medicine without a college degree.
If you **had gotten** an infection,	you **might have died.**
If my father **had** not **met** my mother,	I **wouldn't have been** born.

3.

Mixed Tenses	
Present Condition	Past Result
If she **were** rich,	she **would have sent** her kids to private school.
If I **had** your phone number,	I **would have called** you yesterday.
If I **were** you,	I **would have quit** my job a long time ago.
Past Condition	Present Result
If she **had married** him,	she **would be** very unhappy now.
If I **had stayed** home today,	I **wouldn't be reviewing** this lesson.

Unreal Conditions; Real Conditions; Wishes 459

Summary of Lesson 10

1. **Unreal Conditions—Present** Have students use the examples in the chart to make statements about themselves using unreal conditions in the present: *If I knew more about fixing computers, I would open my own business. If I had a dog, I would name it Rover, after the Mars rovers.*
   If necessary, have students review:
   10.1 Unreal Conditions—Present (p. 426).
2. **Unreal Conditions—Past** Have students use the examples in the chart to make statements about themselves using unreal conditions in the past: *If I had gotten up on time, I wouldn't have been late today. If I had known you were home, I would have asked you to go to the movies with me.*
   If necessary, have students review:
   10.4 Unreal Conditions—Past (p. 442).
3. **Mixed Tenses** Have students work in pairs to write different results for each of the conditions in the chart. Have students use the same tense in the result as that shown in the chart. If necessary, have students review:
   10.5 Mixed Tenses in Condition Statements (p. 444).

Summary Variation

1. Have students work in pairs to ask each other questions about unreal conditions in the present. Model the activity: *If you spoke English perfectly, what would you do? If you were in your country right now, what would you be doing?*

Summary of Lesson 10 (*cont.*)

4. **Real Possibilities for the Future**
Have students make statements about things they might do in the future, such as: *If I do well in this class, I'll take a higher level class next year. If we have a party, I'll bring my guitar.*
If necessary, have students review:
8.6 Condition (p. 346)
10.3 Real Conditions vs. Unreal Conditions (p. 438).

5. **Wishes** Have students use the models in the chart to make three statements with wishes: one about the present, one about the past, and one about something they would like someone to change, such as: *I wish I had really long hair; I wish I hadn't eaten so much last night; I wish my neighbor would get rid of his old car.*
If necessary, have students review:
10.6 Wishes (p. 450)
10.7 Wishing for a Desired Change (p. 454).

Editing Advice

For each item, have students provide the grammar rule behind the Editing Advice. This can be done as an individual, a pair, a group, or a class activity.

1. With an unreal condition, use a past form in the *if* clause and *would* or *could* + base form in the main clause.
2. In the main clause, use *would* or *could* with the base form.
3. For an unreal condition in the past, use *would/could* or *might* + *have* + past participle in the main clause.
4. For unreal conditions and wishes, use the past perfect in the *if* clause and *would have* + past participle in the main clause.
5. For real possibilities in the future, we use the present tense in the *if* clause and the future tense in the main clause.

4.

Real Possibilities for the future	
Condition	Future Result
If we **explore** Mars,	we **will learn** a lot.
If I **go** to New York,	I **will send** you a postcard.
If she **is** late,	she **will miss** the meeting.

5.

Wishes	
Present	Past
I wish I **were** younger.	I wish I **had studied** English when I was younger.
I wish I **could** be a child again.	I wish I **had been** a better student when I was a child.
I wish you **would** cut your hair.	I wish my parents **would have let** me go to the party last week.

EDITING ADVICE

1. Don't use *will* with an unreal condition.
   If I will~~be~~ *were* rich, I would buy a house.

2. Don't include *be* if you have another verb.
   If I knew more English, I would ~~be~~ find a better job.

3. Always use the base form after a modal.
   She would ~~has~~ *have* called you if she had your phone number.

4. Use the past perfect, not the present perfect, for unreal conditions and wishes.
   If she ~~has~~ *had* studied harder, she wouldn't have failed the test.
   I wish I ~~have~~ *had* seen that movie.

5. For a real condition, use the simple present tense in the *if* clause.
   If I will have time tomorrow, I will write my composition.

460   Lesson **10**

PART **1**   Find the mistakes with the underlined words, and correct them. Not every sentence has a mistake. If the sentence is correct, write *C*.

EXAMPLES   What ~~will~~ *would* you do if you had a million dollars?

I wouldn't be able to visit my friends if I didn't have a car. *C*

1. I don't have much money. If I ~~have~~ *had* a lot of money, I'd travel around the world.

2. I ~~will be~~ *would be* happier if my family were here.

3. I don't have any time. If I had time, I'd help my friend today. *C*

4. If I could meet the president, I would tell him that he's doing a great job. *C*

5. I'm unhappy because my daughter can't come here. I ~~will be~~ *would be* happy if my daughter could live with me.

6. I wish I could speak English perfectly. *C*

7. If I ~~will be~~ *were* you, I would buy a new car.

8. If I didn't have to study English, I ~~would be have~~ *would have* more free time.

9. I have a car. I wouldn't be able to find a job here if I ~~don't have~~ *didn't have* a car.

10. If she hadn't repaired the brakes on her car, she might have had an accident. *C*

11. The teacher ~~would has explained~~ *would have explained* the grammar more slowly if she had had more time.

12. I came here when I was 40 years old. I wish I had come here when I was younger. *C*

13. Can you help me?—Sorry. If I could, I would. *C*

14. If I ~~would be~~ *were* young, I would have more energy.

15. I'm sorry I didn't call you yesterday. I ~~would call~~ *would have called* you if I hadn't been so busy.

16. I didn't know about the party so I didn't go. I wish I ~~have known~~ *had known* about it.

17. Mary hates Paul. She wouldn't marry him even if he were the last man on Earth. *C*

18. I wish you would call me more often. *C*

19. If you are late for tomorrow's test, you will not have enough time to finish it. *C*

20. What would you do if you ~~find~~ *found* a wallet with a lot of money in it?

Unreal Conditions; Real Conditions; Wishes   461

Lesson 10 Test/Review

For additional practice, review, and assessment materials, see Assessment CD-ROM with *ExamView Pro, More Grammar Practice* Workbook 3, Interactive CD-ROM, and Web site http://elt.thomson.com/gic

PART 1

1. Part 1 may be used as an in-class test to assess student performance, in addition to the Assessment CD-ROM with *ExamView Pro*. Have students read the direction line. Ask: *Does every sentence have a mistake?* (no) Have students complete the exercise.
2. Collect for assessment.
3. If necessary, have students review: **Lesson 10.**

Lesson Review

To use Part 1 as a review, assign it as homework or use it as an in-class activity to be completed individually or in pairs. Check answers and review errors as a class. Reteach grammar points that students haven't mastered. Then student learning may be assessed using a test generated from the Assessment CD-ROM with *ExamView Pro*.

1. Part 2 may also be used as an in-class test to assess student performance, in addition to the Assessment CD-ROM with *ExamView Pro*. Tell students that this is a conversation between two people about their lives. Review the example. Then do #1 as a class. Have students complete the exercise.
2. Collect for assessment.
3. If necessary, have students review: **Lesson 10.**

---

21. I got an invitation to my sister's graduation. I wouldn't have been able to go without the invitation. *C*

22. I heard you saw a great movie last night. I wish I have gone with you.
    had

23. If he has been more careful, the accident wouldn't have happened.
    had

24. If he will have time next weekend, he will help his brother.
    has

PART **2** Fill in the blanks to complete the conversation.

A: Are you happy you came to the U.S.?

B: Yes, I'm glad I'm here. But I wish I _____ *had come* _____ here when
   (example)

   my brother came here 15 years ago.

A: Why?

B: Well, now I'm 40 years old, and it's harder to learn English and find a good job. I didn't study English when I was a child. I wish I

   _____ *had studied* _____ it when I was younger.
   (1)

A: But your brother learned English quickly.

B: He was only 18 when he came here. Now he speaks English well, has

   a small business, and owns a big house. If I _____ *had come* _____
   (2)

   here when he came here, I _____ *would be* _____ successful
   (3)

   now. But now I have to start everything from the beginning. I wish

   I _____ *didn't have* _____ to start so many new things at my age.
   (4)

A: Did your parents come here too?

B: No. My parents are alone in my country. I've asked them to come

   here. I wish they _____ *would come* _____ here, but they're too old
   (5)

   to make such a big change. If they _____ *came* _____ here,
   (6)

   they _____ *would* _____ have to go to school to learn English.
   (7)

   They're in their late seventies. If they _____ *came* _____ here,
   (8)

   their life _____ *would be* _____ much more difficult than it is now.
   (9)

A: There are a lot of things I wish _____ *were* _____ different
   (10)

   in my life too.

Lesson Review

To use Part 2 as a review, assign it as homework or use it as an in-class activity to be completed individually or in pairs. Check answers and review errors as a class. Reteach grammar points that students haven't mastered. Then student learning may be assessed using a test generated from the Assessment CD-ROM with *ExamView Pro*.

B: What, for example?

A: I got married when I was only 18. I wish I _____*hadn't gotten*_____
(11)
married so young. And I had my first son when I was only 20. I'm attending college now, and it's hard with so many family responsibilities. I wish I _____*had gone*_____ to college when I
(12)
was 18.

B: It's too bad we can't go back and start our lives again. I wish I
_____*could go*_____ back and use the knowledge I have now
(13)
to make better choices.

A: Who knows . . . we may live to be 150 years old and have time to do
all the things we wish we _____*could*_____ do.
(14)

B: If everyone _____*lives*_____ to be 150 years old, the world
(15)
_____*will be*_____ very crowded and there _____*won't be*_____
(16)   (17)
enough food or other resources for everybody.

A: Maybe you're right. We should just do the best we can with the time we have.

PART **3** Some of the following sentences contain real conditions; some contain unreal conditions. Write the latter of the correct words to fill in the blanks.

1. I _____*c*_____ drive to Canada if I had a car.
   a. were **b.** will **c.** would **d.** would be

2. I might go shopping next Saturday. If I _____*d*_____
   shopping next Saturday, I'll buy you a scarf.
   a. will go **b.** went **c.** would go **d.** go

3. If I _____*a*_____ you, I'd move to a different apartment.
   a. were **b.** am **c.** will be **d.** would be

4. I can't help you. I would help you if I _____*b*_____
   a. can **b.** could **c.** will be able to **d.** would

5. I might have to work next Monday. If I have to work,
   I _____*b*_____ be able to come to class.
   a. wouldn't **b.** won't **c.** weren't **d.** wasn't

6. My life would be easier if I _____*a*_____ more English.
   a. knew **b.** know **c.** will know **d.** would know

1. Part 3 may also be used as an in-class test to assess student performance, in addition to the Assessment CD-ROM with *ExamView Pro.* Tell students that this is a multiple choice exercise. Do items 1 and 2 as a class. Have students complete the exercise.
2. Collect for assessment.
3. If necessary, have students review: **Lesson 10.**

Lesson Review

To use Part 3 as a review, assign it as homework or use it as an in-class activity to be completed individually or in pairs. Check answers and review errors as a class. Reteach grammar points that students haven't mastered. Then student learning may be assessed using a test generated from the Assessment CD-ROM with *ExamView Pro.*

7. She has three children. She has no time to study. If she
_____ d _____ children, she would have more time to study.
   a. doesn't have   b. weren't have
   c. wouldn't have   d. didn't have

8. It's raining now. If it _____ c _____ now, I'd go for a walk.
   a. isn't raining   b. doesn't raining
   c. weren't raining   d. wouldn't raining

9. She wouldn't tell you the secret even if you _____ b _____
her a million dollars.
   a. would be pay   b. paid   c. will pay   d. pay

10. If I could live in any city in the world, I _____ c _____
in Paris.
   a. will live   b. would have lived   c. would live   d. live

11. I don't have a house. I wish I _____ a _____ a house.
   a. had   b. will have   c. have had   d. have

12. I can't drive a car. I wish I _____ a _____ a car.
   a. could drive   b. can drive   c. would drive   d. will drive

13. If I had known how difficult it was to learn English,
I _____ d _____it when I was young.
   a. would study   b. would studied
   c. would had studied   d. would have studied

14. He never exercised and was overweight. He had a heart attack and
died when he was 50 years old. If he _____ c _____
better care of himself, he might have lived much longer.
   a. would take   b. took   c. had taken   d. will take

15. He needs more driving lessons before he can take the driver's
license test. If he _____ d _____ the test last week, he
would have failed it.
   a. were taken   b. would take   c. has taken   d. had taken

16. I didn't have time to call you yesterday. I _____ c _____
you if I had had more free time.
   a. would call   b. will call   c. would have called   d. would called

17. He was driving without a seat belt and had a car accident. He
was seriously injured. If he had been wearing his seat belt, he
_____ a _____ such a serious injury.
   a. might not have had   b. wouldn't had
   c. didn't have   d. hadn't had

18. Nobody told me we were going to have a test today. I wish
someone _____ b _____ me.
   a. would tell   b. had told   c. would told   d. were told

Culture Note

Multiple choice tests are very common at all school levels in the U.S., and also on
preemployment exams, certification exams for employment, and driver's license exams.

19. Why didn't you tell me about your move last week? If you had told me, I _____*a*_____ you.
   a. could have helped   **b.** could help
   c. could helped   **d.** could had helped

20. My roommate talks on the phone all the time. I wish he _____*b*_____ on the phone so much.
   a. won't talk   **b.** wouldn't talk
   c. doesn't talk   **d.** wouldn't have talked

EXPANSION ACTIVITIES

Classroom Activities

1. Do you think the world would be better or worse if . . . ? Form a small group and discuss your reasons.

   a. If there were no computers?
   b. If everyone were the same religion or race?
   c. If everyone spoke the same language?
   d. If we could live to be about 150 years old?
   e. If people didn't have to work?
   f. If families were allowed to have only one child?
   g. If every job paid the same salary?

2. Fill in the blanks. Share your sentences in a small group.

   a. If I could change one thing about myself (or my life), I'd change
   _____

   b. If I lost my _____, I'd be very upset.

   c. Most people would be happier if _____

   d. If I could travel to the past, _____

   e. If I could travel to the future, _____

   f. The world would be a better place if _____

   g. I wish I were _____ years old.

3. Fill in the blanks and explain your answers.

   If I had known _____,
   I would (not) have _____

   EXAMPLE   If I had known that I needed computer skills in the U.S.,
   I would have studied computers in my native country.

4. Fill in the blanks and explain your answers.

   a. I didn't _____, but I wish I had.

   b. I _____, but I wish I hadn't.

Unreal Conditions; Real Conditions; Wishes   **465**

Expansion Activities

These expansion activities provide opportunities for students to interact with one another and further develop their speaking and writing skills. Encourage students to use grammar from this lesson whenever possible.

To save class time, assign parts of the activities as homework. Then use class time for interaction and communication. If students do not need additional speaking practice, some of the activities may be assigned as writing activities for homework, or skipped altogether.

CLASSROOM ACTIVITIES

1. Tell students that this activity is about their ideas about the world. Ask: *What do you think would make the world a better place? What would make the world a worse place?* Review with students unreal conditions in the present. Then have students work in groups to discuss one, some, or all of the items in the activity. Have groups share their opinions with the class.

2. Tell students that this activity is about ideas and imagination. Ask students to complete the sentences individually, and then share their sentences with a group. Encourage groups to ask follow-up questions when students present their ideas.

3. Have students complete the activity and then tell a partner or group about their answers. Encourage groups to ask follow-up questions.

4. Have students complete the activity and then tell a partner or group about their answers. Encourage groups to ask follow-up questions.

Classroom Activities Variation

Activity 1 Divide the class into seven groups, and have each group discuss one of the items in the activity. Have each group work together to write a paragraph stating and supporting their ideas. Have each group pass its paragraph to another group; have the second group review the paragraph and say whether or not they agree with the other group's ideas.

CLASSROOM ACTIVITIES(cont.)

5. Have students write as many sentences as they can. When students have finished, have them share their answers with a group.
6. Have students complete the sentence for themselves. Encourage students to write original ideas.
7. Have students work in small groups to take turns making and responding to the requests.

TALK ABOUT IT

Have students work in groups. Either assign or have each group choose one or more of the topics to discuss. Review with students language for agreeing, checking for agreement, and disagreeing (e.g., *I think so too. Are you sure that's right? I'm not sure I agree.*). Set a time limit for discussion. Then have groups talk about their topics. If appropriate, have groups report back to the class; have each group appoint a spokesperson.

---

5. Write some sentences about your job, your school, your apartment, or your family. What do you wish were different? Share your answers in a small group.

   EXAMPLES I have to work on Saturdays. I wish I didn't have to work on Saturdays.

   My son watches TV all day. I wish he would play with his friends more.

6. On a piece of paper or index card, finish this sentence:

   I would be happier if _____

   The teacher will collect the cards or papers and read each statement. The rest of the class has to guess who wrote it. (Many people will write "*if I were rich,*" or "*if I knew more English,*" so try to think of something else.)

7. Name something. Form a small group and discuss your responses.

   EXAMPLE Name something you wish had never happened.
   I wish the war had never happened.

   a. Name something you wish you had done when you were younger.
   b. Name something you wish you had studied when you were younger.
   c. Name something your family wishes you had done differently.
   d. Name something you wish you had known before you came to this city.
   e. Name something you wish your parents had done or told you.
   f. Name something you wish you had never done.
   g. Name something you wish had never happened.

Talk About it

1. If you could meet anyone in the world, who would you want to meet?
2. If you had the brain of another person, who would you be?
3. Since Albert Einstein's death in 1955, his brain has been kept in a jar for study. If it were possible to create a new Einstein from a brain cell, would it be a good idea to do so? Why or why not?
4. If you had the possibility of making a clone of yourself or a member of your family, would you do it? Why or why not?
5. If you could live 200 years, would you want to?
6. If we could eliminate all diseases, would the Earth be overpopulated?

466   Lesson 10

Classroom Activities Variation

Activity 7 Do the activity as a game of truth or lie. Have students in their groups write their names on papers and put them face down in the middle of the table. Have students take turns drawing a name and directing one of the items in the activity to that student. The student who responds may tell the truth or a lie, and should try to fool the other students. Each student says whether he or she thinks the statement is true. Students who guess correctly get a point.

Talk About it Variation

Have students work in pairs. Have members of the pairs interview each other using the questions in the activity, alternating interviewers. Have the interviewers take notes on their partners' responses.

Items 3 and 6 Have students debate item 3 or item 6. Divide the class into two teams. Tell each team to list five reasons supporting its view. Have each team present its arguments. Then give each team an opportunity to respond to the other team's arguments. At the end of the debate, survey the class to see which opinion is more popular.

---

7. In Lesson Six, we read about Tim Berners-Lee, the creator of the World Wide Web. He has never made any money from the Web. Do you think he would have tried to make money on his idea if he had known how popular the Web was going to become?

8. What entirely new things do you think might be possible in the future?

9. Read the following poem and discuss its meaning.

> There was a young lady named Bright,
> Who traveled far faster than light.
> She left one day
> In a relative way
> And returned the previous night.

Write About it

1. Write about personality traits or bad habits you have. Write how your life would be different if you didn't have these traits or habits. (Or you can write about the habits or traits of another person you know well.)

   EXAMPLES If I exercised, my health would be better.
   If my son weren't so lazy, he'd be able to accomplish much more in his life.

2. Write about an important event in history. Tell what the result would or might have been if this event hadn't happened.

3. Write about how your life would have been different if you had stayed in the same place your whole life.

4. Write about some things in your life that you are not happy about. How would you want to change your life?

Outside Activities

1. Ask a native speaker of English to answer the questions in the first classroom activity. Report this person's answers to the class.

2. Rent one of these movies: *Cocoon, Sleeper, Back to the Future, AI (Artificial Intelligence), Contact,* or *Kate and Leopold.* Write a summary.

Internet Activities

1. At a search engine, type in *time travel.* Find an interesting article to bring to class.

2. At a search engine, type in *H.G. Wells The Time Machine.* Find a summary of this 1895 novel.

3. At a search engine, type in *aging.* Find an interesting article to bring to class. Summarize it.

 Additional Activities at http://elt.thomson.com/gic

Unreal Conditions; Real Conditions; Wishes   467

WRITE ABOUT IT

1. If necessary, review unreal conditions in the present. Have students write a paragraph about their trait or habit. Collect for assessment and/or have students review each other's work.

2. If necessary, review unreal conditions in the past. Have students choose an event to write about. Collect for assessment and/or have students present their paragraphs to a group.

3. Have students brainstorm things that might have been different if they had never left the place they were born, and write a paragraph. Collect for assessment and/or have students present their paragraphs to a group.

4. Have students make some notes before they begin, and then write a paragraph. Collect for assessment and/or have students review each other's work.

OUTSIDE ACTIVITIES

1. Have students use the questions in Classroom Activity #1 to interview a native English speaker. Have students share the results of their interviews with the class.

2. If some students are unable to rent and view a movie at home, consider bringing one of the movies to class to view together to complete the activity.

INTERNET ACTIVITIES

1. Have students share the articles they find. Ask: *Do you think the ideas this author talks about are realistic and convincing? Why/why not?*

2. Ask students why they think H. G. Wells's novel has been popular for so long. Ask students if they have seen a movie version of the novel, and if so, what they thought of it.

3. Have students tell the class why they chose the article they did.

Write About it Variation

Have students exchange first drafts with a partner. Ask students to help their partners edit their drafts. Refer students to the Editing Advice on page 460.

Outside Activities Variation

Activity 1 As an alternative, you may invite a guest to your classroom (e.g., an administrator, a librarian, or a service worker at your school) and have students do a class interview. Students should prepare their interview questions ahead of time.

Appendices

Noncount Nouns

The following groups of words are classified as noncount nouns.

Group A. Nouns that have no distinct, separate parts. We look at the whole

air	cheese	lightning	paper	tea
blood	cholesterol	meat	pork	thunder
bread	coffee	milk	poultry	water
butter	electricity	oil	soup	yogurt

Group B. Nouns that have parts that are too small or insignificant to count

corn	hair	rice	sand	sugar
grass	popcorn	salt	snow	

Note: Count and noncount nouns are grammatical terms, but they are not always logical. *Rice* is very small and is a noncount noun. *Beans* and *peas* are also very small but are count nouns.

Group C. Nouns that are classes or categories of things

food (vegetables, meat, spaghetti)	makeup (lipstick, rouge, eye shadow)
furniture (chairs, tables, beds)	homework (compositions, exercises, reading)
clothing (sweaters, pants, dresses)	jewelry (necklaces, bracelets, rings)
mail (letters, packages, postcards, fliers)	housework (washing dishes, dusting, cooking)
fruit (cherries, apples, grapes)	money or cash (nickels, dimes, dollars)

Group D. Nouns that are abstractions

advice	experience	intelligence	nature	trouble
art	fun	knowledge	noise	truth
beauty	happiness	life	nutrition	unemployment
crime	health	love	patience	work
education	help	luck	pollution	
energy	information	music	time	

Group E. Subjects of study

biology	geometry	history
chemistry	grammar	math (mathematics)*

Note: Even though *mathematics* ends with *s*, it is not plural.

Notice the quantity words used with count and noncount nouns.		
Singular Count	**Plural Count**	**Noncount**
a tomato	tomatoes	coffee
one tomato	**two** tomatoes	**two cups of** coffee
	some tomatoes	**some** coffee
no tomato	**no** tomatoes	**no** coffee
(with questions and negatives) **any** tomatoes		**any** coffee
	a lot of tomatoes	**a lot of** coffee
(with questions and negatives) **many** tomatoes		**much** coffee
	a few tomatoes	**a little** coffee
	several tomatoes	**several** cups of coffee
	How many tomatoes?	**How much** coffee?

The following words can be used as either count nouns or noncount nouns. However, the meaning changes according to the way the nouns are used.	
Count	**Noncount**
Oranges and grapefruit are **fruits** that contain a lot of vitamin C.	I bought some **fruit** at the fruit store.
Ice cream and butter are **foods** that contain cholesterol.	We don't need to go shopping today. We have a lot of **food** at home.
He wrote a **paper** about hypnosis.	I need some **paper** to write my composition.
He committed three **crimes** last year.	There is a lot of **crime** in a big city.
I have 200 **chickens** on my farm.	We ate some **chicken** for dinner.
I don't want to bore you with all my **troubles.**	I have some **trouble** with my car.
She went to Puerto Rico three **times.**	She spent a lot of **time** on her project.
She drank three **glasses** of water.	The window is made of bulletproof **glass.**
I had a bad **experience** during my trip to Paris.	She has some **experience** with computer programming.
I don't know much about the **lives** of my grandparents.	**Life** is sometimes happy, sometimes sad.
I heard a **noise** outside my window.	Those children are making a lot of **noise.**

APPENDIX B

Uses of Articles

Overview of Articles

Articles tell us if a noun is definite or indefinite.			
	Count		**Noncount**
	Singular	**Plural**	
Definite	**the** book	**the** books	**the** coffee
Indefinite	**a** book	**(some / any)** books	**(some / any)** coffee

Part 1. Uses of the Indefinite Article

A. To classify a subject

Examples	Explanation
Chicago is **a** city. Illinois is **a** state. Abraham Lincoln was **an** American president. What's that? It's **a** tall building.	• Use *a* before a consonant sound. • Use *an* before a vowel sound. • You can put an adjective before the noun.
Chicago and Los Angeles are cities. Lincoln and Washington were American presidents. What are those? They're tall buildings.	Do not use an article before a plural noun.

B. To make a generalization about a noun

Examples	Explanation
A dog has sharp teeth. **Dogs** have sharp teeth. **An elephant** has big ears. **Elephants** have big ears.	Use the indefinite article (*a / an*) + a singular count noun or no article with a plural noun. Both the singular and plural forms have the same meaning.
Coffee contains caffeine. **Milk** is white. **Love** makes people happy. **Money** can't buy **happiness.**	Do not use an article to make a generalization about a noncount noun.

C. To introduce a new noun into the conversation

Examples	Explanation
I have **a cell phone.** I have **an umbrella.**	Use the definite article *a / an* with singular count nouns.
Count: I have **(some) dishes.** Do you have **(any) cups?** I don't have **(any) forks.**	Use *some* or *any* with plural nouns and noncount nouns. Use *any* in questions and negatives. *Some* and *any* can be omitted.
Noncount: I have **(some) money** with me. Do you have **(any) cash** with you? I don't have **(any) time.**	
There's **an elevator** in the building. Are there **any restrooms** on this floor? There isn't **any money** in my checking account.	*There* + a form of *be* can introduce an indefinite noun into a conversation.

Part 2. Uses of the Definite Article

A. To refer to a previously mentioned noun

Examples	Explanation
There's **a dog** in the next apartment. **The dog** barks all the time.	We start by saying *a dog*. We continue by saying *the dog*.
We bought **some grapes.** We ate **the grapes** this morning.	We start by saying *some grapes*. We continue by saying *the grapes*.
I need **some sugar.** I'm going to use **the sugar** to bake a cake.	We start by saying *some sugar*. We continue by saying *the sugar*.
Did you buy **any coffee?** Yes. **The coffee** is in the cabinet.	We start by saying *any coffee*. We continue by saying *the coffee*.

B. When the speaker and the listener have the same reference

Examples	Explanation
The dog has big ears. **The cats** are sleeping. **The milk** is sour. Don't drink it.	The object is present, so the speaker and listener have the same object in mind.
a. **The teacher** is writing on **the blackboard** in **the classroom.** b. **The president** is talking about taxes. c. Please turn off **the lights** and shut **the door** and **the windows** before you leave **the house.**	a. Students in the same class have things in common. b. People who live in the same country have things in common. c. People who live in the same house have things in common.
The house on the corner is beautiful. I spent **the money you gave me.**	The listener knows exactly which one because the speaker defines or specifies which one.

C. When there is only one in our experience

Examples	Explanation
The sun is bigger than **the moon.** There are many problems in **the world.**	The *sun*, the *moon*, and the *world* are unique objects. There is only one in our immediate experience.
Write your name on **the top** of the page. Sign your name on **the back** of the check.	The page has only one top. The check has only one back.
The Amazon is **the longest** river in the world. Alaska is **the biggest** state in the U.S.	A superlative indicates that there is only one.

D. With familiar places

Examples	Explanation
I'm going to **the store** after work. Do you need anything? **The bank** is closed now. I'll go tomorrow.	We use *the* with certain familiar places and people—*the bank, the zoo, the park, the store, the movies, the beach, the post office, the bus / train, the doctor, the dentist*—when we refer to the one that we habitually visit or use.

Language Note:

1. Omit *the* after a preposition with the words *church, school, work,* and *bed.*

    He's **in church.**

    I'm going **to school.**

    They're **at work.**

    I'm going **to bed.**

2. Omit *to* and *the* with *home* and *downtown.*

    I'm going **home.**

    Are you going **downtown** after class?

E. To make a formal generalization

Examples	Explanation
The shark is the oldest and most primitive fish. **The bat** is a nocturnal animal.	To say that something is true of all members of a group, use *the* with singular count nouns.
The computer has changed the way people deal with information. **The cell phone** uses radio waves.	To talk about a class of inventions, use *the*.
The heart is a muscle that pumps blood to the rest of the body. **The ear** has three parts: outer, middle, and inner.	To talk about an organ of the body in a general sense, use *the*.

Language Note:

For informal generalizations, use *a* + a singular noun or no article with a plural noun.

Compare:

The computer has changed the way we deal with information.

A computer is expensive.

Computers are expensive.

Part 3: Special Uses of Articles

No Article	Article

Personal names:
    John Kennedy
    George Bush
	The whole family:
	    the Kennedys
	    the Bushes

Title and name:
    Queen Elizabeth
    Pope John Paul
	Title without name:
	    the Queen
	    the Pope

Cities, states, countries, continents:
    Cleveland
    Ohio
    Mexico
    South America
	Places that are considered a union:
	    the United States
	    the former Soviet Union
	Place names: the _____ of _____
	    the People's Republic of China
	    the District of Columbia

Mountains:
    Mount Everest
    Mount McKinley
	Mountain ranges:
	    the Himalayas
	    the Rocky Mountains

Islands:
    Coney Island
    Staten Island
	Collectives of islands:
	    the Hawaiian Islands
	    the Philippines

Lakes:
    Lake Superior
    Lake Michigan
	Collectives of lakes:
	    the Great Lakes
	    the Finger Lakes

Beaches:
    Palm Beach
    Pebble Beach
	Rivers, oceans, seas, canals:
	    the Mississippi River
	    the Atlantic Ocean
	    the Dead Sea
	    the Panama Canal

Streets and avenues:
    Madison Avenue
    Wall Street
	Well-known buildings:
	    the Sears Tower
	    the Empire State Building

Parks:
    Central Park
    Hyde Park
	Zoos:
	    the San Diego Zoo
	    the Milwaukee Zoo

Seasons:
    summer   fall   spring   winter
    Summer is my favorite season.
Note: After a preposition, *the* may be used.
    In (the) winter, my car runs badly.
	Deserts:
	    the Mojave Desert
	    the Sahara Desert

Continued

Directions:
   north   south
   east   west
	Sections of a piece of land:
	   the Southwest (of the U.S.)
	   the West Side (of New York)

School subjects:
   history   math
	Unique geographical points:
	   the North Pole the Vatican

Name + *college* or *university*:
   Northwestern University
   Bradford College
	The University (College) of _____
	   the University of Michigan
	   the College of DuPage County

Magazines:
   Time   *Sports Illustrated*
	Newspapers:
	   the *Tribune* the *Wall Street Journal*

Months and days:
   September
   Monday
	Ships:
	   the *Titanic*
	   the *Queen Elizabeth II*

Holidays and dates:
(month + day):
   Thanksgiving   July 4   Mother's Day
	The day of (month):
	   the Fourth of July
	   the fifth of May

Diseases:
   cancer   AIDS
   polio   malaria
	Ailments:
	   a cold a toothache
	   a headache the flu

Games and sports:
   poker   soccer
	Musical instruments, after *play*:
	   the drums the piano
	      Sometimes *the* is omitted.
	   She plays (the) drums.

Languages:
   French
   English
	The _____ language:
	   the French language
	   the English language

Last month, year, week, etc. = the one
before this one:
   I forgot to pay my rent last month.
   The teacher gave us a test last week.
	The last month, the last year, the last
	week, etc. = the last in a series:
	   December is the last month of the year.
	   Summer vacation begins the last
	   week in May.

In office = in an elected position:
   The president is in office for four years.
	In the office = in a specific room:
	   The teacher is in the office.

In back / in front:
   She's in back
   of the car.
	In the back / in the front:
	   He's in the back of the bus.

The Verb *Get*

Get has many meanings. Here is a list of the most common ones:
• get something = receive   I got a letter from my father.

• get + (to) place = arrive
  I got home at six.
  What time do you get to school?

• get + object + infinitive = persuade   She got him to wash the dishes.
• get + past participle = become get accustomed to   get dressed   get scared get acquainted   get engaged   get tired get bored   get hurt   get used to get confused   get lost   get worried get divorced   get married They got married in 1989.
• get + adjective = become get angry   get nervous   get upset get dark   get old   get well get fat   get rich get hungry   get sleepy It gets dark at 6:30.
• get an illness = catch   While she was traveling, she got malaria.

• get a joke or an idea = understand
  Everybody except Tom laughed at the joke. He didn't get it.
  The boss explained the project to us, but I didn't get it.

• get ahead = advance   He works very hard because he wants to get ahead in his job.

• get along (well) (with someone) = have a good relationship
  She doesn't get along with her mother-in-law.
  Do you and your roommate get along well?

• get around to something = find the time to do something   I wanted to write my brother a letter yesterday, but I didn't get around to it.

Continued

• get away = escape   The police chased the thief, but he got away.
• get away with something = escape punishment   He cheated on his taxes and got away with it.
• get back = return   He got back from his vacation last Saturday.
• get back at someone = get revenge   My brother wants to get back at me for stealing his girlfriend.
• get back to someone = communicate with someone at a later time   The boss can't talk to you today. Can she get back to you tomorrow?
• get by = have just enough but nothing more   On her salary, she's just getting by. She can't afford a car or a vacation.
• get in trouble = be caught and punished for doing something wrong   They got in trouble for cheating on the test.
• get in(to) = enter a car   She got in the car and drove away quickly.
• get out (of) = leave a car   When the taxi arrived at the theater, everyone got out.
• get on = seat yourself on a bicycle, motorcycle, horse; enter a train, bus, airplane   She got on the motorcycle and left.   She got on the bus and took a seat in the back.
• get off = leave a bicycle, motorcycle, horse, train, bus, airplane   They will get off the train at the next stop.
• get out of something = escape responsibility   My boss wants me to help him on Saturday, but I'm going to try to get out of it.
• get over something = recover from an illness or disappointment   She has the flu this week. I hope she gets over it soon.
• get rid of someone or something = free oneself of someone or something undesirable   My apartment has roaches, and I can't get rid of them.
• get through (to someone) = communicate, often by telephone   She tried to explain the harm of eating fast food to her son, but she couldn't get through to him.   I tried to call my mother many times, but her line was busy. I couldn't get through.
• get through with something = finish   I can meet you after I get through with my homework.

Continued

- **get together** = meet with another person
  I'd like to see you again. When can we get together?

- **get up** = arise from bed
  He woke up at 6 o'clock, but he didn't get up until 6:30.

APPENDIX D

Gerund and Infinitive Patterns

1. Verb + Infinitive

They need **to leave**.
I learned **to speak English**.

agree	claim	know how	seem
appear	consent	learn	swear
arrange	decide	manage	tend
ask	demand	need	threaten
attempt	deserve	offer	try
be able	expect	plan	volunteer
beg	fail	prepare	want
can afford	forget	pretend	wish
care	hope	promise	would like
choose	intend	refuse	

2. Verb + Noun / Object Pronoun + Infinitive

I want you **to leave**.
He expects me **to call** him.

advise	convince	hire	require
allow	dare	instruct	select
appoint	enable	invite	teach
ask	encourage	need	tell
beg	expect	order	urge
cause	forbid	permit	want
challenge	force	persuade	warn
choose	get	remind	would like
command	help*		

*Note: After *help*, *to* is often omitted: "He helped me (to) move."

3. Adjective + Infinitive

They are happy **to be** here.
We´re willing **to help** you.

afraid	disturbed	lucky	sorry
ashamed	eager	pleased	surprised
amazed	foolish	prepared	upset
careful	fortunate	proud	willing
content	free	ready	wrong
delighted	glad	reluctant	
determined	happy	sad	
disappointed	likely	shocked	

4. Verb + Gerund

I enjoy **dancing**.
They don´t permit **drinking**.

admit	detest	miss	resent
advise	discuss	permit	resist
anticipate	dislike	postpone	risk
appreciate	enjoy	practice	stop
avoid	finish	put off	suggest
can't help	forbid	quit	tolerate
complete	imagine	recall	understand
consider	keep (on)	recommend	
delay	mention	regret	
deny	mind	remember	

5. Expressions with *go* + Gerund

He **goes fishing** every Saturday.
They **went shopping** yesterday.

go boating	go hiking	go sightseeing
go bowling	go hunting	go skating
go camping	go jogging	go skiing
go dancing	go sailing	go swimming
go fishing	go shopping	

6. Preposition + Gerund

Verb + Preposition + Gerund
We talked about **moving**.
I look forward to **having** my own apartment.

adjust to	concentrate on	forget about	refrain from
argue about	depend on	insist on	succeed in
believe in	(dis)approve of	look forward to	talk about
care about	dream about	object to	think about
complain about	feel like	plan on	worry about

Adjective + Preposition + Gerund
I'm fond of **traveling**.
She's not accustomed to **eating** alone.

accustomed to	famous for	interested in	sure of
afraid of	fond of	lazy about	surprised at
appropriate for	good at	proud of	tired of
ashamed of	grateful to . . . for	responsible for	upset about
concerned about	guilty of	sorry about	used to
excited about	(in)capable of	suitable for	worried about

Verb + Object + Preposition + Gerund
I thanked him for **helping** me.
I apologized to him for **forgetting** his birthday.

accuse . . . of	devote . . . to	prevent . . . from	suspect . . . of
apologize to . . . for	forgive . . . for	prohibit . . . from	thank . . . for
blame . . . for	keep . . . from	stop . . . from	warn . . . about

Gerund After Preposition in Certain Expressions
Who's in charge of **collecting** the papers.
What is your reason for **coming** late?

impression of	in favor of	in the middle of	requirement for
in charge of	instead of	need for	technique for
in danger of	interest in	reason for	the point of

7. Noun + Gerund

He has difficulty **speaking** English.
She had a problem **finding** a job.
She spent three weeks **looking** for an apartment.

Use a gerund after the noun in these expressions:

have a difficult time	have a hard time
have difficulty	have a problem
have experience	have trouble
have fun	spend time / money
have a good time	there's no use

8. Verb + Gerund or Infinitive (with little or no difference in meaning)

They like **to sing**.   I started **to read**.
They like **singing**.   I started **reading**.

attempt	intend
begin	like
can't stand	love
continue	neglect
deserve	prefer
hate	start
hesitate	

APPENDIX E

Verbs and Adjectives Followed by a Preposition

Many verbs and adjectives are followed by a preposition.

accuse someone of	(be) ashamed of	count on
(be) accustomed to	(be) aware of	deal with
adjust to	believe in	decide on
(be) afraid of	blame someone for	depend on / upon
agree with	(be) bored with / by	(be) different from
(be) amazed at / by	(be) capable of	disapprove of
(be) angry about	care about / for	(be) divorced from
(be) angry at / with	compare to / with	dream about / of
apologize for	complain about	(be) engaged to
approve of	concentrate on	(be) excited about
argue about	(be) concerned about	(be) familiar with
argue with	consist of	(be) famous for

Continued

feel like	(be) mad about	(be) sorry about
(be) fond of	(be) mad at	(be) sorry for
forget about	(be) made from / of	speak about
forgive someone for	(be) married to	speak to / with
(be) glad about	object to	succeed in
(be) good at	(be) opposed to	(be) sure of / about
(be) grateful to someone for	participate in	(be) surprised at
(be) guilty of	plan on	take care of
(be) happy about	pray to	talk about
hear of	(be) prepared for	talk to / with
hope for	prevent someone from	thank someone for
(be) incapable of	prohibit someone from	(be) thankful to someone for
insist on / upon	protect someone from	think about / of
(be) interested in	(be) proud of	(be) tired of
(be) involved in	recover from	(be) upset about
(be) jealous of	(be) related to	(be) upset with
(be) known for	rely on / upon	(be) used to
(be) lazy about	(be) responsible for	wait for
listen to	(be) sad about	warn someone about
look at	(be) satisfied with	(be) worried about
look for	(be) scared of	worry about
look forward to	(be) sick of	

APPENDIX F

Direct and Indirect Objects

Word Order with Direct and Indirect Objects

The order of direct and indirect objects depends on the verb you use.

$$\underset{\text{IO}}{\underline{\text{He told his friend}}} \quad \underset{\text{DO}}{\underline{\text{the answer.}}}$$

He told his friend the answer.

He explained the answer to his friend.

The order of the objects sometimes depends on whether you use a noun or a pronoun object.

S V IO DO
He gave the woman the keys.

S V DO IO
He gave them to her.

Each of the following groups of words follows a specific pattern of word order and preposition choice. In some cases, the connecting preposition is *to*; in some cases, *for*. In some cases, there is no connecting preposition.
She'll serve lunch *to* her guests.
She reserved a seat *for* you.
I asked him a question.

Group 1 Pronouns affect word order. The preposition is *to*.

Patterns: He gave a present to his wife. (DO to IO)
He gave his wife a present. (IO / DO)
He gave it to his wife. (DO to IO)
He gave her a present. (IO / DO)
He gave it to her. (DO to IO)

Verbs:

bring	lend	pass	sell	show	teach
give	offer	pay	send	sing	tell
hand	owe	read	serve	take	write

Group 2 Pronouns affect word order. The preposition is *for*.

Patterns: He bought a car for his daughter. (DO for IO)
He bought his daughter a car. (IO / DO)
He bought it for his daughter. (DO for IO)
He bought her a car. (IO / DO)
He bought it for her. (DO for IO)

Verbs:

bake	buy	draw	get	make
build	do	find	knit	reserve

Group 3 Pronouns don't affect word order. The preposition is *to*.

Patterns: He explained the problem to his friend. (DO to IO)
He explained it to her. (DO to IO)

Verbs:

admit	introduce	recommend	say
announce	mention	repeat	speak
describe	prove	report	suggest
explain			

Group 4 Pronouns don't affect word order. The preposition is *for*.

Patterns: He cashed a check for his friend. (DO for IO)
He cashed it for her. (DO for IO)

Verbs:

answer	change	design	open	prescribe
cash	close	fix	prepare	pronounce

Group 5 Pronouns don't affect word order. No preposition is used.

Patterns: She asked the teacher a question. (IO / DO)
She asked him a question. (IO / DO)
It took me five minutes to answer the question. (IO / DO)

Verbs:

ask	charge	cost	wish	take (with time)

APPENDIX G

Spelling and Pronunciation of Verbs

Spelling of the -s Form of Verbs

Rule	Base Form	-s Form
Add s to most verbs to make the -s form.	hope eat	hopes eats
When the base form ends in s, z, sh, ch, or x, add es and pronounce an extra syllable, /əz/.	miss buzz wash catch fix	misses buzzes washes catches fixes
When the base form ends in a consonant + y, change the y to i and add es.	carry worry	carries worries
When the base form ends in a vowel + y, do not change the y.	pay obey	pays obeys
Add es to go and do.	go do	goes does

Pronunciation of the -s Form
The -s form has three pronunciations.

We pronounce /s/ if the verb ends in these voiceless sounds: /p t k f/.
hope—hopes   pick—picks eat—eats   laugh—laughs

We pronounce /z/ if the verb ends in most voiced sounds.
live—lives   read—reads   sing—sings grab—grabs   run—runs   borrow—borrows

When the base form ends in s, z, sh, ch, x, se, ge, or ce, we pronounce an extra syllable, /əz/.
miss—misses   watch—watches   change—changes buzz—buzzes   fix—fixes   dance—dances wash—washes   use—uses

These verbs have a change in the vowel sound.
do /du/—does /dʌz/ say /seɪ/—says /sɛz/

Spelling of the *-ing* Form of Verbs

Rule	Base Form	*-ing* Form
Add *-ing* to most verbs. **Note:** Do not remove the *-y* for the *-ing* form.	eat go study	eating going studying
For a one-syllable verb that ends in a consonant + vowel + consonant (CVC), double the final consonant and add *ing*.	p l a n | | | C V C s t o p | | | C V C s i t | | | C V C	planning stopping sitting
Do not double a final *w*, *x*, or *y*.	show mix stay	showing mixing staying
For a two-syllable word that ends in CVC, double the final consonant only if the last syllable is stressed.	refér admít begín	referring admitting beginning
When the last syllable of a two-syllable word is not stressed, do not double the final consonant.	lísten ópen óffer	listening opening offering
If the word ends in a consonant + *e*, drop the *e* before adding *ing*.	live take write	living taking writing

Spelling of the Past Tense of Regular Verbs

Rule	Base Form	*-ed* Form
Add *ed* to the base form to make the past tense of most regular verbs.	start kick	started kicked
When the base form ends in *e*, add *d* only.	die live	died lived
When the base form ends in a consonant + *y*, change the *y* to *i* and add *ed*.	carry worry	carried worried
When the base form ends in a vowel + *y*, do not change the *y*.	destroy stay	destroyed stayed

Continued

Rule	Base Form		-ed Form
For a one-syllable word that ends in a consonant + vowel + consonant (CVC), double the final consonant and add -ed.	s t o p | | | C V C		stopped
	p l u g | | | C V C		plugged
Do not double a final w or x.	sew fix		sewed fixed
For a two-syllable word that ends in CVC, double the final consonant only if the last syllable is stressed.	occúr permít		occurred permitted
When the last syllable of a two-syllable word is not stressed, do not double the final consonant.	ópen háppen		opened happened

Pronunciation of Past Forms That End in -ed
The past tense with -ed has three pronunciations.

We pronounce a /t/ if the base form ends in these voiceless sounds: /p, k, f, s, š, č/.

jump—jumped	cough—coughed	wash—washed
cook—cooked	kiss—kissed	watch—watched

We pronounce a /d/ if the base form ends in most voiced sounds.

rub—rubbed	charge—charged	bang—banged
drag—dragged	glue—glued	call—called
love—loved	massage—massaged	fear—feared
bathe—bathed	name—named	free—freed
use—used	learn—learned	

We pronounce an extra syllable /əd/ if the base form ends in a /t/ or /d/ sound.

wait—waited	want—wanted	need—needed
hate—hated	add—added	decide—decided

APPENDIX H

Capitalization Rules

- The first word in a sentence: **My** friends are helpful.
- The word "I": My sister and **I** took a trip together.
- Names of people: **Michael Jordan**; **George Washington**
- Titles preceding names of people: **Doctor** (**Dr.**) **Smith**; **President Lincoln**; **Queen Elizabeth**; **Mr. Rogers**; **Mrs. Carter**

- Geographic names: the United States; Lake Superior; California; the Rocky Mountains; the Mississippi River

  Note: The word "the" in a geographic name is not capitalized.

- Street names: Pennsylvania Avenue (Ave.); Wall Street (St.); Abbey Road (Rd.)

- Names of organizations, companies, colleges, buildings, stores, hotels: the Republican Party; Heinle Thomson; Dartmouth College; the University of Wisconsin; the White House; Bloomingdale's; the Hilton Hotel

- Nationalities and ethnic groups: Mexicans; Canadians; Spaniards; Americans; Jews; Kurds; Eskimos

- Languages: English; Spanish; Polish; Vietnamese; Russian

- Months: January; February

- Days: Sunday; Monday

- Holidays: Christmas; Independence Day

- Important words in a title: Grammar in Context; The Old Man and the Sea; Romeo and Juliet; The Sound of Music

  Note: Capitalize "the" as the first word of a title.

APPENDIX I

Plural Forms of Nouns

Regular Noun Plurals				
Word Ending	Example Noun	Plural Addition	Plural Form	Pronunciation
Vowel	bee banana	+ s	bees bananas	/z/
s, ss, sh, ch, x, z	church dish box watch class	+ es	churches dishes boxes watches classes	/əz/
Voiceless consonants	cat lip month book	+ s	cats lips months books	/s/

Continued

Word Ending	Example Noun	Plural Addition	Plural Form	Pronunciation
Voiced consonants	card pin stove	+ s	cards pins stoves	/z/
Vowel + *y*	boy day key	+ s	boys days keys	/z/
Consonant + *y*	lady story party	*y* + *ies*	ladies stories parties	/z/
Vowel + *o*	video radio	+ s	videos radios	/z/
Consonant + *o*	potato hero	+ *es*	potatoes heroes	/z/
Exceptions: photos, pianos, solos, altos, sopranos, autos, avocados				
f or *fe*	leaf knife	*f* + *ves*	leaves knives	/vz/
Exceptions: beliefs, chiefs, roofs, cliffs, chefs, sheriffs				

Irregular Noun Plurals

Singular	Plural	Explanation
man woman mouse tooth foot goose	men women mice teeth feet geese	Vowel change (**Note:** The first vowel in *women* is pronounced /I/.)
sheep fish deer	sheep fish deer	No change
child person	children people (OR persons)	Different word form

Continued

Singular	Plural	Explanation
	(eye)glasses belongings clothes goods groceries jeans pajamas pants / slacks scissors shorts	No singular form
alumnus cactus radius stimulus syllabus	alumni cacti OR cactuses radii stimuli syllabi OR syllabuses	*us → i*
analysis crisis hypothesis oasis parenthesis thesis	analyses crises hypotheses oases parentheses theses	*is → es*
appendix index	appendices OR appendixes indices OR indexes	*ix → ices* OR *→ ixes*
bacterium curriculum datum medium memorandum criterion phenomenon	bacteria curricula data media memoranda criteria phenomena	*um → a* *ion → a* *on → a*
alga formula vertebra	algae formulae OR formulas vertebrae	*a → ae*

Metric Conversion Chart

Length

When You Know	Symbol	Multiply by	To Find	Symbol
inches	in	2.54	centimeters	cm
feet	ft	30.5	centimeters	cm
feet	ft	0.3	meters	m
yards	yd	0.91	meters	m
miles	mi	1.6	kilometers	km

Metric

When You Know	Symbol	Multiply by	To Find	Symbol
centimeters	cm	0.39	inches	in
centimeters	cm	0.03	feet	ft
meters	m	3.28	feet	ft
meters	m	1.09	yards	yd
kilometers	km	0.62	miles	mi

Note:
1 foot = 12 inches
1 yard = 3 feet or 36 inches

Area

When You Know	Symbol	Multiply by	To Find	Symbol
square inches	in^2	6.5	square centimeters	cm^2
square feet	ft^2	0.09	square meters	m^2
square yards	yd^2	0.8	square meters	m^2
square miles	mi^2	2.6	square kilometers	km^2

Metric

When You Know	Symbol	Multiply by	To Find	Symbol
square centimeters	cm^2	0.16	square inches	in^2
square meters	m^2	10.76	square feet	ft^2
square meters	m^2	1.2	square yards	yd^2
square kilometers	km^2	0.39	square miles	mi^2

Weight (Mass)

When You Know	Symbol	Multiply by	To Find	Symbol
ounces	oz	28.35	grams	g
pounds	lb	0.45	kilograms	kg
Metric				
grams	g	0.04	ounces	oz
kilograms	kg	2.2	pounds	lb
Note: 1 pound = 16 ounces				

Volume

When You Know	Symbol	Multiply by	To Find	Symbol
fluid ounces	fl oz	30.0	milliliters	ml
pints	pt	0.47	liters	l
quarts	qt	0.95	liters	l
gallons	gal	3.8	liters	l
Metric				
milliliters	ml	0.03	fluid ounces	fl oz
liters	l	2.11	pints	pt
liters	l	1.05	quarts	qt
liters	l	0.26	gallons	gal

Temperature

When You Know	Symbol	Do This	To Find	Symbol
degrees Fahrenheit	°F	Subtract 32, then multiply by $\frac{5}{9}$	degrees Celsius	°C
Metric				
degrees Celsius	°C	Multiply by $\frac{9}{5}$, then add 32	degrees Fahrenheit	°F

Sample temperatures

Fahrenheit	Celsius	Fahrenheit	Celsius
0	− 18	60	16
10	− 12	70	21
20	− 7	80	27
30	− 1	90	32
40	4	100	38
50	10		

Comparative and Superlative Forms

Comparative and Superlative Forms

	Simple	Comparative	Superlative
One-syllable adjectives and adverbs	tall	taller	the tallest
	fast	faster	the fastest
Exceptions:	bored	more bored	the most bored
	tired	more tired	the most tired
Two-syllable adjectives that end in -y	easy	easier	the easiest
	happy	happier	the happiest
	pretty	prettier	the prettiest
Other two-syllable adjectives	frequent	more frequent	the most frequent
	active	more active	the most active
Some two-syllable adjectives have two forms.	simple	simpler	the simplest
		more simple	the most simple
	common	commoner	the commonest
		more common	the most common

Note: These two-syllable adjectives have two forms: *handsome, quiet, gentle, narrow, clever, friendly,* and *angry*.

	Simple	Comparative	Superlative
Adjectives with three or more syllables	important	more important	the most important
	difficult	more difficult	the most difficult
-*ly* adverbs	quickly	more quickly	the most quickly
	brightly	more brightly	the most brightly
Irregular adjectives and adverbs	good / well	better	the best
	bad / badly	worse	the worst
	far	farther / further*	the farthest / furthest
	little	less	the least
	a lot	more	the most

* Note: *Farther* is for distances. *Further* is for ideas.
   I live *farther* from school than you do.
   She doesn't want to discuss the matter *further*.

The Superlative Form

Subject	Verb	Superlative Form + Noun	Prepositional Phrase
Alaska	is	the biggest state	in the U.S.
California	is	the most populated state	in the U.S.

The Comparative Form

Subject	Linking Verb[1]	Comparative Adjective	Than	Noun / Pronoun
She	is	taller	than	her sister (is).
She	seems	more intelligent	than	her sister.

Subject	Verb Phrase	Comparative Adverb	Than	Noun / Pronoun
I	speak English	more fluently	than	my sister (does).
I	sleep	less	than	you (do).

Comparisons with Nouns

Subject	Verb	Comparative Word + Noun	Than	Noun / Pronoun
I	work	fewer hours	than	you (do).
I	have	more time	than	you (do).

Equatives with Adjectives and Adverbs

Subject	Linking Verb	As	Adjective	As	Noun / Pronoun
She	isn't	as	old	as	her husband (is).
She	looks	as	pretty	as	a picture.

Subject	Verb Phrase	As	Adverb	As	Noun / Pronoun
She	speaks English	as	fluently	as	her husband (does).
He	doesn't work	as	hard	as	his wife (does).

Equatives with Quantities

Subject	Verb	As Many / Much	Noun	As	Noun / Pronoun
She	works	as many	hours	as	her husband (does).
Milk	doesn't have	as much	fat	as	cream (does).

Subject	Verb	As Much As	Noun / Pronoun		
Chicken	doesn't cost	as much as	meat (does).		
I	don't drive	as much as	you (do).		

[1] The linking verbs are *be, look, seem, feel, taste, sound,* and *seem.*

Equatives with Nouns

Pattern A

Subject	Verb	*The Same*	Noun	*As*	Noun / Pronoun
She	wears	the same	size	as	her mother (does).
She	isn't	the same	height	as	her brother (is).

Pattern B

Subject & Subject	Verb	*The Same*	Noun
She and her mother	wear	the same	size.
She and her brother	aren't	the same	height.

Similarities using *Like / Alike*

Pattern A

Subject	Linking Verb	*Like*	Noun / Pronoun
Sugar	looks	like	salt.
Regular coffee	tastes	like	decaf.

Pattern B

Subject & Subject	Linking Verb	*Alike*
Sugar and salt	look	alike.
Regular coffee and decaf	taste	alike.

Glossary of Grammatical Terms

- **Adjective** An adjective gives a description of a noun.

    It's a *tall* tree.　　He's an *old* man.　　My neighbors are *nice*.

- **Adverb** An adverb describes the action of a sentence or an adjective or another adverb.

    She speaks English *fluently*.　　I drive *carefully*.

    She speaks English *extremely* well.　　She is *very* intelligent.

- **Adverb of Frequency** An adverb of frequency tells how often the action happens.

    I *never* drink coffee.　　They *usually* take the bus.

- **Affirmative** means *yes*.

- **Apostrophe** ' We use the apostrophe for possession and contractions.

    My *sister's* friend is beautiful.　　Today *isn't* Sunday.

- **Article** The definite article is *the*. The indefinite articles are *a* and *an*.

    I have *a* cat.　　I ate *an* apple.　　*The* president was late.

- **Auxiliary Verb** Some verbs have two parts: an auxiliary verb and a main verb.

    He *can't* study.　　We *will* return.

- **Base Form** The base form, sometimes called the "simple" form, of the verb has no tense. It has no ending (-*s* or -*ed*): *be, go, eat, take, write*.

    He doesn't *know* the answer.　　I didn't *go* out.

    You shouldn't *talk* loudly.

- **Capital Letter** A B C D E F G . . .

- **Clause** A clause is a group of words that has a subject and a verb. Some sentences have only one clause.

    She found a good job.

    Some sentences have **a main clause** and a **dependent clause**.

MAIN CLAUSE	DEPENDENT CLAUSE (**reason clause**)
She found a good job	because she has computer skills.
MAIN CLAUSE	DEPENDENT CLAUSE (**time clause**)
She'll turn off the light	before she goes to bed.
MAIN CLAUSE	DEPENDENT CLAUSE (***if* clause**)
I'll take you to the doctor	if you don't have your car on Saturday.

- **Colon** :

- **Comma** ,

- **Comparative Form** A comparative form of an adjective or adverb is used to compare two things.

    My house is *bigger* than your house.

    Her husband drives *faster* than she does.

- **Complement** The complement of the sentence is the information after the verb. It completes the verb phrase.

    He works *hard*.   I slept *for five hours*.   They are *late*.

- **Consonant** The following letters are consonants: *b, c, d, f, g, h, j, k, l, m, n, p, q, r, s, t, v, w, x, y, z.*

    NOTE: *y* is sometimes considered a vowel, as in the world *syllable*.

- **Contraction** A contraction is made up of two words put together with an apostrophe.

    He's my brother.   *You're* late.   They *won't* talk to me.

    (*He's = he is*)   (*You're = you are*)   (*won't = will not*)

- **Count Noun** Count nouns are nouns that we can count. They have a singular and a plural form.

    1 pen — 3 pens   1 table — 4 tables

- **Dependent Clause** See **Clause.**

- **Direct Object** A direct object is a noun (phrase) or pronoun that receives the action of the verb.

    We saw *the movie*.   You have *a nice car*.   I love *you*.

- **Exclamation Mark !**

- **Frequency Words** Frequency words are *always, usually, often, sometimes, rarely, seldom,* and *never.*

    I *never* drink coffee.   We *always* do our homework.

- **Hyphen –**

- **Imperative** An imperative sentence gives a command or instructions. An imperative sentence omits the word *you.*

    Come here.   *Don't be* late.   Please *sit* down.

- **Indefinite Pronoun** An indefinite pronoun (*one, some, any*) takes the place of an indefinite noun.

    I have a cell phone. Do you have *one*?

    I didn't drink any coffee, but you drank *some*. Did he drink *any*?

- **Infinitive** An infinitive is *to* + base form.

    I want *to leave*.   You need *to be* here on time.

- **Linking Verb** A linking verb is a verb that links the subject to the noun or adjective after it. Linking verbs include *be, seem, feel, smell, sound, look, appear,* and *taste.*

    She *is* a doctor.   She *seems* very intelligent.   She *looks* tired.

- **Modal** The modal verbs are *can, could, shall, should, will, would, may, might,* and *must.*

  They *should* leave.   I *must* go.

- **Negative** means *no.*

- **Nonaction Verb** A nonaction verb has no action. We do not use a continuous tense (*be* + verb *-ing*) with a nonaction verb. The nonaction verbs are: *believe, cost, care, have, hear, know, like, love, matter, mean, need, own, prefer, remember, see, seem, think, understand,* and *want.*

  She *has* a laptop.   We *love* our mother.

- **Noncount Noun** A noncount noun is a noun that we don't count. It has no plural form.

  She drank some *water.*   He prepared some *rice.*

  Do you need any *money?*

- **Noun** A noun is a person (*brother*), a place (*kitchen*), or a thing (*table*). Nouns can be either count (*1 table, 2 tables*) or noncount (*money, water*).

  My *brother* lives in California.   My *sisters* live in New York.

  I get *mail* from them.

- **Noun Modifier** A noun modifier makes a noun more specific.

  fire department   *Independence* Day   *can* opener

- **Noun Phrase** A noun phrase is a group of words that forms the subject or object of the sentence.

  A very nice woman helped me at registration.

  I bought *a big box of candy.*

- **Object** The object of the sentence follows the verb. It receives the action of the verb.

  He bought *a car.*   I saw *a movie.*   I met *your brother.*

- **Object Pronoun** Use object pronouns (*me, you, him, her, it, us, them*) after the verb or preposition.

  He likes *her.*   I saw the movie. Let's talk about *it.*

- **Paragraph** A paragraph is a group of sentences about one topic.

- **Parentheses ( )**

- **Participle, Present** The present participle is verb + *-ing.*

  She is *sleeping.*   They were *laughing.*

- **Period .**

- **Phrase** A group of words that go together.

  Last month my sister came to visit.

  There is a strange car *in front of my house.*

- **Plural** Plural means more than one. A plural noun usually ends with -*s*.

  She has beautiful *eyes*.

- **Possessive Form** Possessive forms show ownership or relationship.

  Mary's coat is in the closet.   *My* brother lives in Miami.

- **Preposition** A preposition is a short connecting word: *about, above, across, after, around, as, at, away, back, before, behind, below, by, down, for, from, in, into, like, of, off, on, out, over, to, under, up, with.*

  The book is *on* the table.

- **Pronoun** A pronoun takes the place of a noun.

  I have a new car. I bought *it* last week.

  John likes Mary, but *she* doesn't like *him*.

- **Punctuation** Period . Comma , Colon : Semicolon ; Question Mark ? Exclamation Mark !

- **Question Mark** ?

- **Quotation Marks** " "

- **Regular Verb** A regular verb forms its past tense with -*ed*.

  He *worked* yesterday.   I *laughed* at the joke.

- ***s* Form** A present tense verb that ends in -*s* or -*es*.

  He *lives* in New York.   She *watches* TV a lot.

- **Sense-Perception Verb** A sense-perception verb has no action. It describes a sense.

  She *feels* fine.   The coffee *smells* fresh.   The milk *tastes* sour.

- **Sentence** A sentence is a group of words that contains a subject[2] and a verb (at least) and gives a complete thought.

  SENTENCE: She came home.

  NOT A SENTENCE: When she came home

- **Simple Form of Verb** The simple form of the verb, also called the "base" form, has no tense; it never has an -*s*, -*ed*, or -*ing* ending.

  Did you *see* the movie?   I couldn't *find* your phone number.

- **Singular** Singular means one.

  She ate a *sandwich*.   I have one *television*.

- **Subject** The subject of the sentence tells who or what the sentence is about.

  My sister got married last April. *The wedding* was beautiful.

- **Subject Pronouns** Use subject pronouns (*I, you, he, she, it, we, you, they*) before a verb.

  They speak Japanese.   *We* speak Spanish.

---

[2] In an imperative sentence, the subject *you* is omitted: *Sit down. Come here.*

- **Superlative Form** A superlative form of an adjective or adverb shows the number one item in a group of three or more.

  January is the *coldest* month of the year.

  My brother speaks English the *best* in my family.

- **Syllable** A syllable is a part of a word that has only one vowel sound. (Some words have only one syllable.)

  change (one syllable)   after (af·ter = two syllables)

  look (one syllable)   responsible (re·spon·si·ble = four syllables)

- **Tag Question** A tag question is a short question at the end of a sentence. It is used in conversation.

  You speak Spanish, *don't you?*   He's not happy, *is he?*

- **Tense** A verb has tense. Tense shows when the action of the sentence happened.

  SIMPLE PRESENT: She usually *works* hard.

  FUTURE: She *will work* tomorrow.

  PRESENT CONTINUOUS: She *is working* now.

  SIMPLE PAST: She *worked* yesterday.

- **Verb** A verb is the action of the sentence.

  He *runs* fast.   I *speak* English.

  Some verbs have no action. They are linking verbs. They connect the subject to the rest of the sentence.

  He *is* tall.   She *looks* beautiful.   You *seem* tired.

- **Vowel** The following letters are vowels: *a, e, i, o, u. Y* is sometimes considered a vowel (for example, in the word *syllable*).

APPENDIX M

Alphabetical List of Irregular Verb Forms

Base Form	Past Form	Past Participle	Base Form	Past Form	Past Participle
be	was / were	been	bid	bid	bid
bear	bore	born / borne	bind	bound	bound
beat	beat	beaten	bite	bit	bitten
become	became	become	bleed	bled	bled
begin	began	begun	blow	blew	blown
bend	bent	bent	break	broke	broken
bet	bet	bet	breed	bred	bred

Continued

Base Form	Past Form	Past Participle	Base Form	Past Form	Past Participle
bring	brought	brought	grow	grew	grown
broadcast	broadcast	broadcast	hang	hung	hung[3]
build	built	built	have	had	had
burst	burst	burst	hear	heard	heard
buy	bought	bought	hide	hid	hidden
cast	cast	cast	hit	hit	hit
catch	caught	caught	hold	held	held
choose	chose	chosen	hurt	hurt	hurt
cling	clung	clung	keep	kept	kept
come	came	come	know	knew	known
cost	cost	cost	lay	laid	laid
creep	crept	crept	lead	led	led
cut	cut	cut	leap	leapt / leaped	leapt / leaped
deal	dealt	dealt	leave	left	left
dig	dug	dug	lend	loaned / lent	loaned / lent
dive	dove / dived	dove / dived	let	let	let
do	did	done	lie	lay	lain
draw	drew	drawn	light	lit / lighted	lit / lighted
drink	drank	drunk	lose	lost	lost
drive	drove	driven	make	made	made
eat	ate	eaten	mean	meant	meant
fall	fell	fallen	meet	met	met
feed	fed	fed	mistake	mistook	mistaken
feel	felt	felt	overcome	overcame	overcome
fight	fought	fought	overdo	overdid	overdone
find	found	found	overtake	overtook	overtaken
fit	fit	fit	overthrow	overthrew	overthrown
flee	fled	fled	pay	paid	paid
fly	flew	flown	plead	pleaded / pled	pleaded / pled
forbid	forbade	forbidden	prove	proved	proven / proved
forget	forgot	forgotten	put	put	put
forgive	forgave	forgiven	quit	quit	quit
freeze	froze	frozen	read	read	read
get	got	gotten	ride	rode	ridden
give	gave	given	ring	rang	rung
go	went	gone	rise	rose	risen
grind	ground	ground	run	ran	run

Continued

[3] *Hanged* is used as the past form to refer to punishment by death. *Hung* is used in other situations:
She *hung* the picture on the wall.

Base Form	Past Form	Past Participle	Base Form	Past Form	Past Participle
say	said	said	swear	swore	sworn
see	saw	seen	sweep	swept	swept
seek	sought	sought	swell	swelled	swelled / swollen
sell	sold	sold	swim	swam	swum
send	sent	sent	swing	swung	swung
set	set	set	take	took	taken
sew	sewed	sown / sewed	teach	taught	taught
shake	shook	shaken	tear	tore	torn
shed	shed	shed	tell	told	told
shine	shone / shined	shone / shined	think	thought	thought
shoot	shot	shot	throw	threw	thrown
show	showed	shown / showed	understand	understood	understood
shrink	shrank / shrunk	shrunk / shrunken	uphold	upheld	upheld
shut	shut	shut	upset	upset	upset
sing	sang	sung	wake	woke	woken
sink	sank	sunk	wear	wore	worn
sit	sat	sat	weave	wove	woven
sleep	slept	slept	wed	wedded / wed	wedded / wed
slide	slid	slid	weep	wept	wept
slit	slit	slit	win	won	won
speak	spoke	spoken	wind	wound	wound
speed	sped	sped	withdraw	withdrew	withdrawn
spend	spent	spent	withhold	withheld	withheld
spin	spun	spun	withstand	withstood	withstood
spit	spit	spit	wring	wrung	wrung
split	split	split	write	wrote	written
spread	spread	spread			
spring	sprang	sprung			
stand	stood	stood			
steal	stole	stolen			
stick	stuck	stuck			
sting	stung	stung			
stink	stank	stunk			
strike	struck	stuck / stricken			
strive	strove	striven			

Note:

The past and past participle of some verbs can end in *-ed* or *-t*.

burn	burned or burnt
dream	dreamed or dreamt
kneel	kneeled or knelt
learn	learned or learnt
spill	spilled or spilt
spoil	spoiled or spoilt

The United States of America: Major Cities

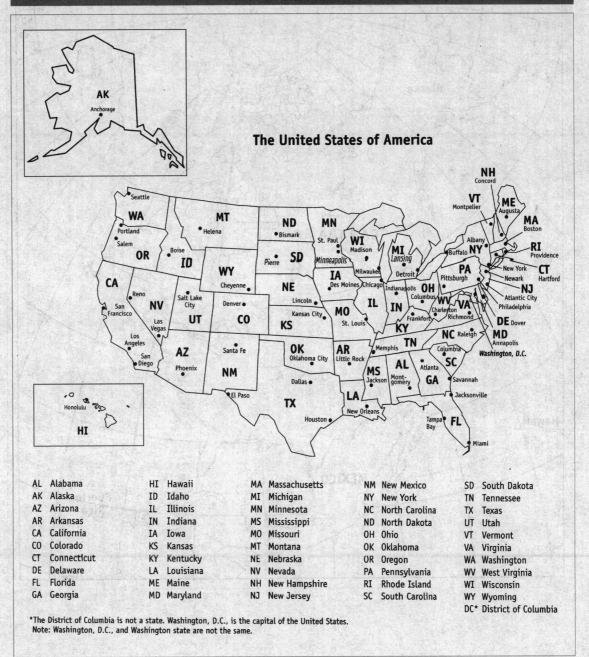

The United States of America

AL Alabama	HI Hawaii	MA Massachusetts	NM New Mexico	SD South Dakota
AK Alaska	ID Idaho	MI Michigan	NY New York	TN Tennessee
AZ Arizona	IL Illinois	MN Minnesota	NC North Carolina	TX Texas
AR Arkansas	IN Indiana	MS Mississippi	ND North Dakota	UT Utah
CA California	IA Iowa	MO Missouri	OH Ohio	VT Vermont
CO Colorado	KS Kansas	MT Montana	OK Oklahoma	VA Virginia
CT Connecticut	KY Kentucky	NE Nebraska	OR Oregon	WA Washington
DE Delaware	LA Louisiana	NV Nevada	PA Pennsylvania	WV West Virginia
FL Florida	ME Maine	NH New Hampshire	RI Rhode Island	WI Wisconsin
GA Georgia	MD Maryland	NJ New Jersey	SC South Carolina	WY Wyoming
				DC* District of Columbia

*The District of Columbia is not a state. Washington, D.C., is the capital of the United States.
Note: Washington, D.C., and Washington state are not the same.

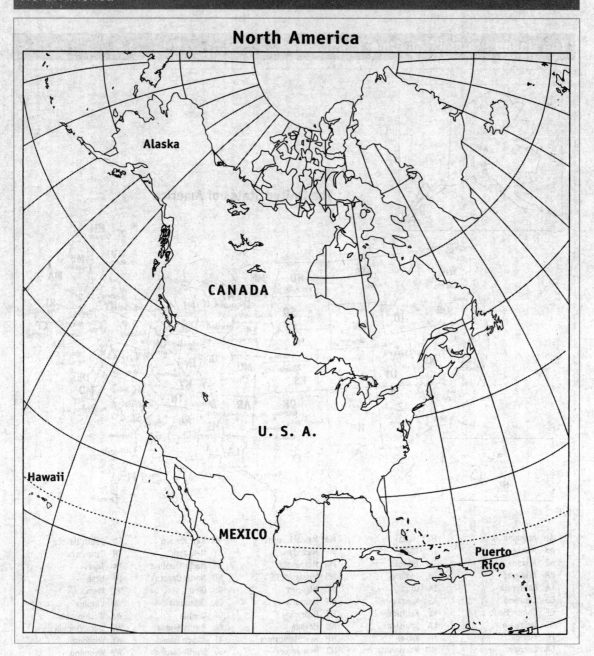

North America

Alaska

CANADA

U. S. A.

Hawaii

MEXICO

Puerto Rico

Index

editing advice for,
319–320

with *enough*, 293–294

examples of, 274

forms of, 274

negative, 279

object before, 279–281

in passive voice, 276

to show purpose, 288–289

as subjects, 290–293,
305–306

with *too*, 293–294

uses of, 274

verbs followed by,
276–279, 304–308

vs. gerunds, 306–308, 318,
AP14

vs. noun clauses, 387–389

-ing. *See also* Present participle(s)

in continuous verbs, 172

in gerunds, 295

in present participles, 76,
340

spelling of, AP18

in time expressions, 340

Intransitive verbs, 71–74

Irregular noun plurals,
AP21–22

Irregular verbs, AP32–34

base form of, 7

past form of, 7

past participle of, 6–7

It

in expressions of importance, 378

with infinitives as subjects, 290, 305

J

Job résumé, 2–3

K

Know how, infinitive after,
387

L

Lately, in present perfect
tense with indefinite
past time, 33, 41–42

Leave, as transitive vs. intransitive verb, 71

Let, as causative verb, 283

Letter, cover, for job résumé, 2, 4

Like/alike, AP27

Logical conclusions

of past, 186–189

of present, 167–170

M

Make, as causative verb, 283

Maps

North America, AP36

United States, AP35–36

May, 138, 140–142, 151–153,
175, 214

May be, 171–172, 175

May have, 189–191, 214

May not, 151, 154, 175

May not have, 189–191

Maybe/may be, 140

Metric conversion charts,
AP23–24

Mexico, map of, AP36

Might, 138, 140–142, 175,
214

with unreal conditions,
442

Might be, 171–172, 175, 214

with continuous verbs,
172–173

Might have, 171–172,
189–191, 214

Might not, 171–172

Might not have, 189–191

Mind, 302

Mistake modals, 198–202

Mixed tenses, in condition
statements, 444–448,
459

Modals, 138–222

with *to*, 146

in active voice, 59, 184

in adverbial clauses, 330

of advice, 146–149

in affirmative statements,
138

of conclusion

in past, 186–189

in present, 167–170

with continuous verbs,
172–174

editing advice for, 146,
216

of expectation, 163–166

forms of, 138–139, 184

may/can, 151–153

may/might/could, 138,
140–142

must/be supposed to,
144–146

must/have to/have got to,
142–144

of necessity or urgency

noun clauses after,
378–379

in past, 205–207

in present, 142–144

negative, 138, 140,
154–160

with *not*, 140, 154

in noun clauses, vs. infinitives, 387

of obligation, 144–146

in passive voice, 59, 138,
184

in past, 184–222

about specific time,
212–213

in active voice, 184

continuous forms of,
212–213

of deduction or conclusion, 186–189

of direction not taken,
193–196

editing advice for, 216

of expected action that
did not happen,
202–203

forms of, 184

of mistakes, 198–202

of necessity, 205–207

in passive voice, 184

of possibility, 189–191

of probability, 186–189

Photo Credits

最新推出

《英语语境语法》(第四版)系列丛书

尊敬的老师:

　　您好!

　　为了方便您更好地使用本套教材,获得最佳教学效果,我们特向使用该套丛书作为教材的教师赠送 CD-ROM 测试题库和教学录像。如有需要,请完整填写"教师联系表",免费向出版社索取。

北京大学出版社

 -

教师联系表

姓名:	性别:		职务:	职称:
E-mail:	联系电话:			邮政编码:
供职学校:		所在院系:		
学校地址:				
教学科目与年级:		班级人数:		
通信地址:				

　　填写完毕后,请将此表邮寄或 EMAIL 给我们,我们将为您免费寄送 CD-ROM 测试题库及教学录像,谢谢!

北京市海淀区成府路 205 号
北京大学出版社外语编辑部负责人
邮政编码:100871
电子邮箱:zbing@pup.pku.edu.cn

邮购部电话:010-62534449
市场营销部电话:010-62750672
外语编辑部电话:010-62765014